BUDDHIST INSIGHT

BUDDHIST TRADITION SERIES

VOLUME 7

Edited by
ALEX WAYMAN

BUDDHIST INSIGHT

ESSAYS BY ALEX WAYMAN

Ed. with an introduction by
GEORGE R. ELDER

MOTILAL BANARSIDASS PUBLISHERS
PRIVATE LIMITED • DELHI

First Published: Delhi, 1984
Reprinted : Delhi, 1990, 2002

ISBN: 81-208-0675-1

Also available at:

MOTILAL BANARSIDASS

236, 9th Main III Block, Jayanagar, Bangalore 560 011
41 U.A. Bungalow Road, Jawahar Nagar, Delhi 110 007
8 Mahalaxmi Chamber, Warden Road, Mumbai 400 026
120 Royapettah High Road, Mylapore, Chennai 600 004
Sanas Plaza, 1302 Baji Rao Road, Pune 411 002
8 Camac Street, Kolkata 700 017
Ashok Rajpath, Patna 800 004
Chowk, Varanasi 221 001

Printed in India
BY JAINENDRA PRAKASH JAIN AT SHRI JAINENDRA PRESS,
A-45 NARAINA, PHASE-I, NEW DELHI 110 028
AND PUBLISHED BY NARENDRA PRAKASH JAIN FOR
MOTILAL BANARSIDASS PUBLISHERS PRIVATE LIMITED,
BUNGALOW ROAD, DELHI 110 007

TABLE OF CONTENTS

Foreword by Alex Wayman vii
Introduction, by George R. Elder 1

Part I. Buddhist Practice
1. Buddha as Savior 11
2. Ancient Buddhist Monasticism 29
3. Aspects of Meditation in the Theravāda and Mahīśāsaka 69
4. The Bodhisattva Practice according to the *Lam Rim Chen Mo* 99

Part II. Buddhist Doctrine
5. The Sixteen Aspects of the Four Noble Truths and Their Opposites 117
6. The Mirror as a Pan-Buddhist Metaphor-Simile 129
7. The Buddhist Theory of Vision 153
8. Dependent Origination—the Indo-Tibetan Tradition 163
9. Nescience and Insight according to Asaṅga's *Yogācārabhūmi* 193
10. The Twenty Reifying Views (*Sakkāyadiṭṭhi*) 215
11. Who Understands the Four Alternatives of the Buddhist texts ? 225
12. The Intermediate-state Dispute in Buddhism 251

Part III. Interpretative Studies of Buddhism
13. No Time, Great Time, and Profane Time in Buddhism 269
14. The Role of Art among the Buddhist Religieux 287
15. Secret of the *Heart Sūtra* 307

Part IV. Texts of the Asaṅga school
16. The *Sacittikā* and *Acittikā Bhūmi,* Text and Translation 327
17. Asaṅga's Treatise, the *Paramārtha-gāthā* 333
18. Asaṅga's Treatise on the Three Instructions of Buddhism 353

Part V. Hindu and Buddhist Studies
19. Two Traditions of India—Truth and Silence 369
20. The Hindu-Buddhist Rite of Truth—an Interpretation 391
21. Significance of Dreams in India and Tibet 399
22. The Significance Mantras, from the Veda down to Buddhist Tantric Practice 413
23. The Goddess Sarasvatī—from India to Tibet 431
24. The Twenty-one Praises of Tārā, a Syncretism of Śaivism and Buddhism 441

Acknowledgments 453
Index 457

FOREWORD

The author of these essays, Alex Wayman, had the good luck of teachers and access to important language materials in the scope of Sanskrit and Tibetan language, and with this background applied his interest to Buddhist topics. Now he shares with readers this unique combination. It seems that various of these essays were conceived in an imaginary bout, as though contending, yet competing with oneself. Even so, such essays, when composed over a period of years, decree the author's non-return to the vanished concatenation of the fortunate circumstances. So it was helpful to have the services of Dr. George Elder to edit the 24 essays. Buddhist treatises, with their non-self theory, insist that the author was not there. Anyway, elsewhere he was able to write more essays. Since the essays can be recommended to the reputed author himself, let them be recommended to other interested readers.

It is planned to issue a companion volume, also of 24 essays, in the next case stressing the untying of knots in Buddhism. Why twenty-four? Indian culture has some famous 24's. The number apparently stands for a complete cycle of some kind. Besides, twenty-four minutes is the water-clock measure, called a *ghaṭaka*, the basic unit for one-pointedness of mind. Forty-eight minutes, the *muhurta*, if the concentration can last that long, is even better.

Alex Wayman

INTRODUCTION

Alex Wayman—Professor of Sanskrit in the Department of Middle East Languages and Cultures and Professor in the Department of Religion at Columbia University—enjoys a world-wide reputation as a truly outstanding scholar in the field of Buddhist Studies. This reputation is founded upon two decades of teaching and writing, with his recent full-length publication entitled *Calming the Mind and Discerning the Real*, a translation from the Tibetan of a portion of Tsoṅ-kha-pa's expansive *Lam rim chen mo*, published in 1978. While Wayman's half a dozen other books have become a standard of quality in this field, it is still a surprise for colleagues to learn that this scholar has also published more than ninety essays to date. These essays have appeared in what are now generally accessible anthologies of other scholars and in the premier journals of the United States. Many have also been written at the request of editors in Europe, India, and Japan. Indexes being what they are, and libraries and one's capacity to keep track being limited, a number of these fine short treatments have not yet been sufficiently known.

Professor Wayman has already attempted to bridge the gap by publishing sixteen of his essays in the collection, *The Buddhist Tantras: Light on Indo-Tibetan Esotericism*, 1973. While that volume focuses upon contributions to tantric Buddhism, the present volume makes more readily available to scholars and the intelligent reader Wayman's contributions to our understanding of non-tantric Buddhism. The twenty-four essays collected here focus almost entirely upon Early Buddhism (what the Mahāyānists refer to as Hīnayāna) and upon Mahāyāna Buddhism in India. Except one, each of these essays has already been published. Their appearance together here has been advised by Alex Wayman himself; and this has allowed the author of the essays the opportunity to make corrections and to provide additional materials. My own emendations have been in terms of regularizing punctuation and diacriticals as much as feasible and seeing to it that the work reads more or less as a coherent statement rather than as so many separate papers. But it is also true that the general consistency of Wayman's translations and his reliance in one article upon positions established in another lend a natural coherence—and, I think, strength—to the book.

The method of scholarship found in this volume has been explained by the author in the preface to his *The Buddhist Tantras.* There, he states: "All those works, whether published or in press or preparation, have a common method which is the subordination of personal opinion about the Tantra to authoritative explanations by the proficients of this cult." Accordingly, the reader will find here some of Wayman's views on the nature of non-tantric Indian Buddhism. But mainly he or she will discover the Buddhists' *own* views on the nature of their religion—and this by way of translations of scripture (fairly literally rendered) illuminated by authoritative commentary. The commentators in this instance are most often Asaṅga (375-430, A.D.), especially his *Yogācārabhūmi* in Sanskrit, and Tsoṅ-kha-pa (1357-1419, A.D.), especially his *Lam rim chen mo* in Tibetan. The felicity of this combination is attested by the fact that the Tibetan reformer often quotes from Asaṅga. While both of these ancient scholars are known to be Mahāyānists by religious persuasion, their works mentioned are encyclopedic in scope and provide a high standard of commentary on virtually all phases of Buddhism. It follows that the essays collected here are also of a high standard with a minimum of mere speculation and with a certain fidelity to the complexity of the materials concerned. Since Buddhism is a rich religion and at times an obscure one, the reader will come upon passages , and perhaps articles, in this work that will seem opaque except to those trained in the issues; but the attentive reader will also find much to inform the intellect and delight the soul. In any case, in the essays assembled here an extraordinary wealth of information, some of it entirely unexpected, is presented in a manner that should give it an enduring value. It might be mentioned also that there is actually a variety of styles in the collection. Most of the articles appeared in the seventies but one as early as 1959 and some as recent as 1980; furthermore, Professor Wayman was writing at different times for different publishers who have had their own purposes.

This brings us to the question of the sort of reader for whom this volume is intended. Wayman, the "scholar's scholar," wrote the essays originally for colleagues in the field; and they, of course, remain the primary audience. Graduate students in Buddhist Studies or Indian religions in general will also find this work invaluable. But I would like to suggest strongly that these essays be considered as a secondary source—alongside scriptures—within the undergraduate curriculum. From my own experience with college students, I know that the surveys of Buddhism now available are useful; but I also know that they provide information of a kind that the professor himself or herself can only too easily provide in lecture. The undergraduate student is left without a bridge between introductory statements and the foreign complexities of Buddhist scripture. With this in mind, these essays have been arranged as a sort of survey of non-tantric Indian Buddhism—by way of in-depth discussion of its most important issues.

Part one, "Buddhist Practice," opens with a treatment of "Buddha as Savior." It is not immediately apparent that this essay has to do with the Path; but it provides an initial focus upon the Indian man who founded Buddhism at the end of the sixth century, B.C. While "Buddha"—"The Awakened One"—can be said to be the chief epithet of Siddhārtha Gautama, we learn here of the many names given this figure in scripture and commentary; and Wayman shows how the various names point to a variety of views of Buddha's activity within the religion. Was Gautama Buddha a "savior" simply because he revealed the truth about reality? Or did he "save" also in the sense of somehow providing others with the power to perceive this truth? In the first instance, disciples would need to "work" out their salvation with diligence; and in the second, they could rely more upon the "grace" of the Lord. Thus, the problem of Buddhist practice is engaged. And Wayman discusses the disciple's "conversion" from an ordinary person to special person—one who has developed his native "insight" and become a "son" in the family of the Buddha. The article that follows, "Ancient Buddhist Monasticism," provides at some length a description of the monastic context in which the process of conversion took place: the kinds of ordination, the rules, the confessions—and stages of progress. Scholars in particular will be pleased to find here a technical discussion of the translation of *prātimokṣa* as "Liberation-

Onset." But there are in Buddhism "Three Trainings" or instructions; and the "morality" emphasized in the essay on monastic life is only one of them. The practice of "meditation is yet another—indeed, it is a mental training which follows upon the right establishment of moral behaviour. And so there follows the informative essay, "Aspects of Meditation in the Theravāda and Mahīśāsaka." Since the Theravāda and Mahīśāsaka are sects of Early Buddhism, the final essay in this section—"The Bodhisattva Practice According to the *Lam Rim Chen Mo*"—turns our attention to the stage of discipleship called the *bodhisattva* within the Mahāyāna.

Part two can be looked upon as a presentation of the third training—training in "insight"—since it takes up the "Doctrine" which must be "discerned" once the mind has been "calmed" by meditation. This is by far the longest section of the book, and it opens with a discussion of "The Sixteen Aspects of the Four Noble Truths and their Opposites." The Four Noble Truths are said to have been taught by Gautama Buddha at his first sermon; and it is interesting to see how the basic doctrine grows with the tradition to encompass eventually four times the "truth" complete with opposites or "coverings" which obscure these truths for ordinary persons. Buddhists ares aying that ordinary reality, called *saṃsāra*, is generally misperceived ; and unless one sees *saṃsāra* correctly, one will not perceive the extraordinary reality called *nirvāṇa*. Having been introduced to the religious use of the symbol of the "wheel" with sixteen aspects or spokes, we encounter the symbol of the "mirror" in the essay, "The Mirror as a Pan-Buddhist Metaphor-Simile." The materials presented are particularly rich, capturing the imagination as religious symbols are intended to do; and the data move through the varied traditions of Buddhism, including the tantric forms. This is all by way of preparation, I think, for the short but important statement, "The Buddhist Theory of Vision." Professor Wayman begins to justify his translation of *prajñā* as "insight" (rather than as "wisdom," a translation preferred by some) toward the close of the essay on "Meditation;" but it is really here that we sense the significance of a translation that preserves a nuance of "seeing." For it is "seeing"—and having the "eye" for it—which serves as the primary symbol of understanding throughout the history of Buddhism.

While the successful *yogin* must "see" the Four Noble Truths in their multiple aspects, he must also see Dependent Origination. There follows, then, the long and complex discussion, "Dependent Origination—the Indo-Tibetan Tradition." Published only recently, this essay is a culmination of the author's previously published research on the subject; and the extensive notes provide a sort of sub-text for the body of this essay. *Avidyā* is the first member of this twelve-member formula for conditioned reality, and Professor Wayman focuses upon it in his article, "Nescience and Insight According to Asaṅga's *Yogācārabhūmi*." Actually, we learn that "nescience" is a general translation of *avidyā* since it might better be rendered "ignorance" as the first member of Dependent Origination so as to preserve an unexpected meaning as a kind of "waywardness" in association with "feelings," the seventh member of the formula. "Insight" opposes "nescience" in any form, and Asaṅga's long list of metaphors for *prajñā*—including the most telling ones that have to do with "light" —can be found here. But the problem of "nescience" for the ordinary person is a persistent one; and so we read next of "The Twenty Reifying Views". These must yield place in favour of the Buddhist view called "non-self" which is, in this instance, the view of the five *skandhas*, each denied in four ways as being "self." As the section comes to a close, we are treated once again to the Buddhist penchant for a four-fold analysis in the essay, "Who Understands the Four Alternatives of the Buddhist Texts?" This is the most philosophical, in some ways the most technical, essay in the volume; it goes directly to problems of logic—and Wayman takes on a number of his colleagues in debate. The subject matter itself includes such ancient problems as this: Does the Tathagata exist after death? And so the section closes with the topic, "The Intermediate-State Dispute in Buddhism." Here, the debate is among Buddhists alone. And the question is whether a person who is not yet Enlightened goes directly to his or her next life upon death, or goes to an "intermediate state," some state in between. I think it is important to see in this essay and elsewhere within the volume that a dispute among Buddhists may exhibit the difference between the Hīnayāna and Mahāyāna forms but may just as readily cut across sectarian lines.

Part three is entitled "Interpretative Studies of Buddhism"

since the author brings to bear upon Buddhist materials in these essays points of view which are not in themselves necessarily Buddhist. The first, "No Time, Great Time, and Profane Time in Buddhism," allows categories more usually associated with the "history of religions" school to inform our understanding of the Buddhist religion; the second, "The Role of Art Among the Buddhist Religieux" blends art history with a fair amount of modern aesthetic theory while relying upon positions already established in the essay on "Dependent Origination." The third, "Secret of the *Heart Sūtra*," is unique. Wayman calls it an "Asian-type commentary composed by a Westerner"—and he is the Westerner. Here, this scholar brings to bear upon a famous Mahāyāna scripture a more or less Yogācāra point of view in opposition to the usual Buddhist commentary from the point of view of the Mādhyamika school. It is a style of scholarship which Wayman also employs in his work, *Yoga of the Guhyasamājatantra*, published in 1977.

Part four, "Texts of the Asaṅga School," provides a change of pace. It contains edited Sanskrit and translated excerpts from the *Yogācārabhūmi* of Asaṅga whose commentary, as already noted, has informed many of the preceding essays. Readers will gain from this section a clear idea of the kinds of materials involved in Buddhist scholarship, and scholars in particular will gain edited materials for their own work along with a clear sense of Wayman's style of translation. The best introduction to these excerpts is actually found in the opening paragraphs of the second essay, "Asaṅga's Treatise on the Paramārtha Gāthā"—and, also, in the opening of the essay entitled, "Nescience and Insight According to Asaṅga's *Yogācārabhūmi*" introduced above. This is because of the preference shown to a presentation in the order of its appearance within the *Yogācārahbūmi* itself. The short text, "The Sacittikā and Acittikā Bhūmi" was previously published only as edited; and Wayman has taken the opportunity to provide the translation here as well. It contains Nos. 8 and 9 of the seventeen *bhūmis* or "stages." The "Paramārtha Gāthā" text already mentioned is a set of verses with commentary by Asaṅga which form a portion of "stage" No. 11; this material, by the way, was previously published as part of Wayman's full-length *Analysis of the Śrāvakabhūmi Manuscript*, 1961. It appears again here with corrections. And, finally, the text "Asaṅga's

Treatise on the Three Instructions of Buddhism" takes up the set of verses and commentary that follow the "Paramārtha Gāthā" within "stage" No. 11. This material in the book has not been published in some form earlier.

Part five extends our appreciation for the range of Professor Wayman's work. It is entitled," Hindu and Buddhist Studies;" and its comparative approach should give a certain feeling for the character of Buddhism in India which was always surrounded, we might say, by Hinduism. The essays can be looked upon as pairs. The first pair is made of : "Two Traditions of India—Truth and Silence" and 'The Hindu-Buddhist Rite of Truth—an Interpretation." They move through the Vedas, Upaniṣads, and Buddhism; and they articulate the tradition of the *muni* or "silent sage" as distinct from the tradition of the sage who verbalizes his truth, especially by way of *mantra*. And the "rite of truth" is shown to be a particular instance of the power of truth spoken. The second pair of essays—"Significance of Dreams in India and Tibet" along with "Significance of Mantras, From the Veda Down to Buddhist Tantric Practice"—are less united in theme. Both, however, focus upon important features of Indian religious life and provide valuable detailed classifications. Finally, it is appropriate that a volume entitled *Buddhist Insight* should end with its attention upon the Feminine since, in Buddhism, "Insight" is sometimes a "Woman." Wayman's treatment, "The Goddess Sarasvatī—from India to Tibet," traces the history of a deity from her form as a river to her many forms within Buddhist meditation; and the translation essay, "The Twenty-One Praises of Tārā, a Syncretism of Śaivism and Buddhism, " brings the volume to a close with a beautiful hymn. Since the last two essays touch upon materials that are ambiguously related to both the non-tantric and tantric forms of Mahāyāna Buddhism, they may serve as an encouragement to continue this "survey" of Buddhism by consulting Alex Wayman's other collection of essays, *The Buddhist Tantras: Light on Indo-Tibetan Esotericism.*

George R. Elder
Hunter College, New York City

PART ONE

BUDDHIST PRACTICE

1

BUDDHA AS SAVIOR

The Buddhist teachings about Buddha as a savior go deep into the meaning of Buddhism, and also involve deep-seated differences in the persons who might be subject to this salvific activity. Our investigation shows one situation during the time of the historical Buddha, another coming to the fore after his passing as the disciples yearned for and received a new dispensation. Fortunately, it is all at hand—the old Buddhist scriptures, the later Mahāyāna developments; and so it is possible to discern some changes in viewpoint as time went on.

A problem in one extensive corpus of Buddhist literature is whether the Buddha's salvific operation is consistent with Buddhist emphasis on individual responsibility and enterprise. But in another branch of Buddhist literature this does not appear to be a problem at all. There are also some highly disputed matters, as to whether such an activity as "grace" is accepted. The old teaching of the Buddha resisted this, and one must pass to Mahāyāna developments to find convincing examples.

Relevant epithets of the Buddha

The celebrated Buddhist dictionary *Mahāvyutpatti* devotes its first section to epithets of the Buddha, and a later section to terms about the greatness of the Tathāgata (a title of the Buddha).[1] From these two sections I have selected certain names that can be arranged in sets as follows:

[1] *Mahāvyutpatti*, edited by Ryōzaburō Sakaki, 2nd edn., Tokyo, 1962, 2 vols.

a. Names indicating the Buddha as refuge and savior: worthy of refuge (*śaraṇya*), the refuge (*śaraṇa*), *protector* (*goptṛ*); savior (*trāyin*, *tāraka*), rescuer of all (*viśvaṃtara*).
b. Buddha's double nature: perfect in clear vision and walking (*vidyācaraṇasaṃpanna*).
c. Names of Buddha as guide and teacher : teacher (of gods and men) (*śāstṛ—devamanuṣyānām*), guide (*nāyaka*, *parināyaka*, *netṛ*); charioteer of persons to be tamed (*puruṣa-damya-sārathi*); caravan leader for the beginners (*sārthavāha—ādikarmikānām*).

Some of those titles are in a scriptural passage of the Pāli canonical collection called *Aṅguttara-nikāya* (Book of Threes):[2]

> Here a Tathāgata arises in the world, an Arahant who is rightly completely enlightened, perfect in clear vision and walking, Sugata, World-knower, incomparable charioteer of persons to be tamed, teacher of gods and men, a Buddha Bhagavat. He proclaims thus: "Come! This is the Path. This is the course I announce: I so mastered it that myself realized directly with supernormal faculty the incomparable yoga-way of brahma-conduct (*brahmacariyogadha*). Come you also! May you so course that having mastered it you too yourselves may directly realize with supernormal faculty the incomparable yoga-way of brahma-conduct, and having acquired it may abide (therein)!" It is in this way that the Teacher teaches the Dhamma, and others course for the thusness goal. You should know, moreover, that these amount to many hundreds, many thousands, many hundred thousands.

My rendition "perfect in clear vision and walking" for the well-known epithet *vidyācaraṇasaṃpanna* is in part verified in the *Mahāprajñāpāramitāśāstra*, which explains the term *vidyā* as possibly the three kinds of visions which the future Buddha had under the tree of enlightenment, namely, the memory of previous lives, the divine eye, and the ending of the fluxes. These are both "clear visions" and supernormal faculties (*abhijñā*), while the remaining three supernormal faculties of the standard Buddhist

[2] The passage was called to my attention in A.K. COOMARASWAMY and I. B. HORNER, *Gotama the Buddha* (London, 1948), p. 43, but the translation is my own.

list are merely supernormal faculties and not clear visions.[3] However, the Chinese *śāstra* takes the *caraṇa* part as practices, while I render it more literally as "walking" to indicate the wanderings during which the Buddha taught his Doctrine that was established in the clear visions.

The *Mahāprajñāpāramitāśāstra*, when explaining the epithet "teacher of gods and men," raises the question of why the title is restricted to two of the five (or six) destinies that also count the animals, hungry ghosts (*preta*), and hell beings. It replies that the Buddha frequently saves beings included among men and gods and rarely saves beings of the "bad destinies," animals, etc. It adds that men have weak bonds and can easily gain detachment, while the gods have sharp insight (*prajñā*), and so both these can easily attain the Path.[4]

The Chinese *śāstra* fortunately also has an entry for the charioteer of persons to be tamed, which partially overlaps the caravan-leader epithet, which, however, it does not explain. The Buddha with his great benevolence (*mahāmaitrī*), great compassion (*mahākaruṇā*), and great wisdom (*mahājñāna*), employs a voice sometimes sweet, sometimes harsh, sometimes of mixed quality, so that the caravan (*sārtha*) does not lose the Path. Verses set forth that the Buddha's Dharma is the chariot, the disciples are the horses, the true *dharmas* are the merchandise, the Buddha is the charioteer. The usual theory of the epithet is that the term "person" (*puruṣa*) refers to males, whether human or animal. The question of why women are not included, although women are also installed in the Path, is answered with the usual Indian remarks that women have detractions—here, that they cannot become a Cakravartin king, or Śakra (=Indra), a Māra king, or have the rank of Brahmā, and so were not intended in the title.[5]

The "caravan-leader" epithet occurs in the early teaching that the Buddha's becoming completely enlightened did not necessitate a proclamation of the Path. Thus the *Majjhima-nikāya* has a celebrated passage that the Buddha at first was not inclined to teach his Doctrine, deeming it too profound for persons imbued

[3] Cf. Étienne Lamotte, *Mahāprajñāpāramitāśāstra*, Tome I (Louvain, 1944), pp. 128-129; and A. Wayman, *Calming the Mind and Discerning the Real* (Delhi, 1979), pp. 42-43.

[4] Lamotte, tr. Tome I, pp. 135-137.

[5] Lamotte, tr. Tome I, pp. 133-135.

with lust, hatred, and delusion. And then Brahmā Sahampati exhorted him to teach, saying among other things:

> Arise, O hero who defeated the troop [of Māra]!
> Caravan-leader without a debt, walk in the world!
> May the Bhagavat teach the Doctrine.
> (Some) will be those who understand (it).

The scripture continued with the Buddha's surveying the world with his Buddha-eye and noticing that persons were of all sorts, of little or much impurity, of keen or dull faculty, like lotuses of different colors and in different stages of development. He decided it would be helpful to preach his excellent Doctrine among men so that the "doors of the Immortal would be opened for them."[6]

The verse shows the early occurrence of the epithet "caravan-leader," which was to be widely used in stories and with varying transcriptions and translation in Central Asia and various Asian languages.[7] The term *sārthavāhin* also means a "merchant," and it is of interest that the early transmissal of Buddhism to China was by merchants and in merchant communities.[8] This meaning seems to agree with the qualification "without a debt," but this may also imply that the Buddha has no debt to requite by walking in the world (cf. the previous epithet, "perfect in clear vision and walking"), i.e. would do it by virtue of his benevolence and compassion. The expression "for the beginners" evidently intends the "novices," in short that they are being brought to a new country (=new sets of doctrines) by the caravan leader who knows the Buddhist route and can avoid the pitfalls and wrong side-paths.

Change from Ordinary Person to Ārya

The preceding section has shown that the Buddha's role as savior amounts to revealing the Path. This in effect separated persons into two groups—the ordinary persons who paid no heed to the Buddha's message, and those who hearkened. The

[6] This directly precedes the *Dhammacakkapavattana* episode of the *Majjhimanikāya*, Vol. I, pp. 218-219, in the Bihar, 1958, edition.

[7] See Albert E. Dien, "The *Sa-Pao* Problem Re-examined," *Journal of the American Oriental Societ*, 82:3, July-Sept., 1962, pp. 335-346, for the details.

[8] Cf. E. Zürcher, *The Buddhist Conquest of China* (Leiden, 1959), p. 59.

ordinary person is called the *pṛthagjana*, while the one who became a disciple is called the *ārya*. The Pāli scripture *Saṃyutta-nikāya* describes the ordinary person (P. *puthujjana*) as the one who has not heard the Doctrine or been disciplined in it, who has not come in contact with the noble ones (*ariya*) or illustrious persons; and this ordinary person identifies his self with the five personal aggregates of form and so on.[9] According to the teacher Asaṅga, the *ārya* person, the Buddha's disciple, views illustrious persons, is skilled in the noble doctrines; he knows, as it truly is, suffering as suffering, the source as the source, cessation as cessation, the path as the path.[10] Thus the disciple knows the four Noble Truths, or Truths of the Nobles, proclaimed by the Buddha in the first sermon, Setting into Motion of the Wheel of Dharma.

While the *ārya* is the one who "enters the stream," and proceeds on the Buddhist path, this does not mean that the "ordinary person" was neglected. According to a Mahāyāna scripture called *Kūṭāgāra-sūtra*, ordinary persons were called "fish."[11]

> Ānanda, "fish" is a term for ordinary persons (*pṛthagjana*).
> The "fishing hook" is a term for the Tathāgata's generating (in them) the root of virtue (*kuśala-mūla*).
> The "line" is a term for the "means of conversion."
> "Fish(erman)" is a term for the Tathāgata.
> "Fish rescue" is a term for installing sentient beings in the Nirvāṇa-fruit.

Thus, much emphasis was put on the change from being an "ordinary person" to being an "*ārya*," installed in the Buddha's family. The Pāli author Buddhaghosa uses a mixed Sanskrit-Pāli term *gotrabhūñāṇa* (knowledge of *gotrabhū*) as the basis of the path aiming at Nibbāna. A recent article about the term *gotrabhū* has decided that it signifies "(one) having the state of the lineage,"[12] while the translator of the Pāli Abhidhamma work

[9] *Saṃyutta-nikāya*, iii (Khandha-Vagga, 42).

[10] A. WAYMAN, *Analysis of the Śrāvakabhūmi Manuscript* (Berkeley, 1961), p. 67.

[11] This scripture, found in both Tibetan and Chinese, was cited in a native Tibetan work by TSOṄ-KHA-PA, his *Saṅsrgyas so Iṅa'i mṅon rtogs daṅ / lha sku'i phyag tshad*, Tashilunpo collected works, Vol. Da.

[12] D. SEYFORT RUEGG, "Pāli *Gotta/Gotra* and the term *Gotrabhū* in

Puggala-paññati under the title *Human Types* takes the term to signify "one become of the Ariya family."[13] A special kind of *ārya* became the "ascetic son of the Buddha," and I will show elsewhere in this volume that this birth in the Buddhist family as a monk coincided with one's taking of the vow called "Pātimokkhasaṃvara."[14]

The Pāli *Saṃyutta-nikāya* hints at the nature of this change to an *ārya* when it points out that the ordinary person does not hear the Doctrine. This is because in Asaṅga's *Yogācārabbūmi* it is taught that persons have a native "insight" (*prajñā*) attained through birth, and which he refers to as "eye of insight." This native insight contrasts with the promoted insight called "eye of insight belonging to the Āryas," which is presumably the three levels of *prajñā*, consisting of hearing, pondering, and cultivation. Hence, the change to being an *ārya* is when this native faculty is promoted to hearing scriptures and so on with faith, whereupon it is called "insight consisting of hearing" (*śrutamayī prajñā*).[15]

The "ordinary persons" also constitute the field for what are called the "four means of conversion" (*samgrahavastu*), that are enumerated in the Pāli canon and undergo a development in Sanskrit Buddhist literature. The first one, giving (*dāna*), coincides with the first of the six Mahāyāna perfections (*pāramitā*). Following the description of a Mahāyāna scripture, the *Akṣayamatinirdeśa-sūtra*, this "giving" means giving any material thing and also giving the Dharma. The second, pleasant speech (*priya-vāditā*) means sweet and attractive words to persons making requests and listening to the Dharma. The third one, promoting aims (*artha-caryā*) means fulfilling the aims of oneself and others in strict accordance with hopes. The fourth one, consistency in advice (*samānārthatā*) means, for example, that whatever the vehicle of teaching that oneself adheres to with the

Pāli and Buddhist Sanskrit," *Buddhist Studies in Honour of I. B. Horner* (Dordrecht, Holland, 1974), pp. 206-207.

[13] B.C. LAW, tr., *Designation of Human Types* (London, 1922), p. 19.

[14] A. WAYMAN, "Ancient Buddhist Monasticism," *Studia Missionalia* 28, 1979, p. 197. This essay appears in this volume.

[15] All the citations from Asaṅga's *Yogācārabhūmi* are in my essay, "Nescience and Insight according to Asaṅga's *Yogācārabhūmi*," appearing in this volume.

attitude that it is meritorious, one installs in that very vehicle persons who accept the material things and Dharma of the first means (*dāna*).[16]

A problem of this theory that one has become stationed in a species (S. *gotra*) with the inherent nature of *parinirvāṇa*, is whether those who are not stationed in the species are incapable of it; and another problem is why those stationed in the species seem still so far away from *parinirvāṇa*. Asaṅga, in common with early Buddhism as indicated in the preceding section, does not appear concerned with the problem of whether some persons are incapable of the change into an *ārya*, thus resident in the species of the Buddhist religious goal, although some Mahāyāna currents felt obliged to treat this problem; and the *Laṅkāvatāra-sūtra* like some other sources employs the term *icchantika* for persons who lack the requisite "root of virtue" (*kuśala-mūla*) (cf. the previous "fish" passage from the *Kūṭāgāra-sūtra*) susceptible of forming the basis for entrance into the "species."[17] Asaṅga does concern himself with why persons with the nature of *parinirvāṇa* have "moved in *saṃsāra* for so long in former times and still have not attained *parinirvāṇa*," and he sets forth four reasons: 1) they were born in unfavorable circumstances; 2) they had the fault of heedlessness; 3) they entered upon a wrong or perverse course; 4) they were hindered; and he proceeds to explain each of the four.[18] Thus Asaṅga's extensive writings were aimed at the persons who were converts to the Buddhist position or had entered the religious life.

BUDDHA AS SAVIOR AND SELF-RELIANCE

It has been usual in Western expositions of Buddhism to bring up the Buddhist stress on "self-reliance." One such passage appealed to is in the Buddhist classic *Dhammapada* (no. 276), in Radhakrishnan's translation: "You yourself must strive. The

[16]This material comes from the ***Akṣayamatinirdeśasūtra*** **itself, of which** I have been preparing a translation. One may consult HAR DAYAL, *The Bodhisattva Doctrine in Buddhist Sanskrit Literature* (Delhi, 1975), pp. 251-259, for more material on the four *vastus*.

[17]For the *icchantika*, cf. D. S. RUEGG, *La theorie du Tathāgatagarbha et du gotra* (Paris, 1969), pp. 75, ff.

[18]Cf. ALEX WAYMAN, *Analysis*, pp. 59-60.

Blessed Ones are (only) preachers. Those who enter the path and practise meditation are released from the bondage of Māra (death, sin)."[19] Along these lines there is a verse of unknown source which I cited elsewhere with annotational expansion:[20]

> The Munis do not wash away the defilements (of the streams of consciousness of the sentient beings) with water (as though it were a matter of washing away dirt). And they do not remove the suffering of beings with a hand (as though it were a matter of pulling out a thorn). They do not shift to another the (features of) comprehension of reality (as though it were a matter of shifting a tool from the right to the left hand). (But rather) they liberate (the beings from the cyclical flow) by the Teaching (provided the beings meditate on its meaning) of the truth of real nature (or absolute truth).

It is possible to overly stress this self-reliance, as though the Buddhas are *only* preachers. This is because all the scriptures begin with "Thus by me it was heard" (*evaṃ mayā śrutaṁ*), admitting that the disciple did not derive the scripture from himself but from another. In Tibet, the author Tsoṅ-kha-pa cited the Tathāgata, "The one who has heard (it) from another, is liberated from old age and death." And the Tibetan author added:[21]

> In that passage, the Teacher clearly explains by personally drawing from his own memory. The words "The one who has heard (it) from another" means that he heard the exposition of nonself from another. Hence he listened previously to illustrious friendly guides for the meaning of nonself; and having done the hearing and pondering, in order to reject the adherence to the notion "It came from within" he states "heard it from another"—of this there is no doubt.

Thus, the cardinal Buddhist doctrine of "non-self" had to be learned from another, since "self" cannot originate the teaching of non-self. But then the important issue is what part of the corpus

19S. Radhakrishnan, *The Dhammapada* (London, 1950), p. 146.

20A. Wayman, "Purification of Sin in Buddhism by Vision and Confession," in Genjun H. Sasaki, ed., *A Study of Kleśa* (Tokyo, 1975) pp. 73-74. The passage is drawn from the annotational edition of Tsoṅ-kha-pa's *Lam rim chen mo*.

21A. Wayman, *Calming the Mind*, p. 175.

must come from others and what part is to be added by oneself. It is not necessary to cite a multitude of passages, since it is easy to get the answer that "right views" (*samyagdṛṣṭi*), first member of the eightfold noble path, is what one must receive from others. This part from others is referred to metaphorically as a "lamp" in the Northern Buddhist expansion of the *Dhammapada* called *Udānavarga* (XXII, 3-6). Here there is first mention of the person who entering a house enwrapped in darkness does not see objects in it even though he has eyes. When he listens he understands the natures that are virtuous or sinful: this is his "lamp", so he is a man who both has eyes and bears a lamp. Having hearkened, he understands the *dharmas*. Finally, having hearkened, he reaches Nirvāṇa.[22] This implication of the borrowed lamp is also in the canonical passages, *Saṃyutta-nikāya* and elsewhere, saying, "he who sees the Dhamma sees me, and he who sees me sees the Dhamma."[23]

Therefore, the Buddha as savior is the one who shows or points out the Path, affords a glimpse (S. *darśana*). When one enters the path, he cannot do it just with a glimpse, but must enter with his body and all its faculties. The trouble is that this self-reliance is premature if it is not preceded by a glimpse of the right hall to enter.

As to the "right views"- -in Pâli, *sammā ditthi*, Nyanatiloka, rendering it "right understanding," has as full a list as could be expected: the four noble truths; merit and demerit in terms of body, speech, and mind; the three characteristics (impermanence, suffering, and non-self); unprofitable questions; five bonds (*saṃyojana*); unwise considerations (e. g. "Have I been in the past?" and other egoistic questions); wise considerations (through hearkening); theory of the "Stream-enterer" and stages of the Path; supramundane "right understanding" when conjoined with the Path; the middle doctrine of Dependent Origination avoiding the extremes of nihilism and eternalism; doctrine of karma and fruit.[24] This, then, usually called the Buddha's Teaching, is also the *darśana*.

22F. BERNHARD, ed., *Udānavarga*, Band I (Göttingen, 1965), Sanskrittexte aus den Turfanfunden.

23COOMARASWAMY and HORNER, *Gotama*, p. 23.

24NYANATILOKA, *The Word of the Buddha* ('Island Hermitage,' Ceylon, 1952), pp. 29-47.

As long as we restrict ourselves to the ancient position of Buddhism, such as found in the early scriptures, and avoid certain novel directions of Mahāyāna Buddhism, we cannot ascribe to the Buddha's role more than this. Still, this role of teaching the "right views" is by no means negligible if we are to understand this situation of ancient Buddhism. Later, such considerations were to be reevaluated as we shall see in the next section.

Even here more could be said. For instance, passing to Āryadeva's *Catuḥśataka*, we notice that he devotes Chap. XII to refutation of wrong views. Verse 1 refers to the "hearer."

> The hearer who is upright (like a post) has discrimination (*buddhimat* = the native insight) and strives, is called the "vessel." Otherwise, there would be no merit of the speaker, nor any in the listener.

Now the hearer comes in for some inspection. We should not forget that there is no point to teaching the "right views" unless there is an appropriate audience. And in the *Jātakamālā*, XVII (The Story of the Jar): "But the speaker of the beneficial words is to be honoured by accepting his words and by putting them into practice (= taking them to heart)." This is advice for the grateful disciple. Finally, the *Mahāyāna-Sūtrālaṃkāra* (i. 16) summarizes his sequence of attainment: "Having based himself first on hearing, there arises here the 'mental orientation' (*manaskāra*); from the 'mental orientation' there arises the knowledge (*jñāna*) whose field is the meaning of reality."[25]

BUDDHA AND ADHIṢṬHĀNA

In the Mahāyāna period, the Buddha had become equipped with multiple bodies; in particular the body with which he appeared on earth was not an ordinary human body but one called a Nirmāṇakāya. This body was credited with various supernormal powers, e.g. *adhiṣṭhāna*, with a frequent verbal form *adhitiṣṭhati*. The appendix to *Vijñaptimātratāsiddhi* summarizes what is attributed to the Buddha by this term, starting with the *Abhidharmakośa*; and La Vallée Poussin here finds Burnouf's rendition "benediction" excellent in many passages. In these passages, there was

[25]The *Catuḥśataka*, *Jātakamālā*, and *Mahāyāna-Sūtrālaṃkāra* passages are selected from among quotations in Tsoṅ-kha-pa's *Lam rim chen mo*, in my quotation notebooks.

especially an ability to conserve the body, make it last for aeons.[26]

Suzuki, *Studies in the Laṅkāvatāra-sūtra*, explains it as the sustaining power of the original vows.[27] This rendition is close to the usage as an architectural term for the Indian temple, where it is the foundation of the superstructure.[28] Thus, the term suggests the sustaining or support for the spiritual component, the part in the "intermediate space" (*antarikṣa*).

It is somewhat of a jump to pass to the usage by way of the Tibetan translation of the noun as "*byin rlabs*." We read in the book, *Tibetan Yoga and Secret Doctrines,* "O Thou, in the Akaniṣṭha Heaven, the emanation of the Pure Realm of the Dharmakāya, vouchsafe me Thy 'gift-waves' (so) that Self-Knowledge, the Immutable State of the Dharma-kāya, may be attained."[29] Here, the rendition "gift-waves" is after the form of the Tibetan words, which, however, themselves render the Sanskrit word *adhiṣṭhāna.* It should be mentioned that the root-guru in the Akaniṣṭha Heaven is understood in Mahāyāna theology as the Saṃbhoga-kāya of the Buddha. The context of the passage, furthermore, agrees with a rendition "spiritual support."

It is clear that the development called Mahāyāna Buddhism, with its theory of the multiple bodies of the Buddha, had made possible a contribution presumably by the Buddha to the disciple that extended beyond the old "showing of the Path." The term in its Tibetan form was frequent in a work which F. D. Lessing and I translated into English under the title *Mkhas grub rje's Fundamentals of the Buddhist Tantras* (Mouton, The Hague, 1968), now reprinted with a new introduction as *Introduction to the Buddhist Tantric Systems* (Motilal Banarsidass, Delhi, 1978.). Here we rendered it usually as 'blessing," and the verbal form as "energize," "empower," and the like.

[26]Louis de La Vallee Poussin, *Vijñaptimātratāsiddhi*, Tome II (Paris, 1929), pp. 771-773.

[27]Daisetz Teitaro Suzuki, *Studies in the Laṅkāvatāra Sūtra* (London, 1930), pp. 277-378.

[28]Cf. Prasanna Kumar Acharya, *A Dictionary of Hindu Architecture* (London, 1927), pp. 17-18, saying, "..it denotes an object on which something stands....it implies the base of the column, being the member between the shaft and the pedestal, if there be any."

[29]Kazi Dawa-samdup, tr., W. Y. Evans-Wentz, ed., *Tibetan Yoga and Secret Doctrines* (London, 1935), p. 264.

Now, the developed theory that the Buddhas or celestial Bodhisattvas like Avalokiteśvara could extend a power to chosen disciples to fortify the latters' limited resources, caused some change in the literature and encouraged the kind of praises and evocation rituals in which the deity is implored to extend this kind of blessing or empowerment (*adhiṣṭhāna*). The theory undoubtedly helped to make the Bodhisattva practice flourish, to extol the possession of compassion (*karuṇā*), and to attribute the intense form of this, "great compassion" (*mahākaruṇā*), to the supramundane Buddhas and Bodhisattvas. So the scripture *Āryagāyaśīrṣa* is cited: "Mañjuśrī, the practice of the Bodhisattvas has what inception, has what spiritual foundation? Mañjuśrī replied: Son-of-the-gods, the practice of the Bodhisattvas has great compassion as its inception, and has the sentient beings as its spiritual foundation (*adhiṣṭhāna*)."

A Mahāyāna *sūtra* called *Ākāśagarbha* says: "By the cognition of insight (*prajñā*) all defilement is cast out of doors. By the cognition of means (*upāya*) all the living beings are given hospitality." Candragomin's *Śiṣyalekhā* (v. 101) compares this nature of the great beings to the sun's impartial radiation and illumination of the worlds; the second half of the verse says: "Such is this nature of the great ones —to have no aim of their own—who delight in the single taste of benefit and happiness for the worldlings." Such passages are very numerous in the Mahāyāna literature, and this sample merely suggests how the Mahāyāna authors were inspired to stress these points with all the beauty of expression they could muster.[30]

I should give still another citation with the word *adhiṣṭhāna* in the sense of a "spiritual foundation," since the *Śikṣāsamuccaya* cites the Sanskrit of this passage from the *Ārya-Ratnacūḍaparipṛcchā*: "Thus, girding himself with the armor of benevolence (*maitrī*) and having based himself on the spiritual foundation of great compassion (*mahākaruṇādhiṣṭhāna*), he works at the meditation (*dhyāna*) which realizes the voidness possessed of all the

[30]The *Āryagāyaśīrṣa*, *Ākāśagarbha-sūtra*, and the *Śiṣyalekhā* passages are selected from among quotations in Tsoṅ-kha-pa's *Lam rim chen mo*, in my quotation notebooks. The line translated from the *Śiṣyalekhā* (I.P. Minaeff's edition) is: / *na sa svārthaḥ kaścit prakṛtir iyam iva mahatāṃ yadete lokānāṃ hitasukharasaikāntarasikāḥ* /.

best aspects. What is the voidness possessed of all the best aspects? The one that does not lack giving, does not lack morality, does not lack forbearance, does not lack striving, does not lack meditation, does not lack insight, and does not lack means."[31]

The foregoing and much more that could be cited in amplification should serve to show that in the Mahāyāna period the new role attributed to the Buddha by virtue of his various bodies could easily have produced teachings that the Buddha exercises a "grace"—to use the Western religious term. And yet, just when the stage is set for such a magnanimous activity by the Buddha, so that such an enlightened being could be regarded as a "savior" in terms comprehensible to Westerners, a reaction that also belongs to the Mahāyāna was to set in. This other development, also a consequence of the theory of multiple bodies, will be clarified in the next section.

Did the Buddha save any beings ?

Early Buddhism was realistic and so took the position that beings were either "rescued" or "not rescued." But a scripture called *Aṣṭasāhasrikā Prajñāpāramitā* that was translated by Edward Conze, and which was probably the earliest of all the Mahāyāna scriptures, takes the "illusionist" position:[32]

> *The Lord:* Here the Bodhisattva, the great being, thinks thus: countless beings I should lead to Nirvana and yet there are none who lead to Nirvana, or who should be led to it. However many beings he may lead to Nirvana, yet there is not any being that has been led to Nirvana, nor that has led others to it. For such is the true nature of dharmas, seeing that their nature is illusory.

Again:

> *Subhuti*: The form of any illusory man is neither bound nor freed. The Suchness of the form of an illusory man is neither

[31]Śāntideva's *Śikṣāsamuccaya*, ed. by P. L. Vaidya (Darbhanga, 1961), text, p. 145.11-13, within the longer passage of similar sentiments. The part I have translated is the *Lam rim chen mo* quotation.

[32]Edward Conze, tr., *The Perfection of Wisdom in Eight thousand slokas* (Calcutta, 1958), Chap. 1, pp. 8-9, 11.

> bound nor freed. Because in reality it is not there at all, because it is isolated, because it is unproduced.

In this first chapter of the celebrated work, the Buddha's early disciple Śāriputra, said to have been the best in "insight" (*prajñā*) of those disciples, put a hard question to Subhuti, saying:

> As I understand the teaching of the Venerable Subhuti, a Bodhisattva also is a non-production. But if a Bodhisattva is a non-production, how then does he go on the difficult pilgrimage, and how can he possibly endure the experience of those sufferings (which he is said to undergo) for the sake of beings?

Subhuti responded:

> I do not look for a Bodhisattva who goes on the difficult pilgrimage. In any case, one who courses in the perception of difficulties is not a Bodhisattva. Because one who has generated a perception of difficulties is unable to work the weal of countless beings....

We see that there is some attractiveness in this position (or non-position) of illusion: it gets rid of the difficulties, because difficulties are a feature of the real world. Even the unknown composer of the *Aṣṭasāhasrikā* had to work at it.

A Japanese Buddhologist Susumu Yamaguchi (then President of Otani University, Kyoto) wrestled with this problem after he read Śāntideva's *Bodhicaryāvatāra* and concluded that the Buddha was always absorbed in contemplation without doing anything for the salvation of the human beings during the half century from his attainment of enlightenment at the thirty-fifth year of age till his entering into Nirvāṇa when he was eighty years old. He further noted: "The Buddha is commonly said to have been preaching to save mankind during that period, but in reality he said no word through these decades." He also noted that the Indian Buddhist scholar Bodhiruci, coming to China in the sixth century A.D., claimed that the Buddha preached using one word only. So Yamaguchi gave lectures about it in Japanese to show the position of his Shin Sect of Japanese Buddhism; and his lectures were translated into English by Shoko Watanabe, a professor at Toyo University, in a book published in 1958. Yamaguchi kindly presented to the present writer on the occasion of an early 1960's visit to Kyoto this book entitled *Dynamic Buddha and Static Buddha*. Professor Yamaguchi noticed that these two forms of Buddha were represented in sculpture. One was the meditating Buddha, contemplating *prajñāpāramitā*, making no audible words; the other was the preaching Buddha, sometimes showing elongated tongue—what he calls the "dynamic Buddha."

These two kinds of Buddha reflect the Mahāyāna teaching of Buddha bodies: the Dharma-kāya is the "static Buddha", and the Saṃbhoga-kāya and Nirmāṇa-kāya the "dynamic Buddha." In the Tibetan tradition, the Dharma-kāya does not teach; only the "bodies of form" (Saṃbhoga and Nirmāṇa) teach.[33] This, however, is a theory that goes back to the early *Parinirvāṇa-sūtra*. Thus, in the *Mahāparinibbāna-suttānta* of the Pāli *Dīgha-nikāya*, the Buddha, giving final instructions, told the gathering that after his passing, the Dharma and Vinaya which he had taught would be their Teacher.[34] Thus this corpus, the Dharma-Vinaya, would be the "teacher" only metaphorically, because it was understood to be the topic of study. However, the Dharma-Vinaya (although composed of words) was silent: it never said a word, never explained itself. This was eventually personified as the "static Buddha" in Yamaguchi's book.[35] However, Mahāyāna Buddhism arose to explain it and thus devised two bodies, the Saṃbhoga-kāya and the Nirmāṇa-kāya, the so-called "dynamic Buddha."

Of course, the Buddha did preach in words. In fact, he taught continuously; and much of what he taught is preserved in the old Buddhist canon, the four Pāli Nikāyas, and the four Chinese Āgamas. The Buddha, while a Bodhisattva, had engaged in many difficult practices and later uttered difficult doctrines—but this happened in the real world, amidst the beings who live and die.

Some Western expounders of Mahāyāna Buddhism speak about Prajñāpāramitā Buddhism as though it were the voidness (*śūnyatā*) —which they render as "emptiness"—devoid of all the best aspects. After all, it is this very author Śāntideva—the one

[33]For the Saṃbhoga-kāya and Nirmāṇa-kāya as teachers, cf. *Mkhas grub rje's Fundamentals of the Buddhist Tantras*, Chapter One.

[34]*The Dīghanikāya* (2. Mahā vagga) (Bihar, 1958), p. 118.15-16.

[35]SUSUMU YAMAGUCHI, *Dynamic Buddha and Static Buddha* (Tokyo, 1958).

who composed the *Bodhicaryāvatāra* that inspired Yamaguchi's somewhat sensational book—who also composed the *Śikṣāsamuccaya* citing the *Ārya-Ratnacūḍaparipṛcchā* about the voidness possessed of all the best aspects. So Śāntideva, if one will read him further, provided the solution to the problem.

The Prajñāpāramitā scripture *Aṣṭasāhasrikā* is a profound work; and it does not help to understand it to translate the term "*prajñāpāramitā*" as the "perfection of wisdom." According to the teacher Asaṅga, man has a native uncultured form of *prajñā*, which certainly is not "wisdom," otherwise why need culture it through the three forms called in Sanskrit *śrutamayī prajñā*, *cintāmayī prajñā*, and *bhāvanāmayī prajñā*, or try to get it to the perfection (*pāramitā*)! So also the future Buddha Gautama is held to have said according to the Mahāyāna biography *Lalitavistara:* "Alas, O charioteer, for the unawaking discrimination of the childish person" (*dhik sārathe abudha bālajanasya buddhiḥ*).[36]

Thus the problem of whether the Buddha "saved" any beings became more confused when persons writing on the topic did not even know the meaning of the main terms.

Transfer of the salvific activity

As though to underline a conclusion that the Buddha's teaching of the Path—valuable as this is—did not constitute "saving" as later followers of this religion would prefer it, there arose other deities to do this job. Thus, there was the Buddha Amitābha or Amitāyus whose "heaven" is called Sukhāvatī, along with scriptures followed by the Chinese and Japanese Buddhists for many centuries. Then in Northern India there arose the cult of the goddess Tārā (the Savioress), popular in Nepal, Tibet, and Mongolia. Twenty-one forms of this deity are presented at the close of this volume. There were other deities too.

In Japan the name Amitābha occurred as Amita or Amida. In the classic of Shin Buddhism, the *Kyogyoshinsho*, we read:[37]

Now the Buddha Meditation Samadhi is the truly superb and

[36] Franklin Edgerton, *Buddhist Hybrid Sanskrit Reader* (Delhi, 1978) p. 14.

[37] Kosho Yamamoto, tr., *The Kyogyishinsho* (Tokyo, 1958), p. 41.

> wonderful gate. With His name as vowed in the forty-eight vows, Amita Buddha, with the vow's power, saves all beings, ...Oh how great! The Law of Thusness that is one with reason is one. It saves and benefits men. This is so because the vows are different. Our Śākyamuni answered the call and took birth in this defiled world and Amita Buddha appeared in the Pure Land. Places differ like as the defiled world and the Pure Land, but salvation is one. It is easy to practice and easy to attain, for truly this is the Way of the Pure Land School.

So the historical Buddha Śākyamuni took birth in this defiled world and announced the difficult practice, because such was his vow; while the Buddha Amitābha stayed in the Pure Land, the Western paradise, and announced the easy practice, because such was his vow. But salvation is one.

Turning to the Goddess Tārā, there are the praises of the White Tārā by Dge-'dun-grub (posthumously the First Dalai Lama), including this:

> I bow to Thee the virtuous Mother of Buddhas
> of the three ages, who protects against all dangers
> such as lion, elephant, fire, poison, snakes; with your
> left hand holding a blue lotus (*utpala*) and making the
> gesture of the "giving of protection."
> I bow to Thee, the locus of all protection, she who guides all beings to the great-ecstasy city of liberation by means of eyes borne on the palms of hands and soles of feet that are the four gates of liberation of voidness and so on.
> I worship Thee who is adorned on the head with Amitāyus, the Lord who mindfully confers long life and knowledge, and who holds the vessel full of immortality nectar.
> I bow to Thee who confers occult powers as desired like immortal life, knowledge, and merit, simply by (our) reciting such incantations as "Tāre."

Those are verses from Dge-'dun-grub's lovely work.[38] By the "Tāre" incantation he means *oṃ tāre tuttāre ture svāhā*, the ten-syllabled evocation of the goddess Tārā. Ratnākaraśānti explains the formula as *Oṃ*, the seed knowledge made clear at the

[38] I translated this work in 1970 while staying in Dharmsala, H. P. India.

end with *svāhā*. Then "Tāre" (O Tārā, who rescues by bringing to the other side—the *pāramitā*); "Tuttāre" (O rescuer from suffering); "Ture" (O Turā, the fast one, who rescues speedily.)[39]

Amitābha and Tārā were not the only deities appealed to. There were the Medicine Buddha (Bhaiṣajya-guru) and the great Bodhisattvas like Avalokiteśvara and Mañjuśrī. It is not necessary to cite more verses, which so often were fashioned with beautiful phraseology. The situation is clear enough. The devotees expected these deities to supply very human wants and fulfil aspirations. In return the devotees supplied all the finances and wherewithal for splendid temples and art in Asia. This does not mean that Śākyamuni was forgotten in the shuffle. He is always there or far off, sometimes shadowy or coming back into focus.

[39]See Chapter 22.

2

ANCIENT BUDDHIST MONASTICISM*

INTRODUCTION

There have been many studies of Buddhist monasticism, oriented both to the ancient forms and to modern features in certain Buddhist countries of Asia and South-east Asia. Many of these studies have been prepared by fine scholars. It is impossible to deal with the manifold aspects in one paper. So the present writer restricts the topic, first of all, to the ancient period, while stressing those particular aspects as appear to be of vital concern in all periods. It is well to admit that there are a number of disputed points in regard to the ancient form of Buddhism portrayed in this paper, and to mention that this writer will not shirk the responsibility when such points deserve fair appraisal and conclusions. In the first part, emphasizing the Prātimokṣa, Vinītadeva's commentary on the Vinaya is employed to suggest a new rendition for the term; the theory of two oral traditions—Vinaya and Dharma—is combined with a division into two Prātimokṣa-s to advance a position that various Vinaya lineages were in Buddhism from the beginning and that the separation into Buddhist sects was due to doctrinal and not Vinaya disagreements. In the second part, emphasizing the monastery inhabitants, there is exposition of well-established facts of monastery life with a comparison to the Brahmanical "stages of life." In the third part, emphasizing the offences, only some of the pre-

*Abbreviations: P. for Pāli language; S. for Sanskrit language; *JBRS* for *The Journal of the Bihar Research Society;* PTT for Peking Tibetan Tripiṭaka, the Japanese photographic reproduction of the Peking Tibetan canon.

vious scholarly findings can be presented. There are a number of selections from Asaṅga's *Yogācārabhūmi*, which appears not to have been utilized by other Western specialists in the topics of this paper.

I. Some early Religious of India, the term Prātimokṣa, Vinaya beginnings

At the time of the Buddha (6th - 5th centuries, B.C.) there were various religious orders, with names that were sometimes obscure in later times. The main classification seems to be into *brāhmaṇa* and *śramaṇa*, with both including the wanderers (*parivrājaka*).[1] While these words were not always used with the same meaning, it appears that the term *brāhmaṇa* stood for persons adhering to the Vedic religion, and who sooner or later would follow four stages of life; and that the *śramaṇas* were ascetic orders. Asaṅga provides a more detailed breakdown: "There are six kinds of persons, as follows: (1) the ascetic (*śramaṇa*), (2) the *brahmaṇa*, (3) the chaste person (*brahmacārin*), (4) the monk (*bhikṣu*), (5) the restrainer (*yati*), (6) the one gone forth (to the religious life) (*pravrājita*)." In further detailing, Asaṅga gives four kinds of ascetics: a. the one victorious over the path (*mārgajina*), who is the Sugata, having achieved, without remainder, the extirpation of lust, hatred, and delusion; b. the teacher of the path (*mārgadeśika*); c. the one who lives by the path, who has entered the stream, etc. (*mārgajīvin*); d. the one who insults the path (*mārgadūṣin*).[2]

Since in the Buddhist religious way, the one gone forth to the religious life (*pravrājita*) and the one called "monk" (*bhikṣu*) had to sever previous social relations and enter into a monasterial situation living with other novices and monks, rules had to be devised both for their daily conduct within the monastery and for their encounters with the lay community, as when seeking alms. The various prohibitions and other rules are in the code called P. *Pātimokkha*-or S. *Prātimokṣa-sūtra*. This contains some one hundred fifty rules called "points of instruction" (P. *sikhāpada*,

[1]Cf. B. C. Law, "A Short Account of the Wandering Ascetics (Parivrājakas) in India in the sixth Century, B.C." *JBRS*, LIII, i-iv, 1967, pp. 17-26.

[2]Alex Wayman, *Analysis of the Śrāvakabhūmi Manuscript* (University of California Press, Berkeley, 1961), p. 103.

S. *śikṣāpada*) emphasizing prohibitions, which are roughly the same in various forms of this Vinaya (discipline) work (some only extant in Chinese translation) that have been handed down; along with extra rules called P. *sekhiya dhamma*, S. *śaikṣa-dharma*, emphasizing positive rules of deportment, which differ considerably in number and kind in the various Vinayas.

Since in the Buddha's lifetime a nun order was started, it was necessary at that early date to make up a separate *Pātimokkha* for the nun, dropping some of the monk rules and adding a further set, especially to define the nun's conduct toward a monk and her attire.

The *Pātimokkha* was rehearsed along with scriptures at the bimonthly meetings of the ordained monks in a meeting called in P. Uposatha ("well-being"), namely on full moon and new moon days, which are traditional days in India picked for festivals. These are the two days, P. Cātuddasī, the 14th day in a lunar fortnight of decreasing phase (= first day of disappearance of the moon), and P. Paṇṇarasī, full moon day. The way it works out according to one explanation is that in the four months of a season, the 3rd and 7th meetings are Cātuddasī, and the others, 1st , 2nd, 4th, 5th, 6th, and 8th are Paṇṇarasī. Hence, most of the Uposatha meetings were on a full-moon day.[3]

The term "Pātimokkha" has been much discussed, and its meaning disputed. Of course, the observance of the prohibitions and precepts of the *Pātimokkha* is independent of knowing the derivation of the term. When the Buddhist Vinayas were translated into Chinese principally in the 5th century, A.D. , there was a difficulty in interpreting the S. "Prātimokṣa." The translators either transcribed the term phonetically or else translated it as though it read Prātimokṣa, with *prati*-understood in the distributive sense ("each one") and *mokṣa* of course rendered as "liberation."[4] This rendition appears to agree with avoiding the prohibited elements of the list, confessing each one as was com-

[3]C. S. Upasak, *Dictionary of Early Buddhist Monastic Terms* (Bharati Prakashan, Varanasi, 1975), pp. 52-53.

[4]My wife (who is Japanese) has read for me the entries on the term in the Buddhist dictionaries by Ono, Hakuju Ui, and Hajime Nakamura; and all sources agree that when the term was translated into Chinese it was always with this distributive meaning of *prati-*, although there are differing interpretations of this distributive meaning "each one."

mitted, and, when indicated, making amends by penance. When the Vinaya was translated into Tibetan starting in the early 9th century, A.D., the term was uniformly rendered as *so sor thar pa*, which understands the distributive sense of *prati-* in agreement with the Chinese translations. When in the 19th century the Pāli scriptures began to be translated into English, an interpretation was made that the term Pātimokkha should be understood with the short *a*, and that P. *pati* (= S. *prati*) should be taken in the "against" sense; and since "against liberation" entails a bond, the translators with this persuasion decided on the rendition "obligation" and have been using this regularly.[5] This rendition appears to agree with the obligation of the monks to recite the list at the Uposatha and to abide by the pronouncements within the text. Of course, these translators knew of the gloss (to be explained below) on the term found in the Vinaya exegesis called *Mahāvagga: pātimokkham ti ādiṃ etaṃ, mukhaṃ etaṃ, pamukhaṃ etaṃ kusalānaṃ dhammānam, tena vuccati p.*[6] It is easy to misunderstand this and think it is a false etymology[7] and so should be disregarded.[8] The reason I am led away from the false-etymology theory is my having found in Vinītadeva's commentary on the *Mūlasarvāstivāda Vinayavibhaṅga* the saying, *so sor thar pa źes bya ba ni daṅ por thar pa'o.*[9] This comment, taking *prātimokṣa* as equivalent to *ādimokṣa* ("liberation at the beginning, *āditas*"), is grammatically justified by understanding *prātimokṣa = pra + atimokṣa.* See Speijer: "The *upasara 'pra'* has sometimes the power of denoting the beginning of the action," citing *Kāś* on P. 1, 2, 21 for the term *pradyotitaḥ* ("He commenced to shine").[10] Now *atimokṣa* is a pre-Buddhist term found in the *Śatapatha-Brahmaṇa*, 14, 6, 1, 8, with identical

[5]Cf. *The Pāli Text Society's Pali-English Dictionary*, ed. by T. W. RHYS DAVIDS and WILLIAM STEDE (The Pali Text Society, London, 1952 reprint), Part V (P-Ph.), p. 73.

[6]*Mahāvagga* (Oldenberg edition), II, 3, 4.

[7]More recently, J. W. DE JONG, review, CHARLES S. PREBISH, *Buddhist Monastic Discipline*, in *Indo-Iranian Journal*, 19 (1977), p. 127.

[8]But this is no excuse for Nathmal Tatia to omit the line from his edition of the *Mahāvagga* in Saṃkhitta-piṭakaṃ, Vol. I (Nava Nālandā Mahāvihāra, 1975), p. 71, circa line 11.

[9]PTT, Vol. 122, p. 304-1-1.

[10]J. S. SPEIJER, *Sanskrit Syntax* (Reprint, Kyoto, 1968), Para. 309, p. 232; here *pra-* is prefixed to the verb.

passage in *Bṛhadāraṇyaka-Upaniṣad*,3.1, 6,[11] and which was presumably replaced in later Sanskrit with the term *mokṣa*. Hence, Vinītadeva's comment—possibly repeated in his Vinaya lineage for a thousand years[12]—understands the term *prātimokṣa* to mean "commencement of liberation," which can be rendered more neatly, "liberation-onset." Now we can return to the *Mahāvagga* gloss (above cited) to render it with fidelity: "As to the 'Pātimokkha,'[13] it is the beginning (*ādi*), *to wit*, it is the orifice (*mukha*) and it is the commencement (S. *pramukha*) of the virtuous natures (S. *dharma*); therefore, one says, 'Liberation-Onset.' "[14]

Furthermore, there is a canonical passage supporting the above conclusion. This is in the *Aṅguttara-nikāya* (Book of Fives), *Rājavagga*, the *Yassamdisam-sutta*. Here a Kṣatriya king is said to have five salient points wherever he abides: (1) being well-born through his father and mother; (2) having bountiful treasuries; (3) mighty through his army; (4) having a wise minister; (5) abiding where he has conquered. The monk also is said to have five comparable salient points wherever he abides. As to the first point, "in that a monk has morality, dwells restrained by the Pātimokkhasaṃvara,...[and so on, much like a *Dīgha-nikāya* passage cited below]—he has the perfection of birth like the consecrated Kṣatriya king." Since the taking of the Pātimokkhasaṃvara (see below) is likened to an illustrious birth, this

[11]Reference from BÖHTLINGK and ROTH *Sanskrit-Wörterbuch* (reprint of Meicho-Fukyū-Kai, Tokyo, 1976).

[12]RANIERO GNOLI, *The Gilgit Manuscript of the Saṅghabhedavastu*, part I (Istituto Italiano per il Medio ed Estremo Oriente, Roma, 1977), General Introduction, p. xix, decides that the compilation of the Mūlasarvāstivāda Vinaya dates back to the times of Kaniṣka, Of course, the content would frequently go back to much earlier times.

[13]AKIRA HIRAKAWA, *A Study of the Vinaya-Piṭaka* (Sankibo-Busshorin, Tokyo, 1970) [in Japanese with a summary including table of contents in English], p. 419, points out that Buddhaghosa in his Vinaya commentary *Kankhāvitaraṇī* analyzed "Pātimokkha" into pa+ita mokkha, understood as "especially excellent liberation." Thus, P. *pa*-S. *pra* was understood only by its classical meaning.

[14]There still remains the problem of why the words *mukha*, *pamukha* were chosen for the gloss. The author of the *Mahāvagga* may have intended, while the words can signify in the manner of my rendition, to have also suggested the "facing" or confrontation as happens in the confessional part of the Pātimokkha, as will be pointed out later in this essay.

supports the rendition "Liberation-Onset.": this onset is a birth in the inner precincts of Buddhism, so the monastic followers were called *samaṇā Sakyaputtiyā*, "ascetics who are sons of the Buddha."[15]

The *Dīgha-nikāya* passage (I, 62) that should now be mentioned is from the well-known scripture *Sāmañña-phala-sutta*:

> When the ascetic (S. *śramaṇa*) has thus gone forth (S. *pravrajita*) he dwells restrained by the Pātimokkhasaṃvara (S. Prātimokṣa-saṃvara). He has the perfection of good behavior and of lawful resort (*ācāragocarasampanna*), views fearfully even the minor things to be avoided. He rightfully takes and learns the "points of instruction" (S. *śikṣāpada*), while accompanied by virtuous acts of body and virtuous acts of speech. With pure livelihood and equipped with morality, he guards the sense doors, accompanied by mindfulness and awareness. He is happy.

This brings up the important expression "Pātimokkhasaṃvara." Here *saṃvara* means a "vow," the solemn promise.[16] As used here, it does not mean "restraint," but conveys the sense of "holding together," i.e. adhering in the stream of consciousness; because a vow is not to be forgotten. The phrase "while accompanied by virtuous acts of body and virtuous acts of speech" raises the question: Why not by virtuous acts of mind, since Buddhism speaks of ten paths of *karma*, three of body, four of speech, and three of mind? This makes up ten, a typical number of the Buddhist Vinaya code. However, morality (*śīla*) *per se* amounts to the seven abstinences, i.e. from the three bad acts of body and four bad acts of speech;[17] so the number seven also is important for Vinaya theory, but detailed variously, as in the citation below. The *Aṅguttara-nikāya* (Book of Sevens, *Vinayavagga*) states that when a monk is possessed of seven natures (*dhamma*), he is a Vinayadhāra (holder, or retainer of the Buddhist discipline, Vinaya), as follows:

15Cf. I. B. Horner, tr. *The Book of Discipline* Vol. I (Suttavibhaṅga) (London, 1949), translator's introduction, p. lii.

16The term *saṃvara* is translated into Tibetan by *sdom pa;* and in this language there are *Sdom gsum* books on the "three vows," namely, the Prātimokṣa, the Bodhisattva, and the Mantra vows.

17Cf. Dipakkumar Barua, *An analytical Study of the four Nikāyas* (Rabindra Bharati University, Calcutta, 1971), pp. 128-129.

> He knows what is a transgression (*āpatti*) and knows what is not. He knows what is a light (*lahuka*) transgression; he knows what is a grave (*garuka*) one. You should know (*kho*) that when both Pātimokkhas are well-handed to him *in extenso,* well-analyzed (*suvibhatta*), well set-in-motion (*suppavatti*), well-determined (*suvinicchita*) according to scripture and according to *anuvyañjana* (? commentary)—having trained, then at will, easily, without trouble, he attains and dwells in the four Jhānas (the four S. *dhyānas* of the Realm of Form), derived from mentals, a comfortable state in the present life; and having extinguished the fluxes, (he attains and dwells) in the liberation of mind (*cetas*) and liberation of insight (*pañña*) which are nonfluxional; and in this life realizes for himself.

While it is not clear how one divides up this passage to get the number seven, the important thing is that the commentary—presumably Buddhaghosa's—cited in Hare's translation (the above is my own), *The Book of Sevens*, says that the expression "both Pātimokkhas" means "of monk and nun." Previously, we observed that the monk and nun have each a Pātimokkha list.[18] However, this interpretation does not appear to fit in the context referring to a monk, not a particular nun (although a nun can also be a Vinayadhāra). Therefore, we may well presume that "both Pātimokkhas" refer to an alternate classification, namely, two kinds of recitation of Pātimokkha: by exhortation (*ovāda*) and by command (*āṇā*).[19] A certain Chinese Vinaya commentary has considerable information about these two Pātimokkhas.[20] We learn that the former Buddhas and then Śākyamuni himself recited only the Pātimokkha of exhortation, such as the lines, "abstain from all kinds of evil; accumulate all that is good;" while the monks (and nuns) only recited the Pātimokkha of command, which is the code recited during the Uposatha. The Buddha announced: "The Tathāgata cannot recite the Pātimokkha at the time of the Uposatha in a congregation

[18]E. M. Hare, tr., *The Book of the Gradual Sayings* (*Aṅguttara-Nikāya*) Vol. IV (London, 1955 reprint), p. 95, n.

[19]Cf. Upasak, *Dictionary*, p. 152.

[20]P. V. Bapat and A. Hirakawa, trs., *Shan-Chien-P'i-P'o-Sha; a Chinese version by Saṅghabhadra of Samantapāsādikā* (Bhandarkar Oriental Research Institute, Poona, 1970), pp. 134-136.

which is not pure." For the Buddhas "know with their own minds the minds of their followers and then instructed them." That is to say, the Buddha knew with superhuman vision the minds of the persons assembled for the Pātimokkha-recitation; but the monks themselves are not able to assess their fellows by this supernormal faculty: they have to rely upon the more obvious acts of body and speech which define "morality" for them. Hence the distinction: the monks will concern themselves in the Pātimokkha of the Uposatha with "morality" in the meaning of the seven abstinences, among others;[21] while the Buddha will do the exhortation which requires knowing the minds of others.

Let us try out the new rendition of the term "Pātimokkha" in two important passages of the scripture "Upāli and the Pātimokkha" (from the *Aṅguttara-nikāya*, Book of Tens):

> In consideration of what purpose were the "points of instruction" prescribed for the disciples (S. *śrāvaka*) by the Tathāgata and the *Liberation-Onset* recited? (Upāli is told, in consideration of ten purposes, to wit:) For the excellence of the Congregation (Saṃgha); for the well-being of the Congregation; for chastising errant persons; for the comfort of the virtuous monks; to restrain the (defiled) fluxes (*āsrava*) of the present life; to prevent the (defiled) fluxes in the future life; to instill faith in those of scarce faith; to promote even more those with faith; to establish the illustrious Dharma; to assist the Vinaya.

Then Upāli asked in what circumstances the *Liberation-Onset* is suspended, i.e. recitation of it postponed; and was told there are ten such, to wit:

> When a "defeated" person is seated in that assembly; when talk of whether one is "defeated" is not finished; when an unordained person is seated in that assembly; when talk of whether one is unordained is not finished; when a person who has repudiated the instruction is seated in that assembly; when talk of whether one has repudiated is not finished; when a eunuch is seated in that assembly; when talk of whether one is a eunuch is not finished; when a seducer of a

[21]Three offences of body and four of speech (as the ten paths of *karma* has it) is not the only classification; cf. BAPAT and HIRAKAWA, *Shan-Chien-P'i-P'o-Sha*, pp. 535-536, for allusion to the Vinaya breakdown of the numbers.

nun is seated in that company; when talk of whether one is a nun-seducer is not finished.

The meaning of "defeated" will be explained later. Meanwhile we observe that the circumstances for suspension of the recitation are in terms of acts of body and speech, as was mentioned previously.

There is little doubt that both kinds of Pātimokkha, i.e. of exhortation and of command, were in existence at the time of the Buddha; although the now extant forms of the Pātimokkha (the "command" kind) in the sense of a text may not be exactly the original one that the monks recited in the Buddha's time, even leaving out the set of Śaikṣa (precept) rules. It has been noticed by scholars that each of the main Vinayas of Buddhist sects had its own *Prātimokṣa-sūtra.*[22] This need not be attributed to a single reason. The fact of different Vinayas has in the past been deemed intimately bound up with the division of the Buddhists into different sects, involving difficult historical matters of what are called the Buddhist Councils. According to Buddhist traditions, the First Council at Rājagaha (S. Rājagṛha), held in the year after the Buddha's passing, rehearsed the Sūtra division according to Ānanda's memory and the Vinaya division according to Upāli's memory. Later, a third division called Abhidharma was added—the three called *tripiṭaka,* often rendered the "Three Baskets." The Second Council, held under the sponsorship of king Kālāśoka about 110 years after the Buddha, concerned the errant Vajjian monks at Vaiśālī who were committing some or all of ten prohibited things, including No. 10, the receiving of gold and silver. It is generally conceded now

22As E. FRAUWALLNER, *The Earliest Vinaya and the Beginnings of Buddhist Literature* (Is. M.E.O., Roma, 1956), pp. 1-2, points out, Vinayas of these schools are preserved: Sarvāstivādin, Dharmaguptaka, Mahīśāsaka, and Mahāsāṃghika in Chinese translation; Pāli school in original Pāli; Mūlasarvāstivādin in Chinese and Tibetan translations. Cf. ETIENNE LAMOTTE, *Histoire du bouddhisme indien* (Louvain, 1958), pp. 181-193, for structure and analysis of the Vinayapiṭaka. Cf. W. PACHOW and RAMAKANTA MISHRA, *The Prātimokṣa-sūtra of the Mahāsāṅghikas* (Ganganatha Jha Research Institute, Allahabad, 1956), pp. 15-22, for concordance tables of several *Prātimokṣa-sūtra,* showing their almost complete agreement, except for the Śaikṣa-dharmas. Cf. HIRAKAWA, *A Study* (n. 13, above), English summary, pp. 15-18, for his conclusions about various *Prātimokṣa-sūtra-s.*

that while earlier (or at this time or later) the Buddhist Sāṃgha (congregation of monks) divided into the Mahāsāṃghika and Sthavira, the Mahāsāṃghika group of monks were not themselves guilty of the ten prohibited things. But that the division was over the errant monks and so is placeable at this time is not necessarily the implication of the Pāli Vinaya text called *Cullavagga*, in its Chap. XII (Oldenberg edition) devoted to this Council of Vaiśālī. While discussing individually the commission of the ten prohibited things, the authors included in the list two items suggesting a rival Uposatha.[23] This appears to have been a defiant act on the part of the errant monks, rather than the independent Uposatha by a separate well-established Buddhist sect. The *Cullavagga* account stops with saying the ten disputed points were brought up at a duly organized Sāṃgha meeting and does not mention the outcome. However, the Mūlasarvāstivāda Vinaya account, as we know from the Tibetan tradition which has only this Vinaya, holds that the errant monks were ejected from the Sāṃgha.[24] The "five theses of Mahādeva"[25] downgrading the "Arhat," about 137 years after the Buddha, could well be the cause of doctrinal splits in Buddhism but hardly capable of generating another Vinaya. Hence, the existence of multiple Vinayas in connection with sectarian splits has been a mystery that attracted various scholarly researches and speculations. Our previous findings suggest that Demiéville has been on the right track in stressing two oral traditions, that of the Vinaya-dharas and the Dharma-dharas, where Dharma really means the *sūtra* class, first gathered by Ānanda.[26] Combining

[23]For the first item, cf. *Cullavagga*, tr. by RHYS DAVIDS and OLDENBERG, *Sacred Books of the East*, Vol. 20, p. 410 (for XII, 2, 8): " 'Is it allowable, Lord, for a number of Bhikkhus who dwell within the same circuit, within the same boundary, to hold separate Uposatha?' 'No, Sir, it is not allowable." '

[24]As one Tibetan source, cf. *Mkhas grub rje's Fundamentals of the Buddhist Tantras*, tr. by FERDINAND D. LESSING and ALEX WAYMAN (Mouton, The Hague, 1968), pp. 63-67.

[25]For a comparison of different textual traditions of the five theses, cf. JANICE J. NATTIER and CHARLES S. PREBISH, "Mahāsāṃghika Origins: The Beginnings of Buddhist Sectarianism," *History of Religions* 16:3, Feb. 1977, pp. 250-257. But the exposition of the present paper does not allow me to accept the conclusions of these writers in their attempt (cf. their p. 238) to fix the schism at year 116 after Buddha and due to a Vinaya quarrel.

[26]Cf. PAUL DEMIÉVILLE, "A propos du Concile de Vaiśālī," *T'oung Pao*,

this with the thesis of two Pātimokkhas, one the Buddha's exhortations and the other the instruction of morality preserved in the Vinaya recited in the Uposatha, a distinct possibility of some of the divergent Vinaya traditions having been in Buddhism from the beginning emerges. Such is the implication of an alternate tradition that not much credence was perhaps hitherto given by reason of obviously faulty features, namely, that the Scripture was recited in four different languages, Sanskrit, Apabhraṃśa, Prakrit, and Paiśācika, accounting for four basic divisions—Mūlasarvāstivādin, using Sanskrit, descended from the son Rāhula; the Mahāsāṃghika, using Apabhraṃśa, descended from Mahākāśyapa; the Saṃmatīya, using Paiśācī, descended from Upāli; and the Sthavira, using Prakrit, descended from Katyāyana.[27] Of course, the sectarian divisions cannot be properly attributed to these dialect differences. Even so, the seemingly arbitrary associations of this tradition are suggestive.[28]

According to Edgerton,[29] the Buddha had allowed and perhaps urged the monk-teachers to preach the scriptures in their own dialects so as to bring the Buddhist teachings to the widest audience. Later King Aśoka sponsored a council in which the scriptures were collected and an attempt made to homogenize them, with perhaps the Māgadha type taken as the basis; and from the homogenization resulted the sacerdotal language of Pāli. This is what the above-mentioned tradition calls Prakrit, claimed to descend from Katyāyana. At about this time, or

Vol. 40, 1951, p. 254, n., mentioning that the compounds *dharma-vinaya* and *sūtra-vinaya* (of course, meaning the same: *dharma*=*sūtra*, and *vinaya*) are frequent in the accounts of the Council of Vaiśālī; and pp. 260-261, agreeing with N. Dutt, *Early Monastic Buddhism*, on the important distinction *dhammadhara* and *vinayadhara*, retainers of the *dhamma* (S. *dharma*) and retainers of the *vinaya*.

27As one Tibetan source, cf. *Mkhas grub rje's Fundamentals* (n. 24, above), pp. 67-69.

28Cf. Lin Li-Kouang, *L'Aide-Mémoire de la Vraie Loi* (Adrien-Maisonneuve, Paris, 1949), pp. 194-228, for a lengthy discussion of these matters; but his sources make somewhat different correlations between schools and languages. As we shall see, this difference, per se, does not matter much: the main thing is that such correlations are made at all.

29Franklin Edgerton, *Buddhist Hybrid Sanskrit Grammar and Dictionary*; Vol. I: Grammar (Motilal Banarsidass, Delhi, 1978), pp. 1-2.

perhaps later, the canon was also rendered into Sanskrit, and this is the language of both the Sarvāstivādin and Mūlasarvāstivādin, supposedly descended from the son Rāhula. But it appears now that the attempt to create a Middle Indic canon in a Prakrit form or the Sanskrit canon of the scriptures was done either with an exemption or a compromise that it would not extend to the Vinaya, the disciplinary code. Hence, the various forms of the *Prātimokṣa-sūtra*. For the other two, first take the Mahāsāṃghika, said to have used Apabhraṃśa and to have descended from Mahākāśyapa. It is of interest that the Vinaya of the Lokottaravādin sect of the Mahāsāṃghika, preserved under the title *Mahāvastu*, uses a kind of language that Edgerton calls "Buddhist Hybrid Sanskrit" and includes in the earliest form of this mixed language. This is not how the word Apabhraṃśa ("fallen-off language") is used nowadays, but conceivably it applies to the language of the *Mahāvastu*. The last one mentioned, the Saṃmatīya, is attributed a dialect called Paiśācī[30] and said to descend from Upāli. This suggests a confused association of names and is hardly identifiable with the remaining extant Vinayas, those of the Dharmaguptaka and the Mahīśāsaka; and it is dubious that Upāli, the great Vinaya-dhara of early Buddhism, would be more associated with a tradition leading to these Vinayas than to the others. This alternate tradition is obviously too neat, with its fourfold description, to suit what is probably a complicated situation. In any case, the partial truth of this tradition cannot account for the doctrinal divisions among the Buddhists: it rather points, albeit confusedly, to a diversity of Vinaya lineages.

It appears then that the division into Buddhist sects, said in some accounts to have amounted to eighteen, is an independent matter from multiple Vinayas; and this lends credence to the position Bareau has argued at length, attributing the initial split to Mahādeva's five theses, which were of doctrinal nature.[31] The

[30]For locales of this dialect, cf. MAURICE WINTERNITZ, *A History of Indian Literature*, Vol. II: Buddhist Literature and Jaina Literature (English translation) (MLBD Delhi, 1980), p. 604.

[31]ANDRÉ BAREAU, *Les premiers conciles bouddhiques* (Presses Universisitaires de France, Paris, 1955), p. 89, by deciding in favor of the date circa 137 after Buddha for the schism, effectively separates the consideration from the Council of Vaiśālī. After careful consideration of the various factors, he

fact of having a slightly different Vinaya—different not by reason of the basic monk and nun prohibitions, but by extra precepts and varying amplitude of associated legends and later of Jātakas (previous-birth stories of the Buddha)—cannot be judged the source of sectarian splits along doctrinal lines unless these doctrinal divisions had somehow invaded one or more of the Vinayas. For the early period there is no evidence of this at all. When we come to the *Mahāvastu* (as a sub-sect Vinaya of the Mahāsāṃghika), we do see some doctrinal intrusion, for example, the early Mahāyāna Buddhist theory of ten Bodhisattva stages; but this text *Mahāvastu* is assembled perhaps five hundred years after Buddha, long after all the old Buddhist councils. Frauwallner's conclusion about the old Skandhaka text (which besides the details of monastic life contains all the legends, including biography of the Buddha) that "It must have been composed shortly before or after the second council," i.e. in the first half of the 4th cent., B.C.,[32] should be accepted. This is because the obviously great challenge to the Sāṃgha by the errant monks of Vaiśālī forced a stock-taking of legends; therefore, the organizers of the Second Council would be responsible for settling the form of the Skandhaka. However, if it is true that some other Vinaya lineages were present in Buddhism from the beginning, these lineages could continue, if not at Vaiśālī, then at Rājagṛha, and so on. That is why legends contained in Vinayas other than the Theravāda (descended from the Sthavira) might conceivably be different for having been accepted from Buddhist beginnings, or for having been added centuries later.

In the light of the preceding—in order to rationalize the Buddhist Vinaya history about the eighteen schools, especially the initial break that was between the groups called the Mahāsāṃghika and the Sthavira—we have simply to assume that the monks at Vaiśālī in a legal Uposatha rehearsed the Vinaya legends. And when the news reached Rājagṛha, this prompted similar rehearsals of legends, not in the spirit of rivalry with Vaiśālī but because it seemed a good thing to do. If some years

---

concludes (p. 109), among other things, that the schism between the Mahāsāṃghika and the Sthavira took place at Pāṭaliputra, capital of Magadha, over the five theses about the Arhat, that the King of Magadha vainly attempted to arbitrate the dispute.

[32]FRAUWALLNER, *The Earliest Vinaya* (n. 22, above), p. 67.

later there should be a divisive quarrel over the status of the Arhat (per the five points of Mahādeva), and the monks who accepted the five points could claim that there were more monks of this persuasion than on the other side, they could then begin to call themselves the Mahāsāṃghika (the great clergy). But this was not because their Vinaya was different in the essentials from the Vinaya of the Sthavira; nor did they differ in the main points of Buddhist doctrine, non-self, impermanence, suffering, dependent origination, and so on, from the other sect. However, the quarrel about the Arhat had profound implications for the theory of the Buddhist path and was later to inaugurate the great movement called Mahāyāna Buddhism. Such sectarian differences would eventually bring some differences in the associated legends of the school, simply because it was a different sect and therefore had differing ability to draw upon the old legends. In this light, while some doctrines—namely, those found in the Pāli canon of the four Nikāyas—are clearly earlier than others, say some of those found in Mahāyāna *sūtras*, it is uncertain to state such "earlier" or "later" in terms of Vinaya legends. As an indication of this, even for the meaning of the term Pātimokkha, I resorted to the Vinaya tradition of the Mūlasarvāstivāda, i.e. Vinītadeva's commentary on its *Vinayavibhaṅga*—which some scholars think arose many centuries after the Theravāda—while specialists in the Vinaya preserved in the Pāli language were unable to come up with such an explanation.

II. The Monastery and Persons in it

Since the monk and nun had to leave home and to give up layman's money transactions, from the beginning there had to be dwellings set aside for such persons, either supported by the community of lay followers or else self-supporting.[33] In India the Buddhist monastery was usually called a *vihāra*,[34] which can also

[33]In the case of Indian and Chinese Buddhist institutions, one may refer to Andre Bareau, "Indian and Ancient Chinese Buddhisme: Institutions Analogous to Jisa," *Comparative Studies in Society and History*, III: 4, July 1961, pp. 443-451; and in the case of Himalayan area and Mongolian institutions, to Robert J. Miller, "Buddhist Monastic Economy: the Jisa Mechanism," in *ibid.*, III: 4, July 1961, pp. 427-438.

[34]See Dipak Kumar Barua, *Vihāras in Ancient India* (Indian Publications, Calcutta, 1969).

mean schools in the monastery.[35] It was also called *saṅghārāma*.[36] This led to the idea of the monastery boundary (*sīmā*); and in various times, places in India and in other countries to which Buddhism travelled, this "boundary" was defined and marked in various ways, by rivers, mounds, walls, etc.[37]

These monasteries were usually on the outskirts of the city, since there are many references in Buddhist stories to the monks rising early, donning religious garb, and going into the nearby city to seek alms. Sometimes the monk cells were cut out of the rock, and there are notable remains of such places in India.[38] The first large Buddhist monastery within a city seems to have been the Jetavana in a park at Sāvatthī (S. Śrāvastī), due to the bounty of Anāthapiṇḍika (or Anāthapiṇḍada), and often mentioned as a place where the Buddha was staying when he preached such and such scripture.[39] That is to say, the Buddhist scriptures normally began: "Thus by me it was heard. The Buddha was dwelling at (such and such a *vihāra*, in or by such and such city)." There was an emphasis on learning in these monasteries, and certain ones grew to university stature, with courses on many topics besides the expected expositions on Buddhism. Probably the most famous one was the Nālandā University, which in an early stage was associated with the illustrious Nāgārjuna and Āryadeva, then developed and lasted through most of the first millenium, A.D.[40]

Relations with the civil authority differed in various times and places. For classical times, perhaps the best source of data has been China. Here we must content ourselves with two brief references. The fourth century, A.D., Buddhist leader Hui-yüan got his point across that the Buddhist monk need not show

[35]FRANKLIN EDGERTON, *Buddhist Hybrid Sanskrit: Grammar and Dictionary:* Vol. II: Dictionary (Motilal Banarsidass, 1968), p. 505.

[36]This term is much employed in H.D. SANKALIA, *The Nālandā University* (Oriental Publishers, Delhi, 1972).

[37]For various boundary-marks see BAPAT and HIRAKAWA, *Shan-Chien-P'i-P'o-Sha*, pp. 514-516.

[38]See, for example, BARUA, *Vihāras*, p. 20.

[39]For a brief account of this monastery, see G. P. MALALASEKERA, *Dictionary of Pāli Proper Names*, Vol. I (London, 1960), pp. 963-966.

[40]Cf. SANKALIA, *The Nālandā University*, Chap. II, Pt. II, "Transformation of 'Sanghārāmas' into Temples of Learning," pp. 26-35.

outer respect to secular authority.[41] But by the seventh century, admission to the priesthood was by public registration.[42]

For some generalities about the lay follower and the one in the monastic life, we turn to the teacher Asaṅga, referring to the teacher converting people to the Buddhist position and what the lay follower does in return:[43]

> What is dissemination of the preserved doctrines? That very person who has fully comprehended the Illustrious Doctrine informs people that there is good fortune and power in the direct perception of the Illustrious Doctrine. With precepts only as he has fully comprehended it and which are in conformity with it, he follows it in teaching and follows it in introducing (people). What is corresponding sympathy from others? "Others" means donors and patrons. They bring the conditions of things useful for living, as follows: religious garb, alms, bedding, seats, medicaments, and whatever utensils may be in point. One is shown sympathy by them.

Just as monks gain merit (*puṇya*) by their practices, so do the laity by their contributions of living materials for the monks, their adornments to the Buddhist structures called *stūpa*, and the like; they gain trusting faith (S. *prasāda*) in the three Jewels (Buddha, Dharma, Saṅgha) and plant the virtuous roots (*kuśala-mūla*) for appropriate results in future lives.[44]

Asaṅga tells how to differentiate the layman and the one gone into the religious life in terms of prevalent defilement:[45]

> Reflections (*vikalpa*), elaboration (*prapañca*), attachment (*saṅga*), and (mundane) ideas (*saṃjñā*) are four kinds of

[41]Cf. LEON HURVITZ, "'Render Unto Caesar' in Early Chinese Buddhism: Hui Yüan's Treatise on the Exemption of the Buddhist Clergy from the Requirements of Civil Etiquette," *Liebenthal Festschrift* (Santiniketan, India, 1957), pp. 1-36.

[42]J. TAKAKUSU, tr. *A Record of the Buddhist Religion by I-Tsing* (Munshiram Manoharlal, Delhi, 1966), p. 98.

[43]ALEX WAYMAN, *Calming the Mind and Discerning the Real;* Buddhist Meditation and the Middle View, from the *Lam rim chen mo* of Tsoṅ-kha-pa (Motilal Banarsidass, Delhi, 1979), p. 34, from Asaṅga's *Śrāvaka-bhūmi*.

[44]LOUIS RENOU, et al., *L'Inde Classique*, Tome II (École Francaise d'Extrême. Orient, Hanoi, 1953), p. 597.

[45]PTT, Vol. 111, p. 238-5-7, 8, in the *Paryāya-saṃgrahaṇī*.

defilements. The former two are on the side of the one in the religious life (*pravrajita*); the other two are on the side of the householder (*gṛhastha*). Those gone-forth have reflections from recalling experience of (mundane) sensory objects; and elaboration from that swaying addiction. The householders have attachment from living amidst (mundane) sensory objects; and (mundane) ideas resulting from adherence to attachment's sign-sources.

Asaṅga reveals the mind of the monk, his fixed ideas in five situations:[46]

(1) the idea when entering a city that one is entering a prison;
(2) when in the monastery, continually having the idea of the monk, e.g. "I have abandoned the home attire and adopted one of bad color, so am not 'good-looking,'" and so on. Twenty-two points were stated in the *sūtra*;[47]
(3) the idea of antidote to the sickness that is continually in food;
(4) the idea when in seclusion, that in regard to forms to be perceived by the eye, the sounds to be perceived by the ear, one is blind and deaf and dumb;
(5) the idea when lying down, that one has stretched out his hands and feet like the deer of the hermitage.

Asaṅga may perhaps speak more for himself than for the generality of monk and nun. There are of course a wide diversity of such persons, who ordinarily started out as a Buddhist layman —male, the *upāsaka*, or female, the *upāsikā*.

In the beginning the Buddha conferred the "going forth" (P. *pabbajjā*) ordination of the male novice (*śramaṇera*), perhaps the first female novice (*śramaṇerikā*), and postulants (*śikṣamānā*); and he conferred the "full ordination" (P. *upasampadā*) of the monks (*bhikṣu*) and perhaps the first of the nuns (*bhikṣuṇī*). But as Buddhism spread to other parts of India, it became necessary for qualified monks to be permitted to conduct these two kinds

[46]PTT, Vol. 111, p. 225-1-2, f., in the *Vinaya-saṃgrahaṇī*.

[47]Asaṅga's list is somewhat larger (his source unknown) than that of the Pāli Vinaya; cf. HORNER, tr. *The Book of Discipline*, Vol. I, p. 42, for the eighteen identifications of "monk." For extended explanations of the eighteen cf. BAPAT and HIRAKAWA, *Shan Chien-P'i-P'o-Sha*, pp. 178-183.

of ordination.[48] Perhaps this shift coincided with the event mentioned in this paper above when the Buddha stopped participating in the Uposatha, and there arose the distinction of two kinds of Pātimokkha. Since this might have led to a large number of unwarranted ordinations by a person seeking to build up a power center, it was prescribed that only a *bhikṣu* of ten years standing and of proven learning could confer the full ordination.[49] These wise rules helped to ensure the integrity of the Sāṃgha; and so, by and large, the main disputes between Buddhist sects in later times were over doctrinal rather than Vinaya matters.

Accordingly, there were different forms of ordination, mainly in terms of complexity. The ones conferred by the Buddha himself were the most simple.[50] The first, later called the *Pañcavargeṇagaṇena upasampadā,* was the ordination of the "fortunate band of five" in the episode of Sarnath; when seeing the Buddha coming from afar their own resolution was broken, and the monk marks—namely, the shaven head, begging bowl, and yellow monk garb—appeared upon them in a miraculous manner, and they became the first disciples.[51] The next one, apparently, is the *Ehi Bhikṣukāya upasampadā,* the "Come, O *bhikṣu!*" formula, addressed to the candidate for ordination. A third form is the *Saraṇāgamana upasampadā,* what is called the *Svam upasampadā,* done by the candidate himself, who first adopted the marks of a monk, shaven head, etc., and appearing before the Buddha thrice uttered, "I take my refuge in the Buddha, I take my refuge in the Dhamma, I take my refuge in the Sangha." But once the ordination process was turned over to the senior monks, a more elaborate procedure was required, involving a formal act of the Sāṃgha.[52] This formal ordination is called P. *Ñatti catutthakamma upasampadā* and S. *Jñapticaturthakarma upasampadā.*

[48]MADAN MOHAN SINGH, "Life in the Buddhist Monastery during the 6th Century B.C.," *JBRS,* XL, Pt. 2, June 1954, pp. 134-135.

[49]MADAN MOHAN SINGH, *ibid.,* p. 135.

[50]For the following names of various *upasampadā,* cf. B. JINANANDA, ed., *Upasampadājñaptiḥ,* Tibetan Sanskrit Works Series, Vol. VI (K. P. Jayaswal Research Institute, Patna, 1961), Introduction, p. 2.

[51]This story is part of the introduction to "The First Sermon" in both the *Mahāvastu* and *Lalitavistara;* cf. FRANKLIN EDGERTON, *Buddhist Hybrid Sanskrit Reader* (MLBD Delhi, 1978), pp. 17, 20.

[52]MADAN MOHAN SINGH, *op. cit.,* pp. 136-137.

As the nun order started later in the Buddha's pilgrimage, it appears that all nun ordinations—with the possible exception of the Buddha's aunt, the first Buddhist nun—took place through a formal Sāṃgha act; but because of certain differences from the monk ordination, it was given a different name, P. *Aṭṭhavācika upasampadā.*[53] There was much emphasis on seniority of "*bhikṣu*-becoming," with respectful devotion extended to the senior monks.

The age of entering the religious life in different countries, where Buddhism established itself with the Sāṃgha, has a lower limit at 15[54] and cases where a boy[55] was ordained. When ordination became formalized, this increased the period between P. Pabbajjā and P. Upasampadā, i.e. the novice and the fully ordained. A period of five years has been mentioned,[56] but this has perhaps not been standard during the many centuries and various countries.

There are various well acknowledged reasons for entering the Buddhist Order. In Buddhist countries orphans frequently entered the Sāṃgha, as did widows the nun order. There are stories about devout parents urging their sons to enter this religious life, even with the background of auspicious dreams.[57] The ancient story "Conversion of Śāriputra and Maudgalyāyana" concerns the "seeker" of the truth, the way, who finally decides to enter the Brotherhood.[58]

While in the beginning the Buddha admitted virtually everybody into the Order, soon exclusions of certain types—criminal element, etc.—had to be enforced. It appears that the more the

[53]Cf. UPASAK, *Dictionary*, p. 50.

[54]MADAN MOHAN SINGH, *op. cit.*, p. 135.

[55]For example, LAMOTTE, *Histoire du bouddhisme indien*, p. 185, mentions that Kumarajīva (350-409) was ordained at the age of six (356). This is known as the Kākuṭṭepaka pravrajyā (the ordination of those who scare away crows), cf. Anukul C. Banerjee, *Sarvāstivāda Literature* (Calcutta, 1957), pp. 179-180.

[56]MADAN MOHAN SINGH, *op. cit.*, p. 137.

[57]Cf. the rather primitive article, ALEX WAYMAN, "The Parents of Buddhist Monks," *Bharati* (Banaras Hindu University), 1966-68, No. X & XI ("Central Asia Number," ed. by A. K. NARAIN), pp. 25-29.

[58]Cf. EDGERTON, *Buddhist Hybrid Sanskrit Reader* pp. 26-33, for his edited text from the *Mahāvastu,* with introductory notes about the versions of the story.

imperial patronage enjoyed by Buddhism, the more it excluded persons—such as deserters from the army, sons lacking the permission of their parents—so as not to offend the civil and military authority. This process appears to have been completed during the patronage of the celebrated King Aśoka.[59] For obvious reasons, persons with contagious diseases were excluded, as were persons with severe sensory afflictions, such as deafness (not allowing the person to hear the precepts).[60]

It seems useful to compare the two ordinations of the Buddhist system with the Brahmanic "stages of life." As well known this is a sequence of the celibate student, followed by the householder, for the first two stages. There followed two stages of homelessness, the Vānaprastha and the Sannyāsa. It has been proposed that the P. Pabbajjā (the "going-forth") or the ordination as a novice somewhat resembles the Vānaprastha stage; while the full-ordination (P. Upasampadā) is equivalent to attaining the Sannyāsa, which is sometimes called the Bhikṣu Āśrama.[61] However, in consideration that the ascetic orders did not recognize the requirement to be a householder, i.e. to repay a debt to the forefathers by procreating progeny, which is essential to the theory of the four stages, the comparison must be done in a different way. Indeed, also in the Brahmanic system, the lad left home to take up the Vedic study with a preceptor who would give him a second birth (make him *dvija*). Hence, the nearest equivalent is to take the Buddhist novice as equivalent to the *brahmacārin* student in the first stage; and to take the fully-ordained monk and nun, because they have loosened their social duties, to be roughly equivalent to the Vānaprastha (forest-hermit) in the third stage. The equivalent to the *sannyāsa* stage can be noticed in the description of this stage in the New Upaniṣads: he only needs strip of cloth, water pot of wood or earth, and staff: sleeps on the ground, with the sky for roof; stays at one place during the rains, rest of the year travels continuously; avoids theatre, families, feasts.[62] This bears some resemblance to the Buddhist

[59]Cf. Radhakrishna Choudhary, "Some Aspects of Buddhism as Gleaned through Aśokan Inscriptions," *JBRS* (Buddha Jayanti Special Issue, Vol. Two), 1956, p. 426.

[60]For a longer list, cf. Upasak, *Dictionary*, p. 138.

[61]Madan Mohan Singh, *op. cit.*, pp. 135-136.

[62]Cf. K. V. Gajendragadkar, *Neo-Upanishadic Philosophy* (Bharatiya Vidya Bhavan, Bombay, 1959), pp. 109-113.

ascetic practices called the *dhutaguṇa* (qualities of a purified man), thirteen in number (*infra*), and the two-week retreats by the monks (*infra*). However, in the Brahmanic theory, the *sannyāsa* stage was in the declining period of life, after complete disengagement from social duties; whereas in the Buddhist case the ascetic practices and retreats could take place when the person was relatively young and in full possession of his strength and sensory faculties.

An important difference to add to the above is that in the case of the *sannyāsin* there was an automatic extinction of his property-rights. But the Buddhist monk or nun did not undergo a "civil death" at ordination. This is because the Buddhist monk could return to the social group if he found the monastic life too hard, or if he experienced a change of heart about this kind of life; and there was no extinction of his property rights in the meantime.[63]

Turning to ordination practices themselves, we note agreement between the Theravāda and the Mūlasarvāstivāda use of the term P. *upajjhāya*, S. *upādhyāya*. In both cases, the Buddha's injunction that a person should seek out a "competent" monk to act as his Upajjhāya refers both to a person ordaining a novice and to a person looking after a disciple (P. *saddhivihārika*, S. *sārdhavihārin*), serving this master who will eventually introduce him to an appropriate meeting of the Saṃgha for the purpose of ordination as a *bhikṣu*.[64] In the Mūlasarvāstivāda practice, for example, the continuance of this Vinaya tradition in Tibet where it was the only Vinaya, the usage of the term can be seen in the biography of Tsoṅ-kha-pa (1357-1419), founder of the Gelugpa seot.[65] "In his seventh year, he 'went forth' to the religious life. The lama Don-grub Rin-chen became his 'principal' (*upādhyāya*), charged with admitting the candidate to the religious order. Gźon-nu Byaṅ-chub became his 'instructor' (*ācārya*). He took the vow of novice (*śramaṇera*), and was given the name Blo-bzaṅ Grags-pa'i-dpal." Notice that a superior called *upādhyāya* and an underling called *ācārya* both played a part in fulfilling the candidate's "going forth" as a novice. Later the biography

[63]Dr. Dev Raj Chanana, "The Vinaya Piṭaka and Ancient Indian Jurisprudence," *JBRS*, Vol. XLIV, Pts. i & ii, March-June, 1958, pp. 22-23.

[64]Cf. Upasak, *Dictionary*, pp. 44-45.

[65]Wayman, *Calming the Mind*, pp. 16, 19.

mentions the persons who directed Tsoṅ-kha-pa's full ordination as a *bhikṣu:* 1) one who was his "principal" (*upādhyāya*, Tib. *mkhan po*), a monastery abbot in spiritual descent from Śākya-śrībhadra (1127-1225), who introduced the third Mūlasarvāstivāda ordination lineage to Tibet; 2) one, happening to be the abbot of another monastery, who was his "counselor" (Tib. *las kyi slob dpon;* S. *karma-ācārya*); 3) a third one, a kind of religious head, who was his "confidant" (Tib. *gsaṅ ste ston pa;* S. *rahonuśāsaka*). Thus, the term *upādhyāya* was used for the principal at the novice vow and at the monk vow and could be two different persons. The Tibetan equivalent to *upādhyāya*, namely *mkhan po*, was regularly used for the head of a monastery.

For the vow of the novice, the following comes from the Mūlasarvāstivāda practice:[66] After the applicant (already a lay Buddhist) before the assembled Sāṃgha has expressed a desire to obtain the "going forth" ordination from an *upādhyāya*, a prearranged monk asks on his behalf if he can be granted the ordination, whereupon the Sāṃgha responds—he can be, if he is pure. After that, the applicant seeks out an *upādhyāya*, who arranges for the person to get his hair and beard shaved; and after bathing, he is furnished by the *upādhyāya* with bowl and yellow robes. Then in front of the *upādhyāya* the applicant takes his refuge in the Buddha, the Dharma, and the Sāṃgha, announces that he is giving up his marks of a householder and accepting those of one "gone forth"—and this is said three times. The *upādhyāya* says something like, "Fine!" The applicant is then turned over to another monk who inquires of the *upādhyāya* if he has ascertained the applicant's purity; and with assent, the applicant again goes through the set formulas as above of refuge and novice's vow. Some monks require the applicant to be able to tell from a shadow the time of the day. Now the "instructor" (*ācārya*) makes the novice state in his presence the ten points of instruction (*śikṣāpada*) which are the ten things he will forego or give up. Of these, he had previously agreed to desist from five during the Buddhist layman's vow, namely, from killing living beings, stealing, unlawful sexual activity, lying, and intoxicants. He now adds desisting from witnessing pleasurable entertainments, from use of beautifying things like unguents,

[66]BANERJEE, *Sarvāstivāda Literature*, pp. 109-113.

using high and big beds, taking meals at wrong times, and accepting gold and silver. The *ācārya* says something like, "Fine!"

For the vow of the monk, the following also comes from Mūlasarvāstivāda practice[67]: The novice having attained an age, of which the minimum is stated as "twenty" (as before, presumably 15+5; and with inevitable exceptions), asks the *upādhyāya* for an alms-bowl and religious robes. He also asks the *karmakāraka bhikṣu* (previously called the *karma-ācārya*) and the *rahonuśāka* to conduct their proper roles in the ceremony and asks some other monks to participate. The information is given that at least five Vinayadharas (retainers of the Vinaya code) had to participate in the *upasampadā* ordination. The candidate makes his salutations, then squatting in front of the *upādhyāya*, three times implores him to act as the *upādhyāya* for his full-ordination. Assenting, the *upādhyāya* provides the candidate with three robes either already made up, or with cloth for the same; and the two go through a robe conferment ceremony with formulas repeated thrice. Then comes exhibition of the bowl, and afterwards the *upādhyāya* confers the bowl. Three times the candidate states the proper use of the bowl. The candidate is moved to the side, standing with folded hands, but in view of the assembled Sāṃgha.

The *karmakāraka bhikṣu* now asks the *rahonuśāsaka bhikṣu* if he is willing to make the confidential inquiries to the candidate with the named *upādhyāya*. Upon getting the assent of the *rahonuśāsaka bhikṣu* the *karmakāraka bhikṣu* makes a *muktikā-jñapti*—apparently meaning his motion to the assembled Sāṃgha, upon his sitting down—that the *rahonuśāsaka bhikṣu* be permitted to make his confidential inquiries to the candidate. There follows the *jñapti-karma* of the *rahonuśāsaka bhikṣu* apparently meaning his questions to the candidate, out of ear-shot of the Sāṃgha (hence as the "confidant") on various private matters, starting with "Are you a man?" "Do you possess the male organ?" "Are you at least 20 years of age?" "Are your three robes and bowl complete ?" and going down to questions of whether he is a thief, a king's soldier, nun-seducer, indebted to someone, afflicted with various illnesses, and so on (in fact,

67 Banerjee, *Sarvāstivāda Literature*, pp. 114-141.

the entire list, which if in any case is not answered properly would drop him from consideration as a monk); and he informs the candidate to stay there until called and not to be shy about revealing to the assembled Sāṃgha his answer to any of the questions. The *rahonuśāsaka bhikṣu* moving within ear-shot of the assembled monks declares that the candidate, after being questioned, speaks of himself as free from all restrictions (to his full ordination). The assembled monks say, "If he is perfectly pure, then let him come." The candidate is now brought before the monks and salutes them. The *karmakarāka bhikṣu* (in his role of "counselor") then directs the novice on what he should say, namely, the formula of asking for the *upasampadā* ordination with the named *upādhyāya*, and that he is willing to answer any question. The *karmakāraka bhikṣu*, after being saluted by the candidate who sits down in front of him, tells the candidate to give answers to the questions without shyness—and then goes through the same list that the *rahonuśāsaka bhikṣu* had asked in confidence. After this, the *karmakāraka bhikṣu* does his *karma* of three times declaring that the candidate is a man with male organ, has completed 20 years of age, has all the robes and begging bowl, and is pure concerning the restrictions; and that if it be the Sāṃgha's convenience and approval, then let the Sāṃgha confer the *upasampadā* ordination on the given candidate with the named *upādhyāya*; and that all in favor should remain silent, and those against speak up. After the third time, he declares that since the Sāṃgha has remained silent (if that was the case), it must be concluded that the Sāṃgha has granted the *upasampadā* ordination on the candidate with such and such name, who has the named *upādhyāya*. This completes the full-ordination of the candidate as a monk (*bhikṣu*). The newly ordained *bhikṣu* is made to measure the shadow and then is informed about the parts of the day and night and about the seasons. This ends the formal ceremony of ordination. He is then told about monastery life, about robes, food, etc., and asked if he is willing to live this way. He is told about the four gross falls, for which he would be ousted from the Sāṃgha. He is told about the four rules about ascetics, i.e. their brotherly conduct, of not reviling others even when reviled, etc. He is told about the moral rules of the Prātimokṣa and his expected service from this day onward to the *upādhyāya*, who is as a father to a son. He is told to study the Buddhist doctrines of the personal aggregates, dependent origination, etc.

The above rituals of "going forth" (Pravrajyā) and "full ordination" (Upasampadā) are called P. *kammavācā*, S. *karmavākya*.[68] According to the Tibetan history text *The Blue Annals*, both Nāgārjuna, founder of the Mādhyamika sect of Buddhism, and Asaṅga, founder of the Yogācāra sect, received their "full ordination" in the Mūlasarvāstivāda Vinaya.[69] Hence, ordination as a monk was independent of doctrinal affiliations, as this paper has already set forth.

As to the newly-ordained monk's learning about parts of the day and the seasons, this is apparently a brief reference to informing him of daily and seasonal observances. There have been doubtless many differences in daily observances in Buddhist monasteries in different countries and centuries. For example, there is description about the daily life of the monks in ancient Ceylon that they arose before sunrise and contemplated the Buddha, loving kindness, impurity of the body, and death; then proceeded to their ablutions, sweeping, dressing according to the rules, meeting with other monks to recite the "Loving-kindness scripture" (*Metta-sutta*); then to the hall for their breakfast.[70] There is a modern publication on the morning and evening chanting in Thai Buddhism.[71]

The Vinayas set forth extensively the main observances in topics frequently called *vastu*. Hence, the Mūlasarvāstivāda Vinaya is called *Vinayavastu*.[72] In this Vinaya, the first book is the Pravrajyāvastu, from which previous material on the ordination of novices and monks was drawn. This book goes also into the

[68] BANERJEE, *Sarvāstivāda Literature*, p. 142. For more information, cf. HERBERT HÄRTEL, *Karmavācanā* (Sanskrittexte aus den Turfanfunden; Akademie-Verlag, Berlin, 1956). For ordination ceremonies of countries other than India, cf. J. P. MINAYEFF, *Recherches sur le Bouddhisme* (Paris, 1894), "La communauté des moines bouddhistes," pp. 296-315.

[69] GEORGE N. ROERICH, *The Blue Annals*, Part One (Delhi, 1978), pp. 34-35.

[70] WALPOLA RAHULA, *History of Buddhism in Ceylon* (M.D. Gunasena & Co., Colombo, 1956), pp. 173-174.

[71] *The Pali Chanting Scripture with Thai & English Translation*, 1962.

[72] The following material on the *Vinayavastu* is summarized from Banerjee, *Sarvāstivāda Literature*, pp. 101-246. FRAUWALLNER, *The Earliest Vinaya*, pp. 70-129, compares all the *vastu-s* of the various Vinayas.

qualifications of the monks chiefly engaged in the ordination rites and the reasons for asking the various questions of the candidate for *bhikṣu.* The second book, the Poṣadhavastu concerns the Prātimokṣa recitation which has been already mentioned by the name P. Uposatha (S. Upavasatha). More details will follow in this paper. This Vinaya then reverses the proper order of two books, the Varṣāvastu, concerning the conduct of monks during the rains—their restriction to one residence, etc.—and the Pravāraṇāvastu, to confess any offences committed during the three-month retreat of the rains in a 1-day ceremony concluding this retreat.[73] The fifth one, the Carmavastu, on footwear; the sixth, Bhaiṣajyavastu, on food and medicaments; the seventh, Cīvaravastu, on the materials and preparation of monk robes; and the eighth, Kaṭhinavastu, on distribution of robes at the end of the rainy season and laymen's gifts—are mainly on the food and clothing needs and the rules for special cases. The ninth, Kośāmbakavastu, on suspension (*utksepanīya*) of a monk, inaugurates chapters showing the internal ecclesiastical law code of the Buddhist monasteries. Then, the tenth, Karmavastu, concerns limitations of monks to perform suspension; the eleventh, Pāṇḍulohitakavastu, gives the disciplinary actions for various serious offences; the twelfth, Pudgalavastu, goes into particular cases of punishment for specific offences; the thirteenth, Pārivāsikavastu, the duties of monks undergoing light punishment (*parivāsa*); the fourteenth, Poṣadhasthāpanavastu, establishing the impurity that would exclude a monk from participation in the Upavasatha (P. Uposatha). The concluding parts in this Vinaya are the fifteenth, Śayanāsanavastu, on construction of monastery buildings and furnishing them; the sixteenth, Adhikaraṇavastu, formation of the nun order and settlement of disputes among the monks; and finally Saṃghabhedakavastu, which should be concerned with splits in the monk community but in fact in this Vinaya goes in to the legendary origin of the Śākya race and the life of Gautama, who became the Buddha, from birth to leaving home for the religious life.

As to the thirteen "qualities of a purified man" (*dhutaguṇa*), or else to be rendered "strands that were shaken off," they consti-

[73]That is, in this Vinaya the Pravāraṇāvastu is the third *vastu*, though logically it should be the fourth one.

tute a movement to adopt more ascetic practices than monastery life was prone to, in consideration that the Middle Path of the Buddha avoided the extremes of mortification of flesh and indulgence in desires but also that the Buddha was called "great ascetic" (*mahāśramaṇa*).[74] In the *Visuddhimagga* the thirteen (called here *dhutaṅga*) are: 1. to wear robes made of refuse rags (*paṃsukūlikaṅgam*); 2. to have not more than three robes (*tecīvarikaṅgam*); 3. to eat only food collected by begging (*piṇḍapātikaṅgam*); 4. to not miss any house in the regular rounds when begging (*sapadānacārikaṅgam*); 5. to sit down for eating only once a day no matter what (*ekāsanikaṅgam*); 6. to be satisfied with whatever is received in one's single bowl (*pattapiṇḍikaṅgam*); 7. to refuse any food after finishing one's meal (*khalupacchābhattikaṅgam*); 8. to dwell in a forest, away from the city (*āraññikaṅgam*); 9. to dwell at the base of a tree (that is not prohibited for the purpose) (*rukkamūlikaṅgam*); 10. to live in an open space (except when raining) (*abbhokāsikaṅgam*); 11. to live in a cemetery (*sosānikaṅgam*); 12. to use whatever bed or seat is offered, without adverse comment (*yathāsanthatikaṅgam*); 13. to take rest at night only by sitting (*nesajjikaṅgam*). Needless to say, a practitioner would adopt a certain one of these ascetic practices, which normally meant a renunciation of certain privileges accorded to the monks in monastery life. Asaṅga explains that these practices are meant to purify the mind and make it fit for dwelling in chastity (*brahmacarya*).[75]

Besides, it appears that the monks dwelling in the usual monastery setting had an opportunity to practice more toward *samādhi* during the three-month retreat of the rains when they did not go begging. There are indications that they may have had to get along with less food than at other times.[76] Indeed, it is said:[77] "If during the three months of summer-retreat, a

[74]Cf. NALINAKSHA DUTT, *Early Monastic Buddhism* (Calcutta, 1960), pp. 155, f., from which the following thirteen *dhutaṅga* are summarized, for the theory that Devadatta's attempt to force certain rigorous practices on the Sāṃgha as a whole—an attempt opposed by the Buddha—attained some measure of success in time in terms of adoption by various monks, although the list was not itself ever incorporated in the Vinaya.

[75]WAYMAN, *Analysis of the Śrāvakabhūmi*, p. 82.

[76]Cf. HORNER, *The Book of Discipline*, Vol. I, on the Fourth Defeat, pp. 153-154.

[77]BAPAT and HIRAKAWA, *Shan-Chien-Pi'-P'o-Sha*, p. 142.

large number of monks who had started practising *samādhi* have not finished their job, the Tathāgata does not observe the Great Pavāraṇā." By "Pavāraṇā" is meant the one-day ceremony, as alluded to above, for concluding the retreat during the rainy season. The Buddha was also mentioned as going into retreats for specified purposes: once in a solitary place for a half-month, except for one bringing food—to enter a *samādhi* for examining the past on a certain matter;[78] at another time for a retreat of three months—apparently to set an example.[79] It appears that the two-week retreat was a favorite of monks, as the writer has observed some Tibetan monks doing the same in present times, for coming to a conclusion on some troublesome point of doctrine, etc.

We should not leave this topic of Buddhist monasterial life with the impression that it just amounted to a big problem of persons adjusting to this sort of life, some obeying injunctions, others committing offences to be censured or deserving ejection from the Sāṃgha. This may be clarified by a cursory comparison of the Brahmin with the Bhikṣu and by an ancient quarrel.

It is well known that when Gautama left home to seek the religious life he undertook an ascetic discipline especially by the River Nairañjanā for six years, perhaps for some time with no more food intake than some ascetics were reported to have taken in those days—a handful of beans every third day.[80] At the end of that time he decided that this course did not lead to the highest goal (the Dharma transcending man's) and he undertook a middle path between mortification of the flesh and indulgence in sensory desires, taking a modest nourishment while meditating at the base of the Bodhi Tree. So also the Hindu *Laws* of *Manu* (II, 100) state: "Keeping the village of the senses in subjection and controlling the mind, he would accomplish all (human) aims without reducing his body through *yoga*." This indicates that when the Buddha decided on the middle path he accepted a certain portion of the Brahmanical "stages of life," and while continuing to uphold the ascetic ideal renounced its more extreme form.

[78]Bapat and Hirakawa, *Shan-Chien-P'i-P'o-Sha*, p. 290.

[79]Bapat and Hirakawa, *Shan-Chien-P'i-P'o-Sha*, p. 434.

[80]Cf. A. L. Basham, *History and Doctrines of the Ājīvikas* (Luzac & Company, London, 1951), 50, for this practice.

What he accepted in common with the Brahmanical course became called in Buddhist terminology "instruction of morality" (*adhiśīla-śikṣā*), amounting, in monasterial language, to adherence to the Pātimokkha (S. Prātimokṣa). Then a Brahmin lad, starting at eight years and taking the Vedic course for twelve years, would become a Brahmin priest in his village at the same age (twenty) that the Buddhist Vinaya gives for "full ordination" as a monk (*bhikṣu*). This Brahmin lad for the normal period of twelve years had been adhering to a standard of continence called *brahmacarya*, which was precisely enjoined upon the entrants to Buddhist monasterial life. However, while the Brahmin proceeded to the next stage of life, the householder who raises a family, the Buddhist monk continued his celibate ways, attempting, as the first part of this article has cited from the *Aṅguttara-nikāya* (Book of Sevens), to surmount the Realm of Desire, dwell in the four Dhyānas of the Realm of Form and then in the liberation of mind and of insight, and have the full realization in this life. And so the quarrel is over how to attain all (human) aims.

It is easier to compare the two systems in terms of a sequence from Asaṅga's *Śrāvakabhūmi:* going forth, restraint of morality, restraint of sense organs, moderation in food, practice of staying awake (in the former and latter part of night), conduct with awareness, solitude, elimination of hindrances, right dwelling in *samādhi.*[81] Thus, in the Brahmanical system, the lad went forth to the preceptor, became twice-born; and the Buddhist monastic followers became "ascetics who are sons of the Buddha." The Brahmanical youth restrained his morality in the code called *brahmacarya* and was supposed to restrain his sense organs in the manner set forth in the *Laws* of *Manu*, Chap. 2; while the Buddhist monasterial novice was supposed also to restrain his morality and then his sense organs, as set forth at length in Asaṅga's *Śrāvakabhūmi.* But then the Buddhist system went on to claim something over and beyond the Brahmanical procedure for attaining the (human) aims. It was claimed that the ascetic in the Buddhist order would proceed to "moderation in food," "practice of staying awake," and so on. In the description of "practice of staying awake" Asaṅga states that when one has

[81]Cf. WAYMAN, *Calming the Mind*, pp. 31-38.

moderation in food in the manner set forth, he goes on to purify his mind from obscuring natures by walking and sitting during the day and during the first watch of the night; and also during the last watch of the night after resting in the middle watch of the night. Notice that Asaṅga claims something for this phase that was not claimed for the restraint of morality or for the restraint of sense organs, namely, a purification of the mind from obscuring natures, as a preparation for entering into *samādhi*. That is not to denigrate those previous observances and behavior restrictions as trivial; indeed, Buddhism puts great stock on this prior base of morality for proceeding to meditation. In short the Buddha's rejection of the extreme of mortification of the flesh should be viewed as a rejection of ascetic practices that are not preceded by a previous moral training involving a continuous discrimination of things to be rejected and things to be accepted (especially by the senses). And the Buddhist rejection of the Brahmanical "stages of life" is an attitude that if one waits until the last period of life before one is an ascetic, there is not much that this asceticism would accomplish in the sense claimed for the asceticism that follows directly upon the restraint of sense organs. It is not the business of the present writer to take sides on this great cleavage between the two systems, except to observe the foregoing as essential for understanding the great movement of Buddhist monasticism. Of course, the training of the Brahmin youth for a number of years with the *brahmacarya* code, followed by the stage of householder, doubtless helped to preserve Hinduism through the many centuries. The non-return to society of the Buddhist monk in the sense of raising a family (except for the person leaving the monkhood) meant a more fragile base in society for the Buddhist monastery.

III. The Offences, Confession, and Penance

Since the offences are listed in the Pātimokkha (S. Prātimokṣa), it should be recalled that this paper already established the meaning of the term as "Liberation-onset." Consistent with my findings, Vasubandhu's *Abhidharmakośa* (IV, 16) states: "The Prātimokṣa path-of-act is the pair, candor (*vijñapti*) and reticence (*avijñapti*), at the outset" (*ādye vijñapty-avijñaptī prātimokṣa-kriyāpathaḥ*). And Vasubandhu comments in part: "Prātimokṣa is the candor and reticence at the commencement, of the person taking the vow (*saṃvara*)" (*saṃvara-samādānasya prathame vijñapty-avijñaptī prātimokṣa ity ucyate*).[82] These terms are in the Mahāsāṃghika listed tenets I have elsewhere cited: No. 60 "virtue caused by a vow increases"; No. 61 "candor (*vijñapti*) is virtue"; No. 62 "reticence (*avijñapti*) is immoral."[83] "Path of-act" apparently refers to the confessional.

The *Prātimokṣa-sūtra*, verse 16, of the Mūlasarvāstivāda Vinaya is cited in Tsoṅ-kha-pa's *Lam rim chen mo* as illustrative of the Instruction of Morality (*adhiśīlaśikṣā*) for the monks:[84]

> This Prātimokṣa (Liberation-Onset) is like the bridle of a hundred sharp nails on the difficult-response mouth of the horse-like mind driven by incessant effort.[85]

According to the context of this verse's citation, the "difficult-response mouth" means the spiritual guide's speech endowment (*vacasā 'bhyupetaṃ*) of *Mahāyāna-Sūtrālaṃkāra*, XVII, 10. The "hundred sharp nails" are presumably the "one hundred *karmas*" of the work *Mūlasarvāstivādanikāyaikaśatakarman*, briefly alluded to by I-Tsing but not listed by him, and apparently all the main monastery rites starting with ordination as a novice.[86] The teacher who has gone through these "*karmas*" is said to have these as a bridle on his mouth, capable of answering the difficult questions of the disciples, while his mind, like a horse, is spurred on. Vinītadeva explains the "hundred sharp nails" as the "points of instruction" (*śikṣāpada*),[87] which might signify the 150-odd

82P. Pradhan, ed., *Abhidharmakośabhāṣyam of Vasubandhu* (K. P. Jayaswal Research Institute, Patna, 1975), p. 207.

83A. Wayman, "The Mahāsāṃghika and the Tathāgatagarbha," *The Journal of the International Association of Buddhist Studies*, Vol. 1, No. 1, 1978, p. 36.

84Tashilunpo ed. of *Lam rim chen mo*, fol. 20b-5, in an introductory section on the topic; reliance on the spiritual guide (*kalyāṇamitra*).

85Anukul Chandra Banerjee, ed., *Prātimokṣa-sūtra* (*Mūlasarvāstivāda*) (Calcutta, 1954), p. 3, mentions that reconstructed passages have been put in brackets in his text. He had to reconstruct a number of lacunae with the help of the Tibetan. However, in the case of verse 16, his reconstruction does not appear to have been successful; and so I have used the rest of the verse (extant Sanskrit) plus the Tibetan translation to arrive at the translation given.

86Takakusu, tr., *A Record*, p. 95.

87PTT, Vol. 122, p. 279-3-2.

prohibitions of the *Prātimokṣa-sūtra* or might conceivably refer to the "one hundred *karmas*."

The Prātimokṣa as a morality (*śīla*) beyond the five layman's vows is called "morality of a day and night," since during the Poṣadha (P. Uposatha) there is no eating after noon for a day and a night, which is the fast (*upavāsa*) accompanied by the eightfold morality (*aṣṭāṅgaśīla*).[88]

The recitation of the Prātimokṣa is ordinarily in full, but it could be cut short to the minimum of the four "defeats" (*pārājika*) alone.[89] These four, mentioned first in the list, are the worst offences, requiring immediate expulsion from the Sāṃgha: 1) sexual intercourse, of any sort; 2) theft of a valuable, with awareness that it does not belong to oneself; 3) murder, or commending it or abetting it; 4) pretending to superhuman powers.[90]

As to the second one, "stealing," it has been wrongly suggested as relevant that the monk upon entering the Order had renounced any claim to private property.[91] Rather, the four "defeats" are related to the Buddhist Genesis story, where—portraying the fall from a superhuman state of the first eon men—sexual intercourse went along with eating of coarse morsel food, requiring crops of same, leading to their theft and mortal blows on that account.[92] Indeed, all the "defeats" have features of "theft", sometimes metaphorical. Thus the first one, sexual intercourse, means taking a sexual partner, who (or even, which) does not belong to the monk for such a purpose since he is supposed to be celibate. The second

[88]Cf. ÉTIENNE LAMOTTE, *Le Traité de la Grande Vertu de Sagesse*, Tome II (Louvain, 1949), esp. pp. 825-832, for this fast, the "eightfold morality," and information about a six days' fast, which may amount to three days at full moon and three days at new moon, or else two days each at full and new, plus two "eighth" days.

[89]B. JINANANDA, ed., *Abhisamācarikā* [Bhikṣuprakīrṇaka] (K. P. Jayaswal Research Institute, Patna, 1969), Introduction, p. viii.

[90]Cf. the extended treatment in BAPAT and HIRAKAWA, *Shan-Chien-P'i-P'o-Sha, op. cit.*

[91]So HORNER, *The Book of Discipline*, Vol. I, introduction, p. xxi. Cf. preceding conclusion, employing the *JBRS* article by DR. DEV RAJ CHANANA, n. 63, above.

[92]Cf. ALEX WAYMAN, "Buddhist Genesis and the Tantric Tradition," *Oriens Extremus*, 9:1, 1962, pp 127-131, for a summary of the story and implication for the "upward" progress of the Buddhist monk. This essay can be found also in A. Wayman, *The Buddhist Tantras* (Samuel Weiser, New York, 1973), pp. 24-29.

one is theft *per se*, especially of material, valuable objects. The third, murder, means *taking* or promoting the *taking* of a life, which belongs to another and has irreplaceable preciousness. The fourth one of pretense to realizations and powers in its explanation has five explicit thieves:[93] i) the big thief in the story about the "defeat": monks living on the bank of the River Vaggumuda near Vesālī (S. Vaiśālī) getting by false pretensions food, medicine, and other valuables. ii) the big thief monk who pretends he learned the Dhamma (S. Dharma) from himself (through his powers of realization) and not from someone else. iii) the big thief evil-minded monk who condemns those monks who are following the path and progressing in meditation, praising himself as the really pure man. iv) the big thief who secretly takes and gives gifts of monastery property in order to get favors and support of certain householder. v) the big thief who acts as though the monastery property belongs to him and freely takes it and uses it or gives it away. The preceding shows that thievery, either concretely or in metaphorical senses, was viewed with particular horror. Perhaps this attitude is behind the Mahāyāna Buddhist emphasis on "giving" (*dāna*) as the first perfection (*pāramitā*), even ahead of "morality" (*śīla*).

The Pātimokkha of the nun (*bhikkhunī*) has eight "defeats," the above four in common with the monk, and four additional ones: 5) enjoying the contact of a male person between the collar-bone and knee; 6) concealing the "defeat" offence of another nun; 7) becoming the follower of a monk who has been suspended; 8) possessing any of eight sexual dispositions.[94] Besides, a nun had to accept the eight *guru-dharma*, which the Buddha enjoined upon the women who would enter the Order, considering that women are also capable of attaining Arhatship, but which doubtless did not encourage them to become nuns:[95]

[93]Cf. Bapat and Hirakaŵa, *Shan-Chien-P'i-P'o-Sha*, pp. 335, ff. for an extended discussion of the five big thieves.

[94]Cf. Upasak, *Dictionary*, p. 158.

[95]For the eight *guru-dharma*, cf. Gustav Roth, *Bhikṣuṇī-vinaya* (K. P. Jayaswal Research Institute, Patna, 1970), Introduction, Chap. III, pp. xxix-xxxii. The association of the number eight with women appears an established matter in the Pāli *Aṅguttara-nikāya* (Book of Eights), where besides the canonical story about Mahāpajāpatī's acceptance of the eight *dharmas*, there is the account that women have eight qualities who after death

i) no matter how old the nun, she should bow her head to the feet of a monk, even one ordained that day; ii) being a virgin of eighteen years she requests the Orders of monks and nuns for two years' training at the end of which she may be fully ordained; iii) nuns may not address monks regarding the true and the false; a monk may address nuns regarding the true but not the false; iv) the nuns must wait until the monks have been supplied with food, bedstead, and lodging before being themselves supplied; v) a nun guilty of a grave offence must apply to the Order of nuns for the severe penance of isolation (*mānatva*) for half a month and certification of rehabilitation from both the Orders; vi) every half month the nuns should desire the coming of the monks on Uposatha day, for instruction; vii) the nuns may not spend the rainy season at a place devoid of a monk; viii) upon the conclusion of the rainy season the nuns should desire to invite each other before both the Orders (to be open about what transpired during the rainy season).

Then for the monks comes a section of thirteen Sanghādisesa offences. One of the traditional explanations for the title—whereby it is rendered "beginning with (*ādi*), and remaining with (*sesa*) the Sangha,"[96] i.e. entirely within the purview of the Sangha—seems confirmed by Vinītadeva's commentary on the *Vinayavibhaṅga*, with the S. Sāṃghāvaśeṣa ("remains in the Sāṃgha"). Thus Vinītadeva: "depends on the Sāṃgha" (Tib. *dge 'dun la rag lus pa*); "entailed by the Sāṃgha" (*dge 'dun daṅ 'brel ba*); "arises from the Sāṃgha" (*dge 'dun las rnam par ldaṅ par 'gyur*); and " 'without a remainder' (would be) because there is no common (shared) means of purification; 'with a remainder' (would be) because there is a common means of purification."[97] Hence, the term Sanghādisesa seems to have been adopted to contrast with the Pārājika ("defeat"), namely, where there is a means of purification within the Sāṃgha for a serious offence and where there is no such means. As to the list, the first five relate to sexual indiscretions short of sexual intercourse. Then come offences relating to construction of monastic dwellings, false

---

are reborn as lovely fairies; and earlier the "Great Chapter" has a passage that a woman enslaves a man in eight ways.

[96]For a discussion of the title, cf. HORNER, *The Book of Discipline*, Vol. I, Introduction, pp. xxix-xxxii.

[97]PTT, Vol. 122, p. 313-4.

accusations, abetting schisms in the Sangha, and polluting the faith of a devout family. The nun had some more possible offences. There was a light punishment of living apart called *parivāsa* and a severe penance of isolation called *manatta* (S. *mānatva*), both requiring the sanction of the Sangha in the beginning and end. By "end" is meant that one becomes ready for restitution (*abbhāna*) by the official act of the Sangha, consisting of at least twenty persons.[98]

Next come the two *aniyata-dhammas* or Indeterminate Offences about the association of a monk with a woman, where the gravity of the offence (whether "defeat", Sanghādisesa, or the lesser fault called Pācittiya) is determined by a reliable witness, especially a reliable female layman (*upāsikā*).[99]

The Theravāda Vinaya now presents thirty Nissaggiya-pācittiyas, offences especially about the religious garb—its measurements, renewals, etc.; and the begging bowl; as well as money transactions with laymen.[100] These are followed by ninety-two infractions (*pācittiya;* Sanskrit uses the term *pātayantika*) of the monk in the Bhikkhu-Pātimokkha, with a hundred sixty-six of the nun in the Bhikkhunī-Pātimokkha. Some of these are heretic views on matters of morality, such as declaring permissible acts that are permissible, and vice versa. Violations of the prohibition on monks to view entertainments, concealing a serious offence of another monk, are among the miscellaneous offences.[101] Various Vinayas differ considerably in the material presented on each of these sins. For example, Pācittiya No. 33 in one list on "taking food successively" is quite short.[102] In the Mūlasarvāstivāda Vinaya this is Pātayantika No. 31, and Vinītadeva's commentary, taking its cue from the basic *Vinayavibhaṅga*, launches into a lengthy description of drawing the "Wheel of Life" (well-known from its Chinese and Tibetan forms),[103] of which there is nothing corresponding in the other account of this offence.

The Pāṭidesanīya are a group of offences to be confessed in a

[98]This summary of the list is based on Upasak, *Dictionary*, pp. 213-214.

[99]BAPAT and HIRAKAWA, *Shan-Chien-P'i-P'o-Sha*, Introduction, p. xxxi.

[100]UPASAK, *Dictionary*, pp. 121-122.

[101]UPASAK, *Dictionary*, p. 151; BAPAT and HIRAKAWA, *Shan-Chien-P'i-P'o-Sha*, Introduction, pp. xxxiii-xxxv.

[102]BAPAT and HIRAKAWA, *Shan-Chien-P'i-P'o-Sha*, pp. 470-471.

[103]PTT, Vol. 123, p. 12-3-3, f.

manner prescribed by the text: "I have fallen into a blameworthy matter, unbecoming, which ought to be confessed, I confess it." They are the offences of requesting food from impoverished persons, four related to monks and eight to nuns.[104]

The group of Sekkiya (S. Śaikṣa) is precepts. The Theravāda Vinaya has 75 such rules, same for monk and nun: 1-2, on proper dress, 3-26 on how to enter a village, town, or house, 27-56 on taking meals, 57-72 on preaching of the Dhamma, 73-75 concerning toilets, etc.[105] The Dharmagupta school is quite different here, with 24 rules dealing with the *stūpa*.[106]

The final entries in the Pātimokkha have to do with settling of disputes.[107]

Asaṅga, in *Vinaya-samgrahaṇī*, says:[108] "One may understand all transgressions (*āpatti*) to be established by the fifteen wickednesses (*duṣkṛta*)," as follows:

1. a grave thing, e.g. the four defeats. But the beginner can have them in a pre-defeat form, which taken care of in time, can avert a "defeat."
2. non-contentment with lack of things one might want more of.
3. creating incidents, or opportunities, to have offensive relations with nuns, etc.
4. acting in such a way among laity as to cause those without faith not to get faith and for those with faith to lose it.
5. trading or trafficking in merchandise and precious things like gold and silver.
6. lust, leading to sexual discharges and to erotic advances.
7. hurting others by calumny, etc.
8. causing injury to others by requiring them to carry excessive loads, etc.
9. interrupting the progress to "heaven" (*sugati*) by breaking the concord in the Sangha.

[104] BAPAT and HIRAKAWA, p. 436; Upasak, *Dictionary*, p. 151.

[105] UPASAK, *Dictionary*, pp. 240-241.

[106] BAPAT and HIRAKAWA, Introduction, p. xxxv, and pp. 487-489.

[107] UPASAK, *Dictionary*, has a good summary, pp. 223-224, and refers to the lengthy description in *Cullavagga*.

[108] PTT, Vol. 111, p. 222-5-5 to p. 223-4-3; in this translation from the Tibetan I have given only the main list with meager expansion for some items.

10. interrupting the way of the ascetic (or novice) by refusing precepts, saying, "Don't tell me!"
11. not eliminating what is to be eliminated; and eliminating what should not be eliminated.
12. dwelling where one should not dwell; and not dwelling where one should dwell.
13. not venerating what one should venerate, e.g. the Prātimokṣa; and venerating what one should not venerate.
14. to tell what should be kept secret, e.g. to express the superior *dharma* (*uttaradharma*) to one not ordained; and to conceal what should be told, e.g. not to tell the neophytes about the transgressions (*āpatti*) that concern them.
15. to rely upon what one should not rely upon, e.g. on not properly examined clerical garb; and not to rely upon what one should rely upon.

Asaṅga was previously mentioned to have been ordained in the Mūlasarvāstivāda Vinaya; therefore, the foregoing and the following from the Vinaya section of his great work should be taken as consistent with that Vinaya. He classifies by their nature (*svarūpa*) ecclesiastical offences (*āpatti*) as minor, middling, and great, where the Defeats are the great transgressions, the Sāṃghāvaśeṣa the middling kind, and any other the minor transgression. He gives another classification where the Defeats and the Sāṃghāvaśeṣa are grave (S. *guruka;* P. *garukāpatti*), the infractions (Pātayantika) and the Prātideśanīya are middling, and the Duṣkṛta is a light one. Classified by agency, he says what is done through ignorance and heedlessness is a minor transgression; what is done through many defilements is a middling transgression; and what is done through (deliberate) disrespect is a great transgression. Classified by intention, whatever one does in a small way when enwrapped by lust, hatred, and delusion, is a small (transgression); does in a medium way, is a medium one; does in a great way, is a great (transgression). Classified by points (of instruction), there are also the minor, the middle, and the great transgression. Classified by the number of monks required for the case, minor transgressions require one to five; middling transgressions require ten, or twenty, or thirty; for the great one, no number given.[109]

[109]PTT, Vol. 111, p. 224-1-6 to 224-3-2; I have taken from Tibetan the main details of Asaṅga's remarks.

Turning to the confessional, it should be observed that certain offences were never admitted to be atoned for by confessing them. We have seen the four Defeats (*pārājika*) as a mandatory expulsion from the Order. The grave sins that could be handled by the Sāṃgha, and called S. Sāṃghāvaśeṣa, required suspension and penance, not expulsion. Any others, i.e. the minor transgressions, could be atoned for by confessing, also referred to as "pacifying" the sin. According to the Pāli Vinaya text *Mahāvagga:* "If a Bhikkhu, after a threefold proclamation, does not confess an existing offence which he remembers, he commits an intentional falsehood.[110] The confessing of sins one by one was a traditional explanation in Asia for the translation of the term *prātimokṣa* by "liberation one by one." Thus I-Tsing writes: "While thus confessing one's own faults and desiring to be purified, one hopes the sins are expiated being confessed one by one. To confess sins all at once is not permitted in the Vinaya."[111] The settlement of sins susceptible of being handled in this manner is referred to in Pāli as *paṭiññatakaraṇa.*[112] The monk admits the offence before the assembled Saṅgha or before a monk. This is a procedure wider than the confession of minor infractions. If one restricts the consideration to these minor ones, this is probably the situation referred to in the often-cited report of a J. F. Dickson (*Journal of the Royal Asiatic Society* for 1875) who was allowed to witness a Pātimokkha in Ceylon and said, among other things: "After we were seated the priests retired two and two together, each pair knelt down face to face and made confession of their faults, one to another, in whispers."[113] Elsewhere I cited sources for the Mahāyāna equivalent to this confession "face to face," pointing out that this abatement of sin, tantamount to a calming of the mind, is involved in facing the Thirty-five Buddhas of Confession and in other forms of "facing" under specified ritual circumstances.[114]

[110]RHYS DAVIDS and OLDENBERG, trs., *The Mahāvagga* (Sacred Books of the East, XIII, Oxford, 1881), II, 3, 4 (Uposatha Ceremony and Pātimokkha), p. 243.

[111]TAKAKUSU, tr., *A Record*, p. 89.

[112]UPASAK, *Dictionary*, p. 130.

[113]Cf. HENRY CLARKE, WARREN, *Buddhism in Translations* (Harvard University Press, 1947), pp. 405-408. For various features of this confessional, see the *Mahāvagga* (RHYS DAVIDS and OLDENBERG, trs.), II 27, 1-15, pp. 282-286.

[114]ALEX WAYMAN, "Purification of Sin in Buddhism by Vision and Con-

However, if the monk is guilty even of minor infractions, it is held that concealment, i.e. failure to confess it in the appropriate circumstances, acts as a hindrance to his success in meditation. He is "sitting on thorns," and the text continues: "If the Vinaya-master goes to his place and asks him: 'Good friend, how is the state of your mind? Did you attain *samādhi* or not?' he replies: 'No *samādhi*.' The Vinaya-master says: 'In this world, one who commits an offence cannot conceal it. If at the time when one commits the offence for the first time, he tries to conceal himself, then the beneficent deities would certainly first come to know it. So also the Samaṇs and Brāhmaṇs who can know the minds of others.' "[115] By "Samaṇs" is meant the ascetics (P. *samaṇa*, S. *śramaṇa*).

Also in the case of the more grave offences called P. Saṃghādisesa or S. Sāṃghāvaśeṣa, it is necessary to approach immediately another monk to inform him of the offence and make arrangement for expiation, in which case the offending monk need only observe the six nights of "Mānatta." But concealment of the offence entails a period of penance called "Parivāsa" equal to the time he concealed the original grave offence, in addition to the six nights of "Mānatta." The Sāṃgha decides on the limitations of his movements, etc. during the period of penance. The nuns were treated differently: whether or not a nun conceals the offence, she only undergoes a Mānatta of a fortnight. The stringency of the limitations on the monk during this penance period is supposed to suffice for the expiation.[116] Again, in the period of Mahāyāna Buddhism, there is a rite of repentance associated with worship of the Bodhisattva Ākāśagarbha, as cited: "Full of shame, like a patient with sores upon his eyes, from one to seven days you must worship Buddhas, and especially the name of the Great Compassionate Bodhisattva Ākāśagarbha, and you must wash your body and burn several kinds of incense. ... Out of compassion with sinners this Bodhisattva in all kinds of shapes appears in their dreams or in *samādhi*, and with the *cintāmaṇi* seal stamps their arms, thus removing the marks of

---

fession," *A Study of Kleśa*, ed. by Genjun H. Sasaki (Shimizukobundo Ltd., Tokyo, 1975), pp. 64-66.

[115] Bapat and Hirakawa, *Shan-Chien-P'i-P'o-Sha*, p. 177.

[116] Cf. the entries 'Parivāsa (I)' and 'Mānatta' in Upasak, *Dictionary*, pp. 142-144 and pp. 183-184.

crime. After having obtained this sign they must return to the congregation of the monks and explain the commandments as before."[117]

[117]WAYMAN, "Purification of Sin in Buddhism by Vision and Confession," pp. 70-71, citing M. W. DE VISSER's translation from the *Kwan Kokūzō Bosatsu Kyō* in his *The Bodhisattva Akasagarbha* (*Kokūzō*) *in China and Japan* (Amsterdam, 1931).

3

ASPECTS OF MEDITATION IN THE THERAVĀDA AND MAHĪŚĀSAKA

INTRODUCTION

> Monks, if a monk should wish: "May I be agreeable to my fellows in the pure life, liked by them, revered and respected," he should be one who fulfills the moral rules (*sīla*), who is intent on calming the mind (*cetosamatha*) within, whose meditation (*jhāna*) is uninterrupted, who is endowed with discerning (*vipassanā*), a frequenter of solitary abodes (*suññāgāra*).
>
> *Ākaṅkheyyasutta* (Dīgha-Nikāya, I, 33)

All Buddhist sects granted that the truths of Buddhism were discovered by the Buddha in the course of his meditations, especially beneath the Bodhi-tree at Gayā in India. Thus meditation has a paramount role in Buddhism for indicating man's own ability to attain to truth. Of those sects, Theravāda is the well-known Buddhism still prevalent in various South-east Asian countries such as Ceylon, Burma, and Thailand. Probably the most famous commentator of this tradition is Buddhaghosa whose fifth century A.D. work the *Visuddhimagga* is arranged in three parts in accordance with the Buddhist categories of three instructions, that of morality forming the basis for the other two: mental training aimed at *samādhi;* and insight, leading to the seeing of things as they really are with full comprehension of Buddhist truth or the discerning of reality.. Bareau has observed that the sect comparable to the Theravāda that remained in India was called the Mahīśāsaka,[1] and I observed that its later form (the Later Mahīśāsaka) had as its most famous son the Buddhist teacher Asaṅga (c. 375-430).[2] Asaṅga did not organize his encyclopedic work the *Yogācārabhūmi* by the three instructions; but he cherished these instructions in voluminous writing that could easily be put under the headings of those three. It is the last two instructions, mental training and insight that properly cover the topic of Buddhist meditation; and this paper must deal with the two topics, although necessarily stressing the mental training, called "calming the mind."

The literature about Buddhist meditation became quite extensive, especially when taking into account the full regime, the various techniques and meditation topics, the promised fruits, and the inevitable controversies. Of the extensive coverages on the textual, rather than interpretive level, Vajirañāṇa's *Buddhist Meditation*[3] may be signalled as representative of the Theravāda exegesis in the Pāli language and for the Indian schools which wrote in Sanskrit the extensive treatment preserved in Chinese and now rendered into French by Lamotte, *Le Traité*,[4] Tome III, and a section in Tome II. When present-day Buddhist monks write on Buddhist meditation the treatment amounts to an exposition of how to do it, rather than of what is going on. A fine example is Buddhadāsa's *Ānāpānasati*.[5] Western writers have various interpretations on behalf of their expected readers. For example, there is Eliade's chapter on "Yoga Techniques in Buddhism,"[6] using the important passages then available and bringing in non-Buddhist movements of the Indian tradition.

1 ANDRE BAREAU, *Les sectes bouddhiques du Petit Véhicule* (Saïgon, 1955), p. 34.

2 ALEX WAYMAN, *Analysis of the Śrāvakabhūmi Manuscript* (Berkeley, 1961), pp. 25-29.

3 PARAVAHERA VAJIRANĀṆA MAHĀTHERA, *Buddhist Meditation in Theory and Practice* (Colombo, 1962).

4 ÉTIENNE LAMOTTE, *Le Traité de la Grande Vertu de Sagesse de Nāgārjuna* (*Mahāprajñāpāramitāśāstra*), Tome II (Louvain, 1949), especially pp. 1013-43; Tome III (Louvain, 1970), especially pp. 1209-1309.

5 BUDDHADĀSA BHIKKHU, *Ānāpānasati* (*Mindfulness of Breathing*) (Bangkok, 1971).

6 MIRCEA ELIADE, *Yoga: Immortality and Freedom* (New York, 1958), pp. 162-99.

An essay by Cousins, "Buddhist *Jhāna*,"[7] is restricted to the second instruction, calming the mind, with some modern observations from Southern Buddhist countries. Another essay, by Goleman, "The Buddha on Meditation,"[8] uses Buddhaghosa's *Visuddhimagga* as a Buddhist textual base to make contact with the "altered states of consciousness" terminology of modern Psychology. These three Western approaches are similar in not purporting to guide anyone in meditation: they are attempts to grapple with certain technical features of the system which most interest the respective authors.

The present article seeks a middle ground: to convey only in summary fashion what is actually done in this classical form of Buddhist meditation in order that there be room to deal with certain matters of considerable contemporary interest, such as whether the meditation brings the yogin to a break with human reason and whether it results in faculties which a person did not have in the beginning.

It is also well to mention that most of the Western works that deal with Buddhist meditation as a major topic have treated rather well the general practices enjoined upon all applicants, such as the seeking out of a spiritual guide (the *kalyāṇa-mitra*, "virtuous friend"), and the various restrictions on daily activities, exemplifying morality as the base for meditation. These works are frequently less useful for defining the specific practices which differ for various beginners and for the various degrees of advancement of a given meditator.

The restrictions on mental and physical acts are ritualistic in the sense that the usual random movements are being cut down. Even so, the meditation practice is a comprehensible human pursuit, since many other persons—for example, athletes—have to follow special regimes with carefulness of diet and sleeping habits, along with unremitting practice. Musicians too must seek out good teachers and spend years of perhaps daily practice, ever attentive to avoid faults of performance. And again, one must take the entire drill; for example, it is no use to stay awake

[7]L. S. Cousins, "Buddhist *Jhāna:* Its nature and attainment according to the Pāli sources," *Religion* III, 2 1973, pp. 115-31.

[8]Daniel Goleman, "The Buddha on Meditation and States of Consciousness", *Journal of Transpersonal Psychology*, IV, 1, 1972, pp. 1-44.

in the former and latter parts of night for meditating, if one is not also to practice moderation in food.

Meditation objects, particularly the "devices"

The specific practices especially relate to different types of persons. The post-canonical Pāli Abhidhamma exegesis compiled a treatise on different classifications of persons (the *Puggala-paññatti*). However, the old passages were sketchy about treating personality differences, and it is likely that the guru lent guidance that was not always spelled out in the texts. The *Visuddhimagga* is content to assign a few meditation objects to certain persons, six in number, in terms of their "disposition" (*carita*). Vajirañāṇa translates :[9] "disposed to lust, to hate, to delusion, to faith, to intellectuality and agitation." Here, instead of "intellectuality" I render *buddhi* as "discrimination," and instead of "agitation" render *vitakka* as "conjecture,"[10] These dispositions are assessed mainly by a person's movements, in his manner of walking, standing, sitting, and lying down (frequently called the four postures).[11] The spiritual guide, having determined by such signs the predominant disposition of the candidate, then steers him to an appropriate meditative object. Vajirañāṇa,[12] following Buddhaghosa's works, tabulates the respective meditative objects. I have elsewhere given Asaṅga's solution,[13] which it should be of interest to compare in part with Buddhaghosa's lineage (Pāli: P., Sanskrit : S.):

[9]*Buddhist Meditation*, p. 98.

[10]It is difficult to assign a good rendition for *vitakka*. My suggestion of "conjecture" (or "speculation") is based on the available evidence that the term (in Sanskrit *vitarka*) is an abbreviation for "inquiry and investigation" (*vitarkavicāra*) (see later, "Progress in the Realm of Form") of the type in the Realm of Desire, hence defiled by lust, hatred, and delusion.

[11]Among Western thinkers, it is especially Hegel who insisted that character is revealed by movement; cf. J. B. Baillie, tr., *Hegel's Phenomenology of Mind* (London, rev. ed., 1949), p. 349: "The true being of a man is, on the contrary, his act; individuality is real in the deed."

[12]*Buddhist Meditation*, p. 110.

[13]Wayman, *Analysis*, pp. 86-7.

Candidate's disposition	*Appropriate meditative objects*	
	Buddhaghosa (Theravāda)	Asaṅga (Mahīśāsaka)
Lust (*rāga*)	Revolting objects (P. *asubha;* S. *aśubhā*);	Revolting objects
ditto	Mindfulness of bodies	——
Hatred (P. *dosa,* S. *dveṣa*)	Four totalities (blue, yellow, red, and white);	——
ditto	four Brahmā-vihāras (love, compassion, sympathetic joy, equanimity)	Love (*maitrī*)
Delusion (*moha*)	Mindfulness while breathing in and out (P. *ānāpānasati,* S. °*smṛti*)	Origination in Dependence of this condition (*idaṃ-pratyayatā-pratītya-samutpāda*)
Conjecture (P. *vitakka,* S. *vitarka*)[14]	ditto	Mindfulness while breathing in and out
Pride (*māna*)	——	Analysis of the elements (*dhātu-prabheda*)
Mixed character (*sabbacarita*)	Six totalities (five elements plus light); Four formless realms	Whichever meditative object on which the yogin has upsurge of rapture[15]
Faith (P. *saddhā*)	Six Recollections (Buddha, etc.)	—
Discrimination (*buddhi*)	Mindfulness of death, etc.	—

In Asaṅga's school, the meditative objects for the persons with predominance of lust, hatred, delusion, conjecture, and pride, are commonly referred to by a word *pratipakṣa*, which, along with other translators, I used to render as "antidote"; but to which I now apply the standard lexical entry of "opponent" or "adversary." In short, the meditation on love is not an antidote for

[14]Cf. BHIKKHU ÑĀṆAMOLI, *The Path of Purification* (*Visuddhimagga*) *by Bhadantācariya Buddhaghosa* (Colombo, 1956), p. 103, for the pairing of *moha* and *vitakka*, including," And just as delusion vacillates owing to superficiality, so do applied thoughts that are due to facile conjecturing."

[15]This is a teaching from Asaṅga's *Śrāvakabhūmi*, as cited in my manuscript translation from Tibetan, *Calming the Mind and Discerning the Real* (Columbia Uuiversity, New York, 1978). Asaṅga refers to "mixed character" by the terminology "addiction of equal parts" meaning that each of the faulty dispositions is of insufficient strength to predominate over the others, and so the meditative object is indeterminate.

hatred, but an adversary meant to supplant hatred in the mind. That is so, because according to this theory the second instruction, calming the mind by way of success with a meditative object, aims to remove the visible tops (the manifestation in the conscious mind); while it is the third instruction, of insight (P. *paññā*, S. *prajñā*), that is required for removing the traces deep down in the mind. But before these traces can be extirpated, it is necessary to supplant the hatred, etc. from the conscious field. Therefore, in Asaṅga's school, the same set would not, as in Buddhaghosa's list, include "hatred," and "faith," and "discrimination"; because "hatred" has a meditative object meant to supplant it, while "faith" and "discrimination" have meditative objects meant to promote them.

It is also necessary to speak about the "totalities" (P. *kasiṇa*, S. *kṛtsna*) frequently referred to as "devices." The *Visuddhimagga* has a lengthy treatment of these "devices," far in excess of what one would expect from the scriptural sources which are quite meagre. The main canonical source is the *Mahā-Sakuladāyi-sutta* of *Majjhima-Nikāya* II, 1, ff., which sets forth then ten "totalities" as one of the meditation techniques taught by the Buddha. The list is also explained in the *Aṅguttara-Nikāya's* Book of Tens, and it occurs twice in the *Dīgha-Nikāya* as a mere list. However, the Pāli term *kasiṇa* does not occur at all in the *Saṃyutta-Nikāya*, which is rich in material on meditation.[16] The standard ten are the four colors, blue, yellow, red, and white; the four elements, earth, water, fire, and wind; space and perception (S. *vijñāna*). The practice was to contemplate the entire world by this "totality" or "device," i.e. all blue, all earth, etc.[17] Such a totality seems to be illustrated by the Fire Sermon: "All things, O monks, are on fire... The eye, O monks, is on fire;..."[18]

[16]Per CAROLINE RHYS DAVIDS, *Samyutta-Nikaya, Indexes* Pāli Text Society, Vol. 54 (London, 1904).

[17]According to the brief Buddhist scripture "The log of wood" in *Aṅguttara-Nikāya* (The Book of Sixes), E. M. HARE, tr., *The Book of the Gradual Sayings* (London, 1952), Vol. III, pp. 240-41, the monk Sāriputta (S. Śāriputra) explained to a group of monks, pointing to a large log of wood, that when someone has learned to control his mind he can be convinced (P. *adhimucceyya*) that the log is earth, or water, fire, air, beautiful, or ugly, because all those elements are in the log of wood.

[18]Cf. HENRY CLARKE WARREN, *Buddhism in Translations* (Cambridge, Mass., 1947), pp. 351-53, translation of "The Fire-Sermon" from the *Mahā-*

Buddhaghosa's generous treatment appears explained by Vajirañāṇa[19] in agreement with the *Visuddhimagga*,[20] mentioning that the "devices" were employed as a means of inducing Jhāna (S. Dhyāna).[21] By this is meant the Jhāna-s of the Realm of Form among the three Buddhist realms (Realm of Desire, Realm of Form, and Formless Realm). As an example, Bapat writes regarding the water device,[22] "He (Upatissa) also agrees with B. (Buddhaghosa) in saying a beginner should not practise on natural sheets of water such as ponds, lakes, rivers, ocean, but should practise on water in a bowl or basin, placed in a quiet, solitary place, neither too dark nor having too much light." C.A.F. Rhys-Davids writes,[23] "We have read of the great lay-mystic, Jacob Boehme, accidentally falling into self-hypnosis by gazing at a surface of shining pewter. Thereupon, so he declares, he seems 'to behold the inward properties of all things in nature opened to him.' By certain similar devices (*kasiṇa*) the Indian sought to obtain similar results systematically." Lounsbery points to their danger:[24] "It will readily be seen that auto-suggestion played an important part in this practice, which has been almost abandoned in Ceylon since the death of a famous Guru three hundred years ago. The Kasiṇas are said to be still used in Burma."

But this use of the "devices" to induce Jhāna, as in Buddhaghosa's tradition and as exposed in the foregoing tabulation for persons of hatred and of mixed character, seems to be a corruption of Buddhist practice. Thus, Asaṅga explains in his exegesis of the

---

vagga of the Pāli Vinaya; and WALPOLA RAHULA, *What the Buddha Taught* (Bedford, 1972 reprint), pp. 95-97, for the equivalent *Sūtra* translated from the *Saṃyutta-Nikāya*.

19 *Buddhist Meditation*, p. 139.

20 ÑĀṆAMOLI, *The Path*, p. 113.

21 So also in Buddhaghosa's Abhidhamma commentary called *Atthasālinī*; cf. Pe Maung Tin, tr., which CAROLINE RHYS DAVIDS edited and revised, *The Expositor*, Vol. I (London, 1958 reprint), p. 248, in reference to the *kasiṇa*, "But why was this method taught? Because it led to the production of *jhāna*."

22 P. V. BAPAT, *Vimuttimagga and Visuddhimagga: A Comparative Study* (Poona, 1937), p. 57.

23 CAROLINE RHYS-DAVIDS, Preface, p. xii, to F. L. Woodward, *Manual of a Mystic* (London, 1916).

24 G. CONSTANT LOUNSBERY, *Buddhist Meditation in the Southern School* (New York, 1936), pp. 43-44.

Samāhitabhūmi:[25] "The bases of Mastery and the bases of Totality are the path of purifying the Liberations. The Liberations are classified by liberation from the hindrance of the knowable; they liberate the mind of *śrāvakas* and *pratyekabuddhas* from whatever hindrance of the knowable." Since the Liberations begin in the Realm of Form, meant for those who have surmounted the Realm of Desire, the bases of Totality must begin with the Dhyānas where the Liberations begin, and therefore cannot serve to induce Jhāna (Dhyāna). *Le Traité*[26] makes the same point, mentioning that the first two Liberations and the first four Masteries are contemplations of revolting objects, i.e. the cadaver in decomposition, and are practiced in the First and the Second Dhyāna. The *Manual of a Mystic*[27] seems to agree because it precedes the use of the "devices" by accomplishment of the "mindfulness while breathing in and out" meditation that takes the meditator out of the Realm of Desire into the Realm of Form; and then the subsequent chapter devoted to the "devices" constantly mentions the Jhānas, which are of course the divisions of the Realm of Form. This is technical but important: it shows the Buddhaghosa's exposition of these "devices" permits them to be used by persons who have not surmounted the Realm of Desire, because using the devices for the very purpose of that surmounting ; and for these persons such "devices" carry some danger, as suggested by Lounsbery. The danger probably amounts to something too strong for the psyche, just as a strenuous physical exercise is dangerous if not worked up to by the gradual strengthening of the muscles.

The reason why Asaṅga does not employ the *kasiṇas* in his *Śrāvakabhūmi* (Stage of the Disciple), although he does have material on these in the *Samāhitabhūmi* of his *Yogācārabhūmi*, seems to be that the main task of teaching Buddhist meditation is to get the disciple over the great hurdle of the Realm of Desire, with its lust, hatred, and delusion, with its five hindrances (*infra*), and its "acts of Māra."[28] There is also no mention of these devices in my

[25]Photographic edition of the Tibetan canons (PTT), Vol. 111, p. 10-5-7 to p. 11-1-1.

[26]LAMOTTE, *Le Traité*, III, p. 1289.

[27]WOODWARD, *Manual*, pp. 67 ff.

[28]See in this connection, JAMES W. BOYD, *Satan and Māra* (Leiden, 1975), especially Chap. Six "The Deeds of Māra," pp. 77-99.

manuscript translation from Tsoṅ-kha-pa's large treatment of "Calming the Mind."[29] Presumably this is also the reason for the silence on the topic in the *Saṃyutta-Nikāya* of the Pāli canon. The theory is that by calming the mind, the yogin may transcend the Realm of Desire in which humanity is plunged; and when he has advanced to the Realm of Form, he can resort to various kinds of meditative objects and "devices" that would be contraindicated for him while he is still a tyro, a slave of ordinary human nabits and appetites. When the yogin advances to the Realm of Form, he has new precepts to observe, especially with the Liberations, the bases of Mastery, and the bases of Totality, which also are involved with the Formless Realm.

But that some persons, by reason of a peculiar constitution can transcend the Realm of Desirc without the regular course of training, has long been recognized. Thus Asaṅga states in the exegesis of his *Śrāvakabhūmi* in the *Viniścayasaṃgrahaṇī* of the *Yogācārabhūmi*:[30]

> The domain of magical power either arises from praxis (*prayoga*) or is attained from birth. Among those, the one arising from praxis is as follows:—the fruit of the cultivation by ordinary persons (*pṛthagjana*), those in training (*śaikṣa*), those beyond training (*aśaikṣa*), and Bodhisattvas, born in this world. The one attained from birth is as follows: —the subsequent attainment from birth after the former recourse to the cultivation, on the part of those born in the Realm of Form; the attainment through the power of merit by the deities and certain men who range in the Realm of Desire, for example, like the [legendary] King Māndhātṛ's. Magical power also belongs to flying creatures [e.g. Vidyādhara-s] incorporated in the same categories [the two Realms] and to certain disembodied men (*preta*). There is also the power of gems, *mantras*, and herbs [respectively], as follows: to create a hypnotic fascination, to lay a curse, or to induce death or a comatose state, and which is called "magical power."

29This is a portion of the encyclopedic work *Lam rim chen mo* by Tsoṅ-kha-pa (1357-1419), referred to above (n. 15).

30This passage is found in the Tibetan canon, Derge Tanjur, *Sems tsam*, Vol. Źi, 259a-1, ff.; with the equivalent statement in the Chinese canon, Taishō, Vol. 30, p. 683c-8, ff. However, the Peking Tibetan canon (PTT) is defective at this point, PTT, Vol. 111, p. 47-2.

A SKETCH OF MEDITATIVE PROGRESS IN ASAṄGA'S SCHOOL

Here I shall construct an abbreviated account of meditative progress according to Asaṅga's *Yogācārabhūmi*. There are these parts: (a) Trying to get beyond the Realm of Desire; (b) Progress in the Realm of Form; (c) Progress in the Formless Realm; (d) Further information on the Form and Formless Realms.

(a) Trying to get beyond the Realm of Desire. In Asaṅga's school, there is what is called the "equipment" (*saṃbhāra*), amounting to thirteen conditions, one chief and twelve subordinate, as detailed in his *Śrāvakabhūmi*, where he sets forth:[31]

> Among those, if persons have the element of *parinirvāṇa*, and lack defective (organs), but have not approached (the spiritual guides), what are their conditions (*pratyaya*) for *parinirvāṇa*? He said: There are two conditons. What are the two? Chief (*pradhāna*) and subordinate (*hīna*). What is the chief condition? He said, as follows— 1. the discourse of others dominated by the Illustrious Doctrine (*saddharma*) and the inner methodical mental orientation (*yoniśo manaskāra*). What is the subordinate condition? He said: There are numerous subordinate conditions, as follows— 2. personal achievement (*ātmasampat*), 3. achievement of others (*parasampat*), 4. virtuous craving for the doctrine (*kuśalo dharmacchandaḥ*), 5. going forth (*pravrajyā*), 6. restraint of morality (*śīla-saṃvara*), 7. restraint of sense organs (*indriya-saṃvara*), 8. moderation in food (*bhojane mātrajñatā*), 9. practice of staying awake (*jāgarikānuyoga*), 10. conduct with awareness (*saṃprajānadvihāritā*), 11. solitude (*prāvivekya*), 12. elimination of hindrances (*nivaraṇa-viśuddhi*), 13. right dwelling in *samādhi* (*samādhisaṃniśraya*).

There is no room to dilate upon each of those conditions; some of them will come into our subsequent discussions. Besides, four of the subordinate conditions are especially pointed out in this literature as constituting the "equipment" for both calming and discerning, i.e. for both the second and third instructions. These are nos. 7-10 "restraint of sense organs" through "conduct with awareness." As to the favorable place to perform the meditations,

[31] WAYMAN, *Analysis*, pp. 59-60.

the *Sūtrālaṃkāra* (XIII, 7) gives the main list:[32] "The place where the wise man accomplishes has the merits 'good access,' 'good settlement,' 'good soil,' 'good companionship,' and 'good usage'."

The theory of overcoming the tremendous power of the realm of desire is especially in terms of the five hindrances (*nivaraṇa*) which are in the standard listing: sensuous lust, ill-will, torpor and sleepiness, mental wandering and regret, and doubt. Ratnākaraśānti states in his *Prajñāpāramitābhāvanopadeśa*,[33] following the *Saṃdhinirmocana-sūtra*, Chap. 8: "Here of the five hindrances, 'mental wandering and regret' is a hindrance to calming; 'torpor and sleepiness' and 'doubt' are hindrances to discerning; 'sensuous lust' and 'ill-will' are hindrances to both."

The yogin, having restrained his senses, being aware of his conduct, in a place suitable for meditation, meditates with folded legs in the former and latter parts of night, resting in the middle part. His spiritual guide had previously advised him on a meditative object, and how to avoid the faults of meditation. He is supposed to stick with this meditative object, without thinking about it or using discursive thought toward it, until some measure of success appears. Of the main faults, the two most troublesome ones are the scattering (*auddhatya*) or fading (*laya*) of the meditative object. The *Bhāvanākrama I* states:[34]

> When, overcome by torpor and sleepiness, and because the apprehension of the meditative object is not vivid, one's mind fades, then he should dispel the fading by the contemplation of the idea of light and by a mental orientation toward a gladdening entity, the merits of the Buddha, and so on. Thereafter, he should apprehend that same meditative object more firmly.

Or, again, from the same work:

> When he notices his mind scattered from time to time through remembrance of former laughter and delight, then he pacifies the scattering through a mental orientation to a sober (mentally aroused) topic, such as impermanence. Thereupon, he should

[32]SYLVAIN LÉVI, ed., *Asaṅga: Mahāyāna-Sūtrālaṃkāra* (Paris, 1907), p. 86.

[33]PTT, Vol. 114, p. 235-3.

[34]The *Bhāvanākrama* citations are drawn from my manuscript translation of Tsoṅ-kha-pa's "Calming the Mind" (n. 15, above). For Kamalaśīla's *Bhāvanākrama I*, see GIUSEPPE TUCCI, *Minor Buddhist Texts, Part II* (Roma, 1958), Chap. 2 "The Contents of the First Bhāvanākrama."

> make an attempt to engage that same meditative object without instigation of the mind.

Also, *Bhāvanākrama II* states:

> At the time there is no fading or scattering, one notices repose of mind toward that meditative object; then one should relax the effort and be equable; then one should abide (in that state) for as long as he wishes.

According to the *Śrāvakabhūmi*, there are nine stages of thought fixation (*cittasthiti*) from the initial fastening of the mind to a meditation object to the point where the mind, after learning to avoid the various major faults, is made to flow one-pointedly (stage no. 8), and finally has a natural concentration (*samādhi*) in an automatic manner with lack of effort (stage no. 9). There are instructions going with each one of the nine stages.[35] But even if one gets to the ninth stage, it does not necessarily constitute a surmounting of the Realm of Desire to arrive at a stage of equipoise (*samāpatti*) in the Realm of Form. Why so? According to the *Bhūmi-vastu* (part of the *Yogācārabhūmi*):[36]

> Why is it that only it is called "stage of equipoise," while any single area (of mind) belonging to the realm of craving is not? As follows—That *samādhi* is accomplished with lack of regret, the highest rapture, the cathartic, and pleasure.[37] However, the one that ranges in craving is not that way. (Still,) there is no lack of thinking-volition that approaches right doctrine in the realm of craving.

But then, how is one to know if he is surmounting the Realm of Desire, if gaining this effortless one-pointedness of mind does not show it?[38] The reply is that it is also necessary to have what is called the cathartic (*praśrabdhi*), especially shown by a serviceability of body—an animation and lightness, and a serviceability

[35]As extensively set forth in "Calming the Mind".

[36]As cited in "Calming the Mind".

[37]Cf. COUSINS, "Buddhist *Jhāna*." pp. 120-22, for an elaborate discussion of the meditative "rapture" (S. *prīti*) by its Pāli form *pīti*.

[38]Therefore one must now correct ELIADE, *Yoga*, p. 169, "Real Buddhist meditation begins with experiencing the four psychic states called *jhānas* (cf. Skr. *dhyāna*)," since one may not have attained the Jhāna states even when having achieved one-pointedness of mind by elimination of faults of meditation.

of mind that prevails without hindrance upon the meditative object by an exchange (*parivṛtti*) of mental-concomitant natures. And this has a portent, as the *Śrāvakabhūmi* states:[39]

> A short time before the obvious cathartic of mind and body and the single area of mind become easy to discern, there occurs a portent (*pūrvanimitta*) of that, the appearance of a weight on the head, and this is not a sign of harm. No sooner does this occur, than the mind contamination in the category of defilements that interrupt the joy of elimination, is (itself) eliminated; and, as its opponent [or, supplantor], the serviceability of mind and the cathartic of mind arise.

And this cathartic is a kind of wind, according to the *Śrāvakabhūmi:*

> As a result of its production, the great elements (*mahābhūta*), urged by the wind, and concordant with the production of the cathartic of body, course in the body. By reason of their coursing, any contamination (*dauṣṭhulya*) of body disappears. Also, the whole body is filled with its opponent, the cathartic of body, as though it were a radiance.

And the same work states:

> Furthermore, when one has emerged (from that *samādhi*) and is occupied with his (ordinary) mind, some measure of the cathartic continues in his body and mind. The mental orientation's marks and signs consistent therewith should be understood as pure.

The late Mongolian Lama, Dilowa Gegen Hutukhtu, once told me that if one does the procedure correctly, it takes about six months to get to this attainment, called the calming of mind (*cetośamatha*) within. This in short is the success in the meditative object, without discursive thought, without deliberating it at all.

(b) Progress in the Realm of Form. According to Buddhist traditions, to become a Buddha one must pass through the four Dhyānas of this realm.[40] The calming already delineated means

[39]The following citations from the *Srāvakabhūmi* are all translated in the context of the manuscript "Calming the Mind".

[40]ANDRÉ BAREAU, *Recherches sur la biographie du Buddha dans les Sūtrapiṭaka et les Vinayapiṭaka anciens* (Paris, 1963), pp. 69-71, points out that all five Buddhist traditions that he examined agree that the four Dhyānas

the yogin has attained the threshold of the First Dhyāna. At that time, he can proceed further through the various divisions of the Realm of Form and the Formless Realm, even up to the summit of existence and still not be liberated from the cyclical flow (*saṃsāra*). But, it is taught, if he combines calming with discerning (the union of the two) he can attain liberation from the bondage of cyclical flow. The value anyway of proceeding to a higher state, even without the wherewithal of liberation from *saṃsāra*, is that the yogin's attainment of a realm gives him the good fortune of possible birth among the gods of that realm.[41]

Now, suppose the yogin proceeds through the various states of the Realm of Form and the Formless Realm. It should be noticed that the basic statements for each state were established in the ancient Buddhist canon, but in post-canonical times, presumably to resolve conflicts of scriptural passages, each one of those states, except for the *bhavāgra* (summit of existence), was divided into two parts, called in Sanskrit the "threshold" (*sāmantaka*) and "main part" (*maula* or *maulī*), and in Pāli the "access" (*upacāra*) and "full concentration" (*appanā*).[42] In such a division the term "attainment" (*samāpatti*)—which I frequently render as "equipoise"—stands for the "main part" of "full concentration," and there are eight of these (four in the Realm of Form, and four in the Formless Realm), with a ninth one sometimes added for the "summit of existence."

The four such two-part states of the Realm of Form are usually referred to as the four Dhyānas (in Sanskrit) or four Jhānas (in Pāli), and Asaṅga includes them under "right dwelling in *samādhi*." I now render the four statements from the old Buddhist canon, along with comments from Asaṅga's school.[43]

"Right dwelling in *samādhi*" (I): *Separated from desires* (*kāma*), *separated from sinful and unvirtuous natures, with inquiry*

(P. Jhāna) are the preparatory phase for the great enlightenment, and then sets forth his reservations about the historicity of the tradition.

[41]Asaṅga's *Srāvakabhūmi*, PTT, Vol. 110, p. 121-3; and Karunesha Shukla, *Srāvakabhūmi of Ācārya Asaṅga* (Patna, 1973), pp. 468-69.

[42]For the Pāli terms, cf. Cousins, "Buddhist *Jhāna*," p. 118 and note; Buddhadāsa, *Anāpānasati*, p. 37.

[43]By Asaṅga's school, I mean especially the treatment in his *Samāhitabhūmi* and *Srāvakabhūmi* (Fourth Yogasthāna), both being portions of his great *Yogācārabhūmi*.

(vitarka) and investigation (vicāra), having attained the First Dhyāna , he dwells in the rapture (prīti) and pleasure (sukha) arising from the separation.

In the *Śrāvakabhūmi*, Asaṅga explains "he dwells" as "up to endeavoring to reach seven days and seven nights,"[44] for which the Japanese translation notes that seven days is the limit for maintaining strength while refraining from morsel food.[45] Also, the chosen meditative object is unsteady (*vyagra*).[46] In the *Samāhitabhūmi* Asaṅga states that in the First Dhyāna the body has an outer light like a gem.[47]

"Right dwelling in *samādhi*" (II): *Through allaying inquiry and investigation, through inward serenity, through continuity of thought, he accomplishes and dwells in the Second Dhyāna which is without inquiry or investigation, and which has rapture and pleasure arising from samādhi.*

Now the meditation object is steady, and the mental orientation is "without interruptions" by avoiding the faults of inquiry and investigation. Caroline Rhys Davids, following the Theravāda, says:[48] "The discursive intellection of the First Jhāna, troubling the *ceto* [the mind], as waves rendering water turbid, has in the Second Jhāna sunk to rest." The *Samāhitabhūmi* explains the "inward serenity" as mindfulness (*smṛti*), awareness (*saṃprajanya*), and equanimity (*upekṣā*). Here, the body has an outer light like that of a flame.[49]

"Right dwelling in *samādhi*" (III): *He dwells with equanimity after losing the feeling of rapture. Mindful and aware he experiences pleasure by way of body, just as the one to whom the nobles referred, "Equable and mindful he dwells in pleasure." He accomplishes and dwells in the Third Dhyāna which is without rapture.*

[44]SHUKLA, *Srāvakabhūmi*, p. 451; *yāvad ākāṅkṣamāṇaḥ saptarātriṃ-divasāni.*

[45]*Kokuyaku Daizōkyō*, Rombu, Vol. 7, p. 144.

[46]SHUKLA, *Srāvakabhūmi*, p. 451-6.

[47]PTT, Vol. 109, p. 278-1.

[48]CAROLINE A. F. RHYS DAVIDS, *A Buddhist Manual of Psychological Ethics* (London, 1900), p. 46, note.

[49]PTT, Vol. 109, p. 278-1.

The *Śrāvakabhūmi* explains the words "he experiences pleasure by way of body": "with the body of form and the body of mind he experiences the pleasure of feelings which is the pleasure of the cathartic."[50] Here he avoids the fault of rapture (*prīti*). The "nobles" are the Buddhas and their disciples. According to the *Samāhitabhūmi*, this is the best place for the *samādhi* of knowledge and vision (*jñānadarśana*) and the Diamond-like *samādhi* (*vajropamasamādhi*).[51] Also, by saying in the same place that love (*maitrī*) best accomplishes the pleasure of the Third Dhyāna, Asaṅga may have hinted at what his brother Vasubandhu was to mention in a comment on a Mahāyāna scripture, namely, that the future Buddha defeated the "son-of-the-gods" Māra by the *samādhi* of love (*maitrī*) during the celebrated assault of Māra.[52] In this case, the "earth-touching gesture" would go with the "body of form" while the "gesture of *samāpatti*" would go with the "body of mind."[53] Besides, Vasubandhu, *Abhidharmakośa*, Chap. VIII, says this Dhyāna is "shaken by its excellent pleasure."[54] And in the legend, earth shook at the future Buddha's touch. This would accord with the general Indian theory that it is precisely when natural forces are inimical that the spiritual victory is possible (thus during the stress of the full-moon, the climactic of sundown, etc.),[55] so also when the Dhyāna is shaken by its excellent pleasure.

"Right dwelling in *samādhi*" (IV): *Through elimination of pleasure, through former elimination of pain and vanishing of*

[50] *Rūpakāyena manaḥkāyena veditasukhaṃ ca prasrabdhisukhaṃ pratisaṃvedayate;* Shukla, *Śrāvakabhūmi*, p. 453-9. improperly separates *vedita* from *sukhaṃ*.

[51] PTT, Vol. 109, p. 278-3.

[52] ALEX WAYMAN, "Studies in Yama and Māra," *Indo-Iranian Journal*, Vol. III, No. 2, 1959, p. 116.

[53] The reference is of course to the celebrated incident in the Buddha's life of the "Assault of Māra," when the Buddha appealed to the "authority" or "measure" (*pramāṇa*) of earth by touching it with his right hand, while his left hand indicated by the "equipoise gesture" (*samāpatti-mudrā*) his meditative attainment, an incident which long ago I attempted to interpret, per "Studies in Yama and Māra," *op. cit.*, pp. 117-18.

[54] LOUIS DE LA VALLÉE POUSSIN, *L'Abhidharmakośa de Vasubandhu*, Septième et huitième chapitres (Paris, 1925), p. 209.

[55] Cf. ALEX WAYMAN, "Climactic Times in Indian Mythology and Religion," *History of Religions* Vol. 4, No. 2, Winter 1965, pp. 295-318.

satisfaction and dissatisfaction, having attained the Fourth Dhyāna, he abides in the purification of equanimity and mindfulness free from both pleasure and pain.

According to the *Śrāvakabhūmi*, this Fourth Dhyāna has eliminated the pleasure that characterized the Third Dhyāna. Formerly, the Second Dhyāna eliminated pain; the Third Dhyāna eliminated satisfaction; the First Dhyāna eliminated dissatisfaction.[56] However, Sthīramati, subcommentary on *Abhidharmakośa*, Chap. VIII, disagrees, presenting an Abhidharma tradition that both pain and dissatisfaction cease in the First Dhyāna.[57] Besides it says in the *Śrāvakabhūmi*: the Fourth Dhyāna is accomplished by avoiding the fault of inhalation and exhalation;[58] and consciousness (*citta*) remains unshaken.[59] *Le Traité* agrees that it is *citta* which is unshaken.[60]

It will be observed that the four Dhyānas divide into two groups of two, since the first two Dhyānas are realized by the mind, and the meditative object is respectively unsteady and steady; while the last two Dhyānas are realized by the body, and are respectively shaken or unshaken by pleasure. For these considerations, it should be recognized that "pleasure" (*sukha*) has both corporeal and mental varictics, while "rapture" (*prīti*) is only mental. Also, the first two Dhyānas, according to the *Abhidharmakośa* and *Le Traité*,[61] go together by their association with the first two Liberations and first four bases of Mastery—in which association their meditation object is the visible form of the realm of desire, especially the revolting object.

Furthermore, according to both the Theravāda and Mahīśāsaka, all four of the Dhyānas have a single area of thought, because that

[56]Cf. Shukla, *Srāvakabhūmi*, p. 454-8-11.

[57]PTT, Vol. 147, p. 265-2.

[58]Shukla, *Srāvakabhūmi*, p. 454.16.

[59]So reads the Tibetan: PTT, Vol. 110, p. 119-1-4, with the word *sems* (consciousness), and included in the Sanskrit as properly edited at this point by Shukla (p. 454.18-19): *cittaṃ...aniṃjyaṃ santiṣṭhate.* But then he gives a wrong reading, *sarvañjitāyatanaṃ*, while the Bihar Society's manuscript which he used (13A-7, last line) reads: *sarvveñjitāpagataṃ*, verified by the Tibetan, *g'yo ba thams cad dan bral bas na*, "being free from all shaking."

[60]Lamotte, *Le Traité*, II, p. 1031.

[61]Lamotte, *Le Traité*, III, p. 1289.

is the meaning of "Dhyāna" (P. Jhāna) here.[62] Besides (*Samāhitabhūmi*), each of the four Dhyānas is "one's partial *nirvāṇa*" (*aṅganirvāṇa*), because it eliminates only the side of defilement and lacks the side of certainty.[63] To avoid the attachment to one of the Dhyānas as "Nirvāṇa," in Asaṅga's school one contemplates the lower planes as "coarse" and the higher ones as "subtle" or "calm"; and is thus motivated to emerge from one plane and go to the next one.[64]

Besides, the Buddhist theory of the realms places at the top of the Fourth Dhyāna what are called the "pure abodes," five in number. The highest one, called Akaniṣṭha, is where certain Buddhist traditions say Śākyamuni was enlightened. Finally, it should be mentioned that each of the four Dhyānas is divided into three degrees corresponding with the gods of the realm being ordered into three groups. Thus, there are twelve such divisions in the basic four Dhyānas, to which the five pure abodes, each with their own gods, are added to make the total of seventeen levels in the Realm of Form.

(c) Progress in the Formless Realm. For the yogin proceeding in the Formless Realm, the states are explained by these passages found in the *Śrāvakabhūmi*:[65]

(1) He (the Lord) said: When one has transcended in every way the ideas of form (*rūpasaṃjñā*), when the ideas of impediment (*pratighasaṃjñā*) have abated, and when one pays no attention to ideas of diversity (*nānātva-saṃjñā*), one perceives space as infinite, accomplishes and dwells in the base of infinite space (*ākāśānantyāyatanam upasampadya viharati*). Now, he said, "when one has transcended in every way the idea of form," because there would be conviction of space when the ideas of color—blue, yellow, red

[62]This is the traditional implication of the expression "dwells" or "abides" used in the traditional statements of the four Dhyānas. More technically, Asaṅga defines the term *dhyāna* in the *Samāhitabhūmi* (PTT, Vol. 109, p. 269-5.1): "Since there is the right directed thinking which purifies consciousness pursuant to the (instruction of) mental training (*adhicitta*), there is the term '*dhyāna*'." Cf. my Introduction.

[63]PTT, Vol. 109, p. 269-5-8, to p. 270-1.

[64]WAYMAN, *Analysis*, pp. 126-29.

[65]SHUKLA, *Srāvakabhūmi*, pp. 455.6, ff.; Bihar Society's manuscript of the *Srāvakabhūmi* 13B-7, ff.; edition in Tibetan canon, PTT, Vol. 110, p. 119-1-6, ff.

and white—disappear,[66] and when one is freed from and transcends the clinging to weariness. He said, "when the ideas of impediment have abated," because when they have abated, one is freed from the numerous and diverse ideas of hindrance (*āvaraṇa-saṃjñā*) that are assembled by colors. He said, "when one pays no attention to ideas of diversity," because when one does not have them, ideas concerned with accumulation (*aupacayikā saṃjñā*), such as ideas of food, drink, vehicles, clothes, adornments, houses, gardens and glades, armies, mountains, etc., and one's possessions in every sense, do not operate. The *Samāhitabhūmi*[67] adds that the best compassion (*karuṇā*) would be in the base of infinite space; since compassion seeks to free the sentient beings from their manifold sufferings.

(2) One gets to the infinity of perception base (*vijñānānantyāyatana*) by that very perception that was convinced of the space with the infinite aspect. The *Samāhitabhūmi*[68] adds that the best sympathetic joy (*muditā*) would be in this base; because here one can perceive whatever beings are happy, have attained, and so on, and have sympathetic joy with them.

(3) One emerges from the base of infinite perception by searching whether there is another object-support (*ālambana*) different from perception (*vijñāna*), whether with form or formless; and not finding such an object-support, one transcends the base of infinite perception with its threshold and basic part. Being convinced that there is no other object-support, one is convinced about only the idea of nothing-at-all (*akiñcana-saṃjñā*). Frequently repeating the conviction of that idea one transcends the threshold of nothing-at-all, accomplishes and dwells in the main part of the nothing-at-all base (*ākiñcanyāyatana*). The *Samāhitabhūmi*[69] adds that this is the outer limit for those with non-fluxional mind (*anāsrava-citta*) and that it is the best place for those with equanimity (*upekṣā*).

(4) Then he emerges from the base of nothing-at-all. As to

66Since "form" (*rūpa*) covers both "shape" (*saṃsthāna*) and "color" (*varṇa*), in the Formless Realm colors also disappear. Observe that these colors in the same order are the traditional mention of the four color *kasiṇa-s*.

67PTT, Vol. 109, p. 278-3-3.

68PTT, Vol. 109, p. 278-3-8.

69PTT, Vol. 109, p. 278-3-8 to 278-3-1. It is worthwhile to give the Chinese reference, Taishō Vol. 30, p. 338b-27.

the idea of the base of nothing-at-all, one possesses the idea of coarseness (*audārika-saṃjñin*) and the idea of (eventual) trouble (*ādīnava-saṃjñin*), so turns away from the idea of the base of nothing-at-all and transcends it. Therefore, there is no idea (*naiva-saṃjñā*) (of the base of nothing-at-all). But also, one proceeds in a subtle manner in an idea whose object-support (*ālambana*) is imageless (*animitta*). Therefore, there is no lack of an idea (*nāsaṃjñā*). Being convinced that it is a base (*āyatana*) one accomplishes and dwells in the base of neither idea nor no-idea (*naivasaṃjñā-nāsaṃjñāyatana*). Asaṅga mentions that the ordinary person (*pṛthagjana*) has the "equipoise without idea" (*asaṃjñi-samāpatti*) in this base; while the noble ones wish for the quiescent abode and so emerge from the base of neither idea nor no-idea, to reach the cessation equipoise (*nirodhasamāpatti*)—and those who reach it are the Arhats. Asaṅga does not identify the cessation equipoise here with the item in other texts of "cessation of feelings and ideas" (*saṃjñāveditanirodha*); but he does mention this, what others call the "ninth *samāpatti*", in the *Samāhita-bhūmi* as the eighth Liberation, with the statement of the ancient scripture: "having directly realized with the body the cessation of feelings and ideas, he dwells therein."

(d) Further information on the Form and Formless Realms. Asaṅga has a remarkable statement in the *Śrāvakabhūmi* about the respective appearance of the body in the realm of form in comparison with the formless realm:[70]

> Among (those states), the appearance shown by the body at the time of equipoise in the Dhyānas is like entering subterranean chambers and at the time of equipoise in the formless realms is like rising to the sky.

This suggests that the usual Western manner of listing the divisions of the Realm of Desire, Realm of Form, and Formless—as though these were successively layered upwards—does not appraise them rightly. One is not really going anywhere, because calming of the mind is an inward process; and still the yogin's body (if one has

[70]Bihar Manuscript, 13A-8. 4b: / tatra dhyānasamāpattikāle adhorasā-talapraveśavat / kāyasaṃprakhyānaliṅgaṃ / ārūpyasamāpattikāle ākāśot-patanavat /. Compare SHUKLA, *Śrāvakabhūmi*, p. 458.16-18. Tibetan at PTT, Vol. 110, p. 119-5-7-8.

the "eye" to see it) exhibits those various features ("like a gem," "like a flame").[71]

The theory of the yogin's attainments in the Realm of Form and Formless Realm is further clarified by ancient Buddhist scriptural passages about the Liberations, bases of Totality, and bases of Mastery.[72] Asaṅga summarizes the Liberations (*vimokṣa*) at the beginning of the *Samāhitabhūmi*:[73]

1. Having form, he sees form. This is the first Liberation.
2. Having the idea (*saṃjñin*) that he is formless personally, he sees exterior forms. This is the second Liberation.
3. Having directly realized with the body the Liberation, he accomplishes it and dwells in it. This is the third Liberation.

4, 5, 6, 7, 8. Having accomplished 4. the base of infinite space, 5. the base of infinite perception, 6. the base of nothing-at-all, 7. the base of neither idea nor no-idea, and 8. having directly realized with the body the cessation of feelings and ideas, he dwells therein. This is the fourth through eighth Liberations.

As to the bases of Totality (*kṛtsnāyatana*), Asaṅga summarizes them in the exegesis of his *Samāhitabhūmi*:[74]

> The cultivation by the yogin of the ten bases of Totality performs five deeds. What are the five?—
>
> 1. By the earth totality, etc. up through the white totality (eight in all) he accomplishes the noble magical power (*ārya-ṛddhi*) of magical manifestation and transmutation of substance.
> 2. By the base of space totality, he accomplishes the noble magical power of coming and going.
> 3. By the base of perception totality, he accomplishes the merits of "*samādhi* purifying others" (*araṇā-samādhi*), "knowledge of aspirations" (*praṇidhi-jñāna*), and the four "special knowledges" (*pratisaṃvid*).[75]

[71]This shows the difficulty of accepting Goleman, "The Buddha on Meditation," Table 1, pp. 30-31, on his imputed physiological differences of these states. For how is one to know which state the *yogin* is in, unless one has the "eye" for it?

[72]For the literature, see LAMOTTE , *Le Traité*, III, Chap. XXXIV, pp. 1281, ff.

[73]PTT, Vol. 109, p. 276-2-5 ff.

[74]PTT, Vol. 111, p. 10-5-3 ff.

[75]Cf. LA VALLÉE POUSSIN, *L'Abhidharmakośa*, Septième, pp. 85 ff. where it is said that the three which Asaṅga mentioned are in common between the

4. Upon accomplishing the base of perception totality, he accomplishes the Liberation in the base of nothing-at-all and the Liberation in the base of neither idea nor no-idea.
5. On the basis of that accomplishment, he is equipoised in the Liberation which is the cessation of feelings and ideas, comprised by the supreme station.

The traditional Buddhist statement of the first base of Mastery (*abhibhvāyatana*) reads:

> Having the idea of form personally, he sees external forms, as small, of good and bad color. He has this idea: "Mastering those forms, I know them; mastering them, I see them." This is the first base of Mastery.

Substituting the expression "large" for "small," one has the statement of the second base of Mastery. According to the *Samāhitabhūmi*,[76] small forms are sentient beings, tools, etc.; large forms, houses, temples, etc. Substituting in the first two statements, "Having the idea that he is formless personally" for "having the idea of form personally" one has the third and fourth bases of Mastery. For the fifth through eighth bases of Mastery, the statement begins with "Having the idea that he is formless personally, he sees external forms as blue" (or yellow, red, and white, respectively).

There are some problems about dovetailing the three lists. According to the *Samāhitabhūmi*,[77] the first Liberation has the mental orientation toward forms, "I was born in the Realm of Desire and achieved freedom of craving toward desires, but am not free from the craving toward forms (of the Realm of Form)."[78] This Liberation is correlated with the first two bases of Mastery.

Buddha and the *āryas*, but here associated with the Fourth Dhyāna, in contrast with Asaṅga's assignment of them to the Formless Realm, the base of infinite perception. Of these terms, the *praṇidhi-jñāna* is a type of knowledge of the future; and the four "special knowledges" are of entities (*artha*), scriptural elements (*dharma*), denotation (*nirukti*), and eloquence (*pratibhāna*).

[76]PTT, Vol. 109, p. 276-4-7.

[77]PTT, Vol. 109, p. 276-2-2,3.

[78]This seems to be involved in a disputed point among the Buddhist sects as Bareau, *Les sectes* p. 267, summarizes, "Il y a *rūparāga* dans le seul, *rūpadhātu*," meaning that craving for forms is restricted to the Realm of Form, which the Andhaka and the Sammatīya sects concurred in, and the Theravāda rejected.

Then, the second Liberation has the idea, "I was born in the Realm of Desire and am free from the craving toward forms, but have not realized the formless equipoise." This Liberation is correlated with the next two bases of Mastery. The correlation with the bases of Totality is more controversial, but Asaṅga states:[79] "Among them, the formal ones (*rūpin*) are totality equipoises of the lower Realm of Form." Now "form" (*rūpa*) in Buddhism is the four elements and their derivatives; thus, it is certain that Asaṅga associates the first four Totalities (earth, etc.) with the first two Dhyānas. Furthermore, the second group of four totalities, the color ones, agree with the fifth through eighth bases of Mastery, involved with the third Liberation. But there was a controversy over placing the third Liberation, since both the Third and Fourth Dhyānas are directly realized by the body. The *Mahā-Parinibbāna-sutta* described this third Liberation as "pleasant" (*subha*), so it would be natural to connect it with the Third Dhyāna whose deities are called the "pleasant' ' (P. *subba*, S. *śubha*) deities. However, Vasubandhu (*Abhibharmakośa*, VIII, 32c) gives the Abhidharma tradition that the Third Dhyāna is shaken by its excellent pleasure and hence is not a place of Liberation; and so this Liberation belongs to the Fourth Dhyāna (at the top of which the Buddha is reputed to have attained Parinibbāna). Asaṅga[80] raises the question of where it is to be located, and associates it with the purification of equanimity and mindfulness, and so places it in the Fourth Dhyāna. On the other hand, Vajirañāṇa[81] points out that the Commentary on the *Mahā-Parinibbāna-sutta* mentions that the Buddha's skillfulness in the particular bases of Mastery that deal with the four color-*kasiṇa* objects "was the basis of his fearlessness even at the sight of Māra." In the light of my previous discussion (based on Asaṅga's and Vasubandhu's Mahāyāna works), associating the Buddha's defeat of the "son-of-the-gods" Māra with the Third Dhyāna, I find here a support (against Asaṅga's and Vasubandhu's Abhidharma-type comments) for associating the third Liberation with the Third Dhyāna. But this solution has the demerit of allotting no Liberation to the Fourth Dhyāna. It seems that a solution which would

[79] *Samāhitabhūmi*, PTT, Vol. 109, p. 276-5-5.

[80] *Samāhitabhūmi*, PTT, Vol. 109, p. 276-3-4, ff.

[81] *Buddhist Meditation*, p. 481.

allow the greatest compatibility with all the foregoing positions, is to allot the third Liberation, with its promotional *yoga* of four bases of Mastery associated with colors, and the equivalent bases of Totality, to both the Third and Fourth Dhyānas. Then there would be Liberations corresponding to all the four Dhyānas as well as to all the formless states.

Another correlation with the Form and Formless Realms, that is apparently independent of the Liberations along with their bases of Mastery and Totality, concerns a remarkable passage in Asaṅga's *Samāhitabhūmi*.[82] He raises the question, "When one has the cessation equipoise, how do the three kinds of 'motivations' (*saṃskāra*) sequentially cease?" And he answers:

> There is both practice (*caryā*) and station (*vihāra*). Among these, at the time one is involved with practice, there is also discourse, because that is the verbal motivation (*vāksaṃskāra*) which is the act of the First Dhyāna. At the time one enterprises stations, since one is equipoised in the Second Dhyāna and subsequent stations in succession, they (the three "motivations") cease successively.

He raises the question, "If the thought (*citta*) and mentals (*caitasikadharma*) of the one in equipoise cessation ceased, how would he avoid a separation of 'perception' (*vijñāna*) and body?" And he answers:

> There is no absence of "store-consciousness" (*ālayavijñāna*) controlled by the seed of evolving perception (*pravṛttivijñāna*) in his non-altering formal sense organs—because this is the true nature of the coming event.

There is no doubt that Asaṅga here refers to the three kinds of "motivation" which the *Arthaviniścaya-sūtra*[83] assigns to the second member of Dependent Origination (*pratītyasamutpāda*). The three, of body, speech, and mind, cease during the succession of "stations" (*vihāra*), which therefore begin with the Second Dhyāna. The manner of ceasing is clear from the traditional

[82]PTT, Vol. 109, p. 281-1-4 ff.

[83]The portion of this *sūtra* that is relevant here is included in the fragment published by Alfonsa Ferrari in 1944 in *Atti Reale Della Accademia D'Italia*, Roma, Serie Settima, vol. V, fasc. 13. In N. H. SAMTANI, *The Arthaviniścaya-sūtra and its Commentary* (*Nibandhana*) (Patna, 1971), the passage is in the text, pp. 7-8.

Buddhist statements of the realms. Thus the Second Dhyāna eliminates the fault of inquiry (*vitarka*) and investigation (*vicāra*) that was present in the First Dhyāna, and so "motivation of speech" ceases. The Fourth Dhyāna eliminates the fault of inhalation and exhalation, so "motivation of body" (*kāya-saṃskāra*) ceases. Finally, the summit of existence (*bhavāgra*) eliminates feelings and ideas, and so "motivation of mind" (*manaḥ-saṃskāra*) ceases.[84] But this third kind of cessation of "motivation" does not constitute a radical separation from ordinary consciousness according to Asaṅga. So Falk is right in saying,[85] "In primitive Buddhist *vijñānavāda* the notion of *ālayavijñāna* is foreshadowed in the conception of *citta* = *mano* = *viññāna* (synonyms in Pāli literature) as origin, source, and essence of all the *dhammas* (Dhp. 1)." She refers to *Dhammapada* 1, including: "The natures (*dhaṃma*, S. *dharma*) are preceded by *manas*, have *manas* as chief, are made of *manas*." By mentioning the "non-altering formal sense organs" Asaṅga alludes to a celebrated Buddhist legend, that at the time of convoking the second Buddhist council the Arhat Kubjita, being in the cessation equipoise, did not hear the gong. Kubjita's ear organ did not alter; and yet when he emerged from his cessation equipoise, a *deva* informed him of the circumstances. Asaṅga's equivalent to the "*deva*" is the yogin's own "store consciousness" (*ālayavijñāna*) controlled by the seed of evolving perception—a seed which holds futurity. The story continues that Kubjita, by virtue of his magical power (*ṛddhi*), then "flew" to the meeting.[86]

The tabulation will show the foregoing correlations, which only in the case of the Third Dhyāna has a contribution of my own.

[84]According to the *Arthaviniścaya-sūtra*, when "motivation of mind" ceases, so must cease the volition (*cetanā*) of an impassioned thought (*rakta*), of a hating thought (*dviṣṭa*), of a deluded thought (*mūḍha*). Moreover, LAMOTTE, *Le Traité*, III, p. 1299, when feelings and ideas cease, the tradition has it that also all thoughts (*citta*) and mentals (*caitasika-dharma*) cease.

[85]MARYLA FALK, *Nāma-rūpa and Dharma-rūpa* (University of Calcutta, 1943), p. 85.

[86]For the story, see for example, Ferdinand D. LESSING and ALEX WAYMAN, *Mkhas grub rje's Fundamentals of the Buddhist Tantras* (The Hague, 1968), p. 65.

Eight successive stations (*vihāra*) of equipoise (*samāpatti*)

VIHĀRA			
8	SUMMIT OF EXISTENCE (*bhavāgra*) (frequently called the "ninth *samāpatti*")		
	Cessation of ideas and feelings = cessation of "motivation of mind" = eighth Liberation.		
	FORMLESS REALM		
7	Base of neither idea nor no-idea = seventh Liberation.		
6	Base of nothing-at-all = sixth Liberation; the best place for those with equanimity (*upekṣā*).		
5	Base of infinite perception = fifth Liberation; perception Totality, with the four special knowledges, etc.		
4	Base of infinite space = fourth Liberation; space Totality, with magic power to come and go.		
	REALM OF FORM		
3	Upper Dhyānas: Fourth Dhyāna: unshaken by pleasure = cessation of "motivation of body"	Third Liberation; bases of Mastery 5-8; bases of Totality 5-8; 5. blue, 6. yellow, 7. red, 8. white	
2	Upper Dhyānas: Third Dhyāna: shaken by pleasure		
1	Lower Dhyānas: Second Dhyāna: meditative object steady = cessation of "motivation of speech"	Second Liberation; bases of Mastery, 3-4	Bases of Totality, 1. earth, 2. water, 3. fire, 4. wind
Caryā samāpatti	Lower Dhyānas: First Dhyāna: meditative object unsteady	First Liberation; bases of Mastery, 1-2	

Asaṅga's *Samāhitabhūmi* presents three degrees of passing through these equipoises:[87] (1) passing through them without skipping, i.e. First Dhyāna up to Summit of Existence, and in reverse order, for a *yogin* who is not pure. (2) leaping over the second one in order, but not over the third which is too far to jump, for example, First directly to Third Dhyāna, to Base of infinite space, to Base of nothing-at-all; and in reverse order in comparable manner—for a *yogin* who is pure. (3) entering any

[87]PTT, Vol. 109, p. 275-4, 5. Cf. Jacques May's entry "Chōjō" in *Hōbōgirin*, Quatrième Fascicule: Chi-Chōotsushō, pp. 353-60, especially p. 358.

of them from any other one as wished, for Tathāgatas and Bodhisattvas who have passed the second incalculable aeon (explained in the Prajñāpāramitā tradition as the last three stages, 8th, 9th, and 10th of the Bodhisattva path).[88]

The Instruction of Insight

The instruction of insight—the third of the three instructions—is frequently set forth by the term "discerning" (*vipaśyanā*). Thus *Sūtrālaṃkāra*, XIV, 8:

> One should know his path of calming and the concise statement of the doctrines; one should know his path of discerning—the deliberation of the meanings of that (concise statement).

As was indicated previously, the path of discerning, which gradually perfects insight (*prajñā*), is meant to eliminate the deep-seated traces (*anuśaya*) of defilements, whereas the training in concentration of the mind aims at a one-pointedness leaving no room in the mind at that time for a defilement. This position, so much stressed in the writings of Asaṅga's school (the later Mahīśāsaka) is also what the Theravāda says.[89]

But, while calming the mind was already set forth as necessary to attain the threshold of the First Dhyāna, one does not continue through the various stations depicted above by calming alone. Thus the Yogācāra sub-commentator Sthiramati states in his commentary on the *Sūtrālaṃkāra* (XVIII, 66-67) that in the first three Dhyānas, discerning is major, calming minor; while in the Fourth Dhyāna there is the pairwise-union (*yuganaddha*) of calming and discerning. He means, starting from the main part (*maulī*) of the First Dhyāna.

The path of discerning, otherwise called the instruction of insight, presents methodical mental orientations in terms of deliberating, investigating the object. Thus the *Visuddhimagga* includes under this instruction such matters as understanding the personal aggregates to be void of self or of what belongs to self, observing impermanence, and the like. It is not necessary to have preceded this path of discerning with calming of the type associated with the cathartic and rapture; because, as was cited, "(Still,)

[88]Cf. Lessing and Wayman, *Mkhas grub rje's*, p. 21.
[89]*Buddhist Meditation*, p. 341

there is no lack of thinking-volition that approaches right doctrine in the realm of craving." What is taught is that it is necessary to calm the mind in order to transcend the Realm of Desire.

Along these lines, Buddhadāsa[90] cites the *Visuddhimagga:* "The wise man, standing firm on the ground, takes up the edged weapon in his hands, sharpens it on the stone, and, working diligently, succeeds in clearing away the thick jungle." And he well explains, "The 'wise man' is anyone with inborn insight (*sahajāta-paññā*) or what is nowadays called intelligence. This is an immature form of insight which has to be developed into true and genuine insight (*vipassanāpaññā*)." In a separate essay,[91] I have cited Asaṅga's explanation of the scriptural "eye of insight" as the native insight (*sahajā prajñā*); and have mentioned his later explanation that the native insight is attained through birth, and that he contrasts the promoted insight possessed by the learned man (*paṇḍita*) with the native insight possessed by the intelligent man (*vijña*). He defines the term *buddhi* as standing for any native insight capable of differentiating (alternatives). Earlier in his great work he shows how the eye of insight is assailed in the Realm of Desire: "For example, smoke is preceded by the element of fire and hurts the eye .... In the same way, craving (*tṛṣṇā*) is preceded by lust, hatred, and delusion and hurts the eye of insight ..." It would be hard to find a more perfect agreement between the Theravāda (as in Buddhadāsa) and the Mahīśāsaka (as in Asaṅga).

Besides, there are numerous references in Buddhist texts to three kinds of "insight." The teacher Atīśa, who was very influential in Tibet starting with his arrival in 1042, A.D., mentions the three in this way:[92] "What is insight? As follows:—native (*sahajā*), or consisting of hearing (*śrutamayī*), consisting of pondering (*cintāmayī*), or consisting of intense contemplation (*bhāvanāmayī*)." *Le Traité*[93] has a different way of referring to kinds of insight, discussing the *prajñā* of the *śrāvaka*, the *pratyekabuddha*, and the Buddha, and also of the heretics; and claims that Prajñāpāramitā (the Perfection of Insight) encompasses all the insights.

[90]Buddhadāsa, *Ānāpānasati*, p. 21.

[91]"Nescience and Insight according to Asaṅga's *Yogācārabhūmi*," published in this volume.

[92]*Bodhimārgapradīpa-pañjikā-nāma*, PTT, Vol. 103, p. 39-4-1.

[93]LAMOTTE, *Le Traité*, II, p. 1066 ff.

Therefore, it is not the position of these schools that in developing a faculty called "insight" (*prajñā*) the yogin has acquired something he did not have before. Rather, it is clear that the process of promoting this insight through the path of discerning is a matter of trading certain defiled concomitants, in the category of lust, hatred, and delusion, for other better concomitants, suiting *prajñā* in a more splendid fashion. The technical word for this trading is *parivṛtti* ("exchange"). While these texts speak of different kinds of *prajñā*, this is necessary because of the undoubted difference in degree and usage of this faculty in different persons. It cannot have been the intention of quite properly mentioning the "*prajñā* of the *śrāvaka* (disciple)" that the Buddha's Prajñāpāramitā excludes and is radically different from that *śrāvaka-prajñā;* for, if this were the case, then *Le Traité* should not have taken the position that Prajñāpāramitā encompasses all insights. Thus, even Prajñāpāramitā cannot be something to acquire as entirely new. Asaṅga makes the same point with his "store-consciousness" theory, namely, that even if the yogin manages to attain the "summit of existence" called equipoise-cessation, this "store consciousness" continues and from it there issues forth at a later time the host of mental natures.

Granted that there are Buddhist scriptural passages suggesting the yogin's radical separation from mankind. Such is this verse, whose Pāli form is in the *Saṃyutta Nikāya*[94] and which the teacher Asaṅga cites from the Sanskrit canon:[95]

> As the tortoise in its own shell withdraws its limbs, so may the monk (withdraw) his mind's (outgoing) conjectures; resortless, not harming another, denouncing no one, proceed to Parinirvāṇa.

Asaṅga explains that this monk is progressing along the seven stations (*vihāra*) which begin with the Second Dhyāna. Along the way, it is taught, he may gain supernormal powers, special

[94]*Saṃyutta-Nikāya*, I, p. 9 (in the India Devanāgarī edition):

kummo va aṅgāni sake kapāle
samodahaṃ bhikkhu manovitakke
anissito aññam ahethayāno,
parinibbuto nūpavadeyya kañcī

[95]*Cintāmayībhūmi*, PTT, Vol. 110, p. 16-4, 5. Asaṅga would naturally be citing the verse from the *Saṃyuktāgama*.

knowledges, and so on. But no matter what the meditative attainment, the yogin should be able to return to society and communicate on mundane matters, even if it is difficult or impossible for him to communicate his visions and meditative success. Indeed, as it was previously cited, "When one has emerged (from that *samādhi*) and is occupied with his (ordinary) mind , some measure of the cathartic continues in his body and mind." Accordingly, the only way the yogin could lose the insight of ordinary men is to lose insight itself.

4

THE BODHISATTVA PRACTICE ACCORDING TO THE LAM RIM CHEN MO

Western readers interested in Buddhism of the Great Vehicle form, and particularly in Buddhism of the Tibetan form, have undoubtedly encountered the great stress that this Buddhism lays on Compassion for the sentient beings. It is of course easy for such teachings to take on a sentimental tone, as though they are simply high-sounding words as "compassion." This may very well have been the case in the past because the usual presenter of such thoughts has sought to spare the Western reader from what he believed would be boring to him. What these books really contain—their wealth of quotations, their lists of subdivisions, their occasional disputes over points, might be difficult for the Westerner to appreciate but which were once burning issues. On the other hand, some scholarly books with no solicitude about boring the reader, and no way of getting to the inside of the subject—dissect it as a corpse in a mortuary.

The present essay seeks a middle ground between those extremes. It will present this remarkable point of view of Buddhism that was preserved and embellished in its Tibetan form and do it with sufficient technical material that the reader can know what the person enrolled in this way of life is actually doing to promote that fine-sounding Compassion. At the same time, it will avoid—on account of brevity—those extended explanations which often confuse the issue. If the reader will bear this in mind, he will begin to appreciate, even without a knowledge of the

Tibetan language, what is actually in the Tibetan books, although only by a sample of an enormous literature.

Tsoṅ-kha-pa (1357-1419, A.D.), founder of the Tibetan Gelugpa sect, finished his great compendium of Buddhism, the *Lam rim chen mo*, in 1402, A.D. This work elaborately presents the stages of the path to enlightenment in extensive amplification of Atīśa's indications in the latter's brief work "A Lamp on the Path to Enlightenment" (*byaṅ chub lam gyi sgron ma*). He is the great Indian pandit who came to Tibet in 1042, A.D. In this work, Atīśa set forth three religious degrees of persons in the verses 3-5:

3. Whoever, by whatever means, pursues only his own aim in just the pleasures of this world, he is known as the inferior person.
4. Whoever, turning his back on the pleasures of phenomenal existence, and averting himself from sinful actions, pursues only his own quiescence, he is known as the mediocre person.
5. Whoever, through the suffering belonging to his own stream of consciousness, completely desires the right cessation of all the suffering of others—that person is superior.

Tsoṅ-kha-pa explains the mental training (*blo sbyoṅ*) for each of those three persons. In the section for the superior person—the *bodhisattva*—it becomes clear that the path here is especially a practice rather than a doctrine, despite the title of a useful book by Har Dayal, *The Bodhisattva Doctrine in Buddhist Sanskrit Literature* (London, 1932).

The emphasis on practice is at the very beginning of Tsoṅ-kha-pa's section. We learn that to serve the aim of others is a possibility of the human condition, not of animals who only work for themselves. The Bodhisattva is not distinguished from the Śrāvaka (auditor), or the Pratyekabuddha (one enlightened for himself), by viewpoint; because as far as Insight (*śes rab*) is concerned, there is no difference between the Lesser Vehicle (Hīnayāna) or Great Vehicle (Mahāyāna). They are distinguished by practice. In the case of the Bodhisattva, the practice is called Means (*thabs*), and the chief Means is the Thought of Enlightenment (*byaṅ chub sems*). This Thought is the door to the Great Vehicle, and when one has it he is called "Son of the Buddha."

The person who would enter this path must generate the Thought of Enlightenment with its double goal—enlightenment for oneself and benefit for others. In order to generate it as a vow, it must be taken ritually. Now it appears to have been the experience of the Indian masters that if one simply went through the laid-down procedure of generating the Thought of Enlightenment, it could easily be dispersed, that is to say, not cohere in the stream of consciousness in the sense of the citation, "Therefore in all his births he loses not the Thought of Enlightenment. Even in dreams he has this Thought: much more if he be awake." Therefore, certain preliminaries are required. First of all, the person must have the right circumstances of life, which are called the four reasons: 1. he should be in this family (*rigs*), 2. taken in hand by spiritual guides (*dge bśes*), 3. be compassionate toward living beings, 4. have zest for austerities. And he should have one or other power to generate that Thought : 1. his own power, whereby he craves the perfect Enlightenment through his own force (of character), 2. another's power, whereby he craves it by way of another's power, 3. the power of a (deep-seated) cause, whereby he generates the Thought through the mere hearing in the present life of praises of the Buddha and Bodhisattvas by reason of having formerly cultivated the Great Vehicle, or 4. the power of praxis, in the course of which he has for a long time been following a path of virtue, seeking out high-minded persons and listening to the Law. Given that the person has such reasons and is endowed with such a power, then he is given a religious exercise to further put his mind in the right frame for generating the Thought of Enlightenment.

Compassion as an Exercise of Mind

Tsoṅ-kha-pa presents two alternate methods of such a religious exercise, one which was handed down from Atīśa, and the other found in the texts by Śāntideva (i.e. his *Śikṣāsamuccaya* and *Bodhicaryāvatāra*;, in Tibetan *Bslab btus* and *Spyod ḥjug*.

A. *Atīśa's precepts of "Seven causes and effects"*. The seven are as follows: perfected Buddhahood arises from the Thought of Enlightenment; that Thought, from altruistic aspiration; that aspiration, from compassion; compassion, from love; love, from gratitude; gratitude, from recollection of kindness; recollection of kindness, from seeing as "mother"—seven in all. The candidate reflects that in the infinite past and in the infinite future, all the uncountable rebirths are possible through a mother's loving care. Every sentient being has sometime or other served as one's own "mother." Thus, the meditator first sees vividly his own mother, and through her passes beyond all bounds of love for all the sentient beings. He dwells on his mother's kindness in taking care of all his needs when he was completely helpless. This recollection arouses gratitude; gratitude arouses love. Having gotten into that frame of mind, he recognizes as his "mother" also his father and friends. He then proceeds to the more advanced task of recognizing as his "mother" the neutral persons. When he is able to regard the latter the same way as he thinks of his friends, he proceeds to the still more advanced task of recognizing as his "mother" all his enemies. When the latter can be seen this way, he recognizes all the living beings of the ten directions as his "mother," expanding his meditations into the boundless state. In this way he brings on the Boundless State of Love. Having come to see all these sentient beings as one's "mother" in the Boundless State of Love, the meditator then reflects on their manifold sufferings in their subjection to transmigration. The intense realization of suffering by empathy with the loved objects—the "mother"—produces Compassion. As applied to all the sentient beings, one enters the Boundless State of Compassion. Having this compassion through realizing the sufferings of these sentient beings, the meditator then aspires to free them from suffering and to bring them happiness—as one wishes to do this for one's mother. Hence, the next stage, called "altruistic aspiration," which expands into the third Boundless State of Sympathetic Joy with all the happiness accruing to those sentient beings. The next stage is reflection on the Thought of Enlightenment itself as having the two aims of Enlightenment for oneself and Deliverance for others. The candidate reflects on the seventh stage as perfect Enlightenment—the final fruition of the sequence.

B. *Precepts based on Śāntideva's texts*. 1. First one reflects on the benefit of changing places with another:

> Whoever desires to speedily rescue oneself and others too,
> Should practice what is the highest secret—changing places between himself and another.
>
> (*Spyod ḥjug*, VIII, 120)

What is meant is that the usual condition of holding oneself as dear must give way to holding others as dear. And if one manages that conversion, then even that person who had been considered one's worst enemy and who caused disagreeable feelings just by hearing his name—becomes converted into a friend who would cause displeasure by his mere absence. This change of heart comes about through cultivating this view of personality interchange. Now, somebody challenges this procedure on the grounds that another's body is certainly not our body, and so it is questionable that anything like our own mentality could be generated therein. The answer given is that we did something analogous when we descended to rebirth in a habitation formed from materials of the father and mother, who are "different" from us, although we speak of "our body." Having come to see the benefit, he then proceeds to 2, the steps of cultivating the interchange between oneself and another. Now, one should not confuse this procedure with the thought, "I am seeing through his eyes," and so on. Rather it is the interchange of feelings, taking on another's suffering, installing in him one's bliss. There are two hindrances to this interchange. (a) One has the thought, "This is mine" and "That is his" much the same way as the colors green and yellow are distinct. One counteracts that with a contemplation given in *Bslab btus* (final verse section):

> Through the repeated cultivation of the sameness of oneself and another, the Thought of Enlightenment would be firmed.
> The relation—oneself-and-another-ness—like this side and the further bank (of a river) is in falsehood.
> Not because of our own is that bank the other one; for, with relation to what is there a "this side"?
> Ego is not proved by our own; in relation to what would there be the other (where the "other" is ourself)?

(b) One has the thought, "His suffering does no harm to me; why try to dispel it?" One counteracts that by contemplating in such a case one should make no provision for old age, because the suffering of the aged does no harm to the youth; and by contemplating that in such a case one should not bother to use a hand to relieve a foot from something distressing, because it is "another." An objection is raised that the old man and the youth have a single stream of consciousness, and the foot and hand are in the same set, while in contrast one cannot say the same of oneself and another. The answer points out that the stream of consciousness is momentary and the set is subject to reformations. Thus it is a similar situation and one could just as well posit oneself and another self in the case of the youth and the old man. Having in that way eliminated the wrong approaches, one can attend to 3. the basic method of cultivation.

> Make sure, O mind, that I belong to the other;
> And except for the aim of all the sentient creatures, henceforth you must not plan.
> These eyes, which are theirs, must no longer see my aim:
> These hands, which belong to another, must not work my aim; so also all the other organs of action.
>
> (*Spyod ḥjug,* VIII, 137-138).

THE THOUGHT OF ENLIGHTENMENT AND THE BODHISATTVA PATH

Assuming that the person with the necessary reasons, and possessed of one or more of the powers, then reflects in the proper manner in one or other of the two religious exercises presented above, he is now prepared to generate the Thought of Enlightenment. Here a distinction is introduced that the Thought has two degrees:

> Precisely the distinction that is made between the one who desires to go and the one who is on the way,
> Just that distinction is to be understood respectively among the two.
>
> (*Spyod ḥjug*, I,16)

The verse refers to the Aspiration Thought (*smon sems*) and the Entrance Thought (*ḥjug sems*), respectively. The Aspiration Thought is understood as the aspiration of thinking, "I shall become a Buddha for the sake of the living beings," or such a formula, and then the practice of the Perfections (*par rol tu phyin pa*) beginning with Giving. The Entrance Thought means that one is holding that Thought as a vow (*sdom pa*), i.e. that it coheres in the stream of consciousness in all circumstances; and then the practice of the Perfections takes on an added significance. It will be noticed that the foregoing religious exercises each have something in common with Aspiration Thought. Indeed, a wide latitude of events and objects is acknowledged as possibly serving the purpose of inspiring the Aspiration Thought. However, the Thought of Enlightenment as the Entrance Thought is a true conversion of the mind; and for taking it, a good *guru* is preferable—as explained by Atīśa: "The *guru* is known as 'good' who is skilled in the procedure of the vow, himself is one who adheres to the vow, and who possesses the forbearance and compassion to impart the vow." Tsoṅ-kha-pa sets forth the elaborate ceremony of Refuge formula and the like, obviously intended to make the occasion memorable. At the appropriate point, the candidate takes the rite of seizing the Thought, by reciting the following thrice:

> All the Buddhas and Bodhisattvas dwelling in the ten directions, pray take cognizance of me! Preceptor, pray take cognizance of me ! I, named so-and-so, have the root of virtue of this and other lives, consisting in the self-existence of Giving to others, the self-existence of Morality, and the self-existence of Contemplation; and by means of that root of virtue consisting of what has been done by me, what has been granted to do, and of sympathetic joy with what is done. Just as the former Tathāgata-Arhat-Samyaksambuddhas and the great Bodhisattvas dwelling on the great earth were made to generate their heart into the Incomparable Right-Perfected Enlightenment,
>
> In the same way, I, named so-and-so, also holding from this time on, up to reaching the precincts of Enlightenment, shall generate my Thought to the Incomparable Right-Perfected Great Enlightenment; shall rescue the unrescued beings; shall save the unsaved; shall encourage the discouraged; shall bring to Nirvāṇa those who have not attained complete Nirvāṇa.

In the case where it is not possible to find a good *guru* or preceptor, an adjustment is made so the person can take it by himself. In fact, he has to imagine the Buddha dwelling in front, go through the rites of bowing and offerings; and when taking refuge and making the above statement, he must omit the entreaty of the preceptor. Tsoṅ-kha-pa continues with the care the person should take so that the vow is not broken; and there is a procedure of broadening the base of the vow by reflecting on its benefits and greatness, because the Thought of Enlightenment is the seed of all the Buddha natures.

In order to appreciate how the Bodhisattva—as he is called by reason of having that vow—is to proceed thereafter, it is necessary to consider some fundamental principles. Tsoṅ-kha-pa quotes a most important passage from the "Revelation-Enlightenment of Vairocana" (*rnam snaṅ mṅon byaṅ*), also known as the "Great Sun Sūtra":

> Master of Secrets! The omniscient knowledge has Compassion for a root, has the Thought of Enlightenment for a motive, and has the Means for a finality.

In that passage, the expression "omniscient knowledge" is equivalent to the Buddha's Insight (*śes rab*). Compassion provides this Insight with a root in the phenomenal world. The Thought of Enlightenment provides this Insight with a motive, the vow as cause. The Means provides this Insight with a finality, its fulfilment. We have seen in the foregoing that the person desiring to embark on this Bodhisattva path had to arouse Compassion, and then to take the Thought of Enlightenment as a vow. Therefore, he has taken care of the first two steps in bringing the "omniscient knowledge" to full expression. He has left to take the third step, called the Means. And this Means consists of the first five Perfections, which are (1) Perfection of Giving (*sbyin pa*), (2) Perfection of Morality (*tshul khrims*), (3) Perfection of Forbearance (*bzod pa*), (4) Perfection of Striving (*brtson ḥgrus*), (5) Perfection of Meditation (*bsam gtan*). This Means must be combined with Insight, which is the sixth Perfection, (6) Perfection of Insight (*śes rab*). The Means must be combined with Insight, because Buddhism of the Great Vehicle is aimed toward the "Nirvāṇa of no-fixed-abode," as Tsoṅ-kha-pa explains:

> What is to be accomplished by the Mahāyānists is the Nirvāṇa of no-fixed-abode. This involves no fixed abode in phenomenal life (*ḥkhor ba*), accomplished by the profound path (*zab moḥi lam*) along with the steps of the path based on Supreme (Truth) (*don dam pa*) with the Insight that fully understands reality, as well as accomplished by the portion of Insight with the collection of knowledge (*ye śes kyi tshogs*). And it involves no-fixed-abode in quiescent *nirvāṇa*, accomplished by the ample path (*rgya che baḥi lam*) along with the steps of the path based on Conventional Truth (*kun rdzob kyi bden pa*) with the Insight that knows the phenomenal side (*ji sñed pa*),

as well as accomplished by the portion of Means with the collection of merit (*bsod nams kyi tshogs*).

The *Lam rim chen mo* cites numerous passages to show in various ways the necessity to combine Insight and Means. For example, from the *Srī-Paramādya* (*dpal mchog dan po*): "Perfection of Insight is his Mother; Skill in the Means is his Father." This happens to occur in the last chapter of that work, where it is seen that they are the Mother and Father of the hierophant (*vajrasattva, rdo rje sems dpaḥ*). Again from the "Questions of Kāśyapa" (*ḥod sruṅ gis ẑus pa*): "Kāśyapa, thus, for example, just as the king who is governed by ministers performs all the acts of a king, likewise the Insight of the Bodhisattva which is governed by the Means performs all the Acts of the Buddha." And in the *Uttaratantra* (*rgyud bla ma*): "The painters who are its aspects are Giving, Morality Forbearance, and the rest. The Voidness (*stoṅ pa ñid*) furnished with the best of all aspects is called the picture." The point of this last citation is that there is no picture if a portion is omitted; therefore, all the Perfections are necessary.

This requirement to practice all the Perfections simultaneously is essential to the theory of ten Bodhisattva stages. For this purpose, on each successive stage all the Perfections are present but with one or more predominant; and so on each stage the "picture" is different. It is the Thought of Enlightenment which is moving upward through these ten stages. With the end of the seventh stage, however, conventional descriptions also conclude, because a mysterious change occurs upon entrance into the Eighth Stage. And great as this new situation may appear, it is not the same as Buddhahood. Therefore Tsoṅ-kha-pa cites the "Sūtra of Ten Stages" (*sa bcu pa*) about the Eighth Stage called "Motionless" (*mi gYo ba*):

> O Prince! You should know concerning the Bodhisattva who has entered this Motionless Bodhisattva Stage, who dwells there adding to the power of his former aspiration, that the blessed Buddhas make for him, in that current at the mouth of natures, a providing of the knowledge of the Tathāgata [an epithet of the Buddha]. And they speak thus to him. "Very well, very well, Son of the Family. This is the supreme forbearance for understanding the Buddha natures. But you

should know, Son of the Family, that our perfection of Buddha natures consisting of the Ten Powers, the Four Confidences, and so forth—that is not in you! So, apply yourself to the quest for perfection of the Buddha natures! Begin your striving!

"Furthermore, Son of the Family, remember your former aspiration—the inconceivable mouth of knowledge and achieving the aim of sentient beings!

"Also, you should know, Son of the Family, that this is the True Nature of all natures. And whether Tathāgatas arise or do not arise, this True Nature abides, this Realm of Natures abides, in this sense: the voidness of all natures, the non-apprehension of all natures. But the Tathāgatas cannot be determined by this alone, for also all the Śrāvakas and Pratyekabuddhas reach this True Nature devoid of discursive thought!"

This is the teaching that in the ascent of the Thought of Enlightenment, the Bodhisattva reaches a decisive point in his career when he attains the True Nature of all natures, which happens to be also the quiescent *nirvāṇa* for those who reach that *nirvāṇa*. But the Bodhisattva should not think he has reached the highest realm, and so he is reminded of his former aspiration and instructed that he must begin all over again in this new manner of existence, and continue onward. The students of the *Lam rim chen mo* are expected to know that the Bodhisattva reaches the end of his career as a Bodhisattva in the Tenth Stage when he is tantamount to a Buddha, but is not a Complete Buddha, for which a further stage, called the Eleventh, is allotted.

The foregoing shows that the six Perfections are the chief kind of Bodhisattva instruction. They can also be grouped under the Three Instructions of Buddhism: Giving, Morality, Forbearance are grouped under the Instruction of Morality; Meditation is included in the Instruction of Mind Training; Insight is included in the Instruction of Insight; and Striving is included under all three Instructions. The first four Perfections (Giving, Morality, Forbearance, and Striving) can be considered as accessories to *samādhi* (*tiṅ ṅe ḥdzin*) because they are different forms of non-swerving, and promote the fifth Perfection, the non-straying meditation; hence, if one cultivates Clear Vision (*lhag mthoṅ*) with them as basis, one comprehends reality.

Reasons are advanced for the traditional order of the Perfections. When there is Giving that is unattached because it does not look to possession, Morality is adopted. When one has Morality well restrained from evil conduct, he has Forbearance toward harm. When there is Forbearance unwearied toward austerity, there is ability to go ahead with Striving that has scarce occasion to turn back. When one enterprises day and night with Striving, there arises the deep concentration (or Meditation) that easily serves a virtuous meditative object of mind. When the mind is stabilized, it rightly understands (with Insight) the way things are. It is also taught that the six Perfections are successively higher or loftier. Besides, they are considered successively more subtle since each later one is found harder to enter and to perform in than the earlier one.

It was primary that the Bodhisattva has two aims, one for himself and one for others. The six Perfections mature the Buddha natures for himself, and what are called the four Persuasions mature the stream of consciousness of others.

MATURING THE BUDDHA NATURES FOR ONESELF

1. *Giving.* From the extensive material on this subject, a few points only: It is said in the *Spyod ḥjug* (III, 11):

> Nirvāṇa is the renunciation of everything; and my mind is intent on Nirvāṇa.
> If I must renounce everything, best it be given to the sentient beings!

And it is said in the *Phar phyin bsdus pa* (*Pāramitā-samāsa*, 1, 11B-12):

> This thing is only yours (*plural*). I have no pride of "mine" with respect to it.
> Whoever he be, having such marvellous reflections—pursuant to the Complete Buddha's mode of being—arise again and again,
> That one, outstanding among enlightenment beings (*bodhisattva, byaṅ chub sens dpaḥ*), the Buddhas (*saṅs rgyas*) who are the inconceivable beings (*bsam gyis mi khyab*), call great being.

There are varieties in the essential nature of Giving: (a) giving of the Buddhist Law (*dharma*), teaching the Sublime Doctrine without error; (b) giving of security against fear of men, fierce animals, and the elements; (c) giving of material things, either concretely or imaginatively. Speaking generally, the household or layman Bodhisattva does the giving of material things, and the Bodhisattva who has entered the religious life does the giving of the Law.

In illustration of how the Bodhisattva practices all six Perfections simultaneously with Giving predominant, the Great Commentary on the "Perfection of Insight in Eight Thousand Units" explains: At the time he practices, say, the Giving of the Law, he has the Morality of restraint against the mental orientation of the Śrāvaka and Pratyekabuddha; he has both the Forbearance with conviction of the Law of the Omniscient One and the Forbearance of mistreatment by another; he has the Striving purposive to promote ever higher that very (Giving); he has the Meditation of one-pointed mind not mixed with the Lower Vehicle, that transfers the merit of the perfected Bodhisattva to other sentient beings; and he has the Insight which knows in the manner of an illusion all three, the gift, the giver, and the receiver.

2. *Morality.* Morality is the abstinent thought that averts the mind from anything involving harm to another. The *Spyod ḥjug* (V, 11) says:

> How lead away all fishes and so on, that I may not kill any? When the abstinent thought is achieved, there is the Perfection of Morality.

Generally in Buddhism this abstinent thought refers to abstinence from the ten evil acts, three of body, four of speech, and three of mind. Morality makes the rest work. The *Phar phyin bsdus pa* (II, 1) says:

> The person whose interest has been aroused to make beings delighted by the Complete Buddha's jewel of Morality,
> Should first of all purify his own Morality, for Morality instills the power of effectiveness.

Without it, one's own aim as well as that of others is out of reach, for the same work (II, 48) says:

> The person who falls from Morality is impotent even in what benefits himself. In what procedure for another's sake is he capable?

Therefore, it is especially improper for one pursuing the aim of others to relax his care in this matter.

There are three kinds of Morality: the morality of restraints, the morality of gathering virtuous natures, the morality of acting for the aim of sentient beings. The morality of restraints covers all the regulations of the Buddhist order, starting from those of the layman and adding until those of the monk and nun are included. The morality of gathering virtuous natures means paying attention to all virtues associated with the six Perfections, developing those not yet developed, and guarding and enhancing those already developed. The morality of acting for the aim of sentient beings means paying attention to the aims of the various kinds of sentient beings, and pursuing those aims, sooner or later, in a sinless manner.

3. *Forbearance*. This is the forbearance of not retaliating in any case of another's harm-doing, the acceptance of suffering in one's own stream of consciousness, and the unshakable conviction while thinking with certainty about the Dharma.

In the first aspect of Forbearance, the Bodhisattva reflects that brutish beings are uncountable—he could never succeed in killing them all. But when angry thought is slain, all enemies are slain! There is not enough leather to cover the earth; but with the leather of a shoe, earth is spanned! So the *Spyod ḥjug*. "The fault of anger hems in the good things of the world like a dam, the waters"—*Phar phyin bsdus pa*. Anger is looked upon as a flash of fire that destroys all the accumulated Perfections of Giving and Morality. So the Bodhisattva notes the benefit of Forbearance: few enemies; few discords; pleasant state of mind; no regrets at the time of death; and certainty of joining the gods in heaven after his death.

The second aspect of Forbearance—the acceptance of suffering in himself—is in fact a solution of the problem posed by the first Noble Truth of Buddhism: "There is Suffering—a Noble truth. The Bodhisattva reflects that in pursuit of worldly desires he was tortured in hell and yet accomplished no worthy aim of himself or others. But it is different with the suffering that accomplishes the great aim. It is ecstatic suffering that dispels the suffering of the whole world. Then the question arises "From what source arises the suffering one should accept?" There are eight such bases, for example, suffering arising from the place where one is practicing the pure life, or arising from the perishable natures of the world, or arising while one is engaged in religious exercises, and so on.

The third aspect of Forbearance amounting to conviction is explained as eightfold. For example, when the field of conviction is the pure-minded trust toward the Three Jewels (the Buddha, the Dharma, the Saṃgha), or when the field is realizable in the sense of two kinds of selflessness, of personality and of natures; and so on.

4. *Striving*. The *Spyod ḥjug* (VII, 2A) says: "What is Striving? Virtuous perseverance." The *Sūtrālaṃkāra* (*mdo sdeḥi rgyan*) proclaims Striving to be chief among the host of virtues because based thereon one subsequently attains that host. So the *Bodhisattva-bhūmi* (*byaṅ sa*) declares that Striving achieves the Incomparable, Rightly-consummated Enlightenment. And the *Phar phyin bsdus pa* says, "There is nothing at all that cannot be reached by the forward step unacquainted with weariness."

Three varieties are set forth: the armored striving, the striving that amasses virtuous natures, and the striving which performs the aim of sentient beings. Armored striving means the striving which is carefully guarded to apply toward Enlightenment (one's own aim); this presents the Bodhisattva in heroic form. He cares not how long it might take, but is confident of the ultimate result. By reason of Compassion for the sentient beings he does not desire to become a Buddha in a short time (which in fact would cause it to take a long time). Having donned such armor, he can practice the kind of striving that amasses virtuous natures in himself, namely the six Perfections; and he can practice the kind of striving which performs the aim of the different classes of sentient beings.

Furthermore, there are favorable circumstances for Striving, especially conviction (*mos pa*), steadfastness (*brtan pa*), joy (*dgaḥ ba*) and giving up (*dor ba*). Longing (*ḥdun pa*) is said to form the basis for Striving; and in this case longing is identified with conviction in the Law, which is the root of all virtuous natures. Steadfastness supports Striving during the term of the Striving, that is, ensures that Striving will not swerve from the goal. Joy should be present from the beginning of the Striving, because it is natural that persons do not want to give up an activity that gives joy to them—so also with Striving. Again, the power of giving up temporarily stops the Striving for a needed rest, whereupon the Striving can resume to reach higher than before.

5. *Meditation*. The essential nature of Meditation is the virtuous one-pointed mind fixed without straying away from the meditative object. Tsoṅ-kha-pa devotes a whole major section of the *Lam rim chen mo* entitled Calming (*ẑi gnas*) for the means of engaging in the cultivation of Meditation. As to varieties in terms of its essential nature, it is mundane, supramundane, in the category of Calming, in the category of Clear Vision. It also has varieties in terms of its results: the Cathartic of body and mind in the one who is stabilized; noteworthy qualities shared with the Śrāvakas, such as the supernormal faculties, and the liberations; and accomplishing the eleven aims serving the sentient beings. The Bodhisattva having himself mastered Meditation, then installs another in it: this is the Giving of Meditation.

It was already mentioned that possession of the first four Perfections (Giving, Morality, Forbearance, and Striving) enables the Bodhisattva easily to master Meditation. Moreover, certain "equipment" or accessories are specified to serve as a foundation for the speedy and pleasant accomplishment of Calming. These are (from the Calming section of the *Lam rim chen mo*): residence in a favorable place (good access, good settlement, good soil, good companionship, good usage); meagre desire; contentment; elimination of multiple activities, such as buying and selling; purity of morality; elimination of discursive thinking, of craving, and so on. Purity of morality, seeing the disadvantages in craving, and residence in a favorable place are the chief ones.

6. *Insight*. The essential nature of Insight is the analysis of the nature of an examined entity, in particular, skill in the five sciences, which are inner science (Buddhism), logic, medicine, grammar, and the arts. Tsoṅ-kha-pa devotes a separate large section of the *Lam rim chen mo* entitled Clear Vision (*lhag mthoṅ*) for the means of engaging in its generation, in fact, the style of thinking of the Mādhyamika School (*dbu ma pa*).

Nāgārjuna (*klu sgrub*) says: "Insight is the root of all this visible and invisible merit; hence, to accomplish both, one must hold on to Insight. It is the great science—the source of (present) nature, (future) purpose, and liberation; hence, with devotion from the outset, one must hold on to Insight, the Great Mother."

Insight has three sources: insight consisting of hearing, insight consisting of pondering, and insight consisting of cultivation. It says in the "Questions of Nārāyaṇa" (*sred med kyi bus žus pa*): "Thus, Sons of the Family, Insight comes to the one who hears. Defilement ceases in the one with Insight. For him devoid of defilement, the tempter (*Māra, bdud*) does not appear."

Also, there are three kinds of Insight: Insight that understands the Supreme (*don dam*), that understands the Conventional (*kun rdzob*), and that understands what will serve the purpose of sentient beings. The first ponders in a general way the meaning of reality of selflessness and ponders by way of direct realization. The second is the Insight skilled in the five sciences. The third knows the sinless way of accomplishing the present and later purpose of sentient beings.

Maturing the Stream of Consciousness of Others

There are four methods of persuasion (*bsdu baḥi dṅos po*) which mature all the sentient beings. They are (1) giving, equal to the Perfection of Giving, already discussed; (2) fine, pleasant speech; (3) acts in accordance; (4) oneself serving as an example. By the first one, the subject becomes a fit vessel, psychologically prepared to listen to the Law. By the second one, faith is aroused in him toward the Law that is taught. By the third one, he is made to exercise in accordance with the Teaching. By the fourth one, he is led to continue training his mind accordingly. Also, the first one involves material things, and the last three involve *dharma* (*chos*).

That stresses the importance of the Perfection of Giving, not only as the first of the six Perfections, but also as the first thing for the Bodhisattva to do in regard to introducing a change for the better in another's stream of consciousness. That is why Tsoṅ-kha-pa devotes such a long section to the Perfection of Giving.

Some idea of the main points in Tsoṅ-kha-pa's treatment of the Bodhisattva practice is presented here. However, I have given only in brief measure what Tsoṅ-kha-pa has explained in great detail and extensively with numerous citations of texts to clarify each point as he goes along.

PART TWO

BUDDHIST DOCTRINE

5

THE SIXTEEN ASPECTS OF THE FOUR NOBLE TRUTHS AND THEIR OPPOSITES

The sixteen aspects of the four Noble Truths are not canonical and are not found in the Abhidhamma of Southern Buddhism.[1] They are a specification resulting from the version of the First Sermon of Buddhism, the Setting into Motion of the Wheel of the Dharma, which, after stating the four Noble Truths, adds a triple turning of the wheel with twelve aspects. This is the *triparivartaṃ dvādaśākāraṃ* of the *Mahāvastu*.[2] The sixteen aspects were possibly represented by the aniconic symbol of the wheel of 16 spokes, four main ones and twelve intermediate spokes. A number of illustrations of these Dharmacakra are collected by Dhanit Yupho in a Bangkok publication.[3] The sixteen aspects are treated in the Northern Abhidharma, as observed in Vasubandhu's *Abhidharma-kośa*, Chap. VII, verse 13, where a number of theories are pre-

[1]Confer Louis de La Vallée Poussin, tr. *L'Abhidharmakośa de Vasubandhu*, Septième...(Paris, 1925), p. 30, note.

[2]Confer Franklin Edgerton, *Buddhist Hybrid Sanskrit Reader* (New Haven, 1953), p. 17, introductory note about the two original parts of the *Dharmacakrapravartana-Sūtra;* and p. 19, triple turning of the wheel in the second part, namely in the *Mahāvastu* version.

[3]Dhanit Yupho, *Dharmacakra or The Wheel of the Law* (The Fine Arts Department, Bangkok, Thailand, B.E. 2511; third edition, 1968). Among the illustrations, the twelve-spoked wheel presumably or possibly symbolizes the twelve-membered dependent origination (*pratītya-samutpāda*); the sixteen-spoked one, the sixteen aspects of the four Noble Truths; the thirty-two-spoked one, the Buddha himself with thirty-two characteristics.

sented.[4] Besides, Asaṅga discusses the 16 aspects in his *Śrāvaka-bhūmi*.[5] I have found the list in a native Tibetan text, lectures by Tsoṅ-kha-pa on Buddhist logic, where he presents a list of sixteen that are the opposites or adversaries of the sixteen aspects, agreeing in large part with one of the theories in the *Abhidharmakośa*[6]. In short, the earliest specification of the sixteen aspects is in the Northern Abhidharma schools, Vaibhāṣika and Sautrāntika. However, if the list of terms originated in these Abhidharma schools, it is curious that some obscurity should still remain after their explanations.

Asaṅga's school contemplates the sixteen aspects in the category of *vipaśyanā* (discerning), i.e. discerning the truth (*satya*), after calming the mind (*śamatha*).[7] This agrees with the *Abhidharmakośa*, which identifies the list with *prajñā* ("insight"),[8] since the term *prajñā* is frequently equated with *vipaśyanā*[9]. Tsoṅ-kha-pa in those lectures refers to Dharmakīrti's *Pramāṇavārttika*, Svārthānumāna chapter, verse 218 (Śastri's ed., but verse 217 in the autocommentary and Tibetan version): "So as to determine the reality of rejecting and accepting together with the means, by virtue of non-deception regarding the chief aim, there is inference (*anumāna*) in terms of the beyond."[10] The autocommentary on

[4]La Vallée Poussin, *op. cit.*, Septième, pp. 30-39.

[5]The lengthy treatment begins with Lokottaramārga and then the exposition of the *vipariṇāma* kind of impermanence (*anityatā*), *Śrāvakabhūmi*, K. Shukla, ed. (Patna, 1973), p. 470, where the sixteen aspects are named.

[6]Tsoṅ-kha-pa, collected works (Tashilunpo edition), Vol. Pha, *Tshad ma'i brjed byaṅ chen mo* (Rgyal-tshab-rje's notes on Tsoṅ-kha-pa's lectures), f. 13b, and following. For the comparable *Abhidharmakośa* theory, confer La Vallée Poussin, *op. cit.*, Septième, p. 38 referred to simply as the "fourth explanation," which was appealed to by Samghabhadra to demonstrate that the aspects are indeed sixteen.

[7]Confer Alex Wayman, *Analysis of the* Śrāvakabhūmi *Manuscript* (Berkeley, 1961). pp. 130-131, for the exposition, in particular, examination of the Noble Truth of Suffering with the kind of discerning (*vipaśyanā*) called "special knowledge" (*pratisaṃvid*) of the characteristics (*lakṣaṇa*).

[8]La Vallee Poussin, *op. cit.*, Septième, p. 39.

[9]Confer Alex Wayman, tr., *Calming the Mind and Discerning the Real* (New York, 1978), p. 28.

[10]*/heyopadeyatottvasya sopāyasya prasiddhitaḥ / pradhānārthāvisaṃvādād anumānaṃ paratra vā //* By "auto-commentary" is meant Dharmakīrti's *Svārthānumāna-pariccheda*, edited independently by Raniero Gnoli and by Dalsukhbhai Malvaniya; and "*vṛtti*" means the one by Manorathanandin.

this mentions the four Noble Truths, and the *Vṛtti* clarifies that the rejecting is of suffering and the source of suffering, that the accepting is of cessation and the path. The beyond means the *parokṣa* (what is beyond sight), namely, the chief aim, Nirvāṇa, which therefore has to be inferred. Tsoṅ -kha-pa takes for granted that his audience knows the sixteen terms and their opposites that are referred to in the *Pramāṇasiddhi* chapter of *Pramāṇavārttika*, namely in the block of verses in Miyasaka's edition 146—283.[11] But Tsoṅ -kha-pa expands to sixteen terms using Abhidharma-type vocabulary, and this is reasonable, since Buddhist logic has an Abhidharma base.[12] The *Abhisamayālaṃkāra* summary of the *Prajñāpāramitā* includes the sixteen aspects of the four Truths as a concentration in the path of the Śrâvaka (as does Asaṅga), and a feature of this path is the identification of Nirvāṇa with the Truth of Cessation (*nirodha-satya*).[13]

While the list of sixteen was included, or generally alluded to, in a variety of texts as mentioned above, there is a question of how viable a classification it is, i.e. to what extent such terms help to explain this cardinal teaching of Buddhism—the four Noble Truths. We should note that not only does the Southern Abhidharma textual tradition not use the sixteen-term system,[14] but also the *Satyasiddhiśāstra* of Harivarman, completely devoted to the four truths, appears opposed to employing this organizational

[11]This is the edition published in *Acta Indologica* II (Naritasan Shinshoji, Japan, 1971/72).

[12]At least this is the case in Tibetan tradition, since according to my observation the chief Tibetan commentators on Buddhist logic also wrote commentaries on either Vasubandhu's *Abhidharmakośa* or Asaṅga's *Abhidharmasamuccaya*.

[13]CONFER E. OBERMILLER, "The Doctrine of Prajñā-pāramitā as exposed in the *Abhisamayālaṃkāra* of Maitreya," *Acta Orientalia*, Vol. XI (1932), pp. 18-19.

[14]The well-known Pāli exegetical work, the *Netti-pakaraṇa* (translated under the title *The Guide*) applies six terms to the four Noble Truths (E. Hardy's edition, p. 8): *Ādīnavo phalañ ce dukkhaṃ, assādo samudayo, nissaraṇaṃ nirodho, upāyo āṇatti ca maggo.* "Trouble and fruit are suffering; gratification is the source; exit is cessation; means and command are the path." Here, "means" and "command" might be equivalent to the two kinds of Pātimokkha, by exhortation (*ovāda*) and by command (*āṇā*); cf. C. S. Uspasak, *Dictionary of Early Buddhist Monastic Terms* (Varanasi, 1975), p. 152; and chapter 2 above.

terminology.[15] To arrive at a conclusion about these matters, it will be necessary to treat each of the sixteen separately, using the above works. The Buddhist dictionary *Mahāvyutpatti* (nos. 1190–1205) gives the individual terms as follows: (Noble Truth of Suffering,) *duḥkham, anityam, śūnyam, anātmakam.* (Noble Truth of Source,) *samudayaḥ, prābhavaḥ, hetuḥ, pratyayaḥ.* (Noble Truth of Cessation,) *nirodhaḥ, śāntaḥ, praṇītaḥ, niḥsaraṇaḥ.* (Noble Truth of Path,) *mārgaḥ, nyāyaḥ, pratipattiḥ, nairyāṇikaḥ.*

Of the sixteen aspects, the easiest are the four of the set going with the Truth of Suffering, mainly because the terms are so celebrated in Buddhist texts. Leaving out the "voidness" (*śūnya*) term, the other three are the well-known set of three characteristics (*lakṣaṇa*) which all constructed things (*saṃskāra*) have: impermanence (*anitya*) pain (*duḥkha*), and non-self (*anātman*). For canonical references, one may consult Nyanatiloka, *Buddhist Dictionary*, under Ti-lakkhaṇa.[16] Asaṅga in the section mentioned writes mostly about this set.[17] He introduces a group of ten aspects (*ākāra*) for treating the Truth of Suffering, namely, aspect of (1) transformation (*vipariṇāma*), (2) destruction (*vināśa*), (3) separation (*visaṃyoga*), (4) closeness (*saṃnihita*), (5) true nature (*dharmatā*), (6) fetters and bondage (*saṃyojanabandhana*), (7) the disagreeable (*aniṣṭa*), (8) no security (*ayogakṣema*), (9) non-apprehension (*anupalambha*), (10) non-independence (*asvātantrya*). He states that the aspect of impermanence is examined by five of these ten aspects, namely, of transformation, destruction, separation, closeness, and true nature. The aspect of pain is examined by three aspects, namely, of fetters and bondage, of the disagreeable, and of no security. The voidness aspect is examined by one aspect, namely, no-apprehension (of a certain object). The aspect of non-self is examined by one aspect, namely, non-independence.

The *Arthaviniścaya-ṭikā* (author unknown, Tibetan Tanjur)

[15]N. Aiyaswami Śastri has reconstructed from Chinese to Sanskrit of the *Satyasidhiśāstra* (Baroda, 1975), and has translated it into English (Baroda, 1978).

[16]Nyanatiloka *Buddhist Dictionary* (Colombo, 1950). (155-6). The late Edward Conze gave his views on the three, calling them "marks" in his *Buddhist Thought in India* (London, 1962), Part I, Chapter 3.

[17]See the references in notes 5 and 7, above.

briefly explains the four in a description of the *saṃskāra* personal aggregate (*skandha*):[18]

> It is impermanent, because it perishes in each instant. It is painful, because possessing the nature (*dharma*) of birth, old age, and so on. It is void, because those *saṃskāras* are not the self imagined by the heretics. It is non-self because precisely those are not the self-existence (*svabhāva*) of self imagined by the heretics.

One should also notice that Harivarman's work attributes the list to an unnamed *sūtra* passage: "*dharmā anityā duḥkhāḥ śūnyā anātmānaḥ pratītyasamutpannā...*" but includes this passage and its discussion not under the first Truth, that of Suffering, but under the third one, that of Cessation![19] Harivarman stresses pursuant to this passage the voidness of *dharmas*, but also insists on voidness of self. Here there is a difficulty shared with the *Arthaviniścaya-ṭīkā*, as cited above, that in the list of four terms including both void (*śūnya*) and non-self (*anātmaka*), to interpret the term "void" as denying a self should make one wonder why the term "non-self" is included as a separate aspect. Asaṅga was apparently appreciative of this point, since for him the voidness aspect is examined just by the aspect of non-apprehension without further qualifying the non-apprehension.

Passing to the coverings or adversaries[20] of these four aspects in Tsoṅ-kha-pa's list,[21] that the covering of impermanence is permanence, of pain is pleasure, of non-self is self—is simple enough. However, the covering he gives for voidness (*śūnya*) is with a term *gcang*, which I correct to *bcang*, "taking hold (of an object)." This agrees with Asaṅga's "non-apprehension" for voidness in the present context. The various explanations in the *Abhidharmakośa* seem not to take account of a requirement to show some adversity for the terms listed under the Truth of Suffering, and in particular the term I render "voidness." Presumably the adversity is the sense of "voidness" that it is here the absence of the thing one hunts and looks for, expects to find, leaving one

[18]Photo edition of Peking Tanjur (PTT), Vol. 145, p. 162-1,2.

[19]AIYASWAMI ŚASTRI, *Satyasiddhiśāstra*, Sanskrit, p. 354.

[20]The 'coverings' are indicated by the word *āropya* in *Pramāṇavārttika*, *Pramāṇa-siddhi* chapter, verse 271 : *ṣoḍaśākārān āropya*.

[21]See the reference in note 6, above.

in a kind of despair. Asaṅga's "non-independence" for non-self does indeed take account of the adversative intention. It might be for the reason which Vasubandhu gives as one tradition:[22] *akāmakāritvād iti* "because there is no performance of what one wishes." Harivarman's placement of the list under the Truth of Cessation of course avoids the implication of adversative sense that placement under Truth of Suffering entails. In support of his placement, there is the set called the four "aphorisms of the Dharma"; cf. *Mahāyāna-Sūtrālaṃkāra*, SVIII, 80, and commentary: "All *saṃskāras* (constructions) are impermanent; all *saṃskāras* (motivations) are suffering;[23] all *dharmas* are non-self; Nirvāṇa is calm (*śānta*)." Observe that this set has an entry "Nirvāṇa" in place of the term "void" of the other list, and that Harivarman practically equates voidness (*śūnyatā*) with Nirvāṇa.[24]

Before leaving the Truth of Suffering, it is well to mention even if briefly the theory of three kinds of *duḥkhatā* (misery). Asaṅga (*Viniścayasaṃgrahaṇī* on *Cintāmayī bhūmi*)[25] identifies the three with the three standard kinds of feelings, painful, pleasurable, and neither painful nor pleasurable. The first *duḥkhatā* is the misery of suffering (*duḥkha*), and as the painful kind of feeling; it is the misery experienced and acknowledged in the world, since the pair "pain and pleasure" (*duḥkha* and *sukha*) are among the eight worldly *dharmas*, of course comprehended by ordinary persons. The *Arthaviniścaya-ṭīkā* (Tibetan Tanjur)[26] describes this kind of *duḥkhatā* consistently with a detailed list that shows it covers the pains people can do something about, as well as those recognized to be outside of one's control. The second *duḥkhatā* is the misery of change (*vipariṇāma*), and as the pleasurable kind of feeling; it is not recognized as misery by ordinary persons. So *Saṃyutta-Nikāya*, Part IV (*Salāyatana-Vagga*):/*yam pare sukhato āhu* / *tad ariyā ahu dukkhato* / "What others call 'happiness' that

[22]La Vallée Poussin, *op.cit.*, Septième, p. 32.

[23]I translate the word *saṃskāra* differently in the first two aphorisms, because when *saṃskāra* is identified with suffering (*duḥkha*) it is variously said to be the five personality aggregates (*skandha*) or to be 'with flux' (*sāsrava*). On the other hand, the *saṃskāra* said to be impermanent means all of the 'constructed natures' (*saṃskrta-dharma*).

[24]See N. Aiyaswami Śastri, *Satyasiddhiśāstra*, Eng. tr., pp. 358-359.

[25]Asaṅga, *Yogācārabhūmi*, PTT, Vol. 111, p. 28-3,4.

[26]See n. 18, above, *op. cit.*, p. 209-2,3.

the noble ones call 'suffering,' "[27] The third *duḥkhatā* is the misery of motivations (*saṃskāra*), and as the feeling that is neither painful nor pleasurable, it is also not recognized as misery by ordinary persons. Asaṅga explains:[28] "It was in connection with the misery of motivations that the Lord said: 'In short, the five grasping aggregates are suffering.' What is the misery of motivations? These and those bodies with motivations generated by *karma* and defilement (*kleśa*) arising,..." He also mentions that this misery is evidenced by the four waywardnesses (*viparyāsa*), i.e., regarding the impermanent as permanent, the painful as pleasurable, the unclean as clean, the non-self as self; and finally, that this misery is the trace (*anuśaya*) of nescience (*avidyā*).

It is clear that the *duḥkha* of the first Noble Truth has a wider scope than the ordinary person can understand, and has a metaphysical side that is comprehensible to the *ārya*, in the ancient use of this word. Some persons accordingly challenged the translation of *duḥkha* as "suffering" or "pain." However, the present translator translates the term in those two ways to accord with the various contexts in which the term is found, sometimes in concrete senses to apply to old age, sickness, and death, and sometimes in a metaphorical way. And to leave the term untranslated, as has been recommended by at least one modern author, would entirely defeat any communication of metaphorical nuance.

As we pass to the remaining three Truths, it turns out that the coverings in the list of sixteen adversaries become of greater importance.

The second set going with "Noble Truth of Source (of Suffering)" has the requirement of providing cause or causes for the suffering without constituting suffering. Here there are the aspects cause (*hetu*), source (*samudaya*), production (*prabhava*), and condition (*pratyaya*). The trouble with the *Abhidharmakośa* explanations in the main is that they define these terms as various kinds of causes without thereby showing their natures as causes for suffering. Asaṅga is quite superior here because he faces up to the necessity that they not only be causes, but cause for suffering.[29]

[27]In the edition of Bhikkhu J. Kashyap, *The Saṃyutta Nikāya*, 4, Salāyatana-vagga, p. 116.16.

[28]See n. 25, above, p. 28-3,4.

[29]See n. 5, above, *op. cit.*, p. 493, where Shukla wrongly edits *duḥkhakṣema-* for *hetu*; read instead: *tṛṣṇāyā duḥkhākṣepakatvād dhetutaḥ*. "By cause (*hetu*)

One of the many explanations he furnishes is especially interesting since it relates these terms to Buddhist Dependent Origination *pratītya-samutpāda*).[30] This particular solution takes the aspect of "cause" to be craving (*tṛṣṇā*), 8th member of Dependent Origination, heading the five members which bring about new destiny. Asaṅga here says it is the cause of "indulgence" (*upādāna*), and casts gestation and suffering. The aspect of "source" is indulgence (*upādāna*), 9th member, which finalizes after the casting. The aspect of "production" is gestation (*bhava*), 10th member, hence embryonic life, prior to the manifestation of suffering. The fourth aspect, of condition (*pratyaya*) is birth (*jāti*), the 11th member, which holds the seed of future suffering, and is the condition for old age, sickness, and death. Notice that in this solution, "birth," 11th member of Dependent Origination, is counted as a cause of suffering and therefore not itself a suffering. The Mādhyamika tradition of the *Pratītya-samutpāda* commentary attributed to Nāgārjuna, and a passage in the *Daśabhūmika-sūtra* along the same lines, disagrees because it counts "birth" as one of the suffering members of Dependent Origination.[31]

Tsoṅ-kha-pa's list of coverings or adversaries of these four seems to amount to non-Buddhist positions.[32] Thus, for the aspect of "cause," from his list, positing that there is no cause of suffering amounts to the position of the ancient materialistic Cārvākas, the position called *ahetuka* ("having no cause"), which Buddhism always denounced. For the aspect of "source," positing the unaffiliated as the cause, or positing only a single cause, might be equivalent to the fourth account in the *Abhidharmakośa*[33] mentioning at this place a Lord (Īśvara), or *pradhāna;* since the Lord could be considered unaffiliated to the effect, and *pradhāna* as the

through craving (tṛṣṇā) which casts suffering." The other three aspects are also explained as sources for suffering.

[30]Since there is further confusion in Shukla's edition (p. 493) at this point, I have consulted the Tibetan translation, PTT, Vol. 110, p. 126--5-4,5,6.

[31]*Daśabhūmikañsūtra* is cited in Śāntideva's *Sikṣāsamuccaya* (Vaidya ed., p. 123.21-22), happening to be in agreement with the *Pratīyasamutpāda* commentary, that of the members of dependent origination, *avidyā*, *tṛṣṇā*, and *upādāna* are defilement (*kleśa*); *saṃskāra-s* and *bhava* are 'action' (*karma*); and the rest are suffering (*duḥkha*). Hence, 'birth' (*jāti*) is counted as a 'suffering.'

[32]See n. 6, above, f. 13b-6 to 14a-1.

[33]La Vallée Poussin, *op. cit.*, Septième, p. 38.

Sāṃkhya *prakṛti* could be considered a single cause. For the aspect of "production," positing (suffering) as created by the evolution of the Śabdabrahman, would be a Vaiṣṇava theory according to S. Dasgupta;[34] while the *Abhidharmakośa* here mentions the evolutionary theory of the Sāṃkhya called *pariṇāma*, in which the effect is pre-existent in the cause. For the fourth aspect of "condition," positing (suffering) as created by a former Īśvarabuddhi (cognition of a Lord), is the same as given in the *Abhidharmakośa*.

When coming to the treatment of the third set under "Noble Truth of Cessation (of Suffering)" and of the fourth set under "Noble Truth of Path (leading to the Cessation)," Asaṅga contents himself with a few neutral remarks for his possible reluctance to enter into the controversies involved in a longer treatment. Let us pass first to the coverings in Tsoṅ -kha-pa's list,[35] namely, for the third set, cessation (*nirodha*), calm (*śānta*), the excellent (*praṇīta*), exit (*niḥsaraṇa*); and for the fourth set, path (*mārga*), principle (*nyāya*), accomplishment (*pratipatti*), way of deliverance (*nairyāṇika*).

For the aspect of "cessation," the covering is the positing by one gone astray that there is no liberation; for the aspect of "calm," positing that there is a special liberation attended with flux of uncalmed defilements; for the aspect of "the excellent" (usually explained as *anuttara,* "the best"), positing that there is a higher liberation than stopping suffering; for the aspect of "exit," positing a temporary liberation and that there is no final liberation.

For the aspect of "path," the covering is the positing that there is no final path of liberation; for the aspect of "principle" (=method), positing that the insight comprehending non-self is not a path of liberations; for the aspect of "accomplishment," positing the situation of the object-scope having gone astray; for the aspect, "way of deliverance," positing that none can put a final end to suffering.

The "coverings" in Tsoṅ-kha-pa's list for the third and fourth sets amount to a paraphrase of the fourth *Abhidharmakośa* explanation. The adversary views do help to bring out the meaning of the aspect terms for these two sets.

[34]Surendranath Dasgupta, *A History of Indian Philosophy* (Cambridge, 1940), Vol. III, p. 58.

[35]See no. 6, above, f. 14a-1 to 14a-4.

Now, a striking feature of the aspects given under "Noble Truth of Path" is that they are not obviously related to the usual statement of the Path, namely, the eightfold members, frequently listed under the three instructions which form the organization of Buddhaghosa's *Visuddhimagga*. These three are the Instruction of Morality, the Instruction of Mental Training of *samādhi*, and the Instruction of Insight. Even though Asaṅga does not organize his *Yogācārabhūmi* along the specific lines of the well-known three instructions (*adhiśikṣā*), these categories are basic for much of his writing. Examining the statements of Tsoṅ-kha-pa's adversaries for the four of this path group in comparison with the four of the cessation set, a suggestive parallel emerges, which may provide an opening for relating the three instructions. By this I mean to call attention to the covering of "cessation" claiming that there is in fact no liberation, while the covering of "path" is the claim that there is no final path of liberation; then, for the aspect of "exit" claiming that there is no final path of liberation, while the covering of "way of deliverance" is the claim that one cannot put a final end to suffering. These seeming affiliations of statement gave me the idea that the two sets of four terms might be correlated in their given order. Following this suggestion, I may propose that the aspect of path (*mārga*) leads to the aspect of cessation (*nirodha*); that the aspect of principle (= method) (*nyāya*) leads to the aspect of calm (*śānta*); that the aspect of accomplishment (*pratipatti*) leads to the aspect of the excellent (*praṇīta*); finally, that the aspect "way of deliverance" (*nairyāṇika*) leads to the aspect "exit" (*niḥsaraṇa*). Then the way of relating the three instructions follows readily, namely, that the instruction of mind training is the principle or method that leads to calm, since *samādhi* is the standard procedure for calming the mind; that the instruction of morality is the accomplishment that leads to the excellent, which is consistent with ancient Buddhism's great stress on morality and extolling of its merit; that the instruction of insight (*prajñā*) is the way of deliverance that leads to the "exit" or "escape" from phenomenal life, constituting the Arhat ideal of early Buddhism[36]. Such a correlation would leave the main terms

[36]TSOṄ-KHA-PA, *brjed byaṅ*, n. 6, above, f. 13a-5, states: "The *ācārya* (i.e. *Dharmakīrti*)...took the *prajñā* that comprehends non-self to be the chief (thing) of the path to liberation from phenomenal life, and the others to be ancillary."

of "cessation" and "path" as headings under which are ranged the respective three aspects that go with the three instructions. This is consistent with the early tradition that takes "cessation" as equal to Nirvāṇa, and with the Tibetan translation of this term as "beyond suffering" (*mya ngan las' das pa*). This is because the thrust of these Abhidharma-type explanations of the four Noble Truths is that liberation amounts to the cessation of suffering (*duḥkha*).

Besides, a feature of the first sermon, Setting into Motion the Wheel of Dharma, in various versions, is to take the four Noble Truths as objects. Thus, the statement is made : "Suffering, a Noble Truth, is to be fully known (*parijñeyam*)." Again, "The Source of Suffering is to be eliminated (*prahātavyaḥ*)." "The Cessation of Suffering is to be realized directly (*sākṣāt kartavyaḥ*)." "The Path leading to the Cessation of Suffering is to be cultivated (*duḥkhanirodhagāminī pratipad bhāvayitavyā*)."[37] This promptly raises a question: If cessation is to be realized directly, i.e., *sākṣāt*, as though before the eyes, then how could this cessation be equated to Nirvāṇa, if Nirvāṇa be taken in Dharmakīrti's sense as something to be inferred rather than seen in direct vision? The resolution here would be to take Nirvāṇa in such usage not to be identified with cessation (*nirodha*). And we note that Dharmakīrti is writing in the mature Mahāyāna Buddhism period, when a Nirvāṇa of no fixed abode (*apratiṣṭhitanirvāṇa*) had come to the fore.

Thus, a consideration of the sixteen aspects of the four Noble Truths, and their sixteen "coverings" or adversaries, does appear to bring out important features of the four Truths, and to make salient certain striking differences of the traditions. The investigation attests to the teaching of the four Noble Truths as basic to the earliest Buddhism and to later disputes of what to place under each of the four. Thus, one strong current of interpretation took the sixteen aspects as a guide, while another was either oblivious of, or uncomfortable with, the neat list.

[37]So in the *Lalitavistara*, as presented in Edgerton, *Buddhist Hybrid Sanskrit Reader* (n. 2, above), pp. 22-23.

6

THE MIRROR AS A PAN-BUDDHIST METAPHOR-SIMILE

INTRODUCTION

The extensive literature of Buddhism contains works of sharply contrasting spirit: some are dry metaphysical treatises; others, inspired sermons; and there are a host of ritualistic works, even on how to conjure rain. If one passes from one work to another collecting material on a given topic, it is easy to amass numerous undigested passages. But the authenticity of the mirror metaphor rests—I believe—on the ease with which one can go from one work to another, written centuries apart, while paying attention to this metaphor and assembling these passages with an overall sense of relevance. In the end I shall express a reservation about bringing together so many passages in one article.

Even so, it is as though—here a metaphor—Buddhist religion and philosophy were an enormous tangle of string, and we should happen to notice among the innumerable loose ends a certain one to pull and thereby begin to resolve the entire tangle. If other scholars—except for a sinologist like Demiéville[1]—have not deemed this study important, they can be excused on the grounds that it looked like just one of many loose ends.

Indeed, the importance of the mirror metaphor was enhanced when Buddhism spread from its native India to various Asian countries. China was fond of mirror symbolism; and Asian

[1] P. DEMIÉVILLE, "Le miroir spirituel," *Sinologica* 1 (1947): 112-37.

forms of shamanism emphasize the mirror, as when it figures on the chest of the Tibetan oracle or is placed on high in the Japanese Shinto worship hall.

So far I have only published two articles dealing with the subject —one on the mirror of ladies (which included a divination section)[2] and one on the mirror-like knowledge of Mahāyāna Buddhism.[3] The material has so increased that it is a matter of selection to present the main ideas in a single essay. Speaking most briefly, there are three parts. First, the early Buddhist use of the mirror as a metaphor of the mind, which becomes dirtied as a mirror collects dust, eventually led to the highly evolved philosophical position of Asaṅga and his school called the Yogācāra, and then in Buddhist tantric ritual to the washing of the mirror while a deity was reflected therein. Second, the rise of the Prajñāpāramitā literature as interpreted by the teacher Nāgārjuna avoids the metaphorical mirror and employs the mirror simile for such illustrative purposes as the theory of *dharmas* (natures, features), and the meaning here is succinctly shown in the brief tantric ritual, initiation of the mirror. Third, the ancient use of a mirror for predictive purposes, as known in the Pāli scriptures and in stories called Jātakas, develops into the representation of mirrors in Buddhist art and eventually into remarkable forms of mirror divination in the Buddhist Tantras. And there is an appendix on the problem of where to include the "*prajñā*-mirror."

It is also necessary to establish the character of the mirror metaphor. The *Saṃdhinirmocana-sūtra*—which is the basic scripture of the Mahāyāna Buddhist Yogācāra school—mentions in its chapter 5 that when conditions are present a clear mirror will reflect one image, two images, and so on, and yet the mirror surface is not changed thereby. The appropriating consciousness (*ādāna-vijñāna*)—practically equivalent to the store-consciousness (*ālaya-vijñāna*) of this system—is compared to this mirror (*ādarśa*) and also to a swift current of water (*ogha*).[4] The swift water

[2] A. Wayman, "A Jotting on the Mirror: Those of Ladies," *Mahfil* 7 (Fall-Winter 1971): 209-13.

[3] A. Wayman, "The Mirror-like Knowledge in Mahāyāna Buddhist Literature," *Asiatische Studien* 25 (1971): 353-63.

[4] É. Lamotte, in his edition and translation of the Tibetan *Saṃdhinirmocana Sūtra* (Louvain and Paris, 1935), reconstructs in part: *tadoghasthānīyam ādarśasthānīyam ādānavijñānaṃ*. It is of interest that Sthiramati, *Triṃśikā-*

current as a metaphor of the mind implies a progression, extending forward and backward but not laterally—that is, a temporal successiveness. In contrast, the mirror as a metaphor of the mind implies a lateral extension, a spacial simultaneity. At first consideration, the two metaphors are inconsistent, and the application of both of them helps the reader to avoid the concretization of either metaphor.

In this light, it is significant that the Yogācāra school prefers the mirror as a metaphor-simile of the mind, while the Mādhyamika is less likely to use it and, when it does, uses the same metaphor-simile in any way except for the mind. Of course, in both Eastern and Western thought, the application of this metaphor to the mind suggests that it will entertain an image for which there is a model somewhere; and this is the dualistic position. The argument was transferred to China, where one branch of the Ch'an school, following the *Laṅkāvatāra-sūtra*, applied the mirror metaphor to the mind; while another Ch'an school, turning to the *Prajñāpāramitā* scriptural position, rejected this metaphor for the mind.

A. The Metaphorical Mirror and the Yogācāra School

Asaṅga, who heads the Yogācāra school, attributes to a *sūtra* or *sūtras* presumably in the old Buddhist canon (the four Āgamas in the northern Buddhist version) the metaphorical identification of a begging bowl (*pātra*), a mirror (*ādarśa*), and a pond (*hrada*) with the three faults that stir up consciousness. The three such faults are "unmethodical mental orientation" (*ayoniśo manasikāra*), "traces" (*anuśaya*), and "entrapment" (*paryavasthāna*).[5] Besides, he mentions in the same place the three gateways to liberation, the place of ambrosia (*amṛta-dhātu*): these are the wishless (*apraṇihita*), voidness (*śūnyatā*), and signless (*ānimitta*) gates. Elsewhere he explains that the wishless gate is the opponent of

bhāṣya, ed. Sylvain Lévi (Paris, 1925), p. 33, has merely *tadoghasthānīyam ālayavijñānaṃ*, in like context. That is, by only mentioning the swift current of water, he may thereby be judging that this metaphor and the mirror one are incompatible.

[5] *Viniścayasaṃgrahaṇī*, photographic ed. of Tibetan canon (PTT), *The Tibetan Tripitaka*, Peking ed. (Tokyo and Kyoto, 1955-61), 110:239-3, 4.

wish for gestation or becoming (*bhava*); the voidness one, of defilement (*kleśa*); and the signless one, of signs.[6] Taking into consideration Asaṅga's further explanations of what he means by "traces" and "entrapment," it is reasonably clear that in his symbolism, the begging bowl, minus its craving, is the wishless gate; the mirror with its traces erased is the voidness gate; and the pond, devoid of entrapment, is the signless gate.

At least one of the *sūtras* which Asaṅga had in mind would be the Sanskrit equivalent of the Pāli *Aṅguttara-Nikāya* [Book of Ones], section 5, where the turbid pool of water stands for the turbid mind (*āvila-citta*). This same section concludes and continues into the next section with the sentence: "Monks, this mind [*citta*] is luminous, but defiled with adventitious defilements." This passage is undoubtedly the reason for the thesis pushed by the Mahāsāṅghika school: "The mind is intrinsically pure." But while in this context the *sūtra* used the pond metaphor, the mirror was later employed in this metaphorical role for the mind that is intrinsically pure but covered by defilements.

A possible reason for the growing importance of the mirror metaphor may come from the early account of Brahmā's urging the Buddha to teach. As recorded in the *Saṃyutta-Nikāya*, volume 1, the Buddha saw with a Buddha's eye sentient beings hardly dusty and sentient beings very dusty,[7] and he compared them to lotuses in different stages of growth from the bottom fo the pool to the surface where they were not adhered to by the muddy water. While the lotus comparison would favor the pond, his observation of the relative dustiness of the sentient being would favor the mirror metaphor.[8] According to the celebrated account called the "conversion of Śāriputra and Maudgalyāyana," the dust collects on the *dharma*-eye—also called the knowledge-eye—directed toward *dharmas*.[9]

Another reason for the ascendancy of the mirror metaphor over the other two (the begging bowl and the pond)) is the association

[6]Ibid., 111:114-4.

[7]See J. J. Jones, trans., *The Mahāvastu, Vol. III* (London, 1956), p. 312, n., for a discussion of the word here translated "very dusty."

[8]This is not to deny the importance in Buddhism of water symbolism, whether of pond, stream, ocean, and so on.

[9]See Franklin Edgerton, *Buddhist Hybrid Sanskrit Reader* (New Haven, Conn., 1953), p. 29; and chapter 7.

with the voidness gate to liberation. Indeed, the growing importance of the mirror metaphor would be fostered by the Prajñāpāramitā scriptures, which emphasized the realization of voidness, even if these scriptures themselves did not feature the mirror metaphor in this manner (the pure and defiled mind).

Still another factor favoring the mirror metaphor was the Mahāyāna Buddhist theory of five kinds of knowledge or wisdom as the content of enlightenment, of which the first one is the "mirror-like knowledge." In Asaṅga's school, this knowledge is achieved through "revolution of the store-consciousness basis."[10] According to the *Laṅkāvatāra-sūtra* this occurs in the Eighth Bodhisattva Stage, where the Bodhisattva lives in a "body made of mind" which is like a current of dreams.[11] Among the most revealing passages which I collected on this subject is one in Abhayākaragupta's *Munimatālaṃkāra*:[12] "The mirror-like knowledge is where consciousness of the infinite three realms and the 'other one'—all the finest atoms of substance—come together individually. The objective domain [*viṣaya*] which is distant and (called) the 'other one,' and temporal states of past, present, and future (there) come together individually, just as a reflected image appears vividly in a mirror." This brings out the sense of the metaphorical mirror's ability to reflect all things without itself being changed, and to display simultaneously both the subjective states of past, present, and future, and all sensory objects. It seems that both the metaphorical swift stream and metaphorical mirror are combined in this particular explanation of the mirror-like knowledge.

Turning to the philosophical position of the Yogācāra school, I have devoted an article to rejecting the common attribution to

[10]Asaṅga in his *Mahāyānasaṃgraha* (trans. É. LAMOTTE [Louvain, 1939], pp. 278-79) merely states that the set of four knowledges beginning with "mirror-like knowledge" are obtained through the revolution of the aggregate of perceptions (*vijñāna-skandha*), while Vasubandhu, in his commentary thereon, clarifies that one obtains the "mirror-like knowledge" through revolution of the "store-consciousness" (*ālayavijñāna*) basis.

[11]See the *Laṅkāvatāra* references in G. Tucci, *Minor Buddhist Texts*, pt. 1 (Rome, 1956), p. 201.

[12]WAYMAN, "The Mirror-like Knowledge," p. 358, n. In 1970 I had a helpful suggestion about this passage from the lama Gonsar Rimpoche of Dharmasala.

the Yogācāra school of the unqualified denial of an external object.[13] In this case, there is the mirror simile of the *Saṃdhinirmocana's* Maitreya chapter, which denies a difference between the image in the mirror and the model of the image.[14] Here the scripture alludes to the situation of *samādhi* when the perceiving mind (the reflecting mirror) that dwells upon a meditative object (the model) is not different from that model and so the latter is called "representation-only" (*vijñapti-mātra*). This passage does not constitute an idealistic denial of an external object, but rather a disinterest in externals; because the yogin has retreated from manifold sense objects and dwells only on the meditative object in his mind.

Moreover, Asaṅga writes in his *Yogācārabhūmi:* "In short, there are two *vijñānas*, 'store-consciousness' [*ālayavijñāna*] and 'evolving perceptions' [*pravṛttivijñāna*]. Among these, the store-consciousness is the place and evolving perception is placed. The latter is sevenfold, the (five) eye, etc. perceptions, mind-based perception, and *manas*. The two are like a body of water and the waves are like a mirror and a reflected image. In that way, this establishment of supreme method establishes the place and the placed."[15] Later, in the exegesis of his *Bodhisattvabhūmi*, Asaṅga discusses the three characters or natures (*svabhāva*) of the Yogācāra school—the perfect (*pariniṣpanna*), the dependency (*paratantra*), and the imaginary (*parikalpita*); and under the rubric "thorough knowledge of the dependency character," he places the similes of natures (*dharma*) that happen to be repeated again and again in the *Prajñāpāramitā* scriptures, to wit: "like an illusion, a dream, a hallucination, an echo, the moon in the waters, a reflected image, a magical materialization."[16] Therefore, Asaṅga intends his likening of the "store-consciousness" and "evolving perceptions" to a body of water and waves, or to a mirror and a reflected image, to constitute metaphoric language appropriate to understanding the dependency characteristic of the Yogācāra system.

[13]A. WAYMAN, "Yogācāra and the Buddhist Logicians," *The Journal of the International Association of Buddhist Studies*, Vol. 2, No. 1, 1979, pp. 65-78.

[14]LAMOTTE, *Saṃdhinirmocana Sūtra*, pp. 211-12.

[15]ASAṄGA, *Viniścayasaṃgrahaṇī*, PTT, 111:16-1.

[16]Ibid., 111:75-4.

Passing to the numerous mirror similes of the *Laṅkāvatāra-sūtra,* we observe a greater interest in describing external objects than is noticed in Asaṅga's school. Now the mirror simile is employed in the problems of identity and otherness, and of error and nonerror. Despite its "mind-only" passages, the philosophical position of the *Laṅkāvatāra-sūtra* is shown by its mirror passages as only somewhat idealistic.[17]

Then there is the theory of the mind as a two-sided mirror—which the Buddhist *tantra* tradition has in common with Kashmir Śaivism.[18] In this case, the phenomenal mind (*manas*), on one side, reflects with error the external world, and the superior discriminating mind (*buddhi*), on the other side, reflects errorlessly because it is devoid of images. Along the same lines the *Mahāyāna-Sūtrālaṃkāra* is cited: "As in a broken water-pot the reflection of the moon cannot be seen, in the same way to those that are evil the Buddha does not manifest himself."[19] In the language of the two-sided mirror, the *buddhi* side of the mirror can represent the Buddha because it is devoid of competing images.

The foregoing directly leads to the tantric ritual of mirror washing preserved in Tibetan Buddhism. The meaning, of course, is washing the mind so it can properly reflect the divine world in the form of a deity's body. This is consistent with the practice, enjoined by the tantric work *Vajramālā*, of contemplating the reflected image of the Lord (= the icon) while washing the mirror.[20] For the rite in brief, Mkhas-grub-rje says.[21]

> Thereupon he reflects the image in a mirror, if he can provide it, and gives an actual bath to the reflected image. If he cannot provide it, such persons as the assistant to the offering or other persons make the seal (*mudrā*) of "washing the body," that is, form a level surface with the backs of their hands, so that the tops of the thumbs and the index fingers touch each

[17]To establish this conclusion would require considerable discussion—beyond the scope of the present article—including the comparison of the Sanskrit and Tibetan versions for certain important passages.

[18]See F.D. Lessing and A. Wayman, trans., *Mkhas grub rje's Fundamentals of the Buddhist Tantras* (The Hague, 1968), p. 210, n.

[19]*Mahāyāna-Sūtrālaṃkāra*, ed. Sylvain Lévi (Paris, 1907), 9:16.

[20]*Vajramālā* (an explanatory tantra of the *Guhyasamāja*), PTT, 3:223-2.

[21]Lessing and Wayman, trans., *Mkhas grub rje's Fundamentals,* p. 181.

> other. He offers a bath, while reciting, OṂ SARVADEVATĀ ACINTYA-AMṚTA SVĀHĀ (*Oṃ*, the inconceivable ambrosia of all the gods, *svāhā*).

A text by Mañjuśrīmitra mentions five perfume drops on the mirror.[22] The reason, as Gonsar Rimpoche of Upper Dharmsala (India) told me, is that the water for washing the icon is always perfumed water. Geshe Rabten, tutor to H.H. the Dalai Lama, explained that in the beginning they draw a square on the mirror to represent the bathing room. The five perfumed drops are in each corner of the square and one in the middle. They signify the five Buddha families, because all Buddhas are included in one or another of those five. Or the five drops stand for the guru, the tutelary deity, the Buddhas, the Bodhisattvas, and the Protectors of the Faith.

The rite in more developed form has been studied extensively by the late F. D. Lessing, who, however, published only one article on the subject.[23] In his summary, he says: "An originally simple devotional act is interpreted symbolically as (a) purificatory, removing sins, both ritualistic and ethical, (b) mystical, conferring gifts, both temporal and spiritual, and (c) consecratory, communicating the three-fold gift of purification, illumination, and mystical union with the deity, as preparation for the attainment of 'gifts of grace' (*siddhi*) and final beatitude."

B. The Mirror Simile and the Mādhyamika School

The mirror simile is rare in Mādhyamika works but found in important contexts. The Mādhyamika follows the *Prajñāpāramitā* scriptures, which stress voidness of *dharmas* and give similes for it in lists, for example, all *dharmas* are like an illusion, a mirage, a dream, a city of *gandharvas*. Nāgārjuna, in his *Mādhyamakakārikā*, has "like an illusion, like a dream, like a city of *gandharvas*"; also, "resembling a mirage" and "like a phantom man and

[22] Manjuśrīmitra, *Ārya-mañjuśrī-nāmasaṃgīti-cakṣur-vidhi-nāma*, PTT, 75: 135-4.

[23] F.D. Lessing, "Structure and Meaning of the Rite Called the Bath of the Buddha according to Tibetan and Chinese Sources", in *Studia Serica Bernhard Karlgren Dedicata* (Copenhagen, 1959), pp. 159-71.

like a reflection [*pratibimba*]."[24] Of these, "like a reflection" may mean as in a mirror, or as the one moon reflects in many waters. Whenever a list in a Mahāyāna scripture was long enough (as though aiming at completeness), it would normally include the "reflected image," but by and large these scriptures preferred to use the language "like an illusion, a mirage, a dream." In time the list grew to ten, as in the two largest *Prajñāpāramitā* scriptures; and these ten similes, including the mirror one, are the occasion for lengthy commentary in the *Mahāprajñāpāramitāśāstra*, chapter 11 (as available in Lamotte's French translation).[25] As I understand the matter, the longer lists are found in the later and larger Mahāyāna scriptures. If for no other reason, I am loathe to agree with the Chinese tradition that attributes the immensely influential *Mahāprajñāpāramitāśāstra* to Nāgārjuna.

The mirror simile is of course more important when a whole sentence or developed idea turns upon it than when it is simply one member in a stereotyped list.

The first case concerns one of the most argued points of early Buddhism—the question of what transfers from life to life, or the manner in which the fruit is ensured for the *karma* as cause. The *Ārya Śālistambha Sūtra* states:[26] "Now, no *dharma* transfers from this world to the other world. Still, there is recognition of karma and fruit on account of the sufficiency of cause and condition. For example, the facial reflection is seen in a clean mirror, but the face does not transfer into the mirror. There is recognition of the face on account of the sufficiency of cause and condition." Nāgārjuna, in his *Śalistambha-kārikā*, writes: "Just as in a well-polished mirror the reflected image of the face is seen, and while the reflected image is in the mirror there is no transfer (to that place), in the same way, the birth manifestation, irrespective of the agent and deed which are mutually without discursive thought, comes in sequence from the previous casting."[27] Along the same lines, Nāgārjuna states in his *Pratītyasamutpādahṛdaya-vyākaraṇa:*

24These similes were collected by the late Richard H. Robinson in his *Early Mādhyamika in India and China* (Madison, Wis., 1967).

25Étienne Lamotte, *Le Traité de la Grande Vertu de Sagesse* (Louvain, 1944), 1:357-90.

26N. Aiyaswami Sastri, ed., *Ārya Śālistambha Sūtra* (Madras: Adyar Library, 1950), Sanskrit text, p. 16.

27PTT, 103:270-3.

"Just as in the case of a flame from a flame, the reflected image in a mirror from a face, an impression from a seal, a fire from a burning crystal, a sprout from a seed...a person is not taught to understand that the one is different from the other, so also in the case of reconnection [*pratisaṃdhi*] of the personal aggregates [*skandha*], the wise person will understand that there is no transfer.[28] Buddhaghosa has a consistent remark in his *Visuddhimagga.*[29]

The Prajñāpāramitā scriptural passages stress that the reflected image has no discursive thought (*vikalpa*), as in the *Aṣṭasāhasrikā prajñāpāramitā* (chap. 26):[30]

> It is also this way, for example, Lord. It does not occur to a reflected image [*pratibhāsa*] that "the support-object which produces the reflected image is close to me, but those that do not approach in the mirror or in the bowl of water are far from me." For what reason? Lord, because the reflected image has no discursive thought. In the same way, Lord, it does not occur to a Bodhisattva great being who is coursing in the Perfection of Insight that "the incomparable complete enlightenment is close to me, but the stage of the disciple [*śrāvaka*] and the stage of the self-enlightened one [*pratyeka-buddha*] is far from me." For what reason? Lord, because the Perfection of Insight has no discursive thought.

It seems possible to associate this passage with the previous ones about no transit of the personal aggregates. That is, it does not occur to the new personal aggregates as a reflected image, "Back there are the old personal aggregates," because the reflected image has no discursive thought, at least not about the old personal aggregates.

But perhaps the most important use of the mirror simile in later Mādhyamika commentary, especially Candrakīrti's *Madhyama-kāvatāra,* is its use to illustrate that the self has no character of its own. In this connection, the Ratnakūṭa scripture *Pitāputra-*

[28]PTT, 103:271-4.

[29]BHIKKHU ÑAṆAMOLI, trans., *The Path of Purification* (*Visuddhimagga*) (Colombo, 1956), p. 639.

[30]U. WOGIHARA, ed., *Abhisamayālaṃkārāloka Prajñāpāramitāvyākhyā* (*Commentary*) *on Aṣṭasāhasrikā-Prajñāpāramitā*): *The Work of Haribhadra,* fasc. 7 (Tokyo, 1935), p. 841.

samāgama [Meeting of father and son] provides a much-cited *passage*:[31] "In the way that an image void of self-existence is seen in a very clean mirror, so Druma, understand these *dharmas*." The passage means that natures (*dharma*) arise dependently, devoid of self-existence (*svabhāva*). Also Nāgārjuna states in the *Ratnāvalī*:[32]

> With recourse to a mirror, one sees the reflected image of one's face, but in reality this (reflection) is nothing at all. In the same way, with recourse to the personal aggregates, the idea of self [*ahaṃkāra*] is conceived, but in reality it is nothing at all, like the reflection of one's face.
> Without recourse to a mirror, one does not see the reflected image of one's face. Likewise, without recourse to the personal aggregates, one does not speak of a self. Having learned the meaning this way, the noble Ānanda gained the *dharma*-eye, and himself repeatedly spoke the same to the monks.

Before proceeding further, it is well to summarize those Mādhyamika uses of the mirror simile. It is used to illustrate the all-important Buddhist theory of nonself, both of personality (*pudgala*) and of natures (*dharma*). It helps to explain the thorny problem in Buddhism, because of its nonself theory, of what, if anything, transfers from life to life. There is an assist to the Buddhist dependent-origination theory, with the natures so arising doing so without self-existence. And since the face in the mirror has no opinions about the person looking in the mirror, this simile shows the meaning of "no discursive thought," a terminology that is frequent in Buddhist works.

Now we can evaluate a passage in the *Mahāprajñāpāramitāśāstra*'s explanation of the mirror simile.[33] "The reflection in the mirror is not produced by the mirror [*ādarśa*], nor by the face [*vaktra*], nor by the holder of the mirror (*ādarśadhara*], nor by itself

[31]As cited in Śāntideva's *Sikṣāsamuccaya*, Vaidya ed. (Darbhanga, 1961), p. 139.17-18, it is in prose, but the Tibetan quotations of it are in verse.

[32]As cited in Candrakīrti's commentary on the *Madhyamaka-kārikā* (chap. 18). See this chapter in translation, J. W. de Jong, *Cinq chapitres de la Prasannapadā* (Paris, 1949), p. 6.

[33]Lamotte, *Le Traité*, 1:378, where the way of talking is traced back to the *Selāsutta* of the *Saṃyutta-nikāya*, and to Nāgārjuna's *Madhyamaka-kārikā* 1,1.

[*svataḥ*]; but it does not exist in the absence of causes and conditions [*hetupratyaya*]." In the explanation there, all the factors—mirror, face, and so on—are required. If one is lacking, the remainder cannot produce the reflection in the mirror. This is a use of the mirror simile not met with hitherto, although admittedly this is merely negative evidence for denying the Indian authorship of this famous work of Chinese Buddhism. On the surface the passage seems to be the way Nāgārjuna writes in his *Madhyamaka-kārikā* 1, 1: "There is no entity anywhere that arises from itself, from another, from both (itself and another), or by chance."[34] Besides, Nāgārjuna says in the *Lokātītastava*:[35] "The sophists claim that suffering is done by oneself, by another, by both, or by chance. But you teach that it arises in dependence. That very thing which arises in dependence you affirm as void. There is no entity self-dependent. Such is your incomparable lion's roar." But the author of the Chinese work goes on to say about the reflection in the mirror: "If it existed without causes and conditions, it would exist eternally. If it existed eternally, it would be produced even in the absence of the mirror and the face."[36] This is a remarkable piece of circular reasoning. According to Candrakīrti's *Prasannapadā* (on chap. 1), the reason is found in Nāgārjuna's own *Madhyamaka-kārikā*, chapter 8, especially verse 4: "If there were no cause [*hetu*], there would be neither effect nor instrument; in such a case, there would be no deed, agent, or way of effecting." Therefore, if the author of the *Mahāprajñāpāramitāśāstra* had been Nāgārjuna, as the legend claims, we would have expected him to explain: If what you call a reflection existed without causes and conditions, it would not be an "effect," and therefore would not be a "reflection" of something.

Moreover, there are the mirror verses of Chinese Ch'an Buddhism. According to the legend, at the time of the Fifth Patriarch the head monk Shen-hsiu wrote a verse to establish his credentials:

[34]L. de La Vallée Poussin, ed., *Prasannapadā Commentaire de Candrakīrti*, Bibliotheca Buddhica, vol. 4 (Saint Petersburg, 1903-13), p. 12.

[35]L. de La Vallée Poussin, "Les quatre odes de Nāgārjuna," *Muséon* 31-32 (1913): 13-14, cites for these verses (*Lokātīta-stava*, 19-20) the Sanskrit for the first one in Candrakīrti's *Prasannapadā* and for the second one in *Bodhicaryāvatārapañjikā*.

[36]Lamotte, *Le Traité*, I:378.

The body is the Bodhi tree,
The mind is like a clear mirror,
At all times we must strive to polish it,
And must not let the dust collect.[37]

We observe at once that this is the tradition going back to early Buddhism, where the mind is intrinsically pure but covered with adventitious defilements, here the "dust"—a view favoring the metaphorical mirror as the mind, a metaphor pushed by the *Laṅkāvatāra* school.

However, a boy (Hui-neng) who in the legend became the Sixth Patriarch wrote his verse:

Bodhi originally has no tree,
The mirror also has no stand,
Buddha nature is always clean and pure;
Where is there room for dust?[38]

This is the switch to the Prajñāpāramitā language. Notice even that the mirror has no stand, recalling the argument in the *Prajñāpāramitāśāstra* that if the holder of the mirror is missing, then there is no reflection in the mirror. But also in the Tun-huang version it is consistent with the theory of the two-sided mirror, with the *buddhi*-side capable of reflecting errorlessly because it has no image in it.

The Mādhyamika employment of the mirror simile is continued in tantric ritual, in particular in the Mirror Initiation of the Akṣobhya Guhyasamāja-tantra tradition; but here we notice that the former theory of the deity appearing in the pure mind—the metaphorical mirror—is also involved. This is an extract from a commentary by the Tibetan author Tsoṅ-kha-pa:[39]

> Having had his eye opened in that manner, (the disciple) should look upon all *dharmas* as reflected images. So (the disciple) may accomplish this, he (the guru) shows a mirror incanted with an ĀḤ, and recites:
>
> All *dharmas* are like reflected images, clear and pure, with-

37Translation by P. B. Yampolsky, *The Platform Sutra of the Sixth Patriarch* (New York, 1967), p. 130.

38Translation by Yampolsky, p. 132.

39The fuller form of this brief ritual is translated in A.Wayman, *The Buddhist Tantras: Light on Indo-Tibetan Esotericism* (New York, 1973), pp. 68-70.

> out turbulence; ungraspable, inexpressible, truly arisen from cause and action [*hetu* and *karma*].
>
> Just like Vajrasattva on a mirror that is clear, pure, without turbulence; so also the Buddhas, universal lords, themselves abide in the heart of thee, my son.
>
> Now that you have so understood the *dharmas* as without intrinsic nature and without location, may you perform incomparably the aim of sentient beings so they may be born as sons of the protectors!

Tsoṅ-kha-pa goes on to explain: "Those verses enjoin (the disciple) to understand in general that all *dharmas* are like a reflected image, and in particular that the Vajrasattva dwelling in one's heart is like a reflected image in a mirror."

C. The Predictive Mirror

In my article on the mirror-like knowledge, I discussed a passage found in the Pāli scripture *Parinibbāna-sutta*:[40] "Therefore, Ānanda, in this world I will reveal the representation of the law called 'mirror of the law,' possessed of which a noble disciple planning would predict for self or selves, 'With no more sojourns in hell, no more animal birth, no more realm of the hungry ghosts, no more disaster, evil destiny, ruin—I have entered the stream, not liable to purgatory, assured, proceeding towards enlightenment.' " The mirror of the law is explained in that Pāli context as the four kinds of "faith with understanding" (*avecca-pasāda*, S. *avetya-prasāda*). The passage scarcely disguises what must have been a current practice in India of using mirrors for divination. It also clearly shows how Buddhism takes prestigious or imposing symbols of secular life and transforms them into religious symbols.

In my previous study on mirrors of ladies, I have alluded to the use of a girl for mirror divination according to the writings of Nāropā connected with the *Kālacakra* cult.[41] Wojkowitz shows that in Tibet a boy was utilized for the purpose.[42] In old Buddhist literature the divining person could be referred to as "mirror-face".

[40] WAYMAN, "The Mirror-like Knowledge," p. 359.

[41] WAYMAN, "A Jotting on the Mirror," pp. 211-12.

[42] R. DE NEBESKY-WOJKOWITZ., *Oracles and Demons of Tibet* (The Hague, 1956), p. 463.

In Pāli there is a Jātaka (previous-birth story of the Buddha), "Story of King Mirror-Face,"[43] which has a Sanskrit counterpart, "Story of King Ādarśamukha."[44] This also appears to be the meaning of the verse in the *Saddharmapuṇḍarīka:*[45] "Just as one sees an image on the surface of a mirror, so also the world is seen on his body. Self-born, he sees no other beings. Just these are the forms on his pure body." The hint is in the line, "Self-born, he sees no other beings." This points to the denial of ordinary vision and agrees with the stress in various passages that one's own face must disappear from the mirror, because that mirrored face is the projection of phenomenal illusions which "dirty" the mirror. And when the face is no longer reflected, it becomes itself the reflector, "so also the world is seen on his body."

The disappearance of the face is implied by the terminology of the void mirror. Presumably one must void his own face, and then the mirror will be clear to reflect other images which the hierophant will then interpret. This magical use of the mirror agrees with the description of the mirror-like knowledge as being free from configuration (*ākāra*) and so able to reflect all forms.[46]

Now, to eliminate the face from the mirror requires that a person appreciate the value of so doing. This was alluded to in the Mahāyāna Nirvāṇa Sūtra as cited in *The Kyogyoshinsho:*[47] "O Great King! This is like a man who takes up a mirror and sees in it his own self. The ignorant will think this is the true face, while the wise will see through and know this is not so." But the realization that the usual face is not the true one does not in itself remove the false face.[48] Then how is one to avoid seeing one's face in the mirror? This is of course easier with the Asian mirrors that are somewhat duller than our modern ones. How-

43H. T. Francis and E. J. Thomas, *Jātaka Tales*, India ed. (Bombay, 1957), pp. 120-28.

44See N. Dutt, *Gilgit Manuscripts* (Srinagar, 1947), 3, pt. 1:114-15, where the story is part of the Bhaiṣajya-vastu of the Mūlasarvāstivāda-Vinaya.

45U. Wogihara and C. Tsuchida, eds., *Saddharmapuṇḍarīka-sūtram* (Tokyo, 1936), chap. 18, verse 62.

46Wayman, "The Mirror-like Knowledge," p. 356.

47Kosho Yamamoto, trans., *The Kyogyoshinsho* (Tokyo, 1958), p. 153.

48See A. Wayman, "Significance of Dreams in India and Tibet," *History of Religions* 7 (August 1967): 9. See chapter 21.

ever, the practice may be what is shown in Maitripāda's *Mahāmudrāsiddhāntopadeśa*:[49]

> First one worships the tutelary deity and goes through the sevenfold rite. Then he gazes at his reflected image in the mirror in front. The constructed colored features of the face are void of entity. The face of the reflected image looks hither; his own face looks thither. Because there is no disagreement of mindfulness, the genuine face is (also) void of entity. According as he manages not to be attached, the appearance of the reflected image is his own mind. He contemplates the color of his mind, for example, the manifestation of lust, thinking it to be void. He contemplates his mind to be a reflected image, and the appearance of body to be his own mind. Body and mind are like reflected images. Denying a person that way, he has become free from attachment by gazing at the reflected image in a mirror.

In this process of transferring the mirror to his own face which is genuine, the *yogin* divests the objective mirror of the false face and replaces it with the colors of his mind, which will be referred to below as the "*karma*-mirror." So this voiding of the false face is a kind of symbolic death.

The disappearance of the face is also an omen of actual death according to the *Sambarodaya-tantra*.[50] The visions which can then appear on the mirror of the mind are properly on what is called the "*karma*-mirror," depicted in judgment scenes in Asian art.[51] Charles Luk translates in the *Śūraṅgama Sūtra:* "The two habits from karma and disputation end in the exposure (of sins); for the mirror and lamp reveal former karmic deeds for (final) judgment."[52] This might be the same passage alternately trans-

[49]PTT, 87:162.

[50]PTT, vol. 2, chap. 19 of the *Sambarodaya-tantra*, p. 212.

[51]Judgment scenes with large *karma*-mirrors are depicted in *The Ancient Buddhist Arts in Central Asia and Tun-Huang* (Kyoto: Hozokan, 1962), pl. 504, A and B. According to the English introduction in a monograph therein by Yūshō Tokushi, "Painted Manuscripts of the Shih-Wang-Shêng-Ts'i-Ching," these are part of the pictures of the ten kings found at the Caves of Thousand-Buddhas, Tun-huang. They belong to the late T'ang, tenth century.

[52]Charles Luk, *The Śūraṅgama Sūtra* (London, 1966), p. 182. This work is probably a native Chinese composition and should not be confused with the

lated: "There is a mirror reflecting a glaring candle. In the daytime it is not able to store the image — the mirror of *karma* and the jewel of a fire, reveal the stored *karma* and make various affairs experienced."[53] The *karma*-mirror is mentioned in a native Tibetan *sādhana* of Yama (lord of the dead) where four fearful goddesses, called "mothers of worldly existence" (Tib. *srid pa'i ma mo*) each hold the *karma*-mirror in their right hands along with the sack of diseases, the destructive ball of thread, and the notched board of the Māras, and in their left hands hold a pair of dice.[54]

One mirror in art representations that is difficult to explain is that depicted as held by the dancing musicians in paradise, for representations of which one may consult Stein's work.[55] Now, it is not impossible that these representations are of the shaman in his mystic flights, who in his frenzy can give prophecy. Also, in the *Veda* the *gandharva* was a musician in the intermediate space, but later on in Buddhism the *gandharva* became the being in the intermediate state (*antarābhava*) between death and rebirth. If the beings depicted in those representations can be construed as *gandharvas*, the suggestion is that the mirror reflects the being's future destiny, which was decreed by the *karma*-mirror.

More particularly about the predictive mirror itself, the theory that the prognostic descends into the divinatory mirror is already in the Pāli scripture *Dīgha-nikāya* 1, which twice has the expression *ādāsa-pañhaṃ* (questions put to the mirror), on which the commentary states: "*ādāse devatan otaretvā pañha-pucchanan.*"[56] Here, *otaretvā* means "having brought down," so "having brought the deity down into the mirror, (then) to ask questions."[57]

Śūraṅgamasamādhisūtra of Indian origin, which É. Lamotte has translated under the title *La Concentration de la Marche Héroïque* (Brussels 1965).

53As a Columbia University student, Shinjō Kawasaki has translated for me, from the same *Śūraṅgama* text in the Chinese Buddhist canon, the Taisho Tripiṭaka, vol. 19, 144a.

54*Sgrub thabs kun btus* (Dehra Dun, 1970). vol. Ta (9), fol. 623, lines 3-4. Also, see Nebesky-Wojkowitz (n. 42 above), pp. 84-85.

55R. A. Stein, *Recherches sur l'épopée et le barde au Tibet* (Paris, 1959), pp. 326, 336, 349, pl. 2, 372-75.

56See s.v. "*adāsa*" in *The Pali Text Society's Pali-English Dictionary*, ed. T.W. Rhys Davids and William Stede, reprint ed. (London, 1952), p. 99.

57As cited in Wayman, "A Jotting on the Mirror," p. 212, Nāro-pā extends the items that can serve the same purpose: "the entrance of the prognostic is said to be in the unreal mirror, sword, thumb, lamp, moon, sun, water, pot,

Besides, I have studied chapter 23 of the Laghu-tantra of Saṃvara, along with Tsoṅ-kha-pa's commentary. In this chapter there is difficult mystical language associated with the spirits called *ḍākinīs*. The questions are put to mirrors, which are apparently one's own consciousness. There are three mentioned: (1) in its own house, like *a vajra* along with a mirror; (2) like a sword along with a mirror; (3) like a banner and like a javelin with a closed-mouth (double) mirror.[58]

As to where in the body itself would be located a divination mirror, there is a suggestion that it is in the heart, because the native Tibetan deity Zhang Blon has a mirror for his heart. The Tibetan author Bu-ston also has a phrase, "mirror and mirror-like in the heart."[59] I have been told that the Tibetan oracles always wear a mirror on their chest to show their ability to capture any desired information; and that when deities are shown by their apparel only, a mirror is regularly placed in the position of the heart. Sometimes the syllable HṚ is put on the mirror—the syllable itself probably an abbreviation of *hṛdaya* (heart).[60] Presumably this heart mirror is intended in a work on the Buddhist goddess Nāro-Ḍākinī in which I found mention of a red two-sided mirror which has the capacity to display brightly all the chiliocosm, because on one side are the five "strands of desire" (the sense objects) and on the other side, the inner forms such as the "beautiful form" (one of the six allotments of the Lord, Bhagavat).[61] Of course, this is an extension of the two-sided mirror with *manas* reflecting the phenomenal world and *buddhi* as the upper or inward side that displays such knowledges as the supernormal faculties.

A divination mirror is especially indicated in Tibetan iconography by accompanying arrow and silk streamer.[62] For

---

or eye." The word "thumb" refers to the thumbnail, according to advice given me in Calcutta in 1970.

[58]TSOṄ-KHA-PA's commentary called "Sbas pa'i don kun gsal ba," PTT, 157: 49-50.

[59]*The Collected Works of Bu-ston*, reprinted. (New Delhi: International Academy of Indian Culture, 1969), vol. 15, no. 66.

[60]Conversation with Gonsar Rimpoche, in Dharmasala, 1970.

[61]The *Dpal nā-ro mkha' spyod dbaṅ mo'i lam rim pa gñis kyi zab khrid ji ltar nos pa'i zin bris śin tu gsaṅ ba gnas mkha' 'gro'i sñiṅ bcud* (paper), fols. 40b-41a.

[62]In Tibetan: *mda' dar me loṅ.*

example, the Tibetan Earth Goddess, Sa'i-lha-mo brtan-ma, has such a divination mirror in her right hand. This is presumably also the meaning of the mirror held by Manene, the goddess of the Tibetan epic Gesar of Ling, who was continually making prophecies to the hero Gesar.[63] The chief tantric deities do not carry a mirror. Hence, there is the suggestion that when a deity does hold a mirror there is a divination cult associated with that deity. In illustration, the deity Kālacakra is depicted as holding a mirror among the objects held by four white hands among his left hands, and in his retinue Amitābha holds a mirror in one of his left hands.[64] But we have previously observed in a commentary by Nāropā that the *Kālacakra* has precisely such a divination subcult.

After those theoretical considerations, it may be useful to give an actual ritual which concerns evocation of the White Tārā to obtain an omen, which I now translate from a native Tibetan *sādhana*:[65]

> Homage to the *gurus*. As to the precept of having an omen arise in immediacy: Previously one has well performed in one session the realization in contemplation of one's tutelary deity. In that state, one has generated himself into the momentary reproduction of the White Tārā. He imagines a white TĀṂ on the center of the opened lotus of his heart, and from that syllable a blazing light which completely fills the empty interior of his body. He sets four silver mirrors in the four directions of the TĀṂ syllable. Reciting A-NU-TA-RA he imagines it [i.e., its four syllables] like a reflected image in the sequence of the four mirrors of East, South, West, and North. With rays emanated from that TĀṂ he invites Tārā from the Akaniṣṭha heaven and he reabsorbs them. Three times he prays that the omen may arise in immediacy. Then he imagines that whatever be his own aim is a white TĀṂ, that from it rays emanate which perform the

[63]Alexandra David-Neel and Lama Yongden, *The Superhuman Life of Gesar of Ling* (New York, 1934), p. 132: "in one hand she held a bow, in the other a mirror."

[64]According to the Kālacakra maṇḍala in B. Bhattacharyya, ed., *Niṣpannayogāvalī of Mahāpaṇḍita Abhayākaragupta* (Baroda, 1949).

[65]*Sgrub thabs kun btus* vol. Ga (3), fols. 438-39.

> aim of all beings of the kingdom, and in particular perform all of one's own aim; and imagines that then the rays of this TĀṂ become like a meteor which penetrates the middle of his forehead. With fierce craving of imploring the *siddhi* [magical success], he imagines that he swallows this TĀṂ and that it is absorbed into the TĀṂ of his heart; and imagines that his desired thing doubtless arises as a dream. Then he goes into deep sleep with the resting posture of the lion [i.e., on his right side]. . . (Later) he prepares a thanksgiving offering[66] to the venerable Goddess.

It is plain that the above rite is tantamount to a yoga state of dream, in which the four silver mirrors become the basis of the prophetic vision, or omen. Combining this with our previous indications, the rite should be preceded by a kind of symbolic death, a yoga state of dreamless sleep, since the diviner has voided the phenomenal dream of his face in the mirror.

Concluding Remarks

After the foregoing sampling of the numerous mirror passages of Buddhist literature, I suppose it would not be possible to find another Buddhist metaphor-simile so enduring through the vicissitudes of religious history, and so revelatory of Buddhist attitudes or instructive on how the educated Buddhist would structure his arguments on crucial issues of his religion and associated philosophies with a metaphor-simile. Even so, these mirror studies are not the most fascinating of study topics, because—I may venture to suggest—the mirror is a static image. And there are sounds to hear, for which a mirror fails. Besides, such a study as I have made tends to place the mirror metaphor in a tiresome role. After all, in their natural habitat these metaphors occur in a spread-out, occasional manner. It perhaps violates their metaphorical integrity to bunch them, jostling their relatives, each of whom would prefer the other to have stayed in his own book!

[66]See F. D. Lessing, "Miscellaneous Lamaist Notes. I. Notes on the Thanksgiving Offering," *Central Asiatic Journal* 2, no. 1 (1956): 58-71.

APPENDIX

THE PRAJÑĀ-MIRROR : DOES IT HAVE AN INDIAN ORIGIN

Walter Liebenthal rendered great service to students of Chinese Buddhism and Buddhism generally by his translation, first published in 1948, *The Book of Chao*; and years later, by his revision of the same, published in 1968, *Chao Lun: The Treatises of Seng-chao*.[67] Seng-chao was a youthful disciple of the famous Kumārajīva in A.D. 401. His wonderful work has many obscure statements about *prajñā* and some in particular about *prajñā* as a dark mirror. It is usually taken for granted that there is non-Buddhist influence on Seng-chao. Can this mysterious *prajñā*-mirror be traced to Indian Buddhism?

Near the end of his *Madhyamakāvatāra*, Candrakīrti employs the mirror simile in the sense of simultaneous appearance of all parts, to show the nature of enlightenment, as well as to show the appearance of a divine body. In Tsoṅ-kha-pa's commentary (the part on the Tenth Stage of the Bodhisattva) the commentarial sentence is as follows.[68] "This Saṃbhogakāya reveals itself only to the attainers of the state [i.e., the Bodhisattva of the Tenth Bodhisattva Stage] who have the mind of enlightenment [*bodhicitta*] free from proliferating imagination [*prapañca*] and have gained the immaculate mirror of *prajñā* from their own two collections [of merit and knowledge]; and it does not reveal itself concretely to the ordinary persons [*pṛthagjana*] attended with proliferating imagination." Passing to the *Laṅkāvatāra-sūtra*, the equivalent language is the mirror wherein the reflections of all forms are seen simultaneously (*yugapat*) and free from discursive thought (*vikalpa*).[69] This *Laṅkāvatāra* passage also speaks of the Niṣyanda-Buddha associated with the Akaniṣṭha mansion, which is obviously this scripture's equivalent to the Saṃbhogakāya of other texts.

Earlier in his *Madhyamakāvatāra* (self-commentary,) Candra-

[67]The 1948 publication was Monograph 13 of *Monumenta Serica* (Catholic University of Peking); the 1968 one was published by Hong Kong University Press.

[68]TSOṄ-KHA-PA'S commentary called "Dgoṅs pa rab gsal," PTT, 154: 105-4.

[69]*The Laṅkāvatāra* Sūtra, ed. Bunyiu Nanjio (Kyoto, 1956), 55, 18.

kīrti (on 6, 174-75) speaks of purifying the face of *prajñā* from nescience (*avidyā*).[70]

Now Seng-chao writes (*Chao-lun*, p. 54): "A perfect void where nothing grows (and decays) such is, perchance, the transcendent realm as it shows in the dark mirror of Prajñā." Again (p. 67): "Prajñā reflects what is totally concealed, yet does so without cognition." Indeed, except for the word "dark" applied to the mirror, these statements agree perfectly with the foregoing materials from the Mādhyamika tradition of Candrakīrti and the Tibetan commentary by Tsoṅ-kha-pa, and with the Yogācāra tradition of the *Laṅkāvatāra-sūtra*, although these particular works were not available to Seng-chao.[71] But as a disciple of Kumārajīva, Seng-chao should have had access to, and would have consulted eagerly, the encyclopedic Buddhist work, the *Mahāprajñāpāramitāśāstra*, which Kumārajīva is credited with having rendered into Chinese; and Seng-chao should have had accessible a number of other Buddhist works already translated into his language. Seng-chao's "perfect void" and "without cognition" are the equivalent for the statements in those other works "*bodhicitta* free from proliferating imagination" and "free from discursive thought." The closest an Indian work comes to calling this Perfection of Insight (*prajñāpāramitā*) a mirror is perhaps Candrakīrti's *prajñā*-face, although we are reminded of the mirror-face of the Pāli Jātakas. It does seem, therefore, that the terminology "dark mirror of *prajñā*" originated in China, while the state to which this terminology applies may have already been described in the Buddhist literature of Indian origin that was available to Seng-chao. That is, for lack of Indian Buddhist texts using this terminology, it may be presumed that Tsoṅ-kha-pa's term "*prajñā*-mirror" derives from earlier Tibetan Buddhism that was influenced in this matter by Chinese Buddhism.

On the other hand, the celebrated Japanese author Kūkai seems not to have received or adopted this dark mirror terminology, for

[70]According to the citation of Candrakīrti's passage in Tsoṅ-kha-pa's *Lam rim chen mo*, namely in the *vipaśyanā* (discerning the real) section in my MS translation, *Calming the Mind and Discerning the Real* (Columbia University, New York, (1978).

[71]In particular, Guṇabhadra translated the *Laṅkāvatāra* into Chinese some years after Seng-chao's passing.

he writes in the same context of the Buddha's enlightenment wisdom: "Just as all the forms are reflected in a clean mirror on a high stand, so it is with the Tathāgata's Mind-mirror. The clean mirror of Mind hangs high on the top of Dharmadhātu, being serene and shining on all without perversion or mistake. What Buddha does not possess such a clean mirror?"[72]

[72]H. Inagaki, "Kūkai's Sokushin-Jōbutsu-Gi (Principle of Attaining Buddhahood with the Present Body)," *Asia Major* n.s. 17 (1971-72): 215.

7

THE BUDDHIST THEORY OF VISION

The Buddhist treatment of vision, especially in terms of eyes, whether meant concretely or metaphorically, is among the most important topics of Buddhist thought from its inception to the present. The stress begins with the first sermon of Buddhism. While the present essay is relatively brief, it is possible to present here the main ideas by means of trenchant passages chosen from a wide variety of sources.

I. The Early Theory of Vision and Consistent Texts

It is well known that every version of the first sermon, "Setting into Motion the Wheel of the Law", has the Buddha's explanation that when he oriented his mind to each of the four Noble Truths, a series of experiences occurred beginning traditionally with the expressions "knowledge arose, vision arose" (Pāli *ñāṇa* and *cakkhu*, Sanskrit *jñāna* and *cakṣus*). The same point is made in other sermons with the expression "knowledge and vision" (P. *ñāṇadassana*, Skt. *jñānadarśana*). A most important passage occrurs in the *Aṅguttara-Nikāya* (Book of Eights, "At Gayā"): "Monks, before my awakening, when being a *bodhisattva* I was not completely enlightened, I conceived (mystic) manifestations (*obhāsa*) but did not see (mystic) forms (*rūpa*). Monks, it occurred to me, 'If I were both to conceive (mystic) manifestations and to see (mystic) forms, in that case knowledge and vision would be better purified in me'." It is quite clear that "knowledge" is going with the conception (*saññā*) of manifestations and that "vision" is going with the seeing of forms.

The copulative interpretation of the compound *ñāṇadassana* is continued down the centuries to the commentary *Ārya-Daśa-bhūmivyākhyāna*, attributed to Vasubandhu in the Tibetan canon (Tohoku Cat. No. 3998), where (Derge ed., *Mdo ḥgrel, Ṅi*, f. 177a-6. ff.) we read: "Four of the supernormal faculties (*abhijñā*) are categorized by knowledge (*jñāna*), the fifth is categorized by vision (*darśana*). The one supernormal faculty of magical ability (*ṛddhi*) purifies the actions of body. The supernormal faculties of both divine hearing and knowing the make-up of others' minds purifies the actions of speech. The supernormal faculties of both the memory of former lives and the (knowledge of) passing away and rebirth purifies the actions of mind". (/mṅon par śes pa rnams las bźi ni śes pas rab tu phye baḥo / lṅa pa ni mthoṅ bas rab tu phye baḥo / rdzu ḥphrul mṅon par śes pa gcig gis ni / lus kyi las yoṅs su dag go / lhaḥi rna ba daṅ / pha rol gyi sems śes paḥi mṅon par śes pa gñis kyis ni ṅag gi las yoṅs su dag go / sṅon gyi gnas rjes su dran pa daṅ / ḥchi ḥpho daṅ / skye ba mṅon par śes pa gñis kyis ni yid kyi las yoṅs su dag go /). This interesting passage agrees with what is well established, namely that the fifth supernormal faculty, the knowledge of passing away and rebirth, is otherwise called the "divine eye" (*dibba-cakkhu, divya-cakṣus*) and so constitutes the category of "vision". The passage furthermore groups this ability with the memory of past lives, suggesting that this memory is an inward-directed knowledge while the divine eye is an associated faculty that is directed outwards in the manner of an eye.

The emphasis on vision was continued in other kinds of terminology: "he who sees the Dhamma sees me, and he who sees me sees the Dhamma" (S. iii. 120; *It.* 91; *Mil.* 73).[1] The Mahāyāna equivalent to this is found in many places, for example in the *Bodhisattva-piṭaka*, part of the Ratnakūṭa collection:[2]

[1]Ananda K. Coomaraswamy and I. B. Horner, *Gotama The Buddha* (London, 1948), p. 23.

[2]The passage occurs in Tibetan in Photo ed., Vol. 23, p. 19-5; and I have included the translation in my "Buddhism", *Historia Religionum* Vol. 2 Brill, Leiden, 1971).

> Whatever is the meaning of Dependent Origination, is the meaning of Dharma; whatever is the meaning of Dharma, is the meaning of Tathāgata. Therefore, whoever sees Dependent Origination, sees Dharma; whoever sees Dharma, sees the Tathāgata. Also, seeing that way, and accordingly fully understanding in the sense of Thusness, still one sees scarcely anything. What is that "scarcely anything"? It is the Signless and the Non-apprehension; the one who sees in the manner of Signless and Non-apprehension, sees rightly.

Besides, the third Noble Truth, of Cessation (*nirodha*), must be realized directly (*sākṣāt*, "before the eyes") according to the ancient Buddhist prescription. Thus, *nirvāṇa* in its oldest sense is attained when it is seen; and it is seen, according to the suggestion of our next section, by the "eye" of insight (*paññā*, *prajñā*).[3]

II. The Three Eyes and the Five Eyes

The three eyes are well-known in Pāli literature as the eye of flesh (*maṃsacakkhu*), the divine eye (*dibbacakkhu*), and the eye of insight (*paññācakkhu*). Falk has discussed these eyes in terms of the bodies which they respectively see. The eye of flesh sees the *rūpa*-personality, the divine eye sees the *manomayakāya* ("body made of mind"), and the eye of insight "sees" Nirvāṇa. She understands from her study of Pāli literature that these eyes constitute the successive spheres or fruits of the Buddhist ascension treated in the three instructions, respectively of morality (*sīla*), meditation (*samādhi*), and insight (*paññā*).[4]

The five eyes are an expansion in Mahāyāna Sanskrit works of the original three (*maṃsa-*, *divya-*, and *prajñā-cakṣus*). The two that are added are the eye of *dharma* and the Buddha eye. Having collected a number of passages on the group of five, I have noticed that some lists have the "eye of knowledge" (*jñāna-cakṣus*) as a substitution for the "eye of *dhamma*."[5] In fact, these books took

[3]"Contributions to the Mādhyamika school of Buddhism", in *Journal of the American Oriental Society*, Vol. 89.1. The same doctrine about Nirvāṇa being of utmost importance for understanding Nāgārjuna's position is held here.

[4]Maryla Falk, *Nāma-Rūpa and Dharma-Rūpa* (University of Calcutta, 1943), pp. 114-115.

[5]Indrabhūti's commentary on the *Śrī-Saṃpuṭatilaka-tantra*, Derge Tanjur,

the "eye of insight" and added the "eye of *dharma*" and "Buddha eye" to make a Mahāyāna set of three eyes. Thus Vasubandhu's commentary on the *Akṣayamatinirdeśa-sūtra* (Derge Tanjur, Mdo ḥgrel, Ci, 15b-6, ff.) states: "The three eyes are 'eye of *dharma*,' 'eye of insight,' and "eye of Buddha"' (/spyan gsum ni chos kyi spyan daṅ / śes rab kyi spyan daṅ / saṅs rgyas kyi spyan no/). Kamalaśīla's commentary on the *Vajracchedikā* (Tohoku No. 3817, Derge Tanjur, Śes phyin, Vol. Ma, 251a-2, ff.) also sets aside these three eyes, defining them as follows: "He has the 'eye of insight' toward the object which is the selflessness of person and nature (*pudgala*-and *dharma-nairātmya*). The 'eye of *dharma*' is toward the realm of *dharma* alone in the conventional sense when there is the appearance only of *dharma* while personality (*pudgala*) is void, there being no personality (in view). The omniscience concerning all forms of the knowable is called the 'eye of Buddha'." (/gaṅ zag daṅ chos la bdag med paḥi yul la ni śes rab kyi spyan mṅaḥo/kun rdzob tu chos tsam du snaṅ ba ñid de gaṅ zag ni ma yin na źes gaṅ zag stoṅ ste / chos tsam gyi yul la chos kyi spyan no / śes bya thams cad rnam pa thams cad du mkhyen pa ni saṅs rgyas kyi spyan źes bya ste/).

A complete explanation of the five eyes from the *Yogācāra* standpoint is in Sthiramati's commentary on the *Mahāyāna-sūtrālaṃkāra* (Bodhipakṣya chapter) from which the essentials are given here:[6]

(a) The eye of flesh sees forms in present time.

(b) The divine eye is of two kinds, both seeing forms in past and future: (1) that born of past action (*karma*), the eye of the gods; and (2) that born of contemplation (*bhāvanā*) in the *samādhi* of a yogin, and which sees the sentient beings passing away from here and going to various destinies in accordance with past actions.

(c) The eye of insight is the non-discursive knowledge which understands the individual and the general characteristic of the *dharmas*, seeing them in the absolute sense (*paramārthatas*).

(d) The eye of *dharma* understands without impediment all

Rgyud ḥgrel, Ga, 75b-6, ff., states the five eyes as eye of flesh, divine eye, eye of insight, knowledge eye, and eye of Buddha, thus omitting the eye of *dharma* and having in its place the knowledge eye.

[6]I have included this summary in my "Buddhism", *Historia Religionum.*

the scripture, understands the stream of consciousness of persons in the sense of discriminating whether it is an ordinary person, or one of the eight classes of disciples (on the four paths or in the fruits of the four paths), or a Bodhisattva and if so then on which of the ten Bodhisattva Stages; and seeing the *dharmas* in the conventional sense (*saṃvṛtitas*).

(e) The eye of a Buddha understands all *dharmas*, whether with or without flux, whether constructed or unconstructed; and realizes directly every knowable field; understands the state of Arhat ensuing from the "diamond-like *samādhi*" and the freedom from fluxes of the Tathāgatas.

It can be observed in Sthiramati's treatment that all three of the eyes which have been grouped above as a Mahāyāna set, turn out to be concerned with *dharma* or *dharmas*. Furthermore, the eyes of insight and *dharma* can be grouped together as constituting two levels of "discriminative knowledge" (*pratyavekṣaṇā-jñāna*), namely in the absolute and in the conventional sense. Since Mahāyāna scriptures insist that in the absolute sense the natures (*dharma*) neither arise nor pass away, no prophecy can be made for them, and so the eye of insight is not prophetic. On the other hand, those scriptures assert that in a conventional sense, those *dharmas* arise void of self-existence (*svabhāva*). Since they "arise" a prophecy can be made for them.[7]

Asaṅga, in his *Yogācārabhūmi-viniścayasaṃgrahaṇī* (Derge Tanjur, Sems tsam, Vol. *Zi*, f. 56b-7, ff.) compares the "divine eye" with the "eye of insight" and explains that the "divine eye" sees all visible forms (*nidarśana-rūpa*), while the "eye of insight" ranges in all forms, namely visible and invisible, whether obstructing or non-obstructing. "All visible forms" includes (cf. *Abhidharma-kośa*, III, 14a-b) the forms of beings in the intermediate state (*antarābhava*), presumably because those beings also have a "visible form" of a sort, ordinarily visible only to beings of the same class. Tsoṅ-kha-pa, in his *Don gsal* commentary on the *Guhyasamāja-tantra* (Lhasa ed., Vol. Cha, f. 23b-1, ff.), basing his remarks also on Asaṅga's *Yogācārabhūmi*, explains that with the "divine eye" one sees the six classes of "passion gods" in the

[7]These remarks about prophecy stem from the *Pitāputrasamāgama-sūtra* (chapter on the Tuṣitā gods), as read in the Tibetan version.

"realm of desire" (*kāma-dhātu*), and all other beings in the "realm of desire," including the sixteen hells.

Following up the previous remark by Falk that the divine eye sees the *manomayakāya*, it is worthwhile to inquire what would be this *manomayakāya* among the three given a prominent place in the *Laṅkāvatāra-sūtra.* I have summarized this Sūtra's treatment of that kind of body in my "Studies in Yama and Māra", *Indo-Iranian Journal*, III:2 (1959), p. 119:

> The Sanskrit text (136-7, f.) sets forth three *manomaya-kāya:* (1) the mental body with stabilization in the pleasure of *samādhi* (*samādhisukhasamāpatti-manomaya*); (2) the mental body which completely comprehends the intrinsicn ature of the *dharmas* (*dharmasvabhāvāvabodha-manomaya*); (3) the mental body which performs the instigations natural to its class (*nikāyasahajasaṃskārakriyā-manomaya*). The commentary by Jñānavajra shows that the first of these, prevalent up through the Seventh Bodhisattva Stage, does not involve transmutation of the basis (*āśrayaparāvṛtti*) of the eightfold set of perceptions (*vijñāna*). The second is prevalent on the Eighth or Superior Stage of the Bodhisattva; and here, with a body comparable to that (of the Buddhas) one proceeds to all the Buddha Realms.

In the *Abhidharma-kośa*, III, 40c-41a, the being of *antarābhava* is called *manomaya*, *saṃbhavaiṣin*, and Gandharva. This particular *manomaya* appears to be the first of the *Laṅkāvatāra-sūtra* set. It would be the one treated by Paravahera Vajirañāṇa as the one of the *Dīgha Nikāya* i, 77, which the meditating monk draws from his own body with identical form.[8] Hence, this would be the *manomaya-kāya* which is seen by the divine eye. Since the second *manomaya-kāya* of the *Laṅkāvatāra-sūtra* comprehends the intrinsic nature of the *dharmas*, this would include both the "eye of insight" and the "eye of *dharma*" as metaphorical eyes. The third *manomaya-kāya* would involve the Buddha eye. This eye of a Buddha is mentioned in a famous passage in the *Saṃyūtta-Nikāya*, Vol. I (the Brahmā Suttas), beginning, "Then the Exalted One, understanding Brahmā's entreaty, because of his compassion

[8]Paravahera Vajirañāṇa Mahāthera, *Buddhist Meditation in Theory and Practice* (Colombo, 1962), p. 440.

toward all sentient beings, looked down with a Buddha's Eye over the world...." This shows that the original conception of a "Buddha's eye" is the eye with which a Buddha looks at the world after his attainment of Complete Enlightenment.

Then the question arises of whether one sees with only one eye at a time or can see simultaneously with more than one of those eyes. For example, what eye or eyes are employed by the celestial Bodhisattva Avalokiteśvara when he surveys the beings in the six destinies (*gati*)? Some years ago, when I was reading Tibetan literature at the University of California I asked the Mongolian Lama named Dilowa Gegen Hutukhtu if Avalokiteśvara looked at the world with the "eye of knowledge." He replied that Avalokiteśvara and every Buddha sees with all five eyes. There is a textual confirmation of this remark in Abhayākaragupta's *Saṃpuṭa-tilaka* commentary called *Āmnāya-mañjarī*, in the Japanese photo edition of the Tibetan canon, Vol. 55, p. 238-1: " 'By gazes' means, by the fleshly, divine, insight, *dharma*, and Buddha eyes". (/śa daṅ lha daṅ śes rab daṅ chos daṅ saṅs rgyas kyi spyan gyis gzigs pa rnams kyis so/). Tsoṅ-kha-pa makes reference to the same point in his commentary on Candrakīrti's *Madhyamakāvatāra*, Photo ed., Vol. 154, p. 238-2: "When one applies eye ointment to the eye and the eye becomes bright, the eye (itself) is not nullified. In the same way, when one applies the eye ointment for seeing voidness and the eye of discrimination (*buddhi*) becomes bright, the eye of knowledge is not nullified. If one understands that (i.e. knows the implication of the foregoing remark), (he realizes that) not rightly applied is the disparaging viewpoint that there is no knowledge (*jñāna*) in *ārya-samāpatti*". (/mig sman bskus pas mig gsal du ḥgro yi/mig ḥdon pa min pa bźin du stoṅ ñid mthoṅ baḥi mig sman bskus pas / bloḥi mig sal du hgro ba gyi/ye śes kyi mig ḥdon pa min par śes na / ḥphags paḥi mñam gzag tu ye śes med ces pahi skur ḥdebs kyi lta bden pa mi gos so/). As previously mentioned, this "eye of knowledge" is the "eye of *dharma*"; it is not nullified when the "eye of insight" is operating. In the Mādhyamika school, this "eye of insight" is said to look upon the voidness, which in the oldest sense is the voidness of self and of what belongs to self.

III. The Eyes in Buddhist Cult and Iconography

In the celebrated story of King Śibi, the generous king received his eyes back through the rite of truth.[9] Ārya-Śūra's formulation of the tale in the *Jātaka-mālā* has this verse in the words of Indra:

> And there will arise an unhindered power of your two eyes to see.
> All around for a hundred *yojanas*, even when interrupted by mountains.

Tsoṅ-kha-pa, in his *Dbaṅ don* ("Meaning of Initiation"), Lhasa collected works, Vol. Ca, f. 45a-2, writes: "By the rite of eye ointment one dispels the obscuration of the nescience film over the eye of discrimination and generates the supernormal power of the 'divine eye'." (/mig sman gyi cho gas blo yi mig ma rig paḥi liṅ tog gis bsgrib pa bsal nas lhaḥi mig gi mṅon śes skyed pa daṅ/). The rite of eye ointment is presented in his *Sṅags rim chen mo* (Peking block print, f. 278b-3. ff.):

> (The guru) places in a gold or silver vessel the golden eye ointment consisting of butter and honey. While the disciple imagines on his eyes the syllable PRAṂ, (the guru) applies (the eye ointment) with a probe (*śalākā*), reciting OṂ VAJRA-NETRA APAHARA PAṬALAṂ HRĪH ("Oṃ. Remove the film that is on the diamond eye! Hriḥ".) And he repeats the verse of the *Vairocanābhisaṃbodhi-tantra*, "Just as the King of Healing (*bhaiṣajya-rāja*) with his probe removed the worldly film, so may the Buddhas dispel your film of ignorance, my son!"

I have also noticed a number of ritual passages about "eye ointment"in the *Amoghapāśakalparājā* (No. 686 in the Tohoku catalog).

There are other tantric rituals about the eyes which involve imagining the syllables MA changing into a sun in the right eye and ṬA changing into a moon in the left eye, and a HO in between the two, radiating light. For example, such a ritual occurs in Kukuri-pā's *Mahāmāyāsādhanamaṇḍalavidhi* (No. 1630 in Tohoku Cat.) and in Jñānavajra's *Karuṇodaya-nāma-bhāvanājapavidhi* (No. 2524 in Cat.)

9"The Hindu-Buddhist Rite of Truth—An Interpretation", *Studies in Indian Linguistics* (Volume presented to Prof. M. B. Emeneau on his sixtieth birthday year), Poona, 1968, pp. 365-369, reprinted here.

Concerning the "diamond eye" (*vajranetra*) the tantric Candrakīrti in his commentary on the *Guhyasamāja-tantra* called *Pradīpodyotana* (Derge Tanjur, Rgyud ḥgrel, Ha, 94a-1) writes: "His eye (i.e. of Mahāvajradhara) sees by means of a perfectly pure bright light; and that is the 'diamond eye'." (/deḥi spyan ni ḥog gsal bas rnam par dag pas gzigs pa gaṅ yin de ni rdo rje spyan te/). In the *Āmnāya-mañjarī* (op. cit., Vol. 55, p. 245-2), Abhayākaragupta quotes the scriptural passage: "O Mañjuśrī, in regard to that, the Tathāgata, by means of the six supernormal faculties which see everywhere, sees the sentient beings passing away and being reborn, also proceeding to a good destiny or a bad destiny. Likewise, the Tathāgata sees with the *uṣṇīṣa;* likewise, he sees with the *ūrṇā-kośa;* so also with each characteristic". The same author quotes the last portion of this passage again in his *Munimatālaṃkāra* (Photo ed., Vol. 101, p. 268-3) and here identifies it as coming from the *Śraddhābalādhāna-sūtra* (No. 201 in the Tohoku cat.). That relates to numerous passages in Mahāyana literature narrating that from the Buddha's *uṣṇīṣa* on the crown of his head, or from the *ūrṇā-kośa* in the middle of his forehead there arose streams of light, illuminating all the worlds, and the like. Hence, the *uṣṇīṣa* and the *ūrṇā-kośa* as well as the remaining thirty-two characteristics (*lakṣaṇa*) function as a sort of eye, answering to the description of the "diamond eye". According to the *Bhadrakalpita-sūtra*, the light emanating from the *uṣṇīṣa* is the fruit of the "perfection of insight" (*prajñāpāramitā*).[10]

The *ūrṇā-kośa* in this sense of an eye is presumably equivalent to the "third eye" depicted frequently on tantric deities in Asian art, especially Tibetan.

[10]As cited by Hjam dbyaṅs bzad paḥi rdo rje in his *Mthaḥ dpyod* of Chapter 8 of the *Abhisamayālaṃkāra* (Tibetan text).

8

DEPENDENT ORIGINATION— THE INDO-TIBETAN TRADITION

INTRODUCTION

In the *Mahā-nidāna-suttanta* of the Dīgha-Nikāya, the Buddha reproved Ānanda for saying that while Dependent Origination looks deep it is clear to him. The Buddha announced that it both looks deep and is deep. In this case the Buddha was on the side of the gods, because the *Bṛhadāraṇyaka-Upaniṣad* (IV, 2, 2) says, "The gods love that which is hinted at darkly, and hate that which is uttered directly." As William Blake puts it, the "dim Windows of the Soul ... leads you to Believe a Lie When you see with, not thro', the Eye"—because Dependent Origination not quite "is" and not quite "isn't".

This signals the difficulties which authors of the past and present have experienced with the Buddhist formula. They considered Dependent Origination as something before their eyes to see in clear relief, as one might see a book. This essay claims that Dependent Origination could not become clear in such a way, since there are two distinct and contrasting interpretations of the series, the first one which I label "discovery and seeing", and the second "lives of a person," and since both interpretations are required for understanding the formula. The first, without concern for particular persons, attempts to develop the Buddhist Doctrine. The second, recognizing individuals, shows the role of defilement and *karma* in successive lives. In order to demonstrate this in continuance of my previous published materials[1] on the subject, it would lead me too far afield to deal with the multitude of theories advanced by sympathetic authors or to counter the hostile criticism that the Buddhist formula does not make sense.[2] I shall report the Indian tradition through the well-known Pāli or Sanskrit works, and for the Tibetan part especially rely on the Dependent Origination section of Tsoṅ-kha-pa's *Lam rim chen mo*.

I. The Two Kinds of Dependent Origination

The essential point of *dependent* (*pratītya*) origination (*samutpāda*) is the requirement of a condition (*pratyaya*) for something to arise.[3] The standard sequence of twelve such conditions in Sanskrit and my English translation is this: 1. nescience (*avidyā*), 2. motivations (*saṃskāra*), 3. perception (*vijñāna*), 4. name-and-form (*nāma-rūpa*), 5. six sense bases (*ṣaḍāyatana*), 6. sense contact (*sparśa*), 7. feelings (*vedanā*), 8. craving (*tṛṣṇā*), 9. indulgence (*upādāna*), 10. gestation (*bhava*), 11. birth (*jāti*), 12. old age and death (*jarā-maraṇa*). I stumbled upon a possibility of two kinds by finding in Asaṅga's *Yogācārabhūmi* that there is a nescience "unmixed with defilement" and in another place that Dependent Origination can be classified in terms of defilement (*kleśa*), *karma*, and suffering (*duḥkha*), where nescience is labelled as a defilement.[4] Even-

[1]Cf. the articles referred to below in notes 38 or 46, and 51; and the work in Note 37.

[2]Among the many treatments, I mention here A. B. Keith, *Buddhist Philosophy in India and Ceylon* (India reprint), pp. 105-109, for some of the older European theories. Edward J. Thomas, *The History of Buddhist Thought* (1933, with reprints), the Causation chapter, for a number of views from Buddhist texts. Shotoru Iida, in a mimeographed paper entitled "Re-turning Gautama's Wheel of Causation—an Interpretation of the dvādaśanidāna", for the Pānadura debate of 1983, and for a number of views of Japanese scholars. L. de La Vallée Poussin, *Théorie des douze causes* (Gand, 1913), for a still valuable survey of the scholastic theories of the causal chain. K. N. Jayatilleke, *Early Buddhist Theory of Knowledge* (London, 1963), esp. pp. 445-457, for a Pāli specialist's evaluation of the theories.

[3]Cf. Jayatilleke, *Early Buddhist Theory*, p. 449, for the basic statements and canonical references: "whenever A is present, B is present" (*imasmiṃ sati idaṃ hoti*), and whenever *A* is absent, *B* is absent" (*imasmiṃ asati idaṃ na hoti*).

[4]Asaṅga expounds two kinds of nescience (*avidyā*) in the part of his *Yogā-cārābhūmi* called *Viniścaya-saṃgrahaṇī*, Japanese photo edition of the Tibetan

tually, I took the first kind as discovered by Gautama Buddha and as unconcerned with particular beings. The second kind is applied to lives of an individual whose *karma* is differentiated or unshared.

My division also follows the implications of Nāgārjuna's *Madhyamaka-kārikā* XXIV, 40: "The one who sees Dependent Origination, sees this (*idam*) precisely (*caiva*) as Suffering and the Source, precisely (*eva ca*) as Cessation and Path." This verse afforded the commentators a splendid opportunity, which they seem not to have taken, to point out that Nāgārjuna's association of voidness (*śūnyatā*) with Dependent Origination makes it possible to see Dependent Origination as any one of the four Noble Truths, i.e., one can see it as the "tree of suffering" (*infra.*) and as any other one of the four Truths.[5] Since Dependent Origination is not a real thing, seeing it one way does not prevent anyone from seeing it another way. Hence I offer this explanation in terms of the present article: The first two Noble Truths of Suffering and Source are associated with the first kind of Dependent Origination that deals with beings as a whole and not with particular ones. The last two Noble Truths of Cessation and Path are associated with the second kind of Dependent Origination concerned with lives of individuals including the specialized ones who follow the Path. As to the "seeing" itself, later I cite various passages.

I.1. *The First Kind of Dependent Origination*

There is a celebrated account in Pāli, Saṃyutta-Nikāya, ii, 25, presenting the twelve members in reverse order: "With the condition of birth, O monks, there is old age and death. With the

---

canon, vol. 110, p. 28-1-5, ff. I gathered materials from many places of his *Yogācārabhūmi* and organized them in a paper "Nescience and Insight According to Asaṅga's *Yogācārabhūmi*", for the volume *Buddhist Studies in Honour of the Venerable Walpola Sri Rahula* (Gordon Frazer, London, 1980), cf. esp. pp. 154-255, and n. 11. This essay is published in this volume.

[5]Among the commentaries that do not face up to the issue is Candrakīrti's *Prasannapadā*, the Chap. XXIV of which is translated into French by Jacques May (Paris, 1959); Bhāvaviveka's *Prajñāpradīpa*, the Chap. XXIV of which is available in a draft translation into English by Ryushin Uryuzu, locally distributed in Madison, Wisc., Nov. 1966, for a seminar in Mādhyamika philosophy; Abhayākaragupta's *Munimatālaṃkāra* photo ed. of Tibetan canon, Vol. 101, pp. 220-223.

condition of gestation, O monks, there is birth..." And then, "Whether Tathāgatas arise or do not arise, there remains this realm (*dhātu*), the continuance of *dhamma*, the rule of *dhamma*, the having of this for condition. This the Tathāgata has discovered; this he fully understands; and having discovered it and fully understood it, he teaches it,..." And finally, the Ārya disciple, having rightly understood it, does not let his mind run to past time, thinking, "Did I live in the past?" and so on. The important feature of this passage is that the discovery and concordant teaching of Dependent Origination is not concerned with whether Tathāgatas arise or whether sentient beings arise, existed in the past, will exist in the future, etc. As to the meaning of such expressions as "continuance of *dhamma*," "rule of *dhamma*," there is also the pithy utterance, "Whoever sees Dependent Origination, sees the Dharma."[6] There is nothing mysterious about this: Once the Tathāgata had discovered Dependent Origination, he taught it, whereupon it became the Dharma. This must be the Dharma among the Three Jewels; so it is the Buddhist Doctrine, or an essential or salient part thereof.

But also the Saṃyutta-Nikāya, ii, 120, says in the *Vakkali-sutta*. "Whoever, Vakkali, sees the *dhamma*, sees me; whoever sees me, sees the *dhamma*." Since Dependent Origination as set forth above is not concerned with whether Tathāgatas arise or not, it follows that it is not concerned with whether *dhamma* (singular or plural) arises or not. A similar identification of *dharma* (the Sanskrit equivalent to the Pāli *dhamma*) with the Tathāgata is made in the Mahāyāna scripture "Meeting of Father and Son" (*Pitāputrasamāgama-sūtra*).[7] Here, after a discussion of Dependent Origination, it teaches: "Therefore, by understanding Dependent Origination, one understands the *dharmadhātu*," and "Lord, the Tathāgata is devoid of characteristics (*lakṣaṇa*), ...; is Dharmadhātu, Thusness, True End (*bhūtakoṭi*). All *dharmas* are also *bhūtakoṭi*. Therefore, all *dharmas* are the Tathāgata." The foregoing suggests that the Buddha's discovery of Dependent

[6]Cf. *Śālistambasūtra* in La Vallée Poussin, *Théorie des douze causes*, p. 70: *yo, bhikṣavaḥ pratītyasamutpādaṃ paśyati sa dharmaṃ paśyati;* while in the Pāli version (Majjhima-Nikāya, I, 191) it is in a discourse by Śāriputra attributed to Buddha.

[7]Photo edition of Tibetan Canon, Vol. 23, chapter on "Instruction of the Bṛhatphala Deities," p. 181-1, ff.

Origination involved no perceptual reach of particular sentient beings, ordinary or advanced; or of particular *dharmas*, ordinary ones like love and hate or supernal ones like Buddha natures. Along the same lines, the discourse to Kaccāyana (Saṃyutta-Nikāya, iii, 134—135) and Nāgārjuna's use of the discourse (with the Sanskrit name Katyāyana) in his *Madhyamaka-kārikā*, show that the middle doctrine or path of Dependent Origination avoids the attributions of "The world exists" or "The world does not exist," hence also avoids such formulations as "The Tathāgata exists" or "The Tathāgata does not exist," or again, such formulations as "He is happy," or "He is unhappy."

To further clarify this kind of Dependent Origination, I shall translate below a Pāli Sutta (Saṃyutta-Nikāya, Nidāna Book, ii, 2) which has no mention of such matters as *karma* and transmigration. In particular, by explaining nescience as ignorance of any of the four Noble Truths, it avoids any direct implications of defilement (*kleśa*). Asaṅga also denies that ignorance of the four Truths is defiled since it does not involve waywardness of thought (*citta-viparyāsa*).[8] Rather, the ignorance of the four Truths is tantamount to not knowing Dependent Origination. The early nature of this Pāli scripture is also confirmed by certain non-standard listings, such as its detailing of "name" in "name-and-form" and of the member "feelings."[9]

When the Buddha was dwelling at Sāvatthī, he said: "Monks, I will teach you, I will analyze Dependent Origination.[10] Listen to

[8]This is in the *Yogācārabhūmi* in the same passage referred to above, Note 4. Here Asaṅga gives two kinds of "unmixed nescience" (i.e., not mixed with defilement), "the confusion of not comprehending" and the "undefiled confusion". He expressly mentions the failure of attention to the Truth of Suffering, etc. under the heading of the "unmixed nescience," and gives the term *cittaviparyāsa*.

[9]That is, this Sutta has for "name" the five items, feelings, ideas, volitions, sense contacts, and mental orientations. It is usual to have, as does the *Śālistambasūtra*, the four "formless" aggregates, of which "feelings" and "ideas" are the first two, followed by "motivations" and "perceptions". More rarely, as in the Dependent Origination section of Buddhaghosa's *Visuddhimagga*, "name" includes only the three middle aggregates, leaving out "perceptions". Again, the detailing of feelings as born from the six sense bases is not standard. It is usual to have three kinds, painful (*duḥkha*), pleasant (*sukha*), and neither painful nor pleasant.

[10]It is of interest that the Buddha's analysis sets forth the last two members,

it, orient your mind well, and I will explain" "Agreed!" those monks responded to the Lord. The Lord spoke as follows: "Monks, with the condition of nescience, there is motivation. With the condition of motivation, there is perception. With the condition of perception, there is name-and-form. With the condition of name-and-form, there is six sense bases. With the condition of six sense bases, there is sense contact. With the condition of sense contact, there is feeling. With the condition of feeling, there is craving. With the condition of craving, there is indulgence. With the condition of indulgence, there is gestation. With the condition of gestation, there is birth. With the condition of birth, then old age and death, grief, lamentation, suffering, dissatisfaction, perturbation, appear together. Such is the source of this entire mass of suffering.

"And what, monks, is old age and death? Whatever, of this and that sentient being, in this and that group, is aging, decrepitude, falling apart, whiteness of hair, wrinkled skin, affliction of life force, spent sense faculties, this is called old age. Whatever, of this and that sentient being, in this and that group, is falling or passing away, separation or disappearance, death which is concrete death, the appointed time, collapse of personal aggregates, laying down of corpse, severance of life faculty, this is called death. Such is this old age and this death, that is called old age and death.

"And what, monks, is birth? Whatever, of this and that sentient being, in this and that group, is birth-process, the begetting, the entrance (into life), definition and differentiation, manifestation of personality aggregates, acquisition of sense organs, this is called birth.

"And what, monks, is gestation? There are three gestations: gestation in the realm of desire, gestation in the realm of form, gestation in the formless realm. This is called gestation.

"And what, monks, is indulgence? There are four indulgences: indulgence in desires (*kāma*), indulgence in (false) views (*dṛṣṭi*), indulgence in (fruitless) rules and vows (S.

---

birth, and old age and death, by sets of terms that are near-synonyms (S. *paryāya*), and the remaining ten members by varieties (S. *prabheda*).

śīlavrata), indulgence in the self-theory (S. *ātmavāda*). This is called indulgence.

"And what, monks, is craving? There are six partite cravings: craving for forms, for sounds, for odors, for tastes, for tangibles, for mental objects (*dhamma*, S. *dharma*). This is called craving.

"And what, monks, is feeling? There are six partite feelings: feeling born from eye-contact, feeling born from ear-contact, feeling born of nose-contact, feeling born of tongue-contact, feeling born of body-contact, feeling born of mind-contact. This is called feeling.

"And what, monks, is sense contact? There are six partite sense contacts: eye-contact, ear-contact, nose-contact, tongue-contact, body-contact, mind-contact. This is called sense contact.

"And what, monks, is six sense bases? The eye-base, ear-base, nose-base, tongue-base, body-base, mind-base. This is called six sense bases.

"And what, monks, is name-and-form? Feelings (S. *vedanā*), ideas (S. *saṃjñā*), volitions (S. *cetanā*), sense contacts (S. *sparśa*), mental orientations (S. *manasikāra*)—this is called name. The four great elements and the forms derived from the four great elements—this is called form. Such is this name and this form that it is called name-and form.

"And what, monks, is perception? There are six partite perceptions: perception with eye, perception with ear, perception with nose, perception with tongue, perception with body, perception with mind. This is called perception.

"And what, monks, is motivation? There are three motivations: motivation of body, motivation of speech, motivation of mind. This is called motivation.

"And what, monks, is nescience? Whatever ignorance (S. *ajñāna*) of Suffering, ignorance of the Source of Suffering, ignorance of the Cessation of Suffering, ignorance of the Path leading to the Cessation of Suffering—this is called nescience.

"Thus, monks, with the condition of nescience, there is motivation; with the condition of motivations, there is perception;... (and so on down to)...perturbation. Such is the source of this entire mass of suffering. But with the utter dispassion and cessation of nescience, motivation ceases. With the cessation of motivation, perception ceases ... (and so on down to)...perturbation. Such is the cessation of this entire mass of suffering.

1.2 *The Second Kind of Dependent Origination*

But also, from its inception Buddhism never denied that a Tathāgata arises, or that *dharmas* arise.[11] It was claimed that anything that arises, arises dependently. Therefore, there must be a usage of Dependent Origination to cover the arising of particular beings or natures. Indeed, some Pāli specialists hold that this is what the Buddhist formula amounts to. For example, Jayatilleke asserts that the formula explains rebirth and *karma* and the arising of suffering while avoiding the extremes of *ātman*-eternalism and nihilism of Materialism.[12] Now rebirth is necessarily the rebirth of a particular being, and so this is the second kind of Dependent Origination as applied to lives of a particular being. This kind of Dependent Origination has been popularized in the West by reproductions of the "Wheel of Life" especially from its Tibetan version.

To further clarify this kind of Dependent Origination, I shall translate below from Sanskrit a passage of the *Madhyāntavibhāga* along with Vasubandhu's comment.[13] Defilement is prominently suggested by the verb *kliśyate* ("is tormented or defiled"). The gloss for "perception" (*vijñāna*) renders it "a conducting" (*nayana*), i.e., to the birthplace, and the comment brings in the "habit-energy of *karma*." This passage is therefore concerned with the past, present, and future life of some person or being:

> The world is tormented by a covering (*chādana*), a quickening (*ropaṇa*), a conducting (*nayana*), a circumscribing (*saṃparigraha*), a finishing (*pūraṇa*), a trisection (*tripariccheda*), an experience (*upabhoga*), an attraction (*karṣaṇa*), a bondage (*nibandhana*), a confrontation (*ābhimukhya*), a sorrowing (*duḥkhana*). (*Madhyāntavibhāga* I, 10)

[11]And see JIKIDO TAKASAKI, *A Study on the Ratnagotravibhāga* (Rome, 1966), p. 35, for the information that a chapter of the Mahāyāna scripture *Avataṃsaka* with title *Tathāgatotpattisaṃbhavanirdeśa* ("Dealing with the Arising of the Tathāgata") was translated into Chinese as an independent Sūtra in the 3rd century, A.D.

[12]JAYATILLEKE, *Early Buddhist Theory*, p. 450.

[13]Cf. GADJIN M. NAGAO, *Madhyāntavibhāga-bhāṣya* (Tokyo, 1964), p. 21.

(Vasubandhu's comment:) The world is tormented (or defiled), among those, by 1.a covering, i.e., by nescience's hindering of the view of how things really are. 2.a quickening, i.e., by motivation's depositing in perception (*vijñāna*) of the habit-energy (*vāsanā*) of karma. 3.a conducting, i.e., by perception's reaching of the birth-place, 4. a circumscribing, i.e., by name-and-form's embodiment (*ātmabhāva*), 5. a finishing, i.e., by six sense bases. 6. a trisection, i.e., by sense contact. 7. an experience, i.e., by feeling. 8. an attraction, i.e., by the craving for re-existence (*punarbhava*) cast by karma. 9. a bondage, i.e., by indulgences in desires, etc., that agree with the occurrence of perception. 10. a confrontation, i.e., by gestation's placing-in-front for yielding the maturation in re-existence of the *karma* previously enacted. 11-12. a sorrowing, i.e., by birth and by old age and death.

This formulation can be traced back to the *Mahā-nidāna-suttanta* of the Dīgha-Nikāya, where the Buddha asks Ānanda (Dīgha, ii, 63): "If perception would not descend into the mother's womb, would name-and-form become consolidated in the womb?" And Ānanda replied that it would not.

II. Discovery and Seeing

In short, the Buddha discovered the formula of Dependent Origination; and when he taught it, the formula became the Buddhist Dharma or Doctrine. The later disciple can repeat the process—discover the formula in the reverse order (12—1) and see the Dharma in the direct order (1—12).

II. 1. *Discovery by the Buddha*

Asaṅga alludes to this first kind of Dependent Origination in his *Paramārthagāthā* along with his own commentary. There are two parts to it: "the *dharmas* possessed of cause" are the first seven members, from "nescience" down through "feelings"—here the creatures are caught by delusion. "The *suffering* possessed of cause" is the last five members, from "craving" down through "old age and death"—here the creatures are caught by craving.[14]

According to the suggestions of the Pāli scripture and later the

[14]Cf. Alex Wayman, *Analysis of the Śrāvakabhūmi Manuscript* (Berkeley, 1961), p. 181.

Lalitavistara, when Gautama was meditating beneath the tree of enlightenment he thought: There is this old age and death and the mass of other suffering. What is its condition for arising? Indeed, it requires birth. And birth requires a gestation (or a pregnancy), and this requires an indulgence (the taking of it, grasping, and so on), and this requires a craving. Thus, Gautama, working backwards, re-discovered the finding of the Vedic seer who, searching with his intelligence (*manīṣā*) for the original principle, found "desire" (*kāma*) as the first-born and as the bond of the existent in the non-existent. Gautama stressed it somewhat differently: It is the first two Noble Truths: the Truth of Suffering, and the Truth of the Cause of Suffering. Here the cause is specified as "craving"—*tṛṣṇā* in Sanskrit, or *tanhā* in Pāli. Even so, the Vedic account is apparently continued in Buddhist dogmatics by the *karma* theory, since "craving" along with the bondage confirmed by indulgence establishes man's free will by permitting a new bondage and so a new *karma* ("gestation"), and could be said to connect the existent habit with the non-existent future.

But Gautama did not stop there. He thought: What is the condition for the arising of craving? And concluded: It is feelings. And this requires sense contact, and this requires the six sense bases, the five outer ones and the mind (*manas*) as the sixth. Searching for the condition enabling the six sense bases to arise, he concluded it was "name-and-form" (*nāma-rūpa*)—an important term of the old Indian Brāhmaṇas and Upaniṣads. As its condition he assigned "perceptions" (*vijñāna*); and for this, "motivation" (*saṃskāra*); and for this, "nescience" (*avidyā*). According to the Pāli scripture, the Third Noble Truth of Cessation is applied to nescience in order to undo the whole series that leads to the mass of suffering. It is a curious feature of Dependent Origination that while "craving" is the source or cause of suffering, once suffering has become the regular thing one can get rid of it only by the cessation of "nescience". But this accords with human experience generally: the broken leg is not healed simply by eliminating the cause of the broken leg. Asaṅga's statement helps with this group because he refers to these seven members as "the *dharmas* possessed of cause." This ties in these members with the Buddhist Abhidharma theory of "all *dharmas*" as included in the five personal aggregates (*skandha*) (="name-and-form"), twelve sense bases (="six sense bases" multiplied for personal and objective bases), and eighteen realms (*dhātu*) (= "contact," the six objects, the six sense organs, and the six perceptions based thereon).[15] Since the *dharmas* are included by members Nos. 4—6, it follows that members Nos. 1—3 are the "cause" of the *dharmas*. Member No. 7, "feelings," also a *dharma* as a personal aggregate, is left over to culminate the deterministic series, or the old bondage.

The following tabulation of the discovery order includes the subdivisions according to Asaṅga's school:

Members	
12. old age and death 11. birth	Suffering
10. gestation 9. indulgence 8. craving	Cause of Suffering
7. feelings 6. sense contact 5. six sense bases 4. name-and-form	Dharmas
3. perception 2. motivations 1. nescience	Cause of Dharmas

Naturally, the Buddhist works do not refer to the pre-Buddhist religion (the Veda and ancillary works); hence they are sketchy and probably incomplete as regards the "discovery" of the series. In a partial unravelling of this discovery, I have already observed that the first four members, starting with "nescience," curiously match the cosmic development of the *Bṛhadāraṇyaka-Upaniṣad*.[16]

II.2. *Seeing by the Disciple*

Since to see Dependent Origination in this sense of "seeing" is tantamount to seeing Dharma, the later writers could fill in. This expansion was conservative at the *sūtra* level, as evidenced in the

[15]Cf. NĀRADA, *A Manual of Abhidhamma* (Kandy, 1968), pp. 348-350, for the comprisal of "all" (*sabba*) in the personal aggregates, the sense bases, and the elements, with the usual translations followed by modern translators from Pāli. Of course, the "all" is the abbreviation for "all *dhamma*" in Sanskrit *sarvadharmāḥ*.

[16]ALEX WAYMAN, "The Intermediate-State Dispute in Buddhism", *Buddhist Studies in Honour of I.B. Horner* eds. L. Cousins *et al.* (Dordrecht, 1974), p. 230. This essay is included in this volume.

several *pratītyasamutpāda*-type scriptures available in Sanskrit.[17] Nāgārjuna's works on the subject are just as brief.[18] The Abhidharma schools of course dilated the members. Vasubandhu, whose early years were devoted to the Abhidharma, has a rather large commentary on *pratītyasamutpāda*, and in the Tibetan Tanjur this is followed by Guṇamati's still larger commentary.[19] These Abhidharma works inevitably introduce differentiated doctrines of Buddhism beyond the primitive Dharma alluded to in the phrase "Whoever sees Dependent Origination, sees the Dharma."

However, the foregoing leaves open the question of whether the "seeing" of *dharma* or *dharmas*, when one "sees" Dependent Origination, is the concrete "seeing" as done with eyesight, or is a way of speaking tantamount to "understanding" or is something else again. The teacher Asaṅga has a section about this in his encyclopedic work *Yogācārabhūmi*, in the portion called *Vastu-saṃgrahaṇī*, second division devoted to analysis of sense bases (*āyatana*). After detailing various superlative benefits, such as calming the mind, to be gained by seeing *dharmas*, Asaṅga explains what is entailed by "seeing" a *dharma*:[20]

> There are two kinds of seeing *dharmas*: seeing constructed natures (*saṃskṛta-dharma*) and seeing unconstructed natures

[17]These are now conveniently collected in P.L. Vaidya, *Mahāyāna-Sūtra-saṁgraha*, Part I (Darbhanga, 1961), namely, two versions of the *Śālistambasūtra* and two versions of the *Pratītyasamutpāda sūtras*.

[18]La Vallée Poussin presents the Tibetan version with a French translation of Nāgārjuna's *Pratītyasamutpādahṛdayakārikā* in *Théorie des douze causes*, pp. 122-14. Nāgārjuna briefly expands upon those seven verses in his *Pratītyasamutpādahṛdayavyākhyāna*, preserved in the Tibetan Tanjur. And just preceding those two works in the Tanjur is his *Ārya-śālistambaka-kārikā*. Besides, he devotes twelve verses to the topic as Chap. XXVI of his *Madhyamaka-kārikā*.

[19]Giuseppe Tucci, 'A Fragment from the Pratitya-samutpada-vyakhya of Vasubandhu', *Journal of the Royal Asiatic Society* July, 1930, pp. 611-623, presents some Sanskrit fragments of Vasubandhu's comments on members 1. nescience, 7. feelings, 8. craving, 9. indulgence, and 10. gestation.

[20]Photo edition of Tibetan Tanjur, Vol. III, p. 175-3-8, ff. The equivalent Chinese is in Taishō Vol. 30, p. 824-C-2, ff. Tibetan and Chinese agree on the term "name-and-form" (*nāma-rūpa*); but where Tibetan continues "called the 'own-nature of a man' " prior to the question "What is truth" the Chinese text has a series of several words beginning with "man".

(*asaṃskṛta-dharma*). Among them, seeing constructed natures (is as follows:) Just as there is here some place of truth, he rightly knows it as it is, and rightly knows as it is the truth (thereof). What is a place of truth? name-and-form, called the "own-nature of a man" (**manuṣya-svarūpa*). What is truth? Conventional truth (*saṃvṛti-satya*) and supreme truth (*paramārtha-satya*). What is conventional truth? Any idea (*saṃjñā*) regarding that place of truth that it is a self, a sentient being, a living being, or a person. Also, the thesis "I see forms with the eye," ... (and so on, down to) ... "I perceive *dharmas* with the mind". Also, the attribution, "Accordingly, his name is called this," ... (and so on, down to, as previously) "His measure of life amounts to this." Anything involving the idea of it, the thesis, the attribution, is conventional truth. What is supreme truth? Attaching to that place of truth that it is impermanent,... (and so on, down to, as previously) it arises in dependence. And thinking that according as there is impermanence, so there is suffering. Any monk who, in regard to a place of conventional or absolute truth, rightly knows the conventional truth as conventional truth and the absolute truth as absolute truth, he is worthy of being called one who sees constructed natures. What is seeing unconstructed natures? Any monk who attaches to a place of truth with skill in the two kinds of truth; and taking recourse to that skill, engages his mind with the view that all the personal aggregates (*skandha*) are exhausted, Nirvāṇa is calm ... (and so on, down to, as previously) there is liberation; and has the thought, "I see unconstructed natures," he is worthy of being called one who sees unconstructed natures. Besides, one should know that there are three kinds of persons who see *dharmas*: (1) the one who engages *dharmas* consistent with *dharmas* of the ordinary person. (2) the one who is skilled in and heedful to equipoise his mind, and methodically courses in *dharma*(*s*), and accordingly sees the points of instruction. (3) the one beyond training whose fluxes are exhausted.

Nāgārjuna's equivalent statement for seeing "unconstructed natures" is in his *Yuktiṣaṣṭikā* (k. 10-11AB):[21] "Having seen

[21]The 1-1/2 verses are translated from the Tibetan version in the Darjeeling publication, *Four Minor Madhyamaka Texts in Tibetan Translation*. Also

with right knowledge (=clear vision) what has arisen with the condition of 'nescience' [i.e. 'motivation'], there is no apprehension at all of either arising or passing away. That very thing is Nirvāṇa as this life (=the *dharma* seen),[22] and the requirement is done (*kṛta-kṛtya*)." Here is a version from the *Bodhisattvapiṭaka-sūtra*, a Mahāyāna scripture.[23]

> Whatever is the meaning of Dependent Origination, is the meaning of Dharma; whatever is the meaning of Dharma, is the meaning of Tathāgata. Therefore, whoever sees Dependent Origination, sees Dharma; whoever sees Dharma, sees the Tathāgata. Also, seeing that way, and accordingly fully understanding in the sense of Thusness, still one sees scarcely anything. What is that "scarcely anything"? It is the Signless and the Non-Apprehension; the one who sees in the manner of the Signless and the Non-Apprehension sees rightly.

Those passages by Asaṅga, Nāgārjuna, and in the *Bodhisattva-piṭaka*, agree that the "seeing" is not the ordinary concrete "seeing." But also, these works persist in using a word meaning "seeing." Sthiramati would explain: because it is without discursive thought (*nirvikalpa*).[24] In the terminology of "eyes" it is ex-

---

I have taken into account the context in which this is cited in Abhyākaragupta's *Munimatālaṃkāra*, *op. cit.*, p. 220-2-2.

[22]Nāgārjuna apparently used in the original Sanskrit the term *dṛṣṭadharma*, which is well known to signify in Buddhist texts "this life". However, since he associated it with the preceding verse which employs the verbal form "having seen," it may be concluded that he intended a double meaning for the term, so *dṛṣṭadharma* also means "the *dharma* that is seen," or "the visible *dharma*." Thus, Nāgārjuna implies the seeing (which amounts to not seeing of the unconstructed *dharma* Nirvāṇa. But since this is the Nirvāṇa of this very life, this *Yuktiṣaṣṭikā* passage helps explain Nāgārjuna's famous verse in the Nirvāṇa chapter of the *Madhyamaka-kārikā* (XXV, 19): "There is no difference between Nirvāṇa and Saṃsāra; there is no difference between Saṃsāra and Nirvāṇa."

[23]Photo edition of Tibetan Tanjur, Vol. 23, chapter on "Inconceivability of the Tathāgata," p. 19-5-2, ff.

[24]Sthiramati's *Abhidharmakośabhāṣyaṭīkā-tatvārtha-nāma*, Photo edition of Tibetan Tanjur, Vol. 147, commentary on Samāpatti chapter of the *Abhidharmakośa*, p. 274-2-1, in the course of explaining the *jñāna-darśana*, comments on the word *darśana* ("vision"): "Vision bears comparison with eye-perception (*cakṣur-vijñāna*), because it is without discursive thought" (mthoṅ ba ni mig gi rnam par śes pa daṅ mtshuṅs par ldan pa ste/ rnam par mi rtog pa phyir ro).

pressly stated to be the "eye of insight" in the *Śālistambasūtra.*[25] In agreement, Buddhaghosa's *Visuddhimagga* places the consideration of Dependent Origination in the Instruction of Insight (*paññā*); and the *bhūmi* theory of Mahāyāna Buddhism includes that consideration in the Perfection of Insight (*prajñāpāramitā*) held to predominate in the Sixth Stage (*bhūmi*). Furthermore, Asaṅga points out that the "seeing" differs according to the person who "sees."

The manner in which a person may "see" Dependent Origination is set forth in the Sixth Stage of the *Daśabhūmika-sūtra.* The presentation here is based on Tsoṅ-kha-pa's citation and discussion of the passage in his Tibetan commentary on Candrakīrti's *Madhyamakāvatāra:*[26]

> (The Bodhisattva on the Sixth Stage) reflects on Dependent Origination (*pratītyasamutpāda*) in the forward direction ... (and so on down to:) Thus he thinks. Only this heap of suffering, this tree of suffering develops, devoid of a creator, a feeler (*kāraka-vedaka*). This occurs to him: Because of the clinging to a creator, activities are known; wherever there is no creator, there also activities are not perceptively reached in the absolute sense. This occurs to him: These three realms are this mind-only; whatever those twelve members of generation, all those, while explained by the Tathāgata in multiple aspect (*prabheda-śas*), in fact depend on a single *citta* (*ekacitta*).

In the Sūtra itself this passage is embedded in a long exposition of Dependent Origination. The Sūtra states that the tree develops devoid of a creator; so Tsoṅ-kha-pa says, "Having denied an eternal self as the creator, (the Bodhisattva) understands that the creator is just the conventional (*saṃvṛti*) mind-only." Or, as Asaṅga mentioned in the previous citation, the conventional mind has the idea of it, the thesis, the attribution. The Bodhisattva

[25]La Vallée Poussin, *Théorie des douze causes*, p. 72. However here it is the Buddha using the *prajñā*-eye that is mentioned.

[26]The passage cited is in Sanskrit original in J. Rahder, ed., *Daśabhūmika-sūtra et Bodhisattvabhūmi*, p. 48 and p. 49; Ryūkō Kondō, ed., *Daśabhūmīśvaro nāma Mahāyānasūtraṃ*, p. 97.13 and p. 98.6—10: (evaṃ hi bodhisattvo) 'nulomākāraṃ pratītyasamutpādaṃ pratyavekṣate /.../ evam ayaṃ kevalo (and so on, down to) sarvāṇy ekacittasamāśritāni/. Tsoṅ-kha-pa's discussion is in Photo edition of Tibetan canons, extra volumes, Vol. 154, p. 71-4 to 72.1.

is said to reflect: "because of the clinging to a creator" which is done by "nescience", "activities" (="motivations") "are known," to wit, by "perceptions," the third member—thus inaugurating the Dependent Origination in the forward direction. Then, to show how the series is eliminated, so that finally, in the absence of "nescience", "perception" does not arise, the Sūtra says: "Wherever there is no creator (i.e., as delusively held by the conventional mind), "there also activities"(=those "motivations") "are not perceptively reached in the absolute sense" (i.e., "perception" does not perceive them). Nāgārjuna's way of stating the same point in that *Yuktiṣaṣṭikā* verse is to deny any apprehension of the arising or passing away of that "motivation," whereupon the Dharma seen is Nirvāṇa.

Besides, Nāgārjuna's *Śūnyatāsaptati* (k. 9-10) states:[27] "When there is neither permanence nor impermanence, neither self nor non-self, neither purity nor impurity, neither pleasure nor pain, then there are not the waywardnesses. In their absence, there is no possibility of the nescience born from the four waywardnesses (*viparyāsa*). In its absence, motivations do not occur, and likewise the remaining members." This agrees with Asaṅga's distinction of "nescience" as defiled (through waywardness) and undefiled. There is the striking conclusion that when the Bodhisattva meditates in the manner prescribed by the *Daśabhūmika-sūtra* he eliminates the defiled nescience that heads the second kind of Dependent Origination, but still has not eliminated the undefiled nescience, wherefor he is still a Bodhisattva[28] and not a Buddha.

[27]The two verses are translated from the Tibetan version in *Four Minor Madhyamaka Texts in Tibetan Translation* (*op cit*.).

[28]La Vallée Poussin, *Théorie des douze causes*, p. v, note, mentions that according to certain sources, which he does not name, the meditation on the twelve causes is reserved to Pratyekabuddhas. Indeed, the attribution of a Bodhisattva meditation in the *Daśabhūmikasūtra* seems to be simply due to this text being a Mahāyāna scripture that expounds the stages of the Bodhisattva. But as far as the exposition of Dependent Origination is concerned, the meditation on it does not seem to require a Bodhisattva. Tsoṅ-kha-pa places his Dependent Origination section in the portion of his *Lam rim chen mo* devoted to the training of the middling person, according to the description in Atīśa *Bodhipatha-pradipa:* "Whoever, turning his back on the pleasures of phenomenal existence, and averting himself from sinful actions, pursues only his own quiescence, he is known as the middling person." This is the second kind of person, and the Bodhisattva is the third kind and called the superior person.

According to Tsoṅ-kha-pa's indications, the Bodhisattva on the Sixth Stage when reviewing the twelve members seriatum emphasizes the subject mind to the neglect of the objective form; thus he is awakening from the dream of defiled nescience. In lotus symbolism this is the budding of the lotus. The Tathāgata, when grasping the whole series with a single thought (*citta*), emphasizes the objective form to the neglect of the subject mind. This is the full-blown state of the lotus. This lotus symbolism is applied to *karma:* and we must observe that in the *Daśabhūmika-sūtra* as in Nāgārjuna's Dependent Origination commentary, the two *karmas* are members No. 2 "motivations" (*saṃskāra*) and No. 10 "gestation" (*bhava*). Tsoṅ-kha-pa maintains in the same place that all the diverse realms (the *bhājana-loka*) of the sentient beings are formed by the shared (*sādhāraṇa*) *karma* accumulated by the mind itself, which must refer to a group *karma*. The sentient beings also have unshared (*asādhāraṇa*) or individual mental *karma*. Tsoṅ-kha-pa employs the metaphor of the "variegated eye of a peacock's tail" (*mecaka* in Sanskrit) for the unshared *karma*, and the metaphor of "variegated petals and colors of lotuses" for the shared *karma* of sentient beings, which generates the variegated receptacle realms. The metaphoric language agrees with the distinction of two kinds of Dependent Origination, because the lotus symbolism, applying as it does to shared *karma* and to the process of enlightenment, must be associated with the first kind of Dependent Origination that is not concerned with particular beings and specialized *karma*. It is the second kind of Dependent Origination whose *karma* would have the metaphor of the "variegated eye of a peacock's tail."

There remains to be explained the Sūtra reference to the development as the "tree of suffering". According to the *Arthaviniścayaṭīkā*[29] the first seven members of Dependent Origination show the development of the tree: 1. "nescience" is the manure covering, 2. "motivations" is the field, 3. fluxional "perceptions", the seed; 4. "name-and-form," the sprout; 5. "six sense bases," the leaves and twigs; 6. "contact," characteristic flowers blooming; 7. "feelings," characteristic fruit matured. In agreement with Asaṅga's attribution to the last five members of the role, "suffer-

[29]The passage is taken from the *Arthaviniścayaṭīkā* (author unknown) in Derge Tanjur, Sna-tshogs, Vol. No. f. 27b-4, f.

ing possessed of cause," the *Arthaviniścayaṭīkā* account continues; Someone craves that fruit ("craving"), takes it (("indulgence"), moistens it with water and eats it ("gestation"), whereupon sharp pains arise ("birth"), he shrivels up and dies ("old age and death").[30] The "tree" thus exhibits the two *karma* members as the "field " into which the seed is cast, and as the "eating" or digestion process.

III. Lives of a Person

This section is much indebted to Tsoṅ-kha-pa's Dependent Origination section in his *Lam rim chen mo*,[31] where he describes the formula as applying to one life, two lives, and three lives of a person. This treatment undoubtedly draws much from Asaṅga's encyclopedic work, the *Yogācārabhūmi* and its summation in Asaṅga's *Abhidharmasamuccaya*. In particular, there is Asaṅga's grouping of the twelve members as available in Sanskrit from the latter work: "The downcasting members are nescience, motivations, and perceptions. The members cast down are name-and-form, six sense bases, contact, and feelings. The producing members are craving, indulgence, and gestation. The members produced are birth, and old age and death."[32] The expression "downcasting" means casting down into the cyclical flow (*saṃsāra*). Besides, the Tibetan treatment accepts Nāgārjuna's brief exposi-

[30]In that Dependent Origination section already mentioned, Tsoṅ-kha-pa refers to the *Śālistambasūtra* as "explaining that the seed of 'perception' (*vijñāna*) is planted in the field of *karma* which has the manure of 'nescience' (*avidyā*); and that is moistened with the water of craving, and then the shoot of 'name-and-form ' in the womb proceeds to completion." The Sanskrit passage is in *Théorie des douze causes*, p. 84 3rd paragraph. Anyway, this associates the metaphorical water with "craving", and this may have also been the intention of the *Arthaviniścayaṭīkā's* account of the 10th member "gestation," to wit, that the fruit's moistening suggests the water of "craving".

[31]The *Lam rim chen mo* is Tsoṅ-kha-pa's encyclopedic exposition of the path to enlightenment for the three orders of persons (cf. n. 28, above). The many quotations in the part containing the Dependent Origination material has numerous quotations from such works as the *Lalitavistara* emphasizing the sufferings and ills of the world, representing it as a kind of prison. One should understand how all this mass of suffering came about, and how to escape. Accordingly, such teachings as that of Dependent Origination are expounded.

[32]Pralhad Pradhan, ed., *Abhidharma-samuccaya*, text, p. 26, lines 20 ff.

tion in his *Pratītyasamutpāda-hṛdaya-kārikā*, in part that three defilements—nescience, craving, and indulgence—give rise to two *karmas*—motivations and gestation—which in turn give rise to the seven sufferings, namely, the remaining members, and that "thus the wheel of becoming (*bhavacakra*) itself revolves again and again." Tsoṅ-kha-pa's treatment introduces the terminology of 2-1/2 and 4-1/2. By 2-1/2 is meant the members "nescience," "motivation," and then the visionary half of "perception" which is called the "causal *vijñāna*". By 4-1/2 is meant the members beginning with the fallen half of "perceptions" which is called the "fruitional *vijñāna*". One should note about all the above terminology that it agrees with the second kind of Dependent Origination, involving *karma* and rebirth of the person.

Besides, it is necessary to clarify the member No. 10 "gestation" (*bhava*) as a *karma*. The ancient explanation by varieties of three worlds (desire, form, and formless) immediately associates the member with the Buddhist theory of food; and it will be recalled that in the detailing of the "tree of suffering" the eating of the fruit was credited to this *karma* member. The Saṃyutta Nikāya, ii, 98, sets forth four kinds of food "for maintaining the sentient beings who have been born or for aiding those who wish to come forth." The standard order of the four is morsel food, coarse or subtle; sense contact (*sparśa*); volition (*manaḥsaṃcetanā*); and perception (*vijñāna*). The *Abhidharmakośa* (Chap. III) explains that the first two foods nourish the being already born—extend its life—and that the last two foods enable the being not yet born to come into existence. The kinds of food that are necessary differ according to which one of the three realms the sentient being aspires to or lives in.[33] Hence, the role of this member as the new *karma* by the act of eating. While I employ the rendition "gestation," the words "digestion" and "brewing" probably also apply. My "gestation" for *bhava* agrees with its representation as a pregnant woman in the Tibetan Wheel of Life. There is partial confirmation from a definition in the *Śālistambasūtra* suggesting that this *bhava* is a self-perpetuating entity. According to the Pāli Abhidharma it both looks behind (Epimethean) and looks ahead

[33]The above discussion of the four foods is based on my treatment in *Analysis of the Śrāvakabhūmi Manuscript*, Chapter V, "Asaṅga's Views on Food," pp. 135 ff.

(Promethean). Perhaps this member gives the mane *bhava-cakra* (Wheel of Becoming) to the whole series of twelve members.[34]

The following, based on Tsoṅ-kha-pa's Dependent Origination section, probably cannot be worked out in the commentarial tradition consistent with the Theravāda. Of course, all these Buddhist schools believed in rebirth.

III. 1. *One Life of a Single Person*

1. Nescience, and 2. motivation, constitute an Intermediate State that forecasts the destiny. Nescience forecasts either a good or bad destiny, to wit, confusion (*sammoha*) about *karma* and its fruit forecasting an evil destiny, confusion about the meaning of reality (*tattva*) forecasting a good destiny. Motivations are virtuous, non-virtuous, and indeterminate.

3. Perceptions, 4. name-and-form, 5. six sense bases, 6. sense contact, and 7. feelings, are a set going with the destiny. Perception (*vijñāna*) is imbued by motivation (*saṃskāra*) with habit-energy (*vāsanā*) either for good or bad destiny. Good destiny is said to be gods and men; bad destiny, animals, hungry ghosts (*preta*), and hell beings.

8. Craving, and 9. indulgence, again and again foster the habit-energy of the destiny. 10. gestation—no information, but presumably it would be a repetition of the realm, whether desire, form, or formless, with the same 'food' being eaten over and over.

11. Birth, i.e. rebirth, means that again and again one repeats in this one life the same destiny.

12. Old age and death; finally one sees the trouble or disadvantage (*ādīnava*) of the destiny.

This explanation of Dependent Origination seems to go with the "tree of suffering" previously mentioned to agree with the phases of seven and five members. The first seven are the growth of the tree. The last five reinforce the habit-energy of the destiny and reap the consequence. Finally, "old age and death" furnishes the realization that the destiny is deplorable, and the being determines to leave it.

III.2. *Two Lives of a Single Person*

(1) The past life = life no. 1.

1. nescience (as defilement)

[34]Of course, "existence" and "becoming" are established meanings of the

2. motivation (as *karma*)
3A. casual *vijñāna* (as suffering = last perception)
8. craving } (defilement, with object not defined) } (death and intermediate state)
9. indulgence }
10. gestation (as *Karma*) = "*karma*-mirror"[35]

(2) The present life = life no. 2, as effect.

3B. resultant *vijñāna*
4. name-and-form
5. six sense bases } (the seed of later suffering)
6. sense contact
7. feelings
11. birth
12. old age and death } (the present suffering)

There are various cases in Buddhist theory to which this for-

---

term *bhava*. Still, where Buddhist tradition calls this *bhava* a *karma* member of Dependent Origination, one wonders how such renderings as "existence" convey the connotation of the warned-of hells and glorified-of heavens for good and bad acts (the *karma*, of course) of laity and monks ! A Tibetan work included in the canon, probably of the early ninth century, with reconstructed title *Pratītyasamutpāda-gaṇanānusāreṇa citta sthāpanopāya*, Japanese photo edition of the Tibetan Kanjur-Tanjur, Vol. 145, p. 278-2-2, mentions that there are four ways to summarize the series, to wit, by count, nature, denotation, and grouping. Under the category of denotation (S. *Nirukti*, Tib. *ṅes pa'i tshig*) the unknown author presents the list that happens to be in the *Śālistambasūtra, Théorie des douze causes*, p. 81; N. Aiyaswami Sastri, ed., *Ārya Śālistamba Sūtra* (Adyar Library, 1950), p. 11; P.L. Vaidya, *Mahāyāna-Sūtra-Saṁgraha*, part I, p. 103-30 to p. 104.2. When the list comes to *bhava*, it has *punarbhavajananārthena bhavaḥ*. "It is *bhava* because it engenders *bhava* again." While the term *punarbhava* is usually rendered "rebirth", such a rendering in the present case would imply that the definition refers to the following member 11. "birth" (*jāti*), for which the definition should have had instead *punarjanma*. However, none of the other "denotation" is in terms of the immediately following member, but is stated in terms of the member itself. Accordingly, this definition of *bhava* is simply a recognition that the word means "existence" but that we should regard it here as signifying the promotion of re-existence (hence my translation of the term in Vasubandhu's comment on the *Madhyānta-vibhāga* verse, *supra*). In short, that *bhava* is a self-perpetuating entity. It both looks to the past and looks to the future according to C.A.F. Rhys Davids in her Hastings' ERE article, Vol. 9, p. 67, giving the Pāli scholastic tradition of two kinds, *kamma-bhava* "fruition of past actions" and *upapatti-bhava* "result in future life".

[35]For the "*karma*-mirror", cf. ALEX WAYMAN, "The Mirror as a Pan-Buddhist Metaphor-Simile", *History of Religions* XIII: 4, May 1974, pp. 264-265. This essay is published elsewhere in this volume.

mulation of the members may apply. For example, there are many popular stories of *karma* where something happening to a person is explained as due to his previous life.[36] There is also the case of the Arhat, who is in his last life, for which reason his preceding life is called "having one more life." Then there is the theory, so much identified with Tibetan Buddhism, of the incarnate Lamas. It was held that certain high Lamas could be immediately reborn, e.g., the Dalai Lama series; and so it would be pertinent to refer to the last life and the present life. The *Śrīmālā-sūtra* has a remarkable specialization of the theory called the "inconceivable transference" of Arhats, Pratyakabuddhas, and Bodhisattvas who have attained power. These beings are held to have a special kind of nescience, presumably undefiled, called the nescience entrenchment (*avidyāvāsabhūmi*); and a special kind of motivation described as non-fluxional *karma* (*anāsrava-karma*). With those two members as conditions, they have a special kind of causal-*vijñāna* referred to as "bodies made of mind," with which they have the "inconceivable transference" to another life.[37] The formulation of members also seems to accord with a tantric description in which the three members 8, 9, and 10, are called "rebirth consciousness" in the sequence, "Gandharva consciousness," "Indulgence-in-desire consciousness", and "Seizing-of-birth consciousness".[38]

III.3. *Three Lives of a Single Person:*

Here there are two solutions.

A. Solution in Tsoṅ-kha-pa's section, with no Intermediate State explicit.

[36]There is an enormous Buddhist literature of the *karma* stories. Besides, the numerous Jātaka tales, there is the *Karma-śataka* (extant in Tibetan). One may signal also the huge *Ārya-Saddharmasmṛtyupasthāna-sūtra* for popular accounts of getting into the heavens and hells. The extensive verse section of this scripture, with numerous *karma* verses, has been edited in Sanskrit, Chinese, and Tibetan versions, and translated into French with title *Dharma-samuccaya* by Lin Li-kouang, 1st part (Paris, 1946); 2nd and 3rd parts posthumously with revisions by A. Bareau, J. W. de Jong and P. Demiéville (Paris, 1969 and 1973).

[37]Cf. Alex Wayman and Hideko Wayman, *The Lion's Roar of Queen Śrīmālā; a Buddhist Scripture on the Tathāgatagarbha Theory* (New York, 1974), pp. 29-31.

[38]Alex Wayman, "Buddhist Dependent Origination", *History of Religions*, 10:3, Feb., 1971, p. 195, in the Table "An 'Eastern' Tradition".

Life No. 1 = the producing life, the previous life. This consists of 8. craving, 9. indulgence, and 10. gestation.[39]

Life No. 2 = the life produced, the present life. It is possible to have a series of these. Each such life consists of 3B. resultant *vijñāna*, 4. name-and-form, through 7. feelings; and these constitute a set included within 11. birth, and 12. old age and death.

Life No. 3 = the forecast life, the future life. This consists of 1. nescience, 2. motivation, 3A. causal *-vijñāna.*

This formulation also can be interpreted to go with a number of Buddhist situations. This essay has previously indicated that 8. craving, which is usually of sullied character and conceivably so in the present formulation, has the decisive role of altering destiny because it leads to a new bondage. But also it might be a virtuous craving for the religious life. For example, in the Indian Buddhist tradition there was a disciple phase called "entering the stream," which would be Life No. 1, when a set number of lives, say seven, could be predicted for progress up to the Arhat-fruit, each of which lives could be counted as Life No. 2, with the Arhat-fruit itself counted as Life No. 3, with the "causal-*vijñāna*" as the "body-made-of-mind" already mentioned. Then, Mahāyāna Buddhism sets forth its hero called the Bodhisattva, whose vow and action in faith would be his Life No. 1; the lives necessary for the first seven Bodhisattva Stages could be counted as Life No. 2; and when he attains the status of a Bodhisattva of the Eighth Stage, this could be his Life No. 3, with the "inconceivable transference" mentioned in the *Śrīmālā-sūtra.* This agrees with the tantric maxim, "By passion the world arises; forecast by passion it goes to its end. By knowledge of the diamond passion, the

[39]Vasubandhu, in Tucci, "A Fragment," *op. cit.*, p. 621, states that in other sūtras the Lord said that *bhava* ('gestation') is the five "grasping aggregates" "(*pañcopadāna-skandha*). Nāgārjuna accepts this explanation in his *Madhyamaka-kārikā* XXVI, 8. This interpretation seems to accord rather well with the present solution of Dependent Origination. And it agrees with the "Promethean" definition of *bhava*, implying "new *karma*". In contrast, the *bhava* in the previous solution "Two Lives of a Single Person" should be understood as the "Epimethean" kind, and agrees with the 'Intermediate-State' (*antarā-bhava*), a variety of *bhava* which Vasubandhu accepts in Tucci, "A Fragment," p. 621, line 6. As the Theravāda denies an Intermediate State, it uses the terminology *kamma-bhava* rather than *antarā-bhava*.

mind becomes the Diamond Being."[40] Besides, Nāgārjuna concludes his *Vigrahavyāvartinī* by bowing to the Buddha "who explained Voidness (*śūnyatā*), Dependent Origination, and the Middle Path (*madhyama-pratipad*) in the same sense." And according to the *Śālistamba-sūtra*, when it was said, "Whoever sees Dependent Origination, he sees the Dharma," the Dharma which he sees is the Eightfold Noble Path.[41] And this is the Path proclaimed in the Buddha's First Sermon as avoiding the extremes of sense indulgence and flesh mortification. Now, in order to treat Dependent Origination as the Middle Path, it appears that this formulation in three lives of one person works out the best for the reasons given above.

B. Solution of the Theravāda, which denies an Intermediate State.[42]

Past Life:
 1. nescience, 2. motivation.
Present Life:
 3. perception, down to 7. feeling. This is rebirth process.
 8. craving, 9. indulgence, 10. gestation. This is *karma* process.
Future Life:
 11. rebirth, 12. old age and death.

The remarkable difference between this solution and the preceding Tibetan solutions, by suggestion of Asaṅga's works, is that while the Theravāda Abhidharma tradition assigns the last two members—birth, and old age and death—to the future life, the Tibetan solutions all place these two members in the category of suffering of the present life.

What they all, including the Theravāda, agree upon is that the sequence of twelve conditions does not by virtue of that order constitute a temporal sequence. There is a time factor, and it is stated in terms of "past life," "present life," and "future life." In Asaṅga's school, as the Dependent Origination section of the *Lam rim chen mo* puts it, there are "two cycles of cause and fruit."

[40]The *Ḍākinī-vajrapañjra*, as cited in the *Subhāṣita-saṃgraha* (Bendall edition).

[41]*Théorie des douze causes*, pp. 71-72.

[42]Cf. Nyanatiloka, *Buddhist Dictionary* (Colombo, 1950), p. 114; and, with more complications, Nārada, *A Manual of Abhidhamma*, Diagrams XVI and XVII.

This means that the chief temporal factor of the series is the alternation of cause (*hetu*) and fruit (*phala*) in terms of lives, while the sequence of conditions (*pratyaya*) is the sufficiency causes for the members to arise. The two cycles are Asaṅga's groupings of the members into "downcasting" (Nos. 1-3A) and "producing" (Nos. 8-10) as against the members "cast down" (Nos. 3B-7) and "produced" (Nos. 11—12).[43] Asaṅga's structuring permits the solutions in the Tibetan tradition to shift blocks of members, differing in this matter from the Theravāda which sticks to the usual order of the twelve terms.

Another difference is that the Theravāda, by not accepting an Intermediate State, was obliged to place nescience and motivation in the past life. A more subtle difference is that the Theravāda had only one solution in comparison with the three from the Tibetan tradition's working over of Asaṅga's teachings. This indicates that the Theravāda insists on a single interpretation of the series, and so followers of that tradition would likely not accept my organization of materials into "two kinds" of Dependent Origination—and in terms of "original Buddhism" they might be right.

IV. THE BUDDHIST FORMULA AND THE SĀṂKHYA

The Buddhist doctrine of Dependent Origination can be further clarified by comparison with a non-Buddhist system, the Sāṃkhya. My foregoing materials have presented two kinds of Dependent Origination; and it turns out that the classical Sāṃkhya and even the kind of Sāṃkhya attributed to the teacher Arāḍa, the older contemporary of the Buddha, are to be discussed along with the second kind of Dependent Origination, as follows.

[43]Thus, TSON-KHA-PA, in the Dependent Origination Section, mentions from Asaṅga's *Bhūmivastu* (the first part of the *Yogācārabhūmi*): "The members reaching from *vijñāna* down to *vedanā* have the characteristic of being mixed with the members birth, old age and death; that being so, why does one teach two kinds? For the purpose of teaching the difference of characteristic as the basis of suffering, and for the purpose of teaching the difference between the downcasting members and the producing members." By further citations of Asaṅga, Tsoṅ-kha-pa shows that the members *vijñāna* (No. 3B) down to *vedanā* (No. 7) are the "seed" of suffering, while *jāti* (No. 11) and *jarā-maraṇa* (No. 12) are the manifest suffering.

The initial comparison is with the third member, "perception" (*vijñāna*). Previously, it was shown that "perception" is referred to metaphorically as the "seed" (*bīja*). So also Āryadeva in his *Catuḥśataka* (XIV, 25): "*Vijñāna* is the seed of phenomenal life; the (inner and outer) objects are its field (of apperception). When it sees the object as selfless, the seed of phenomenal life ceases."[44] That this *vijñāna* is the Buddhist equivalent to the *ātman* or "field-knower" of the pre-Buddhist literature is supported by Aśvaghoṣa's portrayal of the future Buddha's visit to Arāḍa (*Buddhacarita*, Canto XII, 70—73):[45]

> For I deem the field-knower even though liberated from primary matter (*prakṛti*) and secondary characters has the attribute of giving birth and the attribute of being a seed.
> For even if the purified soul (*ātman*) be deemed to be liberated, again it will be bound by reason of the real presence of the conditions.
> It is my belief that just as a seed does not spring up through lack of the season, earth, and water; and springs up by reason of these and those conditions, so also does it (the soul).
> And what is imagined to be liberation through abandonment of (the three things) act, ignorance, and craving (=Buddhist Dependent Origination Nos. 2, 1 , and 8) is ultimately not a complete abandonment of them as long as there is a soul.

Along the lines of the previous finding of this paper, one may infer that when the Buddha denies a true liberation of the purified self it is because the purification is from defilement (*kleśa*), so from defiled nescience and from craving as well as from concordant acts; while there is still no liberation from undefiled nescience which, serving as the condition for an appropriate motivation, provides a condition for the seed—no matter which seed—to again spring up.

Now, I have elsewhere discussed the terminology of 2-1/2 and 4-1/2 members and concluded that the first 1/2 of "perception" is the equivalent to the Sāṃkhya *buddhi* and that the second 1/2 of "perception" is the equivalent to the Sāṃkhya *ahaṃkāra*. They

44Translated in the context of its citation in Tsoṅ-kha-pa's *Lam rim chen mo*, *Lhag mthoṅ* (*vipaśyanā*) section. Cf. V. Bhattacharya, *The Catuḥśataka of Āryadeva*, p. 230.

45E. H. Johnston (ed.), *The Buddhacarita*, Part I (Calcutta, 1935), p. 137.

roughly correspond to the two selves, supreme and individual, of the early Upaniṣads, which stem from the *Ṛg-veda;* although Buddhism does not call those halves of "perception" "selves" or a higher and a lower self, and in fact only counts "perception" (*vijñāna*) once to be the third member of Dependent Origination.[46]

To carry the comparison further, just as "perception" in Buddhism was shown above to be the seed of phenomenal life, in the Sāṃkhya system it is *buddhi* or Mahat that is the initial evolute, inaugurating the phenomenal series. In Buddhism, the "reconnecting perception" (*pratisaṃdhi-vijñāna* of the Abhidharma tradition) first arises as the "appropriating consciousness" (*ādāna-vijñāna* of the *ālayavijñāna* tradition), i.e., the vision of the phenomenal abode (the future parents); this is rather close to the Sāṃkhya Mahat as a field knower (*kṣetrajña*)—the first creation (*sarga*) of the *Anugītā* (of the *Mahābhārata*). Thus the first half of "perception" has the role in Buddhism of establishing the initial division into subject-object by perceiving an object, as does the Sāṃkhya *buddhi* which cognizes "thatness" and which in *Sāṃkhya-kārikā* No. 23 has the function of "ascertainment" (*adhyavasāya*).

The reconnecting "perception" then falls into the womb as the fruitional consciousness (*vipākavijñāna* or *jīvitendriya*), rather close to the Sāṃkhya *ahaṃkāra*—the second creation of the *Anugītā*. The second-half *vijñāna* is followed by name-and-form and the six sense bases, just as in Sāṃkhya the *ahaṃkāra*, according to *Sāṃkhya-kārikā* No. 24, through its function of conation (*abhimāna*) gives rise to the various organs and elements constituting the body. According to the *Vijñaptimātratāsiddhi* the beings take the *ālayavijñāna* ("store consciousness") as their "I" (*svam abhyantaram ātmānam* or *sva adhyātmika ātman*) because of its continuity and homogeneity, but one should not take it as a "self."[47] This text of Yogācāra Buddhism thus makes it equivalent to "calling 'I' " (*ahaṃkāra*), but insists that one should not call it that way.

Now reverting to the first two members of Dependent Origination I shall continue the comparison with the Sāṃkhya in a

[46]Wayman, "Buddhist Dependent Origination", p. 202.

[47]Louis de La Vallée Poussin, *Vijñaptimātratāsiddhi*, Tome I, pp. 150 and 181.

manner employed some years ago, while interpreting the celebrated Yogācāra work *Madhyāntavibhāga* to have two realities: "Thus, the Buddhist text replaces the Sāṃkhya *puruṣa* with the 'imagination of unreality' (*abhūtaparikalpa*) and replaces *prakṛti* with 'voidness' (*śūnyatā*). In this Buddhist system, both the 'imagination of unreality' and 'voidness' are real, co-exist, and are yet distinct."[48] Enforcing my theory, "nescience" and "motivation" are added to the replacement correspondences:

Dependent Origination terminology	*Madhyāntavibhāga* terminology	Sāṃkhya terminology
nescience	imagination of unreality	*puruṣa*
motivations	voidness	*prakṛti*

The Buddhist formula starts with "nescience" (*avidyā*); Sāṃkhya holds that the *puruṣas* emerge in the new development each with their specific *avidyā*.[49] Next Buddhism places "motivations" (*saṃskāra*), the *karma* of body, speech, and mind; here Sāṃkhya has its *prakṛti* (also with three strands, the *guṇas*). *Prakṛti* and *saṃskāra* have the same verbal root, and in both systems have the role of causing a development—in the Sāṃkhya, *prakṛti* as the original cause (*pradhāna*); in Buddhism, *saṃskāra* as the efficacy of former *karma* to attain a fruit. Moreover, the Sāṃkhya sets forth an irreducible duality of Puruṣa (pure consciousness, not the agent) and Prakṛti (pure matter, the impersonal agent); while Buddhism sets forth a primeval duality of *avidyā* (nescience, not the agent, but metaphorically the manure) and *saṃskāra* (motivations, the impersonal agent, but metaphorically the ground).

As to the "voidness," Tsoṅ-kha-pa's great commentary on the *Abhisamayālaṃkāra* helps, because of his section "the subjective knowledge (*yul can ye śes*) and the objective voidness (*yul stoṅ ñid*)," showing that no matter how many the voidnesses, e.g., the list of twenty, they are all objective, the object of the knowledge or insight that discerns them.[50] Thus, the "Imagination of

[48] A. Wayman, "The Yogācāra Idealism (Review Article)", *Philosophy East and West*, XV:1, Jan. 1965, p. 66.

[49] Surendranath Dasgupta, *A History of Indian Philosophy*, Vol. I, p. 249.

[50] Tson-kha-pa, *Bstan bcos mṅon rtogs rgyan 'grel pa daṅ bcas pa'i rgya cher bśad, "Legs bśad gser phreṅ"* (Sarnath, Varanasi, 1970), Vol. I, p. 407.

Unreality" has only voidness (= the void Dharmadhātu) as its object, just as Puruṣa has only Prakṛti as its object.

The "Imagination of Unreality" is definitely a form of nescience; and the *Madhyāntavibhāga* (I, 11) states that from this "imagination" proceed the twelve members of Dependent Origination beginning with "nescience." The "Imagination of Unreality" may therefore be this Yogācāra text's expression for what Asaṅga calls the unmixed nescience, or undefiled nescience. This text, as previously pointed out, counts the series as "defiled" or "afflicted," and Vasubandhu in his comment accordingly explains "nescience" as the first member to be the positive impediment to the view of reality.

In summary, the *Madhyāntavibhāga* agrees with the Sāṃkhya in positing two preexistent realities that are on an equal footing. In contrast, the Buddhist Dependent Origination has the first and subjective member, nescience, serving as the condition for the arising of the second and objective member, motivations. And in any case, it was never my position that correlation and replacement of terms meant identification. One should grant that the Buddhist series, no matter of which Buddhist sect's interpretation, develops quite differently from the Sāṃkhya evolutes, even though there are some striking parallels.

There is another way I compared Dependent Origination with the Sāṃkhya in an early and admittedly speculative effort.[51] Here, partly by suggestion of the *Kālacakra* and other Buddhist Tantric material, I set the first three members of Dependent Origination, namely, nescience, motivations, and perception, in correspondence respectively with the three kinds of Ahaṃkāra of the classical Sāṃkhya system, namely *tāmasika-*, *rājasika-*, and *sāttvika-ahaṃkāra.* This is tantamount to saying that if one succeeded in abolishing the twelve fold Dependent Origination, one would be at the level of Mahat, the cosmic intellectual substance. I do not deny a possible merit of a comparison involving even late works like the Buddhist Tantras, but there is no point in following up this kind of comparison in the present essay.

[51] A. Wayman, "Buddhist Dependent Origination and the Sāṁkhya guṇas", *Ethnos* (1962), pp. 14-22.

V. Conclusion

Certainly much more is written about the formula of Dependent Origination in the Buddhist canon and commentarial traditions than can possibly be conveyed within the limits of this paper. In the application of writings from a long time span, it was inevitable that the "discovery" and "seeing" of the series would be intertwined. It could also be argued about the two kinds of Dependent Origination that if one can "see" Dependent Origination, one can see both kinds in the form here organized, or perhaps "see" just one kind. But if what I have tried to show is indeed the case, much of the past argumentation misses the mark. Those theories were not based on "seeing" Dependent Origination, but rather on the premise that if one theory about the series is right, the others must be wrong.

9

NESCIENCE AND INSIGHT ACCORDING TO ASAṄGA'S *YOGĀCĀRABHŪMI*

The topic treated here is of enormous importance to Buddhism. "Nescience" is adopted as the translation of *avidyā* to include "ignorance" (*ajñāna*) and "waywardness' (*viparyāsa*). For *vidyā* I accept "clear sight," opposed by nescience's blindness. "Waywardness," the second kind of nescience, has its "traces" (*anuśaya*) and "entrapment" (*paryavasthāna*). "Insight" is my usual translation of *prajñā*, and the paper shows its association with light and vision; it is the chief faculty to counteract "nescience"in the sense of ignorance, and to erase the "traces" of "waywardness."

Asaṅga, circa 375-430 A.D., who wrote in Sanskrit, is probably the most famous author of the Buddhist school called the Later Mahīśāsaka; and the views of this school have the most extensive corpus of preservation in Asaṅga's encyclopedic work, the *Yogācārabhūmi*, which also includes some Mahāyāna positions especially based on the scripture *Saṃdhinirmocana-sūtra*[1]. This *Yogācārabhūmi*[2] by Asaṅga has five major divisions (sometimes incorrectly entered in catalogues): *Bhūmivastu* or *Bahubhūmika*, comprised of seventeen *bhūmis; Viniścaya-saṃgrahaṇī*, the exegesis in order of those seventeen; *Vastu-saṃgrahaṇī*, by

[1]Cf. A. Wayman, *Analysis of the Śrāvakabhūmi Manuscript* (Univ. of Calif. Press, Berkeley and Los Angeles, 1961), pp. 25-29.

[2]Paul Demiéville, *La Yogācārabhūmi de Saṅgharakṣa*, *BEFEO*, 44 (1954), shows that there were other works of the same title.

basic Buddhist topics, *saṃskāras*, etc.; *Paryāya-saṃgrahaṇī*, of synonyms, etc.; *Vivaraṇa-saṃgrahaṇī*, miscellaneous explanations. The seventeen *bhūmis* are:

(1) Stage associated with the set of five perceptions (*pañcavijñānakāya-saṃprayuktā bhūmi*).
(2) Stage of mind (*manobhūmi*).
(3) Stage with inquiry and with conclusions (*savitarkā savicārā bhūmi*).
(4) Stage without inquiry and with only conclusions (*avitarkā-vicāra-mātrā bhūmi*).
(5) Stage without inquiry or conclusion (*avitarkā-avicārā bhūmi*).
(6) Stabilised stage (*samāhitā bhūmi*).
(7) Unstabilised stage (*asamāhitā bhūmi*).
(8) Stage with thought (*sacittikā bhūmi*).
(9) Stage without thought (*acittikā bhūmi*).
(10) Stage consisting of hearing (*śrutamayī bhūmi*).
(11) Stage consisting of pondering (*cintāmayī bhūmi*).
(12) Stage consisting of contemplation (*bhāvanāmayī bhūmi*).
(13) Stage of the disciple (*śrāvakabhūmi*).
(14) Stage of the self-enlightened person (*pratyekabuddhabhūmi*).
(15) Stage of the Bodhisattva (*bodhisattvabhūmi*).
(16) Stage of Nirvāṇa with remainder (*sopādhikā bhūmi*).
(17) Stage of Nirvāṇa without remainder (*nirupādhikā bhūmi*).

It is necessary to mention these divisions because various ones will be referred to in my following materials. The entire work is preserved in Tibetan and Chinese translations, and portions are extant in original Sanskrit. Bhūmis 3-5 are grouped as *Savitarkādir bhūmi* in V. Bhattacharya's edition of the Sanskrit text which ends with Bhūmi No. 5.[3]

The Two Kinds of Nescience

The two kinds of nescience are ignorance and waywardness. It is well to include here from Tsoṅ-kha-pa's *Lam rim chen mo* an exceptionally clear explanation identifying the ignorance kind as

3Vidhushekhara Bhattacharya, *The Yogācārabhūmi of Ācārya Asaṅga*, Part I (University of Calcutta, 1957).

the first member of Dependent Origination (*pratītya-samutpāda*), which I now translate from the Tibetan:[4]

> Nescience is as stated in the (*Abhidharma*) *Kośa* (in III, 28): "the contrary of clear sight like enmity and untruth." Besides, one should not regard enmity and untruth as just the negation of friendliness and truth, or as just different from those two; rather, as the opposite side which actively opposes friendliness and truth. Accordingly, nescience should not be regarded in the sense of an opposite as just the negation of clear sight or as just different from it; rather as the contrary side which actively opposes clear sight (*vidyā*). Here, the opposing clear sight is the clear sight with the meaning of right selflessness of person (*pudgala-nairātmya*), so it is the view which destroys its enemy, the positing of self in person (*pudgala-ātmagrāha*)—such was maintained by the great ācārya Dharmakīrti [*Pramāṇavārttika*, I, 215cd-216ab]. Ācārya Asaṅga and his brother (i.e. Vasubandhu) maintained that from among the adhering to waywardness about the right meaning or just the confusion about the right meaning, it is the latter; in short, that from among the deviant reflection and the intellect (*buddhi*) that does not understand, it is the intellect that does not understand. However, this is tantamount to maintaining that the chief opponent to the opposing side is the insight (*prajñā*) which understands selflessness. When one analyzes that confusion, there are two: confusion about *karma* and its fruit, and confusion about the meaning of reality (*tattva*). According to the (*Abhidharma*) *Samuccaya*, with the former, one amasses the motivations (*saṃskāra*) that send one to an evil destiny, and with the latter, one amasses the motivations that send one to a good destiny.

Since this is an explanation of nescience as the first member of Dependent Origination, it emphasizes the first kind of nescience, that of ignorance (*ajñāna*) or confusion (*saṃmoha*), as contrasted with the second kind of nescience, that of deviant reflection or waywardness, as regards Asaṅga's position.[5]

[4]The edition which I use is the Tashilunpo one, and the passage is translated from the Dependent Origination section, as part of the instruction to the "middling person".

[5]For the two kinds of nescience, cf. my early article, 'The Meaning of Un-

Now, Asaṅga includes within the *Cintāmayī bhūmi* these verses of the *Paramārtha-gāthā* (nos. 10-11):[6]

> One finds that creatures lie in two categories.
> They are heedless in sense fields; moreover, deviantly setting out.
> Truly those caught by delusion are those deviantly setting out.
> While those caught by craving are those heedless in sense fields.

Asaṅga's self commentary relates this classification to Buddhist Dependent Origination in two parts: "the *dharmas* possessed of cause" are the first seven members, from "nescience" (*avidyā*) down through "feelings" (*vedanā*) —here the creatures are caught by delusion. "The *suffering* possessed of cause" is the last five members, from "craving" (*tṛṣṇā*) down through "old age and death" (*jarā-maraṇa*)—here the creatures are caught by craving.

That explanation shows that in Asaṅga's position, when one has eliminated "craving" he has overcome "the suffering possessed of cause," while when one has eliminated "nescience" he has understood "the *dharmas* possessed of cause." This implies that in his school, "non-self of personality" (*pudgala-nairātmya*) is a realisation to eliminate "craving," while "non-self of *dharmas*" (*dharma-nairātmya*) is a realisation to eliminate "nescience."[7] This must also be why he states in the *Bodhisattvabhūmi* ((text, p. 3), "Among them, the lineage of all the *śrāvakas* and *pratyeka-buddhas* becomes pure through purification of the hindrance of defilement (*kleśa*), not through purification of the hindrance of the knowable (*jñeya*). However, the lineage of *bodhisattvas* becomes pure not only through purification of the hindrance of defilement, but also through purification of the hindrance of the knowable."[8] This indicates that when Asaṅga mentions that "creatures lie in two categories" he means also those following

---

wisdom (Avidyā),' *Philosophy East and West*, VII: 1-2, April, July, 1957, pp. 21-25. I no longer use the rendition "unwisdom, " but my conclusions there are consistent with the present study.

[6]*Analysis of the Srāvakabhūmi Manuscript*, pp. 169, 180-181.

[7]This observation sets the position of Asaṅga-Vasubandhu in opposition to that of Dharmakīrti, according to the previous passage of Tsoṅ-kha-pa's, where it represents Dharmakīrti as assigning selflessness of person (*pudgala-nairātmya*) the role of countering nescience as the first member of Dependent Origination.

[8]*Analysis*, p. 29.

the religious life in the Buddhist sense. Some (the *śrāvakas* and *pratyekabuddhas*) manage, by non-self of personality, to be not caught by craving with its attendant defilement. Some (the *bodhisattvas*) manage not only that, but also, by non-self of *dharmas*, to be not caught by delusion.

Previously it was mentioned that in Asaṅga's school, the first kind of nescience, that of ignorance, is the first member of Dependent Origination. That leaves the problem of where in Dependent Origination is the emergence of the second kind of nescience, that of waywardness. In this case there is an important passage in the Pāli scripture *Madhupiṇḍika Sutta* of *Majjhima-nikāya* (I, 111), in my translation:

> (*Yaṃ vedeti taṃ sañjānāti, yaṃ sañjānāti, taṃ vitakketi, yaṃ vitakketi taṃ papañceti...*) What one feels, on has an idea about. What one has an idea about, one inquires about. What one inquires about, one develops upon.[9]

This passage shows that the "feelings" member, last of the first seven members, has a concomitant mental state involving discursive thought, with the possibility of "waywardness of idea" (*sáṃjñā-viparyāsa*). Hence, when "craving" arises in dependence on "feelings," these feelings, according to a passage of Asaṅga's I shall later cite, may be associated with the three "poisons," lust, hatred, and delusion; and, to anticipate the later findings, these psychological poisons would be in the form of "traces" (*anuśaya*). Thus while "craving" has the freedom to inaugurate a new bondage, it is usually not a pure "craving" but is sullied with deviant reflection.

Asaṅga himself expounds two kinds of nescience in the *Viniś-caya-saṃgrahaṇī* (PTT,[10] Vol. 110, p. 28-1-5, ff.). Before translating it from the Tibetan, I shall outline the main elements of the passage. And before that, it should be mentioned that Asaṅga evidently means by "nescience" here the *avidyā* of Dependent Origination independent of the life of a single sentient being, since

[9]Compare with the translation by BHIKKHU ÑĀṆANANDA, *Concept and Reality* (Buddhist Publication Society, Kandy, 1971), p. 3.

[10]PTT is the abbreviated reference to the "Peking Tibetan Tripitaka," the photographic reproduction in Japan of the Peking edition of the Tibetan canon.

two types of persons are mentioned, and so there is a nescience without defilement.[11]

A. Unmixed nescience (=ignorance)
   a. The confusion of not comprehending
   d. The undefiled confusion
B. Having the mental concomitants of defilement (=waywardness)
   b. The confusion of heedlessness
   c. The defiled confusion

The translation follows:

> Among them, what is nescience (*avidyā*)? The obscuration (*'gebs par byed pa ñid*) and the hindering (*sgrib par byed pa ñid*) of consciousness in regard to the reality of the knowable that is to be comprehended. Moreover, it is to be understood briefly as four kinds—the confusion (*saṃmoha*) of not comprehending; the confusion of heedlessness; the defiled confusion; and the undefiled confusion. a. The confusion of not comprehending is the ignorance (*ajñāna*) of not seeing and not hearing, and not analyzing the variety, and not perceiving the meaning of the knowable. b. The confusion of heedlessness is the ignorance, when having seen, heard, analyzed the variety, and perceived it (the meaning of the knowable), one has mental straying and forgetfulness. c. The defiled confusion (*kliṣṭa-saṃmoha*) is the ignorance through waywardness of thought (*citta-viparyāsa*). d. The undefiled confusion (*akliṣṭa-saṃmoha*) is the ignorance free from waywardness

[11]This position of Asaṅga's of a nescience that is unmixed with defilement, apparently the nescience which is the first member of Dependent Origination, seems directly opposed to Nāgārjuna's position that the 1st, 8th, and 9th members are *kleśa* (defilement), as set forth in A. WAYMAN, "Buddhist Dependent Origination," *History of Religions*, Vol. 10, No. 3 (Feb. 1971), esp. pp. 188-189. However, in the *Viniścaya-saṃgrahaṇī*, on the first two bhūmis, Asaṅga also states (PTT, Vol. 110, p. 269-4) that the 1st, 8th and 9th members (*avidyā*, *tṛṣṇā*, and *upādāna*) are comprised by *kleśa*. The seeming discrepancy may be resolved by noting that when Asaṅga says, 'creatures lie in two categories,' he is using the formula of Dependent Origination in its *discovery order* by Gautama Buddha and independent of applying it to a single sentient being. When the formula is so interpreted, it is possible to speak of a nescience that is unmixed with defilement. But when the formula is applied to a single life, two lives, or three lives of a sentient being, one then speaks of the 1st member, *avidyā*, being comprised by *kleśa*.

of thought. All those kinds of nescience may be summarised as two kinds: having the mental concomitants of defilement, and unmixed. B. The one having the mental concomitants of defilement is in the case where someone seeks that there be no confusion and that no defilement arise, but still there are present other defilements from the group of lust, etc., and nescience is present. A. The unmixed nescience is in the case of some person of dull insight who, while not entrapped by the other group of defilements, lust, etc., has the wrong method of orienting his mind to the Truth of Suffering, etc. and (the Truths) do not appear to him in the genuine way as they really are; and there is obscuration, hindrance, entrapment, and darkening of consciousness.

It is noteworthy that Asaṅga qualifies the two kinds of nescience in terms of persons following the Buddhist path. This is consistent with my observation that he did not lose sight of the distinction alluded to in the *Paramārtha-gāthā*, "One finds that creatures lie in two categories." In the outline I reversed the order in which he presents these two persons so as to preserve the order in which the two kinds of nescience arise in this interpretation of Dependent Origination. Asaṅga's order is consistent with the passage I cited above from his *Bodhisattvabhūmi*. He scarcely disguises his implication of the *śrāvakas* who seek to eliminate the hindrance of defilement, and yet there are still present other defilements, namely, the "traces" of lust, hatred, and delusion. And then there are the *bodhisattvas*, whose nescience is unmixed with the defilements of lust, etc., and yet their insight is not strong enough to eliminate the hindrance of the knowable. It is this passage which may be the one that led to Tsoṅ-kha-pa's remark that in Asaṅga's position it is insight (*prajñā*) which is the main opponent to nescience as the first member of Dependent Origination.

The foregoing should make it clear that Asaṅga does not refer to the two kinds of nescience when in his *Vastusaṃgrahaṇī* (PTT, Vol. 111, p. 138-1) he says that nescience has two states, former—the state of "traces" (*anuśaya*), and later—the state of "entrapment" (*paryavasthāna*). But then the question arises of which one of the kinds—or is it both?—that has the former and later states mentioned. Asaṅga discusses these two terms "traces" and "entrapment" at length in *Viniścaya-saṃgrahaṇī* on his *Savitarkādir bhūmi*, PTT, Vol. 110, p. 281-4, through p. 282, and to p. 283-1. For example, he says (p. 281-4), "On account of the state of waking, there is entrapment; on account of sleep, there are the traces."[12] Furthermore (p. 281-5), "When one has eliminated entrapment, but has not eliminated the traces, again and again the entrapment arises." Asaṅga (p. 282-4) settles on the number eight for the "traces" in connection with the Truth of Source (*samudaya-satya*). Here he means the eight-fold defilement per Bhattacharya, (ed., text, p. 161), with each defined (pp. 162-164). In the exegetical section he stresses the "exaggeration of views" (*dṛṣṭi-parāmarśa*); and the remaining ones are "deviant views" (*mithyā-dṛṣṭi*), exaggeration of rules and vows (*śīlavrata-parāmarśa*), passion (*rāga*), enmity (*pratigha*), pride (*māna*), nescience (*avidyā*), and doubt (*vicikitsā*). These two states, being forms of defilement (*kleśa*), cannot apply to the first kind of nescience, because as was shown above the first kind is "unmixed," i.e. unmixed with defilement. Therefore, they are states of the second kind of nescience, that of waywardness. Now, the eight "traces" must be a fuller list of possibilities that go along with the seventh member of Dependent Origination, "feelings." This is because at p. 282-2, in the case of the suffering ranging in the "realm of desire," Asaṅga adds to the set of eight, "reifying view" (*satkāyadṛṣṭi*) and "view holding to an extreme" (*antagrāhadṛṣṭi*). This set of ten defilements therefore applies to the five last members of Dependent Origination which Asaṅga described as "the *suffering* possessed of cause." It follows that the kind of meditation that gets rid of the entrapments that are in the nature of those ten defilements has not eliminated the traces of eight defilements that lie deep and are vitalised in sleep, as Asaṅga mentioned. Thus, Asaṅga's scriptural authority, the *Saṃdhinirmocana*, says, "By means of meditation one suppresses the defilements; by means of insight one well erases their traces."[13] Therefore, the power of insight must be applied to eliminate the "traces"

[12]For illustrations of these traces in sleep in terms of the three "poisons", see chapter 21, where Table 1 gives dream defilements of the six senses. This essay is reprinted in this volume.

[13]Étienne Lamotte, ed. and tr. *Saṃdhinirmocana Sūtra* (Louvain, 1935), p. 132 (Tib. text) and p. 244 (French translation).

of the second kind of nescience as well as to counteract the "ignorance" constituting the first kind of nescience.

Nescience as Ignorance

Asaṅga in the latter part of the *Savitarkādir bhūmi* (text, p. 204) presents a list of nineteen entities about which one may be ignorant, each with brief explanation. Then he mentions (text, p. 205.11, ff.: PTT. Vol. 109, p. 260-2-3, ff.) a list of seven ignorances: confusion about time (*adhva-saṃmoha*), confusion about entity (*vastu-°*), confusion about transfer (*saṃkrānti-°*), confusion about the excellent (*agra-°*), confusion about reality (*tattva-°*), confusion about defilement and purification (*saṃkleśavyavadāna-°*), confusion about pride (*abhimāna-°*).

The same group of seven has been subdivided and partially explained in the *Artha-viniścaya-ṭīkā* (author unrecorded), in Tibetan (PTT. Vol. 145, p. 172-3). Here there are seven kinds of confusion (*saṃmoha*):

a. Three degrees of nescience (*avidyā*)—
   1. minor nescience is delusion (*moha*), confusion about reality (*tattva*).
   2. middling nescience is nescience, confusion about defilement and purification.
   3. great nescience is blind obscuration, confusion about pride (*abhimāna*).

b. Four forms of ignorance (*ajñāna*)—
   4. confusion about time (i.e. the three times), is ignorance.
   5. confusion about entity (inner, outer, and both inner and outer), is not seeing (*adarśana*).
   6. confusion about transfer (i.e. karma ... Dependent Origination) is "not understanding" (*anabhisamaya*).
   7. confusion about the excellent (the Three Jewels of the Buddha, Dharma, Saṅgha) is darkness (*tamas*).

This subdivision helps to clarify Tsoṅ-kha-pa's remark as was previously cited: "When one analyses that confusion, there are two: confusion about *karma* and its fruit, and confusion about the meaning of reality (*tattva*)." That *Artha-viniścaya* commentary includes "confusion about reality" as a degree of nescience (*avidyā*), and includes "confusion about transfer" (which involves *karma* and its fruit) as a form of ignorance. This implies that it is the forms of ignorance, here listed as four, that constitute the nescience heading Dependent Origination that is the condition for the second member "motivations" (*saṃskāra*) of the type leading to an evil destiny. And implies that when one is no longer plagued by this ignorance, it is the degrees of nescience, here listed as three, that are the condition for motivations toward a good destiny, and keep one in "cyclical flow" (*saṃsāra*).

Besides, Asaṅga mentions (Sanskrit text, p. 205, 17; PTT, p. 260-2-6) another list with five kinds of ignorance (*ajñāna*), each called a "confusion", which are associated with the list of nineteen ignorances, in the following manner:[14]

a. confusion about view (*dṛṣṭi-saṃmoha*).

1. ignorance of prior limit (the past *saṃskāras*)
2. ignorance of later limit (the future *saṃskāras*)
3. ignorance of prior and later limit (with doubt)
4. ignorance of the personal (one's own *saṃskāras*)
5. ignorance of the other person (the other's *saṃskāras*)
6. ignorance of the personal and the other person (in terms of friend, enemy, and neutral)
7. ignorance of cause (believing in a creator lord, etc.)
8. ignorance of *saṃskāras* generated from cause (the sinful, the sinless, and the mixed)

b. confusion about heedlessness (*pramāda*-°).

9. ignorance of karma
10. ignorance of maturation
11. ignorance of karma and maturation (with waywardness)

c. confusion about the meaning of reality (*tattvārtha*-°).

12. ignorance of the Buddha
13. ignorance of the Dharma
14. ignorance of the Saṅgha
15. ignorance of suffering
16. ignorance of source
17. ignorance of cessation
18. ignorance of path

[14]In the following, occasional extra material within parentheses, e.g. "the past *saṃskāras*," constitutes minimal extra explanation from the definitions of the nineteen ignorances in the Sanskrit text, (p. 204).

d. confusion about pride (*abhimāna*-°).

19. ignorance of the special knowledge of the six sense bases as they really are (with waywardness of consciousness)[15]

c. confusion about the entity (*artha-saṃmoha*). Under this heading one places all nineteen ignorances.

Therefore the comprehensive kind of ignorance called "confusion about the entity" is equal to the previously-mentioned kind of "unmixed nescience" called "the confusion of not comprehending," where the creatures are caught by delusion. But some items add a "waywardness" element.

Nescience as Waywardness

As was previously indicated, the second kind of nescience enters the mind as a concomitant of the "feelings" that are the seventh member of Dependent Origination. With this condition there arises "craving" the eighth member, which is followed by "indulgence" (*upādāna*), the ninth member. It is this ninth member which according to the *Abhidharmakośa* is of four kinds, indulgence in the five strands of desire (the five sense objects), indulgence in any of the 62 views of the *Brahmajālasūtra*, indulgence in rules and vows, indulgence in the self-theory.

Along these lines, Asaṅga explains "waywardness" in the *Savitarkādir bhūmi*, (Sanskrit ed., p. 166):

> There are seven kinds of waywardness (*viparyāsa*), as follows: (1) waywardness of idea (*saṃjñā*-°), (2) waywardness of view (*dṛṣṭi*-°), (3) waywardness of consciousness (*citta*-°), (4) waywardness that considers impermanent as permanent, (5) waywardness that considers pain as pleasure, (6) waywardness that considers impure as pure, (7) waywardness that considers non-self as self. What is the waywardness of idea? It is the discursive thinking (*parikalpa*) of idea that considers the impermanent as permanent, etc. What is the waywardness of

[15]This category regarding confusion about pride especially concerns Asaṅga's discussion of Arhat attainment, as in the *Viniścaya-saṃgrahaṇī* of the Nirvāṇa-with-Remainder and Nirvāṇa-without-Remainder stages, (PTT., Vol. III, p. 119-1, ff.) where he appears to hold that Nirvāṇa-with-Remainder keeps the six sense bases, while Nirvāṇa-without-Remainder lacks the six sense bases. For the implication in terms of *gotra* (species), see chapter 12.

> view? Any acceptance, belief, settling on, or clinging right there to the so-discursively-thought idea. What is the waywardness of consciousness? Any defilement of passion, etc. in precisely that so-clung-to (view). Here one should understand defilement by three aspects—There is defilement, the root of waywardness. There is waywardness. There is the outflow of waywardness. Among them, the "root of waywardness" is nescience (*avidyā*). "Waywardness" is the reifying view (*satkāyadṛṣṭi*); the onesidedness of view that adheres to an extreme; the exaggeration of view and exaggeration of rules and vows; and passion. The "outflow of waywardness" is the deviant view (*mithyā-dṛṣṭi*), the onesidedness of view that adheres to an extreme, enmity, pride, and doubt. Among those, the reifying view is the waywardness that takes non-self to be self. The onesidedness of view that adheres to an extreme is the waywardness that takes the impermanent to be permanent. The exaggeration of view is the waywardness that takes the impure to be pure. The exaggeration of rules and vows is the waywardness that takes pain to be pleasure. Passion involves the pair of waywardnesses, the one that takes the impure to be pure, and the one that takes pain to be pleasure.

As Asaṅga mentions, one should understand defilement by three aspects. By defining the "root of waywardness" as nescience, he means the second kind, as he explains (Skt. text. p. 163): "What is nescience? Any defiled ignorance—whether reflecting upon or not reflecting upon the knowable entity (*jñeya-vastu*), be it (relying on) ignoble persons, [listening to heretic doctrine, orienting the mind in an improper manner, naturally] losing memory (*smṛti*)."[16] It is feasible that by the alternatives "whether reflecting upon or not reflecting upon the knowable entity" he intends the states "entrapment" and "traces." By mentioning "waywardness' in terms of the five "traces" he means them in application to the four "waywardnesses of idea,"as made explicit at the end of the citation. Then, the "outflow of waywardness" includes some other "traces." Since the three aspects of defilement include all ten of the defilements previously mentioned as going with "the suffering ranging in the realm of desire," it is

[16]The portion within brackets was supplied from the Tibetan translation, (PTT, Vol. 109, p. 250-4).

clear that Asaṅga means by that "waywardness" passage "the suffering possessed of cause." It will be recalled that here the creatures are caught by craving.

Insight as an Instruction

The division established previously of two parts of Dependent Origination is consistent with the first sermon of the Buddha, setting forth the four Noble Truths (or Truths of the Nobles, the *āryas*), where the Buddhist path begins with operating on the implications of the last five members of Dependent Origination, and the candidates are those caught by craving and hence heedless in sense fields. So in that sermon the Buddha stressed the avoidance of the extremes of indulgence in sense gratification and mortification. These two extremes may well be what were referred to among the ten defilements as "passion" and "exaggeration of rules and vows."

Furthermore, the Buddhist training was expressed by the three Instructions, of Morality, of Mind-control, of Insight. Asaṅga (*Cintāmayī bhūmi*, PTT, Vol. 110, p. 18-4) says, "Thus the one rightly enterprising, basing himself on the morality set (*adhiśīla*), generates the mind-control set (*adhi-citta*); basing himself on the mind-control set, generates the insight-set (*adhiprajñā*)." In his *Vivaraṇa-saṃgrahaṇī* (PTT. Vol. 111, p. 244-5) he says: "By the Instructions of the morality-set and the mind-control set, there is non-lust, non-hatred, and non-delusion. (Thus,) the absence of the four waywardnesses belongs to the stage of accumulating (merit) (*saṃbhāramārga*) and to the stage of praxis (*prayoga-mārga*). Clear sight (*vidyā*) and liberation (*vimukti*) belong to the Instruction of the insight set, the stage of vision (*darśana-mārga*), stage of contemplation (*bhāvanā-mārga*), and ultimate state (*niṣṭhāgamana-mārga*)." Here Asaṅga combines the early Buddhist theory of three Instructions with the Mahāyāna classification, developed in the Prajñāpāramitā exegesis, of five paths (*mārga*), although the Tibetan word *sa* in each case shows that Asaṅga used the term *bhūmi* rather than *mārga*.[17]

In the *Viniścaya-saṃgrahaṇī*, Asaṅga points out that the four

[17]The theory of five paths is worked out in detail in Eugene Obermiller, "The Doctrine of Prajñā-pāramitā as exposed in the Abhisamayālaṃkāra of Maitreya," *Acta Orientalia*, Vol. XI, 1932.

aspects of the Truth of Suffering serve to oppose the four waywardnesses. That is, the aspect "There is impermanence" opposes the waywardness that the impermanent is permanent; the aspect "There is pain" opposes the waywardness that pain is pleasure; the aspects "There is voidness" and "There is non-self" oppose the waywardness that non-self is self.[18] Here the meditations on voidness and non-self serve to counteract the reifying view (*satkāyadṛṣṭi*) that takes non-self to be self. In Asaṅga's position, the first two Instructions counteract the entrapment state of the defilements during the phase "the suffering possessed of cause." But, as was already pointed out, for liberation from the traces state of nescience, the Instruction of insight is required.

According to Asaṅga's *Śrutamayī bhūmi*, (PTT, Vol. 109, p. 297-1,) among the members of the Eightfold Noble Path, one cultivates Insight with Right Views, Right Conception, and Right Effort. Consistent with assigning Right Views, he says a little previously, (p. 296-5), that the faulty *adhiprajñā* is adopting any of the 62 wrong views (of the *Brahmajāla-sūtra*).

Also, he states in the *Śrāvakabhūmi* (PTT, Vol. 110, p. 70-1): "What is the person liberated by insight? The person who has achieved in every last degree the ending of fluxes (*āsrava-kṣaya*), but who does not dwell accomplishing the eight liberations as a 'witnesser with body' (*kāya-sākṣin*)."

Terminology of Insight

Asaṅga has a rather remarkable list in his *Paryāya-saṃgrahaṇī* (PTT, Vol. 111, p. 232-1, 2, 3). Some corrections were made by consultation of the equivalent Chinese section in Taisho, (Vol. 30. 761).[19] One of the most striking features of what follows is the set of similes emphasizing light, with five entries that are in the Pāli "Book of Fours," Chap. XV. Here five paragraphs have the same form, e.g. "There are four 'lustres' (*ābhā*), that of the moon, sun, fire, and insight, and the last one is greatest." Likewise, four "beams" (*prabhā*), "lights" (*āloka*), "secondary lights" (*obhāsa*), and "lamps" (*pajjota*). But there is no hint in the Pāli scripture that these similes have the implications which Asaṅga makes explicit. This is indeed a mystery of Asaṅga's sources.

[18]"The Meaning of Unwisdom," p. 23.

[19]My wife Hideko aided me at this point.

Taking the order of terms as in Asaṅga's text, I have grouped them by rather obvious headings.

A. (1st group, "insight" as the object, in sūtra passages):

"obtaining insight" means any insight that is virtuous without qualification, or which is purposeful.
"increasing, enhancing, and expanding insight" refers to an ascending scale of small, middling, and great.
"perfectly pure insight" means the maturation at another time of the insight formerly and repeatedly cultivated.
"equipped with insight" means the insight that recognizes defilement of the one which eliminates it.
"fulfilling insight" is the proceeding to the ultimate state.

B. (2nd group, "insight" qualified in various ways, in sūtra passages for *śravakas*):

"non-retreating insight" is the insight that does not retreat, but goes on to the ultimate state.
"speedy insight" is the insight that cannot be overtaken.
"sharp insight"is what well comprehends the phenomenon and noumenon.
"insight that conduces to liberation" (*nairyāṇika-prajñā*) is what well comprehends the natures that conduce to liberation, as well as the freedom from mundane cravings.
"insight that penetrates" (*nairvedhika-°*) is what well comprehends the freedom from supramundane cravings.
"profound insight" (*gambhīra-°*) is what well comprehends the dharma possessed of profound voidness consistent with Dependent Origination, and what rightly reflects on the profound meaning and insight which the Tathāgatas enjoin. It is the great insight enjoined for the disciples (*śrāvakas*), in order that this insight would be for a long time and repeatedly cultivated.
"far-ranging insight" is the one whose domain is boundless and infinite.
"incomparable insight" is the insight unequalled by others.

C. (3rd group, emphasising light):

"jewel of insight" is the insight that is chief of all faculties (*indriya*), because it illuminates with a light like lapis lazuli's

among the gems of the Cakravartin. "Possessing it" means possessing the jewel of insight.
"eye of insight" is the native insight (*sahajā prajñā*).
"lustre of insight" (*ābhā*) is the insight gained from others, or what arises through the generative praxis of others.
"beam of insight" (*prabhā*) is the kind consisting of praxis, i.e. consisting of hearing (*śrutamayī prajñā*) and consisting of pondering (*cintāmayī p.*).
"light of insight" (*āloka*) is the insight consisting of contemplation (*bhāvanāmayī p.*).
"lamp of insight" (*pradyota*) is the kind which establishes the profound scriptures expressed by the Tathāgata, and which illumines.
"torch (or meteor) of insight" (*ulkā*) is the one which goes along only with the time of Teaching of the Dharma [i.e. during Gautama Buddha's teaching career].
"secondary light of insight" (*avabhāsa*) is the one which goes along with subsequent times, when the Dharma is well considered with insight in this and that way, and it is not directly realised by the body [i.e. after the Buddha's Nirvāṇa].
"insight free from darkness" is the one directly realised by the body [i.e. the Buddha's eye of insight].

D. (4th group, emphasising faculty or function):

"faculty of insight" is the insight used to comprehend others.
"power of insight" is the invincible insight about principles and dharma used to comprehend the distinction of former and later of oneself.
"treasure of insight" is the one which generates among lordlinesses the best lordliness, which secures the consecration (*abhiṣeka*) for one's own mind, which is best of all treasures, and which is the basic cause of all mundane treasures.
"sword of insight" and "knife of insight" is what cuts all the bonds of rebirth (*saṃyojana*).
"stake of insight" is the one which dispels the Māras all the way from the "defilement" one to the "son-of-the gods" one.
"reins of insight" is the reins of the horse of mind-organ for virtuous practice.
"expiatory insight" frees the body (of sins) and destroys (them).

"fence of insight" (has only one gate), closes off the innumerable gates to the various defilements.
"ladder of insight" is the path arising from the praxis.
"temple of insight" is the one concerned with the ultimate.

Asaṅga, *Vastu-saṃgrahaṇī*, PTT, Vol. 111, p. 172-3-4, refers to insight's weapon (*mtshon*) for eliminating all defilement. As to the "bonds of rebirth" (*saṃyojana*), Asaṅga lists nine of them, (*ibid.*, p. 152-5) starting with entrapment by clinging to sentient beings and non-sentient entities associated with householder's life, and nine were named (in Bhattacharya, ed., p. 161). The "stake" suggests an impaling of the Māras, who are of course the four, *skandha-°*, *kleśa-°*, *maraṇa-°*, and *devaputra-°*.[20]

It is intriguing that Asaṅga's list seems to have no elements drawn from Mahāyāna literature, although he is generally taken as a Mahāyānist. The list appears based on the four *Āgamas* (the Sanskrit canon roughly equivalent to the four Pāli *Nikāyas*).

Insight as Metaphorical Light

Asaṅga's third group of terms, emphasising light, obviously begins with "jewel of insight" as can be observed by the description "a light like lapis lazuli's". This group agrees with the translation of *prajñā* as "insight."[21]

The "eye of insight" as the native insight (*sahajā prajñā*) deserves more explanation. Asaṅga himself explains a little later (*Paryāya-saṃgrahaṇī*, p. 234-1) that the native insight is attained through birth (*skyes nas thob pa*). He contrasts (*ibid.*, p. 232-4) the promoted insight possessed by the learned man (*paṇḍita*) with the native insight possessed by the intelligent person (*vijña*). He defines (*ibid.*, p. 233-4) *buddhi* (T. *blo*) as any native insight capable of differentiating (alternatives). Therefore, this native insight is present in every rational act of thinking.[22] As such it is usually

[20]Cf. A. Wayman, "Studies in Yama and Māra," Vol. III, No. 2, pp. 112-114.

[21]The noun *prajñā* is rendered into Tibetan as *śes rab* ("superior," *rab;* "knowing," *jñā*), where *pra-* as a nominal prefix has this possible significance in classical Sanskrit. In contrast, *pra-* as in *prajānāti* ("knows about") keeps the old significance of "forth" as a verbal prefix.

[22]In the *Vastu-saṃgrahaṇi* (1st topic, *saṃskārā-pravicaya;* PTT, Vol. 111, p. 137-3), Asaṅga gives five childish states belonging to childish (or foolish)

afflicted. Thus, Asaṅga in *Śrutamayī bhūmi*, PTT, Vol. 110, p. 2-3, gives a simile to show how the eye of insight is assailed:

> For example, smoke is preceded by the element of fire and hurts the eye.... In the same way, craving (*tṛṣṇā*) is preceded by lust, hatred, and delusion; and hurts the eye of insight....

Asaṅga indicates a wide range of possibilities for this "eye" (in *ibid.*, PTT, Vol. 109, p. 290-4): "With the eye of insight one sees all aspects (*ākāra*) of all dharmas, whether with form (*rūpin*) or formless (*arūpin*)." He indicates an inferior and a superior variety in *Vastu-saṃgrahaṇī*, (PTT. Vol. 111, p. 170-4,) speaking of "mundane eye of insight" in contrast with "eye of insight belonging to the nobles (*ārya*)."

A feature of this "mundane eye of insight" is the development of the coarse to the subtle *prajñā* as a discursive series, which Asaṅga mentions in *Viniścaya-saṃgrahaṇī* on *Savitarkādir bhūmi*, (PTT, Vol. 110, p. 281-3); "The coarse *prajñā* based on 'mental murmur' (*manojalpa*) is 'adumbration' (*vitarka*); ... the subtle one is 'thinking with signs' (*vicāra*)." Whether this *vitarka-vicāra* is a member of the First Dhyāna of the "realm of form" or is the kind in the "realm of desire," it always constitutes the development of discursive thought, as speech motivation (*vāksaṃskāra*), starting, as Asaṅga says, with "mental murmur". "Presumably the "ārya" eye of insight is the three levels of *prajñā* , consisting of hearing, pondering, and contemplation.

Asaṅga states (*Paryāya-saṃgrahaṇī*, p. 231-4): " 'Knowledge' (*jñāna*) is any insight arising from supramundane praxis (*lokottara-prayoga*). It is the insight transcending mundane insight. 'Obtaining insight' means any mundane insight obtained after (*pṛṣṭha-labdha*) the supramundane insight." This is illustrated in *Śrutamayī bhūmi*, (p. 16-1): "With that eye of insight, he perceives and witnesses the Tathāgata as the inner Dharmakāya. And when he sees the body of form, a *caitya*, or an external painting, he thinks, 'indeed, in the absolute sense, this is not the right perfected Buddha.' " Thus, after witnessing the inner Dharmakāya, he

persons (*bāla*), namely, 1. not having attained initially the native insight; 2. not having obtained insight arising by reason of others' words; 3. not having attained the insight of the āryas; 4. remaining with entrapment of confusion; 5. conjoined with the traces of that (entrapment). Thus, Asaṅga admits that the irrational person may lack or be deficient in this native insight.

returns to mundane discursive thought, but not with idle verbiage, to deny something "in the absolute sense."

The foregoing involves the theory of final resorts (*pratisaraṇa*), including, in a classical statement, "One should cultivate by resort to knowledge (*jñāna*), not by resort to perception (*vijñāna*)." This points to the superiority of supramundane praxis, and does not intend to deny the value of the mundane praxis. Asaṅga says (*Paryāya-s.*, p. 233-4): "The 'exercise of insight' (*prajñā-pracāra*) means any insight possessed of what is to be perceived higher and higher of perceiving the meaning by way of scripture, its recital in low voice, inquiries, the certainty of cogent discourse, and so forth." These provisional and final resorts are clarified in my previously published note:[23]

For the most obscure set—*jñāna* and *vijñāna*—when we combine the references in de La Vallée Poussin (especially from the *Bodhisattvabhūmi*) with Ratnākaraśānti's explanations, we arrive at the following:

> *jñāna* is supramundane insight (*prajñā*) devoid of discursive thought, namely, insight consisting in creative contemplation (*bhāvanāmayī prajñā*), *vijñāna* is mundane insight, with discursive thought, namely, insight consisting in hearing (*śruta-mayī prajñā*) and insight consisting in pondering (*cintāmayī prajñā*).

As to those three levels of *prajñā*—the first two, consisting of hearing and pondering; and the third consisting of creative contemplation, Asaṅga briefly explains them in *Bhāvanāmayī bhūmi* (PTT, Vol. 110, p. 23-3):

> Taking recourse to the insight consisting in hearing itself, there arise three kinds of trust regarding the path and the fruit of the path which is Nirvāṇa, namely, the trust that it exists, the trust that it has good qualities, the trust that oneself can attain it and learn the means. So as to accomplish the insight consisting of pondering, there is the trust that when one has isolated body and mind, with isolation from hindrances and reflections, and that taking recourse thereto, one is especially certain about the meaning—one accomplishes the *prajñā* consisting of

[23]Alex Wayman and Hideko Wayman, trs. *The Lion's Roar of Queen Śrīmālā* (Columbia Univ. Press, New York and London, 1974), p. 103.

> pondering. Taking recourse to that (i.e. the 2nd level of *prajñā*) when one continually performs contemplation and has the praxis and engagement of devotion, by this sequence one attains in the meantime the *prajñā* consisting of contemplation. Taking recourse to it, one starts the conviction which views *saṃsāra* as base and starts the conviction which views *nirvāṇa* as superb. Repeatedly contemplating this, one attains the comprehension of truth (*satya-abhisamaya*), the path of vision (*darśana-mārga*) which understands directly, the learned liberation (*śaikṣa-vimukti*), and views the essential (*gźi mthoṅ bar 'gyur*). After that, by repeatedly cultivating the *bhāvanā-mārga*, one attains the liberation beyond learning (*aśaikṣa-vimukti*) and completes the liberation. Now, the liberation which has been completed is, namely, only the Nirvāṇa-with-remainder realm (*sopadhiśeṣa-nirvāṇa-dhātu*).

Regarding the "lights" associated with these *prajñā* levels, Asaṅga explains in the *Bhāvanāmayī bhūmi*, (p. 25-2), that the "light" is a variety of the "idea of light" (*ālokasaṃjñā*) meant to counteract one or another kind of darkness, such as the frequent darkening of consciousness when one is trying to keep the mind on a meditative object. He points out that various kinds of "light" are set forth in the *Samāhitabhūmi*. Referring back to this part (PTT, Vol. 109, p. 268-5 to p. 269-1), we find "abstinences" (*an-āhāra*) (from darkness) explained as when there is "light" (*āloka*) and frequent mental orientation thereto. There are three kinds of light—the opponent of darkness, the light of *dharma*, and the light of the body. The "opponent of darkness" means at night the moon and stars, etc.; in daytime, the sun;and at both times, the light of fire, gems, etc. The "light of *dharma*" means reflecting on the doctrines (*dharma*) as they were heard, as they were pondered, and as they were felt, or contemplating mindfulness of the Buddha, etc. The "light of body" means the light which arises from sentient beings themselves (as in certain states of yoga). Asaṅga says (*Bhāvanāmayī bhūmi*, p. 25-2) that in the present context the "idea of light" is meant that is aimed at the "light of dharma". Therefore, in that series in the Pāli "Book of Fours,"—along the lines of *Saṃyutta-nikāya*, (I, 14)—the lights of moon, sun, fire, and insight, refer to the light of nighttime, daytime, both night and day, and the light of *dharma*.

Asaṅga explains in the same place that in the practice of calming the mind (*śamatha*) and discerning (*vipaśyanā*), there are various kinds of faults or darkening; and to counteract these darkenings, there are four "ideas of light" associated with the insight consisting of pondering, and seven associated with the insight consisting of contemplation. Thus, the "beam of insight" (*prabhā*) is the four "ideas of light" that counteract the four damaging factors of the pondering, and the "light of insight" (*āloka*) is the seven "ideas of light" that counteract the seven damaging factors of the contemplation.

It is the hope of the writer that the foregoing not only clarifies some matters of Asaṅga's positions on nescience and insight concerning some of the most fundamental problems of Buddhism, but also gives a taste of Asaṅga's encyclopedic work, the *Yogācārabhūmi*, by excerpts from its great extent.

10

THE TWENTY REIFYING VIEWS
(*SAKKĀYADIṬṬHI*)

The Buddhists were fond of making lists of doctrinal terms and their varieties. Perhaps this bent justifies in part the Theravāda claim, which can be found in the translation of the *Kathāvattnu* (*Points of Controversy*, London, 1913), that the Buddha was a Vibhajjavādin (an "Analyst"). However, it is now difficult to determine which of the many lists found in the Pāli canon were so expressed by the Buddha himself or were added by later "Analysts."

A splendid example of this type of analysis is the Buddhist theory of the "reifying view." This theory stems from the well-known Buddhist stress on "non-self" (*anātman*), especially while analyzing man's make-up as five personal aggregates (*skandha*), and denying in four ways that any of these five is a "self." The commonplace view of man, thus denied, was referred to with a technical term I render "reifying view."

This particular kind of analysis also serves to illustrate how subsequent teachers disagreed about these lists. This is because in this particular case, the opposing positions are well defined and each supported by eminent authorities. To anticipate my findings, on one side there is the scriptural statement in the *Saṃyutta-Nikāya*, the evidence of the *Paṭisambhidāmagga*, and the teacher Nāgārjuna. On the other side there is the Abhidharma work *Jñānaprasthāna*, the Vinaya commentator Vinītadeva, and the Sanskrit-Tibetan Buddhist dictionary *Mahāvyutpatti*. Therefore, study of this topic may reveal a sense in which Nāgārjuna diverged from the Abhidharmists.

There is a valuable article on *sakkāyadiṭṭhi* by J. Rahder,[1] but it seems possible to make a modest advance by considering the various bits of evidence. In the following, 'P' will stand for Pāli, 'S' for Sanskrit, e.g. (S. *satkāyadṛṣṭi*, P. *sakkāyadiṭṭhi*). The portion S. *satkāya* or P. *sakkāya* is variously defined, but the '*kāya*' is frequently explained and provisionally accepted in this paper as referring to the five personal aggregates (S. *skandha*, P. *khandha*).[2] In this acceptance, the full term could be rendered "view that the aggregates are real," but this is an unwieldy translation and I prefer to employ the rendition "reifying view." Translators from Pāli sometimes render it "theory of individuality."[3]

The twenty views (S. *dṛṣṭi*, P. *diṭṭhi*) are variously referred to, in the *Diṭṭhikathā* of the *Paṭisambhidāmagga* part of the *Khuddaka-Nikāya* as an "aspect" (P. *ākāra*), in the *Abhidharmakośa* (Chap. IX) as an "alternative" (S. *koṭika*), in Candrakīrti's *Madhyamakāvatāra* as a "piece" (S. *aṃśa*), in the *Mahāvyutpatti* as a "peak" (*śikhara*).

Those views are applied in four ways to each of the five aggregates to give a total of twenty. Since the listing of the twenty aspects shows in each case an observing of self (*ātman*) in a wrong manner, it amounts to a commentary on the waywardness (S. *viparyāsa*) in the traditional statement, taking as self what is non-self. Asaṅga explicitly states this:[4] "Among those, the reifying view is the waywardness that takes non-self to be self." Furthermore it is a "view" kind of waywardness.[5]

At the scriptural stage, we may consult the Indian edition edited by Jagdish Kasyap of the *Saṃyutta-Nikāya*, sect. 41, "*Citta-*

[1]J. Rahder, "La satkāyadṛṣṭi d'après Vibhāṣā, 8',, *Melanges chinois et bouddhique*, I, 1931-32, p. 227-239.

[2]See *Abhidharmakośa*, Chap. V, La Vallée Poussin tr., p. 15-17.

[3]So Bhikkhu Ñāṇamoli, *The Path of Purification* (*Visuddhimagga*) *by Bhadantācariya Buddhaghosa* (Colombo, Ceylon, 1956).

[4]V. Bhattacharya, ed., *The Yogācārabhūmi of Ācārya Asaṅga* (University of Calcutta, 1957), text, p. 166.19: tatra satkāyadṛṣṭir anātmany ātmeti viparyāsaḥ.

[5]For the three stages of waywardness, including the "view" stage, cf. Alex and Hideko Wayman, *The Lion's Roar of Queen Śrīmālā* (Columbia University Press, 1974), p. 102, note.

saṃyutta," 3. *Dutiya-Isidatta-sutta*, Vol. III, p. 256, for the passage beginning, "Well, then, your honor, how is there the reifying view?" ("kathaṃ puna, bhante, sakkāyadiṭṭhi hotī" ti?). The passage continues with the reply, in my translation:

> In that, householder, the ordinary person (P. *puthujjana*) who does not listen (to the Buddha's teaching), who does not observe the nobles, who is not skilled in the doctrine of the nobles, who is not trained in the doctrine of the nobles, who does not observe illustrious persons, who is not skilled in the doctrine of illustrious persons, who is not trained in the doctrine of illustrious persons, regards form (*rūpa*, or body) as a self, or the self as having a form, or the self as in form, or form as in the self; regards feeling as a self ... or feeling as in the self; ideation as a self ... or ideation as in the self; motivation as a self ... or motivation as in the self; perception as a self ... or perception as in the self. Thus, you should know, householder, there is the reifying view.

The scripture continues' "Well, then, your honor, how is there no reifying view?" And the reply: "In that, householder, the noble disciple, who listens (to the Buddha's teaching) ... (and so on, with the opposite of the foregoing statement, down to). Thus, you should know, householder, there is no reifying view." One may find approximately the same statement in *Majjhima-Nikāya*, (III, 17-18).

The scriptural style continues in the *Diṭṭhikathā* which classifies the views under "nihilistic views" (P. *uccheda-diṭṭhi*) or under "eternalistic views" (P. *sassata-diṭṭhi*).[6] The views, "observes form as a self," observes feeling, ideation, motivation, perception, as a self, constitute "nihilistic views." The views, "observes self as having form," "form as in self," "self as in form," with analogous views for the other aggregates, namely, feeling, ideation, motivation, and perception, constitute "eternalistic views." The point of the classification seems to be that since form (or, body) in time perishes, the identification of self with form (*rūpa*), likewise with the other aggregates, is the nihilistic view. On the

[6]The only edition available to me is ARNOLD C. TAYLOR, Pāli Text Society, *Paṭisambhidāmagga;* Vol. I, 1905, p. 150.

other hand, if self is other than form, by reason of having it, form being in self, or self being in form, likewise self vis-a-vis the other aggregates, then the fact that form perishes, likewise the other aggregates, still leaves self to continue; and so this is the eternalistic view of self. Thus, five of the aspects are nihilistic views, and fifteen are eternalistic views.

The twenty are listed in the *Dhammasangani.*[7] Buddhaghosa's commentary on that work, the *Atthasālinī*, has the remark:[8] "All of them are to be considered as blocking the way to the Path, as not blocking the way to happy rebirth, and as that which is to be slain by the First Path." By "First Path" is meant "Entering the Stream."

For the tradition of Sanskrit Buddhism, we first notice Nāgārjuna's *Madhyamakakārikā*, Chap. XXII, especially verse 1, which on first sight one would think to translate this way:[9]

> The Tathāgata is not the aggregates (S. *skandha*); not other than the *skandhas;* the *skandhas* are not in him; nor he in them; he does not possess the *skandhas.* What, then, is the Tathāgata?

But in the context of Candrakīrti's *Madhyamakāvatāra*, citing this very verse under VI, 144,[10] Candrakīrti points out that when one takes this verse as having five terms, when applied to each of the five aggregates it would yield a total of twenty-five rather than the traditional twenty. He denies that there are more than four terms, and so we are forced to translate Nāgārjuna's verse differently:

> The Tathāgata is not the aggregates; also not other than the aggregates (*skandha*), to wit, the aggregates are not in him, nor he in them, nor does he possess the aggregates. What, then, is the Tathāgata?

Candrakīrti's verses VI, 144-145 are especially devoted to the

[7]Tr. by CAROLINE A. F. RHYS DAVIDS under title *A Buddhist Manual of Psychological Ethics* (London, 1900), p. 259.

[8]Tr. by PE MAUNG TIN under title *The Expositor*, ed. and rev. by MRS. RHYS DAVIDS (London, 1958 reprint), Vol. II, p. 457.

[9]LOUIS DE LA VALLÉE POUSSIN, *Mūlamadhyamakakārikās avec la Prasannapadā*, p. 432: skandhā na nānyaḥ skandhebhyo nāsmin skandhā na teṣu saḥ/ tathāgataḥ skandhavān na katamo 'tra tathāgataḥ.

[10]LOUIS DE LA VALLÉE POUSSIN, *Le Muséon*, 1911, p. 311-312.

topic, and are among the few verses of his *Madhyamakāvatāra* cited in the *Subhāṣitasaṃgraha*:[11]

> The *ātman* is not the *rūpa*, nor does *ātman* have a *rūpa*, *ātman* is not in *rūpa*, the *rūpa* is not in *ātman*. Likewise, know all the *skandhas* in four ways. These are held to be the twenty pieces of the self-view.
>
> These are the high peaks located on the large mountain of reifying views. With the thunderbolt of enlightenment to non-self, the self is rent asunder, and along with them (the high peaks) the mountain of views collapses.

La Vallée Poussin points out in the note what is the first modification of position in comparison with the Pāli Buddhism tradition set forth above. That is to say, there are here two kinds of reifying view; the first, the imagined (S. *parikalpita*), no longer exists among those who have entered the stream, the First Path; but the second kind, the "co-natal" (S. *sahajā*) remains.[12] Tsoṅ-kha-pa, in his native Tibetan commentary on the *Madhyamakāvatāra*, Photo edition, PTT, Vol. 154, p. 89-4, explains that the one who has entered the stream has given up the bad doctrinal systems, and so no longer has the "imagined" kind of reifying view. The more subtle form of "reifying view," is still there.

Now we move to the *Mahāvyutpatti* dictionary, where in the Sakaki edition, item No. 4684 is the title, S. *viṃśati-śikhara-samudgataḥ satkāyadṛṣṭi-śailaḥ* (the mountain of reifying views, high with twenty peaks). The twenty follow:

1. Form (S. *rūpa*) is a self like a prince (*svāmī*).
2. The self has a form like an adornment (*alaṅkāra*).
3. Form belongs to self like a servant (*bhṛtya*).
4. The self is in form like a pot (*bhājana*).
5. Feeling (S. *vedanā*) is a self.
6. The self has feeling.
7. Feeling belongs to the self.
8. The self is in feeling.
9. Ideation (S. *saṃjñā*) is a self.

[11]*Ibid.*, p. 312-313.

[12]See *Abhidharmakośa*, Chap. V, tr., p. 41, for an old Abhidharma theory of the two kinds. Furthermore, Rahder, "La satkāyadṛṣṭi," p. 239, points out that the *Brahmajāla-sūtra* says that the *satkāyadṛṣṭi* is the root of all the sixty-two false views.

10. The self has ideation.
11. Ideation belongs to the self.
12. The self is in ideation.
13. Motivation (S. *saṃskāra*) is a self.
14. The self has motivation.
15. Motivation belongs to self.
16. Motivation is in self.
17. Perception (S. *vijñāna*) is a self.
18. The self has perception.
19. Perception belongs to the self.
20. The self is in perception.

Vinītadeva, in his *Vinaya-vibhaṅga-pada-vyākhyāna*, part of his commentary on the "Fourth Defeat" (PTT, Vol. 122, p. 310-1,2), gives the list of twenty as in the *Mahāvyutpatti*, and, moreover, repeats for each of the aggregates the similes, "like a prince," "like an adornment," "like a servant," and "like a pot." Since his is a commentary on the words of the *Vinayavibhaṅga* (of the Mūlasarvāstivādin Vinaya), it follows that in all likelihood the *Mahāvyutpatti* list stems from this Vinaya, which was the only Vinaya accepted in Tibet. Vinītadeva, p. 310-1-4, explains that the reifying views are said to be like a mountain because they are difficult to shatter. Candrakīrti s expression "thunderbolt of enlightenment" (*bodhakuliśa*) also occurs in Vinītadeva's account by the same Tibetan translation, and with the explanation, "because the defilements that are simultaneously destroyed are eliminated by the path of vision (*darśana-mārga*)."

Notice the difference from the Pāli formulation of the four terms, which obey a pattern of quasi-inflections, "nominative," "genitive," "locative", "locative", as follows:

X is a self,
or the self has X,
or the self is in X,
or X is in the self.

The *Mahāvyutpatti* in common with the Mūlasarvāstivādin Vinaya has a list with a pattern of quasi-inflections, "nominative," "genitive," "genitive," "locative," as follows:

X is a self,
or the self has X,

or X belongs to the self,
or the self is in X.

In short, the *Mahāvyutpatti* reverses the third and fourth aspects, and substitutes "X belongs to the self" for "'X is in the self." While this is a definitely formal departure from the old Pāli Buddhist formulation, still in terms of the division into "nihilistic views" and "eternalistic views" it would make no difference. This is because in the *Mahāvyutpatti* account, the first one would also be "nihilistic view" and the next three, all involving the self as "other," would be "eternalistic" just as in the *Paṭisambhidāmagga*, n.b., if indeed the *Mahāvyutpatti* list belongs to a tradition which is classifying the twenty views, as "nihilistic" or "eternalistic", but this is not borne out.

Rahder's article shows that the *Vibhāṣā* cites the Abhidharma work *Jñānaprasthāna* which takes five of the views to be "view of self" (*ātmadṛṣṭi*), and the remaining fifteen to be "view of what belongs to self" (*ātmīyadṛṣṭi*); that this work mentions that the Buddha expressed the list of twenty views, and that Śāriputra when explaining them did not divide them into *ātmadṛṣṭi* and *ātmīyadṛṣṭi*.[13] It then appears that Śāriputra's explanation is the one found in the *Paṭisambhidāmagga*, with the division into "nihilistic views" and "eternalistic views." The *Jñānaprasthāna* classification also furnishes a reason for the difference between the *Mahāvyutpatti* list and the Pāli literary tradition, which is that the interpretation of the second, third, and fourth aspects as *ātmīyadṛṣṭi* favors the reinterpretation that substitutes "X belongs to the self" for "X is in the self." Hence, the *Jñānaprasthāna* is here consistent with the Mūlasarvastivādin Vinaya tradition preserved in Vinītadeva's commentary and with the *Mahāvyutpatti* list.[14]

We may now conclude that Nāgārjuna in his *Madhyamakakārikā*, Chap. XXII, is faithful to the old Buddhist scripture—he was probably using the canon known as the four Āgamas, including the *Saṃyuktāgama*—in that he uses the four terms, "X is a self," or "the self has X," or "the self is in X," or "X is in the

[13]RAHDER, "La satkāyadṛṣṭi," pp. 228-229.

[14]In agreement with this conclusion, notice that the *Vibhāṣā*, per Rahder, "La satkāyadṛṣṭi," p. 231, uses the terminology, (1) rūpa is the ātman, and so on, including, (2) vedanā is the ornament of ātman, (3) vedanā is the servant of ātman, (4) vedanā is the receptacle of ātman.

self," but of course denies each of them. Furthermore, in my retranslation of his verse XXII, 1, deciding that "not other" is a covering expression for denying the next three terms, we should note that Nāgārjuna has no implication of "not belonging to." Passing to Candrakīrti, he is presumably familiar with the alternate tradition and affected by it sufficiently to employ the terminology of a mountain with twenty peaks that is shattered by the "thunderbolt of enlightenment" (*bodhakuliśa*); but since he is following Nāgārjuna's school, the Mādhyamika, he does not depart from this in favor of the list which made its way into the *Mahāvyutpatti.*

One may appreciate further this distinction by noticing Nāgārjuna's treatment of the topic in *Madhyamaka-kārikā*, XVIII, 1-2. Thus, verse 1: "If the self were the aggregates (S. *skandha*), it would be subject to arising and passing away. If it were other than the aggregates, it would exclude the characteristic of aggregates."[15] And verse 2: "When there is no self, how will there be what belongs to self! By cessation of self and what belongs to self, there is neither 'I' or 'mine.'" Nāgārjuna expresses in these verses two quite different problems. Cessation of self automatically ends what belongs to self, but cessation of self *per se* does not end what is other than self.[16] Therefore, for him, the interpretation of the twenty aspects of the reifying view as a matter of self and other than self is incompatible with interpreting them as a matter of self and what belongs to self.[17] For Nāgārjuna, apparently in agreement with Śāriputra, if indeed he is responsible for what was recorded in the *Paṭisambhidāmagga*, the reifying view is not restricted to self and what belongs to self, but applies to self and what is other than self. Therefore, for him the

[15]For the last part of the verse: *bhaved askandhalakṣaṇaḥ*. Candrakīrti's *Prasannapadā* commentary, text, p. 343.2,3 explains:/*yathā hi gor anyo 'śvo na golakṣaṇo bhavati*/ "Just as a horse, being other than a cow, excludes the cow characteristic."

[16]As in Candrakīrti's illustration, when a cow characteristic passes away, this provides no information on what happens to a horse characteristic.

[17]In short, Nāgārjuna's verse XXII, 1, cited above (note 9) shows a rejection of the Abhidharma position espoused by Vasubandhu, *Abhidharmakośa*, Chap. V. tr., p. 17, who, restricting the *satkāyadṛṣṭi* to belief in "I" and "mine" shows an agreement with the Abhidharma tradition of the *Jñānaprasthāna*, and so on, as was discussed above.

"*kāya*" of the *satkāyadṛṣṭi* is not only the personal aggregates (S. *skandha*), but also anything that is other than those personal aggregates that could be understood as *kāya* (accumulation). This is consistent with classifying the 4X5 views as "nihilistic" or "eternalistic," since "nihilistic views" are *other than* "eternalistic views," and the ending of one set does not entail the ending of the other set, as would be the case when ending the view of self, the view of what belongs to self also ends.

The present writer hopes the foregoing can be considered the modest advance promised at the outset.

11

WHO UNDERSTANDS THE FOUR ALTERNATIVES OF THE BUDDHIST TEXTS?

INTRODUCTION

The Buddhist four alternatives are often referred to by their Sanskrit name *catuṣkoṭi,* and given in the form that something is, is not, both is and is not, neither is nor is not, with observation that each of these terms may be denied. As we proceed we shall see that this is not the only manner of presenting a *catuṣkoṭi.* Since so many authorities and scholars of ancient and modern times have discussed this cardinal matter, sometimes heatedly, it is not possible to deal with all the previous studies. Certain discussions will be considered herein within the scope of my five sections: I. The four alternatives and logic, II. The four alternatives in a disjunctive system, III. The four alternatives applied to causation, each denied, IV. The four alternatives applied to existence, each denied, V. The three kinds of *catuṣkoṭi,* various considerations.

My findings differ from those of the Western scholars that have come to my notice, and the differences stem from my having published a translation of Tibetan work that deals in several places with the formula[1]. In fact, Tsoṅ-kha-pa's separation of

[1]TSOṄ-KHA-PA'S *Lam rim chen mo,* the sections "Calming the Mind and Discerning the Real." The four-alternatives discussion occurs in the "Discerning the Real" section. See A. WAYMAN *Calming the Mind and Discerning the Real* (Columbia University, New York, 1978).

the causation and existence aspects of four alternatives, each denied, goes back to Atīśa (11th century), who in his *Bodhimārga-pradipa-pañjikā-nāma* presents four ways of realizing insight (*prajñā*), as follows:[2]

(1) the principle that denies existence by four alternatives (discussed in section IV herein).

(2) the principle called "diamond grain" (*vajrakaṇa*). He illustrates this in his text by Nāgārjuna's *Madhyamaka-kārikā* (M.K.), I. 1, with alternatives applied to causation (discussed in section III herein).

(3) the principle free from singleness and multiplicity. He appeals to such an author as Śāntideva (especially his *Bodhicaryāvatāra*, Chap. IX).

(4) the principle of Dependent Origination (*pratītyasamutpāda*). Here he means, for example, that the *dharmas* arise dependently and are void of self-existence.

Atīśa's classification is revealing of the meditative use put to the denial of four alternatives when applied to causation or to existence. The fact, then, that his listing does not allude to the disjunctive system of the four alternatives, that I discuss in section II, may be simply because this system was not put to meditative use.

The two topics of causation and existence relate to Buddhist teachings that are essentially distinct. Thus, in Buddhism the problem of how a Tathāgata or Buddha arises by reason of merit and knowledge, that is, the problem of cause, is distinct from the problem of the existence, for example, of the Tathāgata after death. Naturally, the causal topic is first, since a Tathāgata has to have arisen before there is a point to inquiring whether he exists after death. Historically, the first topic represents what the Buddha preferred to talk about, and the second topic includes matters which the Buddha sometimes refused to talk about.

As suggested earlier, my main sources are from Asian languages. I am also indebted to certain Western writers, namely, Hermann Weyl for the limitations of symbolic systems, Bernard Bosanquet for treatment of disjunctive statements, and Willard Van Orman Quine for his use of the world "logic" (bibliography herein).

[2]The passage is in the Tibetan Tanjur, photo edition, vol. 103, pp. 39-4-8 to 40-2-2.

1. The Four Alternatives and Logic

Jayatilleke says, "there is little evidence that Nāgārjuna understood the logic of the four alternatives as formulated and utilized in early Buddhism."[3] This scholar was not content with putting down Nāgārjuna, founder of the Mādhyamika school; for he concludes that scarcely any Western scholars, classical Indian scholars, or modern Indian and Japanese writers have comprehended this logic either. Richard H. Robinson, one of the Western scholars whose theories on the matter were rejected for the most part by Jayatilleke, subsequently replied to him,[4] among other things, questioning the use of the word "logic" to refer to the four alternatives. He had written an article entitled, "Some Logical Aspects of Nāgārjuna's System,"[5] which included a discussion of the four alternatives, and included a section entitled "Nāgārjuna's Logic" in his book (*Early Mādhyamika...*).[6] Chatalian, in turn, asserts that Robinson did not justify his use of the word "logic" in his book.[7] While agreeing with Chatalian thus far, I am still puzzled by Robinson and Chatalian for their overattention to other persons' use of the word "logic." Quine points out that while writers have used the term "logic" with varying scope, a common part of their usage is called "the science of necessary inference", although he admits that this is a vague description.[8] He then states that it is less vague to call *logical* certain locutions, including "if", "then", "and", "or", "not", "unless", "some", "all", "every", "any", "it", etc. Furthermore, he mentions that a set pattern of employing these locutions

[3]K. N. Jayatilleke, "The Logic of Four Alternatives," *Philosophy East and West*, 17: 1967): 82; hereafter cited as Jayatilleke, "Logic".

[4]Richard H. Robinson, book review of Jayatilleke, *Early Buddhist Theory*, *Philosophy East and West* 19, no. 1 (Jan., 1969): 72-81., see especially 75-76; hereafter cited as Robinson, book-review.

[5]Richard H. Robinson, "Some Logical Aspects of Nāgārjuna's System," "*Philosophy East and West* 6, no. 4 (Jan. 1957): 291-308.

[6]Richard H. Robinson, *Early Mādhyamika in India and China* (Madison, Wisc.: The University of Wisconsin Press, 1967), pp. 50-58: hereafter Robinson, *Early Mādhyamika*.

[7]G. Chatalian, "A Study of R. H. Robinson's *Early Mādhyamika in India and China*," *Journal of Indian Philosophy* 1 (1972), section II, Logic and Argument, pp. 315-325.

[8]Willard Van Orman Quine, *Elementary Logic* (New York: Harper & Row, 1965), pp. 1-3.

allows us to speak of the *logical structure*. This is tantamount to saying that every grammatical English sentence in the indicative mood has a logical structure. Then, when Nāgārjuna writes (*Madhyamaka-kārikā*, XVIII, 8), in an English translation, "all is genuine or is not genuine—" this has a logical structure. Indeed, every statement with the pattern, "Every X is an *a* or a *b*," has the same logical structure. Quine further qualifies a statement as *logically true* if its logical structure alone yields truth; and thus his use of the term "logic" involves truth and falsehood in this sense. Other writers have used such terms as "formally valid," "analytic proposition", or "tautology" as closely related to this usage of "logic."[9] Accordingly, the application of symbolic logic to Nāgārjuna's statements, to prove them logically true or false, goes along with such a title as "the logic of the four alternatives": and this application of symbolic logic has been engaged in by H. Nakamura, Robinson, Jayatilleke, R. S. Y. Chi, among others, including Shohei Ichimura in his recent dissertation, "A Study on Nāgārjuna's Method of Refutation." It does seem that both Jayatilleke and Robinson were justified in using the term "logic" in a study of these matters when they employed symbolic logic.

This still leaves the important problem of whether Nāgārjuna's statements are indeed *logically true*, and thus have truth or falseness according to their logical structure regardless of content, regardless of what is given. By "given," what is meant here is the usual "granted, assumed." This involves a problem of translation, because when Nāgārjuna's statements are assumed to be at hand, the mere fact that there are marks on a page in the English language purported to be his statements does not prove that they faithfully relay Nāgārjuna's intention by marks on a page in the original Sanskrit language. Here there are two points: If the statements do not have an easily isolated logical structure, it is hazardous and probably contraindicated to apply symbolic logic. Even if they do have an easily isolated logical structure, one asks if they are also so complicated that one requires a symbolic representation to sift or show truth and falsehood.

[9]Confer, Hermann Weyl, *Philosophy of Mathematics and Natural Science* (Princeton, N. J.: Princeton University Press, 1949), p. 13; hereafter cited as Weyl, *Philosophy*.

We may start to solve this problem with its two points, by recourse to Weyl's remarks regarding "constructive cognition":[10] "By the introduction of symbols the assertions are split so that one part of the [mental] operations is shifted to the symbols and thereby made independent of the given and its continued existence. Thereby the free manipulation of concepts is contrasted with their application, ideas become detached from reality and acquire a relative independence." Thus Weyl, an eminent mathematician, is frank to admit that the pure operations of mathematics are independent of the existence of the given. In the case of the *catuṣkoṭi,* the given is a rather considerable corpus of material in the Pāli scriptures and then in Nāgārjuna's works, not to speak of contributions by later Asian authors. And there is the assumption that this corpus is at hand in a translated form of English sentences that are susceptible, in whole or part, of being converted from their natural form to the artificial language of a symbolic system.

Now to the first point. Let us assume that the *catuṣkoṭi* statements do not have an isolatable logical structure, and yet symbolic logic is utilized. If one would grant the applicability of Weyl's remarks, even if there were a valid utilization of symbolic logic, it could not account for the full corpus of the given, as the "given" has been explicated earlier. So it may be merely a section or subset of the given whose logical structure is not isolatable. But then the application of symbolic logic is a matter of mastering the art of the symbols. And so one may presume that it is an arrogated comprehension of the given—although in fact the symbols are independent, partially or wholly, of the given—whereby an undeniably brilliant writer as Jayatilleke takes the stance that he virtually alone understands "the logic of the four alternatives," while claiming that such a renowned author as Nāgārjuna cannot understand it! Or claiming that a modern writer like Robinson cannot understand, because he does not apply the formal symbolic system right, that is, has not mastered the art. Thus the symbolic system becomes a vested interest, the users jealous of its misuse, while they champion its misapplication to the given, and even to what may not be at hand, for example, a correct translation of a passage from an ancient text.

10WEYL, *Philosophy*, pp. 37-38.

Then to the second point. I do not propose to denigrate, in general, the employment of symbolic systems for representing propositions of Indian philosophy. But are the *catuṣkoṭi* statements so complicated that a symbolic restatement is necessary, with the implication of an understanding already at hand to certify the necessity? Perhaps there is working a psychological factor which could be called "wonder." What mathematics student getting the "right answer" with calculus has not at times felt a wonder at the ability of the mathematics—beyond his native capacities—say, to determine the intercepted volume of the cone? As Buytendijk has been cited: "Wonder is characterized by a halting of the thing observed. This halting, which men call attention, is at the same time permeated by a premonition that light may be shed on this thing."[11] But this premonition of light through the symbolic system is a will-o'-the-wisp, a subtle infatuation. Because light can only be shed on the given, and the symbolic system is independent, in whole or part, of the given as it has been described earlier. It is like a person fascinated by a brilliant lamp and therefore is not seeing anything illumined by the lamp. The master of the art is himself mastered and uses the symbolism willy-nilly: even for the simplest computation, he needs the computer. For centuries the Buddhists believed that the given of the four alternatives, including the traditional exegesis, provides sufficient material for understanding—if a person can understand. Some of the modern writers have rendered the discussions into an artificial language, and then have dwelt on false issues of whether this or that scholar's formulation is a "logic."

II. The Four Alternatives in a Disjunctive System

Here by a "disjunctive system" is meant a system of statements subject to the judgment "A is either B or C." Either B or C is left and one of these two is excluded. Such a judgment appears to be involved in the Indian syllogism, whose "reason" (*hetu*) is relevant to the "thesis" (*sādhya*) when the case referred to in the thesis is agreed to be present in similar cases and absent in

[11]Cornelis Verhoeven, *The Philosophy of Wonder* trans. Mary Foran (New York: The Macmillan Company, 1967), p. 38.

dissimilar cases.[12] Anyway, the disjunctive judgment is a form of inference (*anumāna*), and for a particular system it is necessary to state the rule of the disjunction. Jayatilleke has shown that various systems of four alternatives found in the early Buddhist texts are in a disjunctive system whose rule seems to be that when one of the alternatives is taken as "true" the rest are certainly false. He points to such systems as: "A person is wholly happy... unhappy;...both happy and unhappy;...neither happy nor unhappy". "X is a person who torments himself; ... torments others; ... both torments himself as well as others; ...who neither torments himself nor others".[13] Bosanquet has an apt illustration:[14] "I suppose that the essence of such a system lies in arrangements for necessarily closing every track to all but one at a time of any tracts which cross it or converge into it. The track X receives trains from A, B, C, D; if the entrance for those from A is open, B, C, and D are *ipso facto* closed; if A, B, and C are closed, D is open, and so on."

But the matter is not without complications. The Pāli work *Kathāvatthu* records a dispute between the two Buddhist sects Theravāda and Andhaka about the nature of the meditative state which is called in Pāli *nevasaññānāsaññāyatana* (the base of neither the *saññā* nor non-*saññā*), where *sañā* means something like "idea", and the disagreement was over the presence or absence of *saññā* in that state. The section concludes with an appeal to the case of the "neutral feeling" (the neither-pleasure-nor-pain), thus consistent with the traditional Indian syllogism which uses, as example, something well known to society (*lokaprasiddha*). Just as it would not be cogent to ask if that neutral feeling were either pleasure or pain, so is it not proper to assert there either is or is not *saññā* on the basis of neither the *saññā* nor non-*saññā*.[15] This conclusion agrees with the previous observation that only one of the four alternatives is the case at a

[12]Confer, Th. Stcherbatsky, *Buddhist Logic* (New York: Dover Publication, 1962), vol. 1, pp. 242-245.

[13]Jayatilleke, "Logic", pp. 70-71.

[14]Bernard Bosanquet, *The Essentials of Logic* (London: Macmillan and Co., 1948), p. 125: hereafter Bosanquet, *The Essentials of Logic*.

[15]Confer in translation of the *Kathāvatthu*, *Points of Controversy*, by Shwe Zan Aung and Mrs. Rhys Davids (London: Pali Text Society, 1915), pp. 155-156, where the term *saññā* is rendered "consciousness."

particular time. Besides, we learn that the "neither...nor" alternative points to a neutrality with indeterminate content.

Jayatilleke quite properly explains the third alternative: "S is *partly* P and *partly* non-P".[16] Thus for the content of the third alternative, stated as "the universe is both finite and infinite," the *Brahma-jāla Sutta* explains this as when one has the idea (*saññī*) that the world is finite in the upward and downward directions, and has the idea that the world is infinite across. In agreement, Nāgārjuna states in his *Madhyamaka-kārikā*, XXVII, 17-18:

> If the same place (*ekadeśa*) that is divine were the same place that is human, it would be (both) permanent and impermanent. That is not feasible. If "both the permanent and the impermanent" were proven, one must also grant that the pair "neither the permanent nor the impermanent" is proven.

One should note about this passage (Jayatilleke mistranslates and misunderstands it),[17] that Nāgārjuna does not here deny an alternative of "both the permanent and the impermanent" per se; he denies this for one and the same place. This can be illustrated by his own verse (MK XXV, 14, cited later), implying that *nirvāṇa* is present in the Buddha and absent in ordinary persons, but not present and absent in the same place. Nāgārjuna, in the present verses (XXVII, 17-18), also makes explicit his position that the fourth alternative (neither the permanent nor the impermanent) is derived from the third one, and that the third one (both the permanent and the impermanent) combines the presumed first one (the permanent) and the second one (the impermanent).

This brings up Nāgārjuna's remarkable verse (MK XVIII, 8):

> All (*sarva*) is genuine (*tathyam*),[18] or is not genuine, or is both genuine and not genuine, or is neither genuine nor not-genuine. That is the ranked instruction (*anuśāsana*) of the Buddha.

According to Candrakīrti's commentary "all" means the personality aggregates (*skandha*), the realms (*dhātu*), and the sense bases

[16]JAYATILLEKE, "Logic," p. 79.

[17]Ibid., p. 82.

[18]My rendition "genuine" is close to the dictionary. Confer, the negative forms *atathya* ("untrue, unreal") and *avitatha* ("not untrue, not futile").

(*āyatana*).[19] See, along the same lines, Kalupahana's discussion[20] about the "Discourse on "Everything'" (*Sabbasutta*), available both in the Pāli canon and in the Āgama version in Chinese translation. Therefore the word "all" in Nāgārjuna's verse amounts to "anything," where the "anything" is any entity chosen from the set of "all" entities according to the Buddhist meaning, as just expounded. This agrees with Bosanquet's observation that the content of the disjunctive judgment "A is either B or C" "is naturally taken as an individual, being necessarily concrete."[21]

Next, the interpretation of the word *anuśāsana* as "ranked instruction" comes from observing it among the three "marvels" (*prātihārya*) of the Buddha's teaching. of which the first one is "magical performance" (*ṛddhi*), the second is "mind reading", (*ādeśanā*), and the third, "ranked instruction" (*anuśāsana*), apparently made possible by the preceding "mind reading."[22] This interpretation is confirmed in Vasubandhu's *Buddhānusmṛti-ṭīkā*, saying in part, "...with the three kinds of marvels observing the streams of consciousness of the noble Śāriputra, and so on, and of other fortunate sentient beings, teaches the true nature of the Śrāvakayāna exactly according to their expectations and their potentialities."[23] This only clarifies why Candrakīrti's commentary on the verse interprets it as a ranking, and not why his commentary interprets the ranking as follows:

(a) The Buddha taught to worldly beings the personal aggregates, the realms, and sense bases, with their various enumerations, in a manner that "all is genuine" in order to lead them onto the path by having them admire his omniscience about all these elements. (b) After these beings had come to trust

[19]In translation, see J. W. DE JONG, *Cinq chapitres dela Prasannapadā* (Paris: Paul Geuthner, 1949), p. 27: "il a enseigné que ces agrégats, éléments et bases ... sont vrais." Hereafter cited as de Jong *Cinq chapitres*.

[20]D. J. KALUPAHANA, "A Buddhist Tract on Empiricism," *Philosophy East and West* 19, no. 1 (Jan., 1969), 65-67.

[21]*The Essentials of Logic* pp. 123-124.

[22]See FRANKLIN EDGERTON, *Buddhist Hybrid Sanskrit Dictionary*, p. 392, under *prātihārya*. Here the form *anuśāsanī* is used.

[23]Tibetan Tanjur, photo edition, vol. 104, pp. 33-5-8 to 34-1-1:.. 'phags pa Śā-ri'i bu la sogs pa daṅ/de las gźan pa skal pa daṅ ldan pa.rnams kyi sems can gyi rgyud la gzigs nas cho 'phrul gsum bstan pas bsam pa ji lta ba daṅ/ skal pa ji lta ba bźin du ñan thos kyi theg pa'i chos ñid ston ciṅ...1

the Lord, it was safe to inform them about all those divisions of the world that "all is not genuine", i.e. "all is spurious", because they momentarily perish and change. (c) Certain select disciples could be told 'all is both genuine and not-genuine'. That is, that the same element which is genuine to the ordinary person is not-genuine or spurious to the noble person who is the Buddha's disciple. He tells them this, so they may become detached, i.e. not see it in just one way. (d) To certain advanced disciples, far progressed in viewing reality and scarcely obscured, he taught that "all is neither genuine nor not-genuine", just as in the case of the son of a barren woman, one asserts that the son is neither white nor black (=non-white).[24]

However, he seems to be following, in his own way, the four "allegories" or "veiled intentions" (*abhisaṃdhi*) which are listed and then defined in the *Mahāyāna-Sūtrālaṃkāra*, XII, 16-17.[25] The first one is *avatāraṇa-abhi°* (the veiled intention so they will enter), explained as teaching that form, and so forth, is existent, so as not to scare the *śrāvakas* from entering the Teaching. The second one is *lakṣaṇa-abhi°* (the veiled intention about the character, namely, of *dharmas*), explained as teaching that all *dharmas* are without self-existence, without origination, etc. The third one is *pratipakṣa-abhi°* (the veiled intention about opponents, namely, to faults), explained as teaching by taking into account the taming of faults. So far these terms agree quite well with Candrakīrti's exposition. For example, in the case of the third one, the application to Nāgārjuna's line "all is both genuine and not-genuine" is the opposition (*pratipakṣa*) to the fault of one-sidedness. It is the fourth one whose relevance is obscure: this is the *pariṇāmana-abhi°* (the veiled intention about changeover, namely, to reality). In illustration, the *Sūtrālaṃkāra* cites a verse: "Those who take the pithless as having a pith abide in waywardness. Those who are mortified with the pains [for austere endeavor] [abide] in the best enlightenment." Candrakīrti is at least partially consistent by saying "to certain

[24]I have summarized. In full translation, see de Jong, *Cinq chapitres* pp. 27-28.

[25]*Asaṅga: Mahāyāna-Sūtrālaṃkāra*, édité par Sylvain Lévi (Paris, 1907)., p. 82.

advanced disciples, far progressed in viewing reality," because these ones would take the pithless as pithless.

Jayatilleke[26] refers to the same passage of Candrakīrti's and to a different commentary on Nāgārjuna's verse in the *Prajñāpāramitāśāstra*, both as presented in Robinson's book,[27] to deny that in the verse cited above, the four alternatives are in a "relation of exclusive disjunction" and to claim that they amount to the non-Buddhist relativistic logic of the Jains. However, Candrakīrti's commentary is consistent with Nāgārjuna's MK XXVII, 17-18 (translated earlier, herein) concerning the dependence of the subsequent alternative on the previous one or ones.

Jayatilleke's hostility to Candrakīrti's commentary on the verse may stem from the modern Theravādin's reluctance to attribute a ranked instruction to the Buddha. Ordinarily the canonical passage cited in this connection is, as Thomas renders it: "Buddha replied, "What does the Order expect of me? I have taught the Doctrine without making any inner and outer, and herein the Tathāgata has not the closed fist of a teacher with regard to doctrines.' "[28] From the modern Theravādin standpoint, Candrakīrti's explanation attributes to the Buddha precisely such an inner and outer, because it portrays the Buddha teaching worldly beings (=the outer) in the realistic manner, and then teaching those beings once they had become disciples (=the inner) in the illusional manner. And going on with a still different teaching to certain advanced disciples. But that same scriptural passage from the traditional, last sermon of the Buddha could be taken differently than it usually is, and perhaps consistently with Nāgārjuna's verse as Candrakīrti understood it. That is because the original Pāli (*Dīgha-Nikāya*, ii, 100) reads: *mayā dhammo anantaraṃ abāhiraṃ karitvā* ("By me was the Dhamma preached without inner, without outer"). The phrase "without inner, without outer" can be restated as "with neither an inner nor an outer." And then just as the "neutral feeling" (neither pleasure nor pain) is not either pleasure or pain, so also one could not determine if the Buddha's doctrine was either inner or outer,

26JAYATILLEKE, "Logic," p. 82.

27ROBINSON, *Early Mādhyamika*. pp. 56-57.

28EDWARD J. THOMAS, *The Life of Buddha* (New York: Barnes & Noble, 1952), p. 146.

and one homogeneous character, wearisome by repetition of the same doctrine over and over again. Nāgārjuna's verse, by use of the word *anuśāsana*, seems to mean that the Tathāgata, without the closed fist, would gladly communicate in a graduated manner so that disciples in different stages of progress could have a teaching suited to their particular level. While this position may not be agreeable to some modern exponents of the Theravāda tradition, it is not a "Mahāyāna" quarrel with the earlier "Hīnayāna" school, because also Buddhaghosa of the Theravāda tradition in his *Atthasālinī* insists that the Buddha's teaching was fittingly modified in accordance with the varying inclinations of both men and gods.[29]

III. The Four Alternatives Applied to Causation, Each Denied

Starting with the Buddha's first sermon, the four Noble Truths have been a basic ingredient of Buddhist thinking and attitudes. Of these Truths, the first is the Noble Truth of Suffering; and of the fourth Truth, the Noble Truth of Path explained with eight members, the first member is called "right views" (*samyag-dṛṣṭi*). Sometimes "right views" were established by determining and eliminating the wrong views. So in the Pāli *Saṃyutta-Nikāya* (II, 19-21),[30] the Buddha, replying to questions by Kassapa (Kāśyapa), denied that suffering is caused by oneself, by another, by both oneself and another, or neither by oneself nor by another. Then, in answer to further questions, the Buddha stated that he knows suffering and sees it. Then Kassapa asked the Buddha to explain suffering to him, and was told that claiming the suffering was done by oneself amounts to believing that one is the same person as before, which is the eternalistic view; while claiming that the experiencer of the suffering is different from the one who caused it, amounts to the nihilistic view. Thereupon the Buddha taught the Dharma by a mean, namely, the series of twelve members which begin with the statement "having nescience as condition

[29]*The Expositor* (*Atthasālinī*), trans. Pe Maung Tin, edited and revised by Mrs. Rhys Davids, vol. 1 and 2 (London: Luzac & Company, 1958 reprint), 1:246; 2:318-319.

[30]As cited by I. B. Horner, *Buddhist Texts Through the Ages*, ed. by Edward Conze (Oxford: Bruno Cassirer, 1954), pp. 68-69, and my summary.

the motivations arise" and continue with similar statements through the rest of dependent origination (*pratītya-samutpāda*). The Buddha proceeded to teach that by the cessation of nescience, the motivations cease, and so on, with the cessation of this entire mass of suffering. In agreement, Nāgārjuna's *Madhyamaka-kārikā*, I, 1 states:

> There is no entity anywhere that arises from itself, from another, from both (itself and another), or by chance.

In this case the given element is called the "entity" (*bhāva*). The first two of the denied alternatives have the given element of "cessation" (*nirodha*) in MK VII, 32. The element is "suffering" (*duḥkha*) or "external entity" (*bāhya-bhāva*) in MK XII. The meaning of the denial here is aptly stated by Bosanquet: "Negation of a disjunction would mean throwing aside the whole of some definite group of thoughts as fallacious, and going back to begin again with a judgment of the simplest kind. It amounts to saying. 'None of your distinctions touch the point; you must begin afresh.' "[31] In the discourse to Kassapa, to begin afresh amounts to accepting "dependent origination." This is also Nāgārjuna's position, following the ancient discourse to Katyāyana, as mentioned later in the *Madhyamaka-kārikā*, and as stated in Candrakīrti's *Madhyamakāvatāra*, VI, 114:

> Since entities do not arise by chance, (i.e.) from a lord, and so on (primal matter, time, atoms, *svabhāva*, Puruṣa, Nārāyaṇa, etc.), or from themselves, others, or both (themselves and others) then they arise in dependence (on causes and conditions).[32]

Besides, to begin afresh amounts to the establishment of voidness (*śūnyatā*), for so the *Anavatapta* (*nāgarāja*) *paripṛcchā* is cited: "Any (thing) that is born (in dependence) on conditions, is not born (to wit): The birth of this (thing) does not occur by self-existence (*svabhāva*). Any (thing) that is dependent on conditions, is declared void. Any person who understands voidness,

[31] Bosanquet, *The Essentials of Logic*, p. 125.

[32] Here translated from the Tibetan in the context of Tsoṅ-kha-pa's *Lam rim chen mo*, "Discerning the Real" section. See Wayman, *Calming the Mind and Discerning the Real.*

is heedful."[33] Since Nāgārjuna begins his *Madhyamaka-kārikā* with this theory of causation, it is reasonable to assume that it is essential for the rest of his work. Also, since voidness ((*śūnyatā*) is established in the course of the causal denials, it is taken for granted in the denial in terms of existence, and so the attempt to establish voidness by way of existence becomes a faulty point of view (*dṛṣṭi*), as in MK XXII, 11:

> One should not say "It's void," nor "it's non-void," nor "It's both (void and non-void)," nor "It's neither." But it may be said in the meaning of designation.

One should not say, "It's void," because the four alternatives applied to existence cannot establish voidness. But in the meaning of designation (*prajñaptyartham*), as in the celebrated verses (MK XXIV, 18-19), there is the act of calling dependent origination "voidness" and the *dharmas* so arising "void"; and here Nāgārjuna adds that the act of calling when there is the dependency, is the middle path.[34]

Besides, the denial of the four alternatives in the scope of causation (confer, MK I, 1, earlier) was aimed at four philosophical positions, as follows:[35]

1. The denial of arising from itself is the rejection of the

[33]For the various occurrences of the important verse, see LOUIS DE LA VALLÉE Poussin, *Mūlamadhyamakakārikās de Nāgārjuna avec la Prasannapadā Commentaire de Candrakīrti*, Bibliotheca Buddhica, vol. 4 (St-Pétersbourg, 1903-1913), p. 239.

[34]Here I accept Matilal's correction of my earlier stated position; confer. Bimal Krishna Matilal,*Epistemology, Logic, and Grammar in Indian Philosophical Analysis* (The Hague : Mouton, 1971), p. 148-149; hereafter cited as Matilal, *Epistemology, Logic, and Grammar.* But now my understanding only partially agrees with his, to wit, "Dependent origination=Emptiness= Dependent designation=The Middle Way." Because I would say that as far as Nāgārjuna is concerned, dependent origination is the way things happen and that it is voidness, while the *dharmas* so arising are void, whether one recognizes this to be the case. But while his school designates dependent origination voidness, this is not what every other Buddhist sect does; and Nāgārjuna goes on to add that the act of so designating, when there is the dependence, is indeed the middle path. So it is not voidness that is designation.

[35]Here I have taken suggestions from the context of the *Lam rim chen mo* when *MK* I, 1 is cited, and from the annotational comments of the Tibetan work called *Mchan bźi.*

Sāṃkhya position, which is the *satkāryavāda* (causation of the effect already existent). Murti is certainly right on this point.[36]

2. The denial of arising from another rejects the creator being (*īśvara*), and Kalupahana increases the list from a Jaina source for "caused by another": destiny (*niyati*), time (*kāla*), God (*īśvara*), nature (*svabhāva*), and action (*karma*). The later Buddhist logicians held a theory of "efficiency" that belongs here.[37] Murti incorrectly puts this kind of denial under the heading of *asatkāryavāda* (the non-existence of an effect before its production).[38]

3. The denial of arising from both itself and another is the rejection of the Vaiśeṣika, who say the clay pot arises from itself (clay) and from the potter, wheel, sticks, etc. In fact, this theory is in both the Nyāya and Vaiśeṣika philosophy, which Dasgupta,[39] in agreement with Shastri,[40] calls the *asatkāryavāda*, the opposite of the Sāṃkhya's *satkāryavāda*. Here, the clay is the material cause; the stick, wheel, etc., the instrumental cause.

4. The denial of arising without a cause (or by chance), is the rejection of the Lokāyata (the ancient materialistic school), which espouses the arising from self-nature.[41] That school held that consciousness is just a mode of the four elements (fire,

[36] T. R. V. Murti, *The Central Philosophy of Buddhism* (London : George Allen and Unwin, 1955), pp. 168-169.

[37] Confer, David J. Kalupahana, *Causality : The Central Philosophy of Buddhism* (Honolulu : The University Press of Hawaii, 1975), pp. 5, 46. For the theory of the Buddhist logicians as later expressed by Ratnakīrti, see Surendranath Dasgupta, *A History of Indian Philosophy*, vol. I (London : Cambridge University Press, 1932), 1:158-159. This is a theory that "efficiency" (*arthakriyākāritva*) can produce anything, and so a momentary, efficient entity is the "other" from which something may arise. The stream of consciousness is held to be of this nature, with one "moment" of consciousness giving rise to the next one. Hereafter cited as Kalupahana, *Causality*.

[38] Murti. *The Central Philosophy*, p. 170. misused the term *asatkāryavāda* (for the correct usage, see below).

[39] *A History of Indian Philosophy*. 1:320.

[40] Dharmendra Nath Shastri. *Critique of Indian Realism* (Agra : Agra University, 1964), p. 236.

[41] See now Kalupahana, *Causality*, pp. 25ff, for a valuable discussion of the *svabhāvavāda* in connection with the ancient Materialists, and on p. 31 he admits for them the appelation 'non-causationists' (*ahetuvāda*).

air, water, earth): consciousness is not the effect of another consciousness.[42]

Hence, there is no denial of arising per se, but the alternatives are meant to deny the arising falsely ascribed to certain agencies, to wit, itself, another, both itself and another, or by chance. This, then, is one of the "right views."

V. The Four Alternatives Applied to Existence, Each Denied

The Buddha rejected each of the four alternatives regarding the existence after death of the Tathāgata, because none of the four are relevant (*na upeti*), or defined (*avyākata*).[43] Nāgārjuna devotes *Madhyamaka-kārikā*, chap. XXV to the same topic, saying generally (XXV, 22): "Since all given things (**vastu*)[44] are void, what is endless, what with end, what both endless and with end, what neither endless or with end?" This refers to the celebrated fourteen "undefined given things" (*avyākṛta-vastūni*).[45] So in the chapter, *nirvāṇa* is treated in verses 5, 8, 13, 16; and the Lord before and after cessation, in verses 17, 18. For example, this is verse 17: "One should not infer[46] that the Lord exists after cessation (i.e. in Nirvāṇa). One should not infer that he does not

[42]The *Tattvasangraha of Śāntarakṣita with the Commentary of Kamalaśīla*, trans. by Ganganatha Jha, vol. 2 (Baroda : Oriental Institute, 1939), pp. 887-888.

[43]Cf. Jayatilleke, "Logic," p. 81; and K. N. Jayatilleke, *Early Buddhist Theory of Knowledge* (London : George Allen & Unwin, 1963), pp. 473-474.

[44]While the verse in Sanskrit has the locative plural *dharmeṣu* rather than *vastuṣu*, Candrakīrti's commentary makes it clear that the latter word is intended, because he promptly talks of the fourteen *avyākṛta-vastūni* and does not mention any *dharma-s*: while in the Tibetan translation of the verse, instead of the standard translation for *dharma* (T. *chos*), one finds the term *dṅos po*, which is frequently used to translate *vastu;* confer, Takashi Hirano, *An Index to the Bodhicaryāvatāra Pañjikā, Chapter IX* (Tokyo: Suzuki Research Foundation, 1966), pp. 273-276.

[45]Edward J. Thomas, *The History of Buddhist Thought* (London : Routledge & Kegan Paul, 1963 reprint), p. 124, states that they are actually four, but become fourteen by stating them in different ways.

[46]My translation "should not infer" is for the Sanskrit *nohyate*. The verb *ūh-* has a number of meanings, including "to infer", and the latter meaning is more associated with the verb root when there is the prefix *abhi*, with such a form as *abhyūhya*" having inferred."

exist, or both (exists and does not exist), or neither." Hence the rejections, again, are aimed against all philosophical positions that resort to inference or to ordinary human reason in such matters.[47] The failure of reasoning is clearly expressed in the Mahāyāna work *Ratnagotravibhāga* (chap. I, verse 9) when denying the four alternatives about the Dharma-sun as the ultimate nature:

> I bow to that Dharma-sun which is not existence and not non-existence, not both existence and non-existence, neither different from existence nor from non-existence; which cannot be reasoned (*aśakyas tarkayitum*), is free from definition (*nirukty-apagataḥ*), revealed by introspection, and quiescent; and which, pervasively shining with immaculate vision, removes the attachment, antipathy, and (eye-) cauls toward all objects.[48]

The question arises whether it is proper to interpret this to involve denial in Bosanquet's meaning, what he calls, "contrary negation."[49] "As we always speak and think within a general subject or universe of discourse, it follows that every denial substitutes some affirmation for the judgment which it denies." One could argue that simply to deny one judgment and thereby affirm another judgment would be a process of thinking that is negated by the goal alluded to in the preceding passage, since the Dharma-sun "cannot be reasoned." However, if Bosanquet's statement were altered to read "every denial substitutes some affirmation for the denial," it then appears to suit the state of

[47]This conclusion, however, goes against various speculative solutions that have been advanced to determine particular schools to go with the various denials applied to existence, namely, those of Jayatilleke. *Early Buddhist Theory of Knowledge*, pp. 243ff.: Murti. *The Central Philosophy*, pp. 130-131: K. V. Ramanan, *Nāgārjuna's Philosophy* (Varanasi : Bharatiya Vidya Prakashan, 1971), pp. 155-158. It is noteworthy that there is little agreement between these authors' solutions, and their arbitrariness itself stems from human reason, while to counter such positions Nāgārjuna would also have had to use ordinary human reason.

[48]*The Ratnagotravibhāga Mahāyānottaratantraśāstra*. ed. E. H. Johnston (Patna : Bihar Research Society, 1950), pp. 10-11 : Confer, also Jikido Takasaki, *A Study on the Ratnagotravibhāga* (*Uttaratantra*) Roma : Instituto Italiano per il Medio ed Estremo Oriente, 1966), pp. 163-166.

[49]Bosanquet, *The Essentials of Logic*, p. 129.

affairs alluded to in the passage above. In short, the whole system of four alternatives would be denied in this contrary negation, thus to suggest the retirement of convention (*saṃvṛti*) in favor of absolute truth (*paramārtha-satya*).

In the preceding illustrations, it is the Tathāgata or the Dharma or Nirvāṇa which is affirmed as the affirmation of absolute truth in the process of the denials, because these denials are a meditative act—and acts succeed where theories fail—which downgrades the role of inference and human reason generally, and upholds the role of vision, so—as Atīśa indicated—to promote insight (*prajñā*).

Therefore, it is now possible to evaluate two interpretations which seem to be starkly contrasted: (1) Murti's "The Mādhyamika denies metaphysics not because there is no real for him; but because it is inaccessible to Reason. He is convinced of a higher faculty, Intuition (*prajñā*)...."[50] (2) Streng's, "In Nāgārjuna's negative dialectic the power of reason is an efficient force for realizing Ultimate Truth."[51] One could argue that the disagreement is deceptive, since if reason is to be taken as the mental process of making the denials which substitute an affirmation of the Real or Ultimate Truth, then indeed while the Real is inaccessible to reason, it cannot be denied that reason brought about that higher faculty, the supernal insight (*prajñā*), to which the Real is accessible, This very point is made in the *Kāśyapa-parivarta:*

> Kāśyapa, it is this way: example, for when two trees are rubbed together by the wind, and fire arises (from the friction), (that fire) having arisen, burns the two trees. In the same way. Kāśyapa, (when given things are analysed) by the most pure discrimination (*pratyavekṣaṇā*). the faculty of noble insight is born; and (that Fire) having been born, (it) burns up that most pure discrimination itself.[52]

Hence, the very discrimination which is the kind of reasoning

[50]MURTI, *The Central Philosophy*, p. 126.

[51]FREDERICK J. STRENG. *Emptiness : A Study in Religious Meaning* (Nashville. Tenn.: Abingdon Press, 1967), p. 149.

[52]The passage is translated in the context of its citation in Tsoṅ-kha-pa's *Lam rim chen mo*. It is number 69 in A. Staël-Holstein. ed., *Kāśyapaparivarta*, (Commercial Press, 1926), but original Sanskrit is not extant for this passage.

that denies the alternatives is described metaphorically as a friction which arouses the fire of insight that in turn destroys this kind of reasoning.

Turning to Tsoṅ-kha-pa's section,[53] defending the denial of the four alternatives, this concerns the presence and absence of entities. Tsoṅ-kha-pa states that there are only two possibilities for an entity, that is, accomplished by own-nature, and efficient. Then, if the first alternative is stated in the form, "An entity exists," this is denied—the denial meaning to the Prāsaṅgika-Mādhyamika that, in the case of both truths (*saṃvṛti* and *paramārtha*), one denies that an entity exists accomplished by own-nature, while the efficient entity is denied in the *paramārtha* or absolute sense but not conventionally.

Likewise, the Prāsaṅgika-Mādhyamika rejects the nonexistence of an entity, should someone affirm the nonexistence of an entity accomplished by own-nature among the unconstructed (*asaṃskṛta*) natures (*dharma*).

Likewise, this Mādhyamika rejects the simultaneity of existence of that sort of entity with the nonexistence of the other sort of entity. And he rejects that there are neither, even one accomplished by own-nature.

While I have insisted that the ultimate nature is affirmed by the four denials, it should be granted that the acceptance of this absolute in Nāgārjuna's Mādhyamika is a matter much disputed by Western scholars; de Jong's thoughtful article[54] on the topic deserves consultation. In any case, Candrakīrti's position is clear, as he states in his own commentary on the *Madhyamakāvatāra:*

> Regarding this sort of *svabhāva* (self-existence) as written in particular (*Madhyamaka-kārikā*, XV, 1-2), received from the mouth of the ācārya (=Nāgārjuna), does it exist? (In answer:) As to its authorization, the Bhagavat proclaimed that whether Tathāgatas arise or do not arise, this true nature of dharmas abides, and so on, extensively. The "true nature" (*dharmatā*) (of that text, =*svabhāva*) (necessarily) exists. Which (elements)

[53]Referred to in note 1, herein. There were many Tibetan controversies on this issue.

[54]J. W. DE JONG. "The Problem of the Absolute in the Madhyamaka school," *Journal of Indian Philosophy* 2 (1972): 1-6.

> have this "true nature"? These, the eye, etc. have this *svabhāva*. And what is their *svabhāva*? Their uncreate nature and their non-dependence on another; the self-nature which is to be understood by knowledge (in *āryasamāpatti*) free from the caul of nescience (and its associated habit-energy). When it is asked, "Does that sort of thing exist?" who would answer, "No."? If it does not exist, for which goal do the Boddhisattvas cultivate the path of the perfections? For what reason do the Bodhisattvas, in order to comprehend the true-nature, assume myriads of difficulties that way?[55]

In short, Candrakīrti explains the *svabhāva* of MK XV, 1-2, as the "true nature" of the scriptures, and in a manner equivalent to the *dharma*-sun of the *Ratnagotravibhāga* passage.[56]

Finally, the denials concerning existence are also referred to as the rejection of four "views" (*dṛṣṭi*). So MK XXVII, 13:

> Thus whatever the view concerning the past, whether "I existed," "I did not exist," "I both (existed and did not exist)," "I neither (existed, nor did not exist)," it is not valid.

Such passages undoubtedly support the frequent claim that the Mādhyamika rejects all "views." But note that the views here are of existence, not of causation; and that Nāgārjuna elsewhere adheres to the view of Dependent Origination, which in Buddhism would be counted as a "right view" (*samyag-dṛṣṭi*).

V. The Three Kinds of Catuṣkoṭi, Various Considerations

It might be argued that there are not really three "kinds" of

[55]The passage occurs in the Tibetan Tanjur, photo edition. vol. 98, pp. 151-2-3 to 151-2-7. immediately preceded by Candrakīrti's citation of *MK* XV, 1-2 I have translated it in *Lam rim chen mo* context.

[56]While it is not possible to deal here with the many misconceptions in Ives Waldo, "Nāgārjuna and Analytic Philosophy." *Philosophy East and West* 25, no. 3 (July, 1975), one may observe that Candrakīrti's passage directly contradicts his remarks (p. 283) that the acceptance of "relational conditions" (*pratyaya*) entails a denial both of *svabhāva* and of nonrelational "significant events." Because Candrakīrti accepts, as does Buddhism generally, the *pratyaya* in the causal chain of Dependent Origination, and yet he also insists here upon the *svabhāva* as well as on a significance (the *bodhisattva's* goal) that is perhaps nonrelational.

catuṣkoṭi but simply different applications of *the catuṣkoṭi*. Perhaps an exaggeration of contrast is involved in using the word "kinds." Still I feel the word is necessary to counter the frequent discussion of the *catuṣkoṭi* as though *the catuṣkoṭi* is at hand and the only difficulty is in how to explain it. Hence we may observe that the first kind of *catuṣkoṭi*, in a disjunctive system, is explanatory of the individual propositions, and thus serves as an introduction to the next two kinds or uses of the *catuṣkoṭi*, to wit, to apply to the problem of causation or to the problem of existence. There were disputes concerning each of the three kinds, but it is especially the causation and existence applications of the four alternatives that occasioned spirited disagreements between the two main schools of the Mādhyamika—the Prāsaṅgika and the Svātantrika—disagreements which would require too many technical explanations to be treated in this article.

Moreover, all three kinds of *catuṣkoṭi* are found in early Buddhism and later in the Mādhyamika school. The first case where the four alternatives constitute a disjunctive system, with the individual terms not necessarily denied, was well represented in passages of early Buddhism, as preserved in the Pāli canon; and then was included in Nāgārjuna's *Madhyamaka-kārikā* in the verse about the ranked instruction of the Buddha. The second case, denial of alternatives regarding causation, stating with the discourses to Kassapa and to Kaccāyana, is made much of by Nāgārjuna as the basis of the Mādhyamika, but does not seem to have been stressed as much in other schools of Buddhism. The third case, denial of four alternatives, has important examples in both early and later Buddhism, and, of course, is generously treated in the Mādhyamika. Therefore, when Jayatilleke says, "It is evident that Nāgārjuna and some of his commentators, ancient and modern, refer to this logic with little understanding of its real nature and significance,"[57] these remarks define the limitations of Jayatilleke's own views of these problems, outside of which is his own "little understanding." Robinson answered Jayatilleke in a different way: "And since the *catuṣkoṭi* is not a doctrine but just a form, later writers were at liberty to use it in new ways, doing which does not itself prove that they misunder-

[57]JAYATILLEKE, "Logic," p. 82.

stood the early forms."[58] This is well stated and is meant not only to reject Jayatilleke's criticism of Nāgārjuna and others, but apparently also to justify the application of symbolic logic. However, I have brought up sufficient evidence to show that Nāgārjuna, in the matter of the *catuṣkoṭi*, is heir to and the continuator of teachings in the early Buddhist canon (in Pāli, the four Nikāyas; in Sanskrit, the four Āgamas). Furthermore, I cannot concede that the *catuṣkoṭi* is just a form. Indeed, if Nāgārjuna had used it in new ways, Jayatilleke would have been more justified in his attribution of misunderstanding to Nāgārjuna.

Next, we observe by the foregoing materials that the first kind of *catuṣkoṭi* is a disjunctive system that was used to explain the Buddha's teaching. The second, applied to causation, each of the alternatives denied, is a meditative exercise, and besides serves to classify some of the philosophical positions rejected by the Mādhyamika. The third kind, applied to existence, each of the alternatives denied, is another meditative exercise, and besides serves to establish the absolute by negating the notional activity of the mind (*saṃjñāskandha*) and its net of imputed qualifications.[59]

The priority of the causality to existence treatments—as I have already insisted upon—is consistent with Nāgārjuna's *Madhyamaka-kārikā*, which devotes chapter I to conditional causes (*pratyaya*), beginning with the denial of four alternatives concerning origination of entities, but in the same chapter begins alternatives of existence, nonexistence, etc. So *MK* I, 6: "Neither an existent nor a non-existent entity has a valid condition (*pratyaya*). What non-existent has a condition? What is the use of a condition for an existent?" The next verse (I, 7) shifts to the word *dharma*: "Whenever a feature (*dharma*) neither existent nor non-existent, or both existent and non-existent, operates, in that case how could an operator-cause be valid?" (and it is not valid.) *MK* chapteres III, IV, and V, deal with the

[58] ROBINSON, book review, p. 76.

[59] This is well stated in the Tibetan language by Red-mda'-ba's *Commentary to Āryadeva's "Four Hundred Verses,"* ed. Jetsun Rendawa Shonnu Lodo (Sarnath : Sakya Students' Union, 1974), p. 170: "The form and variety of natures (*dharma*) are posited as different by dint of *saṃjñā* (notions, ideas), but not by reason of the own-form (*svarūpa*) of given things (*vastu*)—because all of them being illusory, it is not possible to distinguish their own-forms."

products of causes, namely, the sense bases, personal aggregates, and elements, that amount to "all entities" (*sarva-bhāva*, IV, 7). Here again, "all entities" presuppose their arising as products, so the causality. The establishment of causality in conventional terms and of existence in absolute terms is therefore implied in *MK* XXIV, 10: "Without reliance on convention, the supreme (*paramārtha*) is not pointed to."

I propose that it was by not distinguishing these uses of the *catuṣkoṭi* that there has been in the past various improper or misleading attributions to this formula. For example, there is the problem of which two kinds of negations is involved: the *prasajya-pratiṣedha* (negation by denial) or *paryudāsa-pratiṣedha* (negation by implication). Matilal concludes that the *catuṣkoṭi* is of the *prasajya* type and that so understood the *catuṣkoṭi* is free from contradiction.[60] Staal after admirably explaining the two kinds of negation (the *paryudāsa* type negates a term; the *prasajya* type negates the predicate) agrees with Matilal that the *catuṣkoṭi* exhibits the *prasajya* type, but disagrees that this frees the formula of contradiction.[61] However, when one considers this along with my preceding materials, one can promptly agree with Matilal and then with Staal that it is the *prasajya* negation which is involved with the *catuṣkoṭi*, nota bene, the four alternatives in their explicit form applied to existence, because the proposition "I bow to that Dharma-sun which is not existence" is of the *prasajya* type (confer, Staal: '*x* is not F'). But when one examines the propositions of the four alternatives in their explicit form applied to causation, one can promptly disagree with Matilal and then with Staal, because the proposition "There is no entity anywhere that arises from itself," is of the *paryudāsa* type (confer, Staal: "not -*x* is F'). And this *paryudāsa* type is of the variety implying action, for which there is the stock example, "Fat Devadatta does not eat food in the daytime." But "fat Devadatta" must eat sometime, so when? The world responds, "at night!"[62] Also, the entities that do not arise from self, another,

[60]MATILAL, *Epistemology, Logic, and Grammar*, pp. 162-167..

[61]FRITS STAAL, *Exploring Mysticism* (London: Penguin Books, 1975), pp. 45-47; hereafter cited as Staal, *Exploring Mysticism*.

[62]Confer, DHIRENDRA SHARMA, *The Negative Dialectics of India* (Leiden : E. J. Brill, 1970), p. 94; note where the example illustrates the Vedānta authority (*pramāṇa*) called 'presumption' (*arthāpatti*).

both, or by chance, must arise somehow, so how? Buddhism responds, "in the manner of Dependent Origination (*pratītya-samutpāda*)." In illustration, the first two members of Dependent Origination are: (1) "nescience" (*avidyā*), and (2) "motivations" (*saṃskāra*). "Motivations" do not arise from self (motivations) or from another (nescience), or from both self and another (motivations and nescience), or without a cause (that is, by chance); "motivations" do arise with "nescience" as condition (*pratyaya*); and since "motivations" are a *karma* member, have a cause (*hetu*) which is *karma*, hence the other *karma*-member, which is (10), "gestation" (*bhava*) or "re-existence" (*punarbhava*)."[63]

But then what of Staal's position that even so (that is, allowing the *prasajya* interpretation for the *catuṣkoṭi* of existence), this does not save the *prasajya* propositions from mutual contradiction? Saying, "In rejecting the third clause, the denial of the principle of non-contradiction is rejected, not the principle of non-contradiction itself,"[64] he interprets the third proposition in its literal form, denial that something both exists and does not exist. However, at least in the Tsoṅ-kha-pa Prāsaṅgika-Mādhyamika explanation that I gave earlier, it is not possible to understand the four denials in terms of existence just by their literal form, because one must bring in the theory of two truths (*saṃvṛti* and *paramārtha*) to understand Nāgārjuna's position. In such a case, the denial of the third proposition amounts in commentarial expansion to: This Mādhyamika rejects, in the absolute sense (*paramārthatas*), the simultaneity of existence by own-nature of that efficient entity with the non-existence by own-nautre of the unconstructed entity. In short, it is here claimed that "existence" and "non-existence" refer contrasting entities. Along the same lines, Nāgārjuna says (*MK* XXV, 14);

> How could Nirvāṇa be both a presence and an absence? Like light and darkness, there is no existence of the two in the same place.

[63]For Nāgārjuna's classification of the two members, nos. 2 and 10, as *karma*, see, for example, A. Wayman, "Buddhist Dependent Origination," "*History of Religions* 10, no. 3 (Feb., 1971): 188. I have gone much more into the cause and effect (*hetu-phala*) side of the formula in my forthcoming "Dependent Origination—the Indo-Tibetan Tradition," (special issue of *Journal of Chinese Philosophy*). See Chapter 8.

[64]Staal, *Exploring Mysticism*, p. 47.

Thus the third alternative of this type of *catuṣkoṭi* can be resolved in various ways, for example, one may deny both a presence and an absence of *nirvāṇa*, adding "that is, in the same place"; or, with a different subject, adding perhaps, "that is, at the same time"; or, with still other subjects, perhaps drawing upon the two truths, "that is, with the same truth." All these additions are consistent with Nāgārjuna's verses in the *MK*. Thus, in such interpretations it is not the intention of the denial, as Staal claims, to save a principle of human reason from default; but rather it is held that such is really the meaning of the third proposition, to wit, that a qualification of place, time, or truth must be added. However, it follows that the denials of alternatives applied to existence, while in their explicit form constituting the *prasajya* type of denial, turn out, by reason of the qualifications added in the Mādhyamika school, to be *paryudāsa* negations. Indeed, study of the two main traditions of the Mādhyamika, Candrakīrti's Prāsaṅgika and Bhāvaviveka's Svātantrika, will show that both of them insist on adding qualifications, especially in terms of the two truths (*saṃvṛti* and *paramārtha*), their disagreement stemming from how such qualifications are made. But that a qualification should be added is consistent with most of the attempts of Westerners to explain the *catuṣkoṭi*, because they usually added something, to wit, their theory of the *catuṣkoṭi*. So the Mādhyamika commentators and the Western writers share this solicitude to rationalize, even in the case of the absolute, which was supposed to cut off the net of qualifications. Even so, as was indicated previously, the Mādhyamika is not against reason as the faculty which denies a self, denies the alternatives, and so on, because this reason leads to the insight which realizes the absolute.

Conclusion

Now we must revert to the initial question: Who understands the four alternatives of the Buddhist texts? It is easier to define the persons who do not understand: as was shown, they are the ones who do not want to understand, or are not confident of their own ability to understand. Besides, no one understands *the* four alternatives, but perchance one does understand the four alternatives in a disjunctive system, or the four alternatives applied to causation, or the four alternatives, applied to existence. The four alternatives, disjunctively considered, constitute a preliminary orientation. The alternatives of causation, each denied, are a meditation with upholding of human reason with its inferences, definitions, and the like. The alternatives of existence, each denied, are a meditation with ultimate downgrading of human reason. Then to answer more along the lines of the way Candrakīrti writes:—Whether one who understands arises or does not arise, "this true nature of *dharmas* abides,"—the *svabhāva* of that sort. So Candrakīrti says in his *Prasannapadā* commentary on *Madhyamaka-kārikā*, chapter XV:

> By *svabhāva* one understands this innate nature, uncreate, which has not deviated in the fire in the past, present, and future; which did not arise earlier and will not arise later; which is not dependent on causes and conditions as are the heat of water, (one or another) of this side and the other side, long and short. Well, then, does this own-nature of fire that is of such manner (i.e. uncreate, not dependent) exist? (In reply:). The (*svabhāva* of such sort) neither exists nor does not exist by reason of own-nature. While that is the case, still in order to avoid frightening the hearers, we conventionally make affirmations (such as "It is *svabhāva*" and "It is *dharmatā*") and say it exists.[65]

[65]La Vallée Poussin, *Mūlamadhyamakakārikās*, pp. 263.5 to 264.4.

12

THE INTERMEDIATE-STATE DISPUTE IN BUDDHISM

The possibility of life after death has always fascinated mankind. India was no exception, even with its metaphysical setting of rebirth theory. Then, with the belief in the extraordinary powers of *yogins* to delve into nature's secrets, it was held that some individuals could communicate what really happened after death: as when the Buddha used a divine eye (*divya-cakṣus*) to observe the sentient beings going from here to various good and bad destinies, and later told his disciples about it.

But is there life between death and rebirth? It is well known that the theory of such an intermediate state (*antarā-bhava*) was a disputed point among the early Buddhist sects. The ones agreeing that there is such a state were the Pūrvaśaila, Sammatīya, Sarvāstivādin, Vātsīputrīya, and the Later Mahīśāsaka. The Buddhist sects that rejected the notion were the Theravādin, Vibhajyavādin, Mahāsāṅghika, Mahīśāsaka, as well as the work *Śāriputrābhidharmaśāstra* (of the Dharmaguptaka sect, which issued from the Mahīśāsaka).[1]

In the Mahāyāna period Vasubandhu's *Abhidharmakośa*, Chapter III, and self-commentary, amassed strong scriptural evidence in support of the intermediate-state theory.[2]

[1]André Bareau, *Les sectes bouddhiques du Petit Véhicule*, Saigon 1955, p. 283.

[2]L. de La Vallée Poussin, in his translation of Vasubandhu's work, gave the main known references of his day, *L'Abhidharmakośa de Vasubandhu*, troisième chapitre, Paris 1926, p. 32, n.

At the outset it should be admitted that the material is abundant on the side of the sects which admitted the intermediate state in this sense, since it allowed a great scope for mythological elaboration. In contrast, the sects which rejected this kind of intermediate state apparently did not make much of a negative position; so their immediate textual contributions to the problem are meagre and their reasoning has mostly to be inferred. It is possible that the Buddhist sects did not always understand the expression "intermediate-state" the same way, and so in some cases there is only a seeming disagreement.

Our considerations promise to relate early Buddhism to certain Brahmanical teachings, to clarify the position of the Buddhist teacher Nāgārjuna, and also to tie in this intermediate-state dispute with Buddhist embryology theory.

I. The Thesis of no Intermediate-State

The Theravāda rejection of the intermediate-state is set forth in *Points of Controversy*,[3] but the space is devoted to rejecting some arguments for the intermediate-state without giving in its stead a coherent alternate position. This is not to deny the relevance of criticism that only three realms are stated in the scriptures, that of desire (*kāma*), of form (*rūpa*), and the formless realm. Perhaps this criticism forced the proponents of the intermediate-state theory—as this paper will show—to treat this state in terms of the three realms. Also, the Theravāda attempted to interpret the scriptural name *antarāparinirvāyin* as "attaining Nirvāṇa before half of his life in a Brahma world has expired."[4] Vasubandhu argues against this, charging that one could then reinterpret the other ones among the five Anāgāmins.[5]

---

[3]Translation of the *Kathā-vatthu* by S. Z. Aung and Mrs. Rhys Davids, London 1915, pp. 212-13.

[4]*Kathā-vatthu* (tr.), pp. 212-13; and *Designation of Human Types* (*Puggala-paññati*) (tr. by B. C. Law), London 1922, pp. 24-25.

[5]de La Vallée Poussin (tr.), III, p. 38. Vasubandhu appears to argue that in such a case, we could say that the *upapadya-parinirvāyin* means one who attains *parinirvāṇa* upon being born in a Brahma world, which is of course absurd. It seems that in his way of disputing, if a term is a member of a standard list, a reinterpretation of such a term has implications for the other members of the list.

How then, does one of the early sects express its denial of an intermediate-state in a positive way? I appeal to the Mahāsāṅghikas, having shown elsewhere that the *Śrīmālā-sūtra* was a product of this school,[6] and it may be cited in this connection even though it belongs among the early Mahāyāna scriptures:

> Lord, as to "cyclical flow" (*saṃsāra*), no sooner do the sense organs for perception pass away than it (the Tathāgatagarbha) takes hold of sense organs for perception, and that is "cyclical flow."[7]

Presumably all the Buddhist sects—the Theravādin, etc.—that posited centers of consciousness other than the *mano-vijñāna* and also denied the intermediate-state, would have some analogous theoretical statement in terms of the sense organs.

Of such sects, the Theravādin have a *bhavaṅga-viññana*, the Vibhajyavādin a *bhavāṅga-vijñāna*, the Mahāsāṅghika a *mūla-vijñāna*, the Mahīśāsaka a *saṃsārakoṭiniṣṭha-skandha*—the forerunner of the *ālayavijñāna* of the Mahāyāna[8]—and the Dharmaguptaka as an offshoot of the Mahīśāsaka inferentially the equivalent.

Passing to the Mahāyāna period in its philosophical sense, three reasons may be advanced for believing that Nāgārjuna did not subscribe to the thesis of an intermediate-state (*antarā-bhava*).

(1) He writes in the *Pratītyasamutpādahṛdaya-vyākaraṇa*:[9]

> Just as in the case of a flame from a flame, the reflected image in a mirror from a face, an impression from a seal, a fire from a burning crystal, a sprout from a seed. . a person is not taught to understand that the one is different from the other, so also in the case of reconnection (*pratisaṃdhi*) of the personal aggregates (*skandha*), the wise person will understand that there is no transfer.

[6]A. Wayman and H. Wayman (trs.) *The Lion's Roar of Queen Śrīmālā; a Buddhist Scripture on the Tathāgatagarbha Theory*, New York 1974, pp. 2-3.

[7]*Ibid*. p. 104.

[8]Bareau, *Les sectes*, pp. 72, 177, 187, and 240.

[9]Photo ed. of Tibetan canon (*PTT*). Vol. 103, p. 271-4: / ji ltar mar me las mar me daṅ / bźin las me loṅ gi gzugs brñan 'byuṅ daṅ / rgya las rgya'i 'bur daṅ / me śel las me daṅ / sa bon las myu gu daṅ / . . / de dag kyaṅ de ñid daṅ de las gźan no źes śes par slob ma yin pa de bźin du / phuṅ po ñiṅ mtshams sbyor ba yaṅ / mi 'pho bar yaṅ mkhas rtogs bya /.

Since the old *skandhas* do not transfer, there is no intermediate-state for them, just as there is no intermediate-state between the two flames in the case of a flame from a flame.

(2) He writes in the *Madhyamaka-kārikā* (XXVI, 20):

> What be the limit of *nirvāṇa* is also the limit of *saṃsāra*. There is nothing, however slight, intermediate (*antara*) between the two.

This shows an aversion for intermediate states.

(3) He does not refer to an intermediate-state in his *Friendly Epistle*.[10] although his description of the bells, and so on, in this work allows him a context to bring in an intermediate-state if this were his sectarian position; and this is the context in which those who espouse the intermediate-state do in fact mention it.

Then what can we decide from this about Nāgārjuna's school? Now, the Mādhyamika school based on Nāgārjuna always maintains that of the *vijñānas*, besides the five based on outer senses, he accepted only the *mano-vijñāna*. We arrive then at the striking conclusion that while Nāgārjuna appears to be in the camp of those rejecting an intermediate-state, he cannot be identified with any one of the known sects which reject it. But since Nāgārjuna is an independent thinker of the early Mahāyāna, there is no reason to insist that he be identified with any early sect.

Perhaps the most important doctrinal effect of the opposition to an intermediate state is the interpretation of the first two members of Dependent Origination (*pratītya-samutpāda*) as pertaining to the previous life. This interpretation is deeply impressed on the Abhidharma literature, both in the Pāli and Sanskrit languages.[11] Of course, birth was standardized in terms of *vijñāna*, third member of Dependent Origination. Therefore, the first two members, nescience (*avidyā*) and motivations (*saṃskāra*) would perforce constitute an intermediate-state, after No. 12, old age and death (*jarāmaraṇa*), *unless* the first two members could somehow be understood to not follow upon death. A solution was to say that those two belong to the previous cycle. We can see this

[10] "Nāgārjuna's *Suhṛllekha*" (tr. by H. Wenzel in *Journal of the Pali Text Society*, 1886, pp. 2-32).

[11] See, for example, Nārada, *A Manual of Abhidhamma*, Kandy, Ceylon, 1968, Diagram XVII; and de La Vallée Poussin (tr.) III, pp. 62-63.

same theory in the Dependent Origination verses of the Mahāyāna biography of the Buddha called the *Lalitavistara*, containing this verse:[12]

> By the wrong procedure engendered by the constructions of imagination, nescience (*avidyā*) arises and there is no originator of it at all. It provides the cause of motivations (*saṃskāra*), and there is no transfer. Perception (*vijñāna*) arises with transference in dependence (on motivations).

This is consistent with Nāgārjuna's statement cited above (from his *pratītyasamutpāda* commentary), because *vijñāna*, not the previous nescience and motivations, now starts the transference by descending into the womb, or other birthplace. Here *vijñāna* depends on the old *saṃskāra* just as the face in the mirror depends upon the model face. Thus the *Lalitavistara* agrees with the theory found in Pāli Buddhism that the first two members of Dependent Origination pertain to the previous life. Hence they are said to be reflected in the new series, started by *vijñāna*, the seed.

But if the first two members of Dependent Origination are attributed to the previous cycle, the question arises: Where? A kind of answer is suggested by the *Pitāputrasamāgama-sūtra*:[13]

> So, great King, a "first perception" (*prathamavijñāna*) arises having two conditions pertaining to "birth" (*aupapatti*)—by reason of the "last perception" (*caramavjñāna*) as predominant condition (*adhipati-pratyaya*) and by reason of *karma* as support condition (*ārambaṇa-pratyaya*).

In fact—as I have shown in a different context[14]—this passage takes "death" to be divided into two phases—expiration as the last perception and death vision as the *karma*. The *karma* is called

[12]F. Edgerton, *Buddhist Hybrid Sanskrit Reader*, New Haven 1953, p. 24 :
saṃkalpakalpajanitena ayoniśena
bhavate avidyā na pi saṃbhavako 'sya kaścit
saṃskārahetu dadate na ca saṃkramo 'sti
vijñānam udbhavati saṃkramaṇaṃ pratītya //

[13]As cited in Śāntideva's *Śikṣāsamuccaya* (ed. by the Mithila Institute), 135, 12-13.

[14]A. Wayman, 'The Fivefold Ritual Symbolism of Passion', in *Studies of Esoteric Buddhism and Tantrism* , Koyasan, Japan, 1965, p. 133. This essay also appears in A. Wayman, *Buddhist Tantras* (Samuel Weiser, New York, 1973).

in Chinese and Tibetan Buddhist mythology the "*karma*-mirror" of Yama's judgment hall.[15] It is well accepted in the theory of Dependent Origination, in the case where the first two members pertain to the previous life, that member No. 2, *saṃskāra*, is the old *karma*, and furthermore that member No. 1, *avidyā*, is the state of previous defilement (*kleśa*). Hence *avidyā* in this context is tantamount to the "last perception" (*caramavijñāna*); and perhaps it is for this reason that Vasubandhu compares this *avidyā* with a king who, when he comes, is accompanied by his courtiers (the host of defilements).[16] Then member No. 3, *vijñāna*, becomes the "first perception " (*prathamavijñāna*) in the new life.

There is a remarkable foreshadowing of this death-fertility—death as the instigator of another life—in the *Bṛhadāraṇyaka Upaniṣad* (I,2,2): "There was nothing whatsoever here in the beginning. By death indeed was this covered, or by hunger, for hunger is death. He created the mind, thinking, 'Let me have a self'. Then he moved about, worshipping. From this, thus worshipping, water was produced." Observe how neatly this fits the first four members of Buddhist Dependent Origination in the interpretation denying an intermediate state:

Bṛhadāraṇyaka statement	*Dependent Origination*
"by death indeed was this covered"	1. nescience (*avidyā*)
"or by hunger, for hunger is death"	2. motivations (*saṃskāra*)
"He created the mind, thinking, 'Let me have a self'"	3. perception (*vijñāna*)
'Then he moved about, worshipping. From him, thus worshipping, water was produced"	4. name-and-form (*nāma-rūpa*) (=*vijñāna* in the womb)

In short, the Buddhist sects that deny an intermediate-state are consistent with the tradition, pre-dating Buddhism, that life comes from death.

II. The Thesis of an Intermediate-State

There must have been fierce argument on the subject to have called

[15] I have included a discussion of this matter in a paper, "The Mirror as a Pan-Buddhist Metaphor-Simile", *History of Religions*, 13: 4, May 1974, pp. 264-65. This essay is included in this volume.

[16] *Abhidharmakośa*, III, 21a-b : / pūrvakleśadasāvidyā saṃskārāḥ pūrvakarmaṇaḥ / And de La Vallée Poussin (tr.), III, p. 63.

forth from Vasubandhu his spirited defence of the intermediate state. He says (*Abhidharmakośa* III, 12, commentary):

> /asaty antarābhave katham antarāparinirvāyī nāma syāt / Were there no intermediate state, how could there be the term [found in the scriptures] "a being who has *parinirvāṇa* in the intermediate state"?

This is part of the teaching that among the five kinds of non-returnees (*anāgāmin*), there is the *antarā-parinirvāyin* who, according to the interpretation which Vasubandhu follows, reaches Nirvāṇa in the intermediate state. He refers to the *Satpuruṣagati-sūtra* for varieties of the *antarā-parinirvāyin* (*infra.*).

Vasubandhu explains the intermediate-state being in two verses (*ibid.*, III, 13-14):

> It [the intermediate-state being] has the configuration of what is to be the configuration of the future being, since it has the same forecasting; to wit, which is subsequent to the moment of birth and prior to death (i.e. the future being has the period of moment right after birth to moment just before death).
> It is seen by the pure divine eye belonging to beings of its class. It has the force of magical power of act. Its sense organs are perfect. It cannot be impeded or turned back. It feeds on odours (*gandhabhuk*).

Vasubandhu's commentary refers to a *Saptabhavasūtra*[17] for the teaching that the five destinies, men, gods, animals, hungry ghosts, and hell beings, have their cause (*sahetuka*), namely the *karma-bhava*, and have their access (*sagamana*), namely the *antarā-bhava*. His commentary explains the term *gandhabhuk* as *gandharva*. He refers to the *Āśvalāyana-sūtra* (presumably from the *Madhyamāgama*) for the reference to the word *gandharva* as some kind of being, to wit (as Miss I.B. Horner translates from the equivalent Pāli scripture, the *Assalāyanasutta* in the *Majjhima-nikāya*): "But do you, sirs, know whether that *gandhabba* is a noble or brahman or worker or merchant?" And this question was preceded by the remark (her translation): "We do know, sir, how there is conception. There is here a coitus of the parents, it

[17]de La Vallée Poussin, II, p. 13, states that the authenticity of this *sūtra* was contested.

is the mother's season and the *gandhabba* is present; it is on the conjunction of these three things that there is conception."[18]

In the Vedic period the *gandharva* is a kind of spirit generally placed in the *antarikṣa* (the intermediate space between earth and sky) along with the Pitaras (ancestors) and Asuras (demi-gods).[19] The intermediate space can be understood as having Indra in the daytime and the Gandharva at nighttime for chief or typical deities.[20] Besides being a musician, the *gandharva* in the Veda could be a cloud,[21] and this meaning was continued into Mahāyāna Buddhism as a simile of illusion (*māyā*) , the often mentioned "city of *gandharvas*", meaning the "castle in the air," a particular atmospheric phenomenon.[22] Even this use of the word continues the association with the midspace. According to Vedic conceptions[23] the *gandharva* was the second of the three non-human deities that married a woman before she married a human male (=one born of woman), the first being Soma (=Candra) in the sky, and the third being Agni (=Yama) on earth.[24] The *gandharva*, in these old Indian ideas, gave the woman her sweetness of voice. Of course, the Vedas did not contain the notion of *gandharva* as a disincarnate entity headed for rebirth; indeed, the rebirth theory has never been traced to the four Vedas.

However, since the theory of *karma* and rebirth has a sympathetic treatment in certain old Upaniṣads, the question arises as to whether the *gandharva* is mentioned therein along the lines of the *Assalāyanasutta*. Such a mention may be intended, although obscurely, in the *Kaṭha Upaniṣad*, which presumably is to be dated at about the same time as that old Buddhist scripture. The *Kaṭha* states (II, 3, 5):

18I.B. Horner (tr.) *The Middle Length Sayings*, Vol. II, London 1957, p. 349.

19Cf. A. A. MacDonell, *Vedic Mythology*, Strassburg 1897, pp. 136-37.

20At least such are my conclusions in "Climactic Times in Indian Mythology and Religion," *History of Religions*, 4:2, Winter 1965, p. 300.

21R. S. Panchamukhi, *Gandharvas & Kinnaras in Indian Iconography* (Dharwar, 1951), p. 3.

22Cf. Étienne Lamotte, *Le Traité de la Grande Vertu de Sagesse*, I, Louvain 1944, pp. 369-73.

23The Marriage Hymn, *Ṛgveda* X, 85, 40.

24My interpretation, "Climactic Times", pp. 298-99, was written with leanings to the "intermediate state" position, generally accepted in Tibetan Buddhism.

As one sees in a mirror, so (Brahman) in the *ātman;*
As (one sees) in a dream, so (Brahman) in the world of the forefathers (*Pitṛloka*);
As (one sees) toward (*pari*) the water, so in the world of the *gandharvas;*
As in light and shade, so in the world of Brahmā.

If we interpret this passage of the *Kaṭha* as a progression, as Radhakrishnan thinks it is,[25] then the similes can be clarified as follows:

simile	*referent*	*progression*
"as in a mirror'	Brahman in the *ātman*	present life
"as in a dream"	Brahman in the world of the forefathers	state after death
"as toward the water"	Brahman in the world of *gandharvas*	heading for rebirth
"as in light and shade"	Brahman in the world of Brahmā	*vijñāna* in the heart[26]

Since "toward the water" (*apsu pari*) implies "toward the female", it follows that the "world of *gandharvas*" may reasonably be identified with the *gandharvas* that are meant by the *Assalāyanasutta.*

Taking these *gandharvas* in the meaning of intermediate-state beings, we notice that a Mahāyāna Buddhist scripture, the *Ārya-Ānanda-garbhāvakrāntinirdeśa*, classifies them so as to be within the Buddhist three worlds. It explains that beings headed for an evil destiny have in the intermediate state a displeasing colour of personal aggregates, namely hell beings have a colour like the burnt stump of a tree; animals, like smoke; hungry ghosts, like water; and that beings headed for a good destiny have a pleasing colour in the intermediate state, namely, men and gods (in the

[25]S. Radhakrishnan, *The Principal Upaniṣads*, New York 1953, p. 643.

[26]So states Asaṅga in the *Yogācārabhūmi* (Part I, ed. by V. Bhattacharya), University of Calcutta 1957, 24.18-19: / yatra ca kalaladeśe tadvijñānaṃ sammūrcchitaṃ so 'sya bhavati tasmin samaye hṛdayadeśaḥ / "At the time that the *vijñāna* becomes unconscious at wherever be the *kalala*, its place is the heart." For the comparable idea in the Pāli commentarial tradition, cf. Y. Karunadasa, *Buddhist Analysis of Matter*, Colombo 1967, pp. 62-66, in a discussion of the term *hadaya-vatthu.* The comparable Upaniṣadic theory is in terms of the *vijñānamaya-puruṣa.*

realm of desire), like the colour of gold; gods in the realm of form, the colour of abiding white; while gods in the formless realm are colourless for the very reason that the realm is formless (and therefore lacks both colour and shape).[27] This is presumably what Vasubandhu means by saying the being has the configuration of the future being, as one of the five destinies.

Asaṅga, who belongs to the later Mahīśāsaka[28] and so accepts the intermediate state, speaks along the lines of that Mahāyāna scripture in his *Bodhisattvabhūmi* when he says that the *antarābhava* is of two kinds, the kind invested with darkness (*tamaḥ-parāyaṇa*) like pitch-black nights, said to have a bad colour (*durvarṇa*); and the kind invested with light (*jyotiḥ-parāyaṇa*) like nights that are lighted, said to have a good colour (*suvarṇa*).[29] The kind of a bad colour leads to a bad destiny; and the kind of a good colour leads to a good destiny.

Asaṅga also explains:[30]

> Besides, there is its synonymous terminology. The term "intermediate state" is used because it manifests in the interval between the death-state and the birth-state. The term *gandharva* is used because it has access (*gamana*) by way of odour and has growth (*puṣṭi*) by way of odour. The term "made of mind" (*manomaya*) is used because the mind, taking recourse to itself, proceeds to the birthplace, but not because its going to a body is going with an object-support (*ālambana*). The "resultant" (*abhinirvṛtti*) is used because it is productive in the direction of birth.

The *Abhidharmakośa* (III, 40c-41a) adds a further name "seeking birth" (*saṃbhavaiṣin*), which Asaṅga apparently includes in "made of mind", according to his explanation.[31] The denial of

[27] In the Tibetan Kanjur, Ratnakūṭa collection, *PTT*, Vol. 23, p. 103-5.

[28] Cf. A. Wayman, *Analysis of the Śrāvakabhūmi Manuscript*, Berkeley 1961, pp. 25-29.

[29] *Bodhisattvabhūmi*, (ed. by Wogihara), II, pp. 390-91.

[30] *Yogācārabhūmi*, I, 20.9-13: / tasya punaḥ paryāyā antarābhava ity ucyate maraṇabhavotpattibhavayor antarāle prādurbhāvāt / gandharva ity ucyate gandhena gamanād gandhena puṣṭitaś ca / manomaya ity ucyate tannisritya manasa upapattyāyatanagamanatayā / śarīragatyā ca punar nālambanagatyā / abhinirvṛttir apy ucyate upapatter ābhimukhyena nirvartanatayā /

[31] Cf. *Abhidharmakośa*, (tr.), III, pp. 122-23.

an object-support seems inconsistent with the explanation for the name *gandharva*.[32] So the proponents of the "intermediate state" also have here a problem that does not appear to be resolved.[33] Anyway, the *gandharva* has perfect sense organs, as Vasubandhu has already been cited.

Besides there are the periods by weeks, found both in the intermediate-state theory and in the theory of intra-uterine development which could therefore be labelled the "lunar route." Thus, Asaṅga states:[34]

> Also, the intermediate state lasts for seven days. But when there is not the condition for rebirth, and when there is the condition for rebirth—is an uncertain matter. And when this [condition] is not attained, then it lasts from seven days to seven times seven days after one has died, while the condition of rebirth is not being attained. When that period has elapsed certainly one attains the condition of rebirth. Sometimes in that very place there is the "resultant" (*abhinirvṛtti*) of the one passed away since seven days. Sometimes, in the case of one with bad fortune (or: who is unlucky) (a "resultant") elsewhere, for if another activity of the *karma* should change the course, it would cause that seed of *antarābhava* to change course.

Presumably what Asaṅga means by the "bad fortune" is that the

[32]That is to say, odour is ordinarily taken as the object-support of the sense of smell. Compare MacDonell, *Vedic Mythology*, p. 137: "The RV. adds the touch that Gandharva wears a fragrant (*surabhi*) garment (10., 123[7]), while in the AV. (12.1[23]) the odour (*gandha*) of the earth is said to rise to the Gandharvas."

[33]One rationalization to avoid the object-support could be that the *gandharva* is "perfumed" by *vāsanā* (habit-energy), so provides its own odour. On the other hand, it would be natural to rationalize that the odour of sexual union is the odour which rises to the *gandharva*, and this ordinarily would be construed as an object-support (*ālambana*).

[34]*Yogācārabhūmi* I, 20.4-8: / sa punar antarābhavaḥ saptāhaṃ tiṣṭhaty asaty upapattipratyayalābhe / sati punaḥ pratyayalābhe 'niyamaḥ / alābhe punaś cyutvā punaḥ saptāhaṃ tiṣṭhati yāvat sapta saptāhāni tiṣṭhaty upapattipratyayam alabhamānaḥ / tata ūrdhvam avaśyam upapattipratyayaṃ labhate/ tasya ca saptāhacyutasya kadācit tatraivābhinirvṛttir bhavati / kadācid anyatra visabhāge / sācet karmāntarakriyā parivarteta tad antarābhavabījaṃ parivartayati //

gandharva has contributed to the conception in the womb, and then has gone away.

In the case of the intra-uterine development, there are the two *garbhāvakrānti* scriptures in both Tibetan and Chinese of the Ratnakūṭa collection. The smaller of these, the *Ārya-āyuṣmannandagarbhāvakrāntinirdeśa,* was translated from Chinese into German by Huebotter.[35] Both of these texts have the teaching that parturition occurs upon 38 weeks.[36] Interestingly, this total of 266 days happens to be exactly the number stated by a modern biological work to be the full term of pregnancy.[37]

As the Mahāyāna developed into tantric Buddhism, there was much made of the intermediate state, with different kinds of *bardo*, as it is now frequently referred to by the Tibetan equivalent (abbreviated) of the word *antarābhava.* My studies in this literature showed me one usage of the term "intermediate state" practically equivalent to the ten lunar months of intra-uterine development.[38] Even the *Points of Controversy* would not have objected to the "intermediate state" if the opponent had said that this is what it is. Indeed, Asaṅga's statement of the periods of seven-day multiples suggests a coordination of this "intermediate state" with the early development of the embryo.

However, the early proponents of the "intermediate state" doctrine necessarily understood this in some way that put them at variance with, and made them opponents of, those who reject the intermediate state. Just as there are doctrinal implications in the case of those who reject the intermediate state, so there are such implications for those who accept it. Perhaps it is in the light of the intermediate-state position that Asaṅga has an alternate way of grouping the members of Dependent Origination, as found in Sanskrit in his *Abhidharma-samuccaya*:[39]

[35]Dr. Med. et Dr. Phil. Huebotter (tr.), *Die Sutra überEm pfängnis und Embryologie* (Deutsche Gesellschaft für Natur-u. Völkerkunde Ostasiens), Tokyo 1932.

[36]Huebotter, p. 21; Tibetan for the same text, *PTT,* Vol. 23, p. 99-3; and Tibetan for the larger text, the *Ārya-Ānanda-garbhāvakrānti-nirdeśa, PTT,* Vol. 23, p. 107-4. But, according to P. V. Bapat, *Vimuttimagga and Visuddhimagga,* Poona 1937, p. 129, the *Vimuttimagga* gives 42 weeks for the same development.

[37]Martin and Vincent, *Human Biological Development,* The Ronald Press Company, New York, 1960.

[38]Wayman, "The Fivefold Ritual Symbolism of Passion", p. 130.

[39]P. Pradhan (ed.) *Abhidharma-samuccaya,* 26.20 ff.

> How are the members grouped—[Into] the groups [called] members which cast downward, members which are cast downward, productive members, and resultant members. What are the members which cast downward? They are nescience, motivations, and perception. What are the members which are cast downward? They are name-and-form, six sense bases, contact, and feelings. What are the productive members? They are craving, indulgence, and gestation. What are the resultant members? They are birth, and old age and death.

Since Asaṅga does not classify the first two members as "past life", it is not possible to make the kind of correlation that was done previously in association with the *Bṛhadāraṇyaka Upaniṣad.* One may conclude that the first three members—those which cast downward—are the intermediate state, although admittedly I have not found Asaṅga stating this explicitly.

Moreover, when speaking of the species (*gotra*) of the religious family, Asaṅga raises the question as to whether it belongs to a single or multiple lineage, and answers in part, "That seed does not have the characteristics of difference as long as it stays apart from the six sense bases (*ṣaḍāyatana*)."[40] This remark immediately contrasts with the position previously cited from the *Śrīmālā-sūtra.* When Asaṅga allows a possibility of the "species" staying apart from the six sense bases, he assumes an intermediate state between the prior set of six sense bases and the later set of six sense bases. Perhaps Asaṅga must take this position because of his emphasis on yoga training, with its premise that one may detach himself from the senses. But usually such detachment would be from the five outer senses, and Asaṅga allows such detachment also from the sixth sense, the *manas.*

Turning now to the three kinds of *antarāparinirvāyin* in the theory of five kinds of *anāgāmin*, long ago Louis de La Vallée Poussin made a comparison of the Sanskrit version from the *Satpuruṣagati-sūtra* cited by Yaśomitra in his *Abhidharmakośa-vyākhya*, with the Pāli version in the *Aṅguttara-nikāya*, vii, 52.[41] For the purpose of the present article, I have edited from the

[40]Wayman, *Analysis of the Śrāvakabhūmi Manuscript*, p. 59.

[41]"Pali and Sanskrit", *Journal of the Royal Asiatic Society*, 1906, pp. 346-51.

Bihar MS of Asaṅga's *Śrāvakabhūmi* his statement about three kinds, which I thereafter translate:[42]

/ antarā-parinirvāyī pudgalaḥ katamaḥ / antarā-parinirvāyiṇaḥ pudgalās trayaḥ /

/ ekāntarā-parinirvāyī pudgalaḥ cyutamātra evāntarābhavābhinirvartikāle antarābhavam abhinirvartayaty abhinirvartate samakālam eva parinirvāti / tadyathā parīttaḥ śakalikāgnir utpannaiva parinirvāti /

/ dvītīyo 'ntarā-parinirvāyī pudgalaḥ antarābhavam abhinirvartayaty abhinirvartate antarābhave tatrastha eva kālāntareṇa parinirvāti / no tu yenopapattibhavas tenādyāpy upanato bhavati / tadyathāyoguḍānāṃ vā ayaḥsthalānāṃ vā dīptāgnisaṃprataptānām ayoghanair *un*mathitā*nām[43] ayaḥprapāṭikā utpataty eva parinirvāti /

/ tṛtīyo 'ntarā-parinirvāyī pudgalaḥ antarābhavam abhinirvartya yenopapattibhavas tenopanamati / upanataś ca punar anupapanna eva parinirvāti / tadyathā / ayaḥprapāṭikā utpadya pṛthivyām apatitā eva parinirvāti / ta ime trayo 'ntarā-parinirvāyiṇaḥ pudgalā ekadhyam abhisaṃkṣipya antarā-parinirvāyī pudgala ity ucyate /

What is the person who attains *parinirvāṇa* in the intermediate state? There are three persons who attain *parinirvāṇa* in the intermediate state.

The first person who attains *parinirvāṇa* in the intermediate state is made to fulfill the intermediate state no sooner has he died, at the time of accomplishing the intermediate state. He accomplishes it at exactly the same time and attains *parinirvāṇa*. For example, a tiny flame of hay arises and immediately disappears.

The second person who attains *parinirvāṇa* in the intermediate state is made to accomplish the intermediate state and accomplishes it, just staying there in the intermediate state and in the intervening time attains *parinirvāṇa*, but where be the state of rebirth (*upapattibhava*) does not just now head toward

[42]This is the manuscript utilized in the work of n. 28 above. The present excerpt is not included in that work. The Tibetan equivalent is found in the Tibetan Tanjur, *PTT*, Vol. 110, p. 69-3ff.

[43]Part of this word was covered by a tack used when R. Sankrityayana photographed the manuscript in Tibet.

> that place. For example, just as when iron balls or iron plates are made burning hot by being violently struck with iron hammers, and the mass of sparks from the irons just ascends and disappears.
>
> The third person who attains *parinirvāṇa* in the intermediate state when he accomplishes the intermediate state does head to where is the rebirth state; and having headed there, without being reborn, attains *parinirvāṇa.* For example, just as when a mass of sparks from the iron ascends and then when falling quite reaching the earth, disappears.
>
> When one takes these three *antarā-parinirvāyin* persons together, the expression "person who attains *parinirvāṇa* in the intermediate state" is used.

So this is the theory repeated by Asaṅga and his brother Vasubandhu centuries after the *Points of Controversy* rejected this interpretation of the word *antarāparinirvāyin.* But, upon inspection of the three kinds of *antarāparinirvāyin* as Asaṅga states them, we find it is actually only the second one that has an *antarābhava* not accepted by the opponents of such a state. This is because all the Indian Buddhist sects agreed that there is a death state followed by a rebirth state within the womb (in the case of human birth), and therefore would not deny the *antarābhavas* which coincide with the death and rebirth states. But they would likely ask, "Then why use the expression 'intermediate state' in these cases?"

III. Final Considerations

My investigation indicates that the old Upaniṣads and the old Buddhist scriptures both present the rival theories of "no intermediate state" and "intermediate state". Perhaps in the Upaniṣads this reflects a contrasting orientation of the "re-death" (per *Bṛhadāraṇyaka*) and the "re-birth" (per *Kaṭha*) positions. In the Buddhist sects the difference is partly temperamental, to wit, those rejecting the state preferring to have a rational control of Buddhist doctrine; and those accepting the state willing to allow mythological exuberance. Once one accepts the intermediate state, there is no end to the elaboration, as evidenced in the *Tibetan Book of the Dead.*

This research also leads to the curious conclusion that the same ancient Buddhist scriptures can lead to opposing doctrines with partisans equally divided among the old Buddhist sects. This should unsettle the all-too-frequent posture among modern exponents of Buddhism where someone claims that he knows better than others the Dharma of the Buddha. Of course, as far as the intermediate-state dispute is concerned, there is no need to attribute one position over the other to early or "original" Buddhism.

PART THREE

INTERPRETATIVE STUDIES OF BUDDHISM

13

NO TIME, GREAT TIME AND PROFANE TIME IN BUDDHISM

This essay maintains that some important Buddhist texts contribute to a neat formulation of man's most treasured modes of thought: No Time as the source of religion, Great Time as the source of myth, and Profane Time as the source of reason. These three forms of Time are not so named in the Buddhist works. The limitation of data to Indo-Tibetan materials makes possible the addition of an expression "No Time" to the two categories "Great Time" and "Profane Timc" utilized by Eliade for worldwide cultural materials, while he marshals the evidence and terminology that facilitate the integration of Eastern and Western spirit.[1] Eliade's ontological interpretation of such modes is well known. The present writer is not thereby released from the obligation to rework the available data according to his understanding of Buddhism. Then—to anticipate the development—without asserting any ontological status for such modes elsewhere in the world, it does appear that in the Buddhist case, in the Indian context, the three modes of thought allude to three modes of being.

There is no claim to involve all of Buddhism in this treatment, although the prevalent Buddhist genesis legend, already studied, will play a significant role.[2] The metaphysical discussion stems

[1]Among the works of Mircea Eliade, the following have been especially important to this paper : *Myths, Dreams and Mysteries* (London, 1960); *The Sacred and the Profane* (New York, 1961).

[2]Alex Wayman, "Buddhist Genesis and the Tantric Tradition," *Oriens Extremus*, 9 (1962): 127-31. The essay also appears in A. Wayman, *Buddhist Tantras* (Samuvel Weiser, New York 1973).

from one celebrated text of Mahāyāna Buddhism—the work called *Madhyānta-vibhāga* which Asaṅga (*ca.* 375-430 A.D.) is held by tradition to have received from the future Buddha Maitreya in the Tuṣitā (a heaven).[3] Asaṅga, a leading exponent of Yogācāra Buddhism, might be the author of the *Madhyānta-vibhāga*, upon which his younger brother (probably half-brother) Vasubandhu wrote a commentary.[4]

Religion, Myth, and Reason in Buddhism

Although the origins of Buddhism have not been fully explained in regard to such modes as "religion," "myth," and "reason," there is little doubt that in its subsequent development, well advanced in the early centuries B.C., Buddhism possessed all these categories of thought.

At the heart of its religion, Mahāyāna Buddhism places the Buddha himself with the body of omniscience called the Dharmakāya ("outside the three worlds"), and adds the two phenomenal bodies called Saṃbhoga-kāya ("at the top of the realm of form") and Nirmāṇa-kāya ("in the realm of desire"). Voidness (*śūnyatā*) means the annihilation of corrupting influences of man's nature, leaving unvoided the Buddha natures. The laws (*dharma*) stem from the void realm of nature (*dharmadhātu*).

Myth in Buddhism includes not only the important genesis legend and the mythical portion of the Buddha's legendary life, but also the extensive literature called the Jātakas ("birth stories"), explained as the illustrious births of the Buddha in his anterior incarnations as a *bodhisattva*, a being striving toward enlightenment while exhibiting exemplary conduct to assist other beings.

The reasoning side of Buddhism played an outstanding role, as the antagonist, in the development of the traditional Hindu schools of philosophy. So well developed is this side of Buddhism that

[3]Alex Wayman, *Analysis of the Śrāvakabhūmi Manuscript* (Berkeley and Los Angeles, 1961), pp. 33-34.

[4]Gadjin M. Nagao, ed., *Madhyāntavibhāga-bhāṣya* (Tokyo, 1964). See also the salient work: Th. Stcherbatsky, *Madhyānta-Vibhanga* ("Discourse on Discrimination between Middle and Extremes"), ascribed to Bodhisattva Maitreya and commented on by Vasubandhu and Sthiramati, translated from the Sanskrit (*Bibliotheca Buddhica*, vol. 30 [Leningrad, 1936]; only the first chapter, with commentary and subcommentary, has been translated herein).

some early Western Orientalists considered Buddhism to be pre-eminently rational.

Creation According to the Madhyānta Vibhāga

Before setting forth the intended structure of three modes of thought, I shall separately treat the rather technical data of the *Madhyānta-vibhāga*, which not only contributes decisively to the present topic but also conveys a rather different picture of the Yogācāra from the way the latter is depicted in current surveys of Indian philosophy.

The *two realities* of the Yogācāra metaphysics are called *abhūta-parikalpa* and *śūnyatā*, here translated respectively as the "Imagination of Unreality" and "Voidness," compatible with Stcherbatsky's respective renditions, the "Universal Constructor of Phenomena" and the "Absolute." The *Madhyānta-vibhāga* states (I, 1):

There was the Imagination of Unreality,
And in it no duality (of subject and object).
There was Voidness in it,
And it was in that (Voidness).[5]

Of the reality called "Imagination of Unreality," what is the "Unreality" (*abhūta*) and what the "Imagination" (*parikalpa*)? The text states (I, 5): "What is imagined is explained as the 'objective thing' (*artha*); what is dependent, as the construction process of unreality; and what is perfect, as the unreality of both (subject and object)."[6] And from the text (I, 3) and Vasubandhu's commentary, we learn that the "Imagination" has its own four characters (*svalakṣaṇa*), called "objective thing" (*artha*), "personal organ" (*sattva*), "self" (*ātman*), and "representation" (*vijñapti*):

Perception was engendered as the projection of (six kinds of) objective things, (five) personal organs, self (=mind), and (six kinds of) representations. The objective thing does not

[5]abhūta-parikalpo 'sti dvayan tatra na vidyate /
śūnyatā vidyate tv atra tasyām api sa vidyate //

[6]kalpitaḥ paratantraś ca pariniṣpanna eva ca /
arthād abhūtakalpāc ca dvayābhāvāc ca deśitaḥ //

> belong to it (i.e., perception). Since the former (the objective thing) is unreal, the latter (perception) is also unreal.[7]

The implication is that when the Imagination of Unreality is not so imagining, its four characters are not grouped in subject-object relation, and that when it is so imagining, the "self" approaches the "personal organ," whereupon the "representation" falsely depicts the "objective thing." As with all such ultimate processes, the *modus operandi* of the primordial subject-object emergence is wrapped in mystery. However, it seems to involve an interaction of the "self" and the "personal organ" with Voidness as Dharmadhātu ("realm of Dharma"), which is the material cause.[8]

The reality called "Voidness" has this character (I, 13*a-b*): "the unreality of both (subject and object), and the reality (subjacent) of this unreality."[9] This translation, following Stcherbatsky, is consistent with Yogācāra definitions in other works as typified by two statements, one of which specifies what is voided and the other of which specifies what remains not voided. The following verse (I, 14) clarifies the sense of the "reality (subjacent) of this unreality" by names of Voidness, justified in the next verse (I, 15):

> Thusness (*tathatā*) because not otherwise, True Limit (*bhūtakoṭi*) because not wrong, Attributeless (*animitta*) because the cessation of attributes, Ultimate State (*paramārthatā*) because the domain of the noble ones, the Realm of Dharma (*dharmadhātu*) because having the noble natures (*dharma*).

Verses I, 8-9 and Vasubandhu's commentary portray the Ima-

[7]artha-satvātma-vijñapti-pratibhāsaṃ prajāyate /
vijñānaṃ nāsti cāsyārthas tad-abhāvāt tad apy asat //
Vasubandhu's commentary (Nagao, *Madhyāntavibhāga-bhāṣya*, pp. 18-19) clarifies the word "self" (*ātman*) as the "corrupted mind" (*kliṣṭamanas*) and the six things as objects grasped by the six sense organs (five by the word *sattva*), including mind as the sixth, in terms of six representations (*vijñapti*).

[8]Such an idea is found near the beginning of Asaṅga's *Śrāvakabhūmi*, in a passage for which original Sanskrit is lacking; here it is translated from Tibetan (Derge edition of Tanjur, *Sems tsam*, *Śrāvakabhūmi*, 2b): "However, that seed does not have the characteristics of difference so long as it stays apart from the six sense bases (*ṣaḍāyatana*). That seed has been handed down in lineage from beginningless time and has states obtained through the six sense bases which are attained by means of 'true nature' (*dharmatā*)."

[9]dvayābhāvo hy abhāvasya bhāvaḥ śūnyasya lakṣaṇam.

gination of Unreality in a new role. Since its own characters (*svalakṣaṇa*) had projected the unreal perception, the younger Imagination of Unreality is now precisely that unreal perception of the unreal objective thing:

> Now the Imagination of Unreality was consciousness (of) and mentals, composing the three realms (of desire, of form, and formless). Perception (= "consciousness of") sees the objective thing itself; its mentals see modifications of the objective thing. The first one is the foundation-perception (= *ālaya-vijñāna*). The other ones pertain to experience. These are the mentals (namely, feelings, *vedanā*) which enjoy, (ideas, *saṃjñā*) which distinguish, and (motivations, *saṃskāra*) which activate (perception).[10]

That passage covers two stages of the process which the present essay intends to keep separate. They are "consciousness of," which sees the objective thing itself, and mentals, which see modifications of the thing. They are preceded by the atemporal state in which the Imagination of Unreality abides with Voidness deprived of the subject-object relationship.

No Time, the Source of Religion

No Time means the revelation of reality, everywhere, always. Man may or may not intuit the dazzling ultimate. It is *other* than Great Time when nature predicts by omens and man obeys. It is *other* than Profane Time when man predicts by reason and nature obeys.

The story of Buddhist genesis alludes to a mode of being prevailing as "men of the first eon" while the lower receptacle worlds are reevolving after the periodic destruction. These men have bodies made of mind, are self-luminous, feed on joy, and are wherever they wish to be. Their actions have immediate fruition, and so involve No Time.[11]

In the *Madhyānta-vibhāga*, No Time is the mysterious truth of a voidness reality subjacent to the unreality of subject and

[10]abhūtaparikalpaś ca citta-caittās tridhātukāḥ /
tatrārtha-dṛṣṭir vijñānaṃ tad-viśeṣe tu caitasāḥ //
ekam pratyaya-vijñānaṃ dvitīyam aupabhogikaṃ /
upabhoga-pariccheda-prerakās tatra caitasāḥ //

[11]Wayman, "Buddhist Genesis."

object—a reality neither joined to nor separate from the creative center called Imagination of Unreality. This Voidness is the goal to which the noble ones (the elect) aspire, because it has the noble natures, called in other Buddhist texts the "Buddha natures" (*buddhadharma*).

Generally, Buddhist texts referred to this state as Nirvāṇa, more properly "Nirvāṇa without remainder." "Nirvāṇa with remainder" is approximately Great Time. The Mahāyāna "Nirvāṇa without fixed abode" (*apratiṣṭhita-nirvāṇa*) is all three Times.

Great Time, the Source of Myth

Great Time is the marvelous beginning of time in the sense of an interval not always progressing in a continuous line, as does Profane Time, which has an anterior past, a present moment, and a posterior future. The interval of time is colored by a glorious quality, because then is the contact with earth by the hero, walking with erect stature. His fabulous and exemplary adventures need only be recounted in myth to inspire the imagination, and possibly also the conduct of men in later Profane Time, especially men who are close to the soil. The myth of the Buddha's life also begins with this walking, as the child leaves his mother's womb by the right side, takes seven steps toward the north, and announces, "I am at the top of the world. . ."[12] The future Buddha's seven steps are (No Time in) Great Time; his announcement is (No Time in) Profane Time.

> All those examples point to the touching of earth as constituting a symbolic moment which we could call Moment 1, as the preliminary moment to mundane life (in case of infant), to spiritual life (in case of Buddha), to the symbolization of the spiritual life (in case of main body of the rite), to acceptance in marriage (in case of the auspicious bride). At Moment 1, the being is not yet alive, but anticipates the whole future life. Astrologically, at the moment of birth the infant is at the center of the universe, in sympathetic communion with the planets and stars, which indelibly impress the being with a sort of centripetal force.[13]

[12]Cf. Eliade, *Myths, Dreams and Mysteries*, pp. 110-15.

[13]Alex Wayman, "Climactic Times in Indian Mythology and Religion," *History of Religions*, 4 (1965): 310-11.

This place where earth is touched is the Center, of which Eliade frequently speaks.

In the Buddhist story of genesis, on the surface of earth there appeared an earth essence—in the Tantric version called an ambrosia (*amṛta*)—which a greedy being tasted with his finger and then ate mouthfuls of. Other beings followed suit. Thus they became dependent on subtle morsel food and no longer fed on joy. They gradually lost the body made of mind as their bodies became heavier and more substantial. The ones who indulged least proudly retained their beautiful form. The sun, moon, and year became known. Hell beings, beings in the embryonic states, and the gods involved with desire (*kāmāvacāradeva*) still have the subtle kind of food which does not give rise to excrement or urine.[14]

According to the *Madhyānta-vibhāga*, in the beginning the world became inner-outer, or subject-object. That is to say, what was always there in No Time continued just the same. But an imaginary relationship was introduced among the four characters, semi-divine beings as it were, of the Imagination of Unreality. Perhaps in a magic square they projected their own being through Voidness into an Imagination of Unreality the younger. This is first the foundation perception called "basic perception" (*ālaya-vijñāna*) which has as object the objective thing itself. Since as yet there are no modifications (*viśeṣu*) of the objective thing, there is no error (*bhrānti*) or specific illusion. Nevertheless, the objective thing is said to be unreal. The unreality here is the cosmic illusion, the beginning of downfall. The fascinating objective thing conceals in its very freshness the specific illusion that is sure to follow in a subsequent remove of Profane Time. From the beginning, the world was pervaded by delusion (*moha*). It is as the Buddha tells: all constructed things (*saṃskāra*) are suffering. In Great Time, the suffering is of transformation.

Profane Time, the Source of Reason

This is horizontality. Man has nature down where it can be handled. But he believes that his inner knowledge stems from outer happenings. Time now, according to Lévy-Bruhl, is what

14Wayman, "Buddhist Genesis."

"our" minds—the minds of us, the "civilized"—take it to be. In his graphic words:

> extending indefinitely in imagination, something like a straight line, always homogeneous by nature, upon which events fall into position, a line on which foresight can arrange them in an unilinear and irreversible series, and on which they must of necessity occur one after the other.[15]

As long as man lives a profane life, his best guide is reason, which is limited and superficial, accompanied by the latest "laws of thought." The remarkable achievements of science fall here. Profane existence proves itself by accumulations such as merchandise and books (religious and secular), and also by desacralized leavings or residues. It is "the rest of life" after Moment 1.

In Buddhist genesis, the beings began to subsist on coarse morsel food, which gave rise to excrement and urine. The distinguishing characteristics of male and female arose, along with sexual desire and relevant acts. Then the idea of "private property" arose with individual rice plots, followed by stealing and consequent violence. Those beings elected a "great chosen one" (*mahāsammata*) to provide security.[16] This shows the emergence of lust and hatred, then private property and the status of ruler and ruled.

The *Madhyānta-vibhāga* alludes to this state of being by "mentals" seeing the modifications of the objective thing. These mentals pertain to experience, and are feelings, ideas, and motivations. They are also called the "evolving perceptions" (*pravṛtti-vijñāna*). This state is full-blown illusion.

Recapitulations

It is a basic feature of Eliade's writings that he denies a purely profane existence. The homogeneity of profane space is interrupted by certain "holy places" dear to the memory of even the profane nonreligious man.[17] While Eliade has not defined the profane life in the terms I have employed above, I see no conflict with his position on this matter. I can therefore go on to agree

[15]Lucien Lévy-Bruhl, *Primitive Mentality* (Boston, 1966), p. 123.

[16]Wayman, "Buddhist Genesis."

[17]So in Eliade, *The Sacred and the Profane*.

with him on this denial of the pure profane. There is no need to repeat here his well-presented justifications. My methods of demonstrating this conclusion are additional. Here there are two kinds of recapitulation—that of childhood and that of the daily life of man.

The Recapitulation in Childhood

In a brief communication[18] I called attention to the Indian theory of life stages, of which the first three are in point now. They are the first year of life under the Moon, the second and third years under Mars, and the fourth through twelfth under Mercury. In the first year—as modern child development study shows—the baby begins with no distinction between himself and his environment, and so is akin to the nondual state of No Time, from which he gradually emerges during the balance of the year. Recently emerged from the primeval waters called the amniotic fluid and still dependent on liquids, the infant is governed by the Moon. For purposes of our correspondences based on Indian classifications, the entire year will be taken conventionally as the "nondual state." About the beginning of the second year, the child starts to walk: this inaugurates the heroic stage of walking on earth. It is a kind of *anabasis*, "advance uphill" (classically used for "military advance"). Also in the next two years the child speaks magic syllables expressing his desires and commanding their fulfillment by parents. Morbid regressions to this state could be called *catabasis*, "retreat to the sea" (classically used for "military retreat"). So the child during those two years is governed by Mars, the commander-in-chief in Indian astrology. This is childhood's type of Great Time. Phylogenetic recapitulation in Profane Time is shown by the last period of childhood, the fourth through the twelfth year, when the lad or girl develops the power of reasoning while playfully dashing hither and yon under the dominion of Mercury. Modern studies show that the child is now a "socialized being" and his games increasingly have rules.[19] The ages assigned to these stages are of course stated with generality and are not meant to deny individual differences.

[18]"The Stages of Life according to Varāhamihira," *Journal of the American Oriental Society*, 83 (1963): 360-61.

[19]Jean Piaget, *Play, Dreams and Imitation in Childhood* (New York, 1962), p. 142.

The Daily Recapitulation

Each day, man's life exhibits modes that disguise the three times. Properly speaking, the disguise is inaugurated by puberty, because the maturation of the sexually differentiated characteristics recalls what in the Buddhist genesis legend inaugurated the last period, corrupted by lust and hatred. In short, dreamless sleep corresponds to No Time, dream to Great Time, and the waking state to Profane Time.

I must stress—and in a similar vein, so does Eliade[20]—that the kind of correspondence referred to in the itemization of recapitulations does not imply identity with the three Times. Indeed, elements in correspondence are both related in some way and differ in some way. No Time, Great Time, and Profane Time each have a universal or shared character. The recapitulations are personal or private. Thus, Great Time is the source of myth as held by a certain society to work out public problems while a dream is a private matter to work out private problems. The dream is also like Great Time in its shortened psychological distance between subject and object, evidenced by the conversion of discursive thinking into nondiscursive imagery, especially in dramatic presentation, and also by its premonitory character (in the sense of showing trends). In contrast, dreaming is mostly inspired by experiences of the waking state, preeminently Profane Time, while Great Time is mostly inspired by No Time. Certain cases of unsuccessful ("unresolved") dreaming even parallel the successful "walking" of Great Time by the striking act of somnambulism. The recapitulations of childhood are more faithful to the three Times (hence the Biblical advice for entering the Kingdom of Heaven). That the third period (ages four through twelve), when the child is allowed to go out and play with other children, establishes Profane Time, is a matter to be justified. Buddhism generally explained that "discursive thought" (*vikalpa*) is the nescience (*avidyā*) , or cause of it, that heads the Dependent Origination (*pratītya-samutpāda*) constituting Phenomenal Life (*saṃsāra*). This "discursive thought" is the basis of human reasoning with its rules. But a child playing by itself does not devise rules for games.[21] Therefore, I understand the third period of

[20]Eliade, *Myths, Dreams and Mysteries*, p. 17.

[21]Piaget, *Play, Dreams and Imitation*, p. 142.

childhood to be involved in the parable of the Buddhist Mahāyāna scripture called *Sāgaramatiparipṛcchā:* "Now suppose this boy, being a child, would fall into a pit of night-soil while playing...." It turns out that this "pit of night-soil" is a term for *saṃsāra.*[22]

While the recapitulations in both childhood and daily life are not identical with the three Times, they do share the universal character in a salient feature. That is to say, we can combine the childhood and daily recapitulations to observe that although the child, and then the child becomes an adult, are in aspects of Profane Time, they do indeed still recapitulate all three Times. They do so irrespective of the degree of religious feeling in particular persons, do so irrespective of such rites as baptism, and do so whether or not people indulge in food and sex sacramentally. In every life the "Moment 1" is Great Time, the rest of life Profane Time, but throughout life there are these recapitulations, echoes, and intimations of the Sacred. This is why no person in Profane Time can be utterly dissociated from No Time and Great Time. In this light, an irreligious as well as a religious person may use with sincerity such expressions as the "sanctity of the home."

Breakthroughs

By "breakthrough" I refer to the numinous experience as described by Otto (*Das Heilige*). It is an irrational revelation of overwhelming majesty or of mysterious power. The complete otherness of the revelation makes it appear as a breakthrough from a superior, nonhuman realm. According to the classification utilized above, this breakthrough would be from No Time into Great Time or from No Time into Profane Time. In the Indian context, the first case—overwhelming majesty of No Time in Great Time—is illustrated in the *Bhagavadgītā* by Krishna's revelation of his cosmic form to Arjuna. This is also the *saṃbhogakāya* of the Buddha preaching to the great *bodhisattvas* in the Akaniṣṭha Heaven. The second case—the mysterious power of No Time in Profane Time—is illustrated by the Hindu-Buddhist Act of Truth. This act is done by Sītā in the Hindu epic *Rāmāyaṇa* and there are many examples in Buddhist scriptures. Here the performer declares the truth of his outstanding acts and

[22]The parable is quoted in Jikido Takasaki, *A Study on the Ratnagotravibhaga*(*Uttaratantra*) (Rome, 1966,) pp. 246-47.

commands the gods to produce the desired miracle. The miracle—an incredible event apparently violating "Nature's laws"—is the breakthrough. Ānandagarbha contains this ritual statement in his *Śrīparamādi-ṭīkā:* "He should recite, 'Oh Bhagavat Vajrasattva, just as it is true that all *dharmas* are like a dream, by virtue of that truth may I be allowed to see and be allowed to hear the such-and-such desired dream!' "[23]

Both kinds of breakthrough have been responsible in numerous cases for the striking religious phenomenon of "conversion." In the category of breakthrough I would also place some debatable religious experiences, of more or less sullied character, all for "ego-defense": battlefield trauma, epilepsy, young man in the whorehouse, psychedelic drugs (as indicated by such images of "shattering" as walls breached by sea-water).

Participations

There is also the attempt to ascend to higher states of consciousness as though to live integrally in them, reified as modes of being—a sort of mystical immersion—or at least to be able to get into and out of those states whenever one wishes. Hence we speak of participation in Great Time or in No Time. Success here can be understood as either discovery or verification of spiritual truth, and also as the acquisition of supernormal powers. Eliade writes:

> Upon the plane of the archaic religions, participation in the condition of the "spirits" is what endows the mystics and the magicians with their highest prestige. It is during his ecstasy that the shaman undertakes, *in the spirit*, long and dangerous mystical journeys even up to the highest Heaven to meet the God, or up to the Moon or down into Hell, etc.[24]

Whatever be the truth in these cases, it is the human mind which so asserts it. It is a wonderful feature of Profane Time that it asserts the truth of religion. The higher Times have truth but do not assert it. Great Time should include the Buddhist search

[23] / bcom ldan ḥdas rdo rje sems dpaḥ bden pa gaṅ gis chos thams cad rmi lam dan ḥdra bar mñam paḥi bden pa des bdag ḥdod paḥi rmi lam che ge mo mthoṅ bar mdzod cig / thos par mdzod cig ces brjod par byaḥo / (Kyoto-Tokyo Photographic reprint [1959-61] of *Kanjur-Tanjur*, vol. 72, pp. 305-3).

[24] Eliade, *Myths, Dreams and Mysteries*, p. 95.

for or experience of suffering as a Noble Truth. For this it is necessary to reduce, even to abolish, psychological distance—man's advancing self-awareness in Profane Time that he is differentiated from the object (nature), which curtails a person's empathy with beings located mentally by that person in other groups. This factitious grouping—the castes of India and the world—is the prejudice engendered during the third period of childhood (see "Recapitulations").

Buddhism, in common with Hinduism, believed that by a regular course of conduct, such as restrictions on food and sex activity, and by finding the proper place and there a *guru*, a person (preferably male) could then undertake the somewhat arduous training for *samādhi* and thus ascend to various levels of consciousness, even the highest, the Incomparable Complete Enlightenment of the Buddha. This meditative ascension is usually stated in terms of sensory experience. The attainment of mental calm gradually brings out certain supernormal faculties, such as divine hearing. Eliade points out, "In short, throughout religious history, sensory activity has been used as a means of participating in the sacred and attaining to the divine."[25] In the *bodhisattva* doctrine of Mahāyāna Buddhism this is also stressed. Thus, in Atīśa's *Bodhipathapradīpa* (verses 35-36):

> Just as a bird with unspread wings cannot fly up to the sky, in the same way the one without the power of the supernormal faculties cannot serve the aim of the sentient beings.
> The merits of a single day that are due to the supernormal faculties would not occur in a hundred births for one lacking the supernormal faculties.[26]

In that way, those *bodhisattvas* who are called "great beings" (*mahāsattva*) are in Great Time, vastly able to serve the aim of sentient beings by dint of the supernormal faculties.

Extraordinary sensory experience is governed by the second instruction of the Buddhist path, which is arranged in three instructions: (1) morality (*adhiśīla-śikṣa*), (2) concentration (*adhisamādhi-śikṣa*), and (3) insight (*adhiprajñā-śikṣa*).[27] The implication

[25]Eliade, *Myths, Dream and Mysteries*, p. 74.

[26]Manuscript translation from Tibetan by Alex Wayman.

[27]The famous Pāli text, Buddhaghosa's *Visuddhimagga*, is arranged in three parts in accordance with three instructions.

of these instructions is that Buddhism is not seeking to attain Great Time or No Time just for the sake of doing so, or for the sake of gaining a striking experience. The old Buddhist aim was of liberation (No Time) and later came the Bodhisattva ideal (Great Time). Since Great Time had the seed of downfall into Profane Time, the Buddhist rationale of reaching that lofty state is to do it in circumstances whereby the concurrent hypnotic delusion is eliminated. And so it was taught that on top of the mental calming, the fruit of the second instruction, there should be the insight which sees things as they really are (what early Buddhism said) or which sees things arising as in a dream (what later Buddhism said).

The order of instructions places morality as the foundation for both mental calming and insight. This is borne out by the assignment of certain rites to Great Time. Ritual action has this in common with the heroic conduct of Great Time: one has to give up all random action and do things with exactitude in the performance of a ritual, and one has to give up all means and timid acts in order to have heroic conduct. That is to say, they both demand the abandonment of the usual human weaknesses exhibited in Profane Time. These rites have features in common with meditation procedures. I have in mind especially the *maṇḍala* rites of Tibetan Buddhism,[28] which are analogous to steps of meditation. Here one has to select the proper site, remove all the stones, potsherds, and other pains of the soil, and meditatively seize the site by vowing to perform the reviewed rite. In Buddhist meditation one must also find the right meditative object, eliminate gross corruptions from the mind, and seize the meditative object by leaving off the usual mental dashing hither and yon to a multitude of sensory objects.

These meditative procedures—the old ways or the "shortcuts" such as the *Tantras* claim to have—are meant to reach an otherworldly condition. It is here that the myth, especially the genesis legend, serves the function of reminding profane man of that mode of being he has lost and even suggesting how he may return. Then, what does Buddhism have to say about participating in Great Time and No Time as modes of being in the senses

[28]See Ferdinand D. Lessing and Alex Wayman, trans., *Mkhas grub rje's* ("Fundamentals of the Buddhist Tantras"), (The Hague, 1968), pp. 279 ff.

suggested by the genesis legend? It was believed in ancient Buddhism that by advanced meditative techniques one could draw from the physical body a duplicate of it called the "body made of mind" (*manomaya-kāya*), as recorded in the *Dīgha-nikāya:*

> Here a monk creates a body from this (his) body, having form mind-made, with all limbs and parts, not deprived of senses. Just as if a man were to pull out a reed from its sheath, he would know: "This is the sheath, this the reed. The sheath is one thing, the reed is another. It is from the sheath that the reed has been drawn forth."[29]

The *Laṅkāvatāra-sūtra* distinguishes three degrees in development of this "body made of mind": (1) its potential separation during stabilization in the pleasure of *samādhi;* (2) its separation due to reversal of the basis of the evolving perceptions and of the basic perception (*ālayavijñāna*), with a reorientation ("alteration of consciousness") toward *dharmas* (natures); and finally, (3) its becoming a body of the Buddha.[30] The second stage, pervaded by "forbearance of the unoriginated natures" (*anutpattikadharmakṣānti*), means living without terror in Great Time; while the third stage, when the "body made of mind" has been initiated as a Buddha, means living in No Time. These three stages of the "body made of mind" appear to reverse the three downward stages of the Buddhist genesis legend and, by mastering the three Times, to prove the myth.

In addition, there are ancient and modern claims that certain drugs, now called "consciousness expanding" (psychedelic), such as the current LSD—possibly the *soma* of the ancient Vedic cult is in the same category—bring one easily to the experience of Great Time. Drugs that arouse striking sensory images have precisely this *intense mindfulness* (*smṛti*) in common with *yoga*. In the case of drugs, however, the experience is of kaleidoscopic and somewhat distorted images rather than the "one pointedness of mind" (*ekāgratā-citta*) of *samādhi* and is uncontrolled by the subject except for some affective preconditioning ("expectancy").

[29]See Paravahera Vajirañāṇa Mahāthera, *Buddhist Meditation in Theory and Practice* (Colombo, Ceylon, 1962), p. 440; and Mircea Eliade, *Yoga; Immortality and Freedom* (New York, 1958), p. 165.

[30]See Alex Wayman, "Studies in Yama and Māra," *Indo-Iranian Journal*, 3 (1959): 119.

Therefore, these drugs cannot supply the mental calm (*śamatha*) necessary for the supernormal faculties. They seem to amount to at least one of the two extremes rejected by the Buddha in favor of the Middle Path—the extreme of indulgence in a riot of sense images; possibly also they represent the extreme of mortification, of body chemistry.

Indeed, an artist of the visionary type is more likely to live in Great Time than any drug-taker. This is because when perception sees the bare objective thing, that object, as "nature," has the upper hand: being the only thing perceived, it has virtual hypnotic value. Notice the words of Picasso:

> There must be darkness everywhere except on the canvas, so that the painter becomes hypnotized by his own work and paints almost as though he were in a trance.... He must stay as close as possible to his own inner world if he wants to transcend the limitations his reason is always trying to impose on him.[31]

Jung writes consistently: "A great work of art is like a dream; for all its apparent obviousness it does not explain itself and is never unequivocal. A dream never says: 'You ought', or: 'This is the truth.' "[32] The breakdown of formal profane structures through shortened psychological distance can bring types of religious experiences to artists and drug-takers as well as to *yogins*. However, there is no special distinction in reaching Great Time or No Time somehow or other, no matter in how disoriented a manner; for, after all, there are the recapitulations which all of us experience normally without risk.

CONCLUSION

If one accepts the terminology of three Times associated with three modes of thought and further accepts that these modes of thought allude to modes of being, he can easily grant that there are various ways of reaching or plunging into those modes of being as a veritable transfer or flight of consciousness to a different

[31]Francoise Gilot and Carlton Lake, *Life with Picasso* (New York, 1965), pp. 110-11.

[32]C. G. Jung, *Modern Man in Search of a Soul* (New York, 1933), p. 171.

field or domain, one that is initially strange and possibly frightening. The three Times themselves, and the corresponding procedure used for dealing with them, are a kind of thinking well known from the ancient *Upaniṣads*, on the background of which Buddhism itself arose. The states of Waking, Dream, and Dreamless Sleep are encompassing categories and are themselves included in the Fourth State (Turīya), which seems to be the forerunner of the Mahāyāna "Nirvāṇa without fixed abode."

The use of the categories "No Time," "Great Time," and "Profane Time" for subsuming disparate features of man's development or states of consciousness is not surprising since the mind of man is structurally the same, though given to different "ways of thought"; and, after all, one can select from various sources the particular material that fits into a prearrangement. The formulation would be outstanding if it should prove to fit well with other salient features of man's thought and life which persons at large might cogently adduce as worthy of inclusion in such schema—that is, if it should turn out to be a more convenient description for worthy data than other schematic descriptions in use. This is for others to judge.

14

THE ROLE OF ART AMONG THE BUDDHIST RELIGIEUX

This paper will first go into some generalities about Buddhist art, then proceed to the aniconic period, the iconic period, and problems of discursive and non-discursive thought and art. An attempt will be made to compare meaningfully with some Western contributors to aesthetics theory, such as Herbert Read and J. P. Sartre. The comparisons are non-historical, with the premise that these problems are common to man, of whatever period of time. The author hopes to communicate his own fascination with the topic as suggesting intriguing implications beyond Buddhist art itself. Among the significant findings is that the term "freedom" is employed in two contrasting senses.

I. Generalities

The term "art" is here employed for the visual arts—namely, architecture, sculpture, and painting—which constitute the greatest artistic achievement of Buddhism. In contrast, most of the versified Buddhist works are of a didactic nature, emphasizing the message rather than poetical finesse. This is not to deny certain outstanding works of Buddhist literature, such as Aśvaghoṣa's early Kāvya and his drama, the works of Mātṛceṭa and Āryaśūra, as well as Śrī Harṣa's dramatic work. Probably others were composed in the early A.D. centuries whose authors were not sufficiently appreciated in monastic circles to have their works repeatedly copied and thus preserved. There is presumably a sizeable body of Buddhist poetry in the various Asian languages; and the Buddhists along with other Indians were fertile in tales, often of an elegant form. Whether or not original, Buddhist music does not appear to have been especially influential. Let us then turn to the visual arts which are our concern here. Many fine Buddhist art objects are preserved in the great museums of the world. Certain monuments and art centers, such as Sāñchi, Ajantā, and Nāgārjunakoṇḍa, are also well preserved at or near their original locations in India. Debala Mitra's *Buddhist Monuments* (Calcutta, 1971) is a satisfactory modern coverage of most of the Buddhist monuments of the ancient India area, including modern Pakistan and part of Nepal. The remarkable outpouring of art was characteristic of Buddhism in every country in which it became followed by a sizeable part of the population. One can gain an idea of how Buddhist art spread through South Asia, Southeast Asia, and the Far East, by consulting the comprehensive catalogue *Guide du Musée Guimet I* (Paris, 1966). Many Buddhist monuments have been irretrievably lost when they lay in the path of invading armies in Northwest India, or in other parts of Asia when they fell to marauders and depredation. As far as this writer knows, the only present-day creativity of Buddhist art is in some of the best Tibetan tankas and carpets; and we should not overlook the continuing artistry of the Japanese.

As to the origins of the art, it seems that the groundwork was laid by instructions attributed to the last sermon of the Buddha to allow a kind of division of labor for the monks and Buddhist laymen.[1] It was the laymen who were to take care of the memorial edifices called *stūpas* which contained the relics. But about a century after the Buddha's passing, there was a schism in the Buddhist order with the splinter group called the Mahāsāṅghika, continuing alongside or geographically separated from the school of the Elders (the Sthavira or Thera, as now called). It seems that the Mahāsāṅghika came in league with these laymen who were probably among the prominent and especially devout of the Buddhist laymen, and began to make theological justifications

[1]The *Mahāparinibbāna-suttanta;* cf. in English translation, T. W. and C. A. F. Rhys Davids, *Dialogues of the Buddha*, Part II (London : Luzac & Company Ltd., 4th ed., 1959), p. 154.

for *stūpa* worship.[2] Be that as it may, the production of Buddhist art now as in past centuries is mainly by well-trained laymen, although of course sometimes monks themselves were artists, as we find these days in the case of some Tibetan lamas. For the Gandhāra Buddha-type, the local Buddhist establishment, or wealthy Buddhist laymen, perhaps hired some sculptors—say, from Rome.[3]

The preciousness of this art is indicated by the depiction of "donors" at various art sites and numerous inscriptions which name the benefactor. Besides, as is well known, gifts of art are made to show appreciation for services rendered. For example, there is the case of Tsoṅ-kha-pa in Tibet, founder of the Yellow-cap sect called Gelugpa, whose new school was sponsored by a powerful hereditary family called 'Ol Kha. Tucci[4] shows how by invitation of the family, Tsoṅ-kha-pa had the worn-away paintings of the local temple done over in accordance with the way those gods had appeared to him in his own *samādhis*. Also, in ancient times temple icons were not saleable (*apaṇya*) according to the grammarian Patañjali's gloss on a Pāṇini *sūtra*,[5] but they were undoubtedly stealable.

In the long history of Buddhist art, the most striking feature is perhaps the shift of subject matter. Basically it is the movement from aniconic to iconic type art, but there is much more to it than that. In the early days it was the historical Buddha Śākyamuni that was stressed, even if the art was aniconic. The former seven Buddhas also appear in the aniconic period. Later, with the first icons, again it was Śākyamuni as the main theme. The artists poured out a deluge of art around all the details of Śākyamuni's life, whether historical or somewhat legendary. But then the theme of heavens came to include the iconic former seven Buddhas, the "Thousand Buddhas of the Fortunate Aeon (*bhadrakalpa*)," and the Buddha Amitābha-Amitāyus. Shadowy

[2]This is my deduction from the materials presented in Akira Hirakawa, "The Rise of Mahāyāna Buddhism and its Relationship to the Worship of Stupas," *Memoirs of the Research Department of the Toyo Bunko*, No. 22 (Tokyo : The Toyo Bunko, 1963).

[3]Cf. Alexander Soper, "The Roman Style at Gandhāra," *American Journal of Archaeology*, LV, 1951, pp. 301-319.

[4]Giuseppe Tucci, *Tibetan Painted Scrolls* (Rome, 1949), Vol. I, p. 41.

[5]B. N. Puri, *India in the Time of Patañjali* (Bombay, 1957), p. 182.

figures called Arhats, standardized as sixteen and then eighteen and appearing even in groups of five hundred, came in for a share of the art. The great Bodhisattvas, such as the future Buddha Maitreya, Avalokiteśvara, and Mañjuśrī inspired many artists. Willetts's table[6] shows that in the century before the T'ang dynasty, near the Chinese Lo-yang capital, Śākyamuni and Maitreya were the chief subjects, but that apparently starting with the T'ang near the same capital the Amitābha-Amitāyus and Avalokiteśvara types were dominant among the new art representations. His data should be compared with Soper's.[7] The Tibetan art school, being later, missed the early stress on the founder, Śākyamuni, and went directly to the Amitābha and Avalokiteśvara types, and then to the host of tantric deities.

The seeming replacement of the founder of Buddhism, Śākyamuni, with these hosts of Arhats, Bodhisattvas, and Buddhas, parallels the emergence of a huge new religious literature, the Mahāyāna scriptures, which seemingly replace the early Buddhism of the Pāli canon. As I have elsewhere suggested, the local differences of Buddhist art involve an adaptation to the particular country, a showing that Buddhism is "at home" there. Doubtless the Southern Buddhist countries are more conservative, both in art representations and in doctrine. In agreement, their art keeps mainly the first state of iconic representation, the Buddha depicted in scenes of his life (such as the Great Departure). In contrast, the Malay Archipelago being subject to later influences also exhibits Chinese-type deities and tantric art of later Indian Buddhism.

But the contact with original Buddhism is not lost to the extent it appears on the surface or at first glance. Deep study of the Mahāyāna scriptures shows not so much a replacement as a reworking and overlay of the early canon. Again, it seems that certain Bodhisattvas began as personifications of high levels of the Buddha's life. Thus, Avalokiteśvara may personify the Buddha's look, i.e. his survey of the living beings when he was seated under the Bodhi tree. Mañjuśrī may be the Buddha's insight (*prajñā*). Amitābha may be Śākyamuni's other-worldly

[6]William Willetts, *Chinese Art* (Penguin Books, 1958), I, pp. 348-349.

[7]Alexander Soper, *Literary Evidence for Early Buddhist Art in China* (Ascona, Switzerland, 1959).

form, the Dharmakāya so called, hence a substitution. No matter what their inception, these Bodhisattvas and other Buddha figures developed a life of their own in the course of time. It is all Buddhist art and can be regarded as the oak tree that does not resemble the acorn, from which by some commonplace miracle it emerged. And yet the art forms become fixed by hieratic standards, such as the proportions and icon size, as though to preserve intact that tree.

II. The Aniconic Period

It is well known that in its first period Buddhist art was aniconic. The founder of the religion, Gautama Buddha, was not at first represented in a human form, but rather by symbols such as: the elephant representing his conception; the auspicious marks such as his footprint representing prophecy; the tree representing the enlightenment as does the empty throne; the wheel as the first teaching set in motion; the parasol as the protective dome; the *stūpa* his Parinirvāṇa. These symbols were images (in Greek, *agalma*) of deity, but not likenesses (Greek, *eidon*).[8] As such they amounted to living embodiments; and this sense is maintained in subsequent centuries by the *stūpa* (or *caitya*). They are also "symbols for the unknown."[9]

That certain images in the above sense were associated with pilgrimage, and so a Buddhist kind of ritual, is well stated by Foucher, quoting from the last sermon of the Buddha:[10] "There are four places, O Ānanda, which an honorable worshipper should visit with religious emotion. What are these four?" Foucher answers : "They are, as we know, those where the Predestined One for the first time received illumination and preached and those where for the last time he was born and died. Now just in the devout practice of the four great pilgrimages resides any hope which we have of at last coming upon the long-sought point of departure. In order that we may grasp at once the germ and

[8]Cf. Francis M. Cornford, *Plato's Cosmology* (New York edition, 1957), p. 99.

[9]Cf. Herbert Read, *Icon & Idea* (New York, 1972 reprint), Chapter III, pp. 53, ff.

[10]A. Foucher, *The Beginnings of Buddhist Art* (Paris, London, 1917), pp. 10-11.

the directing principle of Buddhist art, it is necessary and sufficient to admit that the Indian pilgrims were pleased to bring back from these four holy places a small material souvenir of what they had there seen."

Foucher has an excellent point about these theorized souvenirs, which would have been images (Gr. *agalma*) of deity. They would be invested with an intangible power through the religious zeal of the pilgrim who had travelled to the site—associated with legends of miracles—often with considerable difficulty and sacrifice while filled with faith. Pilgrimage was ordinarily associated with the cyclical return of a certain date of the year, and group visitation at the given place. Thus many persons would participate in this auspicious concatenation of time and space. The image here is involved in a sort of spiritual *synesthesia,* a visual form somehow correlated with the auditory word which is the "insight consisting of hearing" (*śrutamayī prajñā*), the sermon associated with the spot visited.

The aniconic symbols reached triumphal expression in elaborate *stūpas.* The bas-reliefs of Barhut suggest wealthy patrons of Buddhist art already in the 2nd century, B.C. The extraordinary and still-surviving *stūpa* of Sāñchi implies that in the 1st century, B.C., the section of India now called Madhya Pradesh was strongly Buddhist. In the same century (the 1st, B.C.) such Buddhist art, usually in cave and *stūpa* elaboration would be established just south of the Vindhya range in a band that extended clear across India, and has such surviving centers as Ajantā and the more-recently discovered *stūpa* near Nagpur. Sivaramamurti believes that the Amarāvati Stūpa of Āndhra in South India by the Krishna River was founded by King Aśoka in the 3rd century, B.C.[11]

Certain images—the tree, the wheel, and the *stūpa*—were in time rendered banal by appearing on punch-marked coins, the so-called "Buddhist" coins.[12] Perhaps this very multiplication and dispersal of images would eventually result in a weakening of the holiness associated with the images, furnishing a reason for the Buddhist world to become receptive to a new form of art. But even after the iconic art appeared, the aniconic form exerted its

[11]C. Sivaramamurti, *Amaravati Sculptures in the Madras Government Museum* (Madras, 1956), p. 4.

[12]Cf. Foucher, *The Beginnings*, pp. 14-15.

religious fascination. Thus Subramanian says:[13] "As late as the sixth century A.D. and even later, the Buddhist *stūpas* continued to exercise their influence over the Āndhras who visited the holy spots and showed their reverence to them in the shape of benefactions and votive offerings."

Now, let us attempt to fathom some of the aniconic symbolism. At the old Karle cave *stūpa* in present-day Mahārāshtra, on the facade by the entrance, there is a much-reproduced representation of a magnificent male and female pair: the woman depicted with mature sensual corporeality, and the man as a well-built strong male. Inside there is the bare, unadorned *stūpa*. There is evidence that at one time the cave walls were painted with Jātaka-type scenes. It seems that the outside representations—and the cave paintings like the Jātaka sculptures of Barhut would be an extension of them—are meant to show the "realm of desire" (*kāmadhātu*) which is left behind or surmounted when one turns to the plain *stūpa*. This produces a stark contrast between the teeming scenes of "outside" and the spare "inside," and serves for a much greater challenge to the sculptor (and later to the painter of the cave walls) than if he were just to construct the stereotyped central *stūpa*. The symbolism of the one's being detailed and the other one's being plain apparently agrees with Herbert Read's description[14] of the two principles of art: "vital image" or "vitality as an aesthetic factor", and beauty as the "still centre"—because the sculptures and later paintings of the Karle monument are the vital image, and the *stūpa* is the still centre.

Indeed, if it is not stretching the case to attribute "beauty" to the still centre, which is the central *stūpa*, one can find intriguingly applicable Keats's "Ode On a Grecian Urn," at least in Gombrich's interpretation. I would be loathe to cite Keats's line "Beauty is truth, truth beauty," for fear of abusing the poet's intention by quotation here, were not these remarks of Gombrich's at hand: "For beyond the general neo-platonic faith in the truth of the artist's vision such as it is expressed in Keats's letters, the idea that the realm of beauty can be entered by man only at the price of renunciation plays an important part in eighteenth century aesthetics. Thus Schiller's speculations turned round the contrast

[13]K. R. Subramanian, *Buddhist Remains in Āndhra* (Madras, 1932), p. 16.
[14]*Icon*, Chap. I, pp. 17, ff., especially pp. 32, 33.

between the enslavement of our animal nature and the freedom of aesthetic contemplation."[15] Later in this paper I shall revert to the nature of this "freedom," so called. For the present, let us notice that the foregoing ties nicely with Read's two basic principles of art —the principle of vitality and the principle of beauty.[16] If we take Keats's line in the above sense, we can split Buddhist art—as at Karle—into two: the "outer" with the vitality of our animal nature, to be renounced; and the "inner" with the beauty that is truth, where is the so-called freedom. Eventually the Buddhist Mādhyamika school was to represent the "outer" as cyclical flow (*saṃsāra*), referring to the vitalism as "efficiency" (*arthakriyākāritā*); and in this interpretation, the "inner" would be the absolute truth (*paramārtha-satya*), the changeless beauty of what never arose to pass away, like the Lover on the Grecian Urn.

III. The Iconic Period

Buddhism in its inception was not hostile to idolatry, as was Islam. But that early Buddhist texts are simply silent on the matter has been disputed by scholars. Also, Foucher says the idolatry starts with what he calls the "Gandhārian revolution," the consequence of the Greek incursions into India in the early centuries, B.C.; but his theory of the Greek-type has been countered by evidence taking the Gandhāra Buddha rather as a Roman Apollo type.[17] Furthermore, others lean to the native evolution of the Buddha statuary, starting at Mathurā. The provenence is not very important to the role of art; because the main point is that the icons of the Buddha became popular, with their earliest remains belonging perhaps to the 1st century, A.D. The icon, as was suggested above, is lifeless through being a likeness. Precisely because recognized as a similitude, it is not taken as the residence of the Buddha; and so there are meditative practices—as will be illustrated later on—aimed at getting the Buddha to descend into the icon. In contrast, the aniconic symbols, such as the tree, are already the

[15] E. H. Gombrich, "Visual Metaphors of Value in Art," in *Symbols and Values : An Initial Study*, ed. by Lyman Bryson, et al (New York, 1954), p. 271.

[16] Cf. *Icon*, p. 93.

[17] Per Soper (n. 3, above).

seat of deity and so are not associated with meditation but rather with practices of faith, such as the circumambulation of *stūpas*. The artists were not oblivious to the distinction; and in a compromise with the earlier form of art manage to include in the background the aniconic symbols, such as the tree, and a touch of vitalism, as with the hooded serpent-king who serves as a kind of umbrella or sun-shade for the meditating Gautama. The shift from aniconic to iconic art might constitute a movement from impersonal reverence to the kind of personal devotion called *bhakti* (In Hinduism it is easier to trace the *bhakti* movement from its intellectual form in the *Bhagavadgītā* to the more emotional type centuries later in the *Bhāgavata-purāṇa* and later to the erotic forms).

Buddhist doctrine apparently supports the Buddha icon by the insistence on the human state as essential for enlightenment. Asaṅga, doubtless giving the old teaching, defines "personal success" as success of the embodiment and heads the extended list with "human state" (*manuṣyatva*).[18] Nāgārjuna's "Friendly Epistle" states the theory negatively as the "eight unfavorable moments" (*akṣaṇa*): "Adhering to wayward views; being born among the animals, among the hungry ghosts (*preta*), or among the hell-beings; being born when the Buddha's promulgation is not present, or among the heretics in far-off places; having defective organs and stupidity: or birth among the long-lived gods—these are the eight unfavorable moments. If freed from these you should get a favorable moment, exert yourself to avoid the birth (of those eight)."[19] Nāgārjuna mentions the states to be negated in order all the more to affirm the favorable state of being in the presence of the Buddha and, generally, the saints and *gurus*, and being able to listen with human intelligence and good organs. So also there is the ideal human representation in art to symbolize the condition of enlightenment.[20] The iconic type

[18]Cf. Alex Wayman, *Analysis of the Śrāvakabhūmi Manuscript* (Berkeley, 1961), p. 60.

[19]Cf. Nāgārjuna's "Friendly Epistle," Translated from the Tibetan by Dr. H. Wenzel, *Journal of the Pali Text Society*, 1886, p. 19.

[20]Doubtless, once the Buddha became represented iconographically, there would be some textual insertions to justify it. So one may understand the passages mentioning the painting of the Buddha in such works of about the 4th and 5th centuries, A.D., the *Damamūka Nidāna Sūtra* and the Chinese

thus has the role of constantly reminding the devotee of the possibility of consummation by reason of human birth. In the later tantric period a goddess, such as Tārā, as well as the male god, serves the iconic purpose.

Another kind of Buddhist teaching would oppose realistic art-types. This was the instruction to the one in the religious life that he should have sense-restraint (*indriyasaṃvara*), that is, he should avoid taking hold of signs (*nimitta-grāha*) or taking hold of details (*nānuvyañjanagrāha*) from sensory experience that would incite sinful, unvirtuous natures.[21] But hell scenes could be represented.[22] It is feasible that in the old days this favored the aniconic representations. Indeed, the non-realistic form is usual in Buddhist hieratic art, granting the early and temporary exception of the Gandhāra Buddha with the wavy hair. The Buddha is normally represented with the *uṣṇīṣa* on his head and elongated ears, neither of which features are characteristic of the actual male head. These two elements are included among the 32 standard characteristics of the Buddha; and various other characteristics, such as the abnormally long arms, are also non-realistic. In a paper long ago I pointed out that the variant lists of the Buddha's 80 secondary marks favor in one case an interpretation as a great *yogin*, and in another case, as a *kṣatriya* (the Buddha's reputed caste).[23] In fact, the two interpretations give rise to two Buddha types—the seated one in meditation, and the standing one equivalent to the universal emperor (the Cakravartin).

The non-realistic representations of the Buddha in time were combined with meditation exercises. Numerous benefits were set forth to be derived from contemplating the body of the Buddha which brought calming of the mind (*śamatha*), and then from

---

legend of King Aśoka, as are cited in Alexander Soper, "Early Buddhist Attitudes Toward the Art of Painting," *Art Bulletin*, XXXII, 2, June 1950, pp. 149-150.

[21]Wayman, *Analysis*, pp. 61-62.

[22]Nāgārjuna's "Friendly Epistle," p. 24 (verse 84): "But those who, seeing a picture of hell, hearing (of hell), remembering (it), reading (about it), or making images (of it), generate fear (of it), they certainly will experience immense rewards (*vipāka*)."

[23]Alex Wayman, "Contributions Regarding the Thirty-Two Characteristics of the Great Person," *Sino-Indian Studies; Liebenthal Festschrift*, ed. by Kshitis Roy (Visvabharati, Santiniketan, 1957), p. 255.

making offerings thereto, confession of sins, etc., before the so-contemplated Buddha. In this case, the icon serves as a sort of meditative prop to assist in transferring the likeness to the mind, since *samādhi* is not accomplished by what the outer senses are aware of, but rather by what the mind is aware of. So in Kamalaśīla's *Bhāvanākrama* III:[24]

> In regard to that, first the *yogin* fastens his mind on the formal body of the Tathāgata as it is seen and as it is heard, and then is to accomplish calming. He orients his mind continuously on the form of the Tathāgata's body, yellow like the color of purified gold, adorned with the (32) characteristics and the (80) minor marks, dwelling within its retinue, and acting for the aim of the sentient beings by diverse means. Generating a desire for the merits of that (body), he subdues fading, excitement, and the other faults, and should practice meditation until such time as that (body) dwells in front and is seen clearly.

Concerning the remark "dwells in front," as I have written elsewhere, "the god assumes a concrete attitude, reflecting the repose of the Dharmadhātu, or merges with the external icon." Besides, shifting to the tantric literature, we know that showing an icon does not violate tantric secrecy, since the violation does not consist in revealing to the eye, but to the ear.[25]

Coomaraswamy makes a similar point about art creation: "Thus the artist's model is always a mental image."[26] The same author has relevant remarks with some Indian terms.[27] Here the term *pratyakṣa* means "direct sense perception," hence of the icon; while the term *parokṣa* means "beyond the senses," hence beyond vulgar experience. We may appeal now to a great line of the Buddhist logician Dharmakīrti (*Pramāṇa-vārttika*, II, 132b): "When the goal (=cessation of suffering) and its cause (=the means) are out of sight (*parokṣa*), to explain them is difficult." Difficult, but not impossible. Anyway, words rather fail to explain the *samādhi*, the religious goal, and the artist's model.

[24]Alex Wayman, *The Buddhist Tantras; Light on Indo-Tibetan Esotericism* (New York, 1973), p. 58.

[25]*Ibid.*, p. 67.

[26]Ananda K. Coomaraswamy, *The Transformation of Nature in Art* (Dover Publications, New York, 1956), p. 79.

[27]*Ibid.*, Chap. V. on Parokṣa.

However, the icon—and the category includes the tantric icon as well—is exposed to direct sense perception (*pratyakṣa*), and so is the basis for feeling. Buddhism explicitly states this situation in the formula of Dependent Origination (*pratītya-samutpāda*) where the first seven members are understood as the passive unrolling of causes established in the "previous life" and run down to No. 5, "six sense bases," which establish partite experience and serve as the condition for No. 6, "contact", of sense organ, sense object, and partite perception, which serve as the condition for No. 7, "feelings" (*vedanā*), pleasurable, painful, and neutral. Therefore, feelings, and this includes of course the pleasurable feeling aroused by an art object, are not a matter of free will, since they are the culmination of the deterministic series. Besides, Buddhist scriptures insist that feelings are associated with the "naming faculty" (*saṃjñā*), amounting to such particular views or judgments as "It hurts," "The pot is pretty," etc. Hence, one does not *choose* to appreciate art. This is not necessarily in conflict with Sartre's position, as cited in Kaelin: "For this is quite the final goal of art: to recover this world by giving it to be seen as it is, but as if it had its source in human freedom."[28] As this paper will argue later on, the spectator seems to have, although he does not have, freedom.

It is the second part of Dependent Origination, beginning with member No. 8, "craving" (*tṛṣṇā.*, in Pāli *taṇhā*), furnishing the condition for No. 9, "taking" or "indulgence" (*upādāna*), that amounts to free will, if it is at all to be admitted by Buddhism. This is because it is these members which create the new circumstances, prepare the new destiny of the being. Sartre is remarkably parallel: "We have seen that the act of imagination is a magical one. It is an incantation destined to produce the object of one's thought, the thing one desires, in a manner that one can take possession of it. . . . Next, these objects do not appear, as they do in perception, from a particular angle, they do not occur *from a point of view*. . . . For the rest, the object as an image is an unreality. It is no doubt present, but at the same time, it is out of reach."[29] Sartre further

[28]Eugene F. Kaelin, *An Existentialist Aesthetic* (The University of Wisconsin Press, Madison, 1962), pp. 123-124.

[29]Jean-Paul Sartre, *The Psychology of Imagination*, tr. by Bernard Frechtman (Washington Square Press edition, New York, 1968), p. 159.

agrees with the old Buddhist series when he says: "Certainly the unreal always receives and never gives."[30] This is the intention of Buddhist member No. 9, *upādāna*, which always means "taking," and never "giving." Thus the new being is childlike and is free in desire, even though to perception it might look helpless. And like children, art products generally survive best in peacetime.

IV. Discursive and Non-Discursive Thought and Art

This section is quite technical but hopefully will permit some further comparisons with modern aesthetics theory.

The Buddhists more than two millenia ago had gone profoundly into the matter of discursive and non-discursive thought. Was it solely by introspection? In this connection I recall Francis Galton's retort to Max Müller who had claimed that all thought involves language or language-signs: "Prof. Max Müller . . has fallen into the common error of writers not long since, but which I hoped had now become obsolete, of believing that the minds of every one else are like one's own. His aptitudes and linguistic pursuits are likely to render him peculiarly dependent on words. . . ."[31]

Now compare what Śāntideva writes in his *Bodhicaryāvatāra* (IX, 25):

> One illumines himself by seeing someone associated with other conditions. The pot that is seen through the adept's rite of eye-ointment is not just eye-ointment.

Śāntideva's verse points to the supernormal faculty (*abhijñā*) of knowing another's state of mind (*paracittajñāna*), i.e. knowing it as impassioned if it is impassioned, etc. Sometimes this is referred to as a faculty or eye which is opened by the magical eye-ointment; but the object viewed by the supernormal faculty is independent of the "eye-ointment" itself. Thus, one learns from others' minds the nature of one's own mind—just the opposite of Max Müller's procedure of judging everyone else's mind by his own or what he conceives to be his own.

[30]Jean-Paul Sartre, *The Psychology of Imagination*, tr. by Bernard Frechtman p. 178.

[31]*F. Max Müller on the Science of Thought* (Chicago, The Open Court Publ. Co., 1909), Appendix, p. 4.

Modern aesthetics theory has had its own "idealists." Thus Croce rejects the reality of the external world; and refusing to admit an inner and outer in art, insists on the singleness of the intuition-expression. For Bernard Bosanquet's refutation, see his "Croce's Aesthetic."[32] According to Bosanquet, while an art work must originate in an artist's mind, its representation in external or material forms is an essential part of the art process. Langer in turn takes R. G. Collingwood to task, questioning why "he is anxious to deny craftsmanship any role in art and consequently to reject the concept of technique...."[33] Curiously, the Buddhist teacher Asaṅga—whom both Oriental and Western Buddhologists usually associate with the idealist school of Buddhist philosophy—accepts an "outer" part of art when he describes the parallelism of meditation and art technique:[34]

> If he would be convinced regarding the meditative object at a single time, he would not again and again leave off the intense contemplation. His conviction (*adhimokṣa*) does not become ever higher, completely purified, completely cleansed, up to the comprehension with direct perception of the knowable entity. Hence again and again he is convinced; again and again he leaves off the intense contemplation. Hence his conviction becomes ever higher, more completely purified, most completely purified, up to comprehension with direct perception of the knowable entity. A case in point: Suppose the pupil of a painter for the first time is engaged in the work of painting. He, having first had instruction from the master, takes a model and, having looked and looked, makes an image. Having done it and done it, he leaves off the intense contemplation, destroys it, and remakes it. Just as, having rejected and rejected, he makes it, so also one declares his image ever higher, more completely purified, more completely cleansed. Being rightly engaged that way, after some time he becomes the equal of the master or even his superior. Furthermore, if, without having rejected that image, he were to make it

[32]*Science and Philosophy and other Essays by the late Bernard Bosanquet* (Books for Libraries Press, Inc., Freeport, N.Y., reprint 1967), especially p. 417.

[33]Susanne K. Langer, *Feeling and Form* (New York, 1953), p. 383.

[34]Wayman, *Analysis*, p. 119.

> repeatedly by taking a stand on just that, never would that image of his become completely pure. So also in the present case one should understand the method (as that).

The tantric commentator Buddhaguhya writes, "In the manner that a thousand ounces of silver are changed into gold by using gold paint, it is said that one blesses the defilement into purity by using the paint of *samādhi*-knowledge". Both the meditation and the painting art require undivided attention, like being rapt in wonder at an object.[35]

Asaṅga's passage enables us to define one kind of discursive thought that is especially employed in art creation. The improvement of meditation, comparable to the improvement of painting, seems to be what Read[36] calls the "truthful consciousness" which is "the foundation of all genuine art," as when he cites Collingwood: "And this is precisely what every artist is doing when he says, 'This line won't do.' " This is the pursuit of perfection founded on despising one's own imperfection—the imperfect picture. This is apparently the kind of thinking which Asaṅga mentions in his *Śrāvakabhūmi* as when the yogin regards the lower planes as coarser and the higher planes as finer, and thus emerges from a given plane and attains the next higher stage of consciousness. In the last sermon of the Buddha, the *Mahāparinibbāna-sutta*, the Buddha is thus held to have surmounted the "realm of desire," and to have passed successively through the planes of the "realm of form" and "formless realm," then to have proceeded downward to the lowest plane of the "realm of form" and upward to the top of the "realm of form," from which plane he is held to have entered Parinirvāṇa. The emergence from each of these planes would, according to Asaṅga's indications, require this special kind of discursive thought, which is the very kind of thinking as when the artist says, "This line won't do."

Turning to the role of non-discursive thought, Langer says, "Now consider the most familiar sort of non-discursive symbol, a picture."[37] If the word "symbol" here suggests an ontological status, Buddhism would probably not agree with her, since at

[35]Wayman, *The Buddhist Tantras*, p. 94.

[36]*Icon*, p. 92.

[37]Susanne K. Langer, *Philosophy in a New Key* (Penguin Books, 1948), p. 76.

least the Mādhyamika school does not allow such a status for "voidness"; and the picture is voidness in the *Ratnagotravibhāga* (I, verse 92): "Those painters are the aspects, Giving, Morality, Forbearance, and so on; and the voidness, attended with all the best aspects, is said to be the picture (*pratimā*)." The full list of the "painters" (= the act of painting) adds to the three already named Striving and Meditation. The group of five, often called the "means" (*upāya*), is essentially non-discursive; although language can be employed to expatiate upon the individual ones. This use of the word "means" in connection with the painting process agrees with Bosanquet's and Langer's point that technique is an indispensable part of art. But why would "voidness" be said to be the picture, as in that *Ratnagotravibhāga* passage? Perhaps the answer is in a passage of the *Mahāyāna-Sūtrālaṃkāra* (XIII, 17) associated with Asaṅga, as cited by Coomaraswamy,[38] "There is no actual relief in a painting, and yet we see it there" (*citre... natonnataṃ nāsti ca, dṛśyate atha ca*). We find this as well in the *Laṅkāvatāra-sūtra* (text, p. 91), where notice is taken that a painted surface (*citrakṛta-pradeśa*) is observed in relief (*nimnonnata*) though flat (*animnonnata*). Recalling that "voidness" in Mahāyāna literature is associated with illusion (*māyā*), we can get the point: the "painters" who are the Giving, Morality, Forbearance, and so on, are seen in relief, and yet the picture which is voidness is really flat: the "painters" are an illusion. In the earlier period of Buddhism, more given to realism, the relief portion is really there, as Coomaraswamy points out: "in Vinaya, IV, 61, a monk 'raises' (*vuṭṭhāpeti*) a picture (*cittam*) on a cloth; and in *Saṁyutta Nikāya*, Comm., II, 5, a painter 'raises up' (*samuṭṭhāpeti*) a shape (*rūpam*) on a wall surface by means of his brushes and colors."[39] Thus, passages about the artist's techniques suggest the philosophical positions.

Now, reverting to the topic of discursive thought, in Buddhist literature its importance is emphasized by assigning it the rather nefarious role of promoting nescience (*avidyā*). And yet we were introduced previously to a kind of discursive thought that is improvement-oriented, the kind that serves for the Buddhist path, which is of course lauded in Buddhist circles. Sometimes the

[38]*The Transformation*, p. 145.
[39]*Ibid.*, pp. 144-145.

expression "right discursive thought" (*samyag-vikalpa*) is employed for the right kind, observed previously by the illustration "This line won't do." Now a challenge would be apropos : Certainly the goal of the painter and the goal of the Buddhist path are different: Of course, they are sharing this right kind of discursive thought, and their goals are different. In addition to the word *vikalpa* for "discursive thought," previously we met with a kind of discursive thought attributed to the "naming faculty" (*saṃjñā*), which properly belongs to the determined, involuntary part of the psyche. But the philosophical discussions especially involve an archaic pair of terms—*vitarka-vicāra*, terms which occur in the traditional statement of the first meditation plane of the Buddhist "realm of form" (among the three realms), and are assumed for the "realm of desire." It would certainly be a gross digression in the present paper for me to treat this pair of terms with anything like the amplitude of the materials I have collected for a separate study. I should mention my renditions of "adumbration" and "inquiry" for *vitarka*, and "thinking with signs" for *vicāra*; and that the *Arthaviniścaya-sūtra* calls this pair "speech motivation" (*vāk-saṃskāra*). Suffice it to add that according to Asaṅga's *Yogācārabhūmi*, *vitarka* and *vicāra* always amount to discursive thought; but there is a discursive thought outside of *vitarka* and *vicāra*, especially in regard to supramundane knowledge (*lokottarajñāna*). Although Asaṅga does not name this distinguished type of discursive thought, this is surely the improvement-oriented one, or "right discursive thought," which we have already noted to be the one used on the Buddhist path as well as by the good painter, and presumably by inventors, etc.

Dharmakīrti's *Nyāyabindu* (Chap. I, 5) has a term *pratīti* : "Constructive thought (*kalpanā*) is a cognitive dawning (*pratīti*) of a mental reflex able to coalesce with verbalism." The text refers to the initial universal (*sāmānya-lakṣaṇa*) which is the field of inference, subsequent to the series of point-instants, the particulars (*sva-lakṣaṇa*), that are the field of direct perception (*pratyakṣa*); and this *pratyakṣa* may be of the five outer senses, of the mind, of introspection, or of the *yogin*. The verbalism is the "naming faculty" (*saṃjñā*), the idea that something is such-and-such. This *pratīti* (literally: "approach") seems to be the most primitive discursive thought, a sort of bed-fellow to the non-discursive thought, the mental imagery of sound, color, etc. After coalescing with the name, this discursive thought could tend "downward" (hence, "wayward") toward the "realm of desire" in the manner of *vitarka-vicāra*, or tend "upward" (hence, "right") in reference to supramundane knowledge.

Our technical meanderings do have this positive result—to show that Buddhist teachings, based as they are on much meditation and practice, clearly differentiate between passive enjoyment and the creative imagination. This distinction was established by the Buddhist Dependent Origination formula. Here the first seven members develop perception in a determinacy series and wind up with feelings and their associated notions (*vedanā* and *saṃjñā*) in the manner of a syndrome. The last five members are headed by craving (*tṛṣṇā*), which is the freedom to inaugurate a new destiny. An example of this freedom, because issuing from desire rather than perception, is Śāntideva's *Bodhicaryāvatāra* VIII, 120: "Whoever desires (*icchati*) to speedily rescue oneself and others too, should practice what is the highest secrets changing places between himself and another." This is the Mahāyāna Buddhist version of "creative imagination."

Therefore, when I claim that Sartre makes the same distinction, this is not said by way of explaining the Buddhist position. Indeed, this position had to be understood prior to the comparison with a Western theory. The reverse procedure would have amounted simply to a projection on to Buddhism of some system of our culture, an attempt to make Buddhism come out or be in that manner. But that Sartre has a comparable position is clarified by Kaelin: "It will be remembered that for Sartre the perceptive consciousness intends a real object of the spatio-temporal continuum we normally call the real world, while in imaginative experience, consciousness intends an unreal or absent object which may appear only on the margins of the real world."[40] Sartre's perceptive consciousness goes with the Buddhist first seven members of Dependent Origination which develop perception with an imputed realistic object, while what is here called "imaginative experience" (in fact, the creative imagination) goes with the last five members of Dependent Origination, headed by "craving."

The foregoing permits an assessment of the word "freedom" as employed in more than one sense. That is, the "freedom of

[40]*An Existentialist Aesthetic*, p. 364.

aesthetic contemplation"—which was brought up in the discussion of aniconic art—is different from the "freedom" of creative imagination—which was used in treating iconic art. The first kind, of aesthetic contemplation, is not altered essentially by travelling far to a grandiose vista as compared with the lowly gazing appreciatively at the local sunset. Since it involves perception of the object as a real thing, with feelings and the naming function, it reduces to the backyard-garden variety of having passive enjoyment and no creative imagination. We have already noticed that some authors have regarded this "freedom" as really freedom, although it is not. Moreover, we find the "freedom" to be infatuation that the object is controlled by naming it. So Neitzsche in *The Genealogy of Morals* has the "masters' right of giving names . . they say 'this *is* that, and that,' . . and take possession of it."[41] Heidegger, in *What is Called Thinking?*, resumes this position: "By naming, we call on what is present to arrive."[42] To cite Sartre again, it is "as if it had its source in human freedom." That is, while the naming function has an involuntary character, following upon feelings pleasurable, painful, or neutral, these authors arrive at a seeming freedom called "masters' right" to apply names. All the while they demonstrate that they have learned nothing from others, having resorted solely to introspection.

In contrast, the "freedom" of creative imagination is to be taken as the genuine freedom because it is not limited by perception of this and that. Śāntideva's aspiration is of this type, because not directed in particularity to this or that being—in a word, what Buddhist texts called "equanimity" (*upekṣā*). Thus there may be creative imagination as when an actor acts his role, whether or not he enjoys the make-believe, while the spectators enjoy what they take as a real object.

Besides, my study of the Buddhist Dependent Origination, divided as it is into the determinacy and the relatively-free series, indicates that there is neither incompatibility between the two, nor requirement of their conjunction. In this Buddhist sense, one may have both passive enjoyment and creative imagination, as possibly does the creator of a piece of art. Along the same

41In Horace B. Samuel's translation. (The Modern Library), p. 4.

42In the translation by Fred D. Wieck and J. Glenn Gray (Harper Torchbooks), p. 120.

lines, the lack of incompatibility between the first seven and second five members of Dependent Origination (i.e. the Buddhists accept that "nescience", the first member, can cohabit with "craving", the seventh one—called the "father" and the "mother"), permits a Buddhist solution for man's nature as a compound of determinacy and free-will. And, I suppose, this includes a nature with desires and indulgence ever young, and with perceptions and feelings ever older.

Finally, whether it be the seeming freedom of aesthetic contemplation or the genuine freedom of creative imagination, neither are equivalent to the Buddhist "liberation" (*mokṣa*) or "release" (*nirvāṇa*). This is because for this liberation it is necessary to have cessation of Dependent Origination. In contrast, both kinds of "freedom" require Dependent Origination for a platform in cyclical flow (*saṃsāra*). Accordingly, the Vinaya work *Samantapāsādikā* prohibits a monk from holding any of the images of a woman made out of clay, wood, or painting.[43] The monk is of course seeking liberation, not freedom in the aesthetic sense. But when a Tibetan monk keeps a miniature painting of his tutelary deity, the goddess Tārā, and daily offers devotion to it, he has the Mahāyāna ideal of enlightenment. This devotion is not opposed to either of the two kinds of freedom mentioned.

In conclusion, the role of art among the Buddhist religieux involves their appreciation of beauty and creation of great art schools, the occasional monkish avoidance of some art representations, the Buddhist description of the processes of art production in comparison with meditation techniques, and in general a sufficiently detailed and rationalized presentation of their position to permit some comparisons with Western thinkers, provided one is able to make the comparisons. That is, the present writer believes in the feasibility of East-West comparisons on these matters, and that the actual comparisons have clarified some important issues. Unfortunately, such comparisons are frequently made with insufficient background in Buddhist sources.

[43] *Shan-Chien-P'i-P'o-Sha; A Chinese version by Saṅghabhadra of Samantapāsādikā*, by P. V. Bapat and A. Hirakawa (Bhandarkar Oriental Research Institute, Poona, 1970), p. 368.

15

SECRET OF THE HEART SŪTRA

INTRODUCTION

Commentaries on the Heart Sūtra: There are two distinct types of commentaries of the *Heart Sūtra* (*Prajñāpāramitāhṛdayasūtra*): the Asian sectarian commentary, and the Western non-sectarian commentary. Here there is easily a misunderstanding, to wit, that when an Asian talks in the West on the *Heart Sūtra* he communicates his Asian lore, say, as an Asian Buddhist monk. This is not necessarily the case. For example, when Daisetz Suzuki wrote about the *Heart Sūtra*, it must be granted that he wrote out of his knowledge of sources especially in his native Japanese. But what he said, for example,[1] "as far as we can ascertain, the Bodhisattva Avalokiteśvara does not appear in any of the Prajñāpāramitā Sūtras..." is not what would have ever been said in the traditional Asian commentary on the *Heart Sūtra*: it would have been considered impertinent and impugning the validity of the Sūtra. In the Western sense this is a most helpful remark. It is quite apparent that most of what Suzuki writes about the *Heart Sūtra* is not the rendition of Asian commentary but rather what he thinks the Westerner, assumed to be an outsider to the topic, needs to be told so that, hopefully, he will understand this scripture. It is almost inevitable that an Asian (whether Chinese, Japanese,

[1]Daisetz Teitaro Suzuki, *Essays in Zen Buddhism* (Third *Series*) London: Luzac and Company, 1934, p. 195.

or Tibetan), were he to lecture to a Western audience on the *Heart Sūtra* would start by assuming—and ordinarily quite correctly—that his audience members are ignorant of the fundamental teachings of Buddhism; and so, without ever intending to depart from the *Heart Sūtra*, would end up spending the time lecturing on general Buddhism and never really explaining the *Heart Sūtra* itself. Such lectures themselves may be quite informative of other matters.

In contrast, the Asian sectarian commentary is the type found in the Tibetan Tanjur collection, and among Chinese and Japanese native commentaries. A good illustration from the Far East is Kūkai's "Secret Key to the *Heart Sūtra*."[2] In this case also, it is a sectarian commentary filled with allusions to the special tenets of Kūkai's own school (the Shingon)—such as the Diamond Realm and the Lotus Realm, and indicating that portions of the Sūtra refer respectively to the Śrāvakas, Pratyekabuddhas, and the Mahāyāna Bodhisattvas. Hence it is valuable for showing Kūkai's position.

There is easily another misunderstanding, namely, that when a Westerner talks on the *Heart Sūtra* he cannot help but give a Western-type treatment, or could not be expected to speak as an Asian would. But just as the Asian can speak as a Westerner, so also the Westerner can speak as an Asian. My present commentary is probably to be described as an Asian-type commentary composed by a Westerner. That is, it follows a certain type of explanations from sources in Asian languages, and could be understood by persons with the appropriate background. This background is especially in the Buddhist theory of meditation, for which I have used some Yogācāra passages of Asaṅga (who understood), Vasubandhu (who popularized), and Sthiramati (who clarified); but the illustrious Mādhyamika Āryadeva also is helpful, as is the Vinaya master Vinītadeva.

Background of the present commentary: Around the middle 1950's when I was a student at the University of California, Berkeley, the poet Gary Snyder had received a scholarship from the First Zen Institute of New York to participate in the training of a Zen monastery in Kyoto, Japan. After a while he wrote me a note

[2]Yoshito S. Hakeda, *Kūkai* : *Major Works* New York : Columbia University Press, 1972, pp. 262-75.

saying that while the monks recite the *Heart Sūtra* every day, he had been unable to find anyone who could explain what it meant, and asking me if I could find out what it means. In those days I used to spend much time reading in the Tibetan canon, the Kanjur and Tanjur in the Derge edition at Berkeley. So I consulted the Tōhoku catalog of the Derge canon and located the six Tanjur commentaries on this *sūtra* in the section devoted to *Prajñāpāramitā* scripture commentaries. One feature of these commentaries on the *Heart Sūtra* struck me quite forcibly: each commentary seemed so different from the others, and yet they seemed all to show in greater or less degree the influence of the Mādhyamika school of Buddhist philosophy. The writers seemed to be experiencing some difficulty in exposition, as though they were not writing through having inherited a tradition about this scripture going back to its original composition, but rather were simply applying their particular learning in Buddhism to the terminology of the *sūtra*. That would account for the great variety of their comments. Then, for the most part being followers of the Mādhyamika, they would show this sectarian position by their kind of citation. It occurred to me that perhaps the *Heart Sūtra* had a different theoretical basis than what these commentaries were impressing upon it, and that the basis might actually be of Yogācāra nature. Certain commentaries gave explanations of the concluding mantras, and attempted to relate the structure of the *sūtra* to what are called in Buddhism the "three gates to liberation"—voidness, wishless, and non-sign-source. Accordingly, I made my own translation of the *sūtra*, using the Max Müller and Bunyiu Nanjio edition of the shorter version and taking into account some remarks from certain Tanjur commentaries. In those days I communicated my understanding of the *sūtra* to the Berkeley Buddhist Church. Later I incorporated my interpretation of the *Heart Sūtra* within a published paper, "The Buddhist 'Not this, Not this'. "[3] From my present vantage ground, the interpretation of the *Heart Sūtra* in this early essay suffers from various faults, such as a misapplication of the three gates to liberation; and I cannot commend it. There are perhaps only two important points that I saw or rendered correctly in those days, namely, 1) that the Tanjur commentaries, while help-

[3]*Philosophy East and West*, 11:3, *Oct.*, 1961, pp. 109-13.

ful on this or that phrase, still were not really explaining this *sūtra*; and that it would be more fruitful to consult Asaṅga's works; and 2) that the commentary by the author calling himself Vajrapāṇi correctly related parts of the concluding *mantra* to earlier sections of the *Heart Sūtra*. The present interpretation is based on certain findings in my research on Buddhist meditation;[4] and in the case of the concluding *mantra,* based on my essay about *mantras.*[5] Furthermore, I now find Conze's editions of the longer and shorter *Heart Sūtra* preferable to the editions of Müller and Nanjio.[6] For the purposes of my present explanation I have translated the shorter version and added in parentheses certain sentences from the longer version that I deem essential for understanding this *sūtra.*

As to translation of individual words, the rendition that most needs defending is my "afterwards" for *tasmāt*, which is usually and quite properly rendered as "therefore," "hence," and "for this reason" as the "conclusive" interpretation of the ablative *tasmāt*, for which see Speijer.[7] This is the reasoned conclusion, which is a sort of logical afterwards for what went before. As is well attested, the purely temporal interpretation of the ablative in Sanskrit, i.e. as "after, " is rare; but as I have occasionally noticed, when the "after" interpretation is demanded by a context it may be overlooked for that very reason of rarity. Anyway, in the context of the *Heart Sūtra*, the usual translation of the two *tasmāt*-s as "therefore" strikes a jarring note, since there is no obvious antecedent to appeal to as the reason for saying "therefore."

Doctrinal introduction: This commentary of mine, called "Explaining the Difficulties," would not be comprehensible to the usual Western reader, unless prepared by introductory teachings, at least as concerns the Buddhist three worlds and the theory of two *dharmas*.

4*See Chapter* 3.

5*See Chapter* 22.

6For these editions, see Edward Conze, *Thirty Years of Buddhist Studies* (Columbia, S. C.: University of South Carolina Press, 1968), pp. 148-67; F. Max Müller and Bunyiu Nanjio, eds., "The Ancient Palm Leaves.." in *Anecdota Oxoniensia*, Aryan Series, Vol. III (Oxford: Clarendon Press, 1884), pp. 48-50.

7J. S. Speijer, *Sanskrit Syntax* (Kyoto : The Rinsen-Shoten Bookstore, 1968). Para. 444, p. 344.

a. Cessation of "motivations" in the three worlds. The second member of Buddhist dependent origination (*pratītyasamutpāda*) is "motivation" (*saṃskāra*), and one explanation of this member in the old Buddhist canon (the Pāli scriptures) is that it has the varieties of body, speech, and mind. The Buddhist theory of three worlds (desire, form, and formless) is also ancient. In my essay on Buddhist meditation[8] I have gathered the textual sources to show how three kinds of motivation successively cease in various parts of the three worlds. The following lay-out will show the main elements of the solution:

SUMMIT OF EXISTENCE (*bhavāgra*)

3. Cessation of ideas and feelings = cessation of "motivation of mind" (*manaḥ-saṃskāra*); cessation of constructed *dharmas*.

FORMLESS REALM

REALM OF FORM

2. *Fourth Dhyāna:*	free from inbreathing and outbreathing; = cessation of "motivation of body" (*kāyasaṃskāra*).
Third Dhyāna:	pleasure by way of body.
1. *Second Dhyāna:*	free from inquiry (*vitarka*) and investigation (*vicāra*) = cessation of "motivation of speech" (*vāk-saṃskāra*).
First Dhyāna:	inquiry and investigation.

REALM OF DESIRE

b. The two *dharmas*. One may contrast the older and later religious aims of Buddhism. For the ancient view there is the verse in the *Saṃyuttanikāya:*[9]

> As the tortoise in its own shell withdraws its limbs, so may the monk (withdraw) his mind's (outgoing) conjectures; resortless, not harming another, denouncing no one, proceed to *Parinirvāṇa*.

8The one of note 4, above.

9*Saṃyutta-Nikāya*, *I*, p. 9 (in the India Devanagarī edition).

However, with the rise of the Mahāyāna ideal of the Bodhisattva, who has opted to stay in the world for the benefit of other beings rather than pursue the personal aim of liberation, there were in effect two goals—the older one of liberation from the cyclical flow (*saṃsāra*), and the newer one of deliberately postponing this liberation to serve mankind and later to achieve complete enlightenment. The two are stated this way in Āryadeva's *Catuḥśataka*, XII, 23 (=verse 298), available in Sanskrit:

> The Tathāgatas have stated in short that the Dharma is non-harming (of others), and that voidness is Nirvāṇa. Here there are only these two.

As Candrakīrti explains in part this passage, "Non-harming and voidness—these two *dharmas* attain heaven (*svarga*) and liberation (*apavarga*)."[10] The Tibetan author Red-mda'-ba, in his lectures on the *Catuḥśataka*, refers to this very passage along with a citation,[11] "The Nirvāṇa with remainder is explained as the two Formal Bodies [i.e. Saṃbhogakāya and Nirmāṇakāya]; the Nirvāṇa without remainder as the Dharmakāya." Accordingly, non-harm leads to heaven (*svarga*), and in the Mahāyāna sense to the two Formal Bodies; while voidness leads to liberation (*apavarga*), and in the Mahāyāna sense to the Dharmakāya. In the *Prasannapadā*, where the verse is cited amidst the commentary on Chap. XVIII, 4,[12] the discussion appears limited to the voidness *dharma*, since. XVIII, 4, is concerned with this side. The Bodhisattva path is the other one of the pair, with the *dharma* "non-harm." The *Heart Sūtra*, with its stress on voidness, mainly presents the "*dharma* of voidness," but has hints of the other *dharma*.

It is in connection with those two *dharmas* that this essay is entitled "Secret of the *Heart Sūtra*." Jñānagarbha explains the

[10]Vidhushekhara Bhattacharya, *The Catuhśataka of Āryadeva* (Calcutta: Visva-Bharati Book-Shop, 1931), p. 163: *mi 'tshe ba daṅ stoṅ pa ñid ces pa'i chos de gñis ni mtho ris daṅ byaṅ grol thob par byed pa ste.*

[11]Red-mda'-ba Gźon-nu-blo-gros, *Commentary to Āryadeva's 'Four Hundred Verses'*, ed. by Jetsun Rendawa Shonnu Lodo. Sarnath: Sakya Students' Union, 1974, p. 157.

[12]J. W. de Jong, *Cinq Chapitres de la Prasannapadā* Paris: Paul Geuthner, 1949, pp. 10-13.

term "secret": "Because for immature sentient beings, the profound Dharma is secret."[13]

THE PRAJÑĀPĀRAMITĀHṚDAYA-SŪTRA, TRANSLATED FROM THE LONGER AND SHORTER VERSIONS, WITH THE COMMENTARY "EXPLAINING THE DIFFICULTIES"

(And at that time, you should know, the lord was equipoised in the samādhi "profound appearance"). The noble Bodhisattva Avalokiteśvara, while engaged in the practice of profound prajñāpāramitā, inspected and observed that the five personality aggregates are void of "self-existence". (The noble Bodhisattva great being Avalokiteśvara spoke as follows to the venerable Śāriputra).

There are three persons mentioned: *the Lord*, i.e. the Buddha, is the enlightened one, the inaugurator of Buddhism; *Avalokiteśvara*, one of the great Bodhisattvas, the sons of the Buddha, is especially noted for surveying the sentient beings in compassionate manner; *Śāriputra*, one of the great early disciples of the Buddha, is especially noted for preeminence of his insight (*prajñā*, in Pāli, *paññā*). The *Heart Sūtra* represents the Buddha, while in the *Samādhi "Profound Appearance,"* inspiring Avalokiteśvara to instruct Śāriputra. It is claimed in Mahāyāna Buddhism that the Buddha teaches Avalokiteśvara with a body called the Sambhogakāya, and teaches the disciples like Śāriputra with a body called the Nirmāṇakāya. So the Buddhist master Vasubandhu explains in the *Buddhānusmṛtiṭīkā*:[14] "According to the scripture (*āgama*), the Lord (*bhagavat*), with the Sambhogakāya, staying in the abode of the *Akaniṣṭha* [heaven], teaches the Mahāyāna Doctrine to Avalokiteśvara and the other great beings on the Tenth Stage, and with his Nirmāṇakāya, staying in the range of desire for as long as the cyclical flow (*saṃsāra*) lasts, observing the streams of consciousness of the noble Śāriputra, and so on, and of other fortunate sentient beings, with the three kinds of

[13]T. T. Vol. 109, Jñānagarbha's *Āryamaitreyakevalaparivartabhāṣya* (commentary on the Maitreya chapter of the *Saṃdhinirmocanasūtra*), 203b:8 to 203c:1.

[14]T. T., Vol. 104. 33e:5 to p. 34a:1.

marvels (*prātihārya*) teaches the true nature of the Śrāvakayāna exactly according to their expectations and their potentialities." Since Avalokiteśvara teaches Śāriputra, the Nirmāṇakāya is here represented by Avalokiteśvara.

Concerning the *Samādhi* "*Profound Appearance*," the Sanskrit expression is *gambhīra-avabhāsa*. The Pāli equivalent to *avabhāsa* is *obhāsa;* and Gautama Buddha spoke thus to the monks in a passage preserved in Pāli in the *Aṅguttaranikāya* (*Book of Eights*). The additions "profound" and "far-spread" are bracketed in my translation:[15]

> Monks, before my awakening when being a Bodhisattva I was not completely enlightened, I conceived [profound] appearances (*obhāsa*) but did not see [far-spread] forms (*rūpa*). Monks, it occurred to me, "If I were both to conceive [profound] appearances and to see [far-spread] forms, in that case knowledge and vision would be better purified in me."

This expression "knowledge and vision" (S. *jñāna-darśana*) is important in early Buddhism in the theory of advanced meditation. Vinītadeva explains the expression in his commentary on the Fourth Defeat of the Vinaya:[16] " 'knowledge' (*jñāna*) is the insight (*prajñā*) involved in search; 'vision' (*darśana*) is the insight after search." Thus Vinitadeva's comment is directly applicable to that passage from the *Book of Eights*, to help explain the *Samādhi* "*Profound Appearances*." That is, the opening of the

[15]This is in the *Book of Eights*, chapter on Earthquakes, *sutta* called "At Gayā," in *The Aṅguttara Nikāya* (Chakkanipāta, Sattakanipāta and Aṭṭhakanipāta), ed. by Bhikkhu J. Kashyap (Pāli Publication Board, 1960), p. 391. 4-9.

[16]Vinītadeva, *Vinayavibhaṅgapadavyākhyāna*, T. T., Vol. 122-311: *śes pa ẑes bya ba ni rjes su'tshol ba'i śes rab bo|mthoṅ ba ẑes bya ba ni rjes su tshol ba'i śes rab bo|*. Probably the term *rjes su tshol ba* translated a perfect form indicating completed action, even though there is evident clumsiness with a possibility that the second "*rjes su*" meant "after". This is made certain in Yüan-ts'ê's great commentary on the *Saṃdhinirmocanasūtra*, Maitreya chapter, in the Tibetan translation, T. T. Vol. 106:219 when, in the course of giving numerous explanations for the term *jñānadarśana*, he presents one that is the obvious expansion of Vinītadeva's gloss, 219:e: 5-6: "Also, any insight searching the *dharma-s* is knowledge; any insight discriminating (them) after search is vision" / *gẑan yaṅ chos rnams yoṅs su tshol ba'i śes rab gaṅ yin pa de ni śes pa ẑes bya'o|yoṅs su btsal ba la(s) so sor rtog pa'i śes rab gaṅ yin pa de ni mthoṅ ba ẑes bya'o|*.

Heart Sūtra represents the Buddha entering the *Samādhi* "Profound Appearances" to inspire Avalokiteśvara with the pre-enlightenment stages called "knowledge," i.e. when *prajñā* was involved in search, and was assisted by sentient beings.[17]

Besides, Avalokiteśvara as an advanced Bodhisattva has certain abilities in proceeding through what Buddhism calls the "three realms": desire, form, and formless. As meditative attainments the realm of form is divided into the four *Dhyānas* (Pāli, *Jhāna*), and the formless realm with its four "equipoises" (*samāpatti*) is surmounted by the "summit of existence" (*bhavāgra*). Asaṅga's *Samāhitabhūmi* teaches that a yogin who is not pure can do no better than pass through these states sequentially, and likewise in reverse order. But he says that a yogin who is pure can leap over the second one, and not the third which is too far, and comparably in reverse order: for example, jumping from the *First Dhyāna* directly to the *Third Dhyāna*. And finally, Tathāgatas and Bodhisattvas of the last three stages, hence Avalokiteśvara and other great Bodhisattvas, can enter any of these stages from any other one.[18]

Finally, more can be said of Śāriputra from the Pāli canon with his Pāli name Sāriputta in the *Majjhimanikāya* (III, 29): "... speaking rightly he would say of Sāriputta—'He is the Lord's son, born from his heart and his mouth, born from the Dhamma, a creation of Dhamma, an heir of Dhamma, not an heir of material things.' " Asaṅga explains some of the terms of this *sūtra* passage in the *Paryāya-saṃgrahaṇī* of the *Yogācārabhūmi*:[19]

> "Son of the Teacher" is the brief reference. "Born from his heart" means among the inner sons, because omitting ordinary persons (*pṛthagjana*) who are unadvanced. "Born from his

[17]The *Mahāyānasūtrālaṃkāra*, Chap. XVI devoted to the Perfections (*pāramitā*), agrees with this identification of *prajñā* with *jñāna* because in verses 36 through 40 each of the first five Perfections (giving, etc.) is said to stay in the world with the assistance of knowledge (*jñāna*); and when coming to verse 41 to deal with *prajñāpāramitā* the text uses the word *jñāna* instead of *prajñā* and says "with the assistance of sentient beings" (*sattvaparigraheṇa*).

[18]For this leaping of a Bodhisattva, cf. Edward Conze, *The Large Sutra on Perfect Wisdom* (Berkeley: University of California Press, 1975), pp. 71-73, and p. 502, note, containing the reference to J. May's article CHŌJŌ (*Hobogirin* IV, 1970), which also includes Asaṅga's treatment.

[19]T. T. Vol. 111:238a.

mouth" means born from the words which teach the Dharma. "Born from the Dharma" means born from orienting his mind methodically to the Dharma and accomplishing the Dharma accordingly.

Then Avalokiteśvara spoke to Śāriputra about how the Śrāvaka, Pratyekabuddha, and Bodhisattva contemplate the five personal aggregates (*skandha*) to realize "non-self of personality" (*pudgala-nairātmya*):

> *"Here, Śāriputra, form is voidness, and voidness verily is form, voidness is not different from form; form is not different from voidness. What is form, that is voidness; what is voidness, that is form. The same is the case with Feelings, Ideas, Motivations, and Perceptions."*

Here (*iha*) means the *Second Dhyāna* of the "realm of form" where occurs the cessation of "speech motivation" (*vāk-saṃskāra*), since here there is neither "inquiry" (*vitarka*) nor "investigation" (as development of discursive thought) (*vicāra*). And here the yogin especially contemplates revolting objects, such as the cadaver in decomposition, as suggested in the *Mahāyānasūtrālaṃkāra*, XIX, 50, by mention of the sign-source in front; Sthiramati's subcommentary clarifies that this contemplation is meant to destroy the immemorial attachment to the sign-source of location (*pratiṣṭhānimitta*), the "receptacle-realm" (*bhājanaloka*), or sensory objects (*viṣaya*).[20] *Form is voidness* may be understood from Vimalamitra's commentary this way:[21] it is void of self-existence whether form be a mode-of-being (*bhāva*) or a designation (*prajñapti*). The same would apply to the other aggregates—*feelings, ideas, motivations, and perceptions.*

Voidness verily is form means according to Vimalamitra the voidness of the "city of gandharvas"—hence, also the voidness of a dream, of the "moon in the waters (of earth)," and so on. Using his hint, the statement *voidness verily is form* and a like statement for the other personal aggregates, can be illustrated by combining Asaṅga's explanations from two places of his *Yogācārabhūmi* for the similes of the ancient Buddhist canon:[22]

[20]T. T. Vol. 109:99b-c.

[21]*Ārya-Prajñāpāramitā-ṭīkā*, T. T. Vol. 94:280.

[22]*Yogācārabhūmi* in the edition of the Derge Tanjur, *Sems tsam, Vastu-saṃgrahaṇī*, Zi, f. 147b-2 to 6; and *Paryāyasaṃgrahaṇī*, 'i, f. 40a-5 to f. 40b-6.

"a lump of foam" *verily is form.*

Asaṅga: because form (i.e. the body) has arisen from the element of water, appears as though it is a self while it is not a self, and is incapable of behaving as it wishes.

"a bubble" *verily is feelings.*

Asaṅga: by way of a triple association, to wit, by way of cloud (sense object), soil (sense organ), and rain (sense perception).

"a mirage" *verily is ideas.*

Asaṅga: by way of the appearance of a knowable, and as though tormented (by thirst) and deluded.

"a plantain trunk" *verily is motivations.*

Asaṅga: by way of (the noble disciple's) cutting the root which is the reifying view (*satkāyadṛṣṭi*), which amounts to the diverse causes of many kinds of body (" upright shoots"); peeling it (pulling off the various volitions, *cetanā*) he does not find a core.

"an illusion" *verily is perception.*

Asaṅga: by way of perception being a "magician" approaching (motivations) virtuous, unvirtuous, and unshaken; and being the "traveler at the crossroads" based on four stations (i.e. form, feelings, ideas, and motivations).

Voidness is not different from form; *form is not different from voidness* means according to Vimalamitra: there is no respective external entity (*bāhyārtha*) of *form* and *voidness*, that is to say, *voidness* is not external to *form*, and vice versa. This agrees with the Mādhyamika position that positing *voidness* as an external entity would be reifying it. As with *form*, so also in the cases of *feelings, ideas, motivations, and perceptions.* As I take the two statements individually: *voidness is not different from form*—because if different in the sense that *voidness* possesses a *form*, likewise, *feelings, ideas, motivations, and perceptions*—then "*voidness*" would be reified as a self. And *form is not different from voidness*—because if different in the sense that *form* is a lay-out, so also, *feelings, ideas, motivations, and perceptions*, upon voidness as a base—then we could also say that the paints used for painting a picture are different from the picture, stand out as different from the picture which is the reified void base.

Then Avalokiteśvara spoke to Śāriputra about how the

Pratyekabuddha and the Bodhisattva contemplate "all *dharmas*" to realize "non-self of *dharmas*" (*dharma-nairātmya*):

> "*Here Śāriputra, all natures* (*Dharma*) *have the character of voidness*; *are not originated and not destroyed*; *not defiled and not pure*; *without subtraction and without addition*."

Here (*iha*) means the *Fourth Dhyāna*, free from the fault of inhalation and exhalation, i.e. the cessation of "body motivation" (*kāya-saṃskāra*). Vasubandhu's *Abhidharmakośa* (VI, 24) states:

> The Teacher (i.e. the Buddha) and the rhinocerus (i.e. the Pratyekabuddha) up to (their individual) enlightenments at the upper end of (the Fourth) *Dhyāna*, have a single basis (i.e. of the four paths). Before that: what is conducive to liberation (i.e. the path of equipment).

Hence here there are the two *dharmas*—non-harm and voidness, as alluded to in Āryadeva's verse.

The character of voidness: Sthiramati, subcommentary on *Sūtrālaṃkāra*, XIX, 48, uses the term "*character of voidness*" (*śūnyatā-lakṣaṇa*, Tib. *stoṅ pa ñid kyi mtshan ñid*) in connection with the verse's "knowing as they really are" of the Bodhisattva starting with his First Stage.[23] Thus "*character*" (*lakṣaṇa*) points to the "*dharma* of non-harm," because it involves the Bodhisattva's path as contrasted with that of the Pratyekabuddha. The *Madhyāntavibhāga* says: "The unreality of the two (subject and object), and the reality of the unreality, is the character of the void (*śūnyalakṣaṇa*)."[24]

All natures (*dharma*) means the personal aggregates (*skandha*), the elements (*dhātu*), the sense bases (*āyatana*). The Mahāyāna scripture "*Meeting of Father and Son*" (*Pitāputrasamāgama*) has this: "O great king. Thus all *dharmas* are the gateway to liberation."[25] This points to the "*dharma* voidness" for the Pratyekabuddha. According to Asaṅga, *Viniścayasaṃgrahaṇī* of the *Samāhitabhūmi*, the gates to liberation—voidness, wishless, and

[23]T. T. Vol. 109:98d.

[24]*Madhyāntavibhāga-bhāṣya*, ed. by Gadjin M. Nagao. Tokyo: Suzuki Research Foundation, 1964, p. 22: *dvayābhāvo hy abhāvasya bhāvaḥ śūnyasya lakśaṇaṁ/*.

[25]T. T. Vol. 23:208e.

non-sign-source—distinguish the *Fourth Dhyāna.*[26] And further, it says in "*Meeting of Father and son*":[27]

> Great King, when one understands it rightly as it really is, the eye sense-base is void of the eye-sense-base. Why so? This eye-sense-base is a non-sign-source (*animitta*). Why so? When the sign-source of the eye-sense-base is void of the eye-sense-base—this is voidness. When the sign-source of the eye-sense-base is free of sign-source—this is the non-sign-source. When it makes no wish, this is the wishless. Great King accordingly the eye-sense-base is the three doors of liberation. The eye-sense-base is directed toward liberation... Likewise, all *dharmas* are directed toward liberation.

Are not originated and not destroyed means the voidness gateway—because the sign-source is void of the eye-sense-base, i.e. is comparable to a dream.[28]

Not defiled and not pure means the non-sign-source gateway—because it is sign-sources that are defiled or pure.[29]

Without subtraction and without addition means the wishless gateway—because there is nothing to subtract or add for the eye-sense-base to wish for.

Having told the two *dharmas* related to heaven (*svarga*) and liberation (*apavarga*), and since there is no other *dharma* in Buddhism than those two in the sense "born from the *dhamma*" (as was said of Sāriputta), Avalokiteśvara explained to Śāriputra the Truth of Cessation (*nirodhasatya*):[30]

[26]T. T. Vol. 111:11d. I surveyed much of Asaṅga's *Yogācārabhūmi* for various explanations of the gates to liberation, and the particular one here presented seemed most to fit the context of the *Heart Sūtra.*

[27]T. T. Vol. 23:201b, c.

[28]Cf. *Pitāputrasamāgamasūtra,* T. T. Vol. 23:201d:3-4 "O great king, the sense organs are illusory; the sense objects dream-like" (*rgyal po chen po de la dbaṅ po rnams ni sgyu ma lta bu / yul rnams ni rmi lam lta bur śes par bya ste/*).

[29]Cf. A. Wayman, *Analysis of the Śrāvakabhūmi Manuscript*. Berkeley : University of California Press, 1961, p. 61: "he does not take hold of sign-sources (*nimitta-grāhī*) or details by reason of which sinful, unvirtuous natures (*dharma*) would flow in his mind."

[30]*The Pañcaviṃśatisāhasrikā Prajñāpāramitā,* ed. by Nalinaksha Dutt (London : Luzac & Co., 1934), pp. 46-47, sets forth approximately the same material as in the Heart Sūtra under the title "precept of cessation-truth" (*nirodhasatyāvavāda*). Conze, *Thirty Years,* p. 158, calls attention to this similarity.

"*Afterwards, Śāriputra, in voidness there are no form, no feelings, no ideas, no motivations, no perceptions*;
No eye, ear, nose, tongue, body, or mind; no form, sounds, smell, taste, tangible, or mental;
No realm of eye ... [down to] ... no realm of mind-perception;
No nescience, no extinction of nescience ... [down to]—no old age and death, no extinction of old age and death;
No suffering, source, cessation or path;
No knowledge;
No attainment, to non-attainment."

Afterwards (*tasmāt*): In the summit of existence (*bhavāgra*), there is cessation of "mind-motivation" (*manaḥ-saṃskāra*)—referred to in the ancient Buddhist scriptures as "cessation of feelings and ideas" (*saṃjñāvedita-nirodha*). Since here there is cessation of all "constructed natures" (*saṃskṛta-dharma*), this is not the state in which the Buddha discovered 'all *dharmas*' = five personal aggregates (*form* down to *perceptions*), twelve sense bases (*eye* down to *mind*; *form* down to *mentals*), eighteen realms (*realm of eye* down to *realm of mind-perception*); nor in which he discovered the twelvefold dependent origination and the manner in which it is extinguished (*nescience* down to *old age and death*; *extinction of nescience* down to *extinction of old age and death*); nor in which he discovered the four Noble Truths (*suffering* down to *path*); nor in which he had the *knowledge* and the *attainment*. And in this condition there is *no non-attainment* just as one cannot speak of darkness, if there is no light. According to the *Mahāparinibbānasutta*, the Tathāgata took his leave of the monks and attained the *First Dhyāna*, and successively the various equipoises (*samāpatti*) up to the base of neither idea nor no-idea, and emerging from this base, reached the cessation of feelings and ideas. Then, according to the tradition, the venerable Ānanda said to the venerable Anuruddha, "Reverend Anuruddha, the Lord has passed into Nirvāṇa." "Nay, brother Ānanda, the Lord has not passed into Nirvāṇa; he has reached the cessation of feelings and ideas." Thereupon, you should know, the Lord emerging from the cessation, entered the base of neither idea nor no-idea, and successively the equipoises down to the *First Dhyāna*; and emerging from the *First Dhyāna*, proceeded again through the *Dhyānas* to the *Fourth Dhyāna*, and emerging from the *Fourth Dhyāna*, the Lord passed into Nirvāṇa.

Avalokiteśvara explained to Śāriputra that afterwards the Bodhisattva returns to attainment by recourse to *prajñāpāramitā:*

> "*Afterwards, Śāriputra, by reason of the non-attainment, the Bodhisattva takes recourse to prajñāpāramitā, and dwells without obscuration of thought.*"

Afterwards (*tasmāt*): After proving that there is no attainment, and so also no possibility of *non-attainment* in the cessation of feelings and ideas, the Bodhisattva of the upper three stages among the ten returns promptly to the realm of form. The *Mahāyānasūtrālaṃkāra* (XIX, 28, 29), explains:

> For the right praxis of the wise in the six perfections is the giving of the one without wish, the morality of the one without enthusiasm for re-existence, forbearance everywhere, the striving to bring forth all good; likewise meditation (*dhyāna*) apart from the formless realm,[31] and insight (*prajñā*) tied to the means (i.e. the other five perfections).

The Bodhisattva's meditation is apart from the formless realm, for this realm leads to the *non-attainment* summit. Besides, there is a theory that among the *Dhyānas* of the realm of form, the Bodhisattva of the Eighth Stage is in the *First Dhyāna*, the one of the Ninth Stage is in the *Second Dhyāna*, the one of the Tenth Stage is in the *Third Dhyāna*.[32]

takes recourse to prajñāpāramitā, and dwells without obscuration of thought: It is said, "He takes recourse to the wife of another," and explained: 'wife of another' is *prajñāpāramitā*; the "other" is

[31]*vinārūpyaṃ tathā dhyānaṃ.*

[32]This theory is presented in Yüan-ts'ê, commentary on *Saṃdhinirmocana-sūtra*, T. T. Vol. 106:209e where he combines the *Daśabhūmikasūtra's* deifying of the irreversible Bodhisattvas (those of the last three stages) with the *Dhyāna* tradition, since each of the four *Dhyāna* heavens has various types of deities. Thus, in the Eighth Stage the Bodhisattva is Mahābrahmā. This is not necessarily inconsistent with the previous information that Sthiramati associates the "character of voidness" with the First Stage Bodhisattva, and my placement of the information under the *Fourth Dhyāna*. This is because the present reference to the irreversible Bodhisattvas has to do with their *return* to the realm of form, wherein are the four *Dhyānas*.

the Diamond being (Vajrasattva).[33] He dwells without the defilement obscuration, as a Bodhisattva of the upper three stages, although still with obscuration of the knowable. Then, in terms of the two kinds of "insight" previously mentioned from Vinītadeva's Vinaya commentary, the one involved in search called "knowledge" (*jñāna*) and the one after search called "vision" (*darśana*), this one is the "vision." And Gautama Buddha in that passage preserved in the "*Book of Eights*" explained that when he developed the "vision" he saw the forms of the deities (*devatā*) of the different classes.[34]

Avalokiteśvara explained that the Bodhisattva has arrived at the Summit-Nirvāṇa:

> "*Because of the non-existence of thought obscuration, he fearless, having transcended waywardness, is at the Summit-Nirvāṇa.*"

fearless: According to Sthiramati, subcommentary on the *Sūtrālaṃkāra*, there are two kinds of fear: 1) of temporal unexpectedness (*sadyas*), i.e. of rulers, robbers, fire, floods, etc., 2) of objective (spatial) domains (*viṣaya*), such as planes of *yoga*, and *saṃsāra* itself.[35] The Bodhisattva has no temporal fear for the two "afterwards" (*tasmāt*), and no spatial fear for the two "here-s" (*iha*).

Waywardness: Waywardness (*viparyāsa*) means taking the impermanent as permanent, pain as pleasure, nonself as self, and the impure as pure. There are three stages of waywardness, to wit, of ideas (*saṃjñā*), then of views (*dṛṣṭi*) attached to the ideas, and finally of consciousness (*citta*) with secondary defilements going with the view attachment.[36] Since the Bodhisattva does not have thought obscuration (*cittā-avaraṇa*) he cannot have the last stage

[33] *The Collected Works of Bu-ston, Part* 14 (*Pha*) (New Delhi: Indian Academy of Indian Culture, 1969), the abbreviated survey of the Tantras (in Tibetan). Fol. no. 910. Bu-ston goes on to explain that Prajñāpāramitā is the *son mo* ('she who arrives') at the other side of *saṃsāra*, while Vajrasattva is the *son po* ('he who arrives') at the other side of *saṃsāra.*

[34] In the *sutta* called "At Gayā" (cf. note 15, above).

[35] T. T. Vol. 109: 19c: 2, 3, 4, commentary on XVI, 52.

[36] Cf. *The Lion's Roar of Queen Śrīmālā*; *a Buddhist Scripture on the Tathāgatagarbha Theory*, tr. by Alex Wayman and Hideko Wayman (New York : Columbia University Press, 1974). p. 102, and note.

of waywardness, that of consciousness (*citta*); and the sūtra intends this to mean the Bodhisattva has transcended waywardness.

The summit-nirvāṇa: He is at the summit (*niṣṭhā*) where the Buddha entered Parinirvāṇa, i.e. at the upper extreme of the *Fourth Dhyāna*. Besides, *Le Traité* gives the denotation of the word *pāramitā* (perfection) as applied to *prajñā*:[37] "She is called *pāramitā*, because she arrives at the other shore (*pāra*) of the ocean of insight, because she arrives at the extremity (*anta*) of all the insights and attains the summit (*niṣṭhāgata*)."

Avalokiteśvara then made the Mahāyāna identification of Nirvāṇa and enlightenment:

> "*All Buddhas of the past, present, and future, after taking recourse to the perfection of insight, completely realize the incomparable, right complete enlightenment.*"

With the Sambhogakāya, they realize the *Complete Enlightenment* at the top of the realm of form in the Akaniṣṭha heaven.

Avalokiteśvara then summed up all the foregoing by way of an incantation:

> "*Therefore one should know the great incantation of prajñāpāramitā. The incantation of great vidyā, the incomparable incantation, the equal-and-unequal incantation, the incantation which allays suffering, true because devoid of falsehood, proclaimed in the prajñāpāramitā, as follows: gate gate pāragate pārasaṃgate bodhi svāhā.*"

The great incantation of prajñāpāramitā, the incantation of great vidyā is *gate gate pāragate pārasaṃgate bodhi svāhā*, because *vidyā* means the female variety of incantation (*mantra*) and *svāhā* is the final *mantra* of a female formula.[38] Having referred to the *mantra* in general terms, the sūtra now treats the individual terms of the *mantra:*

The incomparable incantation is *gate gate* because this means one has embarked (*tīrṇa*),[39] with cessation of speech motivation in the *Second Dhyāna*.

[37]Etienne Lamotte, *Le Traité de la Grande Vertu de Sagesse*, Tome II. Louvain : Bureaux du *Muséon*, 1949, p. 1066.

[38]Cf. Wayman, "The Significance of Mantras" (note 5, above).

[39]For these terms *tīrṇa*, *pāragata*, and *sthalagata*, see Franklin Edgerton, *Buddhist Hybrid Sanskrit Reader*, New Haven: Yale University Press, 1953, "Conversion of Śāriputra and Maudgalyāyana," p. 31.

The equal and unequal incantation is *pāragate* because this means one is well on the way (*pāragata*), with cessation of body motivation in the *Fourth Dhyāna*. The Pratyekabuddha, and the Bodhisattva, is equal to the Buddha in attaining the cessation of body motivation in the *Fourth Dhyāna*. But these *yogins* are not equal to the Buddha as regards having attained the incomparable enlightenment in the Akaniṣṭha, with the Sambhogakāya.

The incantation which allays suffering is *Pārasaṃgate*, because this means one has reached the dry land (*sthalagata*), beyond the swirling waters of *saṃsāra*. But is this cessation of mental natures to be called "Nirvāṇa"? *True because devoid of falsehood* is *bodhi*. "Enlightenment" (*bodhi*) is true, because devoid of the various falsehoods, by suggestion of Praśāstrasena's commentary and partial adoption of his remarks: devoid of the falsehoods of body, speech, and mind.[40]

Proclaimed in the prajñāpāramitā is *svāhā* because this is the clarification at the end.[41]

Thus Avalokiteśvara finished his instruction to Śāriputra.

(*Then, you should know, the Lord emerged from that samādhi and told Ārya-Avalokiteśvara, "Sādhu Sādhu"*).

According to Vimalamitra,[42] while this *sūtra* was expressed by Ārya-Avalokiteśvara, it was in fact the Tathāgata's promulgation (*ājñā*); accordingly, Avalokiteśvara was empowered (*adhitiṣṭha*) by the Tathāgata in the *Samādhi "Profound Appearance"* (*gambhīra-avabhāsa*). So the Tathāgata, saying *sādhu, sādhu* (It is well, it is well) indicates concurrence with *Avalokiteśvara's* exposition.

So ends the "heart" of noble prajñāpāramitā.

Heart: There are two kinds of "heart" (*hṛdaya*) intended by this scripture. 1) there is the "heart," i.e. the essence of Mahāyāna teaching with reference to Prajñāpāramitā as the mother of the Buddhas and Bodhisattvas. 2) there is the "heart" with reference to the sons of the Buddha, as was Śāriputra, "born from his heart."

So ends the commentary, composed by Alex Wayman, called "Explaining the Difficulties" (*pañjikā-nāma*) of the *Āryaprajñā-pāramitā-hṛdaya-sūtra*.

40Edward Conze, "Praśāstrasena's *Ārya-Prajñāpāramitā-hṛdaya-ṭikā*," *Buddhist Studies in Honour of I. B. Horner*. Dordrecht: D. Reidel Publishing Company, 1974, pp. 58-59.

41This explanation of *svāhā* is from a tantric commentary by Ratnākara-śānti, cited in Wayman, "The Significance of Mantras" (note 5, above').

42T. T. Vol. 94:284e: 5, 6.

PART FOUR

TEXTS OF ASAṄGA SCHOOL

16

THE *SACITTIKĀ* AND *ACITTIKĀ BHŪMI* TEXT AND TRANSLATION

The brief text here edited is from the photographic *Śrāvakabhūmi* manuscript, and is a portion of the encyclopedic work *Yogācārabhūmi* by Asaṅga (circa 375-430, A.D.).[1] The Sacittikā and Acittikā *bhūmis* occupy only one folio side in the manuscript and yet constitute Nos. 8 and 9 of the seventeen *bhūmis*. They have an importance far greater than their length might indicate, since the Sacittikā and Acittikā text is Asaṅga's most extreme summarization of the psychological states that were discussed extensively in the first five *bhūmis* (edited in Sanskrit by V. Bhattacharya), and then discussed from another standpoint in *bhūmis* Nos. 6 and 7 (*samāhitā* and *asamāhitā bhūmis*). Asaṅga then deals with the traditional three levels of *prajñā* (insight)—*bhūmis* Nos. 10-12 (*śrutamayī*, *cintāmayī*, and *bhāvanāmayī bhūmis*). He then exposes the three vehicles (*yāna*)—*bhūmis* Nos. 13-15 (*śrāvaka*–, *pratyekabuddha*–, and *bodhisattva-bhūmis*). He concludes with the fruits (*phala*) of the path—*bhūmis* Nos. 16 and 17 (*sopadhiśeṣā* and *nirupadhiśeṣā bhūmis*).

Sacittikā Acittikā ca Bhūmiḥ

/ sacittikā 'cittikā ca bhūmiḥ katamā / sā dvidhāpi pañcabhir ākārair veditavyā / bhūmiprajñaptivyavasthānato 'pi citta-

[1]Cf. Alex Wayman, "The Sacittikā and Acittikā Bhūmi and the Pratyekabuddhabhūmi (Sanskrit texts)," *Journal of Indian and Buddhist Studies* (Tokyo), 7:1, 1960, pp. 375-379.

bhrāntivyavasthānato 'py utpattyanutpattivyavasthānato 'py avasthāvyavasthānato 'pi paramārthavyavasthānato 'pi //

/ tatra bhūmiprajñaptivyavasthānataḥ pañcavijñānasaṃprayuktā bhūmir manobhūmiḥ savitarkā savicārā ['vi]tarkā vicāramātrā ca bhūmir ekāntena sacittikā / avitarkāyām avicārāyāṃ bhūmau samāpattyupapattikam āsaṃjñikaṃ nirodhasamāpattiṃ ca sthāpayitvā tadanyā sacittikaiva bhūmiḥ samāpattyupapattika [āsaṃ] jñiko nirodhasamāpattiś ca tā (a)cittikā bhūmiḥ //

/ tatra cittabhrāntivyavasthānato yat caturviparyāsaṃ viparyastaṃ cittaṃ tad bhrāntam ity ucyate / yat punaś caturbhir viparyāsenāviparyastaṃ tad abhrāntam ity ucyate / tatra yad bhrāntacitta(ṃ) tad acittam ity ucyate (p)r(akṛti)bhraṣṭ[āt / tadyathā] lokair vacas uktam / unmattakṣiptacittaṃ dṛṣṭvā '[yaṃ puruṣapudgalo 'citta unma]ttaḥ kṣiptacitta iti / tad anena paryāyena yad bhrāntaṃ cittaṃ tad acittikā bhūmir yat punar abhrāntaṃ tat sacittikā //

/ tatrotpattyanutpattito 'ṣṭābhiḥ kāraṇaiḥ cittasyotpādo ['nutpādo] vā / tadyathā indriyaparibhedād viṣayānābhāsam ayanād manasikāravaikalyād apratilabdhād virodhāt prahāṇād nirodhād utpādāc ca / etad viparyayād utpādo draṣṭavyaḥ kṣaya(e)va kāraṇaiḥ / tatra ya utpādakāraṇaiś cittasyotpādaḥ sā sacittikā bhūmiḥ / yaḥ punar anutpādakāraṇair anutpādaḥ sā 'cittikā bhūmiḥ //

/ tatrāvasthāvyavasthānataḥ ṣaḍ avasthāḥ sthāpayitvā sacittikā bhūmir veditavyā / ṣaḍ avasthāḥ katamā tadyathā acittikamiddhāvasthā 'cittikamūrchāvasthā 'saṃjñaṣamāpattir āsaṃjñikaṃ nirodhasamāpattir nirupadhiśeṣanirvāṇadhātur yā punar etāḥ ṣaḍ avasthā iyam acittikā bhūmiḥ //

/ tatra paramārthavyavasthānato nirupadhiśeṣo nirvāṇadhātur acittikā bhūmiḥ / tat kasya hetoḥ / tathā hy ālayavijñānaṃ niruddhaṃ bhavati / tadanyāsv avasthāsu pravṛttivijñānaṃ niruddhaṃ bhavati / yenācittikā bhūmir ity ucyate / ālayavijñānaṃ tu na niruddhaṃ bhavati / paramārthato 'cittikā bhūmir ity ucyate //

/ yogācārabhūmau sacittikā bhūmir acittikā ca samāptā //

Translation of Asaṅga's *Sacittikā* and *Acittikā Bhūmi* with minimal additions from Asaṅga's own comments in *Viniścayasaṃgrahaṇī.*

What is the stage "with thought" and the one "without thought"? Each of these is known under five categories: establishment in terms of stages, establishment of thought delusion and non-delusion, establishment of (thought) occurrence and non-occurrence, establishment of states, establishment of the absolute.

Establishment in Terms of Stages

These stages are in each case a stage with thought: 1. Association with the five (sensory) perceptions (*vijñāna*), 2. Mind (*manas*), 3. With inquiry (*vitarka*) and deliberation (*vicāra*), 4. Without inquiry and with only deliberation. A stage "with thought" must be apart from 5. Without either inquiry or deliberation, under which there are non-ideational equipoise, non-ideational existence, and cessation equipoise. Non-ideational equipoise, non-ideational existence, and cessation equipoise (each) constitute a stage "without thought."

Establishment of Thought Delusion and Non-Delusion

A thought wayward with four waywardnesses is said to be deluded. Any thought not wayward with the four waywardnesses is a non-deluded thought. Among those, the deluded thought is said to be "destitute of intellect" because it has lost its primal nature. For example, when worldly persons see someone of insane, distracted mind, they say, "That person is 'destitute of intellect,' insane, his mind distracted." Hence, in those terms, any deluded thought is a stage "without thought," and any one not deluded is "with thought."

Establishment of Occurrence and Non-Occurrence

Thought occurs or does not occur by eight causes, as follows: 1. impairment of sense organ (six in number), 2. non-appearance of sense object (six in number), 3. lack of attention, 4. non-attainment (of other realms, such as the Dhyāna heavens, by reason of not accomplishing the path), 5. opposition (to a thought by another thought which is present, as when experiencing pleasure one does not experience pain), 6. elimination (of a thought by the path leading to the elimination, as when lust, hatred, and delusion are eliminated by the Eightfold Noble Path), 7. cessation (i.e. states nos. 3-6 in "Establishment of states," below), 8. occurrence already (i.e. having finished occurring, as in momentary theory). The opposites of those constitute origination (of thought), just when there is ending of those causes. Among them, any origination of a thought by causes of origination, is a stage "with thought." And any non-origination by causes of non-origination, is a stage "without thought."

Establishment of States

One should know the stage "with thought" as exclusive of six states. What are the six? As follows: 1. state of sleep devoid of thought (=dreamless sleep), 2. state of faint devoid of thought, 3. non-ideational equipoise, 4. non-ideational existence, 5. cessation-equipoise, 6. Nirvāṇa-realm without residual basis. Furthermore, these six states constitute a stage "without thought."

Establishment of the Absolute

This is the stage "without thought," Nirvāṇa-realm without residual basis. For what reason? For the reason that there is cessation of the "store consciousness" (*ālaya-vijñāna*). In the other (five) states, there is cessation of evolving perception (*pravṛtti-vijñāna*), and consequently they constitute a stage "without thought" (in the conventional sense), but (in those five) there is no cessation of *ālaya-vijñāna*: in the absolute sense, they do not constitute a stage "without thought." Finished is the Stage With Thought and Without Thought in the *Yogācārabhūmi*.

According to Asaṅga, there are four cases for possession of *ālayavijñāna* and/or evolving perception (*pravṛtti-vijñāna*):

1. Possessing *ālayavijñāna* and not possessing evolving perception: persons in states nos. 1-5 in "Establishment of states."
2. Possessing evolving perception and not possessing *ālaya-vijñāna:* Arhats, Pratyekabuddhas, irreversible Bodhisattvas, and Tathāgatas, when in stages "with thought."
3. Possessing both: persons other than those (mentioned above), when in stages "with thought."
4. Possessing neither: Arhats, Pratyekabuddhas, irreversible

Bodhisattvas, and Tathāgatas, when in cessation-equipoise, or in Nirvāṇa-realm without residual basis.

The evolving perceptions are mind (*manas*) and the five sense perceptions. Together with *ālayavijñāna*, they make a set of seven *vijñāna*. The set can also be counted as eight by taking the sixth *vijñāna* as *manovijñāna*, the seventh as "defiled mind" (*kliṣṭamanas*), and the eighth as *ālayavijñāna*. The set of eight is more common.

The associate natures (*caitasika-dharma*) that go with all the *vijñāna*, are: attention (*manasikāra*), contact (*sparśa*), feeling (*vedanā*), idea (*saṃjñā*), volition (*cetanā*). Besides, the mind (*manas*) has many other mental elements associated with it. There are five mental elements never associated with *ālayavijñāna:* longing (*chanda*), conviction (*adhimokṣa*), mindfulness (*smṛti*), one-pointedness (*samādhi*), insight (*prajñā*).

The four waywardnesses are to regard the impermanent as permanent, suffering as happiness, non-self as self, and the impure as pure.

Asaṅga in the foregoing mentioned only "Nirvāṇa without residual basis." Both Nirvāṇas (with and without residual basis) are treated in the comments to the *Paramārtha-gāthā*. The two kinds of Nirvāṇa constitute two stages (Nos. 16 and 17) of the seventeen *bhūmi* of Asaṅga's *Yogācārabhūmi* prior to the exegetical sections.

Regarding the three stages, "non-ideational equipoise," "non-ideational existence," and "cessation equipoise," the essay "Meditation in Theravāda and Mahīśāsaka" above and Asaṅga's *Śrāvakabhūmi* explain the "non-ideational equipoise" (or "equipoise without idea") as that of the ordinary person, and the "cessation equipoise" as that of the *ārya* (noble person), and relate this terminology to the "formless realm." The term "non-ideational existence" (*āsaṃjñika*) refers, according to the *Abhidharmakośa*, II, 41, to a class of deities abiding in the Dhyāna heaven Bṛhatphala, placed as the highest of the three divisions of the "fourth Dhyāna" in the "realm of form." Speaking generally, Asaṅga states in his *Vastusaṃgrahaṇī* (PTT, Vol. 111, p. 134-3) that elimination of ideas (*saṃjñā*) happens in the *samādhi* of "signless mind" (*ānimittacitta*). (See my essay "Secret of the *Heart Sūtra*"). Asaṅga points out there also that some outsiders (wrongly) attributed the two kinds of Nirvāṇa to this Bṛhatphala heaven.

17

ASAṄGA'S TREATISE, THE *PARAMĀRTHA-GĀTHĀ*

The intrusive folios in the unique Bihar *Śrāvakabhūmi* manuscript include a large portion of the *Cintāmayī Bhūmi*, an earlier section of the *Yogācārabhūmi*. The intrusive folios of that *bhūmi* contain the *Paramārtha-gāthā* and the complete text of Asaṅga's comments thereon; the *Ābhiprāyikārtha-gāthā*, with incomplete text of Asaṅga's comments; and the first part of the *Śarīrārtha-gāthā*, small sets of verses with Asaṅga's comments. Long ago I edited and translated the *Paramārtha-gāthā* and commentary in my doctoral dissertation at the University of California, Berkeley, published as *Analysis of the Śrāvakabhūmi Manuscript* (1961).[1] Now I shall present this text and translation with various corrections.[2] Some introductory remarks are necessary.

The bulky work called *Yogācārabhūmi* was composed for persons in the Buddhist religious life. Thus "Yogācāra" in the title "Stages (*bhūmi*) of Yogācāra" does not stand for the Buddhist philosophical school sometimes referred to as "Yogācāra

[1]University of California Publications in Classical Philology, Vol. 17 (University of California Press, Berkeley and Los Angeles, 1961), pp. 163, ff. for details of this text as originally edited and translated, bibliography for the Asian renditions, and so on.

[2]From Franklin Edgerton's generous review in *Language*, Vol. 38, No. 3 (1962), I have adopted all his suggestions except one (on verse 38). Besides, I have made minor improvements throughout the translation as well as major correction of two verses (nos. 4 and 38).

philosophy." Much of the large work is given over to Buddhist *abhidharma*-type doctrinal categories; and, generally speaking, the treatise exposes extensively the doctrine and practice indications for one aiming to follow the Buddhist path, either in the old sense of early Buddhism or in the later sense of the Mahāyāna Bodhisattva. However, the work does contain an early form of what is called "Yogācāra philosophy," especially by Asaṅga's use of the term "store consciousness" (*ālayavijñāna*) and his three *lakṣaṇa*-s or *svabhāva*-s called "imaginary" (*parikalpita*), "dependency" (*paratantra*), and "perfect" (*pariniṣpanna*). The *Paramārtha-gāthā* themselves do not clearly evidence any technical "Yogācāra philosophy," but Asaṅga's comments do bring in some indications of this philosophical position.

The verse that most needs some explanation in this sense is no. 4, with two mentions of the word "self" (*ātman*). The translation of the verse followed commentarial suggestions, especially Asaṅga's use of the word *pariniṣpanna*, which, as a grammatically passive participle is possibly controlled by the instrumental of another word, thus forcing the term *ātmanas* (genitive or ablative) to be interpreted ablatively in overlap of instrumental function. So my translation of *ātmano nāsti* as "is not by way of self." When the verse states that the "self" is imagined in reverse manner, it follows that it is imagined to be "by way of self." Asaṅga's comment with the word *pariniṣpanna* implies the other two terms of the three *lakṣaṇa.* Thus, the "self" is "imagined" in reverse manner—the "imaginary character." The "dependency character" is shown by the phrase "not by way of self," since Asaṅga's *Śrāvakabhūmi* examines the "non-self" aspect of the Truth of Suffering by the one aspect "non-independence" (*asvātantrya*).[3] Finally, the "self" is not the "perfect character" (*pariniṣpanna-lakṣaṇa*). Asaṅga's interpretation of the verse no. 4 is not inconsistent with the *Udānavarga*, I, 20, including: / *ātmeva hy ātmano nāsti kuto putrā kuto dhanam* /, since *kuto* (=Skt. *kutas*) is ablative; thus, "For the self is not through self. Through what the sons? Through what the wealth?" In short, one should realize that the self is not autonomous; that an "independent" self, and one that "possesses" sons and wealth is an illusion.

[3]Cf. Wayman, "The Sixteen Aspects of the Four Noble Truths and Their Opposites," place with n. 17.

For the meaning of the word *paramārtha*, we note that the commentary on *Sūtrālaṃkāra*, VI, 1, says that *paramārtha* ("absolute meaning") is non-two meaning (*advayārtha*). Asaṅga, in his *Vastusaṃgrahaṇī* (PTT, Vol. 111, p. 162-5) says: "By the manner of *paramārtha* one should know the 'world' (*loka*)—arisen by dint of ideas (*saṃjñā*) and cognition (*jñāna*); the means of coming to the end of the 'world'—rightly knowing as it really is the arising-transformation of aspects belonging to the six sense bases of contact; and the end of the 'world'—apprehending the end of 'body,' (after) ending the craving for any sense object."[4] Ending the craving points to Nirvāṇa with residual basis; the end of "body" points to Nirvāṇa without residual basis (cf. *gāthā* 42). Hence "non-two meaning" of *paramārtha* signifies—this way and no other way.

The Paramārtha-gāthās[5]

1. svāmī na vidyate kaścin na kartā nāpi vedakaḥ /
   dharmāḥ sarve 'pi niśceṣṭā atha ced vartate kriyā //
   There is no proprietor at all, no doer, no feeler;
   Although all the *dharmas* are inactive, yet possible activity evolves.
2. dvādaśaiva bhavāṅgāni skandhāyatanadhātavaḥ /
   vicintya sarvāṇy etāni pudgalo nopalabhyate //
   The twelve members of phenomenal life are the aggregates (*skandha*), sense bases (*āyatana*), and realms (*dhātu*).
   Pondering all those, a person (*pudgala*) is not found.
3. śūnyam ādhyātmikaṃ sarvaṃ śūnyaṃ sarvaṃ bahirgataṃ /
   na vidyate so 'pi kaścid yo bhāvayati śūnyatāṃ //
   Void is all within; void all without.
   Nor exists anyone who contemplates voidness.
4. ātmaiva hy ātmano nāsti viparītena kalpyate /

[4] I have condensed Asaṅga's passage, using just his words, from the Tibetan version.

[5] By *gāthā* Asaṅga apparently meant the ancient verses or verse portions that he pieced together to make this set of forty-four. This meaning is certified by his own commentarial conclusion, calling this group of verses "master lineage" (*āptāgama*), i.e. scriptural authority. Hence, the commentarial *āha* (he says) refers to the Buddha.

naiveha sattva ātmā vā dharmās tv ete sahetukāḥ //
For the self is not by way of self; it is imagined in reverse manner. Here there is no being or oneself. But these *dharmas* have their causes.

5. kṣaṇikāḥ sarvasaṃskārā asthitānāṃ kutaḥ kriyā /
bhūtir yeṣāṃ kriyāsau ca kārakaḥ saiva cocyate //
All the *saṃskāras* are momentary; how could there be the activity of transient things?
Precisely their arising is the activity as well as the agent.

6-7. cakṣuḥ paśyati no rūpaṃ śrotraṃ śabdāṃ śṛṇoti naḥ /
ghrāṇaṃ jighrati no gandhāṃ jihvā nāsvādayed rasāṃ /
kāyaḥ spṛśati no sparśā mano dharmān na kalpayet /
nāsti caiṣām adhiṣṭhātā prerako vidyate na ca //
Neither does the eye see form; nor the ear hear sounds.
Neither does the nose smell odors; nor the tongue taste flavors.
Neither does the body feel tangibles; nor the mind conceive *dharmas*.
And these have neither controller nor instigator.

8. na paro janayaty enaṃ svayaṃ naiva ca jāyate /
pratītya bhāvā jāyante niṣpurāṇā navā navā //
Another does not engender this; nor is it engendered of itself.
Entities arise dependently. They are not old, but ever new.

9. na paro nāśayaty enaṃ svayaṃ nāpi ca naśyati /
pratyaye sati jāyante jātāḥ svarasabhaṅgurāḥ //
Another does not destroy this; nor is it destroyed of itself.
When there is the condition, things arise; and having arisen, are perishable by their own essence.

10. pakṣadvaye niśritā hi janatā upalabhyate /
pramattā viṣayeṣv eva mithyā coccalitā punaḥ //
One finds that creatures lie in two categories.
They are heedless in sense fields; moreover, waywardly advancing.

11. mohenāpahṛtās te vai mithyā uccalitās turye /
tṛṣṇayāpahṛtās te tu pramattā viṣayeṣu ye //
Truly those caught by delusion are those waywardly advancing.
While those caught by desire are those heedless in sense fields.

12. sahetukatvād dharmāṇāṃ duḥkhasyeha tathaiva ca /
maulaṃ kleśadvayaṃ kṛtvā dvādaśāṅgo dvidhā kṛtaḥ //
Because *dharmas* have their cause, as does also suffering,

Since one has created the two fundamental defilements, there are the twelve members, of two kinds.

13. svayaṃkṛtā kriyā naiva tathā parakṛtā na ca /
parah kriyāṃ na kārayati na ca nāsti kriyā punaḥ //
The activity is not created by self, nor created by another;
Another (life) does not cause the activity; but also the activity does not fail to exist.

14. nādhyātmaṃ na bahir vā ca nāntarāle tayor api /
anutpanno hi saṃskāraḥ kadācid upalabhyate //
Whether within, without, or between the two,
The *saṃskāra* that has not (yet) arisen is nowhere found.

15. utpanno 'pi ca saṃskāraḥ tenāsau nopalabhyate /
anāgatam nirnimittam atītam tu vikalpyate //
Even when the *saṃskāra* has arisen, it is not thereby found.
The future is devoid of sign. But one imagines the past.

16. kalpyate 'nubhūtaṃ (na) ca nānubhūtaṃ ca kalpyate /
anādimantaḥ saṃskārā ādiś caivopalabhyate //
One imagines not just the experienced, but imagines also the not-experienced.
The *saṃskāras* are beginningless. Still, a beginning is found.

17-18. phenapiṇḍopamaṃ rūpaṃ vedanā budbudopamā /
marīcisadṛśī saṃjnā saṃskārāḥ kadalīnibhāḥ/
māyopamaṃ ca vijñānam uktam ādityabandhunā /
ekotpādāś ca saṃskārā ekasthitinirodhinaḥ //
The solar kinsman has proclaimed formation to be like a lump of foam; feeling like a bubble; ideation like a mirage; motivations like plantain trunks; and perception like an illusion.
The *saṃskāras* arise alike, abide and perish alike.

19. na moho mohayed mohaṃ paraṃ naiva ca mohayet /
na paro mohayaty enaṃ na ca moho na vidyate /
Delusion does not delude delusion, nor does it at all delude any one else; nor does any one else delude it; and yet delusion does not fail to occur.

20. ayoniśomanaskārāt saṃmoho jāyate sa ca /
ayoniśomanaskāro nāsaṃmūḍhasya jāyate //
That confusion is born of unmethodical mental orientation,
And the unmethodical mental orientation is born of one not free from confusion.

21. puṇyā apuṇyā āniñjyā saṃskārās trividhā mataḥ /

trividhaṃ cāpi yat karma sarvaṃ etad asaṃgatam //
Meritorious, demeritorious, and motionless are the motivations (and) held to be threefold; and whichever be the threefold *karma*, all that is disjoined.

22. prabhaṅgurā vartamānā atītā na kvacit sthitā /
ajātāḥ pratyayādhināḥ cittaṃ cāpy anuvartakaṃ //
The present ones are disintegrating;
Those of the past abide nowhere;
The unborn depend on conditions,
And the mind evolves accordingly.

23. atyantikaḥ saṃprayogo viprayogas tathaiva ca /
na ca sarvair hi sarvasya cittaṃ copagam ucyate //
In an absolute sense not all (mind) has association—dissociation likewise—with all (*saṃskāra*).
It is said that mind evolves accordingly.

24. tasmin srotasya vicchinne sadṛśāsadṛśe punaḥ /
ātmadṛṣṭyanusāreṇa saṃvṛtiḥ kriyate tv iyaṃ //
Again, the stream (of consciousness) has similar and dissimilar disruption, but this convention works by following the view that there is a self.

25. bhidyate rūpakāyas ca nāmakāyo 'pi naśyati /
svayaṃkṛto 'pabhogaś ca paratreha nirucyate //
The set of formation breaks up; the set of names also perishes; and the self-done is declared "fruit-eating" both in this and in the other world.

26. paurvāparyeṇa cānyatvāt svahetuphalasaṃgrahāt /
sa eva kartā vettā ca anyo veti na kathyate //
That is the "doer" and the "feeler" through difference of priority and posteriority, and through comprising in itself the cause and the fruit. But one should not explain (that) as "different."

27. hetuvartmānupacchedāt sāmagryā vartate kriyā /
svasmād dhetoś ca jāyante kurvanti ca parigrahaṃ //
Given that the course of causes is not disrupted, activity evolves by reason of the assemblage (of causes). They are born by their individual cause and take control.

28. prapañcābhirati hetu tathā karma śubhāśubham /
sarvabījo vipākaś ca iṣṭāniṣṭaṃ tathā phalaṃ //
When the cause is delight in elaboration, likewise the action (*karma*) is good or evil. When any seed matures, likewise the fruit is desirable or undesirable.

29. sarvabījo vipāko 'bhijāyate ātmadarśanaṃ /
pratyātmavedanīyo 'sau arūpī anidarśanaḥ //
When any seed matures, the view of self is reproduced.
What is to be known of one's own self is that it is formless, invisible.

30. kalpayanty antarātmānaṃ taṃ ca bālā ajānakāḥ /
ātmadarśanam āśritya tathā bahvyaś ca dṛṣṭayaḥ //
And that is what the immature and ignorant imagine to be the self within, having based themselves on the view of self.
Thus there are many (false) views.

31. piṇḍagrāhātmabījāc ca pūrvābhyāsāt sahāyataḥ /
śravaṇād anukūlāc ca jāyate ātmadarśanaṃ //
As a result of the cohering seed of self, the former concomitant habitual practice, and (present) hearing in conformity therewith, the view of self arises.

32. snehas tatpratyayaṃ caiva adhyātmam upajāyate /
anugrahābhilāṣaś ca bahiḥ sneho mamāyitaṃ //
Attachment originates in addition to that condition within;
And attachment craving for acquisition (originates in addition to) the cherished thing without.

33. yato bibheti loko 'yaṃ tan mohātmaṃ haraty asau /
pūrvaṃ niveśanaṃ kṛtvā tenopaiti prapañcitaṃ //
Whatever this world fears, that brings the self of delusion.
Having formerly made an abode, it undertakes the elaborated.

34. yat tan niveśanaṃ kṛtaṃ tad āryā duḥkhato viduḥ /
yena duḥkhitā sadā bālāḥ kṣaṇamātram upaśamito na hi //
Whatever the abode that is made, that the noble ones know as suffering.
Thereby the immature always suffer, for it is not appeased even for a moment.

35. vairūpyaparigataṃ cittam ācinoti duḥkhaṃ tathāvidhaṃ /
yadā cittaṃ bhavati bālānām ahaṃkārasukhaduḥkhapratyayaṃ //
The mind that is filled with variations gathers suffering of like kind. Whenever it is a mind belonging to the immature, it is the condition of egohood, happiness, and suffering.

36. yatra saktāḥ sarvabāliśāḥ paṅke patati kuñjaro yathā /
saṃmohas tatra cādhikaḥ sarvatragaḥ sarvaceṣṭite tatparaḥ //
Where all fools are stuck, as an elephant sinks in a bog,
There is the remaining confusion, proceeding everywhere,

given over to every activity.

37. sarvasrotasāṃ vinirbhedāya yāni loke srotāṃsi viṣamāṇi / naitad asty agnir na vāyur na bhāskaro 'tiśoṣayed anyatra dharmacaryayā //
No fire, wind, or sun could dry up those unbearable streams in the world, so as to destroy all streams—
Nothing but the practice of the Dharma.

38. Duḥkhī duḥkhito 'ham asmīty ātmānaṃ sukhito vā duḥkhaṃ vyavasyati /
parikalpo dṛṣṭisamutthāpakaḥ sa tasmāj jātas taj jānayaty api //
When suffering, one thinks, "I am suffering;" or "I am happy," when he ascertains himself suffering. Imagination is the arouser of (right and wrong) views. It is produced from them and generates them in turn.

39. sahotpannaniruddhaṃ hi kleśaiḥ kliṣṭaṃ manaḥ sadā /
tasya nirmokṣo na bhūto na bhaviṣyati //
The defiled mind always arises and ceases together with defilements.
Its release has not occurred and will not.

40. na tad utpadyate paścāc chuddham anyatra jāyate /
tac ca pūrvam asaṃkliṣṭaṃ kleśebhyo muktam ucyate //
That does not arise later. On another occasion it is born pure. Precisely that which formerly was unstained is called "freed from defilements."

41. yat kliṣṭaṃ tad ihātyantāc chuddham prakṛtibhāsvaraṃ /
na ceha śudhyate kaścit kutaścid vāpi śudhyati //
That which was defiled, here in the end is purified, with its intrinsic light. Anything not purified here would surely not become pure anywhere !

42. sarvabījasamutsādāt sarvakleśaparikṣayāt /
tatraiva cāpy asaṃkleśād dvidhābhinnaṃ pradarśitaṃ //
By reason of the utter destruction of all seeds—the total elimination of all defilement; in the same place, as well, by reason of no stain, a portion of two kinds is specified.

43. pratyātmavedanīyatvād duḥkhamātraparikṣayāt /
tathaiva niḥprapañcatvāt sarvathā na prapañcayet //
Through what is to be known of one's own self, through elimination of suffering only; just so, through no elaboration, one does not elaborate at all.

44. pravāhe pudgalākhyā syād dharmasaṃjñā ca lakṣaṇe /
na veha kascit saṃsartā nirvāty api na kaścana //
The term "person" (*pudgala*) means "continuous stream" and the expression "nature" (*dharma*) means "character." Neither is there any transmigrator here, nor is anything allayed (in *parinirvāṇa*).

COMMENTARY

/ pudgalanairātmyaṃ paramārthatas tadadhikārāt paramārthaṃ gāthā / samāropāpavādāntadvayapratipakṣeṇa / tatra *svāmī* parigrahasya *kartā* kriyāṇāṃ *vedakaḥ* / tat phalānāṃ gāthārddhenārthāntaraparikalpitam ātmānāṃ pratikṣipati / *dharmāḥ sarve 'pi niśceṣṭā* iti dharmāṇām evātmatvaṃ pratikṣipati / etena samāropāntaṃ parivarjayati / *atha ced vartate kriyety* anena dharmāstitvena cāpavādāntaṃ parivarjayati / tatra kriyā trividhā svāmikriyā kārakakriyā vedakakriyā ca / yayā kriyayā svāmī prajñapyate / kārako vedako vā katame te *dharmā* iti noktam ata āha / *dvādaśaive*ti gāthārddhaṃ yathā bhavāṅgakrameṇa ye vartante skandhās tān paridīpayati / skandhadhātvāyatanagrahaṇaṃ / svāmikārakavedakagrāhakapratipakṣeṇa cakṣuḥ pratītya rūpāṇi cotpadyate cakṣurvijñānaṃ phalaṃ *na tu kaścid vedako 'stī*ty aṣṭādaśabhir dhātubhir vedakābhāvaṃ paridīpayati / *svāmī nā vidyata* ity uktaṃ / sa punar yathā na vidyate tat paridīpayati / *vicintya sarvāṇy etāni pudgalo nopalabhyata* iti / *vicintyeti* tribhiḥ pramāṇaiḥ parīkṣya / tasmin na vidyamāne katham ādhyātmikabāhyavyavasthānaṃ sidhyatīty āha / *śūnyam ādhyātmikaṃ sarvaṃ śūnyaṃ sarvaṃ bahirgataṃ* / vyavasthānamātraṃ tv etad iti jñāpayati / kathaṃ parīkṣyaparīkṣakavyavasthānaṃ sidhyatīti /āha/ *na vidyate so 'pi kaścid yo bhāvayati śūnyatām* iti / katham āryapṛthagjanavyavasthānaṃ sidhyatīti / āha / *ātmaiva hy ātmano nāsti viparītena kalpyata* āryapṛthagjanātmaiva tadātmanaḥ pariniṣpanno nāsti viparyāsena tu kalpyata iti jñapayati / kathaṃ parātmavyavasthānam sidhyatīti / āha *naiveha sattvo ātma veti* / kathaṃ saṃkleśavyavadānavyavasthānaṃ sidhyatīti / āha *dharmās tv ete sahetukāḥ* / na saṃkliṣṭā na vyavadātā vā kaścid astīti / *dharmāḥ sarve 'pi niśceṣṭā* ity uktaṃ / na tūktaṃ kathaṃ niśceṣṭā iti / ata āha / *kṣanikāḥ sarvasaṃskārā asthitānāṃ kutaḥ kriyeti* / *atha ced vartate kriyety* uktaṃ / tat katham asatyāṃ kriyāyāṃ kriyā vartata iti āha / *bhūtir yeṣāṃ kriyāsau ca kārakas saiva cocyata* iti / phalatvāt kriyā hetutvāt kārakaḥ / taṃ punar bhūtir yāyatanebhyo vijñānotpattyā sūcayati / tadutpattyā ca / cakṣurādīnāṃ nāntareṇa tatsiddheḥ / *dharmāh sarve 'pi niśceṣṭā* ity uktaṃ / tāṃ niśceṣṭatāṃ saptavidhāṃ darsayati / kāritraniśceṣṭatāṃ *cakṣuḥ paśyati no rūpam* ity evam ādinā / anuvidhānaniśceṣṭatāṃ / *nāsti caiṣām adhiṣṭhātā prerako vidyate na ceti* / svāmikārakābhāvād yathākramaṃ yasyānuvidhānaṃ kuryuḥ/ utpādananiśceṣṭatāṃ *na paro janyaty enam* iti / utpattiniśceṣṭatāṃ *svayaṃ naiva ca jāyata* iti / saṃkrāntiniśceṣṭatāṃ *pratīya bhāvā jāyante niṣpurāṇā navā navā* iti vināśananiśceṣṭatāṃ / *na paro nāśayaty enam* iti vinaṣṭiniśceṣṭatāṃ / *svayam nāpi ca naśyatī*ti / kiyathā pratītya jāyante tathā pratītya vinaśyantīti / āha / *pratyaye sati jāyante jātāḥ svarasabhaṅgurāḥ* / *dharmās tv ete sahetukā* ity uktam / atas tān saṃkleśasvabhāvān gṛhasthapravrajitadharmān sahetukān paridīpayati / *pakṣadvaye niśritā hi janate*ti / dvābhyāṃ gāthābhyām avidyātṛṣṇāhetuparidīpanāt / ataḥ paraṃ pañcabhir gāthābhis tam eva saṃkleśaṃ prabhedataḥ / āśrayataḥ hetutaḥ kālataś ca saṃdarśayati / tatra sahetukā dharmāḥ avidyā yāvad vedanā sahetukaṃ duḥkhaṃ tṛṣṇā yāvad jarāmaraṇa etena trividhaṃ kleśakarmajanmasaṃkleśaṃ darśayati / *maulaṃ kleśadvayaṃ kṛtve*ti / kleśasaṃkleśāt pradhānakleśagrahaṇaṃ darśayati / *svayamkṛtā kriyā naive*ti karmasaṃkleśasya punaḥ pṛthagjanaṃ vacanaṃ tatkṛtatvād vaicitryasya / tadvipākasya cācintyatvāt / tatra na svayamkṛtaiva kriyā pāpakalyāṇamitraparopasaṃhāraś cakṣanān na parakṛtaiva puruṣakārāpekṣaṇāt / *na para eva kriyāṃ kārayati* / pūrvajanmahetvapekṣaṇāt / *nādhyātmaṃ na bahir vety* anayā gāthayā / anāgatāśritasāmkleśāsambhāvaṃ pratyutpannātītasaṃskārāśritasaṃkleśaṃ darśayati / *utpanno 'pi saṃskāraḥ* tenaiva na vikalpyate *'nāgataṃ tu nirnimittatvān* na vikalpyate / idam īdṛṣaṃ vā bhaviṣyatīty anavadhāraṇād anyathā hi / kalpitam ànyathaiva kadācid bhavati / *atītaṃ tu vikalpyate* nimittakaraṇād idaṃ caivaṃ cābhūd iti / na kevalam anubhūtam eva kalpyate / ananubhūtaṃ cānāgataṃ vikalpyate vināpi nimittīkareṇa etena kālpanāhetukaṃ saṃkleśaṃ pratyutpannaṃ saṃskārāśrayaṃ darśayati / *anādimantaḥ saṃskārā ādiś caivopalabhyata* iti / saṃkleśasya kālaṃ darśayati / anādikālānugatatvād abhinavotthāpanāc ca / ataḥ paraṃ vyavadānāpakṣaṃ darśayati / yathā parīkṣyamāno vyavadāyate / svalakṣaṇato rūpādīnāṃ *phenapiṇḍā*dyupamayā sāmānyalakṣaṇataḥ saṃskṛtalakṣaṇasāmānyād *ekotpattisthitinirodha*tayā saṃvṛtiparamārthasatyatas ca / tathā hi na kaścid mohako na ca / moho nāsti pratītya samutpannaḥ saṃvṛtyā ca moho mohayatīty ucyate / yan *nāmūḍhasyāyoni śomanaskāraḥ* tasmād asau *mohaṃ na mohayatī*ti / paridīpayati / tathā hi vijñānaṃ *puṇyādisaṃskāropagam ucyate* saṃvṛtyā paramārthatas tu nopagacchati / *trividhā matā* ity atītānāgatapratyutpannāḥ / *trividhaṃ cāpi yat karmeti* kāyādikarma *sarvam etad asaṃgataṃ* / parasparеṇāsamadhānāt tathā hi *prabhaṅgurā vartamānāḥ* / *atītā na kvacit sthitāḥ* / *ajātāḥ pratyayādhināḥ cittaṃ cāpy anurvartakaṃ* / teṣāṃ yat tat saṃprayuktam / ato yathā puṇyādīnāṃ saṃskārāṇāṃ saṃgamo nāsti / tathā tat saṃprayuktasyāpi cittasyeti kathaṃ tasyopagatatvaṃ bhaviṣyati / yad dhi cittaṃ yena saṃskāreṇa saṃprayuktaṃ vā / viprayuktaṃ vā / na taṃ tena / kadācid asaṃprayuktaṃ vā / aviprayuktaṃ vā bhavati / na ca sarvasya cittasya *saṃprayogo* vā *viprayogo* vā / evaṃ paramārthataś cittasyopagatatvam asiddhaṃ / *cittaṃ copagam ucyate* / saṃvṛtyā yena kāraṇena tad darśayati / *tasmin srotasya vicchinna* iti gāthāyāṃ *saṃvṛtiḥ kriyate tv iyam* ity *upagam* ity eṣā yathā cāsati kārake / vedake ca paramārthataḥ *svayaṃkṛtopabhogaḥ* saṃvṛtyā *nirucyate* / yathā ca punaḥ sa karoti / sa prativedayate / *anyo veti* no vyākriyate / tat paridīpayati / *paurvāparyeṇa cānyatvād* iti / gāthayā evaṃ paramārthataḥ svāminy asati kārake vedake vā hetuphalamātre ca sati codyaparihāraṃ hetuphalalakṣaṇaṃ / tatra cātmaviparyāsaṃ / pañcabhir gāthābhiḥ paridīpayati / tatra yathatmany asati punarbhavo bhavati / nocchedaḥ / yathā ca hetuto yugapat phalaṃ na bhavati / yathā ca sarvataḥ sarvaṃ na bhavati / yathā ca yasya hetuvartmanaḥ ucchedo na bhavati / tad ekayā gāthayā paridīpayaṃś caturvidhaṃ codyaṃ paridīpayati harati / caturbhiḥ padair yathākramaṃ dvitīyayā hetuphalalakṣaṇaṃ / tisṛbhis tatrānātmani hetuphale yathātmadṛṣṭiviparyāsaḥ / tat punar ālambanataḥ / āśrayataḥ phalataḥ hetutaś ca paridīpayati / tasyālambanam ekayā gāthayā / tac ca pratyātmavedanīyatvam arūpitvānidarsanābhyāṃ sādhayaty atarkyatvāt / rūpaṇā hi tarkaṇā sūtra uktā / anidarśanatvāc ca / parebhyo 'deśanayā / āśrayaṃ phalaṃ ca dvitīyayā / bālā āśrayas tadanyā dṛṣṭayaḥ phalaṃ hetuṃ tṛtīyayā / tatra sahajātmadṛṣṭi*piṇḍagrāha*svabījāt ca tadanuśayāj jāyate / parikalpitā tīrthikātmadṛṣṭiḥ *pūrvābhyāsād* iti / sā ca tīrthikadṛṣṭiḥ abhyastā bhavati / ayoniśaś ceha tarkayati / tadanukūlaṃ vāsaddharmaṃ parataḥ śṛṇoti / ity āśrayamanasikārālambanadoṣaiḥ parikalpitasyātmadarśanasyotpattiṃ darśayati / ataḥ paraṃ yathā tad *ātmadarśanaṃ* / samudayānupūrvaṃ duḥkhaṃ nivartayati / yathā ca tad duḥkhaṃ punaḥ sāhaṃkārayor dvayor duḥkhatayoḥ kāraṇaṃ bhavati / yathā ca mokṣasya vibaddhāya bhavati / tat pañcabhir gāthābhiḥ paridīpitaṃ / tatra prathamayā gāthayā samudayaṃ darśayati / dvitīyatṛtīyābhyāṃ duḥkhasaṃskāraduḥkhatāsaṃgṛhītam ālayavijñānam ayaṃ tad *niveśanaṃ kṛtvā / tenopaiti prapañcitaṃ* bhaviṣyāmi na bhaviṣyāmīty evamādi / *niveśanam* ity ātmabhāvaparigrahaṃ / tac ca duḥkhaṃ sarvakālānuṣaktatvāt / *kṣaṇamātram* apy anupaśāntaṃ / caturthyā yathā duḥkham anyayor duḥkhayor ahaṃkārasya ca pratyayo bhavati / pañcamyā yathā punar mokṣasya vibaddhāya bhavati *saṃmohas tatra cādhikaḥ* / itarābhyāṃ duḥkhatābhyām antikāt / sarvatragaḥ sarvaveditānugatatvāt / *sarvaceṣṭite* kuśalākuśalāvyākṛte / tasyedānīm ālayavijñānasaṃgṛhītasya duḥkhasya saraḥsārūpyaṃ darśayitvā viśoṣaṇaṃ *dharmacarya*iva śoṣāt / tatra *viṣamāṇi srotāṃsi* cakṣurādīni ṣaṭ pañca gatayaḥ trayo dhātavas ity evamādīni / tāṃ ca dharmacaryāṃ bandhamokṣaparijñayā darśayati / tatra bandhaparijnā yad evaṃ parijānāti / duḥkham eva vyavasyati / yo duḥkhitaḥ *sukhito* 'smīti ātmanaṃ vyavasyati / sa ca parikalpo dṛṣṭeḥ samutthāpakas tata eva / dṛṣṭer jātas tajjanako bhavati / mokṣaparijñām śeṣābhiḥ ṣaḍbhir gāthābhiḥ paridīpayati / *sahotpannaniruddhaṃ hi kleśaiḥ kliṣṭaṃ manaḥ sadā* kleśebhyas *tasya nirmokṣo na bhūto* yadā kleśais sahotpannaṃ *na bhaviṣyati* / yadā taiḥ sahaniruddhaṃ yadā tarhi *muktam ucyate* tat saṃdarśayati / tad eva *paścāc chuddham* utpadyate 'nyatra śuddhaṃ mano jāyate / tac ca pūrvam evāsaṃkliṣṭatvād muktam ity ucyate / etam evārthaṃ punaḥ sādhayati / *yat kliṣṭaṃ tad ihātyantād* ity anayā gāthayā taṃ ca / mokṣaṃ dvidhaṃ darśayati / kleśamokṣaṃ vastumokṣaṃ ca / sarvabījasamusādena kleśaparīkṣayāt kleśamokṣaṃ / tatraiva cāpy asaṃkleśād vastumokṣaṃ / yo bhikṣavaś cakṣuṣi / chandarāgas taṃ prajahita / evaṃ ca tac cakṣuḥ prahīṇaṃ bhaviṣyatīti / sūtrapadanyāyena / evaṃ sopadhiśeṣaṃ mokṣaṃ darśayitvā nirupadhiśeṣaṃ darśayati / *pratyātmavedanīyata*yā / tasyācintyatāṃ darśayati / abhāvamātragrāhavyudāsārthaṃ *duḥkhamātrakṣaye*nopadhiśeṣāpanayaṃ / tataś ca sarvathāpy aprapañcanīyatvam / anyo vā saḥ ananyo vā bhavati vā / paraṃ maraṇān na bhavati vety evamādi / saty api ca bandhe mokṣe ca / yathā na pudgalo na dharmaḥ saṃsarati vā parinirvāti vā tat paridīpayati / *pravāhe pudgalākhyā syād* ity anayā gāthayā / samāptaṃ ca paramārthagāthānāmāptāgamavyākhyānaṃ //

TRANSLATION OF PARAMĀRTHA COMMENTARY[6]

As an adversary to the extremes of affirmation and denial, there are the Verses of Supreme Meaning, referring to "non-selfhood of a person" (*pudgalanairātmya*) from the standpoint of supreme meaning.

Among them, the "proprietor" is of property; "doer," of activities; "feeler," of the latter's effects. By the half-*gāthā* [la-b] he refutes the self (*ātman*) imagined of other meaning. By saying "Although all the *dharmas* are inactive" [1c], he refutes the possession of self by the *dharmas*. Thereby he removes the extreme of affirmation. By saying "yet activity evolves" [ld), through existence of the *dharmas*, he removes the extreme of denial. Here activity is of three kinds: activity of the proprietor, of the doer, of the feeler. The proprietor is pointed out by the activity, likewise the doer or feeler.

What those *dharmas* are, has not been (so far) stated. Therefore, he says the half-verse "The twelve...."[2a-b] so that he may expound those personal aggregates (*skandha*) which evolve according to the sequence of the members of phenomenal life [i.e. *pratītyasamutpāda*][7]; (expound) the sensory object, that is, "personality aggregates" (*skandha*), "realms" (*dhātu*), and "sense bases" (*āyatana*);[8] and (expound) that the fruitional eye-based perception arises dependently on the eye and forms[9] with exclusion of a subject, that is, "proprietor," "doer," and "feeler."

6Quotations in the commentary of the *gāthās* are here identified by the *gāthā* number and by *pādas*, labeled *a* through *d*.

7The "members of phenomenal life" are the twelve of dependent origination, referred to in *gāthās* 2, 11-12.

8The five personal aggregates are listed by similes in *gāthās* 17-18. The twelve sense bases, six personal (eye, etc.) and six objective (forms, etc.) are listed in *gāthās* 6-7. The eighteen realms, mentioned below in the commentary, are arrived at by adding six "perceptions" (*vijñāna*), e.g. perception based on the eye, to the twelve sense bases, making a total of eighteen *dhātu*.

9Asaṅga here accepts the ancient doctrine, as in the stock Pāli phrase (cf. *Saṃyutta-Nikāya*, Part IV, *Saḷāyatana-Vagga*, 32): / *cakkuñ ca paticca rūpe ca uppajjati cakkhuviññāṇaṃ* / "The eye-based perception arises dependently on the eye and form." Note that Asaṅga admits *vijñāna* is fruitional. This shows that the frequent translation of the term *vijñana* (Pāli *viññāṇa*) as "consciousness" badly misses the meaning, since the word "consciousness" is ordinarily used as a faculty independent of and preceding the function "consciousness of (something)."

By saying "There is no feeler," he expounds the non-existence of the feeler in the eighteen realms. It was said, "There is no proprietor"; and he now expounds how there is none with the words, "Pondering all those, a 'person' (*pudgala*) is not found" [2c-d]. "Pondering" (*vicintya*) means inspecting by means of the three authorities (*pramāṇa*).[10]

In the light that there is none, how does he prove the establishment of inner and outer ? He says [3a-b] : "Void is all within; void all without." (Thus) he teaches the mere establishment. How does he prove the establishment of the thing inspected and the inspector ? He says [3c-d] : "Nor exists anyone who contemplates voidness." How does he prove the establishment of the noble one (*ārya*) and the ordinary person (*pṛthagjana*) ? He says [4a-b] : "For the self is not by way of self; it is imagined in reverse manner." (Thus) he teaches that it is precisely the self of the noble one and of the ordinary person that is not perfect (*pariniṣpanna*) by way of their self, but is imagined in reverse manner. How does he prove the establishment of another and oneself ? He says [4c] : "Here there is no being or oneself." How does he prove the establishment of stain (*saṃkleśa*) and purification (*vyavadāna*) ? He says [4d] : "These *dharmas* have their causes"; that is, there is none either stained or pure.

It was stated, "Although all the *dharmas* are inactive," but it was not stated how they are inactive. Hence he says [5a-b] : "All the *saṃskāras* are momentary; how could there be the activity of transient things ?" It was stated, "yet possible activity evolves." Then, in the light that activity is unreal, how does activity evolve ? He says [5c-d] : "Precisely their arising is the activity as well as the agent." From the standpoint of effect, it is activity; from the standpoint of cause, it is the agent. Furthermore, that arising he indicates by the production of perception (*vijñāna*) at the sense bases (*āyatana*) and by the production of that through accomplishing it in a manner not apart from the eye, and so on.

It was stated, "Although all the *dharmas* are inactive." That inactivity he shows to be sevenfold :

[10]The three "authorities" (*pramāṇa*) are direct perception (*pratyakṣa*), inference (*anumāna*), and master lineage (*āptāgama*), as described in Asaṅga's *hetuvidyā* section of the *Yogācārabhūmi*, a section I have translated ("Rules of Debate") for inclusion in a separate work.

1. Inactivity of agent, by [Gāthā 6] "Neither does the eye see form. . . ."
2. Inactivity of obedient evolving, by (Gāthā 7) "And these have neither controller nor instigator" for which they would make obedient evolving in proper order—because of the non-existence of the proprietor and the doer.
3. Inactivity of generator, by the words [8a] "Another does not engender this."
4. Inactivity of generation, by the words [8b] "Nor is it engendered of itself."
5. Inactivity of transmigration, by the words [8c-d] "Entities arise dependently. They are not old, but ever new."
6. Inactivity of destroyer, by the words [9a] "Another does not destroy this."
7. Inactivity of destruction, by the words [9b] "Nor is it destroyed of itself."

Is it the case that as they arise dependently, so are they destroyed dependently ? He says [9c-d] : "When there is the condition, things arise; and, having arisen, they are perishable, by their own essence."

It was stated, "These *dharmas* have their causes." Hence he (now) expounds the *dharmas*, having the nature of stain, of householder and monk, with their causes, by expounding the nescience-craving causes by means of two *gāthās* [nos. 10, 11] : "Creatures lie in two categories. . . ." Moreover, by means of five *gāthās* [nos. 12-16], he shows this stain in varieties : that of basis (*āśraya*), cause (*hetu*), and time (*kāla*). Among them [12a-b], the *dharmas* possessed of causes are [the seven, viz.] nescience (*avidyā*) through feeling (*vedanā*); the suffering possessed of causes is [the five, viz.] craving (*tṛṣṇā*) through old age and death (*jarāmaraṇa*). Thereby he shows the three kinds of stain (*saṃkleśa*) : defilement (*kleśa*), action (*karma*), and birth (*janma*). With the words [12c] "Since one has created the two fundamental defilements" he shows the chief defilement object by way of 'defilement stain' (*kleśa-saṃkleśa*). With the words [13a] "The activity is not created by self" (he shows) furthermore the ordinary-person parlance of "action stain" (*karma-saṃkleśa*) that is manifold by way of what was (formerly) done and has its maturation in an inconceivable way.[11] Here the activity "not created by self" is what is brought about by others—sinful and beneficial friends, through advice; that "not created by another" is with reference to human effort. The words [13c] "Another (life) does not cause the activity" refer to a cause from a preceding life.[12]

With another *gāthā* [no. 14] he shows the non-origination of stain that is based on the future and of stain that is based on present and past *saṃskāras*. "Even when *saṃskāra* has arisen" [15a] it is not thereby imagined; the "future" one [15c], because "devoid of sign," is not imagined. Since there is no assurance of the type, "This, or similar will occur," it sometimes happens in one way while imagined in another way. "One imagines the past" [15d] through making a sign expressing "So this arose." Not only the experienced is imagined [see 16a-b], but also the unexperienced future is imagined without sign construct. Thereby he shows the stain which is the cause of imagination to be present as the basis (*āśraya*) of motivations (*saṃskāra*). With the words [16c-d] "The *saṃskāras* are beginningless. Still, a beginning is found," he shows the time of stain, by reason of following it for beginningless time and by reason of generating it anew.

Now he shows the category of purification. In the same way as one purifies by inspecting from the standpoints of conventional and absolute truth, that is, (by inspecting) formations and so on from the standpoint of individual characteristic (*svalakṣāṇa*) by the similes of "lump of foam," and the like [Gāthā 17][13] and (by inspecting) the generality of constructed characteristic from the standpoint of generalizing characteristic (*sāmānya-lakṣaṇa*) by "like arising, abiding, and perishing" [Gāthā 18]—

So also [Gāthās 19-20]—there is no deluder at all; there is no

[11]This remark may refer to the popular usage of the word *karma*, as when people speak of "my *karma*," and "your *karma*," as though the unpredictable results must have been due to the different actions of former lives, not of the present life.

[12]In the cases of the human effort and cause from a previous life, Asaṅga accepts the usual Indian terminology of "human effort" (*puruṣakāra*), but substitutes "cause from a previous life" (*pūrvajanmahetu*) for the usual *daiva* (fate, or what is due to the gods).

[13]For Asaṅga's explanations of these similes, cf. Wayman, "Secret of the *Heart Sūtra*," place with n. 22.

delusion arisen dependently, and one says (only) by convention that delusion deludes; hence, the unmethodical mental orientation of one not free from delusion he expounds with the words "It (i.e. delusion) does not delude delusion" [19a]—

So also [Gāthā 21]—by convention it is said that perception evolves after motivations (*saṃskāra*) meritorious, and so on, but from an absolute standpoint it does not evolve. "Held to be threefold" means past, future, and present. "And whichever be the threefold *karma*," that is, *karma* of body, and so on,[14] "all that is disjoined" for the reason of mutual unlike receptacle (*asama-dhāna*)—

So also [Gāthā 22-26]—"The present ones are disintegrating; those of the past abide nowhere; the unborn depend on conditions; and the mind evolves accordingly" [Gāthā 22], associated with them, as the case may be. Still, inasmuch as there is no joining of the motivations meritorious, and so forth, how can the mind associated therewith evolve accordingly ? Since the mind is either associated or dissociated with a motivation, it is neither entirely unassociated nor entirely undissociated with it. And not all mind has either association or dissociation. Thus, from an absolute standpoint, there is no proof that mind evolves accordingly. By convention "it is said that mind evolves accordingly" [23d], for which reason he shows that. In the *gāthā* [no. 24] "Again, the stream has....disruption," the words "this convention works" mean "evolves accordingly." While the doer and feeler is unreal from the absolute standpoint, "The self-done is declared 'fruit-eating'" [in 25c-d] by convention. Moreover, how that creates, experiences, and is not determined as different he sets forth by the *gāthā* [no. 26] "...through difference of priority and posteriority.." Thus, while from an absolute standpoint the proprietor is unreal, likewise the doer or feeler; and, while cause-and-result-only is real, the characteristic of cause-and-effect removes objections.

And among those (*gāthās*), he expounds the delusion of self (*ātman*) with five *gāthās* [nos. 27-31]. Here, (a) how, while the self is unreal, rebirth occurs undisrupted; (b) how the effect does not occur simultaneously with the cause; (c) how nothing at all occurs; and (d) how its course of causes is not disrupted;—setting

[14]The reference is to *karma* of body, of speech, and of mind.

forth that with one *gāthā* (no. 27), he sets forth and removes a fourfold objection with four *pādas* in sequence. With the second (Gāthā 28] he sets forth the characteristic of cause-and-fruit. With three (Gāthās 29-31] he sets forth how, while cause-fruit is without self, there is the delusion of self-view (*ātmadṛṣṭi*); and that he sets forth from the standpoints of consciousness-support (*ālambana*), basis (*āśraya*), fruit (*phala*), and cause (*hetu*). With the first *gāthā* [no. 29] he proves its consciousness-support—what is to be known of one's own self since it is formless and invisible; namely, since it is non-rational; in the *sūtra* "conception of form" (*rūpaṇā*) was declared "rational" (*tarkaṇa*); and since it is invisible : through non-display to others. With the second Gāthā 30] he sets forth the basis (*āśraya*) and the fruit (*phala*) : the immature are the basis; other (false) views are the fruit. With the third [Gāthā 31] he sets forth the cause (*hetu*). In that (verse), it is generated from the self seed—the natural coherence of the self-view, which is its traces (*anuśaya*). "As a result of the former habitual practice," there is the imagined heretic view of self. Not only is that heretic view habitually thought, but also one unmethodically reasons in this world. Or one hears from another a non-illustrious doctrine consistent therewith. Thus he shows the origination of the imagined view of self by the faults of basis, mental orientation, and consciousness support.

Now, with five *gāthās* [nos. 32-36] he sets forth how that view of self arouses suffering following upon its source; how that suffering then becomes the reason for two kinds of misery (*duḥkhatā*) accompanied by egohood; and how it becomes an obstacle for release. Among them, with the first *gāthā* [no. 32] he shows the source (of suffering). With the second and third [Gathas 33-34] he shows the store-consciousness (*ālayavijñāna*) that incorporates the suffering—(*duḥkha*) and motivation—(*saṃskāra*) miseries (*duḥkhata*).[15] That is to say, "Having (formerly) made an abode, it undertakes the (verbally) elaborated" (33c-d]—"I shall be," "I shall not be," and so forth. "Abode" means the

[15]There are three kinds of "misery" (*duḥkhatā*) found in the ancient Buddhist scriptures (cf. *Saṃyutta-Nikāya*, Part IV, *Saḷāyatana-Vagga*, 259), the two that Asaṅga mentions as incorporated by the "store consciousness" plus the "misery of change" (*vipariṇāmadukkhatā*). Perhaps the "misery of change" is incorporated by what the Yogācāra philosophy calls the "evolving consciousness" (*pravṛtti-vijñāna*).

possessions of the embodiment (*ātmabhāva*). And that suffering, by reason of adhering to it in all time, "is not appeased even for a moment" [34d]. With the fourth [Gāthā 35] he shows how suffering becomes the condition for two other sufferings [or, miseries] as well as for egohood. With the fifth [Gāthā 36] he shows that it then becomes an obstacle for release. "There is the remaining delusion" [36c], because close to the other two miseries; "proceeding everywhere," because following after all feelings; "to every activity," that is, to virtue, non-virtue, and the indeterminate.

Now, having shown [Gāthā 37] that this suffering comprised by the store-consciousness compares with a lake, he shows its drying up: just "the practice of the Dharma," for drying it. In that (verse), "unbearable streams" means the six (senses) of eye, and so on, the five destinies, the three realms, and so forth.[16] He shows that practice of the Dharma by complete knowledge of bondage and release. Among these, there is complete knowledge of bondage when one so recognizes: he ascertains it as just suffering. But [38b] he who thinks "I am happy," when he has ascertained himself as suffering, has an imagination that arouses a (false) view; and (imagination) born of just that (false) view is a generator of that (view).

He sets forth the complete knowledge of release in the remaining six *gāthās* [nos. 39-44]. "The defiled mind always arises and ceases together with defilements" [39a-b]. "Its release" from defilements "has not occurred" [39c] when it arises together with defilements, and "will not" [39d] when it ceases together with them. The time when it is called "freed" [40d], he shows that : just that later arises pure. At another time, the pure mind arises; and precisely that, by reason of its prior non-stain, is called "freed." Moreover, he proves precisely this meaning by the *gāthā* [no. 41] "That which was defiled, here in the end. . . ."

And that release he shows [Gāthā 42] to be of two kinds : release from defilements (*kleśamokṣa*) and release from materials (*vastumokṣa*). There is release from defilements by destroying all

[16]The six personal sense bases were previously listed in *gāthās* 6-7. The five destinies are the gods (*deva*) and men (*manuṣa*); and evil destiny (*durgati*) consisting of the animals (*tiryagyoni*), hungry ghosts (*preta*), and hell denizens (*naraka*). The three realms are the realm of desire (*kāmadhatu*), the realm of form (*rūpa-dhātu*), and the formless realm (*arūpadhātu*).

seeds as a consequence of ending defilement; and in the same place, as well, there is release from materials as a consequence of no stain. The *sūtra* says : "O monks, whatever be the sensuous lust in the eye, abandon that ! So also will the eye disappear.":[17] In the manner of that text he thus shows the release with remaining basis and then shows the one without remaining basis.

Because it is "what is to be known of one's own self" [no.43a] he shows the inconceivability of that (release) so as to eliminate the positing of mere absence. He shows the removal of the remaining basis by "elimination of suffering only" [no. 43b]. As a consequence, he shows the condition with nothing at all to be (verbally) elaborated; for example, "He becomes different, or not different, or beyond death does not exist," and so on.

Furthermore, he sets forth how, while there is bondage and release, no "person" (*pudgala*) or "nature" (*dharma*) revolves [in *saṃsāra*] or is allayed [in *parinirvāṇa*]; namely, with the *gāthā* [no. 44] "The term 'person' (*pudgala*) means 'continuous stream...'"

The explanation of the master lineage named *Paramārtha-gāthā* thus ends.

[17]A similar statement occurs in *Saṃyutta-Nikāya*, Part IV (*Salāyatana-Vagga*), 7: / *yo cakkusmiṃ chandarāgavinayo chandarāgapahānam* / *idaṃ cakkussa nissaraṇaṃ* / "That restraint of sensuous lust, that elimination of the sensuous lust in the eye—that is the way of release from the eye."

18

ASAṄGA'S TREATISE ON THE THREE INSTRUCTIONS OF BUDDHISM

The Sanskrit title of this treatise *Ābhiprāyikārtha-gāthā* signifies the *gāthā* set on the meaning of what was intended, or implied (in the Buddha's teaching). It seems that the word *gāthā* is here used for verses that summarize *sūtra* teachings about the three instructions in a way to bring out the *sūtra* intentions—which perhaps amounts to the school called Sautrāntika. Thus, these *gāthā* are not pieced together as were the *Paramārtha-gāthā* that immediately precede the present set in the *Cintāmayī Bhūmi* of the *Yogācārabhūmi*, but are presumably the author's own composition. There are fifty-one *gāthā*, first one for Brahmā's question, then fifty for the Bhagavat's reply. These verses on the three instructions are among the same intrusive folios from which I drew the *Paramārtha-gāthā*. I edited the *gāthā* both from the separate verses and from the partially extant commentary, which cites each of the verses.[1] Some bad places in the manuscript of the *gāthā* required reconstructions of a few terms

[1]The *gāthā* and commentary are on plates 3A-B and 15A-B of the *Śrāvakabhūmi* manuscript, a description of which may be found in Wayman, *Analysis of the Śrāvakabhūmi Manuscript* (1961). The extant commentary (at least one folio is missing) goes from the beginning down through citing verse 8; it resumes with the commentary on verse 30 and continues through verse 51.

that are italicized.[2] I add my translation including commentarial excerpts.

One verse that deserves special mention is no. 38 : "One should not adhere to one's own view, discarding the old lineage (*paurāṇam āgamam*)..." This verse supports a conclusion I made long ago in my *Analysis of the Śrāvakabhūmi Manuscript*, p. 29, that when Asaṅga was converted, according to the legend, to the *Mahāyāna*, he did not forget or reject the four Āgama (sometimes called "Hīnayāna"). The verses also prove that Asaṅga is a "moralist," and believed that the three instructions—of Morality, Mind Training, and Insight—were promulgated for the monks, not for laymen. He evidently considered that of the three instructions it was the morality one that needed the most exposition. Of course, Asaṅga does not neglect the other instructions. His *Paramārtha-gāthā* emphasizes the instruction of insight, and his following extended section in the *Yogācārabhūmi*—the *Śarīrārtha-gāthā*—deals much with Mind Training.

/ tatra ābhiprāyikārthagāthāvyavasthānataḥ // atha khalu brahmā sahāṃpatir yena bhagavāṃs tenopasaṃkrānta upasaṃkramya bhagavataḥ pādau śirasā vanditvā ekānte nyaṣīd(ad) ekāntaniṣaṇṇo brahmā sahāṃpatir bhagavantaṃ gāthābhigītena praśnaṃ pṛcchati sma /

(1) śikṣāsupāramiprāptaḥ sarvasaṃśayanāsaktaḥ /
śikṣām udgṛhīte pṛṣṭo yānuśikṣā suśikṣaṇā //
(2) adhiśīlam adhicittam adhiprajñām ca māriṣa /
tisraḥ śikṣāḥ samāsena śṛṇu yā tā suśikṣaṇā //
(3) bhavet ṣaḍaṅgasaṃpannaś cittasthitisukhānvitaḥ /
caturṣu caturākāra(ḥ) jñānaśuddhaḥ sadā bhavet //
(4) supratiṣṭhitamūlaḥ yaś cittasyopaśame rataḥ /
samyuktavyā visamyuktavyā dṛṣṭyadṛṣṭyāryānāryā //
(5) ādiśuddho dhyānarataḥ satye ca kuśalo bhavet /
utpādayed (vi)varjayed bṛṃhayet satyam eva ca //
(6) śikṣāpadeṣu vidyante catasro gatayas triṣu /
vivarjayitvā dvigatī dvigatī samudānayet //
(7) dve dvayapratyupasthāne ekā nirvāṇagāminī /
anupūrvopaniṣadabhinnasaṃbhinnabhāvitā //

[2]The reconstructions in 16, *vyālambanā*; in 25, *cīvarasaṃtuṣṭa*; in 49. *prīhi*—are certain; while in 29. *ca yācitavyāṃ*—is possibly not the original term.

(8) niṣkaukrtyo bhaved ādau paścāc ca sukhito yataḥ /
ādyāsau sarvaśikṣāṇāṃ yatra śikṣeta paṇḍita(ḥ) //
(9) yato viśodhaye jñānaṃ śucotpattisukhānvitaḥ /
madhyāsau sarvaśikṣāṇāṃ yatra śikṣeta paṇḍitaḥ //
(10) yato vimocayec cittaṃ prapañca(ṃ) ca nirodhayet /
śreṣṭhāsau sarvaśikṣāṇāṃ yatra śikṣeta paṇḍitaḥ //
(11) aśuddhagāminī pratipat tathā sugatigāminī /
ādyā pratipad ukteyaṃ sā ca niṣkevalā matā //
(12) viśuddhagāminī pratipad na sarvātyantagāminī /
madhyā pratipad ukteyaṃ nāpi niṣkevalā matā //
(13) viśuddhagāminī pratipat sarvātyantagāminī /
śreṣṭhā pratipad ukteyaṃ sā naivādvayakevalā //
(14) śikṣeta yo na śikṣeta ubhau tau paṇḍitau matau /
śikṣeta yo na śikṣeta ubhau tau balau saṃmatau //
(15) parigrahaparityāgād dauṣṭhulyāpagamāt tathā /
pratyakṣatvāc ca jñeyasya śikṣādānam tridhā bhavet //
(16) sālambanā v(*yālambanā*) sūkṣmodārikasaṃhitā /
sāmādānaprāvivekyaghoṣaābhogasaṃhṛtā //
(17) eka ekā bhavec chikṣā sadvitīyā paro bhavet /
ekasyātmā tṛtīyaiva tā budhaḥ samatikramet //
(18) ahraṣṭaśīlaḥ śikṣāt(sa) pratijñeyagato bhavet /
agarhitasamācāraḥ pañcasthānavivarjitaḥ //
(19) anāpattaye vyutthātā niṣkaukṛtyo 'tha kaukṛtya /
śikṣām āgamayet tatra pratipadyeta bhāvatas //
(20) pratyākhyānaṃ na kurvīta jīvitārthaṃ na nāśayet /
pratipattau sthito nityaṃ pravṛttavinayo bhavet //
(21) pratijñāṃ śodhayet pūrvam ājīvam api śodhayet /
antadvayaṃ varjayitvā praṇidhānaṃ vivarjayet //
(22) antarāyakarān dharmā(n) nābhigṛdhyet kathaṃ cana /
cittakṣobhakarān dharmān utpannā(n) nādhivāsayet //
(23) nātilīno nātisṛtaḥ sadā sūpasthitasmṛtiḥ /
maulasāmantakaiḥ śuddhaṃ brahmacaryaṃ bhaved api //
(24) bhaved ārabdhavīryaś ca nityaṃ dṛḍhaparākramaḥ /
niṣevatā pramādaṃ ca pañcāṅgasupratiṣṭhitaṃ //
(25) bhavet saṃchannakalyāṇaḥ tathā vivṛtapāpakaḥ /
lūhena vā praṇītena (*cīvarasaṃtuṣṭ*)ādinā //
(26) alpena vartayed mātrāṃ lūhenāpi ca vartayet /
dhūtān guṇān samādāyān samārthaṃ kleśavarjitaḥ //
(27) syād īryāpathasampanno mātrāṃ kuryāt pratigrahe /
tadarthaṃ kalpitām īryāṃ kuryān naiva kathaṃ ca na //

(28) ātmanāś ca guṇan bhūtān na lāpen nāpi lāpayet /
tān guṇān atha cārthitvaṃ nimittena na darśayet //
(29) pareṣām antikāt kramān na yācñāṃ *ca yācitavyāṃ* /
dharmenopagataṃ lābhaṃ lābheneha na saṃcayet //
(30) lābhaṃ naivābhigṛdhyeta satkāraṃ ca kathaṃ cana /
dṛṣṭiś ca nābhiniviśet samāropāpavādikaṃ //
(31) lokāyatāṃs tathā mantrāṇ nirarthān na parāmṛśet /
apārthaṃ dhārayen naiva utsadaṃ pātracīvaraṃ //
(32) gṛhasthaiḥ sahasaṃsargaṃ na kuryāt kleśavarddhanaṃ /
āryais tu sahasaṃsargaṃ kuryāj jñānaviśodhanaṃ //
(33) kuryān mitrakulaṃ naiva śokavyākṣepakārakaṃ /
duḥkhasya janakān kleśān utpannā(n) nādhivāsayet //
(34) śraddhādeyaṃ na bhuñjīta kathaṃ cic ca kṣatavrataḥ /
pratyākhyānaṃ na kurvīta saddharmasya kathaṃ cana //
(35) pareṣāṃ skhalite doṣe anābhogasukhī bhavet /
ātmanaḥ skhalitaṃ doṣaṃ jñātvā vivṛścayāt punaḥ //
(36) āpattiṃ ca tathāpanno yathā dharmaṃ prakalpayet /
tatheti karaṇīyeṣu svayaṃkārī paṭur bhavet //
(37) buddhānāṃ śrāvakāṇāṃ ca anubhāvaṃ ca deśanaṃ /
śrāddho 'vadyadarśī ca nābhyacakṣīta sarvathā //
(38) sugambhīreṣu dharmeṣu atarkāvacareṣu ca /
paurāṇam āgamaṃ tyakṣvo svadṛṣṭiṃ na parāmṛśet //
(39) vyavakṛṣṭavihari syāt prānte hi śayanāsane /
kuśalān bhavayed dharmān dṛḍhavīryaparākramaḥ //
(40) acchadrikaś chadrajāto apraduṣṭo vidūṣaṇaḥ /
nirmiddhaś caiva middhī ca kāle śānto na ca sthitaḥ //
(41) niṣkaukṛtyaḥ sakaukṛtyo niḥkāmkṣvo 'tha ca kāṃkṣati /
sarvathā sarvadā yukto bhavet samyakprayogavān //
(42) nudano bodhanaś caiva tathā samyojanoparaḥ /
naimittika snehanaś ca tathā vilasanoparaḥ //
(43) niṣpīdanas ca paramaḥ snehanaḥ kalpa ucyate /
kāmarāgasya janakas taṃ budhaḥ parivarjayet //
(44) atṛptikarakāḥ kāmā bahusādhāraṇās tathā /
adharmahetavaś caiva tathā tṛṣṇā(ṃ) vivarddhakāḥ //
(45) satāṃ (vi)varjanīyāś ca kṣipraṃ vilayagāminaḥ /
pratyāyeṣv āśritāḥ kāmāḥ pramādasya ca bhūmayaḥ //
(46) karaṅka-sadṛśāḥ kāmāḥ māṃsapeśyupamās tathā /
tṛṇolkāsadṛśāś caiva tathā agniśikhopamāḥ //
(47) āśīviṣopamāś caiva tathā svapnopamāḥ punaḥ /
yācñyālaṃkārasadṛśās tathā vṛkṣaphalopamāḥ //

(48) evaṃ kāmān parijnāya nābhigṛdhyet kathaṃ cana /
saddharmaṃ śṛṇu yo nityaṃ cintayed bhāvayed api //
(49) śānto dārikadarśī prāg yāvan aikāntiko bhavet /
prīhi yo kleśadauṣṭhulyaṃ prahāṇe carato bhavet //
(50) mīmātmakaḥ syān nimitte prayogaparamo bhavet /
kuryāc ca kāmavairāgyaṃ rūpavairāgyam eva ca //
(51) satyābhisamayaṃ kuryāt sarvavairāgyam eva ca /
dṛṣṭe dharme ca nirvāyāt tathā upadhi(ṃ) saṃkṣayāt //

For the following translation of the *gāthā*, I have selected portions of Asaṅga's commentary to go with relevant verses or verse groups. Since half of the Sanskrit commentary is missing, it is practical to add commentarial remarks from the Tibetan version.[3] However, the extant Sanskrit portion was consulted for editing the verses, and will be cited in a few places of the commentarial remarks.

> Then, you should know, Brahmā Sahāṃpati went there where was the Bhagavat, and having bowed with his head to the feet of the Bhagavat, went to one side; and remaining at one side Brahmā Sahāṃpati put a question to the Bhagavat by reciting a verse :
>
> (1) You have been perfected in the Instruction and have cleared all doubt. Whatever be the training and the points of instruction, pray tell how one embraces the Instruction !

(Commentary advances the view that in consideration of persons being fearful of too many rules and tending to laziness, the Buddha presented the Instructions compactly as three kinds :)[4]

> (2) Exalted friend, Morality, Mind Training, and Insight are the three Instructions in short. Listen, what be the training !
>
> (3) One should be equipped with the six members (of mora-

3. Besides, my wife Hideko gave some valuable suggestions for the translation from the Sino-Japanese versions of the text in the *Yogācārabhūmi*, namely, Chinese trans., T30 [no. 1579], pp. 365-67; Japanese trans., *Kokuyaku Daizōkyō*, *Rombo* 6, pp. 462-82.

4. Asaṅga's further commentarial remarks make it clear that he has in mind the Brahmā *sūtras* of the *Saṃyuktāgama* (in Pāli, the *Saṃyutta-Nikāya*, i, 136-138), with the implication that since persons are of widely different character and ability, there should be an appropriate teaching for the lazy person as well as for the enterprising one.

lity), endowed with the pleasure of mind-fixation; and the four kinds among the four should always purify knowledge.

The six members are : 1. one remains in possession of morality; 2. is restrained by the Prātimokṣa vow; 3. has perfection of good behavior (*ācārasaṃpannaḥ*); 4. has the perfection of lawful resort (*gocarasaṃpannaḥ*); 5. views fearfully the major and minor sins; 6. rightly takes and learns the "points of instruction" (*śikṣāpada*). The Instruction of Mental Training is fixation of mind (*cittasthiti*) of four kinds, namely the four kinds of Dhyāna; its pleasure by way of beatific dwelling of present life. The Instruction of Insight is the purification of knowledge by the four kinds for each of the four Noble Truths.

(4) (Namely, respectively,) a) have what is the well-established basis; b) have joy in the pacification of mind; c) take on the noble right view and leave off the ignoble wrong view.
(5) He should be pure from the outset; have the pleasure of Dhyāna; and should have skill in truth, to wit, he should (respectively) generate, eliminate, and promote truth.

He should generate the truth of path; should eliminate the truths of suffering and source of suffering; should promote the truth of cessation by cessation of defilement whether minor, middling, or great.

(6) When there are the three "points of instruction," there are the four destinies, to wit, having warded off two destinies, one should acquire two destinies.

He should ward off two destinies, the bad destiny (*durgati*) and the good destiny (*sugati*) of the realm of desire; and should acquire two destinies, the "upper" destiny of the realm of form and formless realm, and the Nirvāṇa destiny.

(7) Two are based on two; one is the Nirvāṇa-road. One should cultivate them becoming in sequence a basis, unmixed and mixed.

Of the two, Instruction of Morality and Instruction of Mind Training, the first one, Instruction of Morality, is the basis for both the Instruction of Mind Training and Instruction of Insight. The second, middling one, the Instruction of Mind Training, is the basis for the Instruction of Insight and that part of the Instruction of Morality as pertains to the "restraint of meditation." The best one, namely, the Instruction of Insight, is the road to Nirvāṇa. One should cultivate them unmixed (*abhinna*), i.e. consistent respectively, and mixed (*saṃbhinna*), i.e. consistent in leading to the goal.[5]

(8) Wherein the wise one trains, that one should be at first without regret, next happy—this is the first of all instructions.

In sequence, be without regret through the Instruction of Morality; and be happy through the Instruction of Mind Training.

(9) Wherein the wise one trains, whereby knowledge is for purification and one has pleasure in arousing purity—this is the middling one of all instructions.

The Instruction of Mind Training especially promotes the root of virtue (*kuśala-mūla*).

(10) Wherein the wise one trains, whereby one would liberate the mind and destroy verbal elaboration—this is the best one of all instructions.

This refers to the Instruction of Insight.

(11) The path said to be first, namely the impure way, likewise the way to good destiny—this is held to be by itself (*kevala*).

Through failure of the Instruction of Morality, there is the impure way which is the way to bad destiny. Through adherence to the Instruction of Morality, there is the way to good destiny. And either one is accomplished by one instruction alone.

(12) The path said to be middling, namely the path which is the pure way and not the final way—this is held to be not by itself.

This path is pure of the defilements of the realm of desire. But it is not free from the defilements of the realm of form and form-

[5]It appears that the "unmixed" exposition of the three Instructions is presented in the following *gāthā* nos. 8-10, since the three are defined individually without reference to the others. Likewise, it appears that the "mixed" exposition is presented in *gāthā* nos. 11-13, since the three are explained in terms of "path" and in consideration of whether they are *kevala* (by themselves). Hence, the Tibetan translation of the two terms as *so so* "respective" for the *abhinna*, and *'dren mo* "guiding" for the *saṃbhinna*. This information can be added to Franklin Edgerton's *Buddhist Hybrid Sanskrit Dictionary*, p. 580.

less realm, because it has not erased the traces (*anuśaya*) of sensuous lust. It is not the final way, since by itself, i.e. without the first and the best (instructions), it does not fulfil.

> (13) The path said to be best, namely the path which is the pure way and the final way—this is not by itself, i.e. not without the two.

The way freeing from all defilements of the three worlds and finishing off the traces, is not accomplished without the prior two (instructions) or by itself.

> (14) The one who trains and the one who doesn't train, both those are held to be wise (*paṇḍita*). The one who trains and the one who doesn't train, both those are held to be fools (*bāla*).

The one who trains rightly with the three Instructions, and the one who does not train in a wayward manner, is the wise one. The one who trains in a wayward manner, and the one who does not train rightly, is the fool.

> (15) The taking of the Instruction is threefold by way of a) renouncing possessions, b) eliminating contaminations, c) and direct perception of the knowable.

Possessions are home, wife, etc. Contaminations (*dauṣṭhulya*) are the discordant elements to *samādhi*. The knowable are the four Truths. The verse points to the three Instructions in their order.

> (16) They are accompanied with meditative object or devoid of meditative object, are subtle or coarse; and are accomplished by rightly taking, solitude, word, and bent.

The Instruction of Morality does not have a defined meditative object; the other two do have; thus the Instruction of Morality is "coarse," the other two "subtle." The Instruction of Morality is accomplished by rightly taking; the Instruction of Mental Training, by solitude of body and mind; the Instruction of Insight, by the word of another and the bent (*ābhoga*) of rightly orienting the mind within.

> (17) One Instruction (the first) is a single one. The Instruction with a second one is the subsequent one. The third Instruction is the nature of one. The wise person should surmount those.

The Instruction of Morality is single. But the Instruction of Mental Training needs a second one, the Instruction of Morality. The Instruction of Insight should not lack those two. The one "beyond training" (*aśaikṣa*) and the Arhat have surmounted those three Instructions.

(18) His morality should not fall away from the Instruction; he should be possessed of the vow; he should not condemn good behavior; and he should avoid five places.

The Instruction is that of Morality. The vow is the Prātimokṣa. Not condemning good behavior, he does not lose good behavior. The monk adheres to proper resort by avoiding five places, to wit, the royal palace, butcher shop, liquor shop, prostitute quarters, house of outcast.

(19) When he regrets that he cannot again sin, he should rise with no regret. One should rely on the Instruction and practice therein sincerely.

He should view fearfully the major and minor sins, and rightly take the "points of instruction."

(20) One should not repudiate it; not lose it even for life's sake; should always be stationed in the endeavor; should be involved with the discipline (*vinaya*).

These in order are the four "roots" : permanence of morality; firmness of morality; no interruption of it; staying in it continuously.

(21) One should purify his former vow, and should also purify his life. Having eliminated the two extremes, he should reject the (wrong) aspiration.

The two extremes are indulgence in sense desires and ascetic austerity. He should reject the (wrong) aspiration for heaven, for this constitutes merely the pure Instruction of Morality.

(22) One should not at all hanker after natures that create obstacles. One should not acquiesce in natures that have already arisen that disturb the mind.

(23) With mindfulness always present, he is neither over-relaxed nor overly spirited (in mind). His pure conduct (*brahmacarya*) is purified by the main part and threshold (of the four Dhyānas).

(24) He should begin his striving and always have a steadfast forward step by staying close to heedfulness that is well based in five members.

Striving means the kind that is armored and does not retreat from the praxis. Staying close to heedfulness shows distinguished purification of the Instructions. The five members of heedfulness are of 1. past, 2. future, 3. present-time, 4. action from previous (striving), 5. practice in conformity (with striving).

(25) He should be reserved about his virtues and confess his sins; be satisfied with his religious garb, etc. whether inferior or fine.

(26) He should abide the amount, even small; and abide it, even inferior. Rightly adopting the virtues of a purified man, he should eliminate defilements for the purpose of calming.

(27) He should be possessed of dignified posture, and should be judicious in acquisition. On that account, he should in no case ever assume artificial postures.

(28) One should not say one's own merits are real, or induce someone to say it. Besides, one should not reveal those merits by signs in terms of desired objects.

(29) One should not ask for alms forcefully in the presence of others. When what was received came righteously (with *dharma*), one should not speak badly of what was received.[6]

(30) One should not hanker in any way for receiving things or for respect. One should not cling to views that over-emphasize or under-value.

(31) One should not adhere to the meaningless mantras of the Lokāyatas.[7] One should not uselessly bear the begging bowl and religious garb in excess.

[6]As to "should speak badly" for the reading *saṃcayet*, both Tibetan and Sino-Japanese agree on the rendition. While this reading is definitely in the manuscript, it should be understood as though *avaśaṃsiyāt*.

[7]Asaṅga does not employ the name Lokāyata in the ancient sense of the materialist school, but rather in his commentary here as a term of disrespect for authors of worldly treatises that are bad (*kuśāstra*) with bad views (*kudṛṣṭi*), referred to in the *gāthā* as "meaningless *mantras*." To adhere to such treatises prevents the disciple from getting rid of the five *upādānaskandha* (grasping aggregates).

One should not wear the religious garb and begging bowl in excess so as to receive material things and respect.

(32) One should not associate with householders, who promote defilement. One should associate with the nobles, who purify knowledge.

(33) One should not make residence with friends who cause grief and distraction. One should not tolerate the defilements that have already arisen that generate suffering.

(34) One who has lost his vow should not utilize in any case what is to be gained by faith. One should not repudiate in any case the illustrious Dharma.

(35) Should one have thoughtless pleasure in a stumbling fault of others, he should reflect upon his own stumbling fault and in turn confess it.

(36) According as an offence has occurred, one should apply the appropriate Dharma (right act). The wise person should involve himself in duty for the matter concerned.

(37) With faith in the power and teaching of the Buddhas and their disciples (*śrāvakas*), one should never blame by noticing faults.

(38) One should not adhere to one's own view, discarding the old lineage (*paurāṇam āgamam*) regarding the profound doctrines (*dharma*) which are not in the range of logic.[8]

(The *gāthā-s* 18-38 present various aspects for purifying the Instruction of Morality).

(39) Should he be dwelling in solitude, using a resting cot in the outskirts, he should contemplate virtuous natures, with steadfast forward step of striving.

So as to fulfill the praxis, he has solitude of body and mind, a resting cot concordant with his *samādhi*. Contemplating only virtuous natures, he is not oppressed by secondary defilements such as "fading" (*laya*) and "scattering" (*auddhatya*) (of the meditative object). This is a special means of the Instruction of Mind Training.

(40-41) Should he, having been without longing, have long-

[8]The phrase "not in the range of logic" is a frequent one in Buddhist scriptures, starting with the *Brahmajāla-sutta*, para. 28.

ing arise; having not blamed, be blaming; been not sleepy, at this time sleepy; not abiding with calm; been without regret, now regretting; been without lusts, now lusts,—he should get yoked in every way at all times, possessed of the right praxis.

This means he must purify his mind from the five hindrances : 1. sensuous lust, 2. ill-will; 3. torpor and sleepiness; 4. mental wandering and regret; and 5. doubt. This right praxis is the right Instruction of Mental Training.

(42-43) "Stirring" and "awakening"; likewise being fettered; grasping sign-sources and passion; also given to multiple pleasures; being "pressed," and sensual climax—are called "imagination" (*kalpa*), the generator of sensuous lust (*kāma-rāga*). This a wise man should thoroughly eliminate.

There are eight kinds of such imagination : 1. "stirring" (*nudana*) is any imagination that instigates the mind along with an improper mental orientation in a sensual object (*nudano vikalpaḥ yo rañjanīye vastuni / ayoniśo manaskāra saṃprayuktaś ca cittasya prerakaḥ*). 2. "awakening" (*bodhana*) is the being attended with awakening enwrapment of lust toward precisely that object (*bodhanaḥ yat tasminn eva vastuni prabuddharāgaparyavasthāna-saṃprayuktaḥ*). 3. being fettered (*saṃyojana*) is the seeking for precisely that object (*samyojanas tasyaiva vastunaḥ paryeṣakaḥ*). 4. grasping sign-sources (*naimittika*) apprehends various pleasant signs in precisely that object (*naimittikas tasminn eva vastuni vicitraśubhanimittagrāhakaḥ*). 5. passion (*snehana*) is the clinging to this object when it is obtained (*snehanaḥ prāpteḥ tasmin vastuni adhyavasānasaṃprayuktaḥ*). 6. given to multiple pleasures (*vilasana*) is the engagement from various sides in multiple sensuous enjoyment in that object (*vilasanaś ca tasminn eva vastuni vicitraparibhogābhilāṣanānāmukhapravṛttaḥ*). 7. being pressed (*niṣpīdana*) is what is at the time when two unite the two sexual organs (*niṣpīdanaḥ yo dvayadvayendriyasamāpattikāle*). 8. sensual climax (*parama-snehana*) is what is at the time of sexual discharge (*paramasnehanaḥ / yo āsravivipramokṣakāle*)[9].

[9]While this sequence of eight is explicitly stated in terms of sexual attraction and union, a generality for the process of addiction may also have been intended.

(44-45) Desires are not satisfied, and have many cohorts; likewise cause bad conduct (*adharma*) and promote craving (*tṛṣṇā*). They should be avoided by illustrious persons and quickly brought to destruction. Desires are based on conditions (*pratyāya*), and are the stages of heedlessness.

(Commentary indicates that one sees the trouble of desires and avoids them by the eight identifications of the verses 44-45).

(46-48A) Desires are like bones, like a piece of meat, like a torch of hay, like a peaked fire; like a poisonous snake, like a dream, like a borrowed ornament, like the fruit of tree. Having recognized desires in this way, one should not hanker after them at all.

Like bones, because they do not satisfy; like a piece of meat, because they are frequent and common and occasion wrong conduct; like a torch of hay, because if not hurled away, but left in place, they burn one up; like a peaked fire, because while promoting craving, they dry one up; like a poisonous snake, because they are to be avoided by illustrious persons. They are like a dream, because they quickly perish. They are like a borrowed ornament, because they are based on conditions. They are like the fruit of tree, because they are the stages of heedlessness.

(48B-51) Listen to the illustrious Dharma, whoever would ponder it and cultivate it ! First one should be calm and far-sighted, and continue on up to single certitude. Rejoice, whoever is engaged in climinating the contamination of defilement ! Should he analyze the sign-source, he would become uppermost in the praxis. He would eliminate desire of the desire-realm and eliminate desire of the form-realm. He would bring about the clear realization of truth and the dispassion toward everything; would attain Nirvāṇa in the present life; and would erase the (remaining) basis.

The verses 48B to 51 show the pure Instruction of Insight in terms of the seven mental orientations.[10] Of these, the first one, "realization of the characteristics" (*lakṣaṇa-pratisaṃvedī*), is shown

[10]See now Tsoṅ-kha-pa's discussion of these seven mental orientations, based on Asaṅga's exposition in the *Śrāvakabhūmi*, in A. Wayman, translator, *Calming the Mind and Discerning the Real* (Columbia University Press, New York, 1979), pp. 165-169.

by listening to and pondering the illustrious Dharma. The second, "made of conviction" (*ādhimokṣika*), is shown by cultivating this Dharma. The third, "seclusion" (*prāvivekya*), is shown by the expressions "calm" and "far-sighted." The fourth, "attraction of rapture" (*ratisaṃgrāhaka*) is shown by "continue on up to single certitude." The fifth, "orientation with comprehension" (*mīmāṃsā-manaskāra*), is shown by "should he analyze the sign-source." The sixth, "final stage of application" (*prayoga-niṣṭha*), is shown by "would become uppermost in the praxis." The seventh, "fruit of the final stage of application" (*prayoga-niṣṭhaphala*), is shown by "He would eliminate desire of the desire-realm and eliminate desire of the form-realm; would bring about the clear realization of truth and the dispassion toward everything. This seventh mental orientation (*manaskāra*), namely, "fruit of the final stage of application," is the mundane fruit, Nirvāṇa with remainder; and the supramundane fruit, Nirvāṇa without remainder.

PART FIVE

HINDU AND BUDDHIST STUDIES

TWO TRADITIONS OF INDIA—TRUTH AND SILENCE

Elsewhere I cited the *Laws of Manu* : *maunāt satyaṃ viśiṣyate* ("Truth is superior to silence") and turned the citation to my own purpose with the implication, "Now is the time to speak out, because truth is superior to silence."[1] However, admittedly, the celebrated Indian law book had something else in mind with this intriguing maxim. In this study I shall attempt to clarify the two traditions called "truth" and "silence" and to show that they borrow from each other but maintain sufficient contrast to allow the later philosophical schools to treat them as though distinct.

It should be acknowledged that the findings of this article differ rather strikingly from the generality of the surveys of Indian philosophy and religion. Also, the juxtaposition of materials from diverse traditions of India requires a reorganization from the original order of discovery for communication purposes. To justify that these traditions of truth and silence can be treated in contrast, I have prepared individual sections devoted first to the silence and then to the truth which the *Laws of Manu* takes to be superior. As a consequence of these main findings, it turns out that there are two Upaniṣadic traditions, although not in terms of truth and silence; and that some later philosophical formulations, such as "conventional truth" and "absolute truth," take their

[1] "Observations on Translation from the Classical Tibetan Language into European Languages," in *Indo-Iranian Journal* 14, nos. 3-4 (1972): 192.

inceptions in the old Upaniṣads. This shows a sense in which later Indian philosophy develops from the early religion and mythology.

The Muni Tradition

For "silence" the word used was *mauna* (Pāli, *mona*), related to the word *muni* (one who has the vow of silence), used in the *Ṛg-veda* hymn X, 136: "The *munis*, girdled with the wind, wear garments soiled of yellow hue. They, following the wind's swift course, go where the gods have gone before." The word *muni* is important in Buddhism, where the founder has the title *śākya-muni* (*muni* of the *śākya* clan). The Buddha is called "great *muni*," and he adopted for his order (the Saṅgha) the soiled yellow hue of dress that was alluded to in the Vedic hymn.[2]

The *Chāndogya Upaniṣad*, VIII, 5, 2, in the course of its progressive explanation of *brahmacarya* (the pure practice of the student), says: "Now, what they call 'silent asceticism' (*mauna*) is really the pure practice (*brahmacarya*), for only after finding the self by the pure practice, does one think about it."[3] This passage apparently explains *mauna* (ascetic silence) as a thinking about, or contemplation of, the higher self.

The *Udānavarga*, which is the northern Buddhist expansion of the *Dhammapada*, has an important *muni* verse in its *Nirvāṇa* chapter (XXVI, 27): "According as the Muni, with the state of being a *muni*[4] derived from himself, understands in this place

[2]The Sanskrit word *muni*, according to Manfred Mayrhofer (*Kurzgefasstes etymologisches Wörterbuch des Altindischen* Heidelberg: Carl Winter, Universitäts-verlag, 1963, volume 2, pp. 654-655) is cognate with our word "mute" through Greek words, and this cannot be doubted. It has been argued—but the matter is not settled—that it is related to the Greek *maentis*, our word "mantic" (gifted with prophetic powers), this being in the group of words including "mania," from the weak grade of the Indo-Germanic root *men*, which the Oxford English Dictionary says is represented in many words referring to mental states, emotions, etc. In Sanskrit this would be *man-*, the verb meaning "to think, to deem," etc. The Indian grammarians affiliated the word *muni* with the verb *man-*, but a solution cannot be found within the Indian context alone, for it requires a justification of this vowel change in the early Indo-European languages.

[3]. / atha yan maunam ity ācakṣate brahmacaryam eva tat / brahmacaryeṇa hy evā 'tmānam anuvidya manute /.

[4]"State of being a *muni*" translates *mauneya* following Franklin Edgerton,

(i.e., in Nirvāṇa), then is he freed from form and formless, from all suffering."[5] Along the same lines, but not using the words *muni* or *mauna*, Āryadeva states in his *Catuḥśataka*, as cited in the *Prasannapadā* : "He who knows how to ward off at first sin, then to ward off the self, and finally to ward off everything, he is the sage (*buddhimat*)."[6] Also, it appears that the ubiquitous Buddhist terminology of body, speech, and mind, stems from the *muni* tradition. The Recital Sermon (*Saṅgīti Suttanta*, of the *Dīgha-nikāya*, III) allows me to use the word "muted" in the sense "rendered mute, silent, muffled" in this entry among the three-fold items : "There are three states of being a *muni*. (Pāli : *tīṇi moneyyāni*) : muted body, muted speech, muted mind." Elsewhere I cited Vasubandhu's commentary on the *Daśabhūmikasūtra* on how to classify the five supernormal faculties (*abhijñā*) by their respective purification of the acts of body, speech, and mind. The one called magical ability (*ṛddhi*) purifies the acts of body; the divine hearing and knowing the makeup of others' mind, those of speech; the memory of former lives and the vision of the passing away and rebirth, those of mind.[7] Therefore, this is the theory of supernormal faculties consistent with the *muni* tradition.

As to how a *muni* describes himself, the *Udānavarga* has these verses in its Tathāgata chapter (XXI, 1-4)—the words attributed to the Buddha immediately upon his enlightenment (my translation) :

> I know all, have overcome all, am forever unstained by the *dharmas*, have eliminated everything, am free from all fear; having come to fully understand by myself, who can teach me !
>
> I am the Tathāgata, teacher of gods and men; have comprehended enlightenment as a revealer by myself; having reached omniscience, am endowed with the powers; incomparable and unequalled, who can teach me !

Buddhist Hybrid Sanskrit Grammar and Dictionary (New Haven, Conn.: Yale University Press, 1953), p. 441.

[5]Franz Bernhard, *Udānavarga*, Abhandlungen der Akademie der Wissenschaften in Göttingen Philologisch-Historische Klasse, Third Series, Nr. 54 (Göttingen, 1965).

[6]Louis de La Vallée Poussin, ed., *Mūla-Madhyamaka-vṛtti-prasannapadā*, p. 359.

[7]See Chapter 7.

> I am the Arhat in the worlds; I am incomparable in the worlds; and in the worlds with their gods I am the Victor (*jina*), the conqueror of the Māras.
>
> As there is no one like me, none can be my instructor (*ācārya*); alone in this world, I am fully awakened, have attained the ultimate, complete enlightenment.

W. Woodville Rockhill, in the appendix to his translation from Tibetan of the *Udānavarga*, cites the commentary preserved in the Tibetan Tanjur. He says :

> I translate the following lines to show how very nearly the Commentator follows the received Pāli version of the events that occurred shortly after Gautama had become a Buddha. "When he (Bhagavat) had obtained perfect enlightenment, Brahmā the lord of the universe, humbly begged of him to teach the dharma. Then the great Muni thought, 'To whom shall I first teach the law ?' Rudraka had died seven days before that moment, Āḷāra Kalāma had also passed away. Then he thought, 'I will teach the five.' So Bhagavat started for Vārāṇasi, and on his way, an Ājīvaka saw Bhagavat, and said to him, 'Āyuṣmat Gautama, your senses (appear) composed, your complexion is clear, your garments clean; who is your master (*upādhyāya*) ? Āyuṣmat, to what sect do you belong ? In what doctrine do you find pleasure ?' Then he answered, 'I am the Jina who has conquered Māra (the evil one).' 'Then, Āyuṣmat Gautama, you say that you are the Jina ?' 'The Jinas are all like me,' he answered. 'Where are you going, Āyuṣmat ?' 'I am going to Vārāṇasi.' "[8]

Sir John Woodroffe cites the Hindu tradition about the word *muni* to the same effect : "As the Mahābhārata says, 'The Veda differ, and so do the *Smriti*. No one is a *muni* who has no independent opinion of his own (*nāsau munir yasya mataṃ na bhinnam*).' "[9] This practically admits that the only person who could start a new religious movement in India must be, or must have been, a *muni*.

The word *muni* is understood as "the capable one" in Tibetan

[8]*Udānavarga : A Collection of Verses from the Buddhist Canon* (London, 1892), pp. 209-210.

[9]*Introduction to Tantra Shastra* (Madras : Ganesh & Co., 1952), p. 30.

translation. According to Buddhaguhya, "The *munis* are *pratyekabuddhas*: because they have their own religious practice, pledge, and vow, and are capable by themselves while lacking a master, they are the capable ones (*muni*)."[10] This explanation is consistent with the account about the Sanskrit name Ṛṣipatana (Pāli, Isipatana), another name of the Deer Park where the Buddha gave his first sermons:[11]

> Formerly when the time approached for the Buddha Kāśyapa to appear in the world, there lived on that hill five hundred Pratyekabuddhas. They learned from a message given by the devas that the Buddha was to manifest himself. By their magical power they soared up to the sky and equipoised themselves in the element of fire (*tejodhātu*). The fire that issued from their own bodies burned their material bodies, and the ashes fell to the earth. It was said, "The Ṛṣis have fallen," and for this reason the place is called Ṛṣipatana (the falling of the Ṛṣis).

Hence, in consideration of this silence, there are the silent persons called *munis*, who are called *pratyekabuddhas* since they are enlightened by themselves without depending on another teacher, and who are also called Ṛṣis or seers. The association of the *munis* with flying, as mentioned in the Vedic hymn, was contained by other names, *pratyekabuddha* and *ṛṣi*.[12] That the association of the *munis* with the sky or space was not forgotten in later times is apparent in the *Saṃdhivyākaraṇa*, an explanatory *tantra* of the *Guhyasamājatantra*, in a Sanskrit passage I have edited from the Pradīpoddyotana manuscript:

> Thus, the Reality, was heard by me on a certain time extraordinary. The Bhagavat, diamond lord of mysteries, with the supreme pledge of the triple *vajra*,
>
> Was dwelling as the Mahāmuni (great silent one) in the pure heart of the world, in this unique self-existence of sky having

[10]Alex Wayman, "Buddhism," ***Historia Religionum*** (Leiden: E. J. Brill, 1971), vol. 2, p. 397. Buddhaguhya's passage is from his commentary on the *Sarvadurgatipariśodhana-tantra* in the Tibetan Tanjur.

[11]Wayman, "Buddhism," pp. 397-398.

[12]This flight of the ascetic is shown in later Indian art by beings called *vidyādhara* (holders of the mystic science). Also, the Buddhist Tantra had heroes called *ḍāka* or *khecārin* (sky-walkers).

the modes of omniscient knowledge, in the all-Tathāgata gnosis having the inconceivable perfection of merits; beyond existence, non-existence and both, called "place of no location."[13]

While the foregoing has been mainly based on Buddhist sources, it should be observed that the *muni* tradition is part of the great ascetic non-Vedic tradition that became incorporated into Hinduism with worship of the god Śiva, as R. N. Dandekar has well described,[14] although this Śaivitic incorporation apparently takes place after the advent of Buddhism. It is well known that Śaṃkara, the great Advaita Vedāntin, was a follower of Śiva and insisted that knowledge (*jñāna*) is the main thing for liberation (*mokṣa*). His followers use, among other works, the *Aṣṭāvakra Saṃhitā*, in which Aṣṭāvakra says (chap. XVII, 1): "He has gained the fruit of knowledge as well as the practice of *yoga*, who, contented and with purified senses, ever enjoys being alone (*ekākī*)."[15] All this gives a new complexion to the Hindu opponent's challenge to Śaṃkara—that he was a "Buddhist in disguise." This is often misconstrued as having doctrinal implications. In fact, the criticism was a rejection of Śaṃkara's monastic retreat system, which afforded and still affords individuals an opportunity to leave society for seeking divine knowledge in solitude.

There are several forms of the Buddha's silence. First there was his ascetic silence; then upon his enlightenment, when he hesitated to teach, deeming his doctrine too profound for people at large, this was the first withholding type of silence. Later, he sometimes refused to answer certain questions dealing with ultimates, with a selective silence. A certain Buddhist sect had a tenet "The Buddha never said a word."[16] Of course, the Hindu oppo-

[13] / evaṃ mayā śrutaṃ tattvam ekasmin samaye sphuṭe /
bhagavān guhyavajreśas trivajrasamayottama(ḥ) //
sarvatathāgate jñāne acintyaguṇasampadi /
sadasadubhayātīte asthānasthitisaṃjñini //
ākāśaikasvabhāve 'smin sarvajñajñānabhāvini /
jagaddhṛdi viśuddhākhye vijahāra mahāmuniḥ //

[14] "Hinduism," in *Historia Religionum* vol. 2, see especially p. 247.

[15] Swami Nityaswarupananda, trans., *Aṣṭāvakra Saṃhitā*, 3d ed. (Calcutta: Advaita Ashrama, 1969), p. 114.

[16] Cf., A. Bareau, *Les sectes bouddhiques du Petit Véhicule* (Saigon: École

nents of Buddhism would not lose the opportunity to argue cogently that it is a fine thing to know through ascetic silence, but that this does not furnish validity for the Buddha's teachings, since he would have to renounce the ascetic silence in order to teach, and so what proof is there that the teaching itself reflects the omniscience of the silence ? Presumably it was through such attacks that Buddhism was forced into its multiple-body theory, with the Dharmakāya remaining silent and omniscient, and another body, such as the Nirmāṇakāya of the Buddha, doing the teaching.[17] Also the *buddhas* were said to help chosen disciples of a progressed nature with *adhiṣṭhāna* (blessing, empowerment, or spiritual support), a kind of silent power. Thus, in Mahāyāna Buddhism, the Buddha came to have a role tantamount to the solar deity.

The Truth Tradition

For "truth" the ancient Indians generally employed two words, *satya* and *ṛta*, which have respectively a subjective and objective reference. *Satya* is the truth of men and gods; and *ṛta* is the truth of the universe—that the sun will rise and set and that seasonal characteristics will recur.

It is well recognized that in the ancient Vedic tradition the deity Varuṇa was in charge of the *ṛta*, the universal order; and it was believed that liars incurred his punishment in the form of dropsy, presumably because their lies constituted a violation of the world order. In time, Varuṇa's supremacy faded, and a new deity named Indra came to the fore, to be succeeded by Viṣṇu. The latter two deities were not especially associated with preserving the world order; and in time the supreme spirit was generally

Francaise d'Extréme-Orient, 1955), p. 60, among the theories of the Mahāsāṅghikas: The Buddhas never say a word, because they remain eternally in contemplation; but beings, thinking they have pronounced words, leap from joy.

[17]This matter is set forth at length, of course with Buddhist defense, in the *Tattvasaṃgraha* of Śāntarakṣita with the *Pañjikā* commentary of Kamalaśīla, chap. 31, "Examination observing the entity that transcends the senses" (*atīndriyārthadarśi-parīkṣā*), which is the last chapter. The text has been reedited by Dwarikadas Shastri in two volumes (Varanasi: Bauddha Bharati, 1968). The English translation by G. Jha is not available to me at present.

called Brahman. With all these changes of terminology for divinity, the prestige of "truth" by the word *satya* continued unabated.

For the meaning of *satyá*, the adjective, I follow the late H. D. Velankar of the University of Bombay who explained the word in the introduction to his retranslation of Maṇḍala Seven of the *Ṛg-veda.*[18] This *satyá* is the undeniable, after being said, thought, or done by someone; that is, bound to happen.[19] We shall observe that this meaning continues into the *Chāndogya* (below). Accordingly, one should reject the frequent translation of *satyakāmāḥ* in this Upaniṣad as "real desires," as though the word *satya* meant the "genuine," what is simply a fact. Instead, it means a fact that is productive.

The *Bṛhadāraṇyaka Upaniṣad* (III, 5, 1) provides the first answer to what the *Laws of Manu* meant by saying, "Truth is superior to silence" :

> "Therefore, let a *brāhmaṇa*, after being satiated with learning, live as a child. After being satiated with childhood as well as with learning, let him be a *muni* (one vowed to silence). After being satiated with non-silence (*amauna*) as well as with silence (*mauna*), let him be a *brāhmaṇa*." "In what manner (*kena*) is that *brāhmaṇa* ?" "In whatever manner he be, he is just the same in that manner; every thing else is afflicted." Thereupon, Kahola Kauṣītakeya held his peace (*upararāma*).

That is, the state of a *brāhmaṇa*, who is as he is, is claimed to be superior to the state of a *muni*.

The whole verse of the *Manusmṛti* (*Laws of Manu*, II, 83) runs: "The monosyllable (i.e., Oṃ) is the highest Brahman. Suppressions of the breath are the best austerity. But nothing surpasses the Sāvitrī. Truth is superior to silence." My commentarial edition does not help much. It observes that "truth" is verbal, but this is the obvious part. However, it is easy to see the struc-

[18]*Ṛgveda Maṇḍala VII* (Bombay: Bharatiya Vidya Bhavan, 1963), iv-x.

[19]It is of interest that a different way of expressing the adjective "true," to wit, by the Sanskrit word *a-vitatha* "not untrue" (that is, "not contrary to the fact"), has a secondary meaning "not vain or futile"; and so, like the word *satya*, indicates that what is true is not in vain. In contrast, for lying, a prohibition of the ancient five Buddhist layman vows, the expression *mṛṣā-vāda* was used, rather than a negation of the word *satya*.

ture of the verse. When the breath is suppressed, one does not speak—and this is the best austerity. But superior to this is the Sāvitrī, another name of the Gāyatrī, the celebrated *mantra* recited by the Brahmans at their morning and evening devotionals; and this *mantra* is designated as "truth," namely—as we have observed—the undeniable that is not in vain. And so truth is superior to silence. At the same time, the verse shows the preference for the Brahmans who recite the Gāyatrī over the *munis* and other ascetics who engage in such austerities as suppressing the breath. The Gāyatrī (*Ṛg-veda*, III, 62, 10) is translated approximately as follows: "We meditate on or may we attain, the great glory, of the god Savitā, that he may inspire or who inspires, our thoughts or works." It is preceded by the *mantra* Oṃ in the later editions.

That remark in the *Laws of Manu* would equally apply to what is often called the "Act of Truth." This truth act is well known from the Hindu epic *Rāmāyaṇa* and from Buddhist sources. It has a traditional form: the performer announces, if such-and-such be true, then let this or that happen. "Such-and-such" is, according to W. Norman Brown's helpful explanation, the superlative performance of the person's duty (*dharma*), and "this or that" is what the gods are commanded to bring about as a miraculous intervention.[20] In the following essay I point out that it was not sufficient for the person to have been extraordinary in fulfilling his duty, but it was also necessary for the person to verbalize this fact; and so this is a verbal truth that is superior to silence.[21] In short, that a person deserves to be aided by the gods is not sufficient; this person must in addition command the aid.

The preceding makes one issue quite clear. The tradition of "truth" is followed by those who would be inspired by or would command the deity, especially the solar deity. The tradition of "silence" is followed by those who, out of their own resources, would rise to a status beyond ordinary mankind. And certainly

[20]"The Basis for the Hindu Act of Truth," in *Review of Religion* (Nov. 1940): 36-45. His latest article on the subject is "Duty as Truth in Ancient India," in *Proceedings of the American Philosophical Society* 116, no. 3 (June 1972): 252-268.

[21]See Chapter 20.

these routes are distinct and in vivid contrast, and so command divergent allegiance. The *Manusmṛti* definitely insists that the Brahmans who appeal to the sun deity at dawn are superior to the silent ascetics who try, like the Buddha, to be enlightened just prior to dawn.

One complication comes, for example, in the development of Buddhism, where the Buddha began on the *muni* side, the Tathāgata who became enlightened without reliance on another teacher. Then he moved to the other side as the Teacher who inspires the disciples. But when the Buddha did decide to teach and gave his first sermon, what he talked about was *satya*. The Buddha mentioned four kinds of *satya* of the *āryas*, meaning the persons who hearkened to his doctrine and became disciples in contrast to ordinary people (the *pṛthagjana*) who do not hearken. The *satyas*, as was already exposed, are the "undeniables"—that there is suffering, there is the origin of suffering, there is the cessation of the origin, and there is the path leading to the cessation. And sort of analogous to the Vedic and Upaniṣadic usage of the word, there is more to it. So the Buddha in the first sermon (Setting into Motion the Wheel of the Law) made explicit this something more. Suffering is not only undeniable; it is also to be fully known; likewise, its origin is to be eliminated; the cessation of the origin is to be directly experienced; the path is to be cultivated or contemplated.

In the case of the *Laws of Manu*, as a legalistic text, "truth" means the verbal kind; and this kind was observed above as intended in the magical function of truth, illustrated in the "Act of Truth." This amounts to what is often called the *karmakāṇḍa* (section of riteṣ). Indeed, this is the Buddhist sense of the Four Noble Truths, which are the announced truths of Buddhism establishing the norms of conduct, even though early Buddhism opposed the old Vedic ritual.

This is not to insist, however, that "truth" (*satya*) was employed in the old Upaniṣads solely with this verbal sense when, as though by magic, it was undeniable. That it was already used in the more philosophical sense of truths that are understood or realized, and are sometimes inexpressible (*anirvacanīya*), is clear enough in the celebrated Pūṣan verse. This frequently cited verse about truth is the first of four verses that appear both in the *Bṛhadāraṇyaka* (V, 15, 1-4) and the brief *Īśa Upaniṣad* (15-18), and which constitute the prayer to the sun god by a dying person; S. Radhakrishnan mentions, "Even to-day they are used by the Hindus in their funeral rites."[22] The first verse can be translated: "The face of truth is covered by a golden bowl. Unveil it, O Pūṣan, so that I who have truth as my duty (*satyadharma*) may see it !"

This verse foreshadows, on the one hand, the later terminology of absolute and conventional truth (*paramārtha* and *saṃvṛti satya*); and on the other hand, the distinction between direct view (*pratyakṣa*) and the out-of-sight (*parokṣa*). In Buddhist literature, both approaches are explainable in terms of the Four Noble Truths. Thus the Mādhyamika commentator Candrakīrti in chapter 5 of his *Madhyamakāvatāra* explains why the truths of Suffering, Source, and Path are conventional truth, while the Truth of Cessation is supreme truth.[23] In the case of the Upaniṣadic verse, the "face of truth" would represent absolute truth; and "truth as duty," conventional practice of a distinguished type.

The later formulation of view distinction is found, for example, in Dharmakīrti's *Pramāṇavārttika* (II, 132): "The compassionate one applies himself in the means so as to destroy suffering. When the goal (=cessation of suffering) and its cause (=the means) are out of sight, to explain them is difficult."[24] The eminent Tibetan commentator of Buddhist logic, Rgyal-tshab-rje, expands this verse in his brief work "Guidance on the path of authority" (*pramāṇa-mārga*):[25]

> As to the perfection of application:—the person possessed of great compassion at first himself comprehends directly the ultimate condition of the four truths; and in conclusion properly strives in the application. But when the two truths of the causal means and the two truths of the fruitional goal

[22]*The Principal Upaniṣads* (New York : Harper and Bros., 1953), p. 577.

[23]Wayman, "Buddhism," pp. 423-424.

[24] / dayāvān duḥkhahānārtham upāyeṣv abhiyujyate / parokṣopeyataddhetos tadākhyānaṃ hi duṣkaraṃ //

[25]*Tshad ma'i lam khrid* (Varanasi reprint), pp. 36-37: / sbyor ba phun tshogs la sñiṅ rje chen po daṅ ldan pa'i gaṅ zag gi thog mar raṅ ñid bden bźi'i gnas lugs mṅon sum du rtogs pa mthar thug pa la mṅon par sbyor ba'i brtson 'grus mdzad rigs te / thabs rgyu'i bden pa gñis daṅ thabs byuṅ 'bras bu'i bden pa gñis lkog tu gyur pa'am sṅon du gyur kyaṅ blo mi gsal ba'i lhag ma lus na gźan la phyin ci ma log par 'chad mi nus źes pa /.

> are out of sight or are not earlier clear to the intellect, there is no capacity to explain them completely and in errorless manner to others.

Here, the two truths of the causal means must be the truths of suffering and source of suffering; while the two of the fruitional goal must be the cessation of suffering and the path leading to the cessation. Interpreting the Pūṣan verse along the same lines, we see that only when a person first has truth as duty can he subsequently command the exposure of the face of truth.

The Two Traditions of Truth and Silence

In setting forth two traditions of India, as has been done with truth and silence, it is tempting to list various sects under one or another column. One can, for example, place the Brahmanical lineage—faithful to the four stages of life—in the "truth" column, and the ascetic groups (*muni* or *śramaṇa*) in the "silence" column. This runs into the immediate difficulty that the Buddha, who is called "great silent one" (*mahāmuni*) and "great ascetic" (*mahāśramaṇa*), announces the four *ārya* truths and is held to be the teacher of gods and men. His followers never depart from this, eventually—although centuries later—making much of two truths, conventional and absolute. And again, the Brahmanical lineage has its emphatic visionary side; and all sects have their silence, even when merely exclusiveness. Indeed, it may be principally the opponents who classify one or another school under a particular heading, thus to attribute a limitation of action or view to an adversary.

However, it should have already become apparent that the two traditions called "truth" and "silence" are roughly equivalent to the Vedānta classification, the *karma-kāṇḍa* and the *jñāna-kāṇḍa*, where "truth" in its sense of the magical verbal truth amounts to the *karma-kāṇḍa*, and "silence" as the attainment of the withdrawn ascetic amounts to the *jñāna-kāṇḍa*. Expounding the Śaṃkara position, Surendranath Dasgupta says:

> The teachings of the other parts of the Vedas, the *karma-kāṇḍa* (those dealing with the injunctions relating to the performance of duties and actions), were intended for inferior types of aspirants, whereas the teachings of the Upaniṣads, the *jñānakāṇḍa* (those which declare the nature of ultimate

> truth and reaiity), were intended only for superior aspirants who had transcended the limits of sacrificial duties and actions, and who had no desire for any earthly blessing or for any heavenly joy.[26]

But the *Laws of Manu* takes the opposite point of view, declaring that the ritual performance of the Sāvitrī at dawn is superior to the silence—with whatever its knowledge (*jñāna*)—of the *yogī* meditating during the night. The celebrated law book is forced into this position by its defense of *dharma*, the Hindu code of duty.

It has been called to my attention that Kumārila-bhaṭṭa (the seventh-century A.D. commentator on the Mīmāṃsā), when discussing the nonorthodox systems as authority (*pramāṇa*) for *dharma* (*ad* Jaimini-sūtra I 3.11-14), asks whether the Buddhist *dharma*, being as it is a *prayoga-śāstra* (statement of norms for proper performance), is authoritative; and thus deals with the Buddhist *dharma* as an alternative to the brāhmaṇical *karma-kāṇḍa* and not as an alternative to the Upaniṣads.[27] Naturally, this observation is quite consistent with what has been presented, namely, that one can indeed separate the two traditions, especially from how commentators treat the opponent. Consequently, there is a competition as to what properly constitutes the verbal truth (= *karma-kāṇḍa*) as well as to the content of silence (= *jñāna-kāṇḍa*). In illustration, Buddhism not only presents an alternative *dharma*, but an alternative enlightened person (the Buddha as the Mahāmuni). At the same time, it is comprehensible that these Indian systems would not and do not treat themselves in the manner that the opponents do. Therefore, Buddhism does not separate itself into two traditions, the *dharma* and the Buddha; rather it insists that the *dharma* comes from the Buddha and has its authority (*pramāṇa*) accordingly.

THE UPANIṢADIC DISPUTE OVER "TRUE DESIRES"

While my main purpose has been to expose two traditions in

[26] *History of Indian Philosophy* 5 vols. (Cambridge: at the University Press, 1932), 1:436.

[27] Communication from Fred Morgan, lecturer in Asian Religions, University of Bristol, in connection with my article, "The Buddhist 'Not This, Not This'," *Philosophy East and West*, 21, no.4 (Oct., 1961): 99-114.

terms of "truth" and "silence," I must acknowledge that such a classification may imprison the mind in categories and lead to a kind of game in which different schools and sects are mechanically placed within this and that category, irrespective of how those schools are constituted in reality. Categories should not be formulated just for the sake of making them. The importance of a classification is what one learns or brings forward in the course of making it. Now, while collecting materials, as previously organized, on this topic, there was no intention of bringing the *Bṛhadāraṇyaka* and *Chāndogya* into conflict—but this is exactly what happened. According to the *Chāndogya*, when one finds the self, he finds and achieves all desires—which that text qualifies as "true"; according to the *Bṛhadāraṇyaka*, when one finds the self, he overcomes all desires.

Indeed, my analysis agrees with Dasgupta's advice: "It will be better that a modern interpreter should not agree to the claims of the ancients that all the Upaniṣads represent a connected system, but take the texts independently and separately and determine their meanings, though keeping an attentive eye on the context in which they appear."[28] A disagreement between the *Bṛhadāraṇyaka* and the *Chāndogya* was long ago noticed by Paul Deussen : "Between the two great Upanishads, Bṛhadāraṇyaka, which serves as text-book for the students of the (white) Yajur-veda, and Chāndogya, which serves for the students of the Sāmaveda, are to be observed many, often verbal agreements, but side by side with these, certain traces of a thorough-going polemic, which is shown, among other things, by the fact that teachers, who appear in the one Upanishad as the highest authorities, occupy only a subordinate position in the other. Thus, for example, *Ushasta*. . . ."[29] The present essay defines the polemic in terms of the attitude toward the desires (*kāma*) that are "true" (*satya*).

The meaning of the word *satya* as the undeniable is continued into the well-known chapter 7 on the "City of Brahman" in the *Chāndogya*. Within this city of Brahman is contained all creatures (*bhūta*) and all desires (*kāma*); and the Upaniṣad says,

[28]*History of Indian Philosophy*, 1, p. 42.

[29]*The System of the Vedānta*, trans. Charles Johnston (Delhi: Motilal Banarsidass, 1972), pp. 146-147.

"Those who depart hence, having found here the self (*ātman*) and those desires (*kāma*) that are *satya*—for them in all worlds there is engagement with the desires." That is, their desires are undeniable (*satya*), as illustrated in section 2 of the chapter 7, "If he desires the world of the fathers, by his very conception, fathers arise." Likewise, the world of the mothers, the world of brothers, the world of sisters, and so with the world of friends, of perfumes and garlands, of food and drink, of song and music, and finally the world of women. His desires, being *satya*, upon being thought, are bound to happen. Then, in section 3, the Upaniṣad continues, "These same are true (i.e. undeniable) desires, with a covering of the false (*anṛta*, the negation of *ṛta*)." And it goes on to illustrate what is meant by the false : "Just as those who do not know the field walk again and again over the hidden treasure of gold and do not find it, even so all creatures here go day after day into the Brahman-world and yet do not find it, for they are carried away by untruth." This shows that the creatures are carried away by disorder, since *anṛta* is the negation of the objective truth of regularity and universal order.

This *Chāndogya* position was not forgotten in subsequent Upaniṣadic literature. The *Muṇḍaka Upaniṣad* (III 1, 6), coming after the rise of Buddhism, furnishes modern India's motto "Truth alone conquers" (*satyam eva jayate*). This has political overtones and rich slogan-connotation when taken out of its context : "Truth (i.e., the undeniable) alone is victorious, not untruth (*anṛta*, i.e., disorder). By truth is laid out the path leading to the gods by which the seers (*ṛṣi*) who have their desires fulfilled proceed to where is that supreme treasure." This treasure, according to the *Chāndogya*, is in the *Brahman*-world.

But the *Bṛhadāraṇyaka* (III, 5, 1), when setting forth progressive renunciation as the way to know *Brahman*, has a significant opposition to the *Chāndogya's* and the *Muṇḍaka's* emphasis on realizing desires :

> Now Kahola Kauṣītakeya asked him, "Yājñavalkya," said he, "explain to me the Brahman that is directly experienced and not indirectly experienced, which is the self (*ātman*) within everything." "This is your self which is within everything." "Yājñavalkya, which one is within everything ?" "The one which transcends hunger and thirst, sorrow and delusion, old age and death. The *brāhmaṇas*, having recog-

> nized (*viditvā*) that Self, having overcome the desire for sons, the desire for wealth, and the desire for worlds (*loka*), live the life of mendicants (*bhikṣu*). A desire for sons amounts to a desire for wealth; a desire for wealth amounts to a desire for worlds; for both of these amount only to desires.[30]

And if that passage did not sufficiently castigate desires, *Bṛhadāraṇyaka*, IV, 4, 6-7, drives home the point. After mentioning forcefully that the man who desires (*kāmayamānaḥ*) is simply reborn, it gives this verse for the man who does not desire : "When all the desires (*kāma*) that abide in his heart are renounced, then the mortal becomes immortal; he here attains Brahman."

But the question immediately arises : What is in back of this disagreement, the *Bṛhadāraṇyaka* eschewing all desires, and the *Chāndogya* pushing for true desires. The answer appears to be : their creation myths. The two positions of those Upaniṣads probably both have in their background the *Ṛg-veda* "Hymn of Creation" (X, 129), where it was said, "Desire entered the One in the beginning : it was the earliest seed...the bond of being in non-being." Then the question arises : Does one attain the highest state by reverting to the beginning condition ? The *Bṛhadāraṇyaka*, and Buddhism as well, answers, No. The *Chāndogya*, and inferentially any other treatise that lines up with it, answers, Yes.

The *Bṛhadāraṇyaka* would not recommend getting back to the original state because (chap. 1, sec. 2) it says : "There was no particular thing here in the beginning. Only by death was this covered, or by hunger, for hunger is death." The *Chāndogya* (chap. 3, sec. 19) has a different story, called "The Cosmic Egg."

> The Sun is Brahman—so it is taught. This has an explanation: In the beginning this (world) was non-existent (*asat*). It became existent (*sat*). It grew. It changed into an egg. It lay for the extent of a year. It burst open. In the egg-shell there were the silver and the gold. What was the silver, that is this earth. What was the gold that is the sky. What was the outer member (i.e. the chorion) is the mountains. What was the inner membrane (i.e. the amnion) is the mist with the

[30]This passage immediately precedes the previous citation of *Bṛhadāraṇyaka* III, 5, 1.

> clouds. What were the veins are the rivers. What was the fluid of the membranous sac is the ocean. And that which was born, it is yonder sun. As he was being born, shouts and cries were directed toward him, as were also all creatures and all desires. Therefore, at his rise and at his every return, shouts and cries are directed toward him, as are also all creatures and all desires. He who knowing it in this way, repeatedly meditates on the sun as Brahman, is one to whom well-disposed shouts would be directed, and they would gratify him, yea, gratify him.

Therefore, in the *Chāndogya* lineage, it is an appropriate aim to return to the original condition, namely, to find in the City of Brahman all creatures and all desires, to be as the sun when it was being born.

About the true desires, the *Bhagavadgītā* (III, 10) says in apparent agreement: "Of yore when the Lord of Creatures created men with sacrifice, he said: 'By this may you bring forth, and may this be for you the cow which grants desires (*iṣṭakāmadhuk*).'" There were other words in Indian literature: *cintāmaṇi* (the fabulous gem which grants all desires to its possessor), *kalpa-vṛkṣa* (the wishing tree in Indra's paradise). However, K. N. Upadhyaya regards "disinterested action" (*niṣkāma-karma*) as the "crux" of the *Bhagavadgītā's* message.[31] Therefore, it might be the case that the *Bhagavadgītā* was attempting to reconcile the Upaniṣadic dispute exposed earlier with a formula that nonattachment to the desirable is eventually rewarded by all desires. If this possibility has not hitherto been recognized by interpreters of the *Bhagavadgītā*, it may be simply due to the fact that they failed to acknowledge an Upaniṣadic dispute which the *Bhagavadgītā* might try to bridge.

As to schools affiliated to the *Bṛhadāraṇyaka*, I make bold to point to Buddhism, because the Buddhist goal of *nirvāṇa* is also beyond desire. And Buddhism heads its formula of Dependent Origination with nescience (*avidyā*)—a word which is not found at all in the *Bhagavadgītā*.[32] At least once Buddhism says nescience is the father, and craving (*tṛṣṇā*) is the mother (per *Laṅkā*-

[31] *Early Buddhism and the Bhagavadgītā* (Delhi, 1971), p. 146.
[32] Surendranath Dasgupta, *History of Indian Philosophy*, vol. 2, p. 498.

vatāra-sūtra);[33] but the commentary on the *Udānavarga* says nescience is the mother.[34] The Buddhist genesis myth in the Pāli and other scriptures starts out with the sentient beings in bodies made of mind that are wherever they wish to be, and who feed on joy (compare Vedic creation hymn). Their fall begins with greed stemming from delusion; next there is lust arising from eating; and finally hatred due to stealing.[35] Buddhism not only has negative procedures—removal of defiling conditions—for reversion to a superior plane of consciousness, but also a positive requirement for adding knowledge arrived at in *samādhi* attainment. The Vedāntic currents that stress knowledge (*jñāna*) as the main requirement for liberation (*mokṣa*) thereby agree on this particular point that one does not simply return to a primordial condition. Consequently, our previous observation that Buddhism and the Upaniṣads have a rival *jñāna-kāṇḍa* should be modified to admit the possibility that Buddhism shares to some extent the *jñāna-kāṇḍa* of the *Bṛhadāraṇyaka*. At least this is a partial breakthrough in the mystery of the Buddhist relation, if any, to the Upaniṣads.

However, it should be noticed that the categorizing of the old Upaniṣads as the *jñāna-kāṇḍa* in contrast to the preceding *Brāhmaṇa* ritual literature categorized as the *karma-kāṇḍa* is again an oversimplification that becomes strained when one examines the facts. The *Chāndogya* naturally exemplifies the previously exposed connotation of "truth," because it is an appendage to the *Sāma Veda* (meaning the collection of Vedic hymns to be chanted), and the word "Chāndogya" means singer of these chants. This Upaniṣad is therefore concerned in part with the Vedic meters which, by their proper utterance, would satisfy the *Laws of Manu* use of the word "truth" (*satya*); but this belongs to the *karma-kāṇḍa*. The *Bṛhadāraṇyaka* has a *mantra* section and many other topics that are not easily subsumed under a single rubric, so it is by no means to be thoroughly qualified as a *jñāna-kāṇḍa*. Presumably, the over-all inclusion of the Upaniṣads in the *jñāna-kāṇḍa* intends the emphasis or principal object of the

[33]Daisetz Teitaro Suzuki, trans., *The Lankavatara Sutra* (London, 1932), p. 121.

[34]Cf., note 8 herein, pp. 210-211.

[35]Wayman, "Buddhism," pp. 428-430.

Upaniṣads; and, in particular, the part of the Upaniṣads which most interests the Advaita Vedānta.

The subsequent Tantric currents—mainly of Śaivitic or of Buddhist character—also have their two sides. As van Gulik writes : "Above all, they enumerate what desires can be granted by reciting this *dhāraṇī* and how many times it should be recited. Certain rites are required to accompany the reciting in order to obtain the fulfillment of certain desires."[36] But this recitation of *dhāraṇis*, whether incantations or spells, is in the ample category of ritual utterances, including the Sāvitrī, which the *Laws of Manu* plainly counts as "truth".

D. L. Snellgrove, in the introduction to his work, *The Hevajra Tantra*, says, "To dislike the *tantras*, is but to dislike the worst tendencies in man, and of the terrible existence of these tendencies we have ample experience in every generation. The *tantras* claimed to remove like by like, and so of what else should they tell ?"[37] By removing like by like, Snellgrove refers to such lines as the citation in the Dohā commentary, "By passion the world is bound; and precisely by passion it is released" (*rāgeṇa badhyate loko rāgeṇaiva hi mucyate*). His remark about disliking the *tantras* is consistent with what I consider to have been a serious cleavage between the *Bṛhadāraṇyaka* and the *Chāndogya* following. Because—even if modern scholars do not transfer their dislike of the *tantras* to the *Chāndogya Upaniṣad*—the fact still remains that the *Chāndogya* theory of desires in the heart could be paraphrased, "By false desire the world is bound; and precisely by true desire it is released." So, as often happens, people do not know what they dislike.

Conclusions

In the foregoing I have attempted to set forth a rivalry of two traditions, "truth" and "silence," while admitting that the traditions become distinguished especially by the opponent to a sect, who finds it easier to mount a "refutation" by treating somewhat

[36]R. H. van Gulik, *Siddham; An Essay on the History of Sanskrit Studies in China and Japan* (Nagpur International Academy of Indian Culture, 1956), p. 77.

[37]*The Hevajra Tantra : A Critical Study* (London: Oxford University Press, 1959), part I p. 42.

artificially, a single aspect of an opposing sect. Then, while acknowledging that the Upaniṣads themselves are not distinguished by the two traditions, the same investigation shows that the Upaniṣads are indeed distinguished by the attitude to "true desires." The traditions thus made salient appear more fascinating than what T. R. V. Murti sets forth in *The Central Philosophy of Buddhism* as the "two traditions in Indian philosophy"—the acceptance or rejection of the permanent *ātman* or self of the Upaniṣads. Therein Buddhism is characterized as rejecting this permanent *ātman* in favor of a changing, impermanent self. Of course, Buddhism does have its positive disagreements with the Upaniṣadic position, especially as concerns this theory of *ātman*. The Upaniṣads do agree on stressing a Self, even though obviously disagreeing about some matters, such as the role of desire. Murti's classification is faithful to the usual commentarial style of distinguishing the orthodox and the non-orthodox among the Indian schools.

A value of exposing the Indian traditions in the manner of the present article is the readiness of the classification for problem solving, that is, for explaining in contrast to simple portrayal. For example, one can immediately find a plausible solution for the term *satyāgraha* in the modern movement associated with Gandhi.[38] In the light of the rich connotation of such words as *satya* and *anṛta*, Gandhi did not really have to deliver a learned exposition of his term *satyāgraha* (adherence to the truth). In fact, the power of the term depends in part on its not being rationalized or intellectually explained. It insinuated that the produce of the spinning wheel was *satya*, to wit, undeniable and not in vain, and therefore victorious, while the British stuff was *anṛta*, to wit, disordered and a lie, and therefore the sure loser to *satya*. The women doing the spinning—for the most part illiterate—would not have read the Upaniṣads. They were raised in a culture steeped in the connotation of the word *satya*.

Further, the meaning of *satya* as explained by Velankar is its usage in ritual and politics, while the meaning in the Pūṣan verse turns out to be its philosophical usage in subsequent centuries.

Finally, the precious book by Max Picard, *The World of Silence*,

[38]*Gandhi : An Autobiography : The Story of My Experiments with Truth* (Boston : Beacon Press, 1965), pp. 318-319.

reminds us of the spiritual resources that develop in silence, consistent with the Tibetans' translating the word *muni* by the "capable one" (*thub pa*). Picard also writes, in agreement with the *Laws of Manu*, "Language is more than silence because truth is manifested in language."

20

THE HINDU-BUDDHIST RITE OF TRUTH—AN INTERPRETATION

Some years ago at the University of California Professor Murray B. EMENEAU was teaching a class in Āryaśūra's *Jātakamālā*—which it was my privilege to attend—and during the reading of the Śibijātaka called attention to two articles : (1) Eugene Watson BURLINGAME, "The Act of Truth (Saccakiriya) : A Hindu Spell and its employment as a psychic motif in Hindu Fiction," *Journal of the Royal Asiatic Society* 1917, 429-467; (2) W. Norman BROWN, "The Basis for the Hindu Act of Truth," *Review of Religion*, Nov. 1940, 36-45. The contribution of BURLINGAME is to collect many examples of this motif; and for the process involved he goes no further than to assert, "An Act of Truth is a formal declaration of fact, accompanied by a command or resolution or prayer that the purpose of the agent shall be accomplished." BROWN decides that "in every case the basis of the Truth Act is the singleness with which the performer, or some other person used by the performer as a dynamic reference, fulfils his personal duty...In this way the individual achieves personal integrity and fits the cosmic purpose. Life then becomes a sacrificial act, a rite (*kriyā*), and as such, when perfectly executed, it can accomplish any wish, compelling even the gods, as we are taught in the Vedas and the Brahmaṇas is possible through the sacrifice."

There is an obviously different approach in those two articles. BURLINGAME is more interested in the Truth Act and the results credited to it as elements in stories than he is in real life magic.

BROWN treats them as miracles, which, while related in stories, are nevertheless grounded in the religious outlook of the people who therefore regard these miracles as possible even though exceptionally rare. In the "real life" approach, one then wonders why the people think such events might occur, and BROWN well states the case in terms of the person who so succeeds : he has been superlative in doing his duty, the Hindu *dharma*, whatever it may be—as, say, the *dharma* of a king, of a wife, of a courtesan.

BROWN was aware that there is more to it than this, because that person doing the Truth Act must verbalize the fact of his superhuman performance of *dharma.* So BROWN rightfully brings into the discussion "the confession ritual performed at the Varuṇapraghāsas, when the priest asks the sacrificer's wife with whom she consorts other than her husband." And he continues, "It is essential for her to speak, not because speaking lessens the sin, but because it brings exactitude, that is 'truth', into the rite. And it is significant that she speaks out before Varuṇa, who is the Vedic custodian of the *ṛta*, cosmic truth or order." It is of interest that the spoken appeal is also to Varuṇa in the case of the four ordeals—the balance, fire, water, and poison.[1] But in the cases both of the Varuṇapraghāsas and the ordeals the object is the ascertainment of the unknown truth; whereas in the case of the Truth Act, the emphasis is not on ascertainment of the truth however unpleasant, but on telling the truth that is extraordinary, superhuman.

In the Pāli expression *saccakiriyā*, the *kiriyā* (Skt. *kriyā*) is the doing that is here the ritual speaking. HARRISON states that in Latin, Sanskrit, and Greek there are nominal formations based on the verbs "to do, make " that have side meanings of "ritual operations of a magical character," but provides no textual references.[2] For the case of Sanskrit she cites the word *kṛtya.* Our present word *kriyā* also conforms to her view : One of its standard meanings is "rite." Magical aims are certainly behind the performance of many rites in ancient times, while certain social rites, such as those of marriage, may also have had in an-

[1]Dr. Ludo ROCHER, *Vācaspati Miśra*, *Vyavahāracintāmaṇi* (Gentse Orientalistiscle Eljdragen: Gent, 1956), pp. 320 ff.

[2]Jane Ellen HARRISON, *Themis*, Meridian Books, p. 82.

cient times some magical associations. Therefore I employ the rendition "Rite of Truth."

The classical sources of the Rite of Truth are the Hindu *Rāmāyaṇa* and the Buddhist *Milindapañha*. However, the Vedic literature already sets forth the creative nature of truth, especially in these two passages of the *Atharva-Veda* and the *Yajur-Veda* :

तत् सत्यमभवत् तेन प्राजायत् ।।अ० १५, १, ३ ।

"That became Truth, by That was produced (the world)."

सत्यं च मे श्रद्धा च मे...यज्ञेन कल्पन्ताम् ।।य० १८, ५ ।

"May my Truth and my Faith bring about (the wish) through sacrifice !"

The former passage posits Truth in a way comparable to the doctrine of the Logos, an intermediary between the Divine intellect and the created world.[3] The latter passage depicts the method by which man may duplicate the primordial achievement : by sacrifice he will copy the plan of the Divine intellect, by Faith convince himself of the efficacy of the procedure, and by Truth bring about the desired extra-normal results. This tenet of the verbal component acting as an intermediary between mind and the objective world is worked out in a variety of ways in old Indian lore and classical Indian metaphysics. We need only recall the role of Vāk (the female personification of speech) acting as the *śakti*, or power, for the lord to reveal himself in the world. This doctrine was elaborated with Vāk as a group of phonetic powers, the *mātrikā*, and Kashmir Śaivism as well as the Tantric schools wrote extensively on the emanation process of these mediating phoneme mothers.[4]

The verbal form of the Rite of Truth is not a traditional *mantra*. It is rather analogous to the Upaniṣadic expressions called Vidyās,

[3]Cf. H. J. ROSE, *Religion in Greece and Rome*, Harper Torch-books, p. 132.

[4]Cf. André PADOUX, *Recherches sur la symbolique et l'énergie de la parole dans certains textes tantriques*, Publications de l'institut de civilisation indienne Fasc. 21 (Paris, 1963), especially Chap. V, "L 'émanation phonématique".

which are really *upāsanā-s* or meditative exercises.[5] As K. Narayanaswami AIYAR points out,[6] there are three fruits of these Vidyā-s, namely (1) Duritakṣaya, the warding off of calamities; (2) Aiśvaryaprāpti, gaining of the Siddhi-s or occult powers; and (3) Kramamukti, progressive liberation. The standard examples of the Rite of Truth exhibit fruits falling within the first two categories. For example, in Āryaśūra's *Jātakamālā* the first category is exhibited by the Rite of Truth in three *jātakas*, i.e., No. XIV, The Story of Supāraga, to turn a ship back from its perilous position near the fabulous Mare-mouth, site of the submarine fire; No. XV, The Story of the Fish, to call down the rain, thus averting the calamity to the fish in a lake almost exhausted of water; No. XVI, The Story of the Quail's Young, to turn back a forest conflagration. The second category is exhibited in No. II, the Śibijātaka, wherein the Rite of Truth achieves for King Śibi the divine eyes.

Āryaśūra's formulation of the Śibijātaka around fourth century, A.D., not only employs the Upaniṣadic *upāsana* aspect of the rite but also contains elements of considerable interest and relevance to an understanding of this Rite of Truth. In the first part of the story, Indra appears in the form of a blind beggar before the generous King Śibi and asks for the King's eyes, which the King with great delight gives to the beggar. In the second part, the King is seated with crossed legs at a lotus pond, indicating that he is in meditative retirement—his "blindness" suggesting allegorically the blindfold of the candidate for initiation.[7] There is the humming of a swarm of bees (*madhukaragaṇopakūjita*); later on, when the King obtains two eyes of divine sight, large drums (*dundubhi*) of the gods sound forth with deep pleasing sounds—the former and latter sounds suggesting the first and last of the five *anāhata* sounds going with *yoga* success.[8] Indra

[5]Cf. Dr. V. RAGHAVAN's introduction to K. Narayanaswami AIYAR, *The Thirty-Two Vidyā-s* (Adyar; Madras, 2nd ed., 1962).

[6]Ibid., p. 9.

[7]Cf. Giuseppe TUCCI, *Tibetan Painted Scrolls* (Rome, 1949), p. 247.

[8]Śrīśa Chandra VASU, tr. *The Shiva Sanhita* (Allahabad, 1905), Chap. V, verse 27 : "The first sound is like the hum of the honey-intoxicated bee, next that of a flute, then of a harp; after this by the gradual practice of Yoga, the destroyer of the darkness of the world, he hears the sounds of ringing bells

decides it is time for the King to get his eyes back. Why cannot Indra, the powerful one of the Gods (*Devendra*), simply go ahead and restore the eyes ? As a preliminary answer to this question, Indra is now made to say, "Hence I shall endeavour to have his eye produced by showing a way." The word *upāya* is used for this way, or approach, which turns out to be the Rite of Truth. Later, Āryaśūra will give a Buddhist dogmatic answer in terms of the requirement of two causes (*hetu* and *pratyaya*) for a thing to arise. Indra asks Śibi why he still has his mind on the mendicants, suggesting that the answer will remove the condition of blindness. The King replies : "Why is there this urging of your honor that I be made to boast ? (*ko yam asmān vikatthayitum atrabhavato nirbandhaḥ*). But, Devendra, pray lend ear ! Just as at that time and at this time, the mendicants' words, which are certainly expressions of mendicancy, are as pleasing to me as if made of benedictions, so may one eye of mine appear." The narrative continues, "Then, by the king's power of truth blessing (*satyādhiṣṭhāna*) and by his outstanding accumulation of merit (*puṇyopacaya*), no sooner had he expressed those words, than one eye appeared,..."

Let us consider the implications of Āryaśūra's account. First of all, we observe that the Rite of Truth is conducted before Indra, so Buddhism is here preserving a bit of the old Indra religion for the goal of Aiśvaryaprapti. It could be expected that after Indra dethroned Varuṇa as the chief Vedic deity, Indra would have to carry on in some fashion certain functions formerly the business of Varuṇa. While Varuṇa was the upholder of the *ṛta* and *satya*, Indra becomes the one who tests the *satya* and bestows appropriate reward or punishment. However, in the three stories Nos. XIV, XV, and XVI, for the goal of Duritakṣaya there is an indifferent relation to Indra. In No. XIV, the Rite of Truth is done before the sea-traders (visible witnesses) and the gods in the sky (invisible witnesses). In No. XV, it is done before the King of the Devas (*devarāja*), who in this case is probably Indra incorporating the function of the rain-god Parjanya; and the story continues with a eulogy by Śakra, Indra among the *devas*. In No. XVI, it is done before the fire-god, Agni.

---

then sounds like roar of thunder." The original Sanskrit of this text was not available to us at the time of writing.

Next, we observe that the basic cause (*hetu*) of the eye is the accumulation of merit, which Professor BROWN's article enables us to identify as a substitution for the Hindu *dharma*. This is entirely *puruṣakāra*, obvious acts of men, as is also the Rite of Truth, constituting the *upāya* as well as the *anuṣṭhāna* for a corresponding *adhiṣṭhāna*. The blessing (*adhiṣṭhāna*) by the deity is the conditional cause (*pratyaya*) and constitutes a sort of *daiva* dispensation. But note that in the *Milindapañha* account set forth in BURLINGAME's article, pp. 437, ff., the Buddhist monk Nāgasena holds that through the Power of Truth and no other cause, King Śibi received heavenly eyes. Consistent with early Buddhism's rejection of the necessity for an Īśvara or lord, Nāgasena rejects any need for the *adhiṣṭhāna* provided by the deity. Nāgasena's meaning of the word for "truth" implies the creative agency of Vāk incorporated by Truth. This is the implication also in the category of Buddhist scripture said to be promulgated by "mind truth-force," for example, "the words of the doctrine (*dharma*), which proceed from mountains, trees, walls, and so forth, through the force of having been uttered by the Bhagavat mentally with the power of truth (*satya-bala*)."[9] In such case, the successful performer of the Rite of Truth is himself the deity; and truth is not simply the ethical kind, included by the Buddhists in the "accumulation of merit," but has in addition a metaphysical implication of "reality" as the word *satya* is translated in Upaniṣadic contexts by Deussen.[10] In the oldest Vedic literature Nāgasena's position would be untenable because the first mortal to become exemplary in *dharma* was the celebrated Yama and so he received the title Dharmarāja; but in the old tradition he did not become a god : he was tantamount to a *deva* with the commensal relation of drinking with the gods,[11] and presumably also with the interlocutory relation of talking to the gods, as is the situation in the Rite of Truth.

Finally, there is the explicit element of boasting, which long

[9]From the Ms. translation by F.D. LESSING and Alex WAYMAN of *Mkhas grub rje's Fundamentals of the Buddhist Tantras*, (Mouton, The Hague, 1968), Chapter Two.

[10]Paul DEUSSEN, *The Philosophy of the Upanishads*, auth. Eng. tr. by Rev. A. S. GEDEN, (Edinburgh, 1906), p. 162.

[11]Cf. our "Studies in Yama and Māra," *Indo-Iranian Journal*, III (1959), p. 50.

ago attracted my attention. It is a feature of many Vedic hymns that the deity proclaims his prowess in a boasting manner or the poet boasts on the deity's behalf. For example, the goddess Vāk boasts (RV, X, 125, 5) : "I myself announce this thing favorable for gods and men. Whomever the man I love, him I make mighty, him a brahman, him a seer, him a wise man." As long as men believe in gods, they are not held in vain to boast or have their deeds boasted of, because they are believed to perform in fact the acts as stated. But how can puny man claim such superhuman action except with the human fault of boasting ? Āryaśūra suggests that boasting ceases to be a fault, and hence becomes divine, when it is uttered in the Rite of Truth. This feature of boasting seems to have an element in common with what anthropologists call "the breaking of the taboo" in the case of "primitive" societies. For example, the classic exposition by CRAWLEY[12] uses this terminology for marriage breaking the taboo involved in segregation of the sexes. If it is permissible to apply this description to Hindu rites or festivals, certain ones, such as the Holi festival in its older form, and Tantric rites with their striking indulgence in foods and sexual partners—seem to be more appropriately characterized thereby than is the Rite of Truth. In a negative way, the latter Rite exhibits a weak aspect of taboo breaking. In a positive way, the Rite has some feature of what is called a "rite of passage,"[13] to incorporate and confirm an individual in a new group, in this case the society of the gods.

The performer has an intermediary, a meditative utterance, the *vidyā*—which is a goddess (*strīdevatā*),[14] in this case Vāk, the Truth of himself, producing the desired reification.

[12]Ernest CRAWLEY, *The Mystic Rose*, Meridian Books, Inc.

[13]Arnold van GENNEP, *Les rites de passage*, available in English translation, *The Rites of Passage*, a Phoenix Book, University of Chicago Press.

[14]Cf. *Yoginītantra* (Venkateśvara Press, Bombay, 1962), p. 401 : mantravidyāvibhage tu dvividhaṃ jāyate priye / mantrāḥ puṃdevatāḥ proktā vidyāḥ strīdevatāḥ smṛtāḥ //.

SIGNIFICANCE OF DREAMS IN INDIA AND TIBET

Dreams exert a perennial fascination on the waking mind. Whether or not we accept a certain Western theory of dream archetypes, it is certain that in the fact of dreaming itself, in that an individual culture attributes significance to it and makes consequent use of it, we find a common bond of mankind.

The allusions to dreams and the recording and classification of them in India (by the word *svapna*) and in Tibet (by the word *rmi-lam*) usually occur in brief passages in biographies, psychological writings, Mahāyāna Buddhist and Tibetan tantric texts, and in general literature, or at most in chapters of works on medicine and astrology and in Jaina omen books. There are, however, some treatises represented by title to be devoted entirely to dreams, pre-eminently Jagaddeva's *Svapnacintāmaṇi*, which has a German translation, as well as the brief works such as *Svapnādhyāya*, in Sanskrit with Hindi translation, and the *Svapnavicār*, in Hindi. There are undoubtedly such brief tracts on dreams in all the vernaculars of India and of course in the ubiquitous Gypsy dream book in English which one can purchase from sidewalk book displays in large Indian cities.[1]

[1]Dream bibliography for the Vedic literature is referred to in an article by the Japanese Sanskritist N. Tsuji, "On the Adbhuta-brāhmaṇa" (in Japanese), *Annual of Oriental and Religious Studies* (original title in Japanese), No. 1 (1964), p. 41. Indian dreams and their interpretation have a brief popularizing survey in French by Anne-Marie Esnoul, "Les songes et leur

A. DREAMS POPULARLY BELIEVED AND AS THEMES IN LITERATURE

We may cite first the dreams whose importance is independent of whether they were really dreamt, it only being necessary that people at large think so. Thus the dreams of parents establishing sacred mother-son or father-son relations. The dreams attributed to the mother of Mahāvīra, historical founder of the Jaina sect (i.e. , the fourteen, beginning with the white elephant), as well as to the mother of Gautama Buddha (e.g., the white elephant entering her womb) are of this type. It would be difficult to prove that a different social order (polyandry) is responsible for the fact that to both the father and mother of Tsoṅ-kha-pa, founder of the Gelugpa sect in Tibet, are attributed the dreams by which Tsoṅ-kha-pa was regarded as all three *bodhisattvas*, Mañjuśrī, Avalokiteśvara, and Vajrapāṇi.[2]

Again, the dream theme of literature depicts dreams in roles that may or may not have occurred in reality. The parallel dream is illustrated by the tale in *Kathāsaritsāgara* of how king Vikramāditya and the princess Malayavatī first met in dream and were finally united in reality.[3] In the work attributed to Bhāsa, the *Svapnavāsavadatta*, the king goes to Padmāvatī's empty bed, falls asleep on it, and dreams of seeing Vāsavadattā and talking to her, but there in fact she happens not to be dreaming. This example, cited in Bhoja's *Śṛṅgāra Prakāśa*, illustrates the capacity of a dream to breed love and thus serve as a literary theme.[4] In this connection the Tamil classic *Tirukkural* (No. 1216) may be cited :

And if there were no waking hour, my love
In dreams would never from my side remove.[5]

---

interprétation dans l'Inde," in *Les songes et leur interprétation* (Paris : Éditions du Seuil, 1959), pp. 207-47.

There is a psychological treatment from medical, Indian philosophical, and Abhidharma Buddhist sources in a chapter by Jadunath Sinha in his *Indian Psychology : Perception* (London, 1934), pp. 306-23.

[2]These dreams are in the brief biography called *Zur ḥdebs rnam thar legs bśad kun ḥdus* ,in Tsoṅ-kha-pa's Gsuṅ *ḥbum* (Collected Works), Lhasa edition. The identification of Tsoṅ-kha-pa with the three bodhisattvas is in the well-known poem of the Gelugpa sect tradition, *Dmigs brtse ma.*

[3]Esnoul, *op. cit.*, pp. 226-27.

[4]V. Raghavan, *Bhoja's Śṛṅgāra Prakāśa* (Madras : published by author, 1963), pp. 738, 895.

[5]*Tirukkural*, with translations in English by Rev. Dr. G. U. Pope, Rev. W. H. Drew, Rev. John Lazarus, and Mr. F. W. Ellis (Tirunelveli, 1962).

As also Kālidāsa's *The Cloud Messenger* : "Wretch, I saw thee in a dream caressing some woman or other."[6] The ominous dream appears in the *Shilappadikaram :* "The Pāndya queen spoke : 'Alas ! I saw, in a dream..the night devouring the sun....I saw the rainbow shining in the night....Alas !' "[7]

B. CLASSIFICATION OF DREAMS

With regard to dreams in general, the Indian genius for classifying comes into play. There are some differences between the Hindu, Jaina, and Buddhist works as well as much in common. The simplest division is into auspicious (*śubha*) and inauspicious (*aśubha*). The division is seen to be very ancient by the words *svapna* and *duḥsvapna* to mean good and bad dreams and also much later in a chapter of mundane astrology.[8] Esnoul points out that the key words for good dreams and bad dreams stayed fairly constant from the earliest lists down to the twelfth-century work by Jagaddeva.[9] The *Svapnādhyāya* is based on this two-fold division by the words *iṣṭaphala*, "having desirable effect," and *aniṣṭaphala*, "having undesirable effect." This work begins the good dreams by saying (śl. 2-4): "If a man sees a crossing over of a stream or body of water, the sun rising into the sky, a blazing fire, the vision of moon-disk among the asterisms and planets, a mounting in palaces or to the summit of temples, he attains success." It begins the bad dreams (śl. 39-40): "If one sees the sun or moon devoid of light or the asterisms and other stars tumbling down; or sees the Aśoka tree, the Oleander, or the Palāśa tree in full bloom [apparently all of red blossoms], he attains sorrow."[10]

[6]Kālidāsa, *The Cloud Messenger*, trans. Franklin and Eleanor Edgerton (Ann Arbor : University of Michigan Press, 1964), p. 79.

[7]Ilango Adigal, *Shilappadikaram by Prince Ilango Adigal*, trans. Alain Daniélou (New York : New Directions, 1965), p. 126.

[8]Tsuji, *op. cit.*, p. 41. See also the words used in N. P. Subramania Iyer (trans.), *Kālaprakāśikā* (Tanjore : Lawley Electric Printing Press, 1917), chap. xlii.

[9]Esnoul, *op. cit.*, p. 221.

[10]*Svapnādhyāya*, with Hindi commentary (Bombay : Veṅkateśvara Steam Press, 1927):

/ nadī-samudra-taraṇam ākāśa-gamanaṃ yathā /
/ bhāskarodayanaṃ caiva prajvalaṃ taṃ hutāśanam //2//

Nebesky-Wojkowitz reports that in Tibet it is believed that various deities and demons produce dreams : "If one saw a snowy mountain or a soaring white bird, then the *lha* [*deva*] caused this dream....To see snakes, frogs, girls with a pale-blue skin, and mountain-meadows, are mirages caused by the *klu* [*nāga*].... and if one trembles with terror and fear in the sleep, this is due to the influence of the *bdud* [Māra]" (to mention only those due to spirits identifiable with Indian deities).[11]

The Jaina work *Riṣṭasamuccaya* says :

> 112. Dream is twofold. One is that which is told by the god and the other is a natural dream. That dream is a dream told by a god where a *mantra* (sacred formula) is recited.
> 113. The other (viz., a natural dream) occurs when one, void of worries and well-poised body and well-proportioned humours, gets [it], indeed, without (muttering) a *mantra* (sacred formula).[12]

The expression "lacking well-proportioned humours" suggests the threefold division where pathological disorders are explained in the medical works to involve imbalance of the three humours, "wind," "bile," and "phlegm." In the sixty-eighth Pariśiṣṭa of the *Atharva-Veda* men are said to have the temperaments bilious (fiery), phlegmatic (watery), and sanguine (windy). Different dreams are attributed to such persons respectively: for the bilious, dreams, for example, of arid land and of burning objects; for the phlegmatic, dreams, for example, of nature in splendor and burgeoning life; for the sanguine, dreams, for example, of racing clouds and of forest creatures running in terror.[13] In the *Ques-*

/ graha-nakṣatra-tārāṇāṃ candramaṇḍala-darśanam /
/ harmyeṣv ārohaṇāṃ caiva prāsāda-śikhare pi vā //3//
/ evam ādīni saṃdṛṣṭvā naraḥ siddhim avāpnuyāt //4//
/ ādityaṃ vātha candraṃ vā vigatacchavikaṃ yathā //
/ pataṃta cātha nakṣatraṃ tārakādīṃś ca vā yadi //39//
/ aśokaṃ karavīraṃ vā palāśaṃ vātha puṣpitam /
/ svapnān te yas tu paśyeta naraḥ śokam avāpnuyāt //40//.

[11]Rene de Nebesky-Wojkowitz, *Oracles and Demons of Tibet* ('s-Gravenhage : Mouton & Co., 1956), p. 466.

[12]Durgadeva, *Riṣṭasamuccaya*, trans. A. S. Gopani (Bombay : Bharatiya Vidya Bhavan, 1945), p. 56.

[13]Esnoul, *op. cit.*, pp. 215-17.

tions of King Milinda, there are said to be six men who dream : the foregoing three, (4) those under influence of a deity, (5) those who dream under influence of their experiences, and (6) those with prophetic dreams. The text adds that only the last-named dream is true.[14] The basic Jaina classification in the wonderful book of omens, *Aṅgavijjā*, is into *diṭṭha*, "seen"; *na-diṭṭha*, "unseen"; and *avatta-diṭṭha* (Sanskrit : *avyakta-dṛṣṭa*), "inscrutably seen" (or both seen and unseen).[15] Various lists increase the number of sense organs involved. The Buddhist Mahāyāna text "Meeting of the Father and Son" (*Pitṛputrasamāgama*) gives dreams based on all six senses, the usual five plus the mind as the sixth sense; but here again the basic classification is three-fold by the three "poisons," lust (=attraction), hatred (=repulsion), and delusion (=incapacity), because the text gives a sample dream for each of the three in terms of each of the senses, shown in Table 1.[16]

TABLE I

Sense Organ	Lust	Hatred	Delusion
Sight	Sees his sexual play with the belle of the land	Sees himself fighting with an enemy	Sees himself beset upon by a demon (*ḥdre*), and being confused with fear
Hearing	Hears the singing and instrumental music of the belle of the land	Hears lamentation upon mother's or father's death, or upon loss of any pleasant thing	Hears something said, unable to understand the meaning of the words
Smelling	Is anointing his body with sandlewood or other perfumed sub stance	Smells the clinging odor of the carcass of dog, man, or snake	That he has lost sense of smell
Tasting	Hungry, he eats to satiation very savory food	Ravenous he resorts to eating the seeds of pumpkin gourds and other (disagreeable) seeds	That he has lost his sense of taste
Touching	Embraces the waist of the belle of the land	On his lap is a blazing copper slab	That he has lost his body sense organ (touch)
Imagining (ofthe sixth sense)	Dreams that he enjoys the 5 sense objects magically produced by a magician	Along with attendants and retinue, he is carried away by a flood	That he is much inebriated by wine

[14] *Ibid.*, pp. 232-33.

[15] *Aṅgavijjā* (Prakrit Text Society No. 1) [Banaras : Prakrit Text Society, 1957], Introduction, p. 51, and text, pp. 186-91.

[16] *Pitṛputrasamāgama-mahāyānasūtra* (Kyoto-Tokyo photographic reprint of Tibetan canon), XXIII, 201-4 and ff.

The Indian medical text *Carakasaṃhitā* adds the category of dreams as mere past experience (*anubhūta*) though immediately apprehended, and the category as mere imagination (*kalpita*) though based on memory data. Some dreams are wish fulfilment (*prārthita*), the principal category in the Western Freudian classification, and some are prophetic (*bhāvika*). The Buddhist category of recurrent dreams seems to amount to the Vaiśeṣika "dreams due to the intensity of subconscious impressions" (*saṃskārapāṭava*).[17] Accordingly, Śāntideva quotes the *Siṃhaparipṛcchā*, "Therefore in all his births he loses not the thought of enlightenment. Even in dreams he has this thought : much more if he be awake."[18] The Jaina text has a classification of the beings in the dream. Under "gods in dream" are gods and goddesses. In human variety are the dead, the living, the unborn, women, men, and the sexless. Under animals there are five : (1) birds, (2) four-footed animals, (3) reptiles, (4) aquatic creatures, (5) insects.[19] The category of dead persons is consistent with Emeneau's study, "Toda Dream Songs", showing that in Toda belief only dead men sing in the dream.[20]

C. PROPHETIC ASPECT OF DREAM

In the *Atharva-Veda* it was said that the dream comes hither from Yama's world.[21] Yama, the lord of the dead, is stationed in the south. Therefore, we see the reason that the *Adbhuta-brāhmaṇa*, as analyzed by Tsuji, requires that one divine the dream while facing south.[22] Caraka and Suśruta both describe certain dreams as prognostics of impending disease or death.[23] A similar view

[17]Sinha, *op. cit.*, pp. 314-15.

[18]Śāntideva, *Śikṣāsamuccaya*, trans, C. Bendall and W. H. D. Rouse (London : John Murray, 1922), p. 54; and Sanskrit text, ed. P. L. Vaidya (Darbhanga : Mithila Institute, 1961), p. 33.

[19]*Aṅgavijjā* (cited in n. 15).

[20]Murray B. Emeneau, "'Toda Dream Songs," *Journal of the American Oriental Society*, LXXXV, No. 1 (January-March, 1965), 39-44.

[21]William Dwight Whitney (trans.), *Atharva-Veda-Saṃhitā* (Delhi: Motilal Banarsidass, 1962), II, 993-94.

[22]Tsuji, *op. cit.*, p. 41.

[23]Sinha, *op. cit.*, p. 321.

was held by Aristotle.[24] The Indian view is that the prophetic character of the dream is the *adṛṣṭa* (the unseen agency), namely, the merit and demerit (*dharmādharma*) of the dreamer.[25]

Prophetic dreams (*bhāvika*) did not imply a fatalistic belief, because palliative measures were indicated. The *Suśruta-saṃhitā* says : "If one has a sinister dream, he should not relate it to anyone, but should pass three nights in the temple to honor the *pretas* (the deceased). He will then be delivered from the bad dream."[26] In the Mālinī school of Kashmere Śaivism, if the worshipper sees a good dream he may express it to his disciples and if otherwise he should perform the *homa* (burnt offering).[27] In the Buddhist work *Mṛtyu-vañcana* ("Cheating Death"), the author states several portents of death of the dreamer himself, for example, the dream that a shepherd is wandering at night without a companion and is unable to see the moon or stars. To counteract such a portent one performs the ritual of Amitāyus, the Buddha of "Eternal Life."[28] In the above-cited Buddhist text classifying dreams by the three poisons and the six senses, the position is taken that the psychological poison first shows in the dream and subsequently in actions of body, speech, and mind.[29] Similarly, the tantric work *Āryā-Tārā-Kurukulle-kalpa* says, "When the sign appears in the dream, the *siddhi* [occult power or success] will arise automatically."[30] This agrees with other Buddhist tantras, where auspicious dreams that come true indi-

[24]Pedro Meseguer, S. J., *The Secret of Dreams* (Westminster, Md.: Newman Press, 1960), p. 19.

[25]Sinha, *op. cit.*, p. 315.

[26]Esnoul, *op. cit.*, p. 225.

[27]Pandit Madhusūdan Kaul, *Mālinīvijayottara Tantram* (Bombay, 1922), Introduction, p. xxxi.

[28]*Mṛtyu-vañcana* (Kyoto-Tokyo photographic reprint of Tibetan canon), LXXXVI, 121.

[29]This remark occurs in an almost invariant formula after each dream example. Fortunately, one such dream with the standard remarks was cited by Śāntideva, *op. cit.*, Sanskrit text, p. 135, showing how the dream of lust, because for the while believed in, establishes a propensity leading to three bad actions of the body, four of speech, and three of mind : /so 'bhiniviṣṭaḥ sann anunīyate / anunītaḥ saṃrajyate / saṃrakto rāgajam karmābhisaṃskaroti... trividhaṃ kāyena, caturvidhaṃ vācā, trividhaṃ manasā /.

[30]*Ārya-Tārā Kurukulle-kalpa* (Kyoto-Tokyo photographic reprint of Tibetan canon), Vol. III., p. 120, fol. 2: / rmi lam mtshan ma ston źiṅ / dṅos grub raṅ ñid ḥbyuṅ bar ḥgyur /.

cate approach of the tutelary deity and success in the meditative process as contrasted with the bad dreams indicating that the deity stays far away as does the success (*siddhi*).[31] Here the dream, especially the one with psychological poison, reveals the tendency; and Buddhism in common with Hinduism always maintained that one need not follow a portentous inclination because both religions have their regular ways of purifying pollution.[32]

Prophetic dreams are well known in the traditional life of Gautama Buddha. The Pāli text *Aṅguttaranikāya* relates the five dreams Gautama had as premonitory of his full enlightenment.[33] Sixteen dreams are attributed to the King of Kosala in the *Mahāsupina-Jātaka*. For example, No. 2 : "Methought little tiny trees and shrubs burst through the soil, and when they had grown scarce a span or two high, they flowered and bore fruit." Then the Buddha, cast in the role of a dream oracle, explains the dream as foretelling the degenerate times when men will be shortlived and young girls will cohabit with men as mature women do and so conceive and bear children.[34] Here also we see the method of dream interpretation : tiny tree of dream equals young girl in actuality, interpreted in context by the dream oracle. This contrasts with the set meaning of a symbol in lists of good and bad dreams. The dream attributed to a king in the time of the former Buddha Kāśyapa in the Buddhist Sarvāstivādin Vinaya about eighteen men pulling on a piece of cloth and unable to rip it, as a prophecy of Gautama Buddha's doctrine, is obviously fabricated after the rise of the eighteen Buddhist schools, which hopefully could not pull Buddhism apart.[35]

The life of Atīśa, the great Indian paṇḍit who debated the invitation to teach in Tibet, shows him worshipping Tārā to receive a dream advice : "His tutelary gods directed him in a dream to go to the great Tirthika city called Mukhena in the neighborhood of

[31]Mkhas grub rje, *Mkhas grub rje's Fundamentals of the Buddhist Tantras*, trans. F. D. Lessing and Alex Wayman (Indo-Iranian Monographs, Vol. VIII ['s-*Gravenhage* : Mouton & Co., 1966]).

[32]In the Hindu case, the *brahmins* make the expiatory offering (*prayāścitta arghya*), especially in the early morning along with the *gāyatrī* rite. The Buddhist monks have confessional and meditative procedures.

[33]Esnoul, *op. cit.*, p. 237.

[34]H. T. Francis and E. J. Thomas, *Jātaka Tales* (Bombay : Jaico Publishing House, 1957), p. 48.

[35]One of the tales in Mkhas grub rje, *op. cit.*

Vikrama Śilā, at the centre of which there stood on a hillock a small Buddhist temple. He was told that there he would meet with a female ascetic who could tell him all that he wished to know."[36] Also, Tsoṅ-kha-pa's biography contains many prophetic dreams. In some cases he first saw in dream a teacher later to be important in his life, as in the case of the aged lama Khyuṅ-po-lha, repository of the Yoga tantra.[37] Once he and a disciple, Tsha-go-pa, fasted and worshipped near the Jo-bo statue of Śākyamuni in Lhasa, and both had dream omens. Tsha-go-pa saw in dream two great white conchshells descend from the sky and fall into his coat flap. Instantly they merged into one. When he took that in hand and blew upon it, it sounded an unfathomably great sound. This was an auspice of a great spread and enhancement of the Buddha's teaching.[38] It was also a prophecy about Tsoṅ-kha-pa, dreamt by a second person.

In the Appendix to the Tibetan Gesar epic there is a page devoted to each dream analysis in terms of good and bad omens. Among the auspicious ones, if one dreams of the sunrise and dispelling of darkness, this portends happiness of oneself and country. If one dreams of hearing tales of praise while surrounded by a retinue of servants, it is an auspice for moving upward in society. Among the ominous omens, if one dreams that a house caves in or is ruined by fire, one fears for men and others in the house and should call upon Sitātapatrā (the white Umbrella Lady).[39]

The *Atharva-Veda* tradition holds that dreams in the first watch of the night bring their fruit in the year, those of the second watch in six months, while those of the third watch are already half-realized.[40] The *Kālaprakāśikā*, written much later when the night was divided into quarters rather than thirds, says : "The effect of

[36]Sarat Chandra Das, *Indian Pandits in the Land of Snow* (Calcutta : Firma K. L. Mukhopadhyay, 1965), p. 66.

[37]Manuscript of Tsoṅ-kha-pa's biography compiled by Alex Wayman. The card files of the late F. D. Lessing call attention to the story that the Emperor Hsuan-tsung dreamed that he had met an eminent monk of unusual appearance. "The Emperor, applying the paints himself, portrayed (the dream monk) on the wall of his hall. When Shan-wu-woi arrived, he (found him to be) identical with (the monk) of the dream."

[38]Manuscript of Tsoṅ-kha-pa's biography.

[39]Lohpon Tonzin Namdak (ed.). *The Epic of Gesar* (Delhi : Spar khaṅ, 1965), Appendix. See also the list in Nebesky-Wojkowitz, *op. cit.*, pp. 465-66.

[40]Esnoul, *op. cit.*, p. 217.

dreams during the first quarter of the night will be realized in a year; that of dreams of the 2d quarter, in six months; the influence of dreams in the 3rd quarter will be evident in a month; dreams before dawn will be realized in twelve days; dreams before sunrise announce their effects in a day."[41] Again, the *Aṅgavijjā* claims it is important to notice whether the dream occurred in the increasing phases of the moon or decreasing phases and, in each, whether in the first part, middle part, or last part, which each amount to sixty degrees of lunar motion.[42]

D. THE NATURE OF A DREAM

The philosophical treatment of the dream is especially interesting. Mahāyāna Buddhism and Hindu Vedānta compared the world to a dream in the sense that it is unreal but works regardless of whether we understand it. The viewpoint is well stated by Ramakrishna : "It is not easy to get rid of illusion. It lingers even after the attainment of knowledge. A man dreamt of a tiger. Then he woke up and his dream vanished. But his heart continued to palpitate."[43]

The classical schools of Indian philosophy took two basically different interpretations of a dream. Sinha adopts the Western terminology "presentative theory" and "representative theory." The Nyāya-Vaiśeṣika school mostly held to the presentative theory wherein a dream cognition is explained as a perception of the mind itself in retirement when the external sense organs have ceased to function. The Mīmāṃsakas with Prabhākara as spokesman held to the representative theory that dream consciousness amounts to a false recollection. In the Indian philosophical context, Prabhākara's representative theory comes in for weighty blows from many quarters, including Śaṅkara, the great Vedāntin.[44]

To make the two positions clear, I should say that they just involve the belief or disbelief in the mind as a sixth sense, in which the Buddhists generally believed. If the eye as a sense organ enables perception of forms, and not sounds, which require an

[41] This is the way Iyer, *op. cit.*, p. 236, understands the Sanskrit passage.

[42] *Aṅgavijjā*, p. 190, II. 30-33.

[43] Ramakrishna, *Tales and parables of Sri Ramakrishna* (2d ed.; Mylapore : Sri Ramakrishna Math, 1947).

[44] Sinha, *op. cit.*, *pp.* 308-10.

ear, so also the mind—"because it is a sense organ like other sense organs," as Bhāvaviveka stated it[45]—would have its own partite reality of object not shared as object by the other senses. Therefore, when it retires into itself in sleep, the dream is its own object, hence a *presentation* of that perception alone, to which the five external sense organs cannot contribute. Bhāvaviveka explains that the perception that is based on the sixth-sense mind (*manovijñāna*) and that has the *dharmas* ("mentals" or "natures") as object is what perceives the dream.[46] Hence this *manovijñāna* is equivalent to Kashmere Śaivism's *buddhi*, conceived of as mirror-like because it not only reflects external objects as perceived through the five outer senses but also displays the revived traces (*saṃskāras*) "at the time of free imagination, remembrance, and dream."[47] Dandekar explains that in the Hindu view the subtle body (*sūkṣma-śarīra*) is the basis for dream consciousness, having become equivalent to the *prāṇamaya* (vital), *manomaya* (mental), and *vijñāna* (intellectual) sheaths (*kośa*) all taken together.[48] This subtle body of Hinduism agrees with the Buddhist *manovijñāna* as a kind of body that can detach itself from the coarse body and wander, thus perhaps similar in regard to dream as the wandering soul of so-called primitive peoples, although the texts I have seen do not spell out the "wandering."

The philosophical interpretation of dream in India began especially with the Upaniṣadic formulation of four states : waking, dream, deep sleep, and a state that is the first three all in all. Certain later Upaniṣads took a metaphysical and mystically physiological rather than philosophical turn and gave rise in time to the special viewpoints of the tantra. Thus, they teach that the "person" (*puruṣa*) has those four states when dwelling in the four places, namely, waking state in the navel, dream in the neck, dreamless sleep in the heart, and the fourth in the head."[49] The Buddhist tantras explain that the white and red elements of the

[45]Bhāvaviveka, *Tarkajvālā* (Kyoto-Tokyo photographic reprint), XCVI, 92.

[46]*Ibid.*

[47]K. C. Pandey, *Abhinavagupta; an Historical and Philosophical Study* (Benares : Chowkhamba, 1935), p. 252.

[48]R. N. Dandekar, "Man in Hindu Thought," *Annals of the Bhandarkar Oriental Research Institute*, XLIII, Parts I-IV (1962), p. 9.

[49]Mircea Eliade, *Yoga : Immortality and Freedom* (New York : Pantheon Books, 1958), p. 128.

bodhicitta passing up and down the "central channel" of the body generate those respective states and hence stay in the neck at the time of dream.[50] There were also numerous speculations in corresponding terms. So, in the theory of four forms of *Vāc*, or "Speech," the *madhyamā* "middling" form corresponds to dream and, in the southern Śaiva formulation, is the kind of speech dissociated from consciousness.[51] It makes us recall the Jaina verse above cited about the dream being told by a god when a *mantra* is recited. This alludes to the state when the constant repetition of a *mantra* reaches the point where it seems to sound by itself and, being imagined as independent of the mind, is believed to be pronounced or told by a god.[52] In fact, the sound with this life of self-sounding is the dream condition of sound, or "names" as things. This formulation of the situation rationalizes the above-mentioned correspondence of dream to dissociated speech.

This theory of creating a dream state by repeated incantation, thus to evoke a deity, implies that the bulk of Lamaist iconography—those fierce and mild deities—amounts to sets of controlled dreams. Indeed, the production of an artificial dream state is prevalent in the Buddhist tantras and in certain ones is called "purifying or exerting the dream" (*rmi lam sbyaṅ ba*). Furthermore, the tantric machinations aim at a mixing (*sre ba*) of the states of dream, deep sleep, and waking to attain the fourth state. These methods are much practiced by Tibetan lamas, and the method of one of these sects is well set forth by Chen-chi Chang,[53] as also in a work by Tsoṅ-kha-pa showing his standpoint.[54]

The above cursory survey of the subject should attest to (1) a spirited interest in dreams, both in India and Tibet, in regard to their nature and purport and (2) to the attempt to use them widely in literature and even in some techniques of *yoga*. I could have

[50]Alex Wayman, "Female Energy and Symbolism in the Buddhist Tantras," *History of Religions*, II, No. 1 (1962), 84. See also A. Wayman, *Buddhist Tantras* (Samuel Weiser, New York, (1973).

[51]P. T. Srinivasa Iyengar, *Outlines of Indian Philosophy* (Madras : Adyar, 1909), p. 160.

[52]Mkhas grub rje, *op. cit.*, Kriyā and Caryā Tantra section, meditation of "dwelling in the flame and in the sound."

[53]Chen-chi Chang, *Teachings of Tibetan Yoga* (New Hyde Park, N. Y. : University Books, 1963), pp. 88-94.

[54]Tsoṅ-kha-pa, *Dmar khrid* (Kyoto-Tokyo photographic reprint), Vol. CLIX.

stressed more the differences between the Indian and Tibetan traditions, but enough has been presented to suggest that Tibet, despite being swamped by Indian Buddhism in its classical and late forms, has a distinct tradition of its own, perhaps affiliated with the rest of the Himalaya area as well as with China.

22

THE SIGNIFICANCE OF MANTRAS, FROM THE VEDA DOWN TO BUDDHIST TANTRIC PRACTICE

The subject of *mantra* is of course too vast for a single article, although Gonda[1] in one essay has an excellent coverage, especially in terms of secondary sources. I find it possible to treat the principal issues in even briefer compass. The old word *mantra* came in time to have specialized usages, and, in Buddhist literature, to be paired with *dhāraṇī* and sometimes to overlap this latter word. Our procedure will be to lay a foundation of the theme in the old Brahmanical literature, then show that the performance of *mantras* is in terms of varieties, and finally to venture conclusions in the disputed topic of the meaning of *mantras*.

An Old Indian Theory

The old Indian division of the *Veda* was into *Mantra* and *Brāhmaṇa*. Dasgupta writes, "The word Brahman originally meant in the earliest Vedic literature, *mantra*, duly performed sacrifice, and also the power of sacrifice which could bring about the desired result."[2] Therefore, in the standard division of the *Veda*, the *Brāhmaṇas* are texts dealing with the actual performance of the sacrifice, while the Mantra is the sacrifice itself. Pāṇini also

[1] J. Gonda, *The Indian Mantra*, in "Oriens", 1963, pp. 244-295.

[2] Surendranath Dasgupta, *A History of Indian Philosophy*, Cambridge, 1932, Vol. I, p. 211.

opposes the terms "Mantra" and "Brāhmaṇa."[3] The *Śatapatha-brāhmaṇa* states[4] :

> "Make ye Agni's paths to lead to the gods !"—as the text so the meaning;.."making the parents young again"—the young parents, doubtless, are speech and mind, and these two fires are speech and mind.

But the *Śatapathabrāhmaṇa* also records a dispute between speech and mind as to which was the better of the two[5]. In agreement with the other passage that these two are paths leading to the gods, they appealed to Prajāpati for a decision. When he picked mind, saying speech was only its imitator, speech, being dismayed, "miscarried" and refused henceforth to be Prajāpati's oblation-bearer. Hence, in the sacrifice for Prajāpati the performer speaks in a low voice, since the Goddess of Speech refuses to speak out on these occasions.[6] The *Anugītā* of the *Mahābhārata* expands upon the story[7]. When Prajāpati chose the mind, speech reminded him that, after all, it was she who yielded his desires[8].

[3]V. S. AGRAWALA, *India as Known to Pāṇini*, 2d ed., Banaras, 1963, pp. 319-320, says that for Pāṇini the *mantra* means a sacred formula whether a Vedic stanza (*rich*) or in prose (*vajus*), and that the *Brāhmaṇas* are non-*mantra* literature. M. GANGANATHA JHA, *The Pūrva-Mīmāṃsā-Sūtras of Jaimini*, Allahabad, 1911, pp. 163-164, cites *Prabhākara* for *mantra* as including "all those Vedic passages to which the learned men apply that name". The *Sūtras* say that the name "*Brāhmaṇa*" is applied to the rest of the *Veda*. Also both "*Mantra*" and "*Brāhmaṇa*" are referred to as "*vidhi*".

[4]J. EGGELING, tr., *Śatapathabrāhmaṇa*, Part IV, SBE, Vol. XLIII, pp. 123-124, from VIII, 6, 3, 22.

[5]J. EGGELING, tr., *Śatapathabrāhmaṇa*, Part I, SBE, Vol. XII, pp. 130-131, from I, 4, 5, 8-12.

[6]Pt. GANGA PRASAD UPADHyaya, *Śatpatha Brāhmaṇam*, Vol. II, Delhi, 1969, p. 318, mentions for this story particularly *Aum Prajāpataye Svāhā Idam Prajāpataye idam na mama*, as on oblation spoken silently. However, the injunction is general in the *yajña*.

[7]K. T. TELANG, *The Bhagavadgitā with the Sanatsujātīya and the Anugītā*, SBE, Vol. VIII, pp. 263-266. Critical ed., *Aśvamedhaparva*, Section 21.

[8]Cf. ARTHUR BERRIEDALE KEITH, *The Aitareya Āraṇyaka*, London, 1969 reprint, p. 180 : "Speech yields all desires, for by speech man expresses all desires. Speech yields all desires to him who knows this". So from I, 3, 2. Also, *Śatapathabrāhmaṇa*, VI, 1, 2, sets forth Prajāpati's union by his mind (*manas*) with speech (*vāc*) to create creatures, to wit the eight Vasus to inhabit the earth, the eleven Rudras to inhabit the intermediate space, the twelve Ādityas to inhabit the sky, and the All-gods to inhabit the quarters. Thus, Vāc yielded Prajāpati's desires.

Prajāpati mollified the goddess by declaring that there are two kinds of mind, the stationary (*sthāvara*) and the moving (*jaṅgama*). The stationary was his own. The moving, to wit, any *mantra*, or letter (*varṇa*), or sound (*svara*), was in the dominion of the cow-like goddess, from whom comes the twofold flowing. Thus the *Anugītā* says[9]: "It (speech) always proceeds aloud, or noiseless after birth; and of these two, the noiseless one is superior to the one aloud." These two kinds are apparently the twofold flowing. In the later refinement of the *Agnipurāṇa*, chapter CCXCIII (*Mantraparibhāṣā*, verse 28), there would be a "fourfold flowing"[10]:

> The tradition[11] is that one uttered in a low voice is superior in the recitation by tenfold merits that loud ones have. In the case of recitation by tongue, a hundredfold merits (superior), by mind a thousandfold.

The foregoing is instructive of the ancient metaphorical language. Speech was a fire when it was a duly performed sacrifice[12], leading to the gods; and it was a cow when it brought the desired result[13]. Taking the two metaphorical references as a guide, one can separate out the instruction. Thus, when speech is a fire, there is the practice of reciting certain formulas three times, for the gods cannot be contacted by random action. In agreement, Gonda[14] cites the *Maitrāyaṇīsaṃhitā* I, 4, 8, "because the gods are three times in accordance with truth." Also, in Buddhist non-

[9]Critical ed., 14, 21, 16 :

ghoṣiṇi jātanirghoṣā nityam eva pravartate /
tayor api ca ghoṣiṇyor nirghoṣaiva garīyasī // 16.

[10]Ānandāśrama ed., p. 471 :

uccair japād viśiṣṭaḥ syād upāṃśur daśabhir guṇaiḥ /
jihvājape śataguṇaḥ sahasro mānasaḥ smṛtaḥ // 28.

[11]The tradition is alluded to in *Manusmṛti*, ch. II, 85.

[12]Cf. Keith, *The Aitareya Āraṇyaka*, from II, 4, 1 : "From the mouth came speech, from speech fire".

[13]K. N. Aiyar, *The Thirty-two Vidyā-s*, Adyar, Madras, 2d ed., 1962, p. 58, points out that there is no Vidyā devoted to Vāk itself, and then cites *Bṛhadāraṇyaka*, V, 8, 1, for the meditation on speech as Dhenu (milch cow). Two of her udders, (the *bīja-s*) Svāhā and Vaṣaṭ, feed the Deva-s; a third Hanta, feeds men; a fourth one, Svadhā, the Pitṛs. Her bull is Prāṇa and calf Manas. This calf, the *manas*, is presumably *Anugītā's* "moving" mind.

[14]*The Indian Mantra*, p. 267.

tantric as well as tantric practice the vows are repeated three times by the disciple after the preceptor, and this implies that the vow constitutes a sacrificial truth. So also the three times of circumambulation.[15] One recalls here the theory of the "act of truth" (*satya-kriyā*), as has been discussed in several articles by Brown and in one by myself above.[16] This act requires the prior surpassing performance of duty (*dharma*) in the Hindu usage, or to have accumulated much merit (*puṇya*) in the Buddhist usage. But in addition the performer must declare his appeal or command to the deity : the fact that the person desires aid from the deity does not suffice. One may observe that in this "act of truth" there is no implication of relative loudness for expected degree of fruit. Thus, even though the "act of truth" traditionally involved an attempt to derive an extra-normal fruit, the emphasis is on communication with the gods; and so it must be included with speech as a fire.

When it is the case of speech as a cow, there is the emphasis on the role of the *guru*. Accordingly we may understand the *Agni-purāṇa*, same chapter, v. 20B-21A : "A mantra heard by chance, by deceit, by power (i.e. forcibly), found on a leaf, and in *gāthā* form, one would generate in vain". Presumably this is because, v. 20A, "the *guru* should bestow the *mantra*". Hence, getting the *mantra* in any way except from the *guru* renders it worthless. The *guru* is responsible for setting up the ritual circumstances, starting in Vedic times with imparting the celebrated *Gāyatrī* or *Sāvitrī* of the *Veḍa*, according to P.T.S. Iyengar's eloquent remarks[17] :

> By sacramental use is meant the recitation of a *mantra* for producing a *sáṃskāra* conceived as a subtle change in the mind and body of the reciter. A *saṃskāra* renders a man fit to perform some mystic duties...The *Aitareya Brāhmaṇam* (1, i, 3) describes the *dīksha* for *yajñas;* in it the candidate for

[15]Cf. Arthur Berriedale Keith, *Rigveda Brahmaṇas*, Harvard Oriental Series, Vol. 25; Delhi reprint, 1971, *Aitareya Brāhmaṇa*, ii, 5, 5, "Thrice round the sacrifice Agni goeth like a charioteer" (he says), "for he like a charioteer goes round the sacrifice".

[16]W. Norman Brown's most recent article on the subject is *Duty as Truth in Ancient India*, in "Proceedings of the American Philosophical Society", Vol. 116, No. 3, June 1972, pp. 252-268. My own article is Chapter 20.

[17]P. T. Srinivas Iyengar, *The Gāyatrī*, Madras, 1922, p. 11.

initiation is clothed with a skin to symbolize the foetus being encased in the amniotic membrane. The *Sāvitrī mantra* is the chief one used for bringing about Savitā, the generator.

This is the general implication of *mantras* down the ages, namely, that they involve the freedom to alter destiny by ushering in a kind of rebirth. Also the initiate of the Buddhist Vajrayāna enters a new and mysterious world, as suggested by the *Guhyasamājatantra*.[18] "The pledge (*samaya*) and vow (*saṃvara*) said to be liberated from worldly conduct, when protected by all the 'diamonds' (*vajra*), is pronounced 'practice of *mantras*' ".

Varieties in Terms of Fruits

These textual statements of *mantra* varieties exemplify speech as the "cow-of-plenty". The previously mentioned varieties in degrees of loudness of course also belong here.

Turning to the much later Purāṇic classifications, we appeal to the *Agnipurāṇa*, the *Mantraparibhāṣā*, chapter, v.14-15.[19]

> One should imagine them, beginning with the Siddhas, as follows : The Siddha, by reason of surpassing merits. When there is Siddha, the Siddha is through recitation (*japa*). The Sādhya is by way of recitation (*japa*), worship (*pūjā*), oblation (*huta*), etc. The Susiddha by just meditation (*dhyāna*). The

[18] B. Bhattacharya, ed., *Guhyasamāja Tantra*, Baroda, reprint, 1967, p. 156. 16-17.

[19] Ānandāśrama ed., p. 471 :

siddhādin kalpayed evaṃ siddho 'tyantaguṇair api |
siddhe siddho japāt sādhyo japapūjāhutādinā || 14
susiddho dhyānamātreṇa sādhakaṃ nāśayed ariḥ |
duṣṭārṇapracuro yaḥ syān mantraḥ sarvavininditaḥ || 15.

On the occasion of the Second World Sanskrit Conference, Torino, Italy, June 1975, Professor Hélène Brunner informed the writer that these terms, according to various texts, refer to a given disciple. Her position is justified in a valuable work, "*Una tantra du nord : le* Netra Tantra", in BEFEO, Tome LXI, 1974, p. 169. However, in Rasik Vihari Joshi, *Le rituel de la dévotion Kṛṣṇaite*, Pondichéry, 1959, pp. 20-21, the terms are used for magical squares each containing four smaller squares, which the master evaluates to determine how the incantation will work for the disciple. Even here the terms *siddha*, etc., can be understood as types of mantras in agreement with the *Agnipurāṇa*. There seem to be different traditions for the use of these terms, and so the *Agnipurāṇa's* version is justifiably understood at face value.

Ari would destroy the performer (*sādhaka*). Whatever mantra abounds in bad letters should be completely shunned (*sarva-vinindita*).

Here the varieties called Siddha and Sādhya evidently agree with the Vedic *mantra*, according to Haug's description.[20]

The *Agnipurāṇa* chapter (verses 1-3A) starts with the varieties in terms of syllables : "O twice-born one, the 'garland-mantras' (*mālā-mantra*) are said to be mantras with more than twenty syllables. 'Mantras' have more than ten syllables. Less than that (*tadarvāg*), they are called '*bījas*'". The author thereby clarifies that performance is by way of a variety, and points out that the varieties establish the speed and degree of success, namely enjoyment (*bhukti*) and liberation (*mukti*), with the longer the mantra the shorter the time.

The *Agnipurāṇa* continues (verses 3B-5A) with a well-known division by sex or gender[21] : "The species of *mantras* are of three kinds by way of the female, male, and neuter. The female *mantras* end with the wife (*jāyā*) of Vahni (the Fire God) (i.e. Svāhā). The neuter ones end with *namaḥ*. The remaining ones are the masculine ones, and these are approved in the cases of subduing and ruining (of an adversary). The female ones (approved) in the cases of eradication of disease, and minor acts. The neuter ones (approved) in other situations". Here the varieties concern the type of *siddhi* aimed at, the female ones for appealing to inimical forces to desist, the male ones for domineering the opposing side, and the neuter ones otherwise, and so for miscellaneous fruits. Tucci in his 1928 article cites the *Śāradātilaka* (Calcutta ed., 2d *paṭala*, 57-58) for a further clarification of the three genders, saying : ". . . . a *mantra* must end with one of the following words: *huṃ*, *phaṭ*, *svāhā*, *namaḥ*. According as a *mantra* is concluded by the first two syllables or the third or the fourth, it is called masculine, feminine, and neuter."[22] He points out that the Buddhist

[20]Martin Haug, *The Aitareya Brahmanam of the Rigveda*, Vol. I, Bombay, 1863, Introduction, p. 2.

[21]Ānandāśrama ed., p. 470 :

strīpuṃnapuṃsakatvena tridhā syur mantrajātayaḥ // 3
strīmantrā vahnijāyāntā namontāś ca napuṃsakāḥ /
śeṣāḥ pumāṃsas te śastā vaśyoccāṭanakeṣu ca // 4
kṣudrakriyāmayadhvaṃse striyo 'nyatra napuṃsakaḥ /.

[22]Giuseppe Tucci, *Notes on the Laṅkāvatāra*, in "Indian Historical Quarterly", IV-3, 1923; he discusses the *Laṅkāvatāra-sūtra's dhāraṇī-s*, pp. 553-556.

Tantras have a classification of *mantra* and *vidyā*, but of course Hindu *Tantras*, such as the *Yoginī-tantra*, also have this.[23] In this case, the *Agnipurāṇa's* "male *mantra*" (*puṃmantra*) is called simply "*mantra*" : and the "female *mantra*" (*strī-mantra*) is called "*vidyā*".

The Buddhist *Tantra Susiddhikara-mahātantra-sādhanopāyika-paṭala*, extant in Tibetan translation, states[24]:

> Mantras which have few syllables and have *Oṃ* and *Svāhā*, speedily accomplish all propitiatory rites (*śāntika-karma*).
> The *mantras* with a plenitude of vowels and consonants and are equipped with *Hūṃ* as well as *Phaṭ*, are used by the wise for harsh rites (*abhicāruka-karma*).
> The wise should apply *mantras* other than the preceding, and which have the field of the supreme (*paramārtha*) word, for prosperity rites (*pauṣṭika-karma*).

In this description, it is a *mantra* useful for prosperity rites that is the logical candidate for equivalence to the neuter one of the other classification. The third verse of the *Susiddhikara's* exposition does not contain the word *namaḥ*, but possibly alludes to it by the terminology "supreme word" since *namaḥ* is used to express homage to a deity or being superior to the human state.

The preceding and further indications of the present paper for the fruits of the *vidyā* permit an immediate comparison with the Upaniṣadic *vidyā-s*. Thus K. N. Aiyar points out three kinds of fruits of those *vidyā-s* according to the *Vedānta-sūtras* : (1) *duri-*

[23] *Yoginītantra*, Venkateśvara Press, Bombay, 1962, p. 401 : / *mantrāḥ puṃdevatāḥ proktā vidyāḥ strīdevatāḥ smṛtāḥ* /. See also RANIERO GNOLI, *Luce delle Sacre Scritture* (*Tantrāloka*) *di Abhinavagupta*, Torino, 1972, p. 718, but here the *vidyā* is not associated with *SVĀHĀ*; and later (p. 721), when assigning the respective functions or operations of certain *mantras*, *SVĀHĀ is assigned* "l'oblazione" as one would expect for its operation in the old Vedic ritual; and there is no suggestion of its being a female *mantra* as mentioned in the sources which I cite.

[24] Because of textual difficulties with the Peking Kanjur version of the Japanese photo edition, Vol. 9, p. 54-5.3, I also consulted the Narthang Kanjur version, from which I adopted the reading *don dam tshig* (*paramārtha-pada*), "supreme word". Both editions were unsatisfactory for what I translate "vowels and consonants" (the presumed original Sanskrit being *ālikāli*, for which see F. EDGERTON, *Buddhist Hybrid Sanskrit Dictionary*). There was no difficulty with the remainder of the three verses.

takṣaya, warding off of calamities; (2) *aiśvaryaprāpti*, gaining the occult powers which render the possessor invincible; (3) *krama-mukti*, successive release by way of knowledge, thus reaching the Saguṇa Brahman.[25] These fruits appear to go with the female *mantra* now called *vidyā*, and seem also to illustrate the *Agni-purāṇa's Susiddha* type of *mantra* amounting to meditation (*dhyāna*), especially referred to as *upāsanā-s* or meditative exer-cises in the Upaniṣadic context. Therefore, the *vidyā-s* of the *Upaniṣads* may be taken as the forerunner of the later tantric "female *mantra*".

A Tibetan text in my possession with numerous examples of the three kinds of *mantras* (male, female, and neuter), may be cited.[26] This includes the *mantras* of the group called "the four gods of the sublime heart", stressed by Atiśa, the influential Buddhist *paṇḍit* who came to Tibet in 1042 :

1. *Oṃ mune mune mahāmune ye svāhā*. This is the *mantra* of Gautama Buddha, but it is also the *vidyā* of the *Aṣṭasāhasrikā Prajñāpāramitā*, and so the *svāhā* emphasizes the female side, insight (*prajñā*) of the Buddha.
2. *Oṃ maṇi padme hūṃ*, the celebrated six-syllabled *mantra* of the male deity Avalokiteśvara.
3. *Oṃ tāre tuttāre ture svāhā*, the ten-syllabled *vidyā* of the goddess Tārā.
4. *Oṃ caṇḍamahāroṣaṇa hūṃ phaṭ*, the ten-syllabled *mantra* of the fierce male deity, the blue Acala.

In further agreement with the classifications, the formula *Gate gate pāragate pārasaṃgate bodhi* [*ya*] *svāhā*, is the *vidyā* of the goddess Prajñāpāramitā since the formula concludes the cele-brated Heart-*sūtra* (*Prajñāpāramitā-hṛdaya-sūtra*). And when we find the formula for the "Healing Buddha" (*Bhaiṣajya-guru*) to conclude with a *svāhā*, this may be understood as the female healing function, as a fruit of the female formula according to previous citation of the *Agnipurāṇa*.

This same Tibetan text has many illustrations of the *namaḥ* formula, as a third kind. It is intriguing that this so-called "neu-

[25] *The Thirty-two Vidyās*, pp. 9-10.

[26] The book is entitled : *Gzuṅs sṅags daṅ / de bzhin gśegs pa'i mtshan / bka' 'gyur sñiṅ po sogs kha 'don byed rgyu zab mo'i rigs phyogs gcig tu bkod pa don siṅg lhun grub ces bya ba /*.

ter" (*napuṃsaka*) formula was always translated into Tibetan, while the formulas referred to as "male" and "female" were transcribed phonetically. This does show that the fidelity of pronunciation of the "male" and "female" ones is an important issue, while a possible mispronouncing of the "neuter" one seems not to have been an issue. For example, the text includes : "Reciting 'I bow to the Tathāgata Akṣobhya' [completely translated into Tibetan], one purifies all the obscuration of evil *karma* and sin, and is born, by transformation from a lotus, in Akṣobhya's field (*kṣetra*)". Since this text always specifies a fruit from the recitation of a *namaḥ* formula, and only does so for a few cases of the "male" and "female" formulas, the implication is clear that this text agrees with the *Agnipurāṇa* in assuming a well-defined fruit from the "male" or "female" kind; while the "neuter" kind, standing for all the miscellaneous cases, must have a particular fruit specified in each case, since there would be no way of inferring the fruit from the mere fact that it is a "neuter" kind.

Speaking generally, Abhayākaragupta in his *Munimatālaṃkāra* (extant only in Tibetan translation) states : "Furthermore, *man* is knowledge; *traiṇa* is protection. This knowledge (which knows) and compassion (which protects) is referred to by the term *mantra*; and the syllables of such affiliation are also called *mantras*. Those for the purpose of eliminating nescience (*avidyā*) and promoting clear vision (*vidyā*) are the *vidyā-s*".[27]

The overlapping with the word *dhāraṇī* can be observed from Jñānavajra's commentary on the *Vajravidāraṇa-dhāraṇī* (a *Tantra* of the Buddhist tantric deity Vajrapāṇi). Again from the Tibetan: "*Dhāraṇī* is of two kinds : *vidyā-dh.* and *mantra-dh.* Of these, the present work is called a *mantra-dh*".[28] Notice that the varied usage of the word *mantra* resulted in adding the word *dhāraṇī* in this type of classification to indicate the respective evocation of female and male deities, and in the present case, as Jñānavajra mentions, it is a *mantra-dhāraṇī* since the male deity Vajrapāṇi is evoked. An earlier usage of the word *dhāraṇī*, as Tucci mentioned in the 1928 article, was to indicate a long formula made up of a series of *mantras*. Jñānavajra states in agreement, "Be-

27In the Tibetan translation, *Thub pa'i dgoṅs pa'i rgyan*, Tibetan Tanjur, Photo edition, Vol. 101, p. 241-2.2, 3.

28In the photo ed. of Tibetan Tanjur, Vol. 78, p. 169-4.3.

sides, because it retains many meanings and terms, it is called *dhāraṇī*. The *Vajraśekhara* states that the *dhāraṇī* both provides a basis for all virtuous *dharmas*, and renders the meaning unforgotten".[29] Hence, the word *dhāraṇī* practically has the usage of memory", but more generally I render it "retention".[30] Among the two kinds, the *mantra-dh.* is obviously the *dhāraṇī* made up of a string of *mantras*, while the *vidyā-dh.* is perforce a *dhāraṇī* made up of a string of *vidyā-s*. If one were to translate the two expressions—granted the hazard—it could be something like "retention of incantations" (*mantra-dh.*) and "retention of charms" (*vidyā-dh.*)

Elsewhere I translated an explanation of three kinds of *mantra: mantra, vidyā* and *dhāraṇī*. In short, the *mantra* constitutes a non-duality type of recitation, i.e. the non-duality of *insight* upon the void, and *protection* from signs and discursive thought. The *vidyā* opposes nescience (*avidyā*). The *dhāraṇī* holds, i.e. retains, the Buddha-*dharmas*.[31] This classification is consistent with the preceding explanations of this essay except for having *dhāraṇī* as a third kind. The meaning of a *dhāraṇī* as a separate type from both *mantra* and *vidyā* can be observed as a memorial device. For example, there is the *A-RA-PA-CA-NA* formula of the large Prajñāpāramitā scripture of Buddhism.[32] Thus the scripture states, "The syllable *A* is the gate to all *dharmas*, because of their non-birth from the beginning" (*ādy-anutpannatvād*). Each of the remaining syllables is said to be a gate to all *dharmas*, *RA* "because they are free from dirt (*rajas*)"; *PA* "because of the settling of the supreme meaning (*paramārtha*)";

[29]*Ibid.*, Vol. 78, p. 169-5.3, 4, and worth giving : / *yaṅ na don tshig maṅ po 'dzin pas gzuṅs so / rdo rje rtse mo las dge pa'i chos thams cad kyi rten pa byed pas na yaṅ gzuṅs so / yaṅ na mi brjed pa'i don gyis na gzuṅs zhes bya'o* /.

[30]This appears also to be the meaning of *dhāraṇī* as in Asaṅga's *Bodhisattvabhūmi* (U. Wogihara ed., pp. 272-274) where four kinds are given and defined : "retention of doctrine" (*dharma-dh.*). "retention of meaning" (*artha-dh.*) "retention of *mantra*" (*mantra-dh.*), and "retention for acquiring patience" (*kṣāntilābhāya-dh.*).

[31]Alex Wayman, *The Buddhist Tantras; Light on Indo-Tibetan Esotericism*, New York, 1973, pp. 64-65.

[32]The following exposition of the *A-RA-PA-CA-NA* formula is based both on Edward Conze, *The Large Sutra on Perfect Wisdom*, Berkeley, 1975, p. 160; and on the *Munimatālaṃkāra*, Tibetan translation (cf. note 27, above), p. 240-5 to p. 241-1.

CA "because their decease (*cyavana*) and birth are not the object of consciousness"; *NA* "because they are free from names (*nāma*)". The syllables stem from the initials of the respective terms. Therefore, *A-RA-PA-CA-NA* is a formula for remembering in the given order the five statements about all *dharmas*, and thus illustrates *dhāraṇī* as a memorial device.

For other ways of referring to varieties, we may resort to the *Agni-purāṇa*. In its *Mantraparibhāṣā* chapter, verses 8-10, it speaks mysteriously :[33]

> A *mantra* which is sleeping, or has merely been awakened, does not attain success. The time of sleep is the great evocation (*mahā-āvāha*). The waking state is the conveyance by way of the right.
> One should ascertain the waking time of the *Āgneya-Manu* from the opposite of that of the *Saumya-mantra*, i.e. the day of both respectively.
> (The *Svara*) should avoid the Manu-s when there are hostile letters, etc., bad asterisms (*ṛkṣa*) and zodiacal signs (*rāśi*), etc. The *Svara* (should avoid) the Kurus when an enemy has intervened to the purpose of attaining the kingdom.

Here, the term "Manu" is known to mean a *mantra*, but also the Manu-s in Purāṇic tradition represent the solar lineage; while the Kuru-s represent the lunar lineage. Hence, the "Kuru" is also employed for a certain kind of formula, and it is evidently the "female" kind in contrast to the *Manu* as the "male" mantra. This is made certain by the end of the above citation, "when an enemy has intervened to the purpose of attaining the kingdom", at which time the *Svara* should be of the Manu-type that subdues the adversary and not of the Kuru-type, which being female, serves for eradication of disease, etc. On the other hand, when the stellar signs are unfavorable, what is needed is the female-*mantra*, or Kuru, to appease the gods, and not the male-

[33]Ānandāśrama ed., p. 470 :
suptaḥ prabuddhamātro vā mantraḥ siddhiṃ na yacchati |
svāpakālo mahāvāho jāgaro dakṣiṇāvahaḥ || 8
āgneyasya manoḥ saumyamantrasyaitadviparyayāt |
prabodhakālaṃ jānīyād ubhayor ubhayor ahaḥ || 9
duṣṭarkṣarāśividveṣivarṇādīn varjayen manūn ||
rājyalābhopakārāya prārabhyāriḥ svaraḥ kurūn || 10

mantra which would only make matters worse. This interpretation is consistent with the *Śivasvarodaya* (v.100).[34] "During the flow of the Moon, poison is destroyed; the Sun leads to control over the powerful. During Suṣumnā, there is liberation. One *deva* stands in three forms." Here the flow of the Moon is equivalent to the female-*mantra* or Kuru; the flow of the Sun is equivalent to the male-*mantra* or Manu. The "Manu" and the "Kuru" are respectively the *mantra* and the *vidyā* of the previous terminology. Furthermore, the *Agnipurāṇa* apparently intends the fiery *mantra* (*Āgneya-Manu*) to be taken as the male-*mantra*, and the mild (*Saumya*) one to be understood as the female-*mantra*. Hence, when the male one is awake, the female one is asleep, and vice versa. This terminology of "awake" and "asleep" may amount to a striking way of emphasizing the fact that they cannot be simultaneous, since the fiery or male *mantra* and the mild or female *mantra* serve contrasting purposes. But since both are expressions of the goddess Vāc, the goddess herself is neither awake nor asleep.

The phrase "conveyance by way of the right" for the waking state agrees with my citation elsewhere of the Buddhist *Tantra Saṃvarodaya* : "Having entered by the left, the right is the path of leaving".[35] Here expiration of the breath is said to be by way of the right; in-breathing by way of the left. The *Anugītā* (Sect. 21, verse 15) says[36] : "Then the *Prāṇa* appeared, strengthening speech. Therefore, it (*prāṇa*), having reached expiration, speech never speaks up." According to the *Agnipurāṇa*, this is the time when the *mantra* is successful. There must also be what the *Anugītā* calls the "moving" (*jaṅgama*) mind, which is in the dominion of the goddess. In apparent agreement, there is Śrī-Lakṣmī's comment on the Buddhist tantric work *Pañcakrama:* "The cause is *prāṇa*, the effect is *mantra;* and their reality (*tattva*) is the 'reality of *mantra*' ".[37]

[34]The popular edition of Banaras City, Bāhū Thakur Prasād Gupta Bookseller, reads : /

candracāre viṣahate (*sic.* for *-hati*) *sūryo balivaśaṃ nayet* /
suṣumnāyāṃ bhaven mokṣa eko devas tridhā sthitaḥ //

[35]Wayman, *The Buddhist Tantras,* p. 159.

[36]Critical ed. :

tataḥ prāṇaḥ prādurabhūd vācam āpyāyayan punaḥ /
tasmād ucchvāsam āsādya na vāg vadati karhicit //15

[37]This passage is in my *Yoga of the Guhyasamājatantra; the Arcane Lore of Forty Verses,* (Motilal Banarsidass, Delhi, 1977).

Now, the *Anugītā* also says (Sect. 21, verse 14): "Verily, the goddess speech always dwells among the *Prāṇa* and *Apāna*" (*prāṇāpānāntare devī vāg vai sma tiṣṭhati*). The *Anugītā* said earlier (verse 7) : "The *Apāna*, having become lord (*pati*), consequently summons the *apānatā*. That (*apānatā*) (the inhalation) one declares the intelligence (*mati*) of the mind (*manas*). The mind in consequence considers".[38] Accordingly, this mind must be the "stationary" (*sthāvara*) kind, which being Prajāpati's own, is superior to the goddess.

But what does the *Agnipurāṇa* mean by saying, "The time of sleep is the great evocation ?" We suppose that the *ṛṣis* were engaged in the "great evocation" per *Bṛhaddevatā* (i.3): "at the time when the seers had their vision of the *mantras*" (*ṛṣīṇāṃ mantra-dṛṣṭiṣu*).[39] The Jaina work *Riṣṭasamuccaya* (verse 113) says: "That dream is a dream told by a god where a *mantra* (sacred formula) is recited." In an article citing this Jaina passage, I pointed out that the dream level of Vāc is called *madhyamā*, and is the kind of speech dissociated from consciousness; and so the *mantra* by repetition reaches the point where it is objectified as told by a god, as in a dream.[40] Hence, the *mantra* is heard in the normal waking state and is seen (as by the *ṛṣis*) in a *yoga* state of dream. The author of this chapter of the *Agnipurāṇa* apparently wished to reassure the reader that he was not denying that an extraordinary kind of sleep is a "great evocaton" (as would also be the message of the *Māṇḍūkya Upaniṣad*) when he stated that "a *mantra* which is sleeping, or has merely been awakened, does not attain success."

[38]Critical ed. :

tām apānaḥ patir bhūtvā tasmāt preṣyaty apānatām |
tām matiṃ manasaḥ prāhur manas tasmād avekṣate || 7

[39]Various tales of *ṛṣi-s* seeing *mantras* are related in the *Aitareya* and *Kauṣītaki Brāhmaṇas*. There is the celebrated story of Kavaṣa Ailūṣa (the "Śūdra Ṛṣi"), who saw the hymn of fifteen verses called the *Aponaptrīya*. The Gods, because able to see the "silent praise" (*tūṣṇīmśaṃsa*) invisible to the Asuras, were able to defeat their enemy. In the episode of Indra's fight with Vṛtra, when the Gods were frightened away, and Indra's friends, the Maruts, exhorted him saying, "Strike, O Bhagavat ! kill (Vṛtra) ! show thy prowess !"—according to Martin Haug's translation (*The Aitareya Brahmanam*, Vol. II, Bombay, 1863, p. 192) "This saw a *Rishi*, and recorded it in the verse *vṛtrasya* . . . ." KEITH, *Rigveda Brahmanas*, p. 177, agrees but is less clear.

[40]WAYMAN, *Significance of Dreams in India and Tibet*, in "History of Religions", Vol. 7, No. 1 (Aug., 1967), pp. 4, 11. This essay appears above.

THE MEANING OF MANTRAS

The preceding section should have made it clear that when the texts themselves speak of varieties of *mantras*, the intention was to relate them to designated fruits. However, there is another way of classifying *mantras*, and this is in terms of their meaning. The skepticism about the meaning of *mantras* is very ancient in India, but we shall see that the problem involves different species of ritual utterance.

Certain differences of ritual formulas emerge from initial considerations. Thus, there would appear to be an inherent difference between the kind of formulas which abound among the minute details of a ritual, and the kind of formulas which a candidate cherishes and repeats daily. For example, in Buddhist *tantra* ritual the candidate is drawn into the near retinue of the *maṇḍala* deities as he pronounces the so-called "diamond pledge" (*vajra-samaya*), *ĀH KHAM vīra HŪM*[41]; but this does not seem to occur in another ritual circumstance.[42] Among the daily recitation types of formula is of course the *Gāyatrī* of the Hindus and the formula *OM maṇi padme HŪM* of the Buddhists. It can be stated generally that the disciple daily repeats the formula associated with his tutelary deity (*iṣṭadevatā*).

Of a different nature are the three mystical utterances (*vyāhṛti*) which the *Śatapathabrāhmaṇa* ascribed to Prajāpati.[43] He uttered *Bhūr* which became this earth, subsequently to be described by the layers of Pātāla, the underworld. He uttered *Bhuvaḥ*, which became this firmament, subsequently to be described by the stories of the "upon-world," the *bhūmi-s*. He uttered *Svar*, which became that sky, later the pinnacle of existence or heaven (*svarga*). In the Buddhist *Tantras* there is a set of seed syllables, *Oṃ*, *Āḥ*, *Hūṃ*, repeated innumerable times. The three are correlated to

[41]WAYMAN, *The Ritual in Tantric Buddhism of the Disciple's Entrance into the Maṇḍala*, in "Studia Missionalia", Vol. 23 (1974), p. 45.

[42]In Brahmanism probably the most extensive collection of these occasional mantras is now to be found in the *Śrautakośa*, of which the English section has been published in two monumental volumes by the Vaidika Saṁśodhana Maṇḍala, Poona, 1958 and 1962.

[43]According to the *Śatapathabrāhmaṇa*, XI, I, 6, 2-4, Prajāpati was born along with the year, and when first he spoke the words *Bhūr*, etc., did so like a child with words of one and two syllables; cf. J. EGGELING, tr., Part V. SBE XLIV, pp. 12-13.

the three mysteries of the Buddha and to the numerous threefold groups. There is something in common between the three *vyāhṛti-s* of the Brāhmaṇic literature and the three seed syllables of the Buddhist *Tantras*. That is, both sets have an element of the memorial device, the *dhāraṇī*. By this I would suggest that in reciting the sets of three one may recall the associations—in the case of the three *vyāhṛti-s*, the contents and deities of the three worlds;[44] in the case of the three seed syllables, the various threefold sets, as with *Oṃ* remembering the night, with *Āḥ* the day, and with *Hūṃ* the juncture of day and night.[45] So understood, the memorial syllables have no meaning in the ordinary sense; their meaning is in what they intend by way of the respective associations.

On the other hand, numerous *mantras*, and the Vedic ones are principally of this nature, consist of, or include words with meaning to those who understand the language (here Sanskrit). Naturally, even allowing for such meaning, there is occasionally some obscurity with difficulty of interpretation. In the classification of *mantra* as the male formula and *vidyā* as the female one, there are numerous cases with formulas having standard word meanings, with additional syllables at both ends that are of the memorial type. Since the *Tārā vidyā* (*Oṃ tāre tuttāre ture svāhā*) occurs in the *Guhyasamājatantra*, Chap. XIV, *Ratnākaraśānti* in the *Kusumāñjali-guhyasamāja-nibandha-nāma* has a verse (his own ?)[46]:

> Precisely *buddhi* (discrimination) is the root of knowing. It achieves through offering. Hence, at the beginning of the *mantra* is *Oṃ*, and it is made clear at the end with *Svāhā*.

This verse explains the *Oṃ* as associated with *buddhi*, the root of knowing, which comes first; and explains the *Svāhā* as the

[44]To which may be added the three strides of Viṣṇu according to *Śatapatha-brāhmaṇa* I.9,3,10. Viṣṇu strode on earth by means of the *Gāyatrī* meter, in the air by means of the *Triṣṭubh* meter, and in the sky by means of the *Jagatī* meter.

[45]Cf. WAYMAN, *The Buddhist Tantras,* Tables 14 and 15, for a number of threefold sets going with the three seed syllables.

[46]This is in the Tibetan Tanjur, Japanese photo ed., Vol. 64, p. 168-3: */ blo tsam ñid śes rtsa ba yin / mchod pa las ni rab tu byed / des na sṅags kyi thog mar Oṃ / mthar ni Svā-hā zhes gsal byed /*.

clarification or revelation at the end.[47] The same work explains the *Tārā vidyā* : *Tāre* ("O Tārā") because she rescues by bringing to the other side (i.e. is the *pāramitā*). Now *tud-* is pain; *tuttā*, suffering; *Tuttāre* ("O Tārā, from suffering"), because she rescues from pain. Then *Ture* ("O Turā, the fast one"), because she is fast, i.e. rescues speedily. Thus *Ratnākaraśānti* explains the *vidyā* as composed of two kinds of elements, the syllables *Oṃ* and *Svāhā* which have a general intention no matter what the *vidyā*, and then the individual words of the particular *vidyā* which have meanings of the lexicons along with grammatically defined inflexions, in this case the vocatives.

But also, even when the words of the *mantra* appear to have the ordinary meanings of words, there can arise an argument over their meaning and their function, just as happens in the case of any other ancient sentence which now can occasion an argument between prospective translators. For example, in the *Nyāya-Mañjarī* (section translated in "The Calcutta Review", Oct. 1955), the opponent had argued that a *mantra* renders its assistance to a Vedic rite only by its recitation, referring to the case of the *mantra*, "Hear, oh slabs of stone !" (*śṛṇota grāvāṇaḥ*), and observing that stones cannot hear. The author of the *Nyāya-Mañjarī* replied : "*Ṣṛṇota grāvāṇaḥ* is. . a miraculous act by the influence of which slabs of stone can even hear". In this case, both sides of the argument have a point. The opponent could argue that this remark just comes up in the course of the ritual, and evocation is more to be ascribed to the daily-recited formula like the *Gāyatrī*. The *Nyāya-Mañjarī* author is also on good ground, because he is emphasizing the role of faith or conviction, that those going through the ritual should believe that events take place as stated

[47]For some other explanations of *Oṃ*, see K. V. Gajendragadkar, *Neo Upanishadic Philosophy*, Bharatiya Vidya Bhavan, Bombay, 1959, pp. 26-29. It should be understood that Ratnākaraśānti's explanation has been specialized for the case of a *vidyā*, as shown by the *Svāhā* at the end. That is, the *Oṃ* is here the seed from which comes the successes attributed to the *vidyā*. Since the preeminent success of a *vidyā* is the divine knowledge leading to liberation, the *Oṃ* is here explained as the root of knowing. The term *buddhi* is here involved, apparently since it is the process leading to the Buddha, who has been enlightened. While the term is employed in various ways in the Indian texts, the usage here seems about the same as in the *Bhagavad-gītā*, Chap. II, verse 39, including : "associated with which *buddhi*, O Pārtha, you will get rid of the bondage of *karma*".

(whether or not they do), this firm belief ensuring the success of the whole ritual. In any case, this shows that the insiders of a cult frequently do not agree on the meaning or function of a *mantra;* and so, the meaning or use of *mantras* cannot be established by the criterion that all the followers of the cult agree upon it.[48]

Then notice also how some formulas which seem meaningless are ascribed meanings in the commentaries ! Once I noticed in a commentary on the Buddhist *dhāraṇī* of Vimaloṣṇīṣa these *vidyā-s/ kṣaṇa kṣaṇa / kṣiṇi kṣiṇi / kṣuṇu kṣunu /*.[49] As usual these were transcribed into phonetic Tibetan letters. The explanations were translated; and the three pairs were explained respectively : "Guard, guard !" (*sruṅs śig ṣruṅs śig*), "Rescue, rescue !" (*skyobs śig kyobs śig*), "Nourish, nourish !"(*tshos śig tshos śig*). Besides, it appears tnat any *mantra* which is "meaningless" in terms of its constituents might also be considered meaningful in terms of the intended fruits to be derived from the ritual utterance.[50]

Still another case is when a *mantra* appears meaningful, and yet the commentary ascribes an unexpected meaning.[51] Thus a work called *Balimālikā* preserved in the Tibetan Tanjur canon, consists of *mantras* transcribed into Tibetan, and a translation into Tibetan is regularly added. Once I noticed therein the *mantra hana hana*, which we would expect to mean "Destroy, destroy !". But the translator added the Tibetan *snun snun*, which means "Prick, prick !" and seems to preserve a Vedic meaning of the verb *han-*, "to hurl a dart upon".[52]

[48]Cf. JHA, *The Pūrva-Mīmāṃsā-Sūtras*, pp. 43-54, which takes up various arguments by the opponent to the effect that mantras are meaningless and then replies defending the significance of *mantras*.

[49]This *dhāraṇī* has a very long title, and the author of its commentary is known in Tibetan as Lhan cig skyes pa'i rol pa (*Sahajalalita); it has No. 2688 in the Tohoku Catalog of the Kanjur-Tanjur; and the passage is in Derge Tanjur, *Rgyud*, Vol. Thu, f. 285b-1, 2.

[50]JHA. *The Pūrva-Mīmāṃsā-Sūtras*, p. 53, informs us "Examples of the interpretation of apparently meaningless *mantras* are given in the *Tantra-vārtika* (Translation, pp. 100-101)".

[51]Or, again, as Asaṅga's *Bodhisattvabhūmi* (Wogihara ed., p. 273) puts it: "Precisely this meaning of them (i.e. the *mantra* words) is, to wit, fruitlessness" (*ayam eva caiṣām artho yad uta nirarthatā*).

[52]I originally consulted this work in the Derge Tanjur, where it is included in the *Rgyud* (*Tantra* commentary) section but in the Narthang as well as the Peking Tanjur editions it is placed among the miscellaneous works concerned with grammar and lexicography.

In conclusion, the charge that *mantras* are meaningless is to be grouped with the innumerable other charges of meaninglessness that have been traded back and forth in India in past millenia, and the natural retort is that the opponent has either not been in a position, or has not taken pains to ascertain the meaning. And it is also obvious from the present study that later religious practices of India, such as the Buddhist *Tantra*, have a profound debt to the Vedic religion.

THE GODDESS SARASVATĪ—FROM INDIA TO TIBET

In the Vedic period, Vedic lore and learning developed on the banks of river Sarasvatī in North-west India. This river once flowed to the sea, but in time disappeared in the desert sands, as though to bring the Vedic period to an end. Thereafter the goddess of the same name, Sarasvatī, would convey this learning, and as the inspirer of eloquence became called by the Hindus Vāgdevī or the goddess of speech.

Swāmī Prajñānānanda (*Historical Development of Indian Music*)[1] conveniently presents the essentials of the Vedic worship of this deity. She was one of a triad of goddesses who, according to the commentator Sāyana, were conceived as three blazing flames of fire (*agni*); and Sarasvatī in time became preeminent as a fire by which there was communication with the gods. This author writes (p. 51): "In the mytho-historical literature, *Devī Sarasvatī*, the presiding deity of learning and all arts, was described as the tongue of the sacrificial fire (*agni-jihvā Sarasvatī*)". And again, "The ancient authors on music conceived and deified the primal sound, *Nāda*, as a symbol of the goddess *Sarasvatī.*" He refers (p. 56-57) to the *Śatapatha-Brāhmaṇa* (VII, 2.4.1-7), for the legendary association of the goddess with the Gandharvas, the celestial musicians. The Gandharva Viśvāvasu had stolen the nectar Soma from Gāyatrī (which is a certain meter, and also

[1]Published by Firma K. L. Mukhopadhyay, Calcutta, 1960.

the charm, *vidyā*, addressed to the Sun deity at dawn). When the *Devas* learned of the theft of Soma, they sent the beautiful maiden *Vāc* or Vāgdevī to rescue Soma. The Gandharvas are said to be fond of women and beauty, so when Vāgdevī approached, they went to the gods (the *devas*), and said, "Let yours be the Soma and let Vāc or Vāgdevī be ours." Since the Gandharvas had thus secured Sarasvatī for their ranks, from that time they excelled in music. This author also mentions that Śrī or Lakṣmī, the goddess of good fortune, was gradually separated from Sarasvatī though frequently paired with her.

J. N. Banerjea (*The Development of Hindu Iconography*)[2] provides the main details for the classical Hinduism period. As known by the *Purāṇas*, Sarasvatī is sometimes connected with Brahmā, both as his daughter and his consort, and sometimes with Viṣṇu as one of his consorts, Puṣṭi (who thrives). The Jains put her at the head of the Śrutadevatās and the Vidyādevīs. As an independent goddess (i.e. not a consort), she is usually described in such texts as the *Viṣṇudharmottara* as four-armed, white colored, dressed in white garments and decked with many ornaments, holding in her four hands any four of the following objects : manuscript, white lotus, rosary, musical instrument, water-vessel, and so on. The musical instrument is possibly the oldest emblem associated with her, although the manuscript is also old. A late Gupta form shows her in association with Brahmā; she is four-armed, with gift-bestowing gesture (*varamudrā*), the rosary (*akṣamālā*), the musical instrument (*vīṇā*), and the water-vessel (*kamaṇḍalu*) in her four arms. One of her names is Śāradā, which means "she who is autumnal," also the autumn moon; and the name also stands for a kind of Vīṇā or lute.

B. Bhattacharya (*The Indian Buddhist Iconography*)[3] summarizes the forms of Sarasvatī in the late Buddhist period, namely four types of the two-handed goddess, and a form with three faces and six arms. From his work comes the following :

(1) Mahāsarasvatī, resplendent like the autumn moon, rests on the moon over the white lotus, shows the gift-giving (*varada*) gesture in her right hand, carries in the left the white lotus with its stem. She has a smiling countenance (*smeramukhi*), is extre-

[2]Published by the University of Calcutta, 1956.
[3]Published by Firma K. L. Mukhopadhyay, Calcutta, 1958.

mely compassionate, wears garments decorated with white sandal decked in many ornaments; she appears a maiden of twelve years, and her bosom is uneven with half-developed breasts like flower-buds; she illumines the three worlds with the immeasurable light that radiates from her body. She is surrounded by four goddesses who are apparently facets of herself : Insight (*prajñā*) in front, Cleverness (*medhā*) to her right, Memory (*smṛti*) to her left, and backed up by Intelligence (*mati*).

(2) Varavīṇā Sarasvatī. She is distinguished by carrying in her two hands the Vīṇā, and she plays upon it.

(3) As Vajraśāradā (deification of the autumn), she has a crescent in her crown: is three-eyed, and two-armed, carrying the book in the left hand and the lotus in the right.

(4) Āryasarasvatī is also called Vajrasarasvatī, a common name of Sarasvatī among the Buddhist tantrics. She is a maiden of sixteen, in the prime of youth, has white complexion, and in her left hand holds a lotus stalk on which rests the Prajñāpāramitā book. No mention of what is in her right hand is made.

The other form which Bhattacharya found is Vajrasarasvatī, with three faces and six arms, in *pratyālīḍha āsana* (this means right foot bent forward, left retracted), on the red lotus. She is red in color, with right face blue and left face white. In her three right hands she carries the lotus on which is the Prajñāpāramitā book, the sword and curved blade; and in the three left, the skull bowl of Brahmā, the jewel and the wheel (*cakra*). An alternate description has a simple lotus (no mention of book on top) and a simple skull bowl (no mention of its being Brahmā's).

Passing to the Tibetan tradition, I have used the collection *Sgrub thabs kun btus*, Vol. Kha,[4] which is mainly given over to rituals of the three insight deities : Mañjuśrī, Sarasvatī, and the white Acala. The Sarasvatī section has seven works occupying consecutive folio side numbers 394-546, or about 150 folio sides, which I have surveyed for this paper. First some general remarks may be made.

(a) Since there is only one goddess, namely Sarasvatī, among the three "insight" deities, it follows that Prajñāpāramitā (who is occasionally depicted iconographically)[5] is here incorporated

[4]Dehradun. G. T. K. Lodoy, N. Gyaltsen and N. Lungtok, 1970.

[5]See frontispiece in Edward Conze, *Selected Sayings from the Perfection of Wisdom* (The Buddhist Society : London, 1955).

in the Sarasvatī treatment. The reason is suggested by a Mahāyāna scripture that was popular in both Tibet and China, the *Suvarṇaprabhāsa-sūtra*, which devotes a chapter to Sarasvatī setting forth her *sādhana*, together with the rite of expanding insight (*prajñā*) and cognition (*buddhi*).[6] At several places in the Tibetan materials, e.g., at f. no. 472, there is a discussion of the nature of *prajñā*. At f. no. 524, the *Prajñāśataka* is cited.[7] "Prajñā is the root of all merits, whether seen or unseen. Since it accomplishes both, first one should endeavor to promote insight". And the same folio side states : "Among the numerous means for promoting insight, the one that is best is the reliance on Devī Sarasvatī."

(b) There were numerous *sādhanas*, or evocation rituals of deities, translated into Tibetan; and the iconographical descriptions are not always included in Bhattacharya's pioneer and still invaluable work. Thus, he did not include a four-handed type; but in this Tibetan collection the Sarasvatī of the Bo-doṅ school is a four-handed one embraced by a four-handed Mañjughoṣa, although not having in her four hands the four hand symbols of the Gupta form previously mentioned. Both Purāṇic legends are represented in the collection : The white Sarasvatī of the Brahmin Kīla[8] school is called "Brahmā's daughter," although also referred to as a metamorphosis of Ārya Lokeśvara's great tooth, a legend contained in *Mkhas grub rje's Fundamentals of the Buddhist Tantras*.[9] The Sarasvatī in the lineage from Bo-doṅ paṇ-chen phyogs-las-rnam-rgyal makes her an emanation from Viṣṇu (in Tibetan, khyab' jug).

(c) It is of interest that where the age was given I could not find in the iconographical descriptions of this Tibetan collection the age "twelve" that was prevalent in the types Bhattacharya presented. The preference for the 16 yeared Sarasvatī in these *sādhanas* is also evidenced by the description of the breasts, usually "round, firm, high, and large." There is some significance in this switch, because as the *Guhyasamājatantra*, Chap. XV, 66, suggests, the twelve-yeared girl or boy was employed as a vessel for divi-

[6]Cf. Ferdinand D. Lessing and Alex Wayman, *Mkhas grub rje's Fundamentals of the Buddhist Tantras* (Mouton : The Hague, 1968), p. 111.

[7]This work is included in the Tibetan Tanjur, and attributed to Nāgārjuna.

[8]Sanskritized from the Tibetan name, Bram ze phur bu.

[9]See note 6 above.

nation of ritual success.[10] The 16-yeared form loses the possible divination connection, and by the suggestion of nubility fits the form of Viṣṇu's consort, called Puṣṭi ("thriving"). Also, the age of 16 agrees with the well-known Buddhist association of "insight" (*prajñā*) with the sixteen voidnesses (*śūnyatā*); and Sarasvatī's epithet Vāgdevī agrees with the sixteen vowels of the Sanskrit alphabet.

(d) These Tibetan materials help solve a problem alluded to by Madame Mallman[11] in her study of Mañjuśrī's iconography where she mentions (p. 16) that Mañjuśrī's association with Sarasvatī was previously pointed out by A. Foucher and by S. Lévi (the latter in his *Le Népal*), but that so far she has not found this in the Sanskrit text she consulted. In the esoteric *sādhana* of the red Sarasvatī descended from the Kashmirian *paṇḍit* Bhikṣaparama, the statement is made (at folio no. 521. 2) : "Now, here the esoteric evocation of the red Sarasvatī is explained according to the *Kṛṣṇayamāritantra.*" This indicates that the association of Sarasvatī with Mañjuśrī is in the *tantra* devoted to his angry form called *yamāri* or *yamāntaka*. Therefore, it should be in such a Sanskrit text that Sarasvatī would be thus set forth.

(e) These Tibetan *sādhanas* bring up some of their own problems. Thus, the divorce from the original association with the Sarasvatī river seems complete by such remarks as frequently occur, "Sarasvati dwells at the shore of the southern ocean." More fully (f. no. 480): "on the shore of the southern ocean, the dwelling of the *gandharva* maiden, in the pleasure grove of the Vidyādharas." The term "*gandharva*" should be understood by the previous explanation, namely, "heavenly musician." The Vidyādharas seem also to be flying spirits (cf. Kramrisch's illustration "Flying Vidyādhara"[12]).

The Tibetan materials at f. no. 444 call Sarasvatī the wife of the Gandharva Tambura. Now Prajñānānanda when discussing

[10]The reasons, as pointed to in Tsoṅ-kha-pa's annotation of the *Pradīpoddyotana* commentary on the *Guhyasamājatantra*, in the Japanese Photo edition, Vol. 158, p. 126-3-4,5, is the sexual isolation, hence, "puberty crisis" unmixed with the other sex. Chap. XV of the *Guhyasamāja* especially concerns dream and other auspices.

[11]Marie-Thérèse de Mallmann, *Etude iconographique sūr Mañjuśrī* (Ecole francaise d'Extreme-orient : Paris, 1964.)

[12]Stella Kramrisch *The Art of India* (Phaidon Publishers Inc. : London, 1954). Pl.68.

(p. 384) the varieties of *vīnās*, says : *"Tambura, tamburā* or *tānapurā* is known as the *tumburu-veenā"*. Thus, the name "Gandharva Tambura" probably means "Gandharva who plays the *tumburu-vīnā*". In Mallman (p. 94), Pañcaśikha, king of the Gandharvas, is playing a *Vīṇā;* and this entry is followed immediately by reference to "Sarvārthasiddha, king of the Vidyādhara," thus pairing the Gandharvas and Vidyādharas, as in the Tibetan text cited above.

An unsolved problem of the Tibetan *sādhanas* is the epithet of Sarasvatī at f. no. 520-3, 4, "messenger of Sāla."[13]

As to the descriptions of the goddess in this Tibetan collection, there are three basic forms: 1) the independent white goddess; (2) the independent red goddess; (3) the goddess as a consort.

(1) Here there is the white Sarasvatī of the Brahmin Kīla school, f. no. 413 : The officiant goes through the various preliminaries, such as bathing, taking a comfortable seat, taking refuge, generating the mind of enlightenment, and contemplating the four boundless states. Then he purifies the void with the *mantra "svabhāva"*, etc.[14] Thereupon he contemplates that from the realm of the void appears a temple inhabited by the gods and the host of accomplished *ṛṣis* and *gandharvas*, surrounded by delectable herbs of a Mt. Meru grove, within a white and pure ocean of milk. From a PAṂ appears a trunk of white lotus with large petals; and from an A a moon disk, and thereon a white HRĪḤ from which arises Vāg-devī Sarasvatī, with white body, one face, two-armed, her face calm, smiling, and lovely with charming youth of sixteen years, breasts firm and high, narrow waist, in squatting posture; with her hand holding an instrument of many strings of lapis lazuli, and evoking it with the fingers of her right hand, producing an ocean of sounds. The back half of her black glistening hair is tied together, and the remainder freely hangs down. She is beautified on the crown of head with a crescent moon, and on her head is tied a garland of white lotuses; and her tresses of hair are beautified with various jewels. The upper part of her body is covered with white silk, and the lower part

[13]The name "Sāla" was transcribed into Tibetan phonetically.

[14]The *mantra* is given fully on f. no. 541 : / *Oṃ svabhāvaśuddhāḥ sarvadharmāḥ svabhāvaśuddho'ham*/ "Oṃ. All dharmas are intrinsically pure. I am intrinscially pure".

wound around in variegated fashion like a rainbow. She is adorned with strings of gems and jewels and with nets having small bells. Her body, lacking self-existence, emits light rays without end and has in back a shining curtain in the form of a moon. The officiant contemplates in his own heart a lotus stalk with flowers that had been suspended downwards, that becomes directed upwards and takes on the aspect of a red lotus opening up; that within the flower is a moon, and on it a white OṂ. And he contemplates that while he hardly breathes out, the *nāda*[15] of the OṂ (meaning the small circle on top of the OṂ) emits white rays, which pass out through his right nostril, and enter the left nostril of Sarasvatī like the one he has contemplated (in front) but dwelling in the entrancing glade of the Vidyādharas on the shore of the southern ocean, and there entering her heart, attracts Sarasvatī in the gnosic form together with retinue, blazing with light, which leaving via her right nostril, like the rising moon of autumn, in an instant appears in the sky in front (of the officiant), filling the heavens with offering clouds. He offers flowers, etc. with the appropriate mantras, and then invites the goddess, while muttering with barely audible sound, while he holds breath within. He contemplates that the shining circle enters by his left nostril and merges with the OṂ in his heart. Then the OṂ transforms into a white eight petalled lotus with Sarasvatī and retinue.. (and so on down to) pervades his whole body with light, which dispels the darkness of ignorance and expands the light of intelligence directed without hindrance on all the knowable (and so on, for the concluding part of the ritual).

(2) There is the secret evocation of the red Sarasvatī in the lineage from the Kashmirian *paṇḍit* Bhikṣaparama (f. no. 505). The aim is to expand the fulfilment of *prajñā*. After the various ritual preliminaries, much the same as in the case of evoking the white Sarasvatī, the officiant meditatively ascends to the void contemplating all *dharmas* as void and without self. He contemplates that from the realm of the void there appears an eight-petalled lotus, that upon it his own mind changes into a red HRĪḤ, which sends out rays that make offering to the nobles, chase away the darkness of nescience of the sentient beings, and

[15]Compare the previous mention of *nāda* as a symbol of the goddess Sarasvatī.

amount to the light of *prajñā*; then returning, change into a knowledge mirror. That melts into light, and himself (i.e. the officiant) imagines that he becomes the Devī Sarasvatī with body red like the color of coral, with one face, two hands, the right hand holding the wish-granting jewel (*cintāmaṇi*) and the left hand holding the knowledge mirror (*jñānādarśa*), with right leg bent forward and left retracted, breasts firm and large, with head ornament of various jewels, earrings, necklace, hand bracelets, a girdle belt of pearl, a garment of variegated silk that flares out, the maiden aged exactly sixteen, countenance calm, smiling, and charming, (body) sending out innumerable rays; and he imagines that appearances are devoid of self-existence, like reflections on the mirror; and imagines on the head a white OṂ, on the neck a red ĀḤ, and in the heart, a black HŪṂ. (Then the officiant, as in the earlier rite attracts from the shore of the southern ocean Sarasvatī in the gnosic form just as he has imagined her above).

In explanation of the meditation procedures in the above cases of the white and the red Sarasvatī, the officiant first evokes the deity, here the goddess Sarasvatī, as the symbolic being (*samaya-sattva*)—a conventional representation; then attracts the knowledge being (*jñānasattva*)—usually from the sky, but here from the shore of the southern ocean, perhaps meaning the Milky Way; and the entrance of the knowledge being or circle into the officiant to be lodged in his heart, is held to establish the lineage of the deity in that person, who thus unifies the symbolic and knowledge beings.[16]

(3) Here, for the red Sarasvatī as a consort in the Bo-doṅ lineage, the officiant follows preliminaries somewhat along the lines of the preceding evocation of the red Sarasvatī, leading (f. no. 542) to the officiant's becoming meditatively Vajradevī Vāgīśvarī, the venerable Sarasvatī, whose color of body is red, with one face, four arms, of which the two basic ones embrace the male deity; and with the two remaining ones, in the left holds a precious musical instrument of many strings that is resting on her left side, which with the fingers of her remaining right hand she slowly plays, producing an ocean of musical sounds with the

[16]Cf. Lessing and Wayman, *Mkhas grub rje's* index, under "Beings", Symbolic Being and Knowledge Being.

full gamut of notes, gratifying all the Buddhas; while her two feet are in the lotus intertwine. Next to her is the Lord, the venerable Mañjughoṣa, with body red-yellow, one face, and four arms, with the two basic arms embracing the goddess; and with the two remaining ones, in the right wields a sword that blazes with light rays, and in the left holds a blue lotus on top of which is the Prajñāpāramitā book. Both of them have bodies wondrous to see, adored with all manner of jewels, and dwell amidst a furious light display. On the petal to their East is Insight (Prajñā), on the southern one is Intelligence (*mati*), on the western one is Memory (*smṛti*) and on the northern one is Cleverness (*medhā*). Each of these have one face, two arms, hold a sword with the right and a white lotus with the left, are each adorned with silk and jewels, and stand with their two feet together. The central deities and the retinue all have on their forehead an OṂ, on their neck an ĀḤ, in their heart a HŪṂ.

In this case, there was no indication of the goddess's age, although the presumption is that she is here also sixteen years old.

Finally, the elaborate ritual of the white Sarasvatī in the lineage from Bo-doṅ paṇ-chen phyogs-las-rnam-rgyal mentions a role of the goddess's *vīṇā* in the *yoga* of the watches (at f. nos. 473-474). This has to do with the *yoga* procedure of evoking the goddess at the *sandhis*, especially dawn and dusk, taking rest with the goddess's blessing, and being aroused by the sound of her *vīṇā*. The text says : "The great music from the sounding of the *vīṇā*, of the profound and far-reaching *dharma*, awakens him from all the inner and outer sleep; and he sees directly her face".

In conclusion, the powerful goddess personality of Sarasvatī that had developed in the Vedic period continued unabated through the many centuries, even though the iconographic details varied. Despite the adaptation of the goddess to later tantric meditation procedures, the goddess's ability to promote insight and inspiration did not suffer serious detraction even when she advanced from twelve to sixteen years.

THE TWENTY-ONE PRAISES OF TĀRĀ, A SYNCRETISM OF ŚAIVISM AND BUDDHISM

Dr. A. S. Altekar's wonderful and often-moving work named *The Position of Women in Hindu Civilisation from Prehistoric Times to the Present Day* mentions that Tantric writers joined the crusade against the Satī custom. Using the *Mahānirvāṇatantra* (X, 79-80) as authority, "They pointed out that woman was the embodiment of the Supreme Goddess, and boldly declared that if a person burnt her with her husband, he would be condemned to eternal hell." The Buddhist Tantras also stress the sacred nature of all women, and the fourteenth of the fourteen fundamental transgressions (*mūlāpatti*) of the Anuttara-yoga-tantra code is "to disparage women, who are the self-presence of Insight (*prajñā-svabhāva*)".[1] In the latter texts "Insight" (*prajñā*) is a name of the Great Mother.

There is no need here to dwell upon the importance of the Mother-goddess in India or upon the antiquity of the cult.[2] In

[1]Aśvaghōṣa's *Mūlāpattisaṃgraha* is not completely available in Sanskrit, as edited and translated by Sylvain Levi, *Journal Asiatique* (1929), 266-7. The fragment did not go down to the fourteenth one, which, therefore, is translated here from the Tibetan version.

[2]Among the numerous discussions of this subject, one may refer to the treatise by Dr. Dinesh Chandra Sircar, "The Śākta Pīṭhas," J. R. A. S. B. Letters, XIV (1948), 1-108, especially Appendix VI, *Śiva and Śakti in the Orthodox Indian Pantheon*, pp. 100, f.

the West, the analytical psychologist C. G. Jung has pioneered a theory that this is an archetype in the human psyche.

The worship of the Supreme Goddess under the name Tārā began with the Buddhists, and subsequently Tārā was admitted to the Hindu pantheon. This is recognized by Handiqui.[3] The brief text which forms the basis of the present essay covers the various moods, calm and fierce, of the Goddess, and does so with a frank employment of both Śaivitic and Buddhist terminology. It contains a rare use of the word *śakti* (female power) in application to a Buddhist goddess. Such a syncretism is also rare. Ordinarily, Buddhist works, and perhaps the same is the case with other Indian schools, disguise the influence of rival sects by adopting ideas and changing the terminology. The situation is comparable to that of a manufacturer whose product is really not different from that of a rival firm, but who maintains through packaging and advertising a distinct image in the public mind. While there are probably persons in every age who seek the underlying unity or secret resemblance, they usually gain little appreciation for their efforts because these do not appear to serve sectarian interests. Yet, the unknown author of our text managed to strike a winning combination. Waddell, who made a rather unsuccessful attempt to translate the verses from Tibetan,[4] mentions that the hymn is very popular among Lāmaist people in Tibet, Sikkim, etc. The circumstances that originally caused such a text to become prominent are probably those depicted by Dutt in his essay "Buddhism in Kashmir". Speaking of the Chinese pilgrim Hsuan Ts'ang's (or Yuan Chwang's) observations in Kashmir in the 7th cent., Dutt writes, "He saw 100 monasteries, but the religion followed in them, he remarks, was mixed, hinting thereby that the people worshipped both Buddha and Śiva."[5]

The Sanskrit for the text here edited was transcribed in the third chapter of the Tibetan translation of the *Sarvatathāgata-*

[3]Krishan Kanta Handiqui, *Naiṣadhacarita of Śrīharṣa*, Poona, 1956, 548-51.

[4]L. A. Waddell, "The Indian Buddhist Cult of Avalōkita and his Consort Tārā 'the Saviouress,' illustrated from the Remains in Magadha," J.R.A.S. (1894), 71-4.

[5]Nalinaksha Dutt, *Gilgit Manuscripts*, Vol. I (Srinagar, 1939), "Buddhism in Kashmir," 36-7.

mātṛtārāviśvakarmabhavatantra-nāma. The text was also translated as a separate work in the Kanjur collection, which was presumably Waddell's source. This information was found in a native Tibetan text on the Tantras by Khai Dub.[6] Using the transcribed Sanskrit, which is treated in that Tantra as a *dhāraṇī*, and the Tibetan translation, I made a draft edition and translation. Then I compared my materials with Godefroy de Blonay's edition of the text, based on two manuscripts, in his *Matériaux pour servir a l'histoire de la déesse buddhique Tārā* (Paris, 1895). Of course, most of his edition is correct, but many a verse has some serious fault—which may be the reason that he did not present a translation. However, the Kanjur transcription in the Derge edition has several corruptions, and there are also a few places where this transcribed Sanskrit does not agree with the Tibetan translation. Therefore, I was glad to have de Blonay's edition, and it proved helpful in several details. Also the edited colophon is a modification of the one in his edition.

The Tibetan Tanjur collection has a number of works based on this Tārā text. However, they are not true commentaries, but rather ritual works dealing with the twenty-one aspects of Tārā. These are principally by the *ācāryas* Sūryagupta and Candragōmin. The first work by Sūryagupta is the *sādhana*, or iconographic description for evoking the deity, for each of the twenty-one forms of Tārā. This work is presumably the source of the rough descriptions given by Waddell in the same article.[7] It is beyond my present essay to deal with these Tanjur texts. Some of them are important in Tantric Buddhism, but they could contribute little to the type of annotations which would bring out the original syncretic intention of the text. I expect to draw out this intention in annotations to my translation that follows the edited Sanskrit.

नमस् तारायै

नमस् तारे तुरे वीरे क्षणैर्द्युतिनिभेक्षणे ।
त्रैलोक्यनाथवक्त्राब्जविकसत्केसरोद्भवे ॥१॥

[6]This work by Mkhas grub rje, has been translated from Tibetan by Dr. F. D. Lessing and myself in collaboration. It appears as *Mkhas grub rje's Fundamentals of the Buddhist Tantras*, (Mouton, The Hague, 1968).

[7]Waddell (op. cit.), 83-9.

नमः शतशरच्चन्द्रसंपूर्णपटलानने ।
तारासहस्रनिकरप्रहसत्किरणोज्ज्वले ॥२॥
नमः कनकनीलाब्जपाणिपद्मविभूषिते ।
दानवीर्यतपःशान्तितितिक्षाध्यानगोचरे ॥३॥
नमस् तथागतोष्णीषविजयानन्तचारिणी ।
ऽशेषपारमिताप्राप्तजिनपुत्रनिषेविते ॥४॥
नमस् तुत्तारेहूंकारपूरिताशादिगन्तरे ।
सप्तलोकक्रमाक्रान्ति निःशेषाकर्षणक्षमे ॥५॥
नमः शक्रानलब्रह्ममरुद्विश्वेश्वरार्चिते ।
भूतवेतालगन्धर्वगणयक्षपुरस्कृते ॥६॥
नमस् त्रडितिफट्कारपरयन्त्रप्रमर्दिनि ।
प्रत्यालीढपदन्यासे शिखिज्वलाकुलेक्षणे ॥७॥[8]
नमस् तुरे महाघोरे मारवीरविनाशिनि ।
भृकुटीकृतवक्त्राब्जसर्वशत्रुनिषूदिनि ॥८॥
नमस् त्रिरत्नमुद्राङ्कहृद्याङगुलिविभूषिते ।
भूषिताशेषदिक्चक्रनिकरस्वकराकुले ॥९॥
नमः प्रमुदिताटोपमुकुटाक्षिप्तमालिनी ।
हसत्प्रहसत्तुत्तारेमारलोकवशंकरि ॥१०॥
नमः समन्तभूपालपटलाकर्षणक्षमे ।
चलद्भ्रूकुटिहूंकारसर्वापदविमोचिनी ॥११॥
नमः शिखण्डखण्डेन्दुमुकुटाभरणोज्ज्वले ।
अमिताभजटाभारभास्वारकिरणध्रुवे ॥१२॥
नमः कल्पान्तहुतभुग्ज्वालमालान्तरस्थिते ।
आलीढमुदिताबद्धरिपुचक्रविनाशिनि ॥१३॥
नमः करतलाघातचरणाहतभूतले ।
भृकुटीकृतहूंकारसप्तपातालभेदिनि ॥१४॥
नमः शिवे शुभे शान्ते शान्तनिर्वाणगोचरे ।
स्वाहाप्रणवसंयुक्ते महापापकनाशिनि ॥१५॥
नमः प्रमुदिताबद्धरिपुगात्रप्रभेदिनि ।
दशाक्षरपदन्यासविद्याहूंकारदीपिते ॥१६॥
नमस् तुरेपादाघाते हूंकाराकारबीजिते ।
मेरुमन्दारकैलासभुवनत्रयचालिनि ॥१७॥

[8] I have accepted here the reading of the Sanskrit transcription in the Kanjur against both de Blonay's edition, *śikhijvālākulōjjvale*, and the Tibetan which agrees with the latter, *me ḥbar ḥkhrug pa śin tu ḥbar ma.*

नमः सुरसराकारहरिणाङ्ककरस्थिते ।
तारद्विरुक्तफट्कारै रशेषविषनाशिनि ॥१८॥[9]

नमः सुरगणाध्यक्षसुरकिंनरसेविते ।
आबद्धमुदिताभोगकलिदुःस्वप्ननाशिनि ॥१६॥

नमश्चन्द्रार्कसंपूर्णनयनद्युतिभासुरे ।
हरद्विरुक्ततुत्तारेविषमज्वरनाशिनि ॥२०॥

नमस् त्रितताविन्यासशिवशक्तिसमन्विते ।
ग्रहवेतालयक्षगणनाशनि प्रवरे तुरे ॥२१॥

मन्त्रमूलमिदं स्तोत्रं नमस्कारैकविंशकं ।
यः पठेत्प्रसन्नधीमान् देव्यां भक्तिसमन्वितः ॥२२॥

सायं वा प्रातरुत्थाय स्मरेत्सर्वभयप्रदं ।
सर्वपापप्रशमनं सर्वदुर्गतिनाशनं ॥२३॥

अभिषिक्तो भवेत्तूर्णं सप्तभिर्जिनकोटिभिः ।
अस्मिन्महत्त्वमापद्य सोऽन्ते बौद्धपदं व्रजेत ॥२४॥

विषं तस्यं महाघोरं स्थावरं वाथ जङ्गमं ।
स्मरणात्प्रलयंयाति खादितं पीतमेव वा ॥२५॥

ग्रहज्वरविषार्तीनां परमार्तिविनाशानां ।
अन्येषां चैव सत्त्वानां द्वित्रिसप्ताभिवर्त्तिनां ॥२६॥

पुत्रकामो लभेत्पुत्रं धनकामो लभेद्धनं ।
सर्वकामानवाप्नोति न विघ्नैः प्रतिहन्यते ॥२७॥

सम्यक्संबुद्धभाषितं भगवतीतारादेव्यां नमस्कारैकविंशतिस्तोत्रं गुणहितसहितं संपूर्णं समाप्तं । तारे स्वाहा ।

Homage to Tārā

1. Adoration ! O Tārā, the quick one (*ture*), the heroine, bright-eyed with twinklings;
   Who has sprung from the opening flower on the lotus face of the lord of the three worlds ![10]

[9]I have taken the liberty of writing *phaṭkārair aśeṣa*, although both the Kanjur transcription and de Blonay's edition have *phaṭkāra aśeṣa*.

[10]The three worlds in the epic are Bhūrlōka, Bhuvarlōka, and Svarlōka. Possibly these are what Buddhism calls the Realm of Desire (*kāmadhātu*), Realm of Form (*rūpa-dhātu*), and Formless Realm (*arūpadhātu*). In the human body, the three worlds appear to correspond to (1) navel downwards, (2) neck down to navel, (3) head. These divisions of the body were legally recognized in Kauṭilya's *Arthaśāstra*, XIX, 195 (translation by R. Shamasastry,

2. Adoration ! O Lady whose canopy face is full of a hundred autumn moons;
Who blazes with the laughing beams of a thousand starry clusters !
3. Adoration ! O Lady adorned with hand-held lotus colored blue and gold;
Who ranges in giving, striving, austerity, peace, forbearance, and meditation ![11]
4. Adoration ! O Lady of boundless movement in the victory of the Tathāgata's *uṣṇīṣa;*
Who is frequented by the Victor's Sons who have attained every single Perfection ![12]
5. Adoration ! O Lady who fills the quarters, intermediate directions, and space with the sounds of Tuttāre and Hūṃ;
Who presses down the seven worlds with Thy steps and is able to summon all ![13]

---

p. 219). As will be demonstrated more specifically by verse 12, Tārā is the sacred Gaṅgā which flows from Śiva's matted hair. She is the Gaṅgā in heaven, or the Milky Way. According to Indian legend, once Tārā, understood as an asterism, was carried away from her husband Bṛhaspati by Soma or the Moon. When she was recovered after a war, she gave birth to Budha, or the planet Mercury, and confessed that the latter was fathered by Soma, not by Bṛhaspati.

[11]With Śaivitic flavor, austerity and peace here substitute for morality (*śīla*). The Sanskrit word *titikṣā* substitutes for *kṣānti*, both meaning "forbearance". Thus, she who ranges in giving, etc. is the Perfection of Insight (*prajñāpāramitā*). She ranges in the first five Perfections of the Victor's Sons, namely, in Giving, Morality, Forbearance, Striving, and Meditation. In Mahāyāna Buddhism, she is regarded as the Mother of the Buddhas and Bodhisattvas.

[12]She is Uṣṇīṣavijayā, born from the characteristic (*lakṣaṇa*) of the Great Person (*mahāpuruṣa*) called the *uṣṇīṣa*. This is represented in Buddhist images as a spiral hairlock of the Kapardin type on the head of the Tathāgata, one who "has come the same way" or "understood the same" as the former Buddhas. This characteristic reminds us of Rudra, of whom Sir R. G. Bhandarkar writes in "Vaiṣṇavism, Śaivism, and Minor Religious Systems," p. 147 : "He is called [in the śatarudrīya] Kapardin, or the wearer of matted hair, which epithet is probably due to his being regarded as identical with Agni, or fire, the fumes of which look like matted hair." The Victor's Sons are the Bodhisattvas. They unite the sixth Perfection, that of Insight, with the first five, giving, etc. (verse 3). Hence, she (Prajñā or Uṣṇīṣavijayā) is frequented by them.

[13]Regarding the seven worlds, E. Washburn Hopkins, "Mythological

6. Adoration ! O Lady worshipped by Indra, the Fire God, Brahma, the Maruts, and Viśveśvara;
Placed above all by the elementary spirits, vampires, songster spirits, attendants of Śiva, and secret folk !

7. Adoration ! O Lady who defeats with the sounds of Traṭ and Phaṭ the magical diagrams of others,
While Thy left foot is placed forward and Thy right retracted, and Thy wild glance blazes like fire ![14]

8. Adoration ! O thou quick one, most-fearful Lady, who destroys the heroes of the Māras;
Who slays all the enemy by contracting the brows of Thy lotus face ![15]

9. Adoration ! O thou adorned with the heart's "thumb" marked by the seal of the Three Jewels;
The distraught Lady whose own beams in bundles adorn all the directional wheels.[16]

Aspects of Trees and Mountains in the Great Epic," J.A.O.S. Vol. 30 (1909), 373, says : "In the Purāṇas, e.g. VP. 2. 7. 1 f., there is fully developed the idea of the planetary spheres (not Dvīpas) which go by the names Maharlōka, Janalōka, Tapalōka, and Satyalōka, superadded upon the older Bhūrlōka and Svarlōka or Svargalōka (these are epic) with the intermediate *bhuvas* as Bhuvarlōka."

[14]Here we recall the legend that a glance from Śiva's third eye reduced Kāma to ashes and that such a glance destroys the gods and all created things at the ends of certain aeons. In any case, the verse is emphasizing fire in its destructive sense. The second ritual work by Sūryagupta (No. 1686 in the Tohoku Kanjur-Tanjur Catalogue), contains for each of the twenty-one Tārās the rite (*vidhi*) constituting a *karmāṅga*. In the case of the seventh Tārā, the rite is called *Goṅ du ḥpho ba* (Sanskrit *ūrddhva-srōtas*), "going upwards in the stream", Sūryagupta mentions here (Derge Tanjur, Rgyud ḥgrel, Śa, 13a-5) : / ḥchi bdag bdud ni gzom paḥi phyir/ḥgro ba rnams la srog sbyin ziṅ / "So as to defeat the Death Māra (*mṛtyu-māra*), (she) gives life force (*prāṇa*) to the living beings."

[15]There are four Māras in Mahāyāna Buddhism. Their names are usually given as Skandha-māra, Kleśa-māra, Mṛtyu-māra, and Devaputra-māra. I have explained the word *māra* to mean "death" (understood metaphorically) in my essay "Studies in Yama and Māra, "*Indo-Iranian Journal*, Vol. III (1959), Nr. 2, 113.

[16]The Three Jewels are of course the Buddha, his Doctrine (*dharma*), and the Order (*saṃgha*). The "seal" (*mudrā*) of these jewels is their symbolic representation, perhaps as discussed by Tarapada Bhattacharyya, *The Cult of Brahma* (Patna, 1957), 168. The *dharma* jewel is usually represented by a wheel (*cakra*). The heart's thumb is presumably the heart's *liṅga*, understood to be erect.

10. Adoration ! O Lady whose garland is tossed about the diadem as you swell with delight;
Who domineers the world of Māra with the laughing, mocking sound Tuttāre !
11. Adoration ! O Lady able to summon the multitudes of all the Local Genii;
Who liberates all in distress with Thy Hūṃ of shaking contracted brows !
12. Adoration ! O blazing Lady of the diadem ornament with the plumed crescent;
Who is the constancy of radiant beams from Amitābha's mass of braided hair ![17]
13. Adoration ! O Lady who lives amidst the garland blazing like the fire at the aeon's end;
Who overcomes the enemy circle delighted in the circular band of right foot forward and left drawn back ![18]
14. Adoration ! O Lady who strikes with the palm of her hand and pounds with her feet the surface of the earth;

[17]Cf. *Naiṣadhacarita*, XXII, 142 (translated by Handiqui, op. cit., p. 352): "The sixteenth part of the moon is called a digit, but only fifteen digits round off the moon, growing from the new moon to the full moon night. Was then the remaining digit, which had no lunar day allotted to it, taken out of the moon, and made an ornament for Śiva ? And, in its place, do I see in the moon a dark cavity, namely, the lunar spot ?" Jitendra Nath Banerjea, *The Development of Hindu Iconography* (Calcutta, 1956), p. 486, discusses the Gaṅgādharamūrti of Śiva : "Śiva releases Gaṅgā pent up in his matted locks by stretching a coil of his *jaṭās* with his back right hand, while caressing with his front right hand his principal consort Umā. . . ." The Buddha Amitābha, whose name means "infinite light," here substitutes for Śiva. In Tantric Buddhism, Amitābha is the progenitor of the Lotus Clan(*padma-kula*), of which Avalōkiteśvara is the master, and the red-colored Tārā is the Mother. The latter, by reason of white dress, is also known as Pāṇḍarā, and is often described as being "16-yeared".

[18]The Sanskrit for "circular band", *ābaddha* (or is it *ābandha* ?), is here translated into Tibetan by *kun nas bskor*, "completely circumambulating". The Sanskrit expression is a substitution for the *rakṣā-cakra* ("protective circle"), which is the name of the rite for the thirteenth Tārā in the work by Sūryagupta used above (note 14). In this rite, it is customary for the hierophants in the cardinal directions to adopt the egoity and posture of an appropriate wrathful deity (*krōdha*). Thereby, an inner circular region is freed from inimical elements, and the *maṇḍala* may be drawn. It is not clear why the outer enemy circle should be delighted. Perhaps a type of hypnotic fascination is involved.

Who shatters the seven underworlds with the Hūṃ made by her contracted brows ![19]

15. Adoration ! Lady of Calm, Lady of Virtue, Lady of Peace, who ranges in the quiescent Nirvāṇa;
Who is attended by the sounds Svāhā and Oṃ, who destroys the great sin !

16. Adoration ! Lady who crushes the bodies of the enemy delighted in the circular band;
Who is manifested from the Hūṃ of the magical formula consisting in the arrangement of ten syllables ![20]

17. Adoration ! O Lady seeded with the appearance of the Hūṃ syllable, who strikes with the feet of Ture,
Shaking Meru, Mandāra, Kailāśa and the three worlds !"[21]

18. Adoration ! O Lady who stays in the hand aspected by a divine lake and marked by a deer;
Who dispels all poison with a twice-uttered Tārā and the sound Phaṭ ![22]

[19]The seven underworlds (*pātāla*) are of course, in order : Atala, Vitala, Sutala, Pātāla, Mahātala, Rasātala, Talātala. Cf. Fausta Nowotny, *Eine durch Miniaturen erlauterte* Doctrina mystica *aus Srinagar* ('S-Gravenhage, 1958), 30-1. In the same work (p. 21), we read : *saptapātālamayī pṛthvī*, "Earth consists of seven underworlds".

[20]In Tantric-Buddhism, a *vidyā* is a manifestation in female form, or the magical thoughts, utterances, and gestures which produce that manifestation. Hence the word is translated here "magical formula". The ten syllables are in a *sādhana* of Tārā translated by B. Bhattacharyya in *The Indian Buddhist Iconography* (Calcutta, 1958), p. 23 : Om Tārā Tuttāre Ture Svāhā; "This is the lord of all Mantras, is endowed with great powers, and is saluted, worshipped and revered by the Tathāgatas." When the verse speaks of the Hūṃ of the magical formula, it is not clear whether it refers to the entire set of ten syllables as a Hūṃ, or intends the middle term, Tāre Tuttāre Ture, to constitute a Hūṃ. The latter case may be the intention of the next verse.

[21]She is seeded in the sequence depicted by the *Advayavajrasaṃgraha* (edited by Haraprasad Shastri), p. 50, line 7 : śūnyatābōdhitō bījaṃ bījād bimbaṃ prajāyate. "From the realization of voidness proceeds the germ-syllable; from the germ-syllable, the image of the deity."

[22]"Marked by a deer" signifies the moon. Together with "a divine lake", this is the "moon in the water". The reference is presumably to the level hand gesture (*samāhita-mudrā*) which symbolizes the *samāhita-citta* or equipoised mind that sees things as they really are. Therefore, the poison that is dispelled may be understood—besides the external poisons—as psychological poison. Buddhism speaks of the three poisons—hatred (*dveṣa*), lust (*rāga*), and delusion (*mōha*). In connection with the mention of poison here, fever

19. Adoration ! O Lady visited by the superintendent of the host of gods as well as by the gods and the horse-headed men;
Who destroys quarrel and bad dreams with the delightful winding of the circular band !
20. Adoration ! O Lady of bright light in (both) eyes that are filled with the sun and moon;
Who dispels the terrible fever by a twice-uttered Hara and the sound Tuttāre !
21. Adoration ! O Lady endowed with the Power (*śakti*) of Śiva to dispose the state of the Third;
Who destroys the host of possessing spirits, vampires, and secret folk ! Most excellent Lady ! O quick one ![23]
22. With clear cognition and full of reverence toward the goddess, one should recite this Praise, which is both the basic *mantra* and twenty-one adorations.
23. At dusk or rising at daybreak he should remember (this Praise), which grants complete fearlessness, dispels all sin, destroys every evil fate.[24]
24. He would be initiated speedily by seven myriads of Buddhas. Arriving at greatness herein, he would proceed in the end to the rank of a Buddha.
25. If he has eaten or drunk a terrible poison, stationary or locomotive, he dispels it as soon as he remembers (this Praise).[25]

---

in verse 20 and fire elsewhere, one should note that of the *Atharva-veda* Sir Bhandarkar (op. cit., p. 148) mentions, "Rudra is implored not to bring on consumption, poison, and celestial fire (XI, 2, 26)." The deity in whose dominion the particular misfortune lies, is naturally the one who can avert that misfortune. Hence, Tārā ("the Savioress"), as the power (*śakti*) of Śiva, can save one from those dangers.

[23]The third one of the Hindu triad is Śiva. The relation between Śiva and Śakti has been well described by S. K. Das in *Śakti or Divine Power* (Calcutta, 1934), for example, p. 75, "In reply to this Bhairava asserts that Śakti is nothing but His own self (*Svarūpa*) in the aspect of 'one who fashions, sustains and withdraws the world' Bhairava is of course all three—Brahmā, Viṣṇu, Śiva." The present verse refers only to Śiva. Hence, Tārā is the destructive self or ability of Śiva, who withdraws the world.

[24]In Buddhism the three evil fates or destinies (*durgati*) are of animals (*tiryagyōnika*), ghosts (*preta*), and hell-beings (*naraka*).

[25]The two kinds of external poison of classical Indian medicine are meant. For example, poison of plants is the stationary type; poison of snakes is t'ı

26. By repeating it twice, thrice or seven times, he removes the great pains, pains of seizure, fever, and poison, of even other sentient beings.
27. Desiring sons, he obtains sons. Desiring wealth, he obtains wealth. He achieves all his desires and is not frustrated by obstacles.

Completed and ended is the Praise Consisting of Twenty-one Adorations of Her Lordship, Tārā, the Goddess, together with the merit and benefit, expressed by the Samyaksaṃbuddha. Hail, Tārā !

locomotive type. I have pointed out a third external category, created poison, for example that made from quicksilver or from *amṛta*, in my little essay in honor of Leonardo Olschki, "The Concept of Poison in Buddhism," *Oriens*, Vol. X (1957), 107-109.

ACKNOWLEDGMENTS

"Buddha as Savior," *Studia Missionalia*, 29 (1980), pp. 191-207. Reprinted by permission.

"Ancient Buddhist Monasticism," *Studia Missionalia*, 28 (1979), pp. 193-230. Reprinted by permission.

"Meditation in Theravāda and Mahīśāsaka," *Studia Missionalia*, 25 (1976), pp. 1-28. Reprinted by permission.

"The Bodhisattva Practice According to the Lam-Rim-Chen-Mo," *The Tibet Society Newsletter*, 1:2 (July-December 1967), pp. 85-100. Reprinted by permission.

"The Sixteen Aspects of the Four Noble Truths and their Opposites," *The Journal of the International Association of Buddhist Studies*, 3-2 (1980), pp. 67-76. Reprinted by permission.

"The Mirror as a Pan-Buddhist Metaphor-Simile," *History of Religions*, 13:4 (May 1974), pp. 251-269. Reprinted by permission of the University of Chicago Press and Copyright (c) 1974 by the University of Chicago Press.

"The Buddhist Theory of Vision," *Añjali*, Wijesekera volume (1970), pp. 27-32. Reprinted by permission.

"Dependent Origination; the Indo-Tibetan Tradition," *Journal of Chinese Philosophy*, 7 (1980), pp. 275-300. Reprinted by permission of D. Reidel Publishing Company and Copyright (c) by D. Reidel Publishing Co., Dordrecht.

"Nescience and Insight According to Asaṅga's *Yogācārabhūmi*," *Buddhist Studies in honour of Walpola Rahula*, (1980). Reprinted by permission and Copyright (c) 1980 by Gordon Fraser, London.

"The twenty reifying views (sakkāyaditthi)," *Studies in Pali and Buddhism*, Bhikkhu Jagdish Kashyap memorial volume (1979), pp. 375-380. Reprinted by permission of B. R. Publishing Corporation and Copyright (c) 1979 by B. R. Publishing Corporation, Delhi.

"Who Understands the Four Alternatives of the Buddhist Texts," *Philosophy East and West*, 27:1 (January 1977), pp. 3-21. Reprinted by permission of the University Press of Hawaii.

"The Intermediate-State Dispute in Buddhism," *Buddhist Studies in honour of I. B. Horner* (1974). Reprinted by permission of D. Reidel Publishing Company and Copyright (c) 1974 by D. Reidel Publishing Company, Dordrecht.

"No Time, Great Time, and Profane Time in Buddhism," *Myths and Symbols; Studies in Honor of Mircea Eliade* (1969), pp. 47-62. Reprinted by permission of The University of Chicago Press and Copyright (c) 1969 by The University of Chicago Press, Chicago.

"The Role of Art among the Buddhist Religieux," *East-West Dialogues in Aesthetics* (1978), pp. 2-15. Reprinted by permission of State University of New York at Buffalo and Copyright (c) State University of New York at Buffalo.

"Secret of the Heart Sūtra," *Prajñāpāramitā and Related Systems; Studies in honor of Edward Conze* (1977), pp. 135-125. Reprinted by permission of Regents of the University of California and Copyright (c) 1977 by Regents of the University of California.

"The Sacittikā and Acittikā Bhūmi," text and translation, is based on "The Sacittika and Acittikā Bhūmi and the Pratyekabuddhabhūmi (Sanskrit texts)," *Journal of Indian and Buddhist Studies*, 7:1 (1960), pp. 375-379. Reprinted by permission.

"Asaṅga's Treatise, Paramārtha-gāthā," is a corrected version of the text and translation in A. Wayman, *Analysis of the Srāvakabhūmi Manuscript*" (*University of California Publications in Classical Philosophy*, 17 (1961), pp. 167-185. Reprinted by permission.

"Asaṅga's Treatise on the Three Instructions of Buddhism" is simultaneously being published in a volume on Buddhism in India, with different introduction. Reprinted by permission.

"Two Traditions of India—Truth and Silence," *Philosophy East and West*, 24: 4 (October 1974), pp. 389-403. Reprinted by permission of the University Press of Hawaii and Copyright (c) 1974 by the University Press of Hawaii.

"The Hindu-Buddhist Rite of Truth—an Interpretation," *Studies in Linguistics*, Murray B. Emeneau volume (1968), pp. 365-369. Reprinted by permission of the Linguistic Society of India and Copyright (c) 1968 by the Linguistic Society of India, Poona.

"Significance of Dreams in India and Tibet," *History of Religions*, 7: 1 (August 1967), pp. 1-12. Reprinted by permission.

"The Significance of Mantras, from the Veda down to Buddhist Tantric Practice," *Indologica Taurinensia*, III-IV, pp. 483-497, slightly altered from the original in *Brahmavidyā : the Adyar Library Bulletin*, XXXIX (1975), pp. 65-89. Reprinted by permission.

"The Goddess Sarasvatī—from India to Tibet", *Kailash*; *a Journal of Himalayan Studies*, V:3 (1977), pp. 45-251. Reprinted by permission.

"The Twenty-One Praises of Tārā, a syncretism of Śaivism and Buddhism," *Journal of the Bihar Research Society*, A. S. Altekar Memorial Volume, 45:1-4 (1959), pp. 36-43. Reprinted by permission.

INDEX

Abhayākaragupta 133, 159, 161, 165n, 175n, 421
Abhidharma (P., Abhidhamma) 37, 72, 85, 91, 117-119, 127, 172-174, 181, 183n, 186, 189, 216, 221, 222n, 254, 334, 400n
Abhidharmakośa 20, 58, 84-85, 90n, 91, 117-118, 123-125, 157-158, 181, 195, 203, 216, 222n, 251, 251n, 260, 318, 331
Abhidharmakośa-bhāṣya 59n
Abhidharmakośabhāṣyaṭīkā-tattvārtha-nāma 176n
Abhidharmakośa-vyākhyā 263
Abhidharmasamuccaya 180, 195, 262-263
abhijñā (supernormal faculty) 12-13, 20, 36, 97, 113, 146, 154, 160-161, 280-281, 284, 299, 371. See "faculty," "*ṛddhi*."
Ābhiprāyikārtha-gāthā Chapter 18; 333
Abhisamācarikā (*Bhikṣuprakīrṇaka*) 60n
Abhisamayālaṃkāra 119, 161n, 190
Abhisamayālaṃkārāloka Prajñāpāramitāvyākhyā 138n
abhiṣeka (consecration, initiation) 208, 394, 417
abhūtaparikalpa (Imagination of Unreality) 190-191, 271-275
Acala, a deity 420, 433
Acittikābhūmi Chapter 16; 194
Ādarśamukha, a king 143
Adbhuta-brāhmaṇa 404
adhiṣṭhāna (blessing, empowerment, spiritual foundation) 20-23, 324, 375, 395-396
Advayavajrasaṃgraha 449n
Āgama (scripture) 25, 131, 209, 221, 233, 246, 313; = lineage 354, 363
Agni 258, 395, 414, 416n, 446n, 447
Agnipurāṇa 415-421, 417n, 423-425
ahaṃkāra (egohood) 188-189, 191, 339, 348n, 350-351, = self 139
Aitareya Āraṇyaka 414n, 415n
Aitareya Brāhmaṇa 416, 416n, 425n
Ajīvaka sect 372
Akaniṣṭha, a heaven 21, 86, 147, 149, 279, 313, 323
Ākaṅkheyyasutta 69
Ākāśagarbha 67. See "Bodhisattva."
akṣaṇa (unfavorable moment), the eight 295
Akṣayamatinirdeśa-sūtra 16, 156
Akṣobhya 141, 421. See "Buddha."
Āḷāra Kalāma (= Arāḍa) 187-188, 372
ālayavijñāna (store-consciousness, basic perception) 92-93, 97, 130, 133-134, 189, 253, 273, 275, 283, 330-331, 334, 350, 350n. See "*vijñāna*."
Amitābha 26-28, 147, 289-290, 448, 448n; Amitāyus, 405. See "Buddha."
Āmnāya-mañjarī 159, 161
Amoghapāśakalparāja 160
Ānanda 37-38, 139, 142, 163, 171, 291, 320
Ānandagarbha 280
Ānanda-garbhāvakrāntinirdeśa 259, 262n
Ānāpānasati 70
Anavatapta-nāgarāja-paripṛcchā 237
Andhaka sect 231
Aṅgavijjā 403, 404n, 408
Aṅguttara-nikāya 12, 33-35, 35n, 57, 74, 74n, 132, 153-154, 263, 314, 322, 406
Anugīta 189, 414-415, 415n, 424-425
Anuruddha 320
Aristotle 405
Arhat 38, 42, 88, 105, 126, 157, 184-185, 203n, 290, 330-331, 361; the sixteen, etc. 290; as epithet of Buddha 12, 372. See "persons."
Arjuna 279
Arthaśāstra 445n
Arthaviniścaya-sūtra 92, 303
Arthaviniścaya-ṭīkā 120-122, 179-180, 201
Āryadeva 20, 43, 188, 308, 312, 318, 371
Āryadeva's "Four Hundred Verses," Commentary to 247n
Āryagāyaśīrṣa 22
Ārya-prajñāpāramitā-ṭīkā 316n
Āryaśūra 287, 391, 394-395, 397
Ārya-tārā-kurukulle-kalpa 405
Asaṅga. Chapters 9, 16-18; 15-17, 26, 30, 44-45, 55, 57-58, 64-65, 70, 72-74, 75-77, 118-126, 130-136, 157, 164, 168, 171-180, 186-187, 191, 216, 234n, 259n, 260-265, 270, 272n, 295, 300-303, 308, 310, 315-319, 335n, 345n, 422n; meditative progress in Asaṅga's school, 78-95

Aśoka, a king 39, 48, 292, 296n; a tree 401
āsrava (fluxes) 35-36, 125, 157, 175, 184, 206
Aṣṭasāhasrikā Prajñāpāramitā 23-24, 26, 138, 420; Great Commentary on 110
Aṣṭāvakra 374
Aṣṭāvakra Saṃhitā 374
Aśvaghoṣa 188, 287, 441n
Āsvalāyana-sūtra (P., *Assalāyanasutta*) 257-259
Atharva Veda 393, 402, 404, 407, 450n
Atīśa 96, 100-102, 178n, 226, 242, 281, 406, 420
attachment (*saṅga*) 44-45, 144, 339
Atthasālinī 75n 218, 236
Avalokiteśvara 22, 28, 159, 290, 400, 420, 448n. See "Bodhisattva"; Chapter 15
Avataṃsaka 170n
avidyā (nescience, ignorance) Chapters 8-9; 150, 160, 164, 236-237, 244, 254-256, 263, 278, 302, 306, 320, 347, 421, 437; five kinds 202; seven kinds 201; nineteen kinds 202; -craving 374
Āyuṣmannandagarbhāvakrāntinirdeśa 262

Balimālikā 429
Bhadrakalpita-sūtra 161
Bhagavadgītā 279, 295, 385, 428n
Bhāgavata-purāṇa 295
Bhaiṣajya-guru ("Healing Buddha") 28, 420. See "Buddha."
Bhāsa 400
Bhāvanākrama I, 79-80; II, 80; III, 297
Bhāvanāmayī bhūmi 194, 211-212
Bhāvaviveka 249, 409
Bhikṣaparama 435, 437
bhikṣu (monk) 30, 111, 165, 167-169, 175, 183n, 283, 288-289, 302, 306-307, 311, 315, 320, 347, 352, 354, 361, 384, 396, 407n; five salient points of 33; five places avoided by 361; "defeats" of 60-61 (See "offences"); compared to *brāhmaṇa* 56-58, 406n. See "persons"; Chapters 2-3.
bhikṣuṇī (nun) 31, 35, 42-58, 67, 111; "defeats" of 61, 62 (See "offences"). See "persons"; Chapters 2-3.
Bhikṣuṇī-vinaya 61n
Bhoja 400
bhūmi (stage) seventeen 193-194, 327, 333; as stories of the world 426. See "Path," "stages of life."
Bhūmi-vastu 80
Blake, W. 163
Blue Annals 53
Bodhicaryāvatāra (*Spyod 'jug*) 24-26, 101-104, 109-111, 226, 299, 304
Bodhicaryāvatārapañjikā 140n
bodhicitta (thought or mind of enlightenment) 100-108, 149-150, 436; tantric 410
Bodhimārgapradīpa-pañjikā 96n, 226
Bodhipathapradīpa 178n, 281
Bodhiruci 24
Bodhisattva 77, 153, 157, 177-179, 178n, 184-185, 194, 196-197, 244, 244n, 270, 281-282, 312, 446n; great, celestial, supramundane 22-24, 28, 95, 133, 136, 138, 279, 281-282, 290-291, 315n, 321n, 330-331, 400. See "Path," "persons"; Chapters 4, 15.
Bodhisattva-bhūmi 112, 134, 194, 196, 199, 211, 260, 327, 422n
Bodhisattvapiṭaka-sūtra 154-155, 176
Bo-doṅ school 434, 438
body (*kāya, śarīra*) 103, 141, 143-144, 146, 155, 169, 189, 206, 208, 210-212, 217, 260, 283-284, 311, 316-317, 320, 335-336, 349, 360, 363, 373, 402-403, 409, 438; subtle 409; made of mind (*manomayakāya*) 133, 155, 158, 184-185, 273, 275, 283, 386, 409; of the Buddha 20-25, 270, 283, 296, 375 (Nirmāṇa-kāya 20, 25, 270, 312-313, 375; Saṃbhoga-kāya 21, 25, 149, 270, 279, 312-313, 323-324; Dharma-kāya 21, 25, 210, 270, 291, 312, 375); of deity, 135, 149, 433, 436-438; tantric 409-410; *-saṃskāra* 311, 318, 324; = the three worlds 445n; body and mind 360, 363, 416. See "body, speech, and mind"; Chapter 3.
body, speech, and mind (*kāya-vāk-citta*) 19, 110, 154, 190, 311, 324, 350, 371, 405, 405n. See "body," "speech," "*citta*."
Boehme, J. 75
Brahmā 13-14, 252, 252n, 259, 353, 357, 372, 432-434, 447, 450n; as celestial Bodhisattva 321n
brahmacarya, -cārin (brahma-conduct, chaste person) 12, 30, 48, 55, 57-58, 361, 370. See "persons."
Brahmajāla-sūtra 203, 206, 219n; *-sutta* 232, 363n
Brahman 259, 376, 382-385, 413; Saguṇa- 420
brāhmaṇa 30, 376-378, 383; compared to *bhikṣu* 56-58, 406n. See "persons."

Brāhmaṇas 172, 386, 391, 413, 414n. See titles.
Brahmanical tradition 252, 380-381, 413-414, 426n. See "stages of life."
Brahmin Kīla school 434, 436
Bṛhadāraṇyaka Upaniṣad 33, 163, 173, 256, 263, 265, 376, 378, 382-387, 415n
Bṛhaddevatā 425
Bṛhatphala, a heaven 331
Bstan bcos mṅon rtogs rgyan 'grel pa 190n
Buddha Chapters 1, 14; epithets of 11-14; symbols of 291; bodies of (See "body"); the seven, the thousand 289; the Thirty-Five Buddhas of Confession 66; supramundane 22, 26-28, 105-109, 136, 142, 160 (See names); dynamic and static 24-25; as Jina 372; Niṣyanda-Buddha 149; Samyaksaṃbuddha 451; as Vibhajjavādin (Analyst) 215. See "Śākyamuni," "Tathāgata," "Cakravartin," "Arhat," "*Śramaṇa*," "*muni*." See also "eye," "jewel," "persons."
Buddhacarita 188
Buddhaghosa 35, 69, 72-76, 126, 138, 167n, 177, 216n, 218, 236, 281n
Buddhaguhya 301, 373
Buddhānusmṛti-ṭīkā 233, 313
buddhi (intellect, cognition, discriminating mind, discrimination) 20, 26, 72, 96, 135, 141, 146, 159, 195, 209, 427, 428n, 434; *-mat* (sage) 371; in Śaivism 409; in Sāṃkhya 188-189
Buddhist art Chapter 14; 407, 407n, 446n; music 432-433, 438-439
Buddhist Councils 37-38
Buddhist genesis 60, 269-270, 273-278, 282-283, 386
Bu-ston 146, 322n
Byaṅ chub lam gyi sgron ma ("A Lamp on the Path to Enlightenment") 100

Cakravartin 13, 208, 296
Candragomin 22, 443
Candrakīrti 138, 140, 149-150, 159, 165n, 177, 216-222, 222n, 232-235, 237, 240n, 243-244, 244n, 249-250, 312, 379; the tantric 161
Caraka 404
Carakasaṃhitā 404
Cārvākas 124
Catuḥśataka 20, 188, 312, 371
catuṣkoṭi (the four alternatives) Chapter 11
cause (or basic cause) (*hetu*) 123-125, 137, 140-142, 171, 173, 180-183, 186-187, 190, 196, 200, 202, 205-206, 225-226, 236-241, 244-248, 250, 255, 257, 297-298, 336, 338, 346-350, 348n, 379-380, 395-396, 424; the eight 329-330; material cause 239, 272; instrumental cause 239; =reason 229. See "condition."
Chāndogya Upaniṣad 370, 376, 382-384, 386-387
Ch'an school 131, 140-141
Chao Lun: The Treatises of Seng-chao (=*Book of Chao*) 149
characteristics (or characters) (*lakṣaṇa*; P., *lakkhaṇa*) 166, 234, 272n, 318, 348-349, 366; three 19, 120-122, 334; four 271-272, 275; thirty-two 161, 296-297, 446n
Cintāmayi-bhūmi 97n, 122, 194, 205, 327, 333, 353
citta (thought, mind, consciousness) Chapters 3, 6, 16; 167-170, 177, 179, 194, 198, 203-204, 211, 239-240, 245n, 322-323, 338, 339, 358, 360-361, 383, 423, 449n; Aspiration thought 104-105, 107-108; Entrance Thought 104-105; *ekāgratā-citta* 283. See "*manas*," "*bodhicitta*," "*śamatha*."
Cloud Messenger 401
compassion (*karuṇā*) 22, 87, 99-102, 112, 313, 379, 433; great 13, 22-23; Boundless State of 102
condition (or conditional cause) (*pratyaya*) 123-124, 137, 140, 164-166, 168-169, 187-188, 236-237, 244n, 246, 248, 250, 299, 336, 338-339, 347, 349, 351, 365, 395-396. See "cause."
confession 58-59, 66-69, 362, 392, 406n; Thirty-five Buddhas of 66
confidences, the four 108
conversion 103, 105; four means of (*saṃgrahavastu*) 16
"Conversion of Śāriputra and Maudgalyāyana" 323n
craving (or desire) (*tṛṣṇā*; P., *taṇhā*) 96, 113, 124, 148, 196-197, 203, 207, 210, 263, 298, 304, 306, 335-336, 339, 365, 385; nescience-craving 347. See "desire"; Chapter 8.
Cullavagga 38

ḍākinī 146; Nāro-ḍākinī 146; *ḍāka* 373n. See "deity."
Ḍākinī-vajrapañjara 186n
Damamūka Nidāna Sūtra 295n
Daśabhūmika-sūtra 124, 177-179, 321n, 371
Daśabhūmivyākhyāna 154

Dbaṅ don 160
death Chapter 12; 111, 144-145, 148, 154, 161, 168, 196, 226, 291, 320, 347, 352, 383-384, 404-405. See Chapter 8.
deity (*deva, devatā*) 26-27, 135-136, 141-142, 144-145, 163, 258-259, 280, 289, 295-296, 322, 332, 348n, 351n, 370-380, 388, 391, 394-397, 402-404, 409, 414-416, 415n, 419, 423-427, 425n; images of 291-292; Asuras 258, 425n; as irreversible Bodhisattvas 321n, 420; tutelary 144, 306, 406, 426; tantric 290, 421; "passion gods" 157, 275; wrathful 448n; four gods of the sublime heart 420; Divine intellect 393. See names; "*ḍākinī*," "*gati*."
Dependent Origination (*pratītyasamutpāda*) Chapters 8-9; 19, 53, 92, 124, 139, 155, 226, 237-238, 244, 248, 254-256, 262-263, 278, 298, 304-306, 311, 320, 345, 385
desire (*kāma*) 365, 382-388, 414-416, 414n, 451; eight similes of 365; as the god Kāma 447n; sensuous lust (*kāma-rāga*) 352, 360, 364. See "craving," "poison," "*dhātu*."
Dge-'dun-grub 27
Dgoṅs pa rab gsal 149n
Dhammapada 17, 19, 93, 370
Dhammasangani 218
dhāraṇī (retention) Chapter 22; 387, 413, 421-423, 427, 429, 443; four kinds 422n. See "*mantra*."
dharma (P., *dhamma*) (natures, features) 13, 19, 93, 105, 107, 112, 121-122, 130, 134-139, 141-142, 156-158, 166-167, 170-175, 196-197, 207, 210, 234, 238, 243, 246, 246n, 250, 280, 283, 314n, 319-320, 324, 331, 335-336, 341, 345-347, 352, 361, 371, 422-423, 437; seven *dharmas* of a monk 34-35; = mental objects 169, 409; constructed 174-175, 311, 320; unconstructed 174-175, 243; virtuous 33, 111-112, 363, 422; unvirtuous 296; illusory 23; Buddha-natures 105, 107-109, 167, 270, 274, 422; noble 272, 274. See "eye."
Dharma (P., Dhamma) (Doctrine, Teaching, Law) 13, 17-19, 25, 37-38, 61, 64, 101, 109-114, 122, 154-156, 163, 166, 171, 173-178, 186, 207-208, 212, 217, 233-237, 266, 340, 351, 362-363, 365-366, 372, 374, 378-381, 396, 406-407, 447n; = "goal," of two kinds 310-312, 318-319; born from 315-316; as Hindu "duty" 377-381, 392, 396, 416; mirror of 141-142; -sun 241, 244, 247; *dharmādharma* ("merit and demerit") 405; Dharma-kāya (See "body"); Dharmadhara 38; Dharmadhātu 151, 156, 166, 191, 270, 272, 297; Dharmatā 120, 243, 250, 272n; *dharmarāja* 395. See "jewel," "wheel."
Dharmaguptaka sect 40, 64, 251, 253
Dharmakīrti 118, 118n, 195, 196n, 297, 303, 379
Dharma-samuccaya 184n
dhātu (realms), the three (= three worlds) 293, 301, 303-304, 311, 315-316, 321, 321n, 323, 331, 351, 358-360, 365-366, 427, 433, 445, 445n, 447n, 449; defined 351n
Dīgha-nikāya 25, 33-34, 69, 74, 145, 158, 163, 171, 235, 283, 371
dispositions (*carita*) 72-73
Diṭṭhikathā 216-217
Dmar khrid 410n
Dmigs brtse ma 400n
Dohā 387
Don gsal 157
Dpal nā ro mkha' spyod dbaṅ mo'i lam rim pa gñis. . . . 146n
dream (*svapna*) Chapter 21; 101, 133-134, 136-137, 148, 179, 259, 278, 280, 282, 284-285, 316, 319, 330, 365, 425, 435n, 450; Gypsy dream book 399
duḥkha (suffering, pain) 15, 19, 100, 102-103, 111, 120-127, 196, 200-206, 234-237, 275, 280-281, 297-298, 305, 320-324, 330-331, 336, 339-340, 350-351, 358, 363, 371, 378-380, 428, 450-451; sevenfold 179-180; *duḥkhatā* (misery) 122-123, 350-351, 350n; = First Noble Truth (See "truth". See "tree"; Chapter 8.
Dutiya-Isidatta-sutta 217

earth 274-275, 282, 316-317, 373, 406, 414n, 426, 427n, 448, 449n; dirt 422; dry land 324, 351, 402
Egg, Cosmic 384-385
Enlightenment (*bodhi*) 100-101, 105, 112, 133, 138, 142, 149, 153, 159, 219, 234, 270, 295, 306, 314, 318, 323-324, 371-372, 374, 404; (Incomparable) Complete 281, 312, 323, 372; thunderbolt of 219-220, 221. See "*bodhicitta*."
equipment (*saṃbhāra*), as thirteen conditions 78
eye Chapter 7; 19, 27, 103-104, 127, 141, 163, 169, 175, 177n, 179, 241, 244, 297, 299, 336, 345-347, 351-

352, 352n, 382, 394-395, 408; of flesh 155-159; divine 160, 251, 257, 394, 396; of divinity 445, 450; of insight 16, 96, 155-159, 177, 208-210; of knowledge 155, 159; *dharma*-eye 132, 139, 155-156, 158-159; diamond-eye 160-161; Buddha-eye 14, 132, 155-159; threefold or third 433, 447n; -ointment 160, 299

faculty (*indriya*) 193, 399; keen or dull 14, 132; insight as chief 207, 208; supernormal (See "*abhijñā*")
faith (*prasāda*) 142, 185, 263, 292-293, 393, 428
father 103, 107, 306, 383, 386, 400, 403, 415n
faults 397; three 131
fear 371, 403, 450; two kinds 322
feeling (*vedanā*) 197, 200, 203, 217, 219, 231, 235, 263, 273, 276, 276, 298, 304, 305-306, 311, 316-317, 320-321, 331, 337, 351. See Chapter 8.
fire 212, 250, 253, 264-265, 322, 340, 365, 373, 401-402, 431, 446n-447n, 447-448, 450n; sermon 74; speech as 415, 424; of insight 242-243; glance as 447n; ordeal 392. See "Agni," "Vahni," "Sarasvatī."
food 45, 54-57, 60, 62, 64, 87, 276, 279, 281, 383, 386, 397, 403; four kinds of 181-182; subtle 275
forebearance, perfection of 23, 105-106, 108-112, 302, 321, 446, 446n
freedom 287, 294, 298, 304-305, 337, 340, 351, 360, 371

gandharva (P., *gandhabba*) 145, 158, 184, 257-261, 316, 431-432, 435-436
Gandhi 388
Gaṅgā 446n, 448n
gates to liberation, the three 131-133, 309, 318-319
gati (destinies) 13, 124, 142, 156-158, 161, 182, 195, 202, 251, 257, 259, 275, 295, 298, 304, 351, 358-359, 380, 397, 404; defined 351n, 450n; =*niyati* 239; as Nirvāṇa 358
"Gayā, At" (a *sutta*) 314n
Gāyatrī (=*Sāvitrī*) 377, 381, 387, 406n, 416-417, 426, 427n, 428
Gelugpa sect 100, 289, 400
Gesar of Ling 147, 407
giving (*dāna*) 16-17, 61, 104-110, 112-114, 299, 302, 321, 432, 446, 446n. See "perfections."
grace 11, 23, 136. See "*adhiṣṭhāna*."
Guhyasamāja-tantra 141, 157, 161, 373, 417, 427, 434
guṇa (quality, merit) 362; of a purified man (*dhutaguṇa*) 49, 54-55
Guṇabhadra 150n
Guṇamati 174
guru 281, 295, 416
Gzuṅs sṅags daṅ/de bžin gśegs pa'i mtshan/... 420n

Haribhadra 138n
Harivarman 119-122
Harṣa 287
heart (*hṛdaya*) 142, 146-148, 259, 315, 324, 373, 384, 408-409, 420, 437-438; two kinds 324; heart's "thumb" =*liṅga* 447, 447n. See "*Heart Sūtra*."
Heart Sūtra (*Prajñāpāramitāhṛdaya-sūtra*) Chapter 15; 331, 420
Hegel, G. 172n
Heidegger, M. 305
Hevajra Tantra 387
hindrances (*nivāraṇa*), the five 76, 79, 364
householder (*gṛhastha*) 45, 48, 50, 57, 110, 209, 217, 347, 363. See "persons."
Hsuan Ts'ang 442
Hsuan-tsung 407n
Hui-neng 141
Hui-yüan 43
"Hymn of Creation," Vedic 384, 386

ideas (or ideation) (*saṃjñā*) 44-45, 273, 276, 311, 316-317, 320-322, 331, 335, 337; as naming faculty 298, 303, 305
impermanence (*anitya*) 79, 95, 120-123, 175, 178, 203-204, 206, 322, 331. See "characteristics," three.
Indra 258, 375, 394-395, 425n, 447; = Śakra 13
Indrabhūti 155n-156n
insight (*prajñā*; P., *paññā*) Chapter 9; 13, 22, 24, 96-98, 100, 106, 118, 126, 209n-210n, 226, 290, 313-315, 331, 420, 422, 434-435, 438-439; three levels of 16, 26, 96-97, 113-114, 194, 208, 209-212, 292, 327; two kinds 314, 322; terminology of 206-209; noble 242; personified 433, 439, 441; as light 209-213; as jewel 207-209; as ocean 323; eye of (See "eye"); -mirror 130, 149-151; among "three instructions" 69, 74, 95-98, 126, 177, 205-206, 282 (See Chapter 18). See

"perfection of insight," "instructions."
instructions (or trainings) (*adhiśikṣā*), three Chapter 18; 69-71, 74, 108, 126, 155, 205-206, 281-282. See "morality," "meditation," "insight."
intermediate space (*antarikṣa*) 21, 145, 258
intermediate state (*antarābhava*) Chapter 12; 145, 157-158, 182-187; two kinds 259-261
Īśa Upaniṣad 378
Islam 294
I-Tsing 44n, 59, 66

Jagaddeva 399, 401
Jainism 235, 239, 399-404, 410, 425, 432
Jātakamālā 20, 41, 130, 143, 150, 160, 184n, 270, 293, 391, 394, 406
jewel (*maṇi*) 110, 145, 207-209, 433, 436-439; three Jewels (Buddha, Dharma, Saṃgha) 44, 46, 50, 112, 166, 201-202, 447, 447n (See each member); *cintāmaṇi* 67, 385, 438
Jñānagarbha 313
Jñānaprasthāna 215, 221, 222n
Jñānavajra 158, 160, 421
joy 105, 112, 273, 275, 381, 386, 375n; Boundless State of Sympathetic Joy 102
Jung, C.G. 284, 442

Kahola Kauṣītakeya 376, 384
Kālacakra-tantra 142, 147, 191
Kālaprakāśikā 401n, 407
Kālidāsa 401
Kamalaśīla 156, 297, 375n
kalpita (imagination) 336-337, 346, 348, 404, 410, 417, 438; of eight kinds 364. See "*vikalpa*." "*parikalpa*."
karma (act) 19, 123, 137, 142, 144-145, 156, 195, 201-202, 248, 255-258, 261, 338, 347, 348n-349n, 385, 396-397, 421; two 179-181; three 190, 338; one hundred 59; ten paths of 34; -mirror (See "mirror"); Truth Act (See "truth").
Karma-śataka 184n
Karmavācanā 53n
Karuṇodaya-nāma-bhāvanājapavidhi 160
kasiṇa (S., *kṛtsna*) (totalities) 72-77; bases of 76-77, 89, 91-94. See "meditation."
Kāśyapa (P., Kassapa) 107, 236-237, 242, 245, 406
Kāśyapa-parivarta 242
Kathāsaritsāgara 400
Kaṭha Upaniṣad 258-259, 265
Kathāvatthu (*Points of Controversy*) 215, 231, 252, 262, 265
Katyāyana (P., Kaccāyana) 167, 237, 245
Kauṣītaki Brāhmaṇa 425n
Kauṭilya 445n
Keats, J. 293-294
Khanda-vagga 15n
Khuddaka-Nikāya 216
Khyuṅ-po-lha 407
kleśa (defilement) 18 22-23, 81, 95, 114, 123, 125, 132, 141, 163, 167, 170-171, 178-179, 182-184, 188, 191, 196-197, 198n, 199-201, 204-205, 207, 209, 220, 256, 301, 318-319, 322, 331, 337, 340, 346-347, 351, 359-360, 362-365, 386; three 181, 358; four 44-45; eight 200-201; ten 201, 205; *saṃkleśa* (stain) 346-347, 352, 371
knowledge (or cognition) (*jñāna*; P., *ñāṇa*) 210-211, 226, 314-315, 320-322, 335, 351, 358-359, 363, 371-375, 378, 380-381, 385-386, 420-421, 427, 428n, 450; supramundane 303-304; =*vidyā*, five kinds of 133; -*sattva* 438; eye of 155. See Chapters 7, 9.
Kokuyaku Daizōkyō 83n
Kṛṣṇa 279
Kṛṣṇayamāri-tantra 435
kṣatriya 296; five salient points of 33
Kūkai 150-151, 308
Kukuri-pā 160
Kumārajīva 149-150
Kumārila-bhaṭṭa 381
kuśala-mūla (root of virtue) 15, 17, 44, 105, 359, 434
Kusumañjali-guhyasamāja-nibandha-nāma 427
Kūṭāgārasūtra 15
Kyogyishinsho 26n, 26-27, 143

Lakṣmī 424, 432
Lalitavistara 26, 127n, 172, 180n, 255
Lama 184, 289, 410, 442
lamp 19, 144, 206, 208, 230
Lam rim chen mo (including "Calming the Mind and Discerning the Real") Chapter 4; 13n, 18n, 44n, 49n, 57n, 59, 73n, 77n, 79n, 150n, 164, 180, 186, 178n, 180n, 194, 225n, 242n, 365n
languages 228, 288, 299, 302; of scripture 39-40

Laṅkāvatāra-sūtra 17, 131, 133, 135, 141, 149-150, 158, 283, 302, 385-386
Large Sūtra on Perfect Wisdom 315n, 422
Laws of Manu 56-57, 369, 376-378, 381, 387, 389
lay person. See "persons."
liberation (*mokṣa, vimokṣa, apavarga*) 76-77, 88-94, 113, 306, 312, 318-319, 359, 374, 386, 394, 418, 424, 428n; eight 206. See "gates to liberation."
light 230, 259-260, 320, 340, 346, 401, 433, 437-439, 448n, 450; three kinds of 212; insight as 193, 206-213, 438
liṅga 447n
Logos 393
Lokātītastava 140
Lokāyata school 239, 362, 362n
Lokottaravādin sect 40
lotus (*padma*) 14, 27, 132, 179, 394, 421, 426, 432-433, 436-437, 439, 445-447; Realm 308

Madhyamāgama 257
Mādhyamika school 53, 113, 124, 136-141, 150, 159, 221-222, 254, 294, 302, 308-309, 317, 379. See Chapter 11.
Madhyamaka-kārikā 136, 140, 165, 167, 174n, 176n, 185n, 218, 222, 254. See Chapter 11
Madhyamakāvatāra 138, 149-150, 158, 177, 216-219, 237, 243, 379
Madhyāntavibhāga 170, 190-191, 183n, 270-276, 318
Madhyāntavibhāga-bhāṣya 170n, 270n, 272n, 318n
Madhyānta-Vibhaṅga 270n
Madhupiṇḍika Sutta 197
Mahābhārata 189, 372, 414
Mahāmudrāsiddhāntopadeśa 144
Mahā-ṇidāna-suttanta 163, 171
Mahānirvāṇatantra 441
Mahāparinibbāna-sutta 25, 142, 288n, 301, 320
Mahāprajñāpāramitāśāstra (*Le Traité de la Grande Vertu de Sagesse de Nāgārjuna*) 12-13, 60n, 70, 76, 85, 93n, 96-97, 137, 139-141 235, 323
Mahā-Sakuladāyi-sutta 74
Mahāsāṃghika sect 38-40, 59, 132, 251, 253, 288, 375n
Mahāsupina-Jātaka 406
Mahāvagga 32-33, 66, 66n
Mahāvajradhara 161
Mahāvastu 40-41, 117, 132n
Mahāvīra 400
Mahāvyutpatti 11, 120, 215-216, 219-222
Mahāyānasaṃgraha 133n, 174n, 183n
Mahāyāna-Sūtrālaṃkāra 20, 59, 79, 95, 112, 122, 135, 156, 234, 302, 316, 318, 321-322, 315n, 335
Mahīśāsaka sect Chapter 3; 40, 251, 253, 331; the Later 193, 251, 260
Maitrāyaṇīsaṃhitā 415
Maitreya 134, 270n, 290, 314n. See "Bodhisattva."
Maitreyakevalaparivartabhāṣya 313n
maitrī (love) 84, 101-102; Boundless State of Love 102
Maitripāda 144
Majjhima-nikāya 13, 74, 166n, 197, 217, 257, 315
Malayavatī 400
Mālinīvijayottara Tantram 405n
manas (mind, phenomenal mind) 134-135, 146, 172, 194, 208, 263, 271, 299-300, 304, 311, 320, 329, 331, 336, 349, 351, 403, 408-410, 414-415, 415n, 424-425; two kinds 415; *kliṣṭa-* 272n, 340, 351; *-saṃskāra* 311, 320; *manomaya* (made of mind) 260, 409 (See "body"). See "*citta.*"
maṇḍala 282, 426, 448n
Māṇḍūkya Upaniṣad 425
Manene, a goddess 147
Mañjughoṣa 434, 439
Mañjuśrī 22, 28, 161, 290, 433, 435. See "Bodhisattva."
Mañjuśrīmitra 136
Mañjuśrī-nāmasaṃgīti-cakṣur-vidhi-nāma 136n
Manorathanandin 118n
mantra (sacred formula, incantation) Chapter 22; 77, 309-310, 323-324, 462, 386-387, 393, 402, 410, 436-337, 449n, 450; of *prajñāpāramitā* 323-324; Oṃ 377, 419-420, 426-428, 428n, 437-439, 449; *svāhā* 323-324, 418-420, 419n, 427-428, 428n, 449. See "*dhāraṇī*," "*vidyā*"; "seed," syllables.
Manual of Abhidhamma 254n
Manual of a Mystic 76
Manusmṛti 376-378.
Māra 13-14, 18, 91, 114, 145, 158, 372, 402, 447-448; the four 208-209, 372, 447, 447n; "son-of-the-gods" Māra 84, 91, 209; Death Māra 209, 447n; acts of 76
Maruts 447
Mastery, bases of (*abhibhvāyatana*) 76-77, 90-94
Mātṛceṭa 287
Maudgalyāyana 47, 132
means (*upāya*) 22, 100, 106-107, 118, 297, 302, 321, 379-380, 395-396

medicine 399, 400n, 402, 404, 450n
meditation (*dhyāna*: P., *jhāna*) Chapter 3; 200, 206, 226, 231, 242, 246, 250, 281-283, 294-297, 300-301, 303-304, 306, 308-311, 314, 331, 381, 385, 393-394, 397, 406 406n, 415n, 417, 420, 437-438; four Dhyānas 35, 57, 210, 315-316, 320-324, 321n, 329, 331, 358, 361; perfection of 23, 106, 108-109, 113, 302, 446, 446n (See "perfections"); objects of (See "*kasiṇa*"); among "three instructions" 100, 108, 126 (See "instructions").
merit (*puṇya*) 44, 395-396, 415-417
Metta-sutta 53
Mīmāṃsā school 381, 408
mindfulness 76, 83, 91, 144, 212, 283, 331, 361
mind-only (*citta-mātra*) 177
mirror (*ādarśa*) Chapter 6; 253, 255, 259, 409; of the law 142; *karma*- 144-145, 183, 256; knowledge- 438; *prajñā*- 130, 149-151
Milindapañha (*Questions of King Milinda*) 393, 396, 402-403
Mkhas-grub-rje (=Khai Dub) 136, 443
Mkhas grub rje's Fundamentals of the Buddhist Tantras 21, 25n, 38n, 39n, 93n, 95n, 135n, 282n, 396n, 406n, 410n, 434, 434n, 438n, 443n
monastery (*vihāra*) 42-58, 308
monasticism Chapter 2; 374
moon 316, 401, 405, 408, 424, 432, 436-437, 446, 446n, 448n, 449n, 450
morality (*śīla*) 69, 71; three kinds 110-111; six members of 357-358; four roots of 361; as seven abstinences 34-36; perfection of 23, 61, 106-113, 302, 321, 446n (See "perfections"); among "three instructions" 57, 59, 126, 205, 281-282 (See Chapter 18). See Chapter 2.
mother 102-103, 107, 113, 145, 274, 306, 324, 383, 385, 393, 400, 403, 441, 446n. See "*śakti*," "Tārā."
mountain 219-220
Mṛtyu-vañcana (*Cheating Death*) 405
Mūlāpattisaṃgraha 441n
Mūlasarvāstivādanikāyaikaśatakarman 59
Mūlasarvāstivāda sect 38-40, 42, 49-51, 53, 59, 63, 65, 220-221
Mūlasarvāstivāda Vinayavibhaṅga 32, 42, 62-63, 143n, 220
Muṇḍaka Upaniṣad 383
muni (silent sage) 370-375; Buddha as *mahā-muni* 380-381. See "Buddha."
Munimatālaṃkāra 133, 161, 165n, 176n, 421, 422n

Nāgārjuna 43, 53, 113, 124, 130, 136-137, 139-140, 155n, 165, 167, 174-180, 185n, 186, 198n, 215-216, 218, 221-222, 252-255, 295, 296n, 434n. See Chapter 11.
Nāgārjunakoṇḍa 288
Nāgasena 396
Naiṣadhacarita 448n
Nālandā University 43
name-and-form (*nāma-rūpa*) 256, 263. See Chapter 8.
Nāropā 142, 145n, 147
Netti-pakaraṇa 119n
Nietzsche, F. 305
Nikāyas 25, 42, 209, 246. See titles.
Nirmāṇa-kāya See "body", of the Buddha.
nirvāṇa (release) 15, 19, 23, 86, 105-106, 109, 119, 122, 127, 155, 155n, 175, 176n, 178, 194, 208, 211, 232, 240, 242, 248-249, 252, 254, 274, 306, 312, 320, 323-324, 358-359, 365, 370-371, 385, 449; with remainder 203n, 212, 274, 335, 352, 365-366; without remainder 203n, 274, 312, 330-331, 335, 352, 366; without fixed abode 106, 274, 285, 374; Summit- 257; *parinirvāṇa* 17, 78, 91, 97, 252n, 257, 264-265, 291, 301, 311, 323, 341, 352
Niṣpannayogāvalī 147n
Noble Truths, four See "truth."
non-self (*anātman*) 18, 19, 95, 112, 114, 120-125, 139, 178, 188, 195-197, 203-204, 206, 196n, 316-318, 322, 331, 334, 345, 437-438. See "characteristics," three; "*śūnyatā*"; "self"; Chapter 10.
Nyāya-Mañjarī 428
Nyāya school 239; -Vaiśeṣika 408

offences 59-65; the worst as four "defeats" (*pārājika*) 60, 64-65, 314; fourteen transgressions 441
'*Od sruṅ gis žus pa* ("Questions of Kāśyapa") 107
'Ol Kha family 289
ordination 46-54; compared with "stages of life" 48-49

Padmāvatī 400
Pali Chanting Scripture with Thai and English Translation 53n
Pañcakrama 424

Pañcaviṃśatisāhasrikā Prajñāpāramitā 319n
Pāṇini 289, 413, 414n
Pañjikā 375n
paramārtha (absolute sense, supreme, supreme meaning) Chapter 17; 156-157, 177-178, 210-211, 246-247, 329-330, 335, 338, 345, 349, 419, 422; truth 18, 106, 114, 175, 242-243, 248-249, 294, 369, 378-381; *-tā* (Ultimate State) 272
Paramārtha-gāthā (*Verses of Supreme Meaning*) Chapter 17; 171, 196, 199, 331, 345, 352-354
Pāramitā-samāsa (*Phar phyin bsdus pa*) 101-111
parikalpa (imagination) 219, 272, 334, 340, 345, 350; = discursive thinking 203. See "*abhūtaparikalpa,*" "*kalpita,*" "*vikalpa.*"
parinirvāṇa See "*nirvāṇa.*"
parivrājaka (one gone forth) 30, 34, 45, 49-50, 78. See "persons."
Parjanya 395
Paryāya-saṃgrahaṇī 44n, 206, 209-210- 315, 316n
Patañjali 289
Path (*mārga*) Chapters 2-4; 119, 125-127, 165, 199, 202, 205, 212, 218-220, 233, 281, 302-303, 320, 327, 329-330, 334, 359-360, 383, 424; as a ladder 209; the four 318; the five 205; Eightfold Noble Path 19, 126, 186, 206, 236, 330, 358, 378-379; Middle Path avoiding extremes 55-56, 58, 167, 186, 205, 238, 284, 345; stages of Bodhisattva Path 41, 95, 107-108, 149, 157-158, 177-179, 185, 244, 312-315, 318, 321-322, 321n, 333; = Fourth Noble Truth (See "truth.")
Paṭisambhidāmagga 215-216, 221-222
Pavāraṇā ceremony 56
penance 63-68
perception See "*vijñāna.*"
perfection of insight (*prajñā-pāramitā*) 25-26, 96-97, 106-108, 113-114, 138, 150, 161, 177, 313, 321-324, 446n; personified 321-324, 322n, 420,-433, 446n, (See "mother"); *mantra* of 323-324; as a type of literature 130-133, 134, 136-138, 141, 205, 422, 433, 439 (See Chapter 15). See "perfections," "insight."
perfections (*pāramitā*) 244, 323, 428; six Chapter 4; 16, 23, 61, 104-114, 302, 321, 315n, 446, 446n. See "giving," etc.; "perfection of insight."
persons 180-187, 195n; two kinds 198-199, 360, 380-381; three kinds 175, 178n, 202, 264-265, 402; six kinds 403; six religious kinds 30; three degrees of religious 99; of six dispositions 72-73; five childish 209n-210n; ordinary (*pṛthagjana*) 14, 17, 77, 88, 122, 149, 157, 167, 175, 217, 232, 234, 315, 331, 346-347, 377-378; lay (*upāsika, -kā*) 44-45, 50, 63, 110, 183n, 228, 354, 376n (See "householder"); novice 14, 30, 45, 47-53; directing ordination 49-52; noble (*ārya*) 14, 17, 84, 123, 166, 205, 210, 217, 234, 272, 331, 339, 346, 363, 378, 434, 437; lazy 357, 357n. See titles.
persuasions, four 109, 114
Picasso, P. 284
Pitāputrasamāgama-sūtra (*Meeting of Father and Son*) 138-139, 157n, 166, 255, 319, 403
Platform Sutra of the Sixth Patriarch 141n
poison 392, 424, 449-451, 450n-451n; the three Poisons (lust, hatred, delusion) 14, 30, 76, 96-97, 197, 205, 210, 330, 386, 403, 405, 449n (among "dispositions" 72-74)
postures, four 72; "walking posture of the Buddha 12-13
powers, ten 108
Prabhākara 408
Pradīpoddyotana 161, 373, 435n
prajñā See "insight."
Prajñāpāramitābhāvanopadeśa 79
Prajāpati 414-415, 414n, 425-426, 426n
Prajñāpradīpa 165n
Prajñāśataka 434
prakṛti (primal nature) 190-191, 237, 329
pramāṇa (authority) 381; three 346, 346n
Pramāṇavārttika 118-119, 195, 297, 379
Prāsaṅgika-Mādhyamika school 243-245, 249
Prasannapadā 139n-140n, 140, 165n, 222n, 233n, 250, 312, 371
Praśāstrasena 324
praśrabdhi (cathartic) 80-81, 84, 95, 98, 113
Prātimokṣa (P., Pātimokkha) (Liberation-Onset) 30-42, 52-54, 58-68; two kinds 35-37, 119n; *-saṃvara* 16, 33-34, 59, 358, 361 (See "vow").
Prātimokṣa-sūtra 30-42, 59-60
Pratītyasamutpāda-gananānusāreṇacittasthāpanopāya 183n
Pratītyasamutpāda-hṛdaya-kārikā 18
Pratītyasamutpādahṛdaya-vyākaraṇ 137, 253; *-vyākhyāna* 174n

Pratītyāsamutpāda Sūtra 174n
Pratītyasamutpāda-vyākhyā 174n
pratyakṣa (direct perception, direct view) 297-298, 300, 303, 346n, 360, 379
pratyekabuddha (self-enlightened one) 76, 96, 100, 108, 110, 138, 184, 178n, 194, 196-197, 308, 316, 318, 324, 330, 373; as rhinocerus 318. See "persons."
pudgala (person, personality) 139, 156, 175, 195-196, 196n, 264-265, 316, 335, 341, 346, 352
Puggala-paññati (*Designation of Human Types*) 16, 72, 252n
Purāṇic tradition 417, 423, 432, 434, 447n
Pure Land (Sukhāvatī) 26-27
puruṣa (person) 190-191, 237, 396, 409; *mahā-* 446n
Pūrva-Mīmāṃsā-Sūtras 429n
Pūrvaśaila sect 251
Pūṣan 378-380, 388

Rājavagga 33
Rāmāyaṇa 279, 377, 393
Ratnacūḍaparipṛcchā 22, 26
Ratnagotravibhāga 241, 244, 302
Ratnākaraśānti 27, 79, 211, 324n, 428, 428n
Ratnakīrti 239n
Ratnakūṭa 138, 154, 260n, 262
Ratnāvali 139
ṛddhi (magical power) 77, 89, 93, 154, 233, 257, 371, 373. See "*abhijñā*," "*siddhi*."
reasons, four 101
Red-mda'-ba 246n, 312
refuge (*śaraṇa*). Buddha as 12; the taking of 46, 50, 105. See "jewel."
Ṛg-*veda* 189, 370, 376-377, 384
Rgyal-tshab-rje 379
Riṣṭasamuccaya 402, 425
rite (*kriyā*, *vidhi*) 291, 378-381, 386-388, 397, 406n, 417-419, 426-429, 433-439, 447n-448n; of truth Chapter 20; of passage 397; of eye ointment 160, 299; of mirror washing 135-136; confession 392; *homa* 405, pilgrimage 291-292; sacrifice 381, 385, 391, 393, 413-416, 416n. See "*maṇḍala*"; Chapter 22.
Rnam snaṅ mṅon byaṅ ("Revelation Enlightenment of Vairocana") 106
Ṛṣi (Seer) 373, 383, 397, 425, 425n, 436
Rudra 446n, 450n; -ka 372

Sabbasutta (*Discourse on "Everything"*) 233
Sa bcu pa ("Sūtra of Ten Stages") 107
Sacittikābhūmi Chapter 16; 194
sādhana (evocation) 145, 147-148, 410, 428, 434-439, 449n; defined 443; Sādhya 417-418; *sādhaka* 418;= *āvāha* 423, 425
Saddharmapuṇḍarīka 143
Saddharmasmṛtyupasthāna-sūtra 184n
Sāgaramatiparipṛcchā 279
Sahajalalita 429n
Sa'i-lha-mo brtan-ma (Earth Goddess) 147
Śaivism Chapter 24, 135, 374, 387, 393, 405, 409-410, 442, 446n
śakti (power) 393, 442, 450, 450n. See "mother," "Tārā."
Śākyamuni 27-28, 35, 54, 56, 289-290, 370
Saḷāyatana-Vagga 122, 345n, 350n, 352n
Śālistambaka-kārikā 137, 174n
Śālistambasūtra 137, 166n-167n, 174n, 177, 180n, 181, 186
samādhi (concentration, one-pointedness, meditation) 55-56, 67-69, 78-84, 89, 98, 109-110, 126, 155-158, 281, 283-284, 289, 297, 301, 313-315, 324, 331, 360, 363, 386; Diamond-like 84, 157; of "knowledge and vision" 84; of "love" 84
Samāhitabhūmi 76, 83-84, 86-90, 92, 94, 194, 212, 315, 318, 327
Sāmañña-phala-sutta 34
Samantapāsādikā (*Shan-Chien-P'i-P'o-Sha*) 35n-37n, 45n, 55n-56n, 61n, 63n, 64n, 67n, 306
samāpatti (equipoise) 80, 82, 84, 88, 90, 92-94, 97, 159, 175, 313, 315, 320, 329-331, 373, 449n
śamatha (P., *samatha*) (calming) 66, 77, 81, 88, 113, 118, 174, 281, 284, 296-297, 362, 364-366, 436, 442, 449; combined (=*yuganaddha*) with "discerning" 82, 95, 213; among three "instructions" 69-71, 74, 78, 95, 125-126. See "meditation," "*vipaśyanā*"; Chapter 3.
Sāma Veda 382, 386
saṃbhavaiṣin, a being 158
Saṃbhoga-kāya See "body", of the Buddha.
Saṃdhinirmocana-sūtra 79, 130, 134, 193, 200, 314n, 321n
Saṃdhivyākaraṇa 373
Saṃgha (P., Sangha) (Congregation, Order) 235, 370, 447n; eighteen early sects 40, 406 (See names). See "jewel"; Chapters 2-3.
Sāṃkhya-kārikā 189

Sāṃkhya school 125, 187-191, 239
Sammatīya 39-40, 251
Saṃpuṭa-tilaka-tantra 155n, 159
saṃsāra (cyclical flow, phenomenal life) 17-18, 82, 106, 176n, 180, 188-189, 202, 212, 253-254, 278-279, 294, 306, 312-313, 322, 322n, 352; as swirling waters 324
saṃskāra (motivations) 92-94, 120-123, 194-195, 202, 217-220, 237, 248, 254-256, 263, 273, 276, 303, 311, 316-317, 320, 336-338, 346, 348-350, 404, 409, 416 (See "*skandha*"; Chapter 8); =traces 409; =constructions 120, 122, 174-175, 275 (See "*dharma*")
Saṃvarodaya Tantra 144, 146, 424
saṃvṛti (conventional) 157, 242, 247, 330, 338, 349, 438; truth 106, 114, 175, 243, 248-249, 348, 369, 379; mind 178
Saṃyuktāgama 221, 357n
Saṃyutta-nikāya 15, 16, 19, 74, 77, 97, 122, 132, 158, 165-167, 212, 215-216, 236, 302, 311, 345n, 350n, 352n, 357n
Saṅghabhadra 118n, 306n
Saṅghabhedavastu 33n
Saṅgharakṣa 193n
Saṅgīti-Suttanta (*Recital Sermon*) 371
Śaṅkara 374, 381, 408
Saṅs rgyas so lṅa'i mṅon rtogs. . . . 15n
Śāntarakṣita 240n, 375n
Śāntideva 24-26, 101-102, 124n, 1?9n, 226, 255n, 299, 304-305, 404, 405n
Saptabhavasūtra 257
Śāradātilaka 418
Sarasvatī Chapter 23
Śāriputra (P., Sāriputta) 24, 47, 132, 166n, 221-222, 233. See Chapter 15.
Śāriputrābhidharmaśāstra 251
Śarīrārtha-gāthā 333, 354
Sarvadurgatipariśodhana-tantra 373n
Sarvāstivāda 40, 251, 406
Sarvatathāgatamātṛtārāviśvakarmabhavatantra 442-443
Śatapathabrāhmaṇa 32, 414, 426, 426n-427n, 431
Satpuruṣagati-sūtra 257, 263
Satyasiddhiśāstra 119
Sautrāntika sect 118, 353
Savitā 377, 417
Savitarkādir-bhūmi 194, 200-201, 203, 210
Sāyaṇa 431
Sbas pa'i don kun gsal ba 146n
Schiller, J. 293
sciences, five 113
seal (*mudrā*) 67, 135, 138, 253, 447, 447n, 449n
secret Chapter 15; 313, 331, 442
"Secret Key to the *Heart Sūtra*" 308
seed (*bīja*) 179, 183, 187n, 188-189, 253, 255, 261, 263, 272n, 282, 338-340, 350, 352, 449; syllables 418, 426-427, 427n-428n, 437-439, 449n. See "*mantra*."
self (*ātman*) 18, 95, 102,104, 121, 138, 142-143, 159, 169-170, 175-178, 188-189, 195, 203-204, 206, 247-249, 271-271, 317, 322, 331-340, 345-350, 350n, 352, 370-371, 382-384, 388, Upaniṣadic 256, 259; as *kliṣṭamanas* 272n; =*ahaṃkāra* 139. See "non-self"; Chapter 10.
Seng-chao 149-150
sense bases (*āyatana*) 169-172, 175, 179-180, 182-183, 203, 233, 247, 263, 272n, 298, 318-320, 335, 345-346, 345n
Sgrub thabs kun btus 145n, 147n, 433
shaman 130, 145, 280
Shan-Chien-P'i-P'o-Sha See "*Samantapāsādikā*."
Shen-hsiu 140
Shilappadikaram 401
Shingon school 308
Shin school 24, 26
Shintō 130
Shiva Sanhita 394n
Śibijātaka 391, 394
Siddha 417-418, 417n
siddhi (success, magical success, occult power) 136, 148, 394, 405-406, 418. See "*abhijñā*," "*ṛddhi*," "Siddha."
śikṣāpada (P., *sikhāpada*) (points of instruction) 30-31, 34, 50, 59, 175
Śikṣāsamuccaya 22, 26, 101, 124n, 139n, 255n, 404n
śīla See "morality."
Siṃhaparipṛcchā 404
Śiṣyalekhā 22
Sītā 279
Sitātapatrā (White Umbrella Lady) 407
Śiva 374, 442, 446n, 447, 447n-448n, 450, 450n
Śivasvarodaya 424
skandha (personal aggregates) 15, 53, 95, 121, 123, 138-139, 168, 172-173, 232-233, 246-247, 253, 259, 313, 316, 320, 335, 345, 362n. See Chapter 10.
smṛti (memory) 283, 372; personified 433, 439
Sṅags rim chen mo 160
soma 283; personified 259, 432, 446n
speech (*vāc*), and mind 414, 414n; -*saṃskāra* 210, 303, 311, 316, 323;

as fire or cow 415-417, 415n; personified 393, 396-397, 410, 414, 414n-415n, 424-425, 431-432, 435-436. See "*mantra*," "body, speech, and mind"; Chapters 19-20, 22.
Śraddhābalādhāna-sūtra 161
śramaṇa (P., *samaṇa*) (ascetic) 30, 34, 55-57, 67, 361, 374-375, 378, 380; of four kinds 30; Buddha as *mahā*- 380; female 407. See "persons."
Śrautakośa 426n
śrāvaka (disciple) 30, 36, 76, 96-97, 100, 108, 110, 113, 119, 138, 157, 173, 194, 196-197, 199, 207, 217, 233-236, 251, 308, 313, 316-317, 363, 416; =hearers 250. See "persons."
Śrāvakabhūmi 15n, 17n, 30n, 55n, 57, 70n, 72n, 76-78, 80-86, 88, 118, 171n, 181n, 194, 193n, 196n, 206, 264, 260n, 263n, 270n, 272n, 295n, 296n, 300n, 301, 319n, 327, 331, 333-334, 353n, 354, 365n
Sred med kyi bus ẓus pa ("Questions of Nārāyaṇa") 114
Śrīmālā-sūtra (*The Lion's Roar of Queen Śrīmālā*) 184-185, 211n, 216n, 253, 263, 322n
Śrīparamādi-ṭīkā 280
Śrī-Paramādya 107
Śṛṅgāra Prakāśa 400
Śrutamayī-bhūmi 194, 206, 210
stages of life 277; Brahmanic 380 (compared with life of a Bhikṣu 56-58; compared with Buddhist ordination 48-49). See "*bhūmi*."
Sthavira sect 38-39, 288
Sthiramati 85, 95, 130n, 157, 176, 270n, 308, 316, 318, 321n, 322
stream 340-341, 349, 351-352, 401, 447n; -enterer 15, 19, 30, 142, 185, 218-219; of consciousness 99-104, 109, 111, 114, 157, 233, 313, 338 (cf. mind as water 130-131)
striving 108, 362, 363; three kinds 112; perfection of 23, 106, 108, 113, 302, 321, 446, 446n (See "perfections")
stūpa 44, 64, 288-289, 291-292; see *caitya* 291
Subhāṣita-saṃgraha 186n, 219
Subhūti 23-24
Suhṛllekha (*Friendly Epistle*) 254, 295
śūnya (void) or *śūnyatā* (voidness) 22, 25, 27, 107-108, 120-121, 131-133, 136, 139-140, 143-144, 148, 150, 157, 159, 165, 186, 190-191, 206-207, 237-238, 240, 270-274, 275, 302, 309, 312-313, 316-320, 321n, 335, 346, 348, 422, 436-437; sixteen kinds 435. See "gates to liberation."
Śūnyatāsaptati 178
Śūraṅgamasamādhisūtra 145n
Śūraṅgama Sūtra 144
Sūryagupta 443, 447n-448n
Susiddhikara-mahātantra-sādhanopāyika-paṭala Tantra 419-420
Suśruta 404
Suśruta-saṃhitā 405
Suttavibhanga 34n, 45n, 55n, 60n, 62n. See "Vinaya."
Suvarṇaprabhāsa-sūtra 434
svabhāva (self-existence, intrinsic nature, own-nature, nature) 121, 134, 139, 142, 157-158, 174n, 226, 234, 237-244, 244n, 248, 250, 316, 334, 373, 438; as *mantra* 436, 436n
Svapnacintāmaṇi 399
Svapnādhyāya 399, 401
Svapnavāsavadatta 400
Svapnavicāra 399
Svārthānumāna-pariccheda 118n
Svātantrika-Mādhyamika school 245, 249
symbol (*samaya*) 117, 117n, 206-209, 291, 293, 294-295, 301, 406, 417, 431, 434, 437n, 447n, 449n; *-sattva* 438. See "Buddhist art"; Chapter 6-7.

Tantra 130, 135-136, 141-142, 146-147, 160-161, 184-185, 191, 262, 275, 282, 290, 296-298, 301, 322n, 373, 373n, 387, 393, 399, 405, 409-410, 433-435, 439-443, 449n; Caryā 410n; Kriyā 410n; Yoga 407; Anuttarayoga 441. See titles; Chapter 22.
Tantravārtika 429n
Tārā Chapter 24; 26-28, 296, 306, 406, 420; White Tārā 27-28, 147; *vidyā* of 320, 427-428; as Gaṅgā 446n; as Pāṇḍarā 448n. See "mother," "*śakti*."
Tarkajvālā 409n
Tathāgatagarbha 253
Tattvasaṃgraha 240n, 375n
Theravāda sect Chapter 3; 41-42, 49, 63, 182, 186-187, 185n, 215, 231, 235, 236, 251-252, 288, 331
Thusness (*tathātā*) 12, 155, 166, 176, 189, 272
Tibetan Book of the Dead 265
time (*kāla*) Chapter 13; 201, 239, 323, 347-348, 362, 369, 373, 395, 406-408, 439
Tirukkural 400
"Toda Dream Songs" 404

tree 242, 259, 291-292, 294, 317, 365, 396, 401, 406; wishing- 385; *bodhi-* 12, 56, 141, 172, 290; of suffering 165, 177, 179-180
Triṃśikābhāṣya 130n-131n
tripiṭaka (Three Baskets) 37
truth (*satya, ṛta*) 175, 195, 212, 228-231, 279-280, 284, 293-294, 323-324, 358, 376n, 403; the two truths (See "*saṃvṛti*," "*paramārtha*"); the Four Noble Truths 15, 19, 111, 153, 155, 199, 202, 205-206, 236, 281, 319-320, 334, 358, 360, 378-380 (See Chapters 5, 8); and silence (See Chapter 19); rite or Act of 160, 279, 377-378, 416 (See Chapter 20)
Tshad ma'i brjed byaṅ chen mo 118n
Tshad ma'i lam khrid ("Guidance on the Path of Authority") 379
Tsha-go-pa 407
Tsoṅ-kha-pa Chapter 4; 15n, 18, 49-50, 59, 77, 118-119, 121, 125-126, 141-142, 146, 149-150, 157-160, 164, 177-182, 177n, 178n, 180n, 184, 187n, 190, 194, 196n, 201, 219, 225, 225n, 237n, 242n, 243, 248, 289, 365n, 400, 407, 410, 435n
Tathāgata 155, 176, 218; defined 11, 446n
Tuṣita, a heaven 270

Udānavarga 19, 334, 370-372, 386
Upāli 36-37, 39-40
Upaniṣads 172, 189, 258-259, 265, 369-370, 376-388, 393, 420, 327; four states of 409-410 (Turīya 285). See titles.
Upasampadājñaptiḥ 46n
Uposatha (S., Upavasatha) 31, 35-36, 38-39, 46, 54, 60, 62. See Chapter 2.
uṣṇīṣa 161, 296, 446, 446n
Uttaratantra (=*Ratnagotravibhāga*) 107

Vācaspati Miśra 392n
Vahni 418
Vaibhāṣika sect 118
Vairocana 106. See "Buddha."
Vairocanābhisaṃbodhi-tantra 160
Vaiśeṣika school 239, 404
Vaiṣṇava tradition 125
vajra (diamond, thunderbolt) 185-186, 226, 417; triple 373; -lord 373; Realm 308; -pledge 426; cf. *kuliśa* (thunderbolt) 219-220, 221. See "Vajrasattva."
Vajracchedikā 156
Vajramālā 135
Vajrapāṇi 310, 400, 421
Vajrasarasvatī 433, 438
Vajrasattva (Diamond Being) 142, 186, 280; husband of Prajñāpāramitā 322, 322n
Vajraśekhara 422
Vajravidāraṇa-dhāraṇī- Tantra 421
Vajrayāna See "Tantra."
Vakkali 166
Vakkali-sutta 167
Varāhamihira 277n
Varuṇa 375, 392, 395;- praghāsas 392
vāsanā (habit-energy) 170-171, 182, 244, 261n
Vāsavadatta 400
Vastusaṃgrahaṇī 174, 199, 209n, 209-210, 316n, 331, 335
Vasubandhu 58, 84, 91, 117, 122, 154, 156, 170-171, 174, 191, 183n, 185n, 195, 196n, 222n, 233, 251-252, 256-257, 260-261, 265, 251n, 252n, 270n, 270-272, 308, 313, 318, 371
Vātsīputrīya sect 251
Vedānta 247n, 380, 386, 408; Advaita 374, 387
Vedānta-sūtras 419
Vedas 145, 172-173, 258, 261n, 283, 370, 372-376, 378, 380, 386, 391-393, 395-397. See Chapters 22-23.
Vibhajyavādin 251, 253; =Buddha 215
Vibhāṣā 221
vidyā (clear vision, clear sight; charm, magical formula) 12, 193, 195, 205, 393, 422, 432; three fruits of 394, 419-420; *-dhara* 373n, 435-437; as female *mantra* 323, 397, 415n, 419-422, 424, 427-429, 428n, 449, 449n; of Tārā 420, 428, 449n. See "*avidyā*," "knowledge," "*mantra*."
view (*dṛṣṭi*; P., *diṭṭhi*) 168, 200, 238, 322, 338-339, 350, 354, 379; four 244; bad, false, deviant 200, 203-204, 350-351, 358, 362n; reifying 200, 204, 206, 317 (See Chapter 10); holding to an extreme 200, 204; right 19-20, 206, 237, 240, 244, 358 (See "Path," "eightfold)
Vigrahavyāvartinī 186
vijñāna (perception, consciousness) 74, 87, 158, 194, 209-211, 217-220, 253-256, 259, 259n, 263, 271-273, 283-284, 298, 303-306, 316-317, 320, 329, 337, 345-346, 345n, 408-409; *pravṛtti-* 134, 254, 276, 283, 330-331, 349, 350n; *ādāna-* 130; causal 181-185; fruitional 181-185, 189, 345n; *mano-* 253-254, 409; *-koṣa* 409. See "*ālayavijñāna*"; Chapter 8.
Vijñānavāda See "Yogācāra."

vijñapti (representation) 137, 271-272
Vijñaptimātratāsiddhi 20, 189
vikalpa (discursive thought) 108, 113, 137-139, 149-150, 176, 197, 210-211, 278, 287, 299, 301, 302-304, 316, 422; right 303; =imagination 337. See "*kalpita*," "*parikalpa*."
Vikramāditya 400
Vimalamitra 316
Vimaloṣṇīṣa 429
Vimuttimagga 262n
Vinaya (discipline) 24, 30-42, 215, 220-221, 302, 306, 314, 322, 361, 406; -dhāra 34, 38, 40, 51. See titles; Chapter 2.
Vinayavastu 53
Vinaya-vibhaṅga-pada-vyākhyāna 220, 314n
Vinaya-saṃgrahaṇī 45n
Viniścayasaṃgrahaṇī 77, 122, 131n, 134n, 157, 164n, 197, 198n, 200, 203n, 205, 210, 318, 328
Vinītadeva 32-33, 42, 59, 62-63, 215, 220-221, 308, 314, 322
viparyāsa (waywardness) 216, 234; three stages of 322; four 123, 178, 322, 329, 331; seven 203. See Chapter 9.
vipaśyanā (P., *vipassanā*) (discerning, clear vision) 69, 108, 113, 118, 176, 190; among three "instructions" 78, 95; combined (*-yuganaddha*) with "calming" 82, 95, 213. See "*śamatha*"; Chapter 3.
vision (*cakṣus*; P., *cakkhu*) (*darśana*; P., *dassana*) Chapter 7; 314, 322, 380. See "eye," "insight."
Viṣṇu 375, 427n, 432, 434-435, 450n
Viṣṇudharmottara 432
Visuddhimagga (*Path of Purification*) 55, 69, 72-76, 73n, 75n, 95-96, 126, 138, 167n, 177, 216n, 262n, 281n
Viśveśvara 447
Vivaraṇa-saṃgrahaṇī 205
vow (*saṃvara*) 168, 200, 204, 282, 361, 363, 373, 376n, 416-417; Bodhisattva vow 101, 104-106. See "Prātimokṣa."

wheel (*cakra*) 291-292, 433, 447; of Dharma 15, 117, 117n, 127, 153, 378, 447n; of Life or Becoming (*bhavacakra*) 63, 170, 182; spinning 388; *rakṣā-cakra* 448n. See "Cakravartin."
wickednesses (*duṣkṛta*), the fifteen 64-65
woman 306, 383, 388, 401-402, 404-406, 432; sacred nature of 441; detractions of 13. See "*bhikṣuṇī*," "mother."

Yājñavalkya 383
Yajur-veda 382, 393
Yama 145, 158, 256, 258, 396, 404
Yassamdisam-sutta 33
yati (restrainer) 30. See "persons."
yoga 56, 212, 263, 283, 322, 374, 394, 394n, 410, 425, 439. See "Path"; Chapters 2-3.
Yogācārabhūmi Chapters 9, 16; 16n, 70, 76-77, 126, 157, 164, 164n-165n, 167n, 175, 187n, 216n, 259n-261n, 303, 315-316, 333, 315-316, 333, 346n, 353-354, 357n; meditative progress in 78-96
Yogācāra school 53, 95, 130-134, 150, 156, 189-191, 270-273, 308-309, 333-334; as *vijñānavāda* 93
yogin 251, 284, 297, 301, 303, 315-316, 324, 381
Yoginītantra 397n, 419
Yüan-ts'ê 314n, 321n
Yuktiṣaṣṭikā 175, 178

Zen school 308
Zhaṅ Blon, a deity 146
Zur 'debs rnam thar legs bśad kun 'dus 400n